The fall of the house of labor

The fall of
the house of labor

The workplace, the state, and American labor activism, 1865–1925

DAVID MONTGOMERY

YALE UNIVERSITY

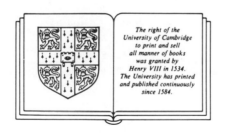

The right of the
University of Cambridge
to print and sell
all manner of books
was granted by
Henry VIII in 1534.
The University has printed
and published continuously
since 1584.

CAMBRIDGE UNIVERSITY PRESS
Cambridge
New York   New Rochelle   Melbourne   Sydney

EDITIONS DE LA MAISON DES SCIENCES DE L'HOMME
Paris

Published by the Press Syndicate of the University of Cambridge
The Pitt Building, Trumpington Street, Cambridge, CB2 1RP
32 East 57th Street, New York, NY 10022, USA
10 Stamford Road, Oakleigh, Melbourne 3166, Australia
and
Editions de la Maison des Sciences de l'Homme
54 Boulevard Raspail, 75270 Paris, Cedex 06, France

© Maison des Sciences de l'Homme and
Cambridge University Press 1987

First published 1987

Printed in the United States of America

Library of Congress Cataloging-in-Publication Data
Montgomery, David, 1927–
The fall of the house of labor.
Includes index.
1. Labor and laboring classes – United States – History.
2. Trade-unions – United States – History.   I. Title.
HD8072.M73   1987   331.88'0973   86–21530

British Library Cataloguing in Publication Data
Montgomery, David
The fall of the house of labor: the
workplace, the state, and American labor
activism, 1865–1925.
1. Labor and laboring classes –
United States – History
I. Title
322'.2'0973   HD8072

ISBN 0 521 22579 5
ISBN 2 7351 0210 6 (France only)

TO DOUGLAS, NICHOLAS, LINDSAY, AND ELIZABETH

Contents

Acknowledgments

The research for this book was made possible by generous grants from the John Simon Guggenheim Memorial Foundation, the American Council of Learned Societies, and the Whitney Humanities Center of Yale University. Typing of the manuscript was assisted by an A. Whitney Griswold Faculty Award at Yale University.

Many people have taken an interest in this research over the years and have suggested ideas or guided me to sources that have contributed significantly to my understanding of the topic. Among them are James Barrett, Neil Basen, John Bennett, Iver Bernstein, Jeremy Brecher, Cecelia Bucki, Paul Buhle, Mark Erlich, Dana Frank, Patrick Fridenson, Carter Goodrich, Andrea Graziosi, Julia Greene, Maurine Weiner Greenwald, Gregory Kealey, Patrick Lynch, Martel W. Montgomery, Priscilla Murolo, Bryan Palmer, George Pearlman, Michelle Perrot, Lewis Perry, Linda Pickard, Gordon E. Sands, Steven Sapolsky, Ronald W. Schatz, Joan W. Scott, Erroll Wayne Stevens, H. Shelton Stromquist, and Paul Worthman. David Brody, Eric Foner, Steven Fraser, Peter Friedlander, Herbert Gutman, James Hinton, and E. P. Thompson all offered valuable criticisms of early drafts of the manuscript. Portions of later drafts benefited from the comments and advice of Barbara J. Fields, Priscilla Murolo, Margaret Nelson, Steve Nelson, and Donald Tormey. The entire manuscript was read critically by David Brody. I am deeply grateful to all of them for their suggestions, even those with which I continue to disagree.

Without the help of able archivists and librarians, no historical research could be brought to a successful completion. Among those who lent special assistance to this effort are Philip Mason, Dione Miles, and George Tselos of the Archives of Labor History and Urban Affairs at Wayne State University; Moreau B. C. Chambers of the Department of Archives and Manuscripts of the Catholic University of America; Sandra Keith, Lynn S. Toscano, and Rudolph Vecoli of the Immigration History Research Center in St. Paul, Minnesota; Joseph Howerton of the National Archives of the United States of America; the staff of the Manuscripts and Archives Division of the New York Public Library; Josephine

Harper of the State Historical Society of Wisconsin; and Susan Steinberg of Yale University's Sterling Memorial Library.

Special thanks are due to Sheila Brewer, Sheila Klein, and Mary Whitney for their able contributions to the typing of the manuscript.

Abbreviations used in text and notes

ACWA	Amalgamated Clothing Workers of America
AFL	American Federation of Labor
AIU	American Industrial Union
ARU	American Railway Union
ASE	Amalgamated Society of Engineers
ASME	American Society of Mechanical Engineers
BLE	Brotherhood of Locomotive Engineers
CCF	Central Competitive Field
CFI	Colorado Fuel and Iron Company
CIA	Citizens' Industrial Association
CIO	Congress of Industrial Organizations
CND	Council of National Defense
CPI	Committee on Public Information
CPPA	Conference for Progressive Political Action
FMCS	Federal Mediation and Conciliation Service
GE	General Electric Company
IA	*Iron Age*
IAM	International Association of Machinists
IBEW	International Brotherhood of Electrical Workers
ILA	International Longshoremen's Association
ILGWU	International Ladies' Garment Workers' Union
IMU	International Machinists' Union
ISR	*International Socialist Review*
IWA	International Workingmen's Association
IWM	Interchurch World Movement
IWPA	International Working People's Association
IWW	Industrial Workers of the World
La. BSL	Louisiana Bureau of Statistics of Labor
LUPA	Longshoremen's Union Protective Association
Mass. BSL	Massachusetts Bureau of Statistics of Labor
MBIU	Machinists' and Blacksmiths' International Union
MLR	*Monthly Labor Review*

MMJ	*Machinists' Monthly Journal*
MTD	Metal Trades Department
NAM	National Association of Manufacturers
NCF	National Civic Federation
NICB	National Industrial Conference Board
N.J. BIS	New Jersey Bureau of Industrial Statistics
NLT	*National Labor Tribune*
NMTA	National Metal Trades Association
NR	*New Review*
NUTW	National Union of Textile Workers
NWLB	National War Labor Board
N.Y. BSL	New York Bureau of Statistics of Labor
OBU	One Big Union
Ohio BLS	Ohio Bureau of Labor Statistics
Pa. BIS	Pennsylvania Bureau of Industrial Statistics
R.I. CIS	Rhode Island Commissioner of Industrial Statistics
SLP	Socialist Labor Party
SPA	Socialist Party of America
SUR	*Seattle Union Record*
TUEL	Trade Union Educational League
UMWA	United Mine Workers of America
USCIR	United States Commission on Industrial Relations
WIIU	Workers International Industrial Union
YMCA	Young Men's Christian Association
YSA	Yugoslav Socialist Alliance

Introduction

To write about the working class is to discuss many disparate individuals. At any moment in the American past the researcher encounters such variety in personal aspirations, talents, and sense of self among working people as to defy stereotypes. Moreover, socially prescribed differences in gender, race, religion, and nationality have influenced various workers' behavior in powerfully different ways. Instead of listening for the "voice of the working class," therefore, we must be attuned to many different voices, sometimes in harmony, but often in conflict with one another.

Nevertheless, it remains not only possible but imperative to analyze the American experience of the late nineteenth and early twentieth centuries in terms of conflicting social classes. The human relationships structured by commodity production in large collective enterprises devoted to private gain generated bondings and antagonisms that were, in one form or another, the daily experience of everyone involved. "As a worker yourself, you're 'inside' with a vengeance," noted Smith College graduate Alice Kimball of her sojourn in a Paterson silk mill.

> You face the same sense of wearing monotony. You too swallow your injured pride when you have to kow-tow to the boss. You rage like the others at any attempt to overthrow the precious eight hour day. And just like the rest you sit around when unemployed and watch your savings ooze away and wonder why industry runs on such a stupid basis when you want work and can't get it.[1]

Although the modern experience of class had its origin in the encounter with wage labor described by Kimball, class consciousness permeated social intercourse outside the workplace as well as within it. Married women caring for their children in bleak, congested neighborhoods and facing creditors, charity officials, and the ominous authority of the clergy were reminded of their class as regularly as were their husbands, daughters, and sons in the factories. Children learned early the differences be-

---

1. Alice Kimball, "In the Silk," *The World Tomorrow*, 6 (January 1923), 51.

tween their parents' attire, bearing, and patterns of speech and those of
the gentlemen and ladies who seemed to move with such grace and ease
through the corridors of power and the emporiums of abundance.

Those daily experiences and visible social distinctions taught many
workers that although others might wield social influence as individuals,
workers' only hope of securing what they wanted in life was through
concerted action. Although the personal bondings of families, migrant
groups, young wage-earning women, craftsmen, strikers, voters, and rioters
defined people's loyalties in different and often conflicting ways, all attachments were rooted in the shared presumption that individualism was
appropriate only for the prosperous and wellborn. Nevertheless, to organize concerted action and to fashion a sense of social goals shared by
all workers required deliberate human agency. Class consciousness was
more than the unmediated product of daily experience. It was also a
project. Working-class activists, and some individuals from other social
strata who had linked their aspirations to the workers' movement, persistently sought to foster a sense of unity and purposiveness among their
fellow workers through the spoken and printed word, strikes, meetings,
reading circles, military drill, dances, athletic and singing clubs, and cooperative stores and to promote through those activities widely shared
analyses of society and of paths to the "emancipation of labor." Both
"history from the bottom up" and the common fixation on great leaders
have obscured the decisive role of those whom twentieth-century syndicalists have called the "militant minority": the men and women who
endeavored to weld their workmates and neighbors into a self-aware and
purposeful working class.

The development of that project during the six decades between the
abolition of chattel slavery and the closing down of mass immigration
from Europe and Asia is the subject of this book. Its three basic points of
reference are the human relationships that wage labor generated at the
workplace, the changing structures of economic and political power fashioned by the evolution of nineteenth-century competitive industrial capitalism into twentieth-century imperialism, and the diverse styles of thought
and activity by which working-class activists sought to interpret and improve the society in which they lived. No attempt is made here to offer a
comprehensive history of American labor struggles. Indeed, some of the
most familiar and important episodes, such as the strikes of 1877, the
Haymarket affair, the Pullman boycott, the 1902 anthracite strike, the
garment workers' uprisings of 1909–11, and the steel strike of 1919, will
receive only passing mention. They have had well-deserved attention lav-
ished on them by other historians in the past and will, I hope, enjoy still

more research in the future. The narrative history found in these pages is devoted primarily to less well-known chapters in American workers' experience, such as the struggles of textile and garment workers before 1900 and of railroad, mining, and electrical workers after that time. If famous events like the 1892 Homestead strike and the 1914 Colorado miners' strike are treated in detail, it is to learn from them how the relationship between the state and conflict in the workplace was changing.

Even when this study carries us into the chambers of Washington's decision makers, however, its primary concern remains working life. The Belgian sociologist Henri de Man noted that the European workers he studied after World War I disagreed among themselves on many fundamental issues but spoke in remarkably similar ways about work. "As workers, the Christians felt exactly like the infidel socialists whose material conditions of life they shared," he wrote.[2] Both the shared sentiments and the fact that some workers were Christians and others infidel socialists, whereas still others disavowed both faiths, pose questions for historical analysis. As the self-educated coffin maker Ethelbert Stewart argued, history often witnessed a "transformation of [workers'] sentiments into customs" and of "trade interests into 'union principles,'" which "goes on so gradually before our eyes [when we study union] minute books that we can understand them better." Conversely, he added, the principles enshrined in the bylaws of early unions "have since become a part of the subconscious thought life of the 'union man,' and no longer printed or stated [in the twentieth century], because nobody in the union supposes it necessary to state basic principles."[3] Those customs, principles, and rules composed what Selig Perlman called "Labor's own 'home grown' ideology."[4]

The ethical norms governing workplace behavior, whether they were explicitly codified or covertly expressed at a given time or place, thus provide our first clues to the meaning of class for nineteenth-century workers. My analysis of those clues, however, has not led me to agree with Perlman's dictum: "It was from the intellectual that the anti-capitalist influences in modern society emanated."[5] On the contrary, as labor re-

2. Henri de Man, *Joy in Work*, translated by Edan and Cedar Paul (London, 1929), 64.
3. Ethelbert Stewart, *Documentary History of the Early Organization of Printers* (U.S. Department of Commerce and Labor, Bulletin of the Bureau of Labor, No. 61, Washington, D.C., 1905), 859.
4. Selig Perlman, *A Theory of the Labor Movement* (New York, 1929), 6.
5. Ibid., 5.

former George E. McNeill wrote at the century's end, "The organization of laborers in Trades Unions recognizes the fact that mutualism is preferable to individualism."[6] That mutualism was the ethical seedbed for both the efforts of some workers to reform capitalism and the proposals of others to overthrow it. Even workers' reception and interpretation of social analyses and proposals that emanated from "intellectuals" can best be understood by reference to the workers' own codes of ethical behavior.

Nineteenth-century trade unions provide only a limited perspective on workers' codes and beliefs, however, because their adherents were usually from the ranks of craftsmen. In the two decades following the Civil War, trade-union activists endeavored simultaneously to organize members of their own crafts in defense of their wages and work rules and to act as the voice of the working class as a whole in a dialogue with bourgeois intellectuals and reformers concerning the future of America's republican institutions, a dialogue sometimes friendly but often acrimonious. Rarely could they succeed for long in the first task: Employers' resistance was all too often made effective by technological changes, periodic economic crises, and the arrival of new workers. And trade unionists' claims to be the voice of the producing classes were regularly mocked by politicians' firm grip on the votes of working-class constituencies and by angry protesting crowds of the working poor taking to the streets in defiance of the admonitions of labor organizations. Consequently, the work cultures of factory operatives and common laborers must be studied, as well as those of the skilled crafts, if the late-nineteenth-century working class is to be understood. The working lives of the operatives turn out to have been fashioned by their youth and by the socialization of the large numbers of women among those working youth. Examining their codes and solidarities carries us irresistibly into the neighborhoods. The working lives of laborers bore the stamp of their rural origins. Their exploration leads us into the relationship between the industrialized world and its rural periphery and into society's definitions of race and citizenship.

Craftsmen, operatives, and laborers alike were caught up, along with their employers, in a prolonged deflationary crisis between 1873 and 1897 that generated endemic conflict over wages and costs of production. Although workers' efforts to unify their own ranks during this conflict enjoyed only transitory success at best, their workplace, craft, and neigh-

6. George E. McNeill, "Philosophy of the Labor Movement," in Trades Council of New Haven, *Illustrated History of the Trades Council of New Haven* (New Haven, 1899), 212–13.

borhood solidarities presented formidable obstacles to business's goals and prompted industrialists to attempt reforms of both work relations and political life that might strengthen their hand. The increasingly militant assertiveness in many crafts made this quest for reform ever more urgent by the century's end, and the reorganization of business enterprise by the great merger movement made its realization possible.

At the dawn of the present century the practice of scientific management, which had long gestated in the American Society of Mechanical Engineers, gained widespread popularity among business executives and blended harmoniously with the ideals of "rationalization," "organization," "efficiency," and "science in the service of democracy" that dominated the public discourse of the time. The phrase "Drift and Mastery"[7] coined by the young Walter Lippmann captured the spirit in which business leaders who uprooted nineteenth-century working-class practices and codes celebrated their own reforms. But if employers' conflicts with craft practices had prepared them to welcome scientific management, their encounters with the rapidly expanding numbers of machine operatives led them to embrace personnel management as well. The role of the state also changed. Its task in industrial disputes during the earlier age of laissez-faire had been essentially one of repressing disorder and guaranteeing owners the use of their property without interference from protesting workers. In the new age of rationalized and consolidated enterprise, that repressive task remained important, but it was supplemented by the need to devise solutions. That undertaking politicized industrial conflict in the minds of all participants. It also prompted men of affairs to experiment with the National Civic Federation and then to marshal their forces behind the promise of the Rockefellers' Colorado Industrial Plan as formulas for industrial peace that would not inhibit the drive of business enterprises for efficiency and mastery within their own domain.

The labor movement assumed a new shape at the same time. With the abrupt quadrupling of union membership between 1897 and 1903, the American Federation of Labor (AFL) for the first time secured its place as the "House of Labor." During the previous decade and a half it had been, at best, one of several important centers of labor organizing. Most city trades assemblies had included union locals that bore no AFL affiliation, as well as those that were affiliated. Dual unionism had been not an offense against the labor movement but standard practice. Although many unions large and small continued to function independent of the AFL after 1900, and the Industrial Workers of the World openly chal-

7. Walter Lippmann, *Drift and Mastery: An Attempt to Diagnose the Current Unrest* (New York, 1914).

lenged its right to speak for America's workers, the federation not only dwarfed the independent organizations in size but also came to represent in the minds of most union activists the arbiter of what was or was not "bona fide" trade unionism. No government agency then determined what unions were to be certified, what bargaining units recognized, and what practices tolerated or banned. The federation claimed for itself authority to define legitimate union behavior, and it fiercely contested court injunctions and proposed legislation that threatened that claim.

Before the 1920s the house of labor had many mansions. Although most of its leading officers endorsed Samuel Gompers's vision of "pure and simple unionism," its ranks teemed with socialists, Catholic activists, single taxers, and philosophical anarchists. All of them agreed that their hopes of reshaping the American republic in accordance with the aspirations of its working class could best be achieved by working within labor's own, self-legitimizing federation. There were others who disagreed, believing the conservative hand of craft-union practice an intolerable impediment to the organizing of mass-production workers. After 1909, strikes and union membership grew rapidly both inside and outside the bounds of legitimacy defined by the AFL.

The tensions within and surrounding the federation were magnified by the outbreak of world war. Mobilization of the economy for war production locked the administrative structures of business and government tightly together, while full employment augmented workers' ability to win strikes and improve their terms of employment. Simultaneously, the temporary ascendancy of the Democratic Party in Washington had made it solicitous of working-class votes and spurred the formation of a labor bloc within the party. Workers of all types gained a new sense of power, and with it new (or newly articulated) desires. New styles of organization within the workplace, often energized by radicals, challenged the scientifically managed enterprise on its own turf and threatened the "bona fide" practices of craft unions at the same time. Between 1916 and 1922, when levels of strike participation soared far above those of any other period thus far in the country's history, workers' demands became too heady for the AFL or even the Socialist Party to contain and too menacing for business and the state to tolerate.

By the end of the depression of 1920–2, American workers' militancy had been deflated, trade unionism largely excluded from larger corporate enterprises, and the left wing of the workers' movement isolated from effective mass influence. Rationalization of business could then proceed with indispensable government support, and the very composition of the labor force could be subjected to federal management by the immigration-restriction laws. Although AFL membership had shrunk by a third be-

tween 1920 and 1923, the federation remained considerably larger than
it had been before the war. The battles through which it had passed,
however, had imposed a new orthodoxy on its counsels. Wartime demands for nationalization of industries, a six-hour day, government
guarantees of union rights, a labor party, and strikes to demand freedom
for political prisoners, never favored by Gompers, now disappeared from
the federation's proceedings altogether. Dissidents faced expulsion. The
federation program adopted in 1923 proclaimed a vision at once grandiose and timid, of workers gathered into unions as "the conscious organization of one of the most vital functional elements for enlightened
participation in a democracy of industry," and as a bulwark against "state
invasion of industrial life."[8] Despite the proud example of union-
management cooperation on the Baltimore and Ohio Railroad, however,
corporate executives remained convinced that they could organize the
cooperation of all "functional elements" and fend off "state invasion"
without the AFL's help.

Although American workers as a class had never become revolutionary
during this half century of struggle, they had attempted to give their social and political life a very different character from what confronted
them in the 1920s. Modern America had been created over its workers'
protests, even though every step in its formation had been influenced by
the activities, organizations, and proposals that had sprung from working-
class life. Moreover, the decade after 1923 was a remarkable hiatus in
the evolution of the labor movement itself. With strike activity falling
to an all-time low, the many workers radicalized by the war years isolated and able to influence only occasional struggles, and workers' aspirations turning inward upon family and ethnic ties, corporate mastery
of American life seemed secure. Those AFL officials who had once been
vociferous reformers now believed they had to bide their time until a
more favorable political climate would allow them to lead a union resurgence. As it turned out, when that time came, the petrified house of
labor split in two.

The history of American workers has not been a story of progressive
ascent from oppression to securely established rights, nor has it offered
us a past moment of democratic promise that was irretrievably snuffed
out by the consolidation of modern capitalism. Their movement has grown
only sporadically and through fierce struggles, been interrupted time and
again just when it seemed to reach flood tide, overwhelmed its foes only
to see them revive in new and more formidable shapes, and been forced

8. "Industry's Manifest Duty," in American Federation of Labor, *History, Encyclopedia, Reference Book* (2 vols., Washington, D.C., 1919, 1924), II, 99.

to reassess what it thought it had already accomplished and begin again. The taproot of its resilience has been the workers' daily experience and the solidarities nurtured by that experience, which have at best encompassed a lush variety of beliefs, loyalties, and activities within a common commitment to democratic direction of the country's economic and political life. The becalmed and beleaguered trade unions of the 1920s had made their peace with a most undemocratic America, one whose economic underpinnings were soon to give way. When working-class activists sought a path out of the depression of the 1930s, they revoked that settlement, reopened controversy over what had been considered accomplished, and began to organize anew on the basis of the ways America's heterogeneous working people actually experienced industrial life.

1

The manager's brain under the workman's cap

The regular Saturday-night meeting of Lodge No. 11 of the Rollers, Roughers, Catchers and Hookers Union stirred with excitement on June 27, 1874. There had been no work for its members since mid-April, when they had finished rolling a few thousand tons of iron rails for which they had contracted with their employer, the Columbus Rolling Mill Company, in January. Through two months of unemployment, between eleven and twenty-six of the members (who had once numbered fifty-two) had faithfully appeared at the weekly meetings and paid not only their dues but also a two-dollar weekly assessment to aid their brothers who were on strike against the giant Cambria Iron Works in Johnstown, Pennsylvania. Only Daniel Childs had refused to pay, protesting, "I don't believe in any Society that is going to take half a man earns to keep it up." He had been expelled.[1]

That evening a committee of four members had brought before the meeting a report of utmost importance. They had met with superintendent Christopher Lewis of the rolling mill to discuss a contract for what was described in the lodge's minutes as "the new mode of working: namely Reheating." After sections of iron "muck bar" had been heated in gas-fired soaking pits under the watchful eyes of experienced heaters, they would be wheeled on buggies to the rolling mills on which these workers would fashion them into rails. Handling the bars with large tongs, as they were forced back and forth through the rolls a dozen or more times (with occasional trips back to the pits for further heating), would require full crews of thirteen men, and the superintendent had offered the men $1.13 per ton to do the work.

1. Lodge No. 11, Rollers, Roughers, Catchers and Hookers Union, Minute Book (July 14, 1873–April 28, 1876), January 26, April 18, May 30, June 21, June 27, 1874, in William Martin Papers, University of Pittsburgh. The quotation is from May 30, 1874. For strike assessments, see Rollers, Roughers, Catchers and Hookers Union of the United States, Grand Lodge Cash Book (1874), 57–81.

The minutes of the discussion that followed that report reveal a great deal about work relations in late-nineteenth-century heavy industry. The union members soon accepted the company's offer (that was no season to be choosy about possible work) and turned to the major task of dividing up the tonnage rate of $1.13 among themselves. Each worker stated his own price. When those prices were added up, they produced a total that was 3¾ cents higher than the company's tonnage offer. By careful revision of the rates for the buggymen, whose work was to transport the materials to and from the rolls, a complete scale was finally devised. The roller, who adjusted the space between the middle roll and those below and above it for each successive pass and also checked the product's size and shape as it developed, was to receive 19¼ cents per ton, and the rougher down, who helped him hurl the hot bars into the mill's front end, got 10 cents. The two men on the other side of the rolls, who caught the emerging bar and forced it back through the upper set of rolls, were the catcher, who got 9 cents, and the rougher up, who earned 13. The hookers, who helped move the bars to alignment before the proper grooves on the rolls, were to earn 8½ cents each. The runout hooker and the two runback buggymen, who moved bars about off the mill, got only 5 cents apiece, but more was to go to the gang buggyman and his helper, whose task it was to bring the heated blooms into position to be rolled. They were accorded 13¾ cents, to be divided between themselves.[2]

Thus, the team of men who performed the work also devised the payroll structure in open meeting, where everyone voted. It was far from egalitarian: The highest pay was almost four times the lowest. It is also evident that the lodge was kept informed about wage scales elsewhere in the industry by regular correspondence with other lodges, by transfer of new members from other localities, and by its practice of sending observers to conventions of rail manufacturers.[3] Thus, both the customs of the trade and market forces shaped the claim that each worker made for his own part of the tonnage rate. Moreover, the plant superintendent did intervene in the process, after the meeting at which the scale had been adopted. He persuaded a union committee to raise the rate for the general buggyman and his helper to 8 cents apiece, by taking ¼ cent from the rougher up and each of the hookers and ¾ cent from the rougher down. At a union meeting the next night, the hookers protested against the

2. Lodge No. 11 Minute Book, June 27, 1874. On the development and operation of three-high rolls, see Robert W. Hunt, "The Evolution of American Rolling Mills," *Transactions of the American Society of Mechanical Engineers*, 13 (1892), 47–51.
3. Lodge No. 11 Minute Book, September 6, 1873, November 15, 1873, January 13, 24, 26, 1874.

change, but they finally yielded and allowed the meeting's consent to the new scale to be unanimous.[4]

In effect, the Columbus iron rollers had subcontracted the entire job from their employer. Unlike many other subcontracting workers of that time, however, they had taken the contract as a group, not as individuals, and they had decided collectively on the terms of the arrangement. That this was their regular practice is evident from earlier agreements with the company by which tonnage rates had been pegged to the fluctuating selling price of rails (a "sliding scale" of wages), and the company had agreed to consult with union committees on the terms of any new orders it undertook.[5] Moreover, at union meetings the workers fixed the limit for a day's work at six rounds on the rolls and allocated overtime and special work assignments by group decision. At a meeting in March 1875, for example, Henry Meyers claimed the right as the oldest hand to any extra turns at hooking that might come open. His assertion precipitated a general discussion of the problem. The lodge president, David Plant, declared that brother Meyers had forfeited claim to extra turns "on account of drinking," which led him to neglect his regular work. Controversy among the hookers as to who should "take the tongs" on "standing turns" and for "rough and tumble hooking" culminated in a general agreement to raise the hookers' share of tonnage rates during the hot summer months and to deputize a committee of hookers to devise a plan of job allocation, subject to the approval of the whole lodge at its next meeting.[6]

The roller himself was a figure of great authority. He both directed the highly coordinated team effort involved in rolling iron rails and customarily hired and promoted his helpers. Nevertheless, the constitution of the roll-hands union, to which Lodge No. 11 was affiliated, specified that "all workmen in the mill who are capable of working around the rolls be taken into the union."[7] Even its very exclusive rival, the Associated Brotherhood of Iron Heaters, Rollers and Roughers, had admitted at least roughers and catchers to the fraternity by 1876.[8] Moreover, the Amalgamated Association of Iron and Steel Workers, into which both unions

4. Ibid., June 30, 1874.
5. Ibid., January 26, 1874. Inside subcontracting will be discussed in Chapter 4.
6. Lodge No. 11 Minute Book, March 22, 27, 1874.
7. Hunt, "American Rolling Mills"; John H. Ashworth, *The Helper and American Trade Unions* (Johns Hopkins University Studies in Historical and Political Science, Series XXXIII, No. 3, Baltimore, 1915), 90.
8. Associated Brotherhood of Iron and Steel Heaters, Rollers and Roughers of the United States, "Report on Communications. The Year's Term having closed July 10th 1875" (hereafter cited as Heaters' Correspondence), April 11, 1876.

merged in 1876, specified in its constitution that, subject to such local rules as may govern "the hiring of standard turn men," rollers and heaters "having charge of trains of rolls or furnaces shall be compelled to give the next job in line of promotion to the oldest hand, provided he is a member in good standing of the association."[9]

What is evident, therefore, is that both the management of the production process and the craft union of the workers rested on the same social basis. Rolling iron or steel was a collective operation that involved then, as it does now, a highly coordinated team effort.[10] Each person toiling in the heat and sparks around the monstrous machinery had to work in close harmony with all the others in order to avoid disaster, let alone to make money. The machinery belonged to a company, which sold the workers' output for its own profit in intensely competitive markets. To survive and grow within that market, a company was obliged not only to hold its labor costs as low as possible but also to introduce new machinery to raise output and eliminate workers. By the end of the century, lifting tables, hydraulic pushers, power-operated tables, and other innovations would reduce the average size of a rolling-mill crew to only five men, mainly by eliminating hookers and buggymen.[11] Yet the roller of 1874 was not a supervisory worker – not a part of management, as his twentieth-century counterpart would be.[12] He was an inside contractor, and often a prominent member of a union that regulated the terms under which work was subcontracted from the employer by collective decisions of the workers involved, reached in open meetings. The discipline their job required was self-discipline.

The meetings of Lodge No. 11 usually took place on Saturday evenings, following a half-day's work, as was the case with most unions of ironworkers and steelworkers during the 1870s and 1880s. They were small because the lodges were small, not because members were absent, and they were conducted with decorum appropriate to the self-discipline and responsibilities of the workers. Each new candidate for membership had to be personally approved by the entire lodge, unless he held a withdrawal card from another lodge in the same union. The rules of order were painstakingly followed until the minutes could record that the gathering finally "by motion Closed in Peace and Harmony" to meet again two weeks later. A New Year's Eve ball, arranged for the entertainment

9.   John A. Fitch, *The Steel Workers* (New York, 1911), 283.
10. On teamwork in today's steel rolling, see William Kornblum, *Blue Collar Community* (Chicago, 1974), 37–47.
11. Hunt, "American Rolling Mills," 54–60; Steven R. Cohen, "Steelworkers Rethink the Homestead Strike of 1892," *Pennsylvania History*, 48 (April 1981), 170.
12. See the discussion of the sequel to the Homestead strike later in this chapter.

of delegates to the roll-hands union's national convention, when it met in Columbus, was planned with the same precision. Thirty dances were scheduled: twenty square and ten round. Committee members sported red, white, or blue roses, depending on their assignments. And the lodge resolved that any member

> ... Presenting himself at the Ball in Such a condition as Be a hinderance or a nuicense to the guests Who may Be Preasant Shall Be fined the Sum of 5 Dollars ... and Should any Party or Parties conduct themselves in any improper way [they] Shall upon the Refunding of there money Be expelled from the Room.[13]

The very men who appear here managing collectively the productive operations of the rolling mill, regulating relations among themselves, and arranging their own social affairs were also pioneers of the late-nineteenth-century labor movement. David Plant, their president, soon became national head of the roll-hands union and was a prime mover in bringing about the formation of the Amalgamated Association of Iron and Steel Workers in 1876. William Martin, a member since September 1873, became the first secretary of the Amalgamated Association and, ten years later, a member of the Executive Council of the AFL.[14] The Columbus lodge not only adopted wage scales and job allocations but also resolved to build a "thorough Unification of Labor" in order to fend off the "recent alarming onslaughts" on their conditions by the iron masters and "to compete with the Aggression of Combined Capital."[15]

What this glimpse into the records of the Columbus iron-rollers union reveals is that within the context of mechanized industry and hired wage labor, some skilled craftsmen exercised an impressive degree of collective control over the specific productive tasks in which they were engaged and the human relations involved in the performance of those tasks, and these same workers stamped their own distinctive mark on the character of the labor movement of the age. They exercised this control because they fought for it, and their position in that struggle drew strength from the workers' functional autonomy on the job, from the group ethical code that they developed around their work relations, and from the organizations they created for themselves in order to protect their interests and values.[16]

---

13. Lodge No. 11 Minute Book, December 23, 1873.
14. John Jarrett, "The Story of the Iron Workers," in George E. McNeill, ed., *The Labor Movement: The Problem of To-Day* (New York, 1887), 281, 285. For proceedings of the merger convention to form the Amalgamated Association, see *National Labor Tribune*, August 5, 12, 1876.
15. Lodge No. 11 Minute Book, July 20, 1874.
16. See David Montgomery, "Workers' Control of Machine Production in the Nineteenth Century," *Labor History*, 17 (Fall 1976), 485–509; Benson Soffer,

These three aspects of their struggle (the autonomy, the code, and the organizations) deserve closer examination.

Four groups of skilled workers joined forces to create the Amalgamated Association of Iron and Steel Workers in 1876: rollers, puddlers, heaters, and nailers. The workers in all four crafts enjoyed broad autonomy in the direction of their own work and that of their helpers. Their work required technical knowledge, judgment, stamina, and strength. Although there was no apprenticeship in any of the trades, workers acquired their knowledge of the highly variable qualities of hot or molten iron (no two charges were exactly alike) by assisting experienced craftsmen. As James Davis, a puddler who later became Warren Harding's secretary of labor, described his experience of the 1890s in Sharon, Pennsylvania, "None of us ever went to school and learned the chemistry of it from books. We learned the trick by doing it, standing with our faces in the scorching heat while our hands puddled the metal in its glaring bath."[17]

Puddlers were far more numerous than any other type of craftsmen in the industry. For example, in 1875 at the Pittsburgh Forge and Iron Company of Allegheny, Pennsylvania, the iron needed to supply three trains of rolls was supplied by fifteen puddling furnaces running two shifts, and manned by thirty puddlers and thirty helpers.[18] The process was a second step in the refining of the pig iron produced by blast furnaces, and it was necessary in order to make good wrought iron out of most ores – all but the very finest iron ores. It was used in virtually all American iron production.[19] "Pigs" were melted in the hearth of a furnace and stirred with a long iron rod (a "rabble") to keep little glowing spikes of pure iron, which appeared atop the molten froth of slag, moving to the bottom and to knead them there into a pasty mass that slowly "came to nature." After the slag, which contained most of the impurities that had risen to the top, had been poured off the furnace, the puddler shaped the spongy mass remaining into two or three balls of equal size (some 200 pounds apiece, which he judged by eye). These balls were then removed by tongs and a chain hoist from the furnace and put through a squeezer, to force out most of the surplus slag from the "blooms," which were subse-

"A Theory of Trade Union Development: The Role of the 'Autonomous' Workman," *Labor History,* 1 (Spring 1960), 141–63.

17.   James J. Davis, *The Iron Puddler: My Life in the Rolling Mills and What Came of It* (Indianapolis, 1922), 91.

18.   John W. Bennett, "The Iron Workers of Woods Run and Johnstown: The Union Era" (unpublished Ph.D. diss., University of Pittsburgh, 1977), 10.

19.   Peter Temin, *Iron and Steel in Nineteenth Century America: An Economic Inquiry* (Cambridge, Mass., 1964), 101.

quently rolled into flat sections known as "muck bar."[20] That was the product sent forward to the heaters, rollers, and nailers, who fashioned the mill's finished products from it.

Despite persistent efforts of mill owners to reduce their dependence on puddlers by doubling up furnaces, installing mechanical rabbles, and other equally futile innovations, masters and metallurgists alike were forced to agree with the labor paper that boasted that all these devices "lacked one feature of the human puddler – brains."[21] And muck balls of uniform size and consistency, which would later pass through the rolls without breaking, could not be created without brains. The expansion of the nation's production, therefore, meant a rapid and steady increase in the number of puddlers. B. F. Jones reported that his American Iron Works employed 158 puddlers and an equal number of helpers in 1884 (one-tenth of his total force).[22]

As late as the 1890s, when James Davis learned the trade in Sharon, the rights to puddling furnaces were often passed from father to son. Puddlers hired and trained their own helpers and told them what to do: stoking the furnace, pouring off the impurities, helping lift out the muck balls, and spelling the puddler during the arduous task of working the rabble through the blistering heat of the furnace's door.[23] In return for his efforts, the helper received a portion of the puddler's earnings, a portion that union practice had fixed at one-third plus 5 percent by the end of the 1870s. The close working relationship that was necessary between the two men made the privilege of selecting his own helper precious to the craftsman. The British practice of hiring two helpers was seldom duplicated in America except by older workers. Puddlers, who were considered "old at forty," prolonged their days at this man-killing trade at

20. Bennett, "Iron Workers," 2–3; Davis, *Iron Puddler,* 106–12. "Boiling" was a variant of puddling in which the molten cinder was kept on top of the iron, rather than being poured off as it formed, thus changing the oxidation process. For the purposes of this study, puddling and boiling are used interchangeably, but the reader will notice reference to both processes in the workers' poetry.
21. *National Labor Tribune,* August 26, 1882, quoted in Bennett, "Iron Workers," 12.
22. Benjamin Franklin Jones, diary (unpublished), January 7, 1885. For an outsider's impressions of puddling on the eve of the Civil War, see Rebecca Harding Davis, "Life in the Iron Mills," *Atlantic Monthly,* 7 (April 1861), 430–51.
23. Davis, *Iron Puddler,* 106–12; "Journal of Working of Gas Puddling Furnaces," *Bulletin of American Iron and Steel Association,* 1 (June 26, 1867), 342–3.

the expense of their earnings, by dividing their tonnage with yet a third man or boy. It was just such an older puddler who initiated the twelve-year-old Davis into the art of puddling in the 1890s.[24]

Under these conditions, a puddler could treat his furnace as his personal domain. Although Davis had left the trade by 1900 because his father had not been ready to give up his furnace, the young man used to take over his father's furnace during the afternoons of his visits home, allowing the elder Davis some time off.[25] Similarly, nailers, who tended many cutting and shaping machines at once, taught newcomers the trade by letting them run some of their machines. Because nailers were paid according to the number of machines they tended, the trainees for whom they made such sacrifices were usually relatives.[26] Often the trainee would pay the journeyman a fee to compensate for the latter's lost earnings. In general, however, puddlers' helpers were in such a good position to learn the trade while they worked that many rose to puddlers' jobs. In fact, the rapid multiplication of puddling furnaces between the 1860s and the 1880s brought about a dramatic shift in the ethnic composition of the craft: from English and Welsh puddlers with Irish helpers in the 1860s to numerous Irish-Americans at all levels in the 1880s.[27]

Although the autonomy of the puddlers in the operation of their fur-

24.   On helpers' pay, see B. F. Jones's diary, May 23, 1877; Jesse S. Robinson, *The Amalgamated Association of Iron, Steel and Tin Workers* (Johns Hopkins University Studies in Historical and Political Science, Series XXXVIII, No. 2, Baltimore, 1920), 13, 132–3; Davis, *Iron Puddler*, 85, 92–3. On morbidity and mortality among puddlers in the United States and Europe, see Mary Ellen Freifeld, "The Emergence of the American Working Classes: The Roots of Division, 1865–1885" (unpublished Ph.D. diss., New York University, 1980), 461; Peter N. Stearns, *Lives of Labor: Work in a Maturing Industrial Society* (New York, 1975), 61–4. The Sharon Mills, where Davis worked, must have run nonunion at the time, because Amalgamated Association rules prohibited a puddler from hiring a helper under fifteen years of age and prescribed a charge 50 pounds lighter than the 600 pounds described by Davis. See Fitch, *Steel Workers*, 283.

25.   Davis, *Iron Puddler*, 227.

26.   B. F. Jones's diary, November 22, 1876; Margaret Johnston to John Johnston, December 8, 1856 (Public Record Office of Northern Ireland, file D 1047/2); U.S. Commissioner of Labor, Thirteenth Annual Report, *Hand and Machine Labor* (2 vols., Washington, D.C., 1899), II, 1322–3.

27.   No quantitative data on ethnic composition in the iron trades are available, but for suggestive discussions, see Bennett, "Iron Workers," Chapters 3 and 4; Bruce Laurie, Theodore Herschberg, and George Alter, "Immigrants and Social History: The Philadelphia Experience, 1850–1880," *Journal of Social History*, 9 (Winter 1976), 219–67.

naces and in the selection and direction of their helpers provides an indispensable clue to their social behavior (as does that of the rollers, heaters, and nailers), it does not by any means offer a full explanation. Around
their autonomous work the craftsmen wove an ethical code to govern
their own conduct, and that code clashed at many points with both the
interests of the iron masters and the strictures of acquisitive individualism. The code governed the craftsmen's conduct toward their fellow
workers and toward their bosses. Its content was clearly manifested in
the strike issues and union work rules of the late nineteenth century.
Because temptations and inducements for craftsmen to violate its norms
were ever present, workers applied severe sanctions to those of their number
who did so.

The most important component of this code was the "stint." As was
the case with virtually every other craft in the late nineteenth century,
workers in the skilled iron trades made their own collective definitions of
a reasonable day's work.[28] Because iron puddlers, heaters, and rollers all
labored by the "heat" or "charge," and because the sometimes perverse
nature of iron could lead to considerable variability in the length of time
required for a single heat, these craftsmen were less concerned to fix the
number of hours of labor in a working day than they were to fix the
number of heats and the quantity of iron to be handled per heat. As
unions developed, they enacted work rules to regulate these limits. What
is important to notice is that these rules were not negotiated with the
employers, but were unilaterally adopted by the workers. Each union
adherent was bound by his oath of membership not to violate these norms.
In the language of the labor movement, work rules were "legislated" by
the union. He who upheld them in his daily work was "honorable" or
"manly." He who exceeded the stints was a "hog," a "rooter," a "chaser,"
a "blackleg," a "swift," or a "boss's pet."[29] Unlimited output, the craftsmen argued, led to irregular employment, slashed piece rates, drink, and
debauchery. Rationally restricted output reflected "unselfish brotherhood," personal dignity, and "cultivation of the mind."[30]

Abram Hewitt testified in 1867 that the puddlers in his large New
Jersey works, who apparently were not unionized, had decided that a
puddler should charge his furnace with no more than 450 pounds of iron

28. On stints in other trades, see Montgomery, "Workers' Control of Machine
    Production," 489–494, and see Chapter 4.
29. U.S. Commissioner of Labor, *Eleventh Special Report, Regulation and Re-
    striction of Output* (Washington, D.C., 1904), 18.
30. See, e.g., "What One Trade Has Done," *John Swinton's Paper*, March 23,
    1884; Bryan D. Palmer, *A Culture in Conflict: Skilled Workers and Indus-
    trial Capitalism in Hamilton, Ontario, 1860–1914* (Montreal, 1979).

at a time, work no more than three charges per turn (or half day), and work no more than eleven turns per week ($5\frac{1}{2}$ days).[31] That was no easy pace: An account of puddling in England at the same time described the same number of charges, but with 420 pounds maximum weight and two helpers (rather than one, as in America).[32] The journalist James Parton described Pittsburgh's "aristocracy" of puddlers and rollers, "performing labors so severe that they have to stop, now and then, in summer, take off their boots, and *pour the perspiration out of them.*"[33] By 1870, the puddlers' union, the Sons of Vulcan, had fixed the daily stint at five charges of 550 pounds each. The same standard was still to be found in the Special Rules of the Amalgamated Association of Iron and Steel Workers forty years later, although many exceptions were allowed for various types of improved furnaces.[34]

Rollers handled their stint in the manner of the men at Columbus. Because heating pits before the mid-1880s could prepare only one batch of iron at a time (putting in cold iron would spoil the temperature control for the hot bar already in the pit), rolling crews enjoyed a rest from their ferocious exertions between the time they finished one heat and the time the next was ready for them. As new furnaces increased the sizes of heats and new rolling mills were able to handle ever larger blooms, union legislation reduced the number of heats per day. In the Carnegie works, just before the union was defeated in 1892, rollers worked from 5 A.M. to about 2 P.M., with one heat before breakfast, two between breakfast and dinner, and a final heat before going home. Within fifteen years after the union's defeat at Homestead, the company had tripled its output through more and larger heats and thus a much longer working day.[35]

The stint, however, was not the whole of the craftsmen's ethical code. Equally important, in the language of the Sons of Vulcan constitution, was the provision that "every member conduct themselves in a proper

31. United Kingdom, Parliament, *Second Report of the Commissioners Appointed to Inquire into the Organization and Rules of Trade Unions and Other Associations* (Parliamentary Sessional Papers, 1867, xxxii, c3893, hereafter cited as *Royal Comm. on Trade Unions*), 4–6.
32. *Bulletin of the American Iron and Steel Association*, 1 (June 26, 1867), 342–3.
33. James Parton, "Pittsburgh," *Atlantic Monthly*, 21 (January 1868), 33.
34. Fitch, *Steel Workers*, 282–3. Francis G. Couvares argues that the five-heat day was won during the 1880s: "Work, Leisure, and Reform in Pittsburgh: The Transformation of an Urban Culture, 1860–1920" (unpublished Ph.D. diss., University of Michigan, 1980), 18–19.
35. Cohen, "Steelworkers Rethink," 171.

manner toward each other."[36] This meant that workers would support each other's grievances, contribute to special solicitations for a disabled brother or for the widow of a dead brother (the Amalgamated never adopted a union insurance fund in the nineteenth century), "not tolerate any man holding more than one job," proclaim any bad iron that a union member could not work up within specified times a "grievance," and refrain from "undermining or conniving" at a brother's job.[37]

Often this obligation caused disputes with employers over whose orders and whose code of conduct were to prevail in the mill. During the depression years 1874 to 1876, three strikes on the records of the roll-hands union, three heaters' strikes, and sixteen strikes by the Vulcans involved "administration of the works," and such strikes graphically illustrate the ethical dimension of the struggle for control on the job.[38] For example, the William Penn Lodge of the heaters' union reported to the "Grand Recording Secretary" in February 1875 that a wage dispute had escalated into a battle over the life of the union at a Philadelphia mill. A three-week strike over the scale for a new job, which had earned rollers only $1.80 for eleven hours of work, had ended in a raise for the workers. But within a few days of the resumption of work, the report continued, a guide-mill roller named Springman was discharged "for dissatisfaction in regard to his management of the mill and a quarrel he has had with the Sup^td at the time of the strike." Although Springman packed his tools, "not wishing to stay where he was not wanted," his workmates soon learned that while the strike had still been in progress, one of their number (named Hannigan) had "undermined" Springman with the superintendent and been promised Springman's job. Furious, the union members expelled Hannigan and, for good measure, a friend who had defended him, then struck the mill, refusing to work by the side of such delinquents.[39]

Three issues had been at stake here: Springman's authority over "his" train of rolls, Hannigan's unconscionable behavior, and the work group's discipline against the deviant. On all three points they disputed not only their employer's pretensions to control the use of his property but also the related belief of such leading ideologues of the age as E. L. Godkin that "when a man agrees to sell his labor, he agrees by implication to sell

36. Sons of Vulcan, *Constitution and By-Laws of the Puddlers and Boilers' Union* (Pittsburgh, 1866), Article VI, Section 1.
37. Fitch, *Steel Workers*, 258–96.
38. McNeill, *Labor Movement*, 307; Heaters' Correspondence, passim; Rollers, Roughers, Catchers and Hookers, Grand Lodge Cash Book.
39. Heaters' Correspondence, February 25, 1875.

his moral and social independence."[40] Disputes arising around such issues were invariably fierce and often ended in defeat for the workers.
Thus, a letter to the same Grand Recording Secretary from the heaters'
lodge in Mountain City, Maryland, not five months later, related that a
new puddler, named "three fingered Bill" Williams, had recently been
hired. On checking his background in Troy, New York, the puddlers
learned that he was "a notorious Scoundrel [and] Black Lege." When a
puddlers' committee approached the superintendent to protest the man's
presence, the boss replied that before he would fire Williams, "He would
Discharge the committee & all Puddlers first." Knowing that times were
hard and the company already had a large stack of muck bar on hand
for rolling, the puddlers "Dampered" the case while they approached the
heaters and rollers to learn if the latter would "Stand By them." The
upshot was that all walked out together. Six months later another letter
reached the secretary from Mountain City bearing the sad news that the
strikers had lost their battle, and the mill was working nonunion. Nevertheless, wrote the correspondent, the union members were "among the
Living yet" and "had a few good Brothers Left – But Idle two thirds of
the time."[41]

One clear sign that union standards and the craftsmen's ethical code
had been vanquished at any particular moment was the flourishing of
inside subcontracting by individual workers. There was no way that late-
nineteenth-century employers in the iron industry could dispense with
the functional autonomy of the craftsmen, but they could make use of it
as a managerial instrument, provided they could induce a sufficient number of craftsmen to place their own individual material advantage above
every other consideration. The most common technique was to allow or
request an individual craftsman to contract with the company for the
entire output of several furnaces or trains of rolls (or of one furnace on
two or three shifts), then to hire his own helpers as cheaply as possible.
The subcontractor thus combined his own toil with general supervision
of others' work and derived his income from the margin between his
wage bill and the tonnage payment he received from the company.

So widespread was this practice that its discussion must be postponed
until such time as its manifestations in many different industries can be
examined simultaneously.[42] Suffice it to say that the Amalgamated As-

40. [E. L. Godkin], "The Labor Crisis," *North American Review*, 105 (July
    1867), 186.
41. Heaters' Correspondence, July 15, 24, 1875; January 3, 1876.
42. For a thorough discussion of inside contracting, with an interpretation dif-
    ferent from mine, see Dan Clawson, *Bureaucracy and the Labor Process:
    The Transformation of U.S. Industry, 1860–1920* (New York, 1980).

sociation of Iron and Steel Workers and its predecessors fought a running battle against inside subcontracting from the 1860s to the early twentieth century. President Joseph Bishop denounced those puddlers who hired "green men" at less than the standard helper's scale, forcing "men who have grown grey in the business . . . into idleness and want simply because other men are too greedy and too selfish to pay them full wages."[43] At its second convention, the Amalgamated Association decreed that it would "not tolerate any member holding more than one job. One furnace, one train of rolls, to constitute one job, and where practicable members are expected to enforce this rule."[44] The very wording of the rule, however, revealed the persistence of the practice and the difficulty of stamping it out. A union vice-president, denouncing "Jim Grabs" among the workers in 1880, could ask, "Is it right for a roller to have three or four sets of rolls, hire men by the day to work them, while he gets the benefit from the rolls?" But not until seven years later did the Amalgamated feel strong enough to stigmatize any such subcontractor as a "blacksheep" and decree his presence in the mill legal cause for a strike.[45]

During the long depression of the 1870s, some rolling mills, faced with imminent bankruptcy if they could not find an immediate way to reduce costs, actually subcontracted the entire operation of their mills to their workers collectively. The practice was especially common in Ohio, where mills in Bellaire, Bridgeport, Ashtabula, Girard, Niles, Sharon, and Hubard leased their operations to their employees, on the condition that the company could withhold 20 percent of the year's earnings until the end of the year, to be paid to the workers only if the ledgers showed a net profit. Although John Jarrett of the Amalgamated Association denounced the plan as a simple wage cut, it was revived in Ohio during the crisis of 1883–4 and was widely used during the depression of the 1890s.[46]

In general, however, the Amalgamated Association waxed strong during the economic boom of 1878–82 in the iron-rolling mills between Pittsburgh and St. Louis. East of the Appalachians, where the largest iron mills were to be found before 1880 (especially in Trenton, Phoenixville, Bethlehem, Danville, Steelton, and Johnstown), trade unionism had been snuffed out during the 1870s depression and never revived until World War I. Many of those mills coupled wrought-iron production with Bessemer steel production, and even in the Midwest, as John Jarrett wrote

43. Amalgamated Association, *Proceedings* (1878), 132, quoted in Freifeld, "Emergence," 444.
44. Bennett, "Iron Workers," 35.
45. Amalgamated Association, *Proceedings* (1880), 414, quoted in Freifeld, "Emergence," 447; Fitch, *Steel Workers*, 98–100.
46. Freifeld, "Emergence," 580–90.

in 1887, the giant steel mill had brought with it "complete subjugation of labor."[47]

Workers' control: the craftsmen's style

The depression of the 1870s was a watershed in the development of craft unionism among ironworkers and steelworkers. As we have seen, the union rules that codified craftsmen's norms concerning the stint and "manly conduct" toward one's boss and toward one another did not run back to time immemorial but, rather, had been forged in the fire of conflict during the depression of the 1870s. They represented new collective efforts to defend the autonomy and dignity of the craftsman against the growing power of the company. The large eastern mills had proved too big to defeat. As early as 1866, the country's largest manufacturing establishment, the Cambria Iron Works of Johnstown, had denied its hundred or so puddlers authority to hire their own helpers, and then defeated them when they struck over wages. Six years later, visitors found Cambria's puddlers unaware even of the tonnage rate at which they were being paid, and afraid to ask. When they did re-form their union and mount a desperate strike, along with the mill's other workers, in 1874, they went down to such total defeat that only those who pledged never again to join a union were even considered for reemployment.[48]

Union members elsewhere were faced with continual wage cuts after 1873, and such reductions were the most frequent causes of strikes until 1878. Most commonly, a company that had been closed a month or more for lack of work would try to reopen a mill at tonnage rates less than those at which the men had last worked. Union records reveal seven such strikes by the heaters, three by roll hands, and nearly eighty by the Sons of Vulcan, including a huge strike in Pittsburgh, between 1873 and the formation of the Amalgamated Association in 1876.[49] Most of them lasted about two weeks and ended in compromise settlements. A few ended with the companies rehiring only those who renounced their union. All of them spurred on the efforts to amalgamate the industry's craft unions. A poem in the *National Labor Tribune* captured the new spirit of the iron and steel craftsmen. The poet must have been Welsh, for he modeled his poem on the rousing battle song "Men of Harlech":

47. McNeill, *Labor Movement,* 309.
48. Bennett, "Iron Workers," 15–35, 160–2; Herbert G. Gutman, "Two Lockouts in Pennsylvania, 1873–1874," *Pennsylvania Magazine of History and Biography,* 83 (July 1959), 307–26.
49. See footnote 38 for sources on the strikes of 1870s.

> Rouse, ye noble sons of Labor,
> And protect your country's honor
> Who with bone, and brain, and fibre,
>   Make the nation's wealth.
>
> Lusty lads with souls of fire,
> Gallant sons of noble sire,
> Lend your voice and raise your banner,
>   Battle for the right.
>
> Heater, roller, rougher,
> Catcher, puddler, helper,
> All unite and join the fight
> And might (for right) encounter;
> In the name of truth and justice
> Stem the tide of evil practice
> Mammon's sordid might and avarice,
>   Our land from ruin save.[50]

Amalgamation! With all crafts standing together, strikes could be won, wages held high, and the workers' code of conduct enforced. More than that, as the *National Labor Tribune* editorialized on the occasion of the new union's founding convention,

> The great aim of our amalgamation is to render strikes and lockouts, unnecessary and impossible. That will be done by rendering it impossible to make a break in our ranks. We have been driven into strikes merely because we had a large element who would give their labor away for less than it is worth.[51]

In search of this goal, the militants of the new union battled relentlessly against craft jealousies and against lodges that excluded or slighted helpers. To the original quadrumvirate of puddlers, heaters, rollers, and nailers they added new crafts year by year – spike makers, hammermen, roll turners, annealers, picklers, wire drawers, spring makers, axle turners, water tenders, shearmen, Bessemer chargers, vesselmen and spiegel makers, and so on – until by 1891 the constitution simply solicited "all men working in and around Rolling Mills, Steel works, Nail, Tack, Spike, Bolt and Nut factories, Pipe mills, and all works run in connection with the same, except laborers, the latter to be admitted at the discretion of the Subordinate lodge to which application is made for membership."[52]

---

50. *National Labor Tribune,* March 30, 1878. The poem is reproduced in Freifeld, "Emergence," 453–4.
51. *National Labor Tribune,* August 12, 1876.
52. Amalgamated Association of Iron and Steel Workers, *Constitution* (Pittsburgh, 1891), Article I, Section 1. On the earlier detailed eligibility list, see Amalgamated Association, *Proceedings* (1882), 968. The active role of union

During the 1880s, the effort to consolidate workers' strength through the route of amalgamation was rapidly made both more urgent and more difficult in two interrelated ways. The first is suggested by the new union's noteworthy exclusion: "except laborers." In iron and steel mills this referred to the large numbers of workers who were employed by the day or by the hour to carry materials about, shovel ores, clean up, stack finished goods or load them for shipment, or perform other types of indirect gang labor. Unlike the craftsmen, they were not engaged directly in "making" iron and steel, and they were not paid by the ton. They were ancillary, but indispensable. The problem with their omission was twofold. First, as new iron and steel technology allowed smaller production crews to produce constantly more output, the proportion of the labor force who were common laborers grew rapidly. In contrast to a large iron mill of 1877, where only 76 employees out of 380 (or 20%) were laborers, in an integrated steel mill of 1887 with 2,426 workers, 850 (or 35%) were laborers, and another 272 boys. No union could safely ignore such a presence in the workplace it hoped to control.

Common laborers engaged in numerous strikes during the late nineteenth century, sometimes on their own initiative and sometimes organizing on their own behalf after the craftsmen had struck and thrown them out of work. During their heyday (1886–7), the Knights of Labor formed many local assemblies of laborers in iron and steel mills. As the struggle over the very existence of unions in steel mills grew in intensity between 1887 and 1892, some lodges of the union also opened their doors to laborers. But such developments were rare. The Amalgamated Association's concern was with the wage scales and work rules for the "tonnage men" – the skilled trades and their helpers.[53]

Second, and more fundamental, the strong arms and backs that performed the mill's laboring chores belonged to men whose backgrounds were very different from those of the craftsmen. They were overwhelmingly of rural origin. In the large eastern mills, such as the Cambria works, Lackawanna Steel, and the Pennsylvania Steel Company, they were mostly farm lads from the Pennsylvania countryside around 1880. In the South, where most mills had been set in motion by immigrant craftsmen, furnace laborers were 90 percent Afro-Americans, as were more than one-third of the rolling-mill laborers by the 1890s. By the mid-1880s, many

militants in the struggle for amalgamation is a central theme of Bennett, "Iron Workers."

53. Andrea Graziosi, "Common Laborers, Unskilled Workers: 1890–1915," *Labor History*, 22 (Fall 1981), 515; Robinson, *Amalgamated Association*, 48–50; John Bodnar, *Immigration and Industrialization: Ethnicity in an American Mill Town, 1870–1940* (Pittsburgh, 1977), 40–3.

black laborers inhabited the wretched laborers' shanties in Steelton, Pennsylvania, as well. By that time, however, the common labor force in northern mills was rapidly becoming dominated by eastern and southern Europeans. Although no exact ethnic breakdown for steelworkers is available, an estimate made twenty years later by the United States Immigration Commission called some 55 percent of the 142,588 ironworkers and steelworkers of the 1890 native-born whites (most of them probably sons of immigrants), 4 percent of them black Americans, and 41 percent foreign-born whites. Three-fourths of the 57,574 foreign-born were from Germany, Britain, or Ireland. The remaining quarter, however, represented the most rapidly growing segment of the work force. Their peasant backgrounds set the new roustabouts sharply apart from the other workers, in the mind of President Jarrett of the Amalgamated Association. He described them scornfully to a Senate committee in 1883 as "Hungarians, Poles, Italians, Bohemians, men that really don't know the difference . . . between light work and heavy work, or good and bad wages." He had been "disgusted to find that those people can live where I think a decent man would die."[54]

Jarrett was by no means speaking only for himself. The craftsmen's definition of who could live up to their code of "manly" behavior was usually cast in ethnic and racial terms. Witness the "Puddler poet" Michael McGovern's description of workers' unity at the celebration of the signing of the puddlers' scale:

> There were "Johnny Bulls" and "Paddies," and some sturdy men
>   from Wales
> Who are nicknamed after animals that wear contracted tails;
> Americans from every state took sets 'mongst Dutch and Scotch,
> And all appeared as friendly as if they'd never made a "potch."
> There were no men invited such as Slavs and "Tally Annes,"
> Hungarians and Chinamen with pigtail cues and fans.
> No, every man who got the "pass" a union man should be;
> No blacksheep were admitted to the Puddlers' Jubilee.[55]

What then of the black workers? This question is so central to the emerging consciousness of the labor movement that a complete answer

54. On rural migrants, see Bennett, "Iron Workers," 138–9; Bodnar, *Immigration and Industrialization,* 15, 24. Figures on ethnic composition are from James Holt, "Trade Unionism in the British and U.S. Steel Industries, 1880–1914: A Comparative Study," *Labor History,* 18 (Winter 1977), 16. Jarrett quotations are from U.S. Congress, Senate, *Report of the Committee of the Senate upon the Relations between Labor and Capital* (5 vols., Washington, D.C., 1885, hereafter cited as Senate, *Labor and Capital*), I, 1139.

55. Michael McGovern, *Labor Lyrics, and Other Poems* (Youngstown, Ohio, 1899), 27–8.

must be postponed until the many contradictory links between the working class and the social order as a whole have been examined. At this point it is possible only to make some very specific observations about the practices of ironworkers and steelworkers. The helpers whom puddlers and rollers hired, and thus put in a position to learn the crafts, were usually white, preferably their own blood relatives. The immigrants who filled the skilled trades in Birmingham, Alabama, for example, saw to it that there was scarcely a black puddler or roller in the city. Similarly, in Knoxville, where all the white craftsmen were migrants from the North, they refused to work with black helpers.[56] Nevertheless, there were some experienced black puddlers. The historic centers of their employment were the Tredegar Iron Works and the Old Dominion Works in Richmond. There, black craftsmen not only were a well-established part of the mills' work force but also had developed their own trade and benevolent organizations during the 1860s and early 1870s.[57] Consequently, they confronted the white trade unionists directly with the question of whether experienced members of the very trades they sought to amalgamate were to be excluded simply because they were Afro-Americans.

By 1881, the growth of the southern iron industry had spread the controversy far beyond Richmond. Black puddlers were working in Atlanta, Knoxville, and even Pittsburgh.[58] Those in Knoxville had found employment when a company fired all whites who had refused to work with Afro-Americans and staffed its skilled trades almost entirely with black workers. Those in Pittsburgh had arrived during the bitter 1875 lockout of the Sons of Vulcan and had gone to work escorted by a company of soldiers, in defiance of angry crowds of strike supporters. A book of labor poems, published by the local *National Labor Tribune,* had responded with a scurrilous lampoon of the "brudder darkies" who had come to "show de white man how to boil."[59]

56. Paul B. Worthman, "Working Class Mobility in Birmingham, Alabama, 1880–1914," in Tamara K. Hareven, ed., *Anonymous Americans: Explorations in Nineteenth-Century Social History* (Englewood Cliffs, N.J., 1971), 175–80; H. S. Chamberlain testimony, Senate, *Labor and Capital,* IV, 133–4.

57. Peter J. Rachleff, "Black, White, and Gray: Working-Class Activism in Richmond, Virginia, 1865–1890" (unpublished Ph.D. diss., University of Pittsburgh, 1981), 27–9, 195–211, 551–2, and passim.

58. *People's Advocate* (Washington, D.C.), October 1, 1881, in Philip S. Foner and Ronald L. Lewis, eds., *The Black Worker: A Documentary History from Colonial Times to the Present* (6 vols., Philadelphia, 1978–82), III, 70–1.

59. On Knoxville, see Senate, *Labor and Capital,* IV, 133–4. On Pittsburgh, see Pennsylvania Bureau of Industrial Statistics, *Annual Report of the Sec-*

By 1881, however, the activists of the Amalgamated Association had concluded they could no longer afford such disdain for the black crafts-men, and the union's convention voted to admit Afro-Americans to membership. That hardly ended the question. During the many bitter strikes in the steel industry in the early 1880s, black workers (usually laborers) were often brought north as strikebreakers, and late in 1882 President Jarrett reported that the union's all-black Sumner Lodge in Richmond had been disbanded because its members had been "perse-cuted by the whites." Nevertheless, when a motion was made at the 1885 convention to restrict membership to whites again, it was defeated by a large majority.[60] Eligibility for union membership remained officially de-fined on the basis of occupation, not race.

The second problem facing those who wished to solidify the crafts-men's power through an amalgamation of craft strength was the rapid growth of steel production after the mid-1870s. The crafts that had brought the new union into existence were those of the iron-rolling mill. Bessemer converters for refining steel had appeared at the Cambria Iron Works in the 1860s, then been installed in many new mills for fabrication of steel rails during the early 1870s (e.g., the Pennsylvania Steel Company and the Edgar Thompson works), opening the way for the dramatic displace-ment of iron wares by steel. In 1872, only 4 percent of the country's pig iron had been converted into Bessemer steel; in 1880, 28 percent became steel, and by 1892 more than 50 percent. By 1913, steel absorbed 93 percent of the country's pig iron.[61]

"The Building of Steel works & the manner in which they work Where [*sic*] a Curse to the cause," wrote Secretary Spangler of the heaters' union to its members in the Vulcan Iron Works of Carondolet (South St. Louis), who had just disbanded their lodge.[62] The lodge had been organized in 1874 by two veterans of defeats in the East: James Lapsley of Johnstown, Pennsylvania, and Henry Miners of St. Albans, New York. For almost two years they had held the fledgling union together through a strike, two wage cuts, and the discharge of its negotiating committee. But now the company had made its first charges from new Bessemer converters and had begun rolling steel rails. The lodge secretary, John Thomas, wrote Spangler of the plant manager's decision not to "Engage or Employ any

retary of Internal Affairs of the Commonwealth of Pennsylvania. Part III, *Industrial Statistics, 1880–1881* (Harrisburg, 1882, hereafter cited as Pa. BIS, 1880–1), 312; Isaac Davis, *Labor Poems* (Pittsburgh, n.d.), 6–7.

60. Freifeld, "Emergence," 518–26; the quotation is on p. 526.
61. My calculations from statistics in Bennett, "Iron Workers," 18; David Brody, *Steelworkers in America: The Nonunion Era* (Cambridge, Mass., 1960), 8–9.
62. Spangler to John Thomas, April 3, 1876 (Heaters' Correspondence).

of them in the manufactureing of steel Except thoes who have Heated by the Gas Process Beforehand [*sic*]." On the very eve of the founding of the Amalgamated Association these members were returning their union seal and books and "would have to Seek Employment Elsewhere."[63]

Steel mills were a "Curse to the cause" for three reasons: They were significantly larger than iron-rolling mills, they were characterized from the outset by a different style of organizing work, and their competition stimulated animosities among the older iron crafts by affecting different crafts in different ways. For all three reasons they simultaneously magnified the need for strict craft-union rules and increased the employers' power to oppose such rules. They not only intensified the workers' struggle for control through craft amalgamation but also revealed the inadequacies of that project itself.

Steel mills were vast – both those like Carnegie's Edgar Thompson works at Braddock, Pennsylvania, which were built to make steel, and those like the Cambria and Vulcan works, which were gradually or abruptly converted from iron rails to steel. As early as 1880 the average Bessemer mill had a capacity of 114,000 tons per year, as compared with 12,000 tons for the average iron-rolling mill.[64] That year the Cambria Iron Works had 4,200 employees on its payroll, Lackawanna Iron and Steel 3,000, Bethlehem Iron 2,900, and the Edgar Thompson works 1,500. By 1900, when only four manufacturing concerns in the United States employed more than 8,000 workers apiece, three of them were steel mills (Cambria, Homestead, and Jones and Laughlin). Consolidation of ownership also appeared quickly, especially in the form of vertical integration from mines to rolling mills, so that the scale and capitalization of steel-making companies grew even faster than the mills themselves. Steel manufacture thus shared with railroads the distinction of being the original locale of the huge business enterprise. And the link was more than coincidental: More than 80 percent of all the steel poured from Bessemer converters in 1880 went into railroad track.[65]

It was not only with respect to size that mills rolling steel rails differed from those fabricating rails from iron. The division of labor within an

63. John Thomas to Spangler, September 3, 5, 20, 23, 30, 1874; October 7, 15, 21, 1874; July 26, December 24, 31, 1875; March 16, April 1, 1876. The quotations are from letters of March 16 and April 1, 1876 (Heaters' Correspondence).

64. Freifeld, "Emergence," 472.

65. Daniel Nelson, *Managers and Workers: Origins of the New Factory System in the United States, 1880–1920* (Madison, Wisc., 1975), 6–7; Alfred D. Chandler, Jr., *The Visible Hand: The Managerial Revolution in American Business* (Cambridge, Mass., 1977), 258–69; Freifeld, "Emergence," 469–85.

iron mill had created, on the one hand, common laborers, who fetched and pushed at the command of their gang bosses, and, on the other hand, large groups of craftsmen, who learned their trades by doing and who clearly directed their own work and that of their immediate helpers. In sharp contrast to that dichotomy, a Bessemer steel mill not only required many more laborers and (with new rolling technology) much smaller rolling crews but also, and more important, required a swarm of specialists involved in the Bessemer process itself, each of whom had to be highly competent at a particular task and work in close cooperation with other crew members, but none of whom mastered an entire process in the flow of production. A charger filled the converter with the proper amounts of iron, spiegeleisen, and other materials. Regulators moved the converter to a vertical position for the "blow" and a horizontal position for charging and emptying. The blower, usually trained by the company in the new metallurgy, regulated the flow of air through the converter, assessing the progress of the refining by the size and color of the flame, and deciding when the process was finished. Ladle crews then moved the molten steel to the ingot molds, which were set in molds in the floor. Another crew then moved the ingot molds to the soaking pits, by means of the dinkey train. Others then operated mechanical strippers to remove the molds, so that they could be turned over to the heater, who prepared them for rolling.[66] Not only did each step in the process require of the worker less judgment and autonomy than did the puddling of iron, but the whole process, as one manufacturer explained, "is so combined and arranged that the management of it by the party superintending conversions is not at all difficult."[67] It provided the opportunity, wrote a Cambria engineer, of "breaking away from . . . arbitrary shop-rules . . . and limited output."[68]

Nevertheless, breaking away from workers' control of output did not prove to be easy. In the first place, even though academically trained engineers and company metallurgical laboratories increased the ability of the superintendent to direct Bessemer processes, that method of refining steel remained notoriously cantankerous. Unanticipated chemical reactions and temperature changes made at least the blower's judgment indispensable.[69] More important, the close cooperation required of various work crews in the process bred intense solidarities within the small work

66. Bennett, "Iron Workers," 14–15.
67. *Bulletin of the American Iron and Steel Association*, September 10, 1874, quoted in Bennett, "Iron Workers," 17.
68. John E. Frey, "The Bessemer Steel Industry: Johnstown's Contribution to It," *Johnstown Daily Democrat Souvenir Edition* (Autumn 1894), 10, quoted in Bennett, "Iron Workers," 17.
69. Freifeld, "Emergence," 181–3.

group. The power of such groups, even in nonunion settings, could be formidable, as is evidenced by the fact that Bessemer crews quickly established the eight-hour day as their own standard, while many tonnage crafts working by the heat or charge continued to toil approximately ten hours, and those on such continuous processes as work with blast furnaces were forced, by the 1890s, to toil twelve hours a day, and often seven days a week. Actually, the eight-hour day on Bessemer converters had been decreed by the Amalgamated Association at its 1881 convention (a gathering charged with optimism and the spirit of amalgamation, at which Afro-Americans had been admitted and many new categories of tonnage workers invited to join, although blast-furnace laborers had been rejected). What is noteworthy, however, is that the shorter day remained the practice among Bessemer crews, despite the consistent defeats of the union in steel over the next twenty years, and despite the longer hours decreed for other workers in the same mills. By the end of the century, employers had ratified the shorter day, forced on them by the solidarity of the Bessemer crews, by acknowledging that Bessemer work allowed less rest time than most other work in steel.[70]

Occasionally (probably on rare occasions), other steel-mill crews were able to establish their own patterns of hours without a union. Around 1900, the chargers, bottom makers, and helpers at the soaking pits of Jones and Laughlin, where everyone had been forced to sign a nonunion pledge in 1897, demanded and were granted an eight-hour day. Five years earlier the crew of Rail Mill No. 1 at Illinois Steel had struck for an eight-hour (rather than twelve-hour) day, in defiance of the mill's two boss rollers. They won, and as late as 1919 the boss rollers on Rail Mill No. 1 worked twelve hours daily, as did the entire crew of the newer Rail Mill No. 2, but the *crew* of No. 1 changed every eight hours.[71]

Those small-group struggles all developed after the defeat of the Amalgamated Association. Between 1878 and 1892, however, the story had been different. The craftsmen's drive for control through amalgamation then led to a frontal union assault on the new steel industry itself. The first phase of this struggle began with the end of the great depression in 1878. Unusually high European demand for American farm products triggered an upward leap in grain exports, and with it a new surge of

70. McNeill, *Labor Movement*, 291; Charles R. Walker, *Steel: The Diary of a Furnace Worker* (Boston, 1922); Fitch, *Steel Workers*, 301.
71. Interviews with Dave Hollingsworth (Pittsburgh), Patrick Elliott (Pittsburgh), and Victor Roberts (South Chicago), in David Saposs Papers, State Historical Society of Wisconsin, Box 26. Compare Brody, *Steelworkers*, 35–7, where the explanation offered for variations in hours is technological.

railroad building in the American West. As the price of rails soared, and both iron- and steel-rail mills expanded rapidly during the last two years of the decade, many union members found work in the Bessemer mills – so many, in fact, that in December 1880 the Amalgamated Association could convene a meeting of delegates from lodges in steel mills, which adopted a scale of minimum tonnage rates for the entire industry. Victory in a bitter strike at the Springfield (Illinois) Iron and Steel Company inspired the formation of seven successful lodges in steel. Although the union lost a major strike at the Cleveland Rolling Mills in 1882, it won its scale at the Homestead mills, which were about to be purchased by Andrew Carnegie. The decisive test came, however, at the end of 1882, when the railroad construction boom collapsed, the price of steel fell abruptly, and the midwestern companies demanded that the union agree to a one-third cut in tonnage rates. Despite President Jarrett's advice to compromise, the steel lodges went on strike in 1883. Defeat followed in Springfield and Bethlehem, then the next year in Joliet, Beaver Falls, Pennsylvania, Belleville, Illinois, and elsewhere. The depressed condition of the trade also opened the way to a general assault on Amalgamated Association lodges in iron mills, with the overall result that the union's membership fell from 16,003 in 1882 to 5,702 in 1885, and seventy-six of its lodges had been broken – twenty-five of them in steel mills. Of the fifteen steel-rail mills operating in 1885, only three did not require "iron-clad oaths" of nonunionism from their employees, and the exceptions included Carnegie's Edgar Thompson and Homestead works.[72]

As was noted, however, the union's crisis also touched the iron-rolling mills. In part this was because the strike defeats created a pool of drifting, experienced craftsmen, blacklisted from their former employment and often eager to obtain jobs on any terms available. More important, however, was the differential effect of the new technology on the older iron crafts. Puddlers suffered most: The swollen labor supply of craftsmen who were no longer in great demand both depressed tonnage scales and closed all opportunities for promotion among helpers – except for scabbing. Embattled puddlers responded by demanding that their fellow union members support puddlers' wage struggles and by legislating increasingly draconic rules concerning their own stints and workplace behavior.[73]

72. Freifeld, "Emergence," 477–534; Robinson, *Amalgamated Association*, 21. Freifeld makes a major contribution to our knowledge of steel workers' history by discussing these early defeats of the union, which go virtually unmentioned in Fitch, Robinson, Brody, and other standard works. Curiously, she, in turn, underestimates the resurgence of unionism in steel between 1886 and 1892.

73. Bennett, "Iron Workers," 48–9.

The problem was that for the "finishers," especially for the nailers and rollers, things were different. When the first steel sheets were rolled for cutting into nails in the major nail center, Wheeling, West Virginia, chalk graffiti marked them "puddlers' tombstones." Puddlers, who dominated the Amalgamated Association, demanded that the nailers charge a higher price for cutting steel than for iron sheets, but many nailers replied that cutting steel was, if anything, easier than making nails from iron, and they withdrew from the Amalgamated Association to form their own union. Those loyal nailers who did strike to enforce the new differential scale found themselves replaced by machinery that made nails not from sheet steel, which required their cutting, but from steel wire![74]

As for the rollers, the newer rolling mills so increased their output and so reduced the number of helpers that even though rollers' tonnage rates were slashed, their earnings soared. As early as 1882, a puddler from Woods Run (near Pittsburgh) complained with considerable justice that while he and his fellows were earning $3.00 to $3.50 per day, rollers were raking in $10.00 to $15.00.[75] Ten years later the Carnegie company offered its rollers annual salaries of $3,500 if they would work during the Homestead strike.[76] Although many of them then refused, by 1919 it was standard company practice to put rollers on annual salaries, and many of them agonized over whether they should join that year's strike now that they were "part of management."[77]

Consequently, amalgamation was a project that demanded tireless dedication and deliberate endeavor by thousands of activists among iron-workers and steelworkers. Tendencies toward division and disunity had to be overcome by incessant exhortations from the labor press, huge solidarity rallies, union band concerts, dances, picnics, wide distribution of inspirational songs and poetry, and the spread-eagle oratory of friendly politicians, journalists, and social reformers. Especially effective were the farewell dinners, at which activists leaving town or leaving the trade were celebrated for their "manly virtues" and steadfast adherence to the craftsmen's moral code. Large funeral processions followed by stirring eulogies also served to instruct the young and reconfirm the living in the union principles by which the departed brothers had lived.[78]

74. Ibid., 19–21; McNeill, *Labor Movement,* 295–7.
75. *Pittsburgh Post,* April 14, 1882.
76. Cohen, "Steelworkers Rethink," 164.
77. Interviews with Robert Allen (New Kensington), Jack Pfeifer (Braddock), Blair Hedridge (Gary), Victor Roberts (South Chicago), and George V. Sterling (South Chicago), in Saposs Papers, Box 26.
78. Bennett, "Iron Workers," is especially rich and insightful in its discussion of the role of activists in creating a movement culture; see pp. 42–4, 86ff. See also Couvares, "Work, Leisure," 137–9.

In the Pittsburgh district, the annual spring reunions of the Amalgamated Association drew crowds of men, women, and children varying in number from fifteen thousand to twenty-five thousand. The first such gathering was actually a demonstration for higher tariff protection, organized by the union in 1880. In subsequent years, however, the tariff theme gave way to the message of workers' solidarity, and speeches were supplemented by singing groups and races. The atmosphere of the 1891 reunion was vividly described in a report in the *National Labor Tribune:*

> There were tents and side shows containing jubilee singers and the
> strong man and wizard, . . . two dancing platforms . . . crowded with
> people. Fakirs, . . . machines to test the lungs and muscles . . . ; [a]
> phonograph giving the songs sung by popular singers and played by
> the grand orchestras; dolls to knock down for a cigar. . . . Vendors
> of every description. . . . Bands were sending forth their best music.
> . . . A pleasant day renewing old acquaintances and making new ones.[79]

All these devices for cultivating a mutualistic ethic and a movement culture strong enough to offset corporate power and the diversities of craft interests alike were put to the acid test in the great strike of 1882 and its sequel. During the prosperous years of 1880 and 1881 the union had both improved the sliding scale for puddlers and won a raise of 10 percent for most finishers. In the spring of 1882 it responded to the demand of its puddlers for an additional raise, to help them recoup their losses of the 1870s, by calling out all tonnage men in the Pittsburgh district. The rolling-mill owners responded with unprecedented unity of their own: They locked out all union mills as far west as Illinois. Some 150 mills were shut down, at the very time the union was also engaged in some of its earliest strikes in steel. As President Jarrett had warned his members, they had chosen a bad time to strike. The market for iron rails was shrinking rapidly, leaving employers with huge inventories.

As the strike dragged on for five months, many western lodges collapsed. Finishers in the Pittsburgh region complained increasingly about the sacrifices they had been asked to make on the puddlers' behalf, and some eventually seceded to form their own union. As John Bennett described so vividly in the case of the rolling mills of Woods Run, heaters and rollers who were prominent in the Amalgamated Association exhorted and cajoled their fellow finishers unceasingly to hold them in line. The union's national convention in August was the largest it had ever held (213 delegates from eighty-one lodges met in Chicago for nine days), and it devoted itself assiduously to the detailed work necessary to carry amalgamation through its test of fire. Other unions and the Knights of Labor rallied to the side of the Amalgamated Association, joining in a

79. Bennett, "Iron Workers," 100–2. The quotation is from *National Labor Tribune,* June 13, 1891.

parade in Pittsburgh that turned out twenty-five thousand participants despite a pouring rain. The vast, orderly ranks and ornate banners of that procession challenged that year's first Labor Day parades in New York and elsewhere for the distinction of producing the best-known lithographs of the nineteenth-century labor movement.[80]

In spite of all these efforts, the strikers had to return to work in September with no raise in pay and many lodges lost. Defeats in steel and dissension among the iron crafts both increased during the next three years, as union membership fell from 16,003 in 1882 to 5,702 in 1885.[81] By and large, iron-rolling mills never recovered from the hard times of 1883–5, and by the early 1890s many mills that had not merged with, or converted to, Bessemer steel mills were going out of business throughout the Pittsburgh region. As the industry contracted, disputes over questions of promotion became increasingly chronic and bitter in union lodges. Unemployed puddlers seeking jobs at vacated furnaces clashed with helpers already on the payroll and anxious for promotion to the same jobs. At the Pork House Mill of Woods Run, an old union stronghold, helpers struck to obtain promotions, and the puddlers voted to fire them all and stay on the job.[82]

Similarly, the tension between the rollers and other union members grew worse. Reports from the Pennsylvania Bureau of Industrial Statistics indicated that in contrast to 1874, when rollers' pay averaged 1.5 times the average earnings of puddlers, by 1887 their pay averaged three times that of the puddlers. Worse yet, the differential between rollers and their own helpers was also widening (from 2 to 3.5 times in the case of roughers, for example), and rollers not only were resurrecting the practice of inside contracting but also were arbitrarily promoting whichever helpers they pleased and even using the power of their own union offices to block protests against their violations of union rules. The combined effects of huge wage differentials and displaced puddlers trying to move into the more prosperous "finishing" trades, in competition with the children and friends of established rollers and heaters, sapped the Amalgamated Association's morale. "The rollers used to run the union and saw to it that their friends were promoted," a former union activist at Homestead told John Fitch in 1908. Others grumbled that the Welsh craftsmen "always stood together and worked for one of their own race." The complaint of yet another veteran revealed his loss of faith in the union's se-

80. Bennett, "Iron Workers," 42–5, 87, 99. Pictures of the Pittsburgh parade may be found in M. B. Schnapper, *American Labor: A Pictorial Social History* (Washington, D.C., 1972), 172.
81. Robinson, *Amalgamated Association*, 21.
82. Bennett, "Iron Workers," 48–9.

niority rule: "I had a puddling furnace of my own at age 16. I then became a rollhand, but never worked up to a chance on the rolls. This is largely a matter of favoritism. The roller is in a position to promote whom [he] will."[83] This degeneration explains the bitter tone of the poem "Woods Run," which appeared in 1893. It ran, in part:

> Listen to the sound of gladsome laughter,
> 'Tis the Amalgamated members after
> Envelopes filled with crisp dollar bills;
> Pay day it has come.

> Picnic day is here again.
> All hearts are filled with joy as when
> Friend meets friend with pleasure and beaming,
> "Old acquaintances" renew. . . .

> Puddler and finisher look on with delight
> As steelman tells sheet worker he don't think he's right.
> Too light are the new weights and measures, he's sure,
> A chainmaker delegate told him. . . .

> But hark to that distant rumbling sound
> As if spirits troubled 'neath the ground.
> The scene to hide the clouds hang low;
> Dissension's done his work.

> Truth protests, then blushes with shame
> At falsehoods uttered in her name;
> Duplicity tells honesty he's too slow,
> To Progress (?) please make way. . . .

> No longer is heard the friendly greeting,
> Now each one's bent on his own good seeking;
> Beyond healing rends the gaping wound,
> A generation's work destroy.[84]

It was, however, precisely in this setting of internal dissension that the Amalgamated Association waxed the strongest in its entire history, and the struggle of the tonnage men for collective control over their conditions of work was waged with the greatest intensity. With the revival of the steel industry between 1888 and 1892, the union began to grow rapidly once more. At the 1891 convention, 294 delegates transacted business for 24,068 members (the largest union of ironworkers and steelworkers in the world and the largest number to belong to the Amalgamated Association until 1934), about one-fourth of the eligible tonnage men in the country. Delegates to this and other conventions during this militant

83. Couvares, "Work, Leisure," 25; Cohen, "Steelworkers Rethink," 160.
84. *National Labor Tribune*, September 28, 1893. The poem is reprinted in Bennett, "Iron Workers," 114–15.

half decade responded to the decay of their trades with draconic work rules: ordering promotion by seniority in rolling crews, "blacklegging" inside contractors, reducing the amount of iron that could be puddled per heat by any one member, and banning overtime turns where anyone was out of work.[85] "Corruption" at the local level was thus challenged by the adoption of uniform and rigid rules at the union's national level. Moreover, because the technology, the managerial controls, and the very size of the new steel mills made such self-discipline increasingly difficult to enforce, the union members had to resort to ostracism, boycotts, and threats of violence against deviants, and when strikes came, they used mass picketing, sympathetic strikes, and even armed force. As this happened, the employers appealed increasingly to the community at large to support the freedom of property owners and of individual workers from "union tyranny," and to support "law and order." Thus, the battle for control between craft and managerial authorities within the mill spilled over into a social and political confrontation of social classes and of social ideals. At the Homestead works in 1892, that confrontation assumed legendary proportions.

The lockout that gripped Andrew Carnegie's Homestead works from the beginning of July to the end of November 1892 put the amalgamation movement to the acid test. Of the thirty-eight hundred workers in the mill, roughly eight hundred tonnage men belonged to one of eight Amalgamated lodges on the eve of the lockout. Not only had they won a strike in January 1889, forcing the company to deal with the Amalgamated Association and pay according to its sliding scale of tonnage rates for the next three years, but also they formed the keystone in the structure of ninety-four lodges in the district, which constituted one-third of all the lodges in the union. They also dominated the borough's government, Burgess John McLuckie himself being a mill worker and a union leader. When the county sheriff had led a posse into Homestead during the 1889 strike, he and his men had simply been chased away by the strikers, and the sheriff had concluded that the better part of valor was to offer his services as a mediator in effecting a settlement.[86]

In the spring of 1892, however, the situation was quite different. For three years the Carnegie company had made careful preparations for a showdown over the question of who controlled the mills. Henry Clay Frick had assumed direction of the works, bringing with him a reputation

85. Robinson, *Amalgamated Association,* 21; Holt, "Trade Unionism," 16; Bennett, "Iron Workers," 48–9; Freifeld, "Emergence," 446–7.
86. Robinson, *Amalgamated Association,* 20; Arthur G. Burgoyne, *Homestead* (Pittsburgh, 1893), 18–19.

for having smashed strikes in the coal and coke end of the industry, and he promptly erected fortifications around the plant. Moreover, the latest boom in railroad construction had clearly ended; rail prices were falling and many mills in the Midwest were laying off or shutting down. The manufacturers' association in the iron-rolling mills rejected the union's proposed scale and demanded major wage cuts. In steel, however, the union did not deal with an association, but simply and directly with Frick. He brooked no compromise with the drastic tonnage reductions he proposed, and when the negotiators for the Amalgamated Association refused to accept his terms, Frick began closing down parts of the mill. On July 2 the company discharged all its workers and served public notice: "Hereafter, the Homestead steel works will operate as a non-union mill."[87]

The union lodges rallied the workers with enthusiastic mass meetings, elected an advisory committee of thirty-three members to direct their struggle, and set up special committees that patrolled the streets, warned tavern keepers to allow no drunkenness, and cut down effigies of company officials, with which inhabitants had liberally decorated the town. As the Pittsburgh journalist Arthur Burgoyne concisely put it:

> The government of Homestead had now passed absolutely into the hands of the advisory committee of the Amalgamated lodges, and the committee was determined to use its arbitrary authority for the preservation of order and decency and the protection of life and property as well as the exclusion from Homestead of non-union men, better known to the unionists as "scabs" or "black sheep."[88]

Four days later, two barges filled with Pinkerton detectives arrived at the waterfront entrance to the mill, and on their refusal to obey the committee's instructions to depart, the great battle of July 6 began. While the Pinkertons fired through gun slits in the armor plating of their barges, the populace of Homestead hastily erected steel barricades of their own and assaulted the invaders with rifle fire, dynamite, flaming oil, cannon fire, and fireworks left over from the Fourth of July. When the detectives surrendered to the advisory committee toward the end of the day, they were forced to run a bloody gauntlet of men, women, and children and were saved from death only by the efforts of the committee members.

87. Hunt, "American Rolling Mills," 61; Burgoyne, *Homestead*, 22–39; the quotation is on p. 39. See also Leon Wolff, *Lockout, The Story of the Homestead Strike of 1892: A Study of Violence, Unionism, and the Carnegie Steel Empire* (New York, 1965).

88. Burgoyne, *Homestead*, 39. The analysis that follows relies heavily on Burgoyne's splendid firsthand account of the strike, which has been republished under the title *The Homestead Strike of 1892* (Pittsburgh, 1979), with an afterword by David P. Demarest, Jr.

The "Fight for Hearth and Home," through which the steelworkers cleansed their town of the hated lackies of capital, was soon celebrated in song and legend in working-class homes throughout the land:

> Now the man that fights for honor, none can blame him,
>   May luck attend wherever he may roam,
>   And no son of his will ever live to shame him,
>   Whilst liberty and honor rule our home.[89]

The "Battle of Fort Frick" had projected the contest for control of Carnegie's mills into the community for all America to observe. Newspaper reporters who swarmed into Homestead remarked on the prominence of the borough's women in the armed confrontation with the Pinkertons and in the bloody gauntlet the detectives had to run after their surrender. They were equally impressed by the way the mill hands who did not belong to the Amalgamated Association supported the union. A committee of mechanics and laborers had approached management on the eve of the strike with proposals for a scale of wages for their work and had been rebuffed. That committee ardently endorsed the strike of the tonnage men on July 2, and its adherents remained off the job until November 18. In the ominous calm that followed the battle of July 6, the union's advisory committee was absolute master of the community. Its representatives patrolled the streets and the silent mill, organized huge funeral processions in collaboration with local churches and lodges, and even arrested a group of anarchists who came from Pittsburgh to distribute leaflets. No one expressed the craftsmen's image of themselves better than the Reverend J. J. McIlyar of the Fourth Avenue Methodist Episcopal Church, who pronounced John Morris, slain in the battle with the Pinkertons, "a perfect citizen; an intelligent man; a good husband who was never lacking in his duty; a brother who was devoted and loyal and who will surely find his reward."[90]

Three days after Reverend McIlyar's eulogy, eight thousand soldiers of the Pennsylvania National Guard arrived in Homestead to begin ninety-five days of military occupation. It was the army, not the Pinkertons, that allowed Frick gradually to reopen the mill with strikebreakers. But its commander, General George R. Snowden, envisaged his mission as far more important than simply deciding the outcome of an industrial dispute. As he explained in his official report, "Philadelphians can hardly appreciate the actual communism of these people [in Homestead]. They believe the works are their's [sic] quite as much as Carnegie's."[91]

89. Michael McGovern, "The Homestead Strike," in Philip S. Foner, *American Labor Songs of the Nineteenth Century* (Urbana, Ill., 1975), 244.
90. Burgoyne, *Homestead*, 36, 58, 83–5, 91–4; the quotation is on p. 93.
91. Report of General Snowden, quoted in Philip S. Foner, *History of the Labor Movement in the United States* (6 vols., New York, 1947–82), II, 212.

That view was seconded by Chief Justice Edward Paxson of the Pennsylvania Supreme Court. Coming to Pittsburgh in September for the court's annual session, after 167 Homestead residents had already been indicted on charges of murder, riot, and conspiracy for the events of July 6, the chief justice handed down a further bill of charges against the union's advisory committee, that they did "unlawfully, falsely, maliciously and traitorously compass, imagine and intend to raise and levy war, insurrection and rebellion against the Commonwealth of Pennsylvania." Proof of their treasonous intent was found by Justice Paxson in the fact that they had not participated in "a mob driven to desperation by hunger as in the days of the French Revolution," but were rather "men receiving exceptionally high wages . . . resisting the law and resorting to violence and bloodshed in the assertion of imaginary rights." Their act had been "a deliberate attempt by men without authority to control others in the enjoyment of their rights."[92]

This crisp and firm declaration that workers' control was illegal – that the group discipline in the workplace and community by which workers enforced their code of mutualism in opposition to the authority and power of the mill owners was tantamount to insurrection against the republic – clearly illuminated the ideological and political dimensions of workplace struggles. It also made clear to Justice Paxson himself the "diseased state of public opinion" regarding the respective rights of labor and capital that "finds expression in the assurances of demagogues who pander to popular prejudices and in the schemes of artful politicians."[93]

Indeed, the "artful politicians" were drawn to the Homestead strike like moths to a flame. While leading Republicans pursued private negotiations with some leaders of the Amalgamated Association in quest of a formula to end the embarrassing conflict before election day, Pennsylvania's Democrats (undaunted by the fact that the governor who had dispatched the troops was one of their own) staged gala parades in both Pittsburgh and Homestead to identify their partisan cause with that of the strikers. The Pittsburgh parade featured a contingent of six hundred strikers, from Homestead and from other Carnegie mills where workers had struck in sympathy. As they passed the county jail, the marchers raised loud cheers for Hugh O'Donnell and other imprisoned leaders. Although Homestead itself had long been a Republican stronghold, prominent local Republicans joined with strikers in a Democratic dem-

92. Quoted in Burgoyne, *Homestead*, 198, 204–5. No one was found guilty of either the riot or the treason charges, but Hugh Dempsey, Master Workman of District Assembly 3 of the Knights of Labor, and two other men were sentenced to seven years in prison on charges of conspiring to poison scabs. Burgoyne, *Homestead*, 259, 262–3, 275, 290, 294.
93. Quoted in Burgoyne, *Homestead*, 205.

onstration that moved through the borough's streets on the night of October 23 (ten days after the Pennsylvania National Guard had withdrawn). Emblems and illuminated transparencies carried by the marchers mixed attacks on Carnegie and the Pinkertons with the traditional Democratic themes of free trade and white supremacy. On one float, which featured the slogan "This is Protection," stood a live sheep painted black and a white man arrayed as a black woman. The scab, imprisoned trade unionists, the McKinley Tariff, and Senator Henry Cabot Lodge's bill for federal enforcement of the rights of black voters were thus symbolically joined to represent the Republicans as foes of popular liberties. Even though the imprisoned O'Donnell continued to remind the citizens that both Paxson and the governor were Democrats, enough voters had been persuaded by this symbolism to give the Democrats a resounding victory on election day and to bear out the defiant prediction of one popular transparency that referred to the Democratic emblem, the rooster:

> The cock will crow in '92
> Over Fort Frick and the Pinkerton crew.[94]

At the very moment the Democrats were carrying the local elections, however, the strike was crumbling. Enough strikebreakers were already in the mill to permit a high level of operation, and thirty deputy sheriffs patrolled the town. Assaults on scabs by small groups became commonplace, and a hotel where newcomers were housed was mysteriously blown up. As if in response to Democratic rhetoric, half a dozen Afro-Americans were fiercely assaulted by a crowd the Sunday after Election Day. As early as mid-October, the *Homestead News,* voice of the borough's elite, which had consistently supported the strikers, had begun to editorialize that the struggle was lost and should be abandoned. Mounting anxiety among the laborers that all their jobs were being taken by newcomers led a mass meeting of mechanics and laborers a week and a half after the Democratic triumph to vote to ask for their jobs back. Defeat now being certain, a mournful gathering of tonnage men voted to "declare the mill open" by the narrow margin of 101 to 91.[95]

In the eight years after the defeated workers seeking reemployment filed past two hiring clerks under the watchful eye of Superintendent Charles Schwab, steel production in Carnegie's mills tripled – from 878,000 tons to 2,870,000 tons. "Ashamed to tell you profits these days," Andrew Carnegie wrote a friend in 1899. His word for them was "Prodigious!" In place of the $4 million net return of 1892 stood a profit of $21 million that year (and almost $40 million the next).[96] The 2,663,412-

94. Burgoyne, *Homestead,* 212–14, 222–3; the quotation is on p. 213.
95. Ibid., 211, 214–19, 224–7.
96. Quoted in Gerald G. Eggert, *Steelmasters and Labor Reform, 1886–1923* (Pittsburgh, 1981), 28. See also James H. Bridge, *The Inside History of the*

ton output of Carnegie's Monongahela Valley plants (Homestead, Duquesne, Braddock, etc.) in 1899 surpassed Great Britain's world-historic record of 1885 by 35 percent.[97] No longer, to use the words of Carnegie's one-time colleague James H. Bridge, was "the method of apportioning the work, of regulating the turns, of altering the machinery, in short, every detail of working the great plant . . . subject to the interference of some busybody representing the Amalgamated Association."[98] Tonnage rates were slashed, twelve-hour turns were extended to at least one-third of the workers, breaks in the working day that had once been prescribed by union rules were eliminated, and workers were reassigned at management's discretion, while new charging machines, heating furnaces, automatic roll tables, and other equipment eliminated an estimated five hundred jobs in Homestead alone by the end of the decade.

Simultaneously, the company gradually but systematically devised a new managerial structure. Blowers, melters, rollers, and other craftsmen were, in the words of Mary Freifeld, "grafted . . . onto the bottom of [the firm's] own management structure, with their traditional supervisory work roles, and scientific and technical knowledge intact."[99] They usually selected their own crew members, assigned men to tasks at their own discretion, and transferred men among one another's teams as they saw fit. It was no uncommon event at the turn of the century for men who had already worked twelve hours to be ordered to stay for another twelve, if their replacements had not shown up. The arbitrary nature of the authority of craftsmen/gang bosses over lesser workmen is well illustrated by the case of Paul Korchnak of the Homestead works. As a hook man, he earned relatively good wages by raising ingots from a heating furnace. That is, he did in the summertime. Every winter for twelve years, when cold weather made the furnace almost bearable, the heater pulled Korchnak off the job and gave it to some favored man.[100]

Carnegie Steel Company: A Romance of Millions (New York, 1903), 296–7.

97. Bridge, *Inside History*, 297.   98. Ibid., 202.
99. Cohen, "Steelworkers Rethink," 167–74; Freifeld, "Emergence," 540–53; the quotation is on p. 551. Katherine Stone's influential article "The Origins of Job Structures in the Steel Industry," *Review of Radical Political Economy*, 6 (1974), 115–70, seriously overestimates both the pace and the extent of the steel industry's adoption of a job hierarchy based on "scientific management" principles.
100. Interviews with James Conn (Pittsburgh), A. J. Cottrell (Pittsburgh), John Wasko (Homestead), J. W. Hendricks (Bethlehem), and Paul Korchnak (Homestead), in Saposs Papers, Box 26; Walker, *Steel*, 30–41; Whiting Williams, *What's on the Worker's Mind, By One Who Put on Overalls to Find Out* (New York, 1921), 182–3.

This style of supervision, in one sense, did not represent a radical break with the past. It was built on both the technical knowledge of skilled workers, which remained indispensable, and the tradition of promotion within gangs. What had been eliminated was collective, deliberate control from the workers' end. In its place the company cultivated a hierarchy of fiercely competing individuals, held together, as John Fitch observed, "by the ambition of the men lower down," and secured by the vast differentials in earnings that still existed despite draconic slashing of tonnage rates after the strike, by craftsmen's fear of losing their jobs, and by the graft they could glean from their subordinates. The sense of distance, and even of animosity, between the skilled workers on one side and the workers they supervised on the other intensified as the industry resumed its rapid expansion after 1897. Despite the dramatic increase in productivity per worker between 1890 and 1910, the total production force grew by 129 percent (to 326,000). According to the estimates of the United States Immigration Commission, however, the number of native-born white workers rose by only 55 percent during those two decades, and the employment of immigrants from Germany and the British Isles had actually decreased by 18 percent. Although Afro-Americans had become a larger proportion of steelworkers' ranks by virtue of an increase of 165 percent, the decisive shift had been toward immigrants from southern and eastern Europe. An increase of 227 percent in their numbers had made them the largest group in the industry. In contrast to 1890, when southern and eastern Europeans constituted less than 10 percent of the industry's labor force, these immigrants, whom the amalgamation cause had slighted, constituted almost one-half (47.5 percent) of all America's steelworkers by 1910.[101]

At the apex of the mill hierarchy were Frick, Corey, Dickson, Schwab, and the other zealous managers brought up through the company's ranks by Carnegie, who devoted their waking hours to cutting costs and setting

101. Fitch, *Steel Workers*, 142 and passim; Peter B. Doeringer, "Piece Rate Wage Structures in the Pittsburgh Iron and Steel Industry – 1880–1900," *Labor History*, 9 (Spring 1968), 262–74; Peter R. Shergold, "Wage Differentials Based on Skill in the United States, 1899–1914: A Case Study," *Labor History*, 18 (Fall 1977), 485–508. The calculations of ethnic composition and its changes are mine, based on data in W. Jett Lauck and Edgar Sydenstricker, *Conditions of Labor in American Industries: A Summarization of the Results of Recent Investigations* (New York, 1917), 6–7; Holt, "Trade Unionism," 16; U.S. Bureau of the Census, *Sixteenth Census of the United States: 1940. Population. Comparative Occupation Statistics of the United States, 1870–1940* (Washington, D.C., 1943, hereafter cited as U.S. Census, *Occ. Stat.*), 106.

production records. Twice a year they ran the mills flat out for "record months," whose output was then made the basis for calculating tonnage rates and "normal" production for the coming year. When William Corey was general superintendent at Homestead, he routinely leafed through the order books to pull out orders on which output records could most easily be set, regardless of delivery dates. One consequence was that large orders clogged the yards, while others were simply ignored. Orders on which records had been set were often buried under other such lots, then rolled a second time when customers asked for delivery. Only the Spanish-American War saved the plant from disaster. The government, manager William Dickson reported, "sent men to Homestead and bought practically all the duplicate plates at high prices, thus cleaning up the entire mess."[102]

The founding of United States Steel Corporation and the mighty efforts of Judge Elbert H. Gary and the House of Morgan to rationalize the steel industry still lay in the future. But the age in which the men who actually produced iron and steel had struggled, at times with noteworthy success, to rationalize production from below through their own knowledge, their own ethical code, and their own organizations and rules had effectively ended with the defeat of the Amalgamated Association in its western Pennsylvania strongholds. There had never been a Golden Age in which "the steel industry was controlled by the skilled workers."[103] In every industrial country of the world, except England, the steel industry was notorious for the weakness of its unions before World War I. But the work practices and moral codes of America's nineteenth-century craftsmen had given them the strength to wage a formidable and persistent battle to oppose the employers' power with their own collective regulation of the industry. This had been the essence of the amalgamation movement. James Holt is probably right in asserting that in 1891–2, "the strength of trade unionism in the U.S. iron and steel industry overall was in some respects greater than it was in Britain."[104] But the situation by the end of the 1890s was better described by Michael McGovern:

102. Bridge, *Inside History*, 293–9; Eggert, *Steelmasters*, 23.
103. Katherine Stone, "The Origin of Job Structures in the Steel Industry," *Radical America*, 7 (November–December 1973), 19. The same view is held by Couvares, "Work, Leisure."
104. Holt, "Trade Unionism," 14. On the weakness of unionism in basic steel in France, Germany, and Italy, see Stearns, *Lives of Labor*, 172–86; Michael Hanagan, *The Logic of Solidarity: Artisans and Industrial Workers in Three French Towns, 1871–1914* (Urbana, Ill., 1980); Stefano Merli, *Proletariato di fabbrica e capitalismo industriale: il caso italiano, 1880– 1900* (2 vols., Florence, 1976); Dieter Groh, *Negative Integration und*

He stood before his workingmen
        As ruler of the mills;
Who lived among the 'upper ten'
        And sneered at labor's ills,
And bid them come to meet him in
        His office one by one,
To sign a new "agreement;" "then,"
        He said, "the mills will run." . . .

"I tell you he's an anarchist
        Who'd slash at freedom's throat,
Who'd call a meeting and insist
        This matter put to vote:
For I shall deal with each alone
        As with a Slav or Hun,
For 'neath no scale except my own
        Shall these industries run.

"So sign at once my ironclad,
        And by its laws be bound,
For scabs in numbers can be had,
        Who now are tramping round;
Renounce your foolish sentiment,
        And labor unions shun,
Then strikes shall never more prevent
        These mills a steady run."[105]

The crisis of competitive capitalism

Our brief look at work relations and strife in the iron and steel industry of the late nineteenth century has suggested some of the most important characteristics of the workers' movement of the epoch. The line of battle did not run between "industrialism" (or "modernity") and its foes. On the contrary, class conflict was an inherent part of industrial life. The production of iron and steel was a collective undertaking, involving the coordinated teamwork of thousands of workers, whose technical expertise and intense physical exertion were applied to ever more imposing furnaces, rolling mills, molds, and transfer machinery, all of which were legally owned by other men and set in motion in such a way, and only such a way, as to earn a profit for the owners.

The industry's rapid development, therefore, involved simultaneous social accumulation of capital and of knowledge. The former legally be-

revolutionärer Attentismus: Die deutsche Sozialdemokratie am Vorabend des ersten Weltkrieges (Frankfurt am Main, 1973).

105. "Squeezing His Lemons," in McGovern, *Labor Lyrics*, 6–7.

longed to the firms' partners and shareholders, and its perpetual increase was their driving ambition. But to whom did the knowledge belong? From the vantage point of society's real wealth, Karl Marx argued that

> ... the accumulation of the skill and knowledge (scientific power) of the workers themselves is the chief form of accumulation, and infinitely more important than the accumulation – which goes hand in hand with it and merely represents it – of the *existing objective* conditions of this accumulated activity. These objective conditions are only nominally accumulated and must be constantly produced and consumed anew.[106]

The process of accumulation involved social conflict not only because workers and owners disputed over the division of the product between wages and profits but also because the social character of production clashed with the private nature of ownership. The "skill and knowledge" accumulated by workers assumed decisive importance in determining the outcome on both levels of conflict, and indeed in determining the way in which capital itself was "constantly produced and consumed anew." Such "prodigious" profits as had made Carnegie himself "ashamed" could not have been earned without Carnegie's triumph over workers' power that had its roots in their accumulated "skill and knowledge."

This contest placed the skilled workers of late-nineteenth-century industry in a position of unique importance. They were producers, whose "mass of rule-of-thumb or traditional knowledge," in the words of Frederick Winslow Taylor, was their "principal asset or possession" and made their "initiative" indispensable to the operation of the enterprise.[107] The craft workers' initiative was both indispensable to the employers and a source of controversy for them. Because the firm was an agency for the generation of profits out of money invested in buildings, land, machinery, raw materials, and labor power, its success depended on management's exploitation of all those factors of production in the generation of salable products. But because that process involved the creation of goods needed by society, the "manager's brains," to quote Bill Haywood and Frank Bohn, were "under the workman's cap."[108] By the turn of the century,

106. Karl Marx, *Theories of Surplus Value* (translated by Emile Burns, 3 vols., Moscow, 1963–71), III, 266–7. In this statement, Marx is paraphrasing Thomas Hodgskin. His basic agreement with Hodgskin's argument is evident in the tenor of Marx's discussion, and it is made explicit in Volume III, p. 295.

107. Frederick Winslow Taylor, *Principles of Scientific Management* (New York, 1967), 31, 32.

108. William D. Haywood and Frank Bohn, *Industrial Socialism* (Chicago, n.d.), 25.

the steelmasters' quest for greater and more secure profits had led them
not only to integrate "backward" for control of every operation from the
iron or coal mine to the rolling mill but also to attack the menace of
collective workers' control over any part of those operations and ultimately to search for ways in which to cut the taproot of nineteenth-
century workers' power by dispossessing the craftsmen of their accumulated skill and knowledge.

To understand the scope and nature of that development, however, it
is necessary to look beyond the iron and steel craftsmen and their amalgamation struggle. They have served to bring to our attention the interlocking character of the skilled workers' "managerial" role, the social
structure of the mill, the craft basis of nineteenth-century trade unionism,
the mutualistic culture and ideology of the epoch's labor movement, and
the workers' increasingly aggressive drive for collective control in the
face of the increasingly awesome ability of the firms' owners to impose
their will in the workplace. Moreover, their workplace conflicts spilled
over into community and political life, raising fundamental questions about
the nature of the American republic itself, and reached a climax in the
century's last decade, which revealed profound structural changes under
way in the social order as a whole. Finally, the failure of the steelworkers'
struggle for control of their conditions of work through amalgamation
underscored the shortcomings of an attempt to forge working-class unity
under the hegemony of skilled craftsmen. The laborers and machine operatives, who already dominated the work force numerically in many
industries and were assuming that importance in steel, were offered only
the role of supporters to the craftsmen's initiatives; family and community networks that bound working people together (in grossly unequal
solidarities) were considered only as they bore upon conflicts at the point
of production. The dominance of the skilled crafts blended all too easily
with a national ideology that proclaimed the supremacy of the white
race.

All these developments, however, belonged to a large economic and
social context that must now be considered. The long upswing of American industrial growth in the nineteenth century had different characteristics before and after the depression of the 1870s. Before that decade lay
the formative years of the American working class. The ranks of wage
laborers had grown hand in hand with rapid accumulation of capital for
more than half a century to the point that they represented more than
half of those counted by the census of 1870 as gainfully employed. Per
capita output had also grown steadily, at least since the 1830s. The 1850s
had represented something of a nodal point in this growth: Along with
the iron ship, the telegraph, and the consolidation of railroad trunk lines,

that decade had brought aggressive working-class activity in both economic and political life and had closed with America's achievement of second place in manufacturing output among the nations of the world and a genuine industrial depression.

After the early 1870s, industrial growth continued, but at a more erratic tempo. On the one hand, the web of commodity markets and wage labor spread from its source in the Northeast to all but the most remote corners of the land. Steel rails and ubiquitous telegraph wires were the web's visible fibers. Within its domain the number of nonagricultural wage earners increased more than twice as rapidly as the country's population. On the other hand, economic crises appearing in ever shorter intervals, and major depressions only twenty years apart (1873 and 1893), dried up the source of wages for millions of people. Although manufacturing output continued to rise, the rate of growth slowed after 1870, selling prices fell quite steadily, and the resulting downward pressure on profit margins generated, simultaneously, a record rate of business failures by the 1880s, the consolidation of large-scale enterprises, and chronic conflict between employers and workers over the costs of production.

These developments marked the end of the era of competitive industrial capitalism in America. Experiments with business consolidation, with overseas markets for products and investment, with the use of laborers from peasant communities outside the world's industrialized zones, and with more systematic management of workers and work relations (all of which were evident in the example of the steelworkers) were previews of a new stage of industrial development that was to mature rapidly after the depression of the 1890s. The amalgamation struggle of the iron and steel craftsmen and Michael McGovern's poetry belong to the final, spasmodic phase of industrial development on the basis of highly competitive capitalist relationships. The character of that period's labor movement was indelibly stamped by the spastic, deflationary character of its economic growth and by the variety of conditions under which different groups of wage earners turned out and distributed its industrial wares.[109]

The downward drift of prices during this epoch was exactly what leading economists of the age (from John Stuart Mill to Alfred Marshall) had predicted: As agricultural and industrial expansion increased the supplies of most commodities, their prices fell. Incessant attempts by manufacturers to reverse the steady decline of prices by means of pools, trusts, and other measures seem to have had little long-term effect. The index of

109.   My analysis of this epoch is deeply indebted to David M. Gordon, Richard Edwards, and Michael Reich, *Segmented Work, Divided Workers: The Historical Transformation of Labor in the United States* (Cambridge, 1982).

nineteenth-century wholesale prices constructed by George F. Warren and Frank A. Pearson (with 100 set at the level of 1910–14) declined from 111 in 1857 to 82 in 1890. The descent had not been smooth and even. On the contrary, it was interrupted by severe inflation during the Civil War, followed by a rather steady, steep reduction of prices to their 1857 levels by 1876 (the middle of the depression). The boom of 1879–82, fueled by simultaneous increases in farm exports, railroad building, steel production, immigration, and building construction, pushed the index from the 1879 low of 90 back almost to 1876 levels (i.e., to 108) before the downward trend resumed for the rest of the decade. Recurrent recessions at consistently shorter intervals starting in 1883 helped assure that prices would continue to fall steadily. It was only after the depression of 1893–7 that wholesale prices began to climb steadily. The fact that their ascent was seriously interrupted only once (by the depression of 1920–2) before the world depression of the 1930s reveals the important structural changes in the economy that had matured by the turn of the century.[110]

With every sign of economic recovery, entrepreneurs raced to capture potential markets, often investing heavily in new equipment and hiring every available worker. Labor, and especially immigrant labor, proved to be acutely responsive to every upsurge in demand and also very mobile geographically. Consequently, not only did immigrants flood into the United States every time business revived, but also they moved quickly to all corners of the land, creating enclaves of foreign-born factory or railroad workers that stood out sharply against the native-born population of the adjacent shops, offices, and farms. Workers whose parents had been born in America remained numerous in eastern Pennsylvania, in the smaller towns of the Ohio, Mohawk, and Hudson valleys, and in three midwestern cities (Dayton, Columbus, and Indianapolis), according to the calculations of Herbert Gutman and Ira Berlin, but elsewhere in the country – from New England's mill towns to Rocky Mountain mining camps – immigrants and their children provided the overwhelming majority of industrial wage earners. In Ansonia, Stamford,

110.	U.S. Department of Commerce, Bureau of the Census, *Historical Statistics of the United States, Colonial Times to 1970. Bicentennial Edition* (2 vols., Washington, D.C., 1975), hereafter cited as *Hist. Stat. U.S.*, I, 200–1. The index, which is explained in Volume I, p. 186, is heavily biased toward New York City prices and unfortunately does not separate the prices of manufactured goods from those of other commodities. On business failures and the intervals between business cycles, see Gordon, Edwards, and Reich, *Segmented Work*, 41–7, 101–2.

Wheeling, Joliet, Creston, Dubuque, and Saginaw the ambiance on the industrial side of the tracks was that of transplanted Britons, Germans, Scandinavians, and Irish. Indeed, the cities of the Midwest, which became the "Corliss engines" of industrial growth after 1870, displayed markedly European characteristics. In the Detroit of 1890, for example, 77 percent of the entire population had at least one foreign-born parent, and nearly 60 percent of the manual workers had personally migrated from Europe. Germans dominated the local working-class life, as they did in St. Louis, Milwaukee, and Chicago. In all, 2,855,000 immigrants landed between 1880 and 1885. Of them, 1,045,000 were from Germany, 457,000 from Britain, and roughly 417,000 each from Ireland and Scandinavia.[111]

It was primarily because most immigrants were of working age that the labor force increased much faster than the population during the late nineteenth century. Substantial numbers of black and white farmers also devoted part of the year to railroad construction, mining, dock work, or textile mills; and some gave up farming altogether to drive a wagon, switch freight cars, or build houses in town. The number of female wage earners rose sharply, while their most common occupation changed slowly from domestic service to factory work and then office work. Children under fourteen found work in mines and factories on an unprecedented scale during the 1878–82 boom, although the rate of increase in child labor subsequently began to subside. In all, the percentage of people sixteen years of age or older who were listed by the census as in the non-agricultural labor force rose from 23.2 percent in 1870 to 32.3 percent in 1900 (and, for males alone, from 35.9 percent in 1870 to 48.3 percent in 1900). The key to industrial growth in the middle and late nineteenth

111.   Ira Berlin and Herbert Gutman, "Osztályszerkezet és az amerikai munkásososztaly fejlödése 1840–1890 között (A bevándorlók és gyermekeik, mint bérmunkások)," *Történelmi Szemle*, 26 (1983), 224–37; Estelle Feinstein, *Stamford in the Gilded Age, 1868–1893* (Stamford, Conn.), 8–23; Cecelia F. Bucki, *Metal, Minds and Machines: Waterbury at Work* (Waterbury, Conn., 1980), 44–54, 70–4; Richard J. Oestreicher, "Solidarity and Fragmentation: Working People and Class Consciousness in Detroit, 1877–1895" (unpublished Ph.D. diss., Michigan State University, 1979), 48–54; John B. Jentz and Hartmut Keil, "From Immigrants to Urban Workers: Chicago's German Poor in the Gilded Age and Progressive Era, 1883–1908," *Vierteljahrschrift für Sozial- und Wirtschaftsgeschichte*, 68 (1981), 52–97. On the role of large urban centers in growth after 1870, see Gordon, Edwards, and Reich, *Segmented Work*, 88–9. The immigration figures are my calculations from *Hist. Stat. U.S.*, I, 106.

Table 1.1. *Manual wage earners by industry*

Industry	1870		1910	
	Number (000)	% of total	Number (000)	% of total
All industries	3,546	100	14,234	100
Construction	795	22.4	2,662	18.7
Metalworking	310	8.7	1,664	11.7
Clothing	276	7.8	1,190	8.4
Textiles	253	7.1	804	5.7
Mining	186	5.3	917	6.4
Shoes	173	4.9	209	1.5
Railroads	157	4.4	1,158	8.1
Woodworking	129	3.6	565	4.0
Team and truck	106	3.0	558	3.9
Food processing	87	2.5	300	2.1
Printing	50	1.4	237	1.7
Iron and steel	25	0.7	326	2.3
Chemical, oil, rubber	10	0.3	200	1.4

Sources: U.S. Census Office, *Statistics of the Population of the United States. Ninth Census* (1870), I, 704–15; U.S. Bureau of the Census, *Sixteenth Census of the United States: 1940. Population. Comparative Occupational Statistics for the United States, 1870–1940*, 104–11.

century was more people devoting more of their lives to working harder than ever before.[112]

The major sectors of the industrial economy in which they worked are indicated in Table 1.1. The thirteen industries listed there accounted for 71 percent of industry's manual wage earners in 1870 and 75.3 percent in 1910. The figures were derived from the detailed occupational listings

112. The data on labor-force growth are calculated from figures in *Hist. Stat. U.S.*, I, 127. On the importance of labor-force growth, see Gordon, Edwards, and Reich, *Segmented Work*, 81–5. On child labor, see Edgar S. Furnis, *Labor Problems* (Boston, 1925), 186–9; Gordon, Edwards, and Reich, *Segmented Work*, 121; Katherine A. Harvey, *The Best-Dressed Miners: Life and Labor in the Maryland Coal Region, 1835–1910* (Ithaca, 1969), 49–55; Fernand Harvey, *Révolution industrielle et travailleurs: une enquête sur les rapports entre le capital et le travail au Québec à la fin du 19ᵉ siècle* (Montreal, 1978), 124–5. On women workers, see Alice Kessler-Harris, *Out to Work: A History of Wage-Earning Women in the United States* (New York, 1982), 108–19; *Hist. Stat. U.S.*, I, 129.

in the 1870 census and from the Census Bureau's historical tabulation of American occupations, which was developed in 1940. It is, unfortunately, not possible to use data from 1900 for comparison with 1870, because the 1940 study lumped occupational figures for decades before 1910 into aggregates that are inappropriate to the comparisons being made here (e.g., placing iron molders, agricultural-implement workers, and many others together with basic ironworkers and steelworkers).

What is evident is that the number of manual wage earners in industry rose by 301 percent during these four decades, at a time when the population increased by only 132 percent. Moreover, there were many wage earners not included in these figures at all. In 1870, for example, female domestic servants (902,000) outnumbered construction workers, and by 1910 male and female clerical workers (1,718,500) were more numerous than metalworkers. The point here is simply that the rising output of the century's last decades was fed by the entry of millions of new production workers, especially into building construction, metalworking, clothing and textile manufacture, mining, and railroading.

Even more important, all this influx of new wage earners failed to sustain the high rate of growth enjoyed by American industry between the 1830s and the 1870s. According to the calculations of David Gordon, Richard Edwards, and Michael Reich, industrial output had grown at a rate of 6.5 percent annually between 1839 and 1874, but between 1874 and 1899 the rate slowed somewhat to 5.5 percent. Other measures (real gross national product, capital formation, and inventories) showed similar deceleration of growth. Above all else, the boom periods became shorter and the recessions more frequent than they had been before the 1870s.[113] All this does not mean that the United States was experiencing a prolonged depression of the sort England suffered between the 1870s and the 1890s. On the contrary, expansion still characterized American industry, and, as Brinley Thomas has argued, both capital and labor moved steadily and massively from Britain to America during these years, so that for the Atlantic economy as a whole, there was no "long depression."[114] Two points are important here: First, in this final stage in the develop-

113. Gordon, Edwards and Reich, *Segmented Work*, 51, 101. Census figures on value added by manufacture reveal the same trend Gordon, Edwards and Reich describe, but produce large growth figures for both phases. Between 1849 and 1869, value added grew 10% annually. From 1879 to 1899 it grew 8.9% annually. These figures include neighborhood and hand manufacture, as well as factory output, as is only appropriate for the epoch. *Hist. Stat. U.S.*, II, 666.

114. Brinley Thomas, *Migration and Economic Growth: A Study of Great Britain and the Atlantic Economy* (Cambridge, 1954), 108–9 and passim.

ment of competitive industrial capitalism, ever larger inputs of human toil failed to generate corresponding increases in output. Second, chronic deflation and staggering cycles of boom and bust forced employers to undertake an intensive search for labor that was cheaper and could be more tightly controlled. In that quest they encountered a working class that was becoming not only steadily larger but also more articulate and self-assertive.

It is important to note, however, that those workers still toiled in a variety of settings. Important though factories employing hundreds or thousands of workers were during the late nineteenth century, only a minority of wage earners labored in them. In a thorough analysis of manufacturing in Philadelphia between 1850 and 1880, Bruce Laurie and Mark Schmitz found five distinctive forms of manufacturing. Artisan production remained important there, as elsewhere, into the 1880s. Using hand methods, such as would have predominated in the early decades of the century, artisans who labored alone or in small workshops constituted 8 percent of the city's labor force in 1880, but almost half of its butchers, bakers, and light metal tradesmen. Outwork and sweatshops were noteworthy in the fabrication of shoes, caps, glassware, and furniture. Outworkers used hand tools or foot-powered machines in their homes to work up materials provided them from central shops, and the sweating system arose (especially in clothing) when an outworker hired others, thus becoming an outside contractor. Manufactories provided a fourth, and still very widespread, type of workplace. They gathered many workers under one roof and subjected them to close supervision and often detailed division of labor, but they used no power to drive machinery other than that of human muscle. Almost half of Philadelphia's clothing firms of 1880 used neither water power nor steam power, nor did more than half its furniture factories and glassworks, or more than 70 percent of its boot and shoe establishments. A special feature of the 1870s in Philadelphia, as in New York, was the employment of thousands of needle women within the back rooms of large department stores, like Wanamaker's and A. T. Stewart's. By the 1880s, however, most department stores abandoned the manufacture of the attire they sold, in favor of large staffs of buyers, who managed the acquisition of goods for each department.[115]

115. Bruce Laurie and Mark Schmitz, "Manufacture and Productivity: The Making of an Industrial Base, Philadelphia, 1850–1880," in Theodore Hershberg, ed., *Philadelphia: Work, Space, Family, and Group Experience in the Nineteenth Century* (New York, 1981), 43–92. On the role of buyers in department stores, see Susan Porter Benson, "The Clerking Sisterhood," *Radical America,* 12 (March–April 1978), 41–55.

By 1880, factory production in Philadelphia employed more than 80 percent of the workers in textiles, iron and steel, machine tools and hardwares, shipbuilding, gasworks and other fuels, and chemicals. Fully half of those workers, however, were contributed by textiles and metallurgy (which together accounted for one-third of the city's industrial workers).[116] Even in textiles, the eclipse of the hand-loom weaver by power looms had occurred only after 1850, and in the city's important carpet industry, only during the later part of the 1870s.[117] Moreover, in every metal-fabricating factory, much of the work was still done without power-driven machinery. Files and chisels and sledgehammers remained indispensable supplements to lathes, milling machines, and annealing furnaces. Nevertheless, mechanized factory production was quite advanced in Philadelphia in comparison with many other manufacturing centers. In 1880 in Poughkeepsie, for example, only 9 percent of the male workers and 13 percent of the females were machine tenders in factories.[118]

As Table 1.2 reveals, however, it was the capital-intensive industries that had the nation's highest rates of growth in the number of workers they employed. The new recruits to the army of labor fed not only a proliferation of small firms but also the new giant enterprises, whose hegemony was unmistakable after the crisis of the 1890s. In the midst of protracted deflation of the century's last decades, entrepreneurs in these industries were creating the firms of the future: consolidating their control over workers in a wide variety of related activities, experimenting with new ways of subordinating those workers directly to management's control, and thus inserting themselves into the front lines in the confrontation with workers' control. The chemical and oil industries led the way in the development of continuous-flow processes. Raising capital, driving out competitors, and distributing the products of high-volume technology were the greatest challenges facing these employers. Their manual workers were almost exclusively common laborers, and such challenges from crafts as the coopers posed in turning out the industries' barrels were ruthlessly overcome as early as the 1870s by Standard Oil's smashing of the coopers' union.[119]

116. Laurie and Schmitz, "Manufacture and Productivity," 45, 53, 59.
117. Susan Levine, "Their Own Sphere: Women's Work, the Knights of Labor and the Transformation of the Carpet Trade, 1870–1890" (unpublished Ph.D. diss., City University of New York, 1979), 81–3.
118. Clyde Griffen and Sally Griffen, *Natives and Newcomers: The Ordering of Opportunity in Mid-Nineteenth-Century Poughkeepsie* (Cambridge, Mass., 1978), 7; U.S. Commissioner of Labor, *Hand and Machine Labor.*
119. Chandler, *Visible Hand,* 253–7, 290–8; Herbert G. Gutman, "La politique ouvrière de la grande enterprise amèricaine de 'l'âge du clinquant':

Table 1.2. *Rates of increase in*
manual workers, 1870–1910

Industry	% increase
Chemical, oil, rubber	1,900
Iron and steel	1,204
Railroads	638
Metalworking	437
Team and truck driving	426
Mining	393
Printing	374
Woodworking	338
Clothing	331
All industries	*301*
Food processing	245
Construction	235
Textiles	218
U.S. population	*132*
Shoes	21

Sources: Same as for Table 1.1.

Quite different was the case of the railroads. They were the first of the giant enterprises. In the mid-1870s, when Cambria Iron's four thousand employees made it the country's largest manufacturing firm, the Pennsylvania Railroad and its affiliated lines had between fifty thousand and fifty-five thousand wage earners, managed by one thousand company officials. Railroads pioneered in the development of management by salaried officials (rather than by the owners personally), as well as in alliances with investment banks to raise the funds needed for building seventy-five thousand new miles of track in the 1880s. The intervention of investment houses in the affairs of bankrupt lines established the pattern of consolidating competing firms, a practice that spread to many industries during the 1890s. Moreover, railroad companies promoted standardization of equipment, gauges, accounting methods, and even the time of day (through zones of uniform standard time, established in 1883). Nevertheless, the line-and-staff form of management, by which these far-flung networks were all directed after the Civil War, produced no standardized labor policy or direction. There were many different types of work on a railroad: running trades, construction, switching and setting up trains in

le cas de la Standard Oil Company," *Le Mouvement Social,* 102 (January–March 1978), 67–99.

yards, repair of cars, telegraph operation, and handling records and receiving and dispensing funds at hundreds of thousands of different locations. Each type was handled separately by separate officials, except during the strikes of 1877 and the upsurge of the Knights of Labor and American Railway Union with their gospel of all-grades unionism between 1885 and 1894. Then certain elements of a labor system began to appear, especially on western lines. Slowly and unevenly until 1894, rapidly thereafter, railroad managers introduced centralized payroll and discharge lists, personnel records with all infractions of discipline noted, contributory accident insurance, and cooperation among lines to defeat strikes and to standardize wages. As was the case in steel, the systematic personnel policies of the railroads were forged in the furnace of industrial conflict and ultimately were made possible by the decisive intervention of the government in suppression of strikes.[120]

Major metalworking firms, like Philadelphia's Baldwin Locomotive Company, usually were linked to railroad building in the late nineteenth century just as tightly as the steel industry was. But two other groups of large metal firms had appeared by the end of the 1880s. One group included the builders of intricate machinery such as harvesting machines or sewing machines, which needed a widespread network of sales and repair people if they were to be used by hundreds of thousands of individual customers. As Alfred D. Chandler has shown, firms that created such networks (competitive capitalism's counterpart to the state's machine-tractor stations amid Soviet collective farms) readily dominated both national and world markets and thus had an outlet for ever expanding productive capacity. The second group is typified by the electrical industry, which saw its competing firms quickly consolidated by investment houses, and tightly linked to all levels of government, because they needed capital and franchises to create customers. Power stations, transmission lines, street railways, and urban electrification were all public projects. State capitalism created the markets; productive capacity, concentrated in large modern plants, followed.

Such metalworking industries, together with the machine-tool industry, which remained in relatively small firms, selling to larger ones, could not introduce continuous-flow processes. Metalworking firms did not enjoy economies of scale. Quite small plants were the most efficient. Large and small alike were hopelessly dependent on the skills of labor, in a

120. Chandler, *Visible Hand,* 106–87; H. Shelton Stromquist, "A Generation of Boomers: Work, Community Structure, and the Pattern of Industrial Conflict on Late Nineteenth Century American Railroads" (unpublished Ph.D. diss., University of Pittsburgh, 1981), 414–73.

multitude of different crafts: machinists, pattern makers, molders, black-smiths, metal polishers, fitters, electricians, sheet-metal craftsmen, and others. This was the domain of the most bitter and protracted struggles of the epoch to change work practices, the cradle in which scientific management was born. Here managers sought, first through piecework and inside contracting, to induce "each workman to use his best endeavors, his skill, his ingenuity, and his goodwill – in a word, his 'initiative,' so as to yield the largest possible return to his employer,"[121] and subsequently, through standardization of the tasks themselves, to eliminate reliance on the workers' initiative altogether.

Finally, the growth rates shown in Table 1.2 draw attention to the continuing importance of textiles and clothing, mining, and construction. The first of these was the classic habitat of the machine tender. As Carroll D. Wright wrote in 1880, looking backward from that date, "the history of the factory system becomes the history of the textile industries."[122] In 1870, cotton goods and worsted goods still led all other industries in the average number of workers per plant, and the numerous power-loom weavers in these mills were the archetypal factory operatives of the nineteenth century.[123] Paid by the yard of cloth or pick of the shuttle, these women and men tended several machines at once, refilling bobbins and watching for breaks, while the mechanisms themselves controlled the tempo of work. Although unions had little staying power in the industry (outside of Fall River, Massachusetts), they were often formed, and strikes were numerous. By way of contrast, the manufacture of clothing was a citadel of outwork and the sweatshop. Factory production grew in several cities (often simply by bringing subcontracting practices indoors) without expelling the older forms. Despite major strikes against the subcontracting system, especially in the 1880s, and despite some growth of factory production, the production of clothing remained subject to uncontrolled, labor-intensive competition past the end of the century.

Building construction and coal mining also remained labor-intensive and fiercely competitive. Although the building trades went through many changes, as standardized wood, metal, and plumbing parts were made in factories, steel girders and electrical power transformed downtown

121.   Taylor, *Principles,* 32. On the diseconomies of scale, see Laurie and Schmitz, "Manufacture and Productivity," 66–78.
122.   Carroll D. Wright, "Report on the Factory System of the United States," 1, quoted in Edward C. Kirkland, *Industry Comes of Age: Business, Labor, and Public Policy, 1860–1897* (New York, 1961), 171.
123.   Nelson, *Managers and Workers,* 4. Workers in the metal trades, textiles, clothing, mining, and construction will all be discussed in detail in the pages to come.

buildings, and speculative contractors began to erect large tracts of uniform housing, the swelling volume of construction was brought about largely by putting hammers, saws, and trowels into the hands of more and more men. In no other industrial country was so large a proportion of the working class made up of building workers. Similarly, despite the introduction of undercutting machinery, especially in the Midwest, the soaring demand for coal was met here, as in Europe, basically by putting ever growing numbers of men underground at the coal face. In fact, it was only after 1920 that the combined impact of rival fuels and mine mechanization reversed the upward spiral in the employment of coal diggers. Construction workers and coal miners together constituted half of the country's union members by the first decade of the twentieth century. Their activities decisively shaped the house of labor, particularly its response to business consolidation and management reform after the 1890s.

These workers, whose numbers were growing so remarkably as competitive industrial capitalism entered its crisis decades, are the historical actors to be examined in the chapters to come. The patterns of struggle found in the iron and steel industry reveal much about late-nineteenth-century craftsmen, but they do not explain all labor activism by any means. Common laborers, factory operatives, and skilled workers in other industries generated their own distinctive challenges to employers' authority during these years. On occasion, workers of all three types acted together, if not in unison. Both their separate initiatives and their concerted class struggles profoundly influenced the responses of industrial managers and government officials to the declining rate of capital accumulation.

2

The common laborer

The toil of the common laborer is the most elementary form of wage dependence and one that has largely escaped the attention of historians. Seemingly in defiance of industrial society's celebration of incessant change and of mechanical power, the men who wielded shovels and pushed wheelbarrows on twentieth-century construction projects bore an uncanny resemblance to those who had dug canals and erected fortifications two hundred years earlier. Their work gangs were totally male, as those not constituted of slaves or serfs had long been in western Europe and North America. They had shoveled between sixteen and nineteen tons per day when they were studied by Sébastienne Vauban in seventeenth-century France, by early Victorian contractors of English navvies, and by Frederick Winslow Taylor at the dawn of the twentieth century.[1] They exchanged simple physical force for a daily wage, whose level changed only gradually over the course of the nineteenth century. What changed, and changed significantly, was the place of origin of America's laborers. Both the timeless quality of laborers' work and the changing geography of their recruitment profoundly influenced their relationship to the nation's labor movement.

Laborers seldom formed durable unions. Their life-style made a mockery of social reformers' efforts to promote habits of "thrift, sobriety, adaptability, [and] initiative."[2] In the researches of quantitatively ori-

1. Andrea Graziosi, "Lavori comuni e concetto di lavoro nelle primi analisi del lavoro umano, con alcune osservazioni relative alla produttività dei primi e alle consequenze che ne derivana," *Studi Economici* (Falcotà di Economia e Commercio dell'Università di Napoli, 1984); Terry Coleman, *The Railway Navvies: A History of the Men Who Made the Railways* (London, 1965); Taylor, *Principles*, 71. For descriptions of early laboring, see Merritt Roe Smith, *Harpers Ferry Armory and the New Technology* (Ithaca, 1977), 43–4; Michael Chevalier, *Society, Manners, and Politics in the United States* (Boston, 1839), 108.
2. W. H. Beveridge, quoted in Don D. Lescohier, *The Labor Market* (New York, 1919), 268.

ented students of social mobility, they simply disappeared in droves between one census and the next. They moved continually, and unlike the
iron puddler or railroad machinist who might also rove about in search
of work, laborers belonged to no particular industry. On the contrary,
they were necessary to nearly all forms of manufacturing, transportation,
and commerce. Even an effort to distinguish between industrial and agricultural laborers is thwarted because most of them were of rural origin,
and consequently they persistently quit steel mills or road construction
in the heat of summer in order to harvest sugar beets, wheat, or cotton.
Nor were they assigned to perpetual repetition of the same task, as was
the textile-mill operative, who is so often regarded as the archetypal worker
of industrial capitalism. In building a new aqueduct for New York City's
water system, as an observer noted, "the same gang of men may work in
the stone quarry one day, on concrete work the next, or in moving the
track for the dirt trains the following day."[3]

It is not even possible to say with any confidence or precision how
many men supplied the country's portable muscle power. The last three
censuses of the nineteenth century used a classification system that categorized occupations according to sectors of the economy, as they were
then defined by political economists: agriculture; professional and personal service; trade and transportation; and manufactures, mechanical
and mining industries. Laborers could be found in all four of them, but
within the last two categories census directors did not distinguish them
from other employees. Many were explicitly grouped, however, under
the general heading of "personal and professional service," because, as
Margo Conk has explained, they were "assumed to be in a personal,
almost feudal relationship either to an artisan (a mason's laborer, for
example), or to the society as a whole (a road laborer or a day laborer)."[4]
According to this method, the census of 1870 classified 1,031,666 people
(or 8 percent of the gainfully employed population) as "laborers (not
specified)." By 1910 a new classification scheme was in use, but one that
was even less helpful. In place of economic sectors, the census takers had
substituted three general categories (trades, operatives, and laborers) based
more on the Census Bureau's assessment of each job's socioeconomic
status than on any effort to evaluate the work's technical content. Using
this classification, the 1910 census put 4,478,000 individuals (or 12 per-

3. U.S. Immigration Commission, *Immigrants in Industry* (in 25 parts, 61st
    Cong., 2nd Sess., Senate Document No. 633, Washington, D.C., 1911), Part
    22, 398.
4. Margo Anderson Conk, *The United States Census and Labor Force Change:
    A History of Occupational Statistics, 1870–1940* (Ann Arbor, 1978), 30.

cent of the gainfully employed) under the heading "laborers, except farm and mine."[5]

Although the changing definitions make any conclusions about trends hazardous, and even though both definitions ignored the ubiquity and transience of laborers' working lives, these figures reveal that the demand for portable muscle power had by no means been eclipsed by the much-heralded triumph of "labor-saving machinery." On the contrary, the nineteenth century expended human physical exertion more prodigiously than any other epoch in the country's history.[6] The 1910 figure represented fully one-third of the manual wage earners in manufacturing and transportation. When Alba Edwards, director of the 1910 census, reconsidered its data, he concluded that 32 percent of all male employees in this modern, corporation-dominated economy deserved to be called laborers (9,595,000 men).[7] Moreover, the nature of their toil had changed at only a glacial pace over the preceding century. And the attitude of polite society toward laborers had changed equally little. Eighteenth-century intellectuals could easily have written the description penned by Edith Abbott in 1905: "a dangerous class: inadequately fed, clothed, and housed, they threaten the health of the community, and, like all the weak and ignorant, they often become the misguided followers of unscrupulous men."[8]

But common laborers were not an archaic vestige of preindustrial society. In fact, their largest employers included the most highly capitalized industries: railroads, steel, chemicals, mining, and metal fabricating. The wonders of urban reconstruction – the subway, the suspension bridge, and the skyscraper – also required their strong backs and arms in vast numbers. Disciples of Taylor set out to measure the work and endurance of men and horses, just as physicists and military engineers had done so assiduously in the 1700s.[9] We find, in a series of articles written by the International Harvester executive H. A. Worman, describing his experi-

---

5. *Hist. Stat. U.S.*, I, 139; Conk, 41–2.
6. See Raphael Samuel, "Workshop of the World: Steam Power and Hand Technology in mid-Victorian Britain," *History Workshop*, 3 (Spring 1977), 6–72.
7. Whitney Coombs, *Wages of Unskilled Labor in Manufacturing Industries in the United States, 1890–1924* (New York, 1924), 18.
8. Edith Abbott, "The Wages of Unskilled Labor in the United States," *Journal of Political Economy*, 13 (June 1905), 324. On the eighteenth century, see Gary B. Nash, *The Urban Crucible: Social Change, Political Consciousness and the Origins of the American Revolution* (Cambridge, Mass., 1979).
9. Frederick W. Taylor and Sanford E. Thompson, *Concrete Costs* (New York, 1912); Graziosi, "Lavori comuni."

mental findings on the hiring of various categories of workers, the following definition of laborers: "men of mighty thews and sinews under poor control, lacking the brain development, experience or training which would fit them for anything but routine muscular effort."[10] Although scientific interest in laborers was not new, eighteenth-century scholars had detected aspects of laboring work and its significance that were lost to Worman (and to Taylor and his colleagues). On the one hand, their thoughts about the "human machine" had led off simultaneously toward physics, political economy, and moral philosophy. Considering this elementary form of wage labor, Desaguiliers, Diderot, Adam Smith, and others had identified a point of departure for analyzing the "natural force" of the human being, the income necessary to reproduce that force (or "natural wage"), and the relationship between expended labor and the value of the commodity produced (or "natural price"). Their basic conception of work was derived from Newtonian mechanics: a determinate push or pull (i.e., the transference of force from one body to another, measured by the product of the force and the amount of displacement along the line of force). Nevertheless, these early thinkers were also keenly aware that the "human machine" brought to his task more than physical force. As Charles Augustin de Coulomb wrote in 1778 of his experiments in the human capacity to move earth:

> Although human strength is quite limited, it is sometimes employed in preference to that of animals, even in the most simple and uniform movements, because under some circumstances it is easy to provide through numbers what is lacking in the force of each individual; because [men] often occupy less space than other agents providing the same results; because they can always operate with machines which are more simple and easier to transport than those with which animals are used; [and] because, finally, their intelligence enables them to economize their strength [and] to moderate their work to suit the obstacles which they have to overcome.[11]

Note how much more subtle and accurate Coulomb's sense of laborers' work was than that of International Harvester's Worman. More than "mighty thews and sinews under poor control" had appeared in the French physicist's comparison of men with horses. Teamwork, adaptability, and the use of such fundamentals of mechanics as inclined planes, pulleys, and levers also entered his description, not to mention the laborers' in-

10. H. A. Worman, "Recruiting the Workforce. IV – Hiring the Unskilled Workman," *Factory,* 1 (February 1908), 158.
11. Charles Augustin de Coulomb, *Théories des machines simples, en ayant égard au frottement de leurs parties et à la roideur des cordages* (Paris, 1821), 255; my translation.

telligence and their experience in pacing themselves against the tasks at hand. Worman's reduction of laboring to "routine muscular effort" implicitly denied any significance to the very qualities of work that scientific management sought to eliminate: the workers' initiative and collectivity. Those very attributes, however, hold the keys to understanding laborers' behavior and aspirations.

Because both the force and the talents of "human machines" were easily transferred from one task or location to another, they were exercised in many different contexts. It is possible, however, to identify two general categories of laboring that gave rise to somewhat different experiences on the job, despite the movement of many men back and forth between the two spheres of work between 1860 and 1910. One category involved jobs on which the laborers themselves were the producers. In constructing and repairing railway tracks, drilling tunnels, and loading ships and lighters, for example, the laborers' own exertions directly added value to the product. A glance at their work, therefore, brings vividly to mind Karl Marx's observation that under capitalism, to "be a productive laborer is . . . not a piece of luck, but a misfortune."[12] They toiled in gangs under the arbitrary direction of gang bosses, who drove them with curses, threats, or entreaties, and who were as often as not armed with ax handles and shotguns, as ominous reminders of their authority. John White, a visitor from England, caught the essence of such production when he observed Irishmen laying track for the Union Pacific across Wyoming at a pace of four miles per day:

> Unlike the same race at home, the men were working too hard to talk much, and were too thoroughly drilled into precision to have much to say of their work. Foremost went the carts, tumbling out wooden ties upon the roadway [which had been raised above ground level]. Then came a gang of men, carrying long poles with iron hooks at their ends. By sticking these hooks into the ties, the men could push them or pull them into any position required, after they were tumbled out on the roadway. Then a gang followed, throwing down rails upon the ties. Then came other gangs to arrange the rails in their places and set two lines of them at just the right gauge apart; and lastly, a gang to drive in the iron bolts and fix the rails firmly on the ties.[13]

The availability of such jobs fluctuated drastically with the seasons and with business cycles. After months of futile searching for odd jobs in Chicago early in 1892, Walter Wyckoff found that spring came "like the

12. Karl Marx, *Capital. A Critique of Political Economy* (3 vols., Chicago, 1906), I, 558.
13. John White, *Sketches from America* (London, 1870), 266–7.

heralding of peace and plenty after war." Jobs were everywhere to be had. On the railroads, far and away America's largest employers, laborers like those John White had described constituted almost 30 percent of the total work force during the construction boom of 1880 (122,500 men). Thirty years later they again composed 26 percent of the force, and they numbered 449,000. In hard times, no new construction was undertaken. Trainmen then often were sent out on fewer runs each week, and shopmen suffered reductions in pay, but laborers were simply dismissed.[14] Although craftsmen such as carpenters, masons, coopers, and engineers could be found at their work sites, it was the laborers who not only provided the main body of employees but also set the tone on the job. In such settings, work styles, social life, and strikes were fashioned by the laborers themselves.

In the other category, laborers performed ancillary tasks. In manufacturing and in building construction, laborers fetched and carried, loaded or cleaned up, whatever, wherever, and whenever they were told, while the actual production (the direct addition of value) was carried on by skilled workers or by machine tenders. John Fitch called the puddlers, rollers, and other tonnage men in steel mills "the men who give character to the industry." His invidious comparison reflected both the economic thinking of the age and the attitudes of the craftsmen themselves.[15] Laborers' toil, their unions, and even their strikes in these industries tended to be subject to the dominance of the skilled trades.

The dominance was especially clear where lines of occupation coincided with lines of race. In railroad switchyards in the South, for example, both black and white workers could be found in switching gangs, but no Afro-Americans were foremen, let alone engineers or brakemen. Switchmen had to follow complex instructions in lining up boxcars on several tracks of differing lengths according to their destinations and cargoes, and their mistakes might be costly to a load of glass or furniture – not to mention to themselves. As a veteran Savannah switchman put it, "Now when you worked on the railroad switching boxcars, it is a known fact [that] if you lost on the railroad you lost. If you lost in a skin game you had a chance to win tomorrow. But if you lost anything on the rail-

---

14. Walter A. Wyckoff, *The Workers. An Experiment in Reality. The West* (New York, 1898), 248; U.S. Industrial Commission, *Report of the Industrial Commission* (19 vols., Washington, D.C., 1901), XVII, 719–21; Walter Licht, *Working for the Railroad: The Organization of Work in the Nineteenth Century* (Princeton, 1983), 34; Frank Julian Warne, *The Workers at War* (New York, 1920), 88.
15. Fitch, *Steel Workers*, 9.

road, you lost a hand, leg, arm, life, or eye. You can't get that back."[16]

The same man testified that the highest position any black worker attained in the Savannah yard was "bottoming," that is, leading an engine. And it was on this very job that the white engine drivers' sense of themselves as "the real workers" was most keenly felt. The black switchman had to scramble on and off locomotives that never slowed down — charging ahead with the "real work" of the yard.

The availability of jobs for ancillary laborers was also seasonal and varied sharply with business cycles. There was, however, a long-term trend in many industries for the number of laborers to increase in both absolute and relative terms over the half century before World War I. As our earlier examination of iron and steel craftsmen revealed, nineteenth-century technological innovations most sharply reduced the number of men working at tonnage jobs around rolling mills and converters, so that the proportion of workers who were day laborers rose from the general range of 10–20 percent in the 1870s to more than 40 percent by the 1890s. Peter Shergold has estimated that by 1907, 42 percent of the workers in Allegheny County's steel industry were common laborers, and another 7 percent earned no more than the common-labor rate. Whitney Coombs's calculations based on the years 1910–15 confirm Shergold's estimates. There were many men in tonnage gangs, Coombs pointed out, whose work consisted essentially of handling materials or cleaning up, and whose earnings were superior to those of men in the labor pools, if at all, only because their work was steadier. Among them were stockers, cinder pitmen, and bottom-makers' helpers in Bessemer crews and third-melters' helpers and switchmen in open-hearth crews.[17] The available data for building laborers are more exact, because census takers counted them separately from building tradesmen in both 1870 and 1910. During those forty years, the number of laborers rose by 408 percent — from 184,000 to 936,000 — and that increase was more than double the rate of growth for the construction labor force as a whole. Prefabrication of building materials in planing mills and other factories had retarded the growth of

16. Kimathi Mohammed, interview of Mr. Sanford (transcript in possession of author). Compare Robert Asher, "Machines, Accidents, and Working Class Consciousness" (unpublished paper presented at the Organization of American Historians convention, April 17, 1975); Carl Gersuny, *Work Hazards and Industrial Conflict* (Hanover, N.H., 1981).

17. Graziosi, "Common Laborers"; Peter R. Shergold, *Working-Class Life: The "American Standard" in Comparative Perspective, 1899–1913* (Pittsburgh, 1982), 17; Coombs, *Wages*, 49, 72–4. See also the report on a Department of Labor survey of steel-industry employment in *IA*, 88 (August 10, 1911), 336.

the skilled trades, but mechanization of lifting and hauling, which became so evident by the 1980s, had not yet had much impact on the way materials were prepared and moved about building sites.[18]

No matter which of these two contexts provided laborers with their new employment, most of the men had come originally from farms. Even for those who resided, or at least wintered, in cities and traveled out to the country for work, farms had been their places of birth. To be sure, yard laborers, janitors, and watchmen aplenty could be found around mills and factories who had once been craftsmen but had become too old to ply their trades. Among switchmen in New Haven's terminal yards in 1902 were seven men who had served the same railroad in various jobs since the 1870s (in one case since 1858). Unemployed craftsmen sought laborers' jobs during hard times. Youngsters from very poor circumstances sought the immediate income of laborers, in preference to the low starting wages for apprentices or other trainees to crafts. Even such youngsters, however, more often became machine operators than members of labor gangs. It was not by chance that laborers of the early twentieth century seldom quizzed a native white American who joined them about his origins. They took it for granted that he was either a drunkard or someone on the run from the law or from his family.[19] A "normal" laborer was a foreign-born or black farm youth.

The hoe and the shovel

Consider the name American society has given those who carried out its most spectacular feats of engineering – the railroads, dams, subway tunnels, and sewer systems. In Britain they were called *navvies;* in France, *terrasiers;* in Italy, *terrazzieri;* in Germany, *Streckenarbeiter.* In the United States, a "navvy" was an earth-moving machine of the middle of the nineteenth century.[20] These men had no name, except perhaps the colloquial *ditchdigger.* What does this lack of a suitable name tell us about the place of such laborers in America? It reminds us that wherever they worked, they were strangers. Sedentary Americans knew songs and legends about them, but shunned personal encounter. Yankee residents of

18. U.S. Census, *Occ. Stat.,* 105.
19. Williams, *Worker's Mind,* 15–26, 33. On older yard laborers, see *New Haven Union,* June 19, 1902. On poor urban youth becoming laborers, see Frank Roney, *Frank Roney, Irish Rebel and California Labor Leader,* edited by Ira B. Cross (Berkeley, 1931), 351. On German farm laborers and Chicago, see Jentz and Keil, "From Immigrants to Urban Workers," 73.
20. Coleman, *Navvies,* 50.

Wareham and Shoreham, Massachusetts, first met the 300 Italians who were digging the Cape Cod Canal in October 1880, when the Italians quit work and marched through the town to protest the failure of their employers to pay them for over a month. The response of the townspeople was to swear in special deputies to defend their communities against the alien invasion.[21]

During the middle decades of the century, local farmers might be hired temporarily to help build railroads or canals, especially if they came with horses and wagons, but far more often the farmers locked up their wagons, along with their chickens and their daughters, and made contact with these rude sojourners only when harvest needs tempted them to lure some workers off the railroad or canal for their own use. The payroll of the Titusville Railroad in rural Pennsylvania during 1870 and 1871 contained only Swedish and Irish names.[22] Charles Nordhoff found that most of the men laying track in West Virginia's Kanawha County during the following year were black field hands from eastern Virginia, and the remainder were Irish immigrants. Although Afro-Americans deserted the work in droves during harvest times and at Christmas, Nordhoff reported that labor contractors sought them out because they "had a wider experience than these roadside white people, who do not stir out of their woods."[23] During the New Mexico Territory's railroad boom of the 1880s, workers recruited in the Republic of Mexico constituted between 70 and 90 percent of the section crews. In fact, Juan Gómez-Quiñones has argued that such laborers, who subsequently fanned out all over the southwestern United States in search of farms or work in mines, were the largest group of late-nineteenth-century Mexican immigrants.[24] Nine hundred

21. Edwin Fenton, *Immigrants and Unions, A Case Study: Italians and American Labor, 1870–1920* (New York, 1975), 200–1. To be sure, laborers were also shunned as "heathens in a Christian country" even where their occupation had a proper name. Coleman, *Navvies*, 21–2. Italian laborers were violently assaulted in the 1880s in France. See Michelle Perrot, *Les ouvriers en grève. France, 1871–1890* (2 vols., Paris, 1974), I, 165–73.

22. J. S. and D. T. Casement Payroll, Union and Titusville Railroad, September 1870–January 1871, Historical Society of Western Pennsylvania, Box MSS, BB.

23. *American Missionary*, 16 (January 1872), 2–4; the quotation is on p. 4.

24. Juan Gómez-Quiñones, "The Origins and Development of the Mexican Working Class in the United States: Laborers and Artisans North of the Rio Bravo, 1600–1900," in Elsa Cecelia Frost, Michael C. Meyer, and Josefina Zoraida Vasquez, eds., *El Trabajo y los Trajabadores en la Historia de Mexico* (Mexico, D.F., 1979), 495. See also Mark Reisler, *By the Sweat of Their Brow: Mexican Immigrant Labor in the United States, 1900–1940*

miles to the north, popular legend has James J. Hill proclaim: "With enough Swedes and enough snuff, I could drive a railroad clear to Hell." Swedes were not alone, however, in laying his tracks. At the dawn of the twentieth century, the firm of W. H. Remington and Tanaka Chuschirici alone provided the Great Northern and the Northern Pacific with twenty-five hundred to three thousand Japanese laborers at a time.[25]

No other railroad builders ever accomplished feats of labor as spectacular as those of the Chinese. After the Central Pacific began hiring them by the thousands in 1865, Chinese workers drove a railbed from San Francisco to Promontory Point in Utah. They carved a path out of the perpendicular cliffs above the American River by lowering one another in wicker baskets to drill holes, set powder, and fire it off. Because the size of the Central Pacific's subsidies from the federal government depended on the track mileage laid before it encountered the westward-moving Union Pacific, President Charles Crocker kept his Chinese laborers at work in the dead of winter – even drilling a tunnel through the Donner Summit while their camps were buried in snow. Many of those who were killed in snowslides were not found until the following summer.[26]

Although few in America were aware of it at the time, these particular strangers also staged, in June 1867, one of the largest-scale strikes of the century. One Saturday, a document listing demands was circulated through the camps, which together housed almost ten thousand Chinese workers. The demands were remarkable in that they encompassed several historical epochs of workers' struggles. A pay scale of forty-five dollars per month was specified, to match the thirty-five dollars per month plus board received by white workers; over the weekend that demand was scaled down to forty dollars. A working day of ten hours was requested for toil on open ground, and a day of eight hours for tunneling. Finally, the document called for abolition of whipping and freedom for any worker to quit, if and when he chose.

On Monday morning, no Chinese reported out to work. Throughout

(Westport, Conn., 1976); Lawrence A. Cardoso, *Mexican Emigration to the United States, 1897–1931: Socio-Economic Patterns* (Tucson, 1980).

25. Yuji Ichioka, "Japanese Immigrant Labor Contractors and the Northern Pacific and Great Northern Railroad Companies, 1898–1907," *Labor History*, 21 (Summer 1980), 325–50.

26. Victor G. Nee and Brett de Barry Nee, *Longtime Californ': A Documentary Study of an American Chinatown* (New York, 1972), 40–1; Yen Tzu-kuei, "Chinese Workers and the First Transcontinental Railroad of the United States" (unpublished Ph.D. diss., St. John's University, 1977); Maxine Hong Kingston, *China Men* (New York, 1977), 122–49.

the week that followed, they remained in their camps, staged no demonstrations, committed no violence. It was, President Crocker later recalled, "just like Sunday all along the work." By the following Monday, however, Crocker had broken the strike. First, he had stopped all food trains headed for the camps. Then he went to the sites and "made a little war speech," reminding the strikers of the rule under which anyone who missed work on any day was fined for the expenses of his gang's underused horses and carts. Having forgiven all fines for the week just passed, Crocker announced he would enforce them without mercy against anyone who failed to report on the coming Monday, to show that "no one made laws here but me." Finally, he made it known that among his "laws" was a decision, which he assured his listeners he had reached before the trouble began, to raise the wages of Chinese to forty dollars per month. At six o'clock Monday morning, Crocker later told a congressional committee, "the whole country swarmed" with working Chinese.[27]

Not only this strike, but also the very existence of the Chinese who had built the railroad, was soon obliterated from the American consciousness. When the famous photograph of the joining of the lines from east and west was taken at Promontory Point, all Chinese workers were ushered out of the camera's range. And back in San Francisco, Judge Nathaniel Bennett orated on the achievement of a transcontinental railroad, saying it was a testimonial to the "impetuous daring and dash of the French, the philosophical spirit of the German, the unflinching solidity of the English, and the light-hearted impetuosity of the Irish."[28]

As the Chinese experience suggests, however, to understand the interaction of rural origin and laboring experience, one must consider how the rural periphery of the nineteenth-century industrial world became the primary source of supply for "human machines" and how that interaction contributed to, and in turn was molded by, the ideology of racism. As early as the 1850s, railway builders complained frequently about a "deficiency of hands." As Walter Licht has shown, railroads in the middle of the century tended to be "deluged with applicants" for the prestigious and relatively steady positions of engineers, conductors, machinists, clerks, and telegraph operators, but they always found it difficult to

27. Ping Chiu, *Chinese Labor in California, 1850–1880. An Economic Study* (Madison, Wisc., 1963), 46–8. The strike demands were reported in the *San Francisco Dispatch,* July 1, 1867, and reprinted in the Boston *Daily Evening Voice,* August 5, 1867, but no organization of white workers made any comment on the strike.

28. Quoted in Nee and Nee, *Longtime Californ',* 42. The same contempt for the Chinese is still to be found in today's historical writings on the subject: e.g., Schnapper, *American Labor,* 65.

Table 2.1. *Index of daily money wages for laborers and others*
(1859–60 = 100)

Years	Laborers	Average in manufacturing	Factory unskilled
1858–60	100 ($0.97)	100 ($0.96)	100 ($0.81)
1872–3	166 ($1.64)	155 ($1.49)	170 ($1.36)
1876–8	133 ($1.23)	138 ($1.32)	143 ($1.13)
1887–9	140 ($1.39)	157 ($1.50)	150 ($1.21)
1891	141 ($1.39)	159 ($1.53)	151 ($1.22)

Sources: Edith Abbott, "The Wages of Unskilled Labor in the United States, 1850–1900," *Journal of Political Economy,* 13 (June 1905), 321–67, for wage rates and indices of laborers and factory unskilled; Robert Ozanne, *Wages in Practice and Theory,* 134–5, for average wage rates in manufacturing. The index numbers provided by Abbott were generated by different tables than those that provided the absolute wages, and so the two figures do not exactly correspond. The wages for unskilled factory workers are for males only. The averages in manufacturing include all workers.

attract the number of tracklayers they needed at the prevailing wages for unskilled workers. Southern lines, which had depended heavily on slave labor before the Civil War, had found even the price of slaves rising out of their reach during the cotton boom of the 1850s. At times during the 1850s, the Illinois Central Railroad, in spite of the efforts of its recruiting agencies in eastern ports, found itself obliged to raise the summertime wages of track laborers to the level earned by skilled tradesmen.[29]

Nevertheless, the soaring demand for laborers after the Civil War did not stimulate a continuous rise in laborers' wages. Although seasonal and regional variations in laborers' daily pay make generalizations hazardous, it is possible to contrast the best available index of changes in laborers' wages with that for wages in manufacturing. Such a comparison is shown in Table 2.1, and it reveals that laborers' daily earnings advanced more rapidly than the average wage in manufacturing during the late 1850s and the inflationary boom of the 1860s. After that, all wages fell sharply, especially during the depression of 1873–8. Only the wages of unskilled workers failed to regain their 1872 levels before the end of the century.

Heavy demand for laborers drove their average daily wages up to two

29. Licht, *Working for the Railroad,* 60–7; the phrases quoted are on pp. 60 and 61.

subsequent peaks, one in 1887–9 and the other in 1891–2. In neither of these peak periods, however, did laborers' wages approach those of 1872–3. Nor did they rise to that level before 1900, when Edith Abbott's calculations show them slightly lower than they had been in 1892.[30] More important, the average wage in manufacturing – a calculation that serves our purposes here for the very reason that makes it unreliable elsewhere, that is, it blends everything from children's rates to those for the most skilled crafts into a single figure – moved upward with noticeably greater speed then did laborers' wages after the depression of the 1870s. So did the wages of male unskilled factory hands. By the first decade of the twentieth century, as Peter Shergold had argued, what distinguished American earnings from those in England was not so much their general level as the size of the differential in the United States between the skilled and the unskilled. A British laborer of 1900 stood to gain very little, if anything, by moving to the United States.[31]

There were others with much to gain. What slowed down the improvement in laborers' wages under conditions of high demand after 1878 was the newfound mobility of rural people from the periphery of capitalist development. By the 1870s, industrial society had generated distinct but interlocking geographic regions that were to remain essentially fixed until after World War I. An industrial core, throbbing with manufacturing activity at continually rising levels, was roughly bounded by Chicago and St. Louis in the west, by Toronto, Glasgow, and Berlin in the north, by Warsaw, Lodz, and later Budapest (as rather isolated outposts) in the east, and by Milan, Barcelona, Richmond, and Louisville in the south. Surrounding that core, and indeed enveloping its urban outposts, lay a vast agricultural domain in which capitalist development shattered long-established patterns of economic activity, without cultivating more than scattered pockets of extractive and processing industry. Modernization thus appeared on the periphery more as an alien, destructive force than as an integrated pattern of growth. That region encompassed Quebec and Canada's Maritime Provinces, much of Scandinavia, European Russia (or, more precisely, the domain that Poland had embraced before the eighteenth-century partitions), the Kingdom of Hungary, Croatia-Slovenia, Greece, Italy, Sicily, Andalusian Spain, the defeated Confederate States and Great Plains of America, central and northern Mexico, the hinterland of Canton, and later the southern islands of Japan. Although this

30. Abbott, "Unskilled Labor," 365, Table XV.
31. Shergold, *Working-Class Life.*

territory shipped agricultural produce, minerals, and forest products to the industrial core, it also exported people.[32]

Beyond the periphery lay an even larger third world that became increasingly tightly integrated into the economy of the core as the nineteenth century drew to a close, although it sent forth few emigrants. On the contrary, capital investment as well as workers migrated from western Europe and North America into that portion of the world to develop mines, plantations, railroads, and ports. A vast export network there was based increasingly on the wage labor of local residents, who were put to work in their own countries, and of migrant laborers from other parts of the third world, especially India and China, during this period of history. Accompanying that investment and migration were warships and soldiers, staking out spheres of influence and colonies and embroiling the great powers of the core itself in an ascending spiral of armament and diplomatic controversies.[33]

Although social developments differed considerably between one portion of the periphery and another, certain common patterns served to integrate large portions of this region into the industrial economy of the United States and to make it especially important as a source of laborers. In the periphery, nineteenth-century capitalism destroyed established patterns of bondage and communal life that had tied much of the population to the land, made the quest for money wages imperative, intensified national and religious persecution, and provided the railroads and steamships by means of which tens of millions of men and women could engage in what Frank Thistlethwaite has graphically called "proletarian globe-hopping."[34]

This is not to say that the immigrants to the United States either were or became all laborers. Quite the contrary. Those who came in family

32. The terms "core" and "periphery" are borrowed from Immanuel Wallerstein, *The Modern World-System: Capitalist Agriculture and the Origins of the European World-Economy in the Sixteenth Century* (New York, 1974), and are adapted here to my own purposes. My concept of the geographic boundaries of the core in the nineteenth century has been strongly influenced by Frank Thistlethwaite, "Migration from Europe Overseas in the Nineteenth and Twentieth Centuries," *XI. Congrès international des sciences historiques. Rapports* (Stockholm, 1960), 32–60; and by Iván T. Berend and György Ránki, *The European Periphery and Industrialization, 1780–1914* (Budapest, 1982).

33. The implications of imperialism and militarization of the state for American workers will be examined in Chapters 7 and 8.

34. Thistlethwaite, "Migration."

units tended to seek out cities where employment for women was abundant, either in factories or through work carried home. Young Finnish, Swedish, and Irish women came independently and were readily hired as domestic servants. Skilled Britons and Germans crossed the ocean in search of better pay for their trades. Journalists, shopkeepers, lawyers, physicians, and even sons of great landowners often joined the procession. From towns of the Italian *Mezzogiorno* came representatives of all strata of their complex social structures, which almost reproduced themselves in urban American settings. Moreover, through the mid-1880s, rural Ireland and Germany continued to provide the greatest flow of laborers. Immigrants who arrived between 1871 and 1882 had brought with them no higher general level of urban-industrial skills than did those of 1899–1909. During the earlier period, which encompassed the two great migratory waves of 1870–2 and 1878–82, among those who declared their occupations on arrival (mostly adult men), 66 percent of the Irish, 50 percent of the Germans, and 74 percent of the Scandinavians called themselves common laborers, farmers, or farm laborers. Among the arrivals from southern and eastern Europe in the later period, 69 percent listed themselves in those categories.[35] As Julianna Puskás wrote in her study of the regions of the Kingdom of Hungary that sent forth 3.5 mil-

35. Paul H. Douglas, "Is the New Immigration More Unskilled than the Old?" *American Statistical Association Publication*, 16 (June 1919), 393–403. This brief description of patterns of emigration is drawn from the following studies: Thistlethwaite, "Migration"; Julianna Puskás, *From Hungary to the United States (1880–1914)* (Budapest, 1982); Anna Maria Martellone, *Una Little Italy nell'Atene d'America: La Communità italiana di Boston dal 1880 al 1920* (Naples, 1973); Berend and Ránki, *European Periphery;* Cardoso, *Mexican Emigration;* Arnold Schrier, *Ireland and the American Emigration, 1850–1900* (Minneapolis, 1958); Zoltán Krámar, *From the Danube to the Hudson: U.S. Ministerial and Consular Dispatches on Immigration from the Hapsburg Monarchy, 1850–1900* (Atlanta, 1978); Caroline Golab, *Immigrant Destinations* (Philadelphia, 1977); Joseph J. Barton, *Peasants and Strangers: Italians, Rumanians, and Slovaks in an American City, 1890–1950* (Cambridge, Mass., 1975); J. S. MacDonald, "Agricultural Organization, Migration and Labour Militancy in Rural Italy," *Economic History Review*, 2nd series, 16 (1963), 61–75; John W. Briggs, *An Italian Passage: Immigrants to Three American Cities* (New Haven, 1978); Arthur Liebman, *Jews and the Left* (New York, 1979); Michael G. Karni, Matti E. Kaups, and Douglas J. Ollila, eds., *The Finnish Experience in the Western Great Lakes Region: New Perspectives* (Turku, 1975); Varpu Lindström-Best, *The Finnish Immigrant Community of Toronto, 1887–1913* (Toronto, 1979); David M. Katzman, *Seven Days a Week: Women and Domestic Service in Industrializing America* (Urbana, Ill., 1978).

lion Magyars, Slovaks, Ruthenians, Romanians, and others between 1871
and 1913:

> The first groups to emigrate, then, were miners and artisans. They
> were joined by young day laborers and jobless journeymen who could
> not find work in small industry or in the depleting mines. Later, and
> in ever increasing numbers, came the agricultural day laborers, cot-
> ters, and servants, and the bankrupt small landowners. After the turn
> of the century, the occupational distribution of the emigrants tipped
> heavily toward agricultural day laborers, who made up a much greater
> proportion of the emigrants than they comprised of the Hungarian
> population.[36]

One thing was clear to immigrants from the periphery. Their own world
had become monetized. Common lands had been privatized from Fin-
land and Galicia to Mexico and Japan, while population increased rapidly. Both those who had been rendered landless and those who struggled
to improve and enlarge minuscule plots desperately needed to earn cash.
The selling prices received by agricultural producers fell in Europe and
the Americas alike after 1870, but the remedies pursued by large landowners – orienting all production toward exports, turning off excess hands,
lobbying for tariff protection – paradoxically served to drive up the prices
local working people paid for food, especially in Hungary, Italy, and
Mexico. By the turn of the century, however, rural laborers in those
countries knew well that they could earn in one day in the United States
what they could in five or six days at home.[37]

Here was the source of what Anna Maria Martellone has called *la
rivolta dell'emigrazione.* Refusing to accept their impoverished lot, unable to change it by insurrection, and having become connected with the
wide world by the lines of transportation that had played a central role
in altering their home communities, they set out to the heartland of the
new industrial world. Not everyone did. Wladyslaw Benda, visiting the
Tatra Mountains of Galicia in 1907, found that in some villages no one
so much as mentioned emigrating, whereas in other nearby villages, going
to America was a mania, and many men could already describe their
experiences there. By that time, most of those who crossed the Atlantic
had contacts. The U.S. immigration reports of 1910 reveal that 82 percent of those arriving from Austria-Hungary named friends or relatives
waiting for them in America. As the visit to Galician villages also sug-

36. Puskás, *From Hungary,* 35.
37. Ibid., 52–6; Berend and Ránki, *European Periphery,* 28–43; Martellone,
    Little Italy, 49–51; Cardoso, *Mexican Emigration,* 10–15; Reisler, *Sweat
    of Their Brow,* 14. See also [Jan Slomka], *From Serfdom to Self-Govern-
    ment: Memoirs of a Polish Village Mayor, 1842–1927* (London, 1941).

gested, however, many of the emigrants returned home, usually after less than five years in America, with money to buy some land. To be sure, the more people who did this, the more land prices rose, helping to persuade many people to make yet another visit to America to earn more money. Nevertheless, intense competition for passengers between the government-sponsored steamship companies of England and Germany kept fares low and people moving. All in all, when the increases in population in the United States between 1900 and 1910 are compared with the numbers of immigrants who disembarked here, the decade shows a turnover rate of 238 percent for Italians and 281 percent for subjects of the Dual Monarchy. In this sense, large portions of the peripheral countryside not only were sending people to the United States but also had become integral parts of its economy – as it had of theirs.[38]

This structural interlocking of the industrial core and its periphery explains the discoveries of the U.S. Immigration Commission when it investigated laborers who constructed and maintained railroad track in the summer of 1909. The variety of regional patterns described in its reports provides a panorama of the bonds that linked laborers to distant lands. Less than 4 percent of all these workers were American-born children of immigrants. They were either immigrants or native-born Americans, but in either case they stemmed from and remained linked to capitalism's rural periphery. When investigators distinguished among different regions of the United States, however, significant variations on this theme appeared.[39]

A sample for the Northeast was taken from the rolling, well-settled farming country of upstate New York and northern New Jersey, where thirty camps varying in size from three hundred to two thousand workers were surveyed. A scattering of Irish-Americans, almost half of them over thirty-five years old, was linked to a larger group of recent immigrants from Ireland itself. Their presence is remindful of the period, then three decades past, when Irish immigrants had dominated the track work in this region, as they had in the West.[40] By 1909, however, the Irish-Americans and Irish immigrants together held virtually all the jobs paying more than two dollars per day. They were all literate, and most of

38. Martellone, *Little Italy,* 57–8; Wladyslaw T. Benda, "Life in a Polish Mountain Village," *The Century Magazine,* 76 (July 1908), 323–32; Puskás, *From Hungary,* 61, 80–85. The turnover figures are my calculations from data in *Hist. Stat. U.S.,* I, 105, 117.

39. Except where otherwise noted, the following account of track laborers is based on U.S. Immigration Commission, *Immigrants in Industry,* Part 22, 332–460.

40. Licht, *Working for the Railroad,* 221–2.

the Irish-born workers who were eligible had become citizens. Only 10 percent of the laborers of this region were whites of native parentage, and 6 percent were Afro-Americans. Almost half were Italians in their twenties, and the rest were Slavic or Hungarian. Less than one-third of the latter groups of immigrants had been in the United States as long as five years, and hardly any were citizens.

Few of the jobs lasted through the winter. During the building season, laborers boarded in long, unpartitioned bunkhouses and bought their food at commissaries, where food prices were only slightly above those in towns in the area, although shoes, clothes, liquor, and other wares sold at 50 to 75 percent higher prices. The men took turns cooking for themselves, used pits for toilets, and generally lived in squalor, except for a small number of Italians who resided with their families in shanties that stood out because of their cleanliness, curtains, and flower beds. Evenings were given over to playing cards, pitching quoits, playing musical instruments, stealing rides on handcars, playing baseball, and drinking – mainly a cheap brew called "Italian beer."[41]

The prominence of Italians involved a paradox, which appeared in other parts of the land as well as the East. Contractors and labor agents alike told the investigators that they wanted most to hire Croats and Bulgarians; failing that, they preferred anyone else to southern Italians. Immigrants from the *Mezzogiorno*, claimed one contractor after another, were less strong than Slavs because of the lack of meat in the Italians' diet, spent less money at the commissaries (a major source of contractors' profits), and were more likely to walk off the job together if any one of them had a grievance. Despite all these denunciations, young southern Italians and Sicilians far outnumbered any other group among the track laborers. Although young Slavs in great numbers were also found in railroad work, it was among the laborers in steel mills and urban factories generally, as well as in coal mines, that they outnumbered Italians. Monika Glettler estimated that although as many as one in four of the world's 3 million Slovaks came to America before 1913, four-fifths of them headed for the mining and mill towns of Pennsylvania.[42]

41. Compare Vera Lysenko's description of leisure hours on western Canadian railroads: *Men in Sheepskin Coats: A Study in Assimilation* (Toronto, 1947), 53.

42. John Bodnar, "Immigration, Kinship, and the Rise of Working-Class Realism in Industrial America," *Journal of Social History*, 14 (Fall 1980), 45–65; Virginia Yans-McLaughlin, *Family and Community: Italian Immigrants in Buffalo, 1880–1930* (Urbana, Ill., 1982); Puskás, *From Hungary*, 129–31; Golab, *Immigrant Destinations*, 25–41; Monika Glettler, *Pittsburg-Wien-Budapest: Programm und Praxis der Nationalitätenpolitik bei*

The reason offered by contractors for this anomaly was that Italian *padroni* in cities like New York and Syracuse, where laborers spent the winter, could provide hundreds and even thousands of their countrymen on demand, quickly, at no expense to the contractors, and at low daily wages. Here was a system of hiring deeply rooted in Italo-American communities that permitted sedentary urban centers to be the locales for rapid ·recruiting and wide dispersal of "human machines." The practice was of little value to large manufacturers, who readily found as many laborers as they needed at their plant gates or among the kin and acquaintances of their current employees. But in mobilizing manpower for such vast projects as subways, aqueducts, and railways, as well as for unskilled building work, the *padrone* system was ideal.

The pivotal figure in this efficient entrepreneurial link between Italian immigration and American construction was a *banchiere,* usually an immigrant himself who had acquired some capital as a grocer, barber, or saloonkeeper and who instituted a wide range of services for fellow Italians. The *banchiere* acted as travel agent, moneychanger, moneylender, marriage broker, scribe, legal advisor, and transmitter of funds to the old country – all for a fee. As Anna Maria Martellone has shown, such bankers dominated the immigrant communities through a combination of important services, prominence in Italian mutual-aid and fraternal societies, and old, familiar, personal forms of exploitation. Some rose to great wealth, like Naples-born Thomas Marnell of Syracuse, who had graduated in 1891 from railroad foreman to owner of a saloon, chief of the Italian Exchange Bank, court interpreter and notary public, and owner of a grocery store and steamship agency. Many more *banchieri* duplicated his activities on a more modest scale. It was to them that *padroni* turned with orders for some specific number of Italian workers, whom the *padrone* would organize into a work crew, escort to the site, and provide with groceries and supplies, the primary sources of his profit. The *banchiere* charged a fee (*"la bossatura"*) to each job applicant, and often he also charged full passenger fare to each laborer, while obtaining a lower group rate from the railroad, thus supplementing the many other fees on which his income was based.[43]

der Auswanderung der ungarischen Slowaken nach Amerika in 1900 (Vienna, 1980), 18–23.

43. Martellone, *Little Italy,* 120–30; Fenton, *Immigrants and Unions,* 89–92; Luciano J. Iorizzo, "A Reappraisal of Italian Leadership in Central New York Immigrant Communities – Some Preliminary Observations," in Istituto di Studi Americani, Università degli Studi di Firenze, *Gli Italiani negli Stati Uniti* (Florence, 1972), 207–32; Robert F. Harney, "Montreal's King of Italian Labour: A Case Study of Padronism," *Labour/Le Travailleur,* 4

Several attributes of the *padrone* system kept it flourishing despite increasingly vociferous attacks after 1900 from middle-class reformers, American bankers and grocers, the Italian government and its consuls in the United States, trade unionists, and ultimately many laborers themselves. Young men in search of a few years' work in America found the *banchieri* familiar with jobs all over the continent; many an immigrant arrived carrying a *banchiere*'s business card that had been distributed in Italy. Through elaborate personal connections with each other, agents in search of men in, say, Syracuse could quickly and effectively contact others in New York, New Haven, Boston, or Montreal, not to mention shipping companies in Europe, to help fill any urgent order. Contractors involved in construction work found such networks especially useful when workers abruptly quit a job, perhaps to join in the harvesting of crops or to go on strike. So, despite the contempt for southern Italians that they freely and universally expressed, contractors hired them by the thousands, segregated them carefully in separate bunkhouses under the control of the *padrone*, and if the laborers did happen to strike or quit en masse, had the suspected ringleaders arrested and jailed for disturbing the peace, thereby persuading the rest to return to the job. Failing that, the *padrone* would be sent off looking for replacements.

Outside of the Northeast, the Immigration Commission found different patterns of recruiting. In the West, its investigators examined the states of Minnesota, North and South Dakota, Kansas, and Missouri. From July 1908 through June 1909, they found, labor agencies in Chicago had dispatched fourteen thousand Americans, fifteen thousand Slavs and Hungarians, and perhaps nine thousand Scandinavians to construction projects of various sorts, the Americans and Scandinavians to jobs in and around Chicago, the Poles largely to logging camps, and the others primarily to railroad section work. Few Italians were among those dispatched by the Chicago agencies, although many were to be found in the railroad camps. They had been brought by *padroni,* as they were in the East. Chicago, however, was not the West's only source of recruits for the summer's work. Agencies in St. Louis sent forth forty-five thousand men, and those of St. Paul and Minneapolis shipped off twenty-three thousand

(1979), 57–84. The following advertisement from *Il Corriere del Connecticut,* October 18, 1902, typifies the work of a *banchiere*:

RICERCA DI OPERAI

Si cercano 200 uomini operai e 4 "bosses," per un lavoro continuo in costruzione di ferrovie per carri electrici. Paga pei bosses $45 al mese e per gli operai $1,35 al giorno. Pagamenti settimanali. Lavoro garantito.

Gli operai hanno abitazione gratuita carbone, legna e stufa. Dirigersi al Banchiere sig. Guiseppe Fagostino, 422 East st. City.

Scandinavians, twenty-two thousand American-born laborers, nine thousand Greeks and Italians, and seven thousand Magyars, Slovaks, Poles, Bulgarians, and Herzogovenians. A total of 106,000 men were shipped from these four cities during the year, and still others went out from Kansas City, Duluth, and other minor centers.

Grace Abbott conducted a careful examination of Chicago's labor agencies in 1914 (a leaner year by far than 1909). She found that railroad work began in March or April and continued until November or December, unless a particular project was completed earlier. About one-third of the workers dispatched by the agencies were "hoboes," or English-speaking veterans of construction work, and the others were from southern, central, and eastern Europe. The hoboes, or "white laborers," as they were then called, to distinguish them from the others, seldom stayed on a job for more than ten to fifteen days. They paid employment agencies' fees, which were fixed by law at two dollars, but in fact varied from fifty cents, when contractors were desperate for hands, to ten dollars, when jobs were scarce. Those fees got them transported to the job sites, from which they later hopped freights to other jobs. So often did they move that one railroad that needed 4,593 men estimated that it had transported fifteen to twenty times that number to workplaces. Winter found most of the Americans back in Chicago, cutting ice, shoveling snow, and doing odd jobs, while a minority went to lumber camps. Theirs was the enduring world Nelson Algren would later capture vividly for his readers in *A Walk on the Wild Side*. Few went south, despite the longer building season there. Southern tracklaying was for Afro-Americans.[44]

The dependable section hands on western railroads were Slavic, Hungarian, Greek, or Italian farm youth, only recently arrived in the United States and with no intention of staying long. Many of them were married, the Immigration Commission discovered, but none had wives in this country. They boarded in freight cars, buying food from commissaries and cooking it themselves, rather than partaking of the wretched fare for which Americans at the site paid board, and they returned to Chicago, in Abbott's words, "much better off than the hoboes," having "earned more, spent some less for better food and much less for liquor."[45] Although many, perhaps most, of the Slavs moved on to the Pacific Coast in search of winter work, a large minority of the immigrants returned to

---

44. Grace Abbott, "Railroad Gangs," in *Report of the Mayor's Commission on Unemployment* (Chicago, 1914), 69–72. I am indebted to Steven Sapolsky for this source. See also Mary R. Coolidge, *Chinese Immigration* (New York, 1909), 387.
45. Abbott, "Railroad Gangs," 71.

the city for the winter, where they might invest in peddlers' wagons, carry shovels around town in quest of casual employment, or join the crowds outside stockyard and factory gates in the mornings. By spring, their savings were drained, and they scanned the windows of the *banchieri* and employment agencies once more for notices of far-off jobs.

To the west and southwest of the territory selected for study by the Immigration Commission, still different patterns of hiring could be found. In the 1860s and 1870s, immigrants from China had contracted with Chinese merchants for a term of service in repayment for transportation across the Pacific. "In addition to providing employment, merchant contractors," wrote Victor Nee and Brett de Barry Nee, "were also the source of provisions, imported rice and so forth, for the laborers, and as elders within the [clan and district associations of Chinese communities] they controlled all decision-making which affected the group as a whole."[46] The Exclusion Acts and the violent "abatement" movement of the 1880s brought to an end the large-scale employment of Chinese workers on railway tracks, and the Japanese who came in the 1890s appear to have been recruited by agencies that were more overtly and exclusively commercial undertakings than the companies dominated by Chinese merchants had been, and to have been run jointly by Japanese and Anglo-Saxon businessmen. The firm of W. H. Remington and Tanaka Chuschirici, which earned as much as twenty-five hundred dollars per month by providing Japanese laborers to northwestern railroads, assessed each laborer ten cents per day from a daily wage of $1.15 in 1892 and also withheld another dollar per month to pay its interpreters; in addition, the firm retailed provisions, charged for remission of money to Japan, and charged a monthly medical fee of fifty cents.[47] In the Southwest, an elaborate network of agents called *enganchadors* recruited *braceros* in Mexican border towns and turned them over to other agents on the U.S. side of the line, who in turn passed them on to railroad contractors. Each step along the way was supported by new fees and commissions, although, as everywhere, selling commissary provisions to the workers provided the main source of the agents' profits, and often a source of debt bondage for the laborer. From the railroad work sites, where Mexicans were clearly in the majority, they often moved on to mines, agricultural work, or growing terminal cities for the lines, such as Los Angeles.[48]

Western railroad construction and maintenance were a domain of

46. Nee and Nee, *Longtime Californ'*, 40–1.
47. Ichioka, "Japanese Immigrant," 336–7.
48. Cardoso, *Mexican Emigration*, 27–9.

transient immigrants and even more transient Americans encamped across the sparsely populated plains. Because most work in the region was track repair, rather than new construction, by the time of the commission's survey, jobs tended to last for shorter periods than they did in the East and South. But the region offered one real advantage to laborers: Every summer, other jobs also beckoned them. In April 1909, laborers were being recruited for $1.25 per day. By July they could get $1.65 from the same railroad. It was harvest time, and wheat alone needed seven thousand men each season. This competition was nothing new to railroad builders. In 1886, amid a great construction boom, a correspondent from Laramie, Wyoming, had written of the situation facing the Union Pacific: "Laborers have been in good demand the past month as many were wanted to go out on the ranches haying. Many of the ranch hands are now through and men have become more plentiful [for the Union Pacific]."[49]

Twenty years later, Canadian railway builders complained that their Ukrainian hands were homesteading in the prairie provinces. Half the Japanese laborers in the Cascade divisions of both the Great Northern and Union Pacific quit to take jobs in sawmills in April 1906, and later that year another two hundred of them went off to harvest sugar beets.[50] By 1909, contractors on northwestern lines reconciled themselves to the closing of immigration from Japan by replacing Japanese everywhere with Italians and Greeks, who, they hoped, would prove to be "easier to handle than the Japanese and steadier workmen."[51] Turnover in western railway track crews seems to have been lowest among those workers who intended to spend the least time in the United States.

Finally, one more important group of insights is provided by the commission's study of track labor in the Southeast. Major construction activity on new trunk lines in the Piedmont and Appalachians, as well as the laying of many spurs to mines and mill villages, made the South a region of intense railway building early in this century. In West Virginia and western Virginia, many Italians were brought in by *padroni* from New York, in the manner previously described. Farther south, however, in Tennessee and the Carolinas, another pattern prevailed. Whereas white engineers, mechanics, and carpenters could be found there, the tracklaying crews were young, unmarried Afro-Americans. Contractors hired them in preference to all others. The bosses attributed prodigious output to

49. *Union Pacific Employees Magazine* (September 1886), 253, quoted in Stomquist, "Generation of Boomers," 117.

50. Donald Avery, *"Dangerous Foreigners": European Immigrant Workers and Labour Radicalism in Canada, 1896–1932* (Toronto, 1979), 19–37; Ichioka, "Japanese Immigrant," 345–6.

51. U.S. Immigration Commission, *Immigrants in Industry*, Part 22, 341.

their black workers, claiming that even those who went on three- or four-day binges after payday moved more earth in the remaining days than did immigrants who always showed up. Moreover, most of the wages paid out to them returned to the contractors because of the exorbitant prices they charged at the commissaries.

In the South, all gang bosses were armed. They marched workers back to the barracks each evening, paid them only once a month, locked up their belongings, and patrolled the sites, in order to assure that transportation and store debts were repaid. In boom times, when other jobs were abundant, they were especially watchful of their section hands. Not only might workers leave for other jobs, but also, because most of them had left families on cotton or tobacco farms while temporarily seeking out "public work" (wage earning), Afro-Americans worked least when pay rose highest. Having earned the sum they wanted, they went home. Conversely, in hard times, when daily earnings fell, the number of men seeking work each day rose. In this context, open coercion played a special role in holding down turnover. Local sheriffs were sometimes called on to arrest black workers who had quit, on charges of violating boarding-house laws, and the sheriffs did so willingly. In general, however, gang bosses considered it a sign of personal weakness to call in the law. They maintained camp "order," recaptured runaways, and sold the bootleg booze in dry counties themselves.[52]

Our kind of people

The southern evidence brings vividly into focus the decisive importance of the ideology and practice of racism in the experience of laborers. In one sense, American culture at the turn of the century categorized all the strangers who filled the laborers' ranks as "lesser breeds," except those who were native white Americans, and they were "bums." When John Watson, a shipping-company executive, was being questioned by a government investigator, Charles Barnes, in 1914, the following revealing exchange was recorded:

> Mr. Barnes. I know the name on the water front; a white man is not an Italian?
> Mr. Watson. That is the idea; or a Polack.[53]

52. Ibid., Part 22, 445–69. For a revealing analysis of the relationship between sharecropping and "public work," see Peter Gottlieb, "Making Their Own Way: Southern Blacks' Migration to Pittsburgh, 1916–30" (unpublished Ph.D. diss., University of Pittsburgh, 1977), 56–79.
53. U.S. Commission on Industrial Relations, *Final Report and Testimony Submitted to Congress by the Commission on Industrial Relations* (11 vols.,

The distinction drawn so sharply in the dominant culture reflected daily work practice and found repeated echoes in popular discourse. "I don't approve of Italians much myself," said one dock boss, who never called any of them from the shape-up. A foreman on Brooklyn's Bush Docks testified that in discharging cargoes, only Italians were employed, but in loading, "all white men." That, he explained, was simply the way things were done there.[54] And a congenial Irishwoman, who fed jobless Walter Wyckoff in return for some chores in 1892, expressed a thought then so common among working people: "There should be a law . . . to give a job to every decent man that's out of work. . . . And another law . . . to keep all them I-talians from comin' in and takin' the bread out of the mouths of honest people."[55]

In this view, newcomers from the periphery were seen to be transient and unassimilable, bearers of political and social corruption who simply could neither understand nor become a part of the American way. Certainly, as the puddler poet Michael McGovern had written, such a person was unfit to be a "union man." "These fellows have no pride," a skilled Pittsburgh worker protested about recent immigrants, "they are not ruled by custom. When the foreman demands it they will throw down the saw and hammer and take up the wheelbarrow." A decade and a half earlier, Terence V. Powderly had concurred in this sentiment. A man like his own father, who had emigrated from Ireland, he said, "must have had a strong heart, he must have been determined to work out his own salvation, and he did not come with the prospect ahead of him of taking some other man's place, or of reducing wages. . . . The class of immigrants that come now are not as good as those of twenty years ago."[56]

Neither the popular prejudices nor the learned writings of the epoch, both of which drew a sharp and invidious contrast between the "Old Immigrants" and the "New Immigrants," suffice to explain the decisive role of racism in shaping the experience of laborers.[57] On the contrary,

64th Cong., 1st Sess., Senate Document No. 415, hereafter cited as U.S. CIR), III, 2069.

54. Ibid., III, 2171.
55. Wyckoff, *West*, 94. Compare John Higham, *Strangers in the Land: Patterns of American Nativism, 1860–1925* (New York, 1963).
56. On McGovern, see footnotes 55 and 89 in Chapter 1. Paul U. Kellogg, ed., *Wage-Earning Pittsburgh* (New York, 1911), 41; Powderly quoted in New York *Daily Tribune*, May 4, 1890. Compare the exposés of Hungarian and Italian immigrants' conditions in *Journal of United Labor*, May 3, 1883 (3 pages), July 10, 1885, p. 1024, and July 25, 1885, p. 1040.
57. See Higham, *Strangers*, 131–93; Richard Hofstadter, *Social Darwinism in American Thought* (rev. ed., Boston, 1955), 170–211.

the interrelationship between agricultural life and industrial life that made "human machines" from the periphery available to American industry in abundance also shaped their social position within industrial society. If we consider briefly the experiences of European, Asian, and black laborers from this perspective, we may understand some of the significant differences in their struggles and their relationships with other workers.

Immigrants from the European periphery were not all laborers, as has been noted. Hundreds of thousands of Swedes, Poles, Croats, Italians, and Magyars became factory operatives, domestic servants and commercial-service workers, seamstresses or cigar wrappers in domestic industry, peddlers, storekeepers, labor agents, fraternal-order executives, carpenters, molders, priests, and lawyers. Even the most transient of laborers, spending only a few years in America before returning to their European villages, became part of larger or smaller urban communities. The city itself provided a reservoir of mutual support, as well as a locus of exploitation – a domain of sociability as well as of squalor. Women were there as well as men. Parishes and localities fashioned tight social units, socialists and anarchists made regular appearances at the halls of national groups, and even those American trade unionists who were most contemptuous of the newcomers often found no alternative to organizing them into their own ranks. The urban counterpoint of transiency, self-organization, and assimilation most immediately affected the factory operatives. Even though the working lives of laborers kept most of them on the margins of this process, they could not completely avoid being drawn into it. On the docks they developed relatively sedentary neighborhoods. Passing through a large mill or mine exposed them to a polyglot but tightly knit environment in which there were virtually always some men and women of broad political vision, and even those who toiled through the summer on great rural construction projects often wintered in the city. In short, for all its timeless quality, the world of immigrant laborers was changing. Their ties to the land in Europe, as well as the transient nature of their work here, kept them the most marginalized members of immigrant communities, who were regarded with fear and contempt by the dominant society. Nevertheless, through the city, and in particular through the networks built by their own peoples in the cities, they were inexorably becoming incorporated into their adopted society.

Urbanization followed a different path for black Americans. In the first place, the rural periphery from which they emigrated lay not overseas but within the United States. But theirs was a region that two centuries of chattel slavery had stamped indelibly with the mark of white supremacy. After their emancipation, thousands of Afro-Americans had become wage earners in coal and iron mines, in the tobacco and furniture industries, on the railroads, and on the waterfronts, either temporarily or permanently. For those who remained on the land, the urgent quest for money income had driven women to take in washing or go out to perform household labor, and men to seek employment off the farms during seasons when cotton or tobacco required little effort. In short, by the 1880s, Afro-Americans in the South were thoroughly immersed in a money and wage economy.[58]

Both the rural and urban components of this economic nexus contributed to the system of racial segregation that had matured by the first decade of the twentieth century. In the countryside, the post–Civil War development of sharecropping and debt peonage was reinforced by legal regulation of relations between workers and planters. The region's industrial growth was founded on extractive and manufacturing enterprises, which could yield a good return on investment only if the wages paid were much lower than those in the North. Systematic exclusion of black workers from supervisory or machine-operating positions confined them to a pool of jobs for which the lowest wages of all were paid. Moreover, after the black population had been excluded from political participation, municipal and state governments fashioned codes for legal separation of the races. It was, as John Cell has argued, especially in the most modern, urbanized parts of the South that legally codified "separate racial development" played its most distinctive role and found its most articulate champions.[59] The outcome was a social order that not only saw black track laborers marched to and from their barracks under armed guard but also imposed both legal and informal impediments against any common efforts of white and black workers, or even any efforts to unite them in common causes. Working-class efforts did circumvent the barriers of racial separation during the 1880s in many parts of the South – and even after disenfranchisement and legal segregation of Afro-Americans

58. See C. Vann Woodward, *Origins of the New South, 1877–1913* (Baton Rouge, La., 1951); Roger L. Ransom and Richard Sutch, *One Kind of Freedom: The Economic Consequences of Emancipation* (Cambridge, 1977); Jay R. Mandle, *The Roots of Black Poverty: The Southern Plantation Economy after the Civil War* (Durham, N.C., 1978); Harold D. Woodman, "Sequel to Slavery: The New History Views the Post-Bellum South," *Journal of Southern History*, 43 (1977), 523–54.

59. John W. Cell, *The Highest Stage of White Supremacy: The Origins of Segregation in South Africa and the American South* (Cambridge, Mass., 1982). See also Howard N. Rabinowitz, *Race Relations in the Urban South, 1865–1890* (Urbana, Ill., 1980); C. Vann Woodward, *The Strange Career of Jim Crow* (third edition, New York, 1974).

had been fully accomplished – in the coal mines of Alabama and West Virginia, on the New Orleans docks, and in the timber camps of Louisiana. All such efforts, however, had to confront not only the economic power of employers and the mutual suspicion of white and black workers but also the ultimate bulwark of white supremacy and segregation: the state.

The racism encountered by Asian immigrants differed somewhat from what confronted either European immigrants or black laborers. White workers and farmers who flocked to the Pacific Coast in search of high wages and fertile valleys quickly and virtually unanimously came to look on first the Chinese and later the Japanese as the carriers of poverty and social decay. They were imagined to be the hirelings of grasping corporations, bonanza farms, and urban sweatshops that prospered only because Asians could be hired for so little, and thus they threatened the whole fabric of economic opportunity and small enterprise for whites. White politicians, playwrights, songsters, journalists, and preachers joined the chorus of denunciation of the Asians as heathens who corrupted whatever they touched. The labor movement itself played a leading role in the struggle to exclude Chinese and Japanese from American life altogether. George McNeill's famous treatise on the workers' movement, written in 1887, explicitly denied that white and Chinese workers could make common cause: "From his cradle, the Chinese serf is disciplined in the doctrine of nonentity. . . . It does not require much knowledge of human nature to arrive at the conclusion that an element trained in such a school cannot possibly sympathize with our plan of co-operation."[60]

The unions and the Knights of Labor in the Far West not only lobbied for legal prohibition of Chinese immigration but also, after passage of the Exclusion Act of 1882, unleashed an "abatement" campaign to drive Chinese by force away from mines, ships, and lumber camps and formed a League of Deliverance, which attempted to compel all San Francisco employers to replace Chinese workers with white union members. Despite the opposition of employers of Chinese workers, labor's exclusion strategy was warmly supported by local merchants, by both political parties, and by the Workingmen's Party of California in the 1870s, as well as by San Francisco's governing Union Labor Party of the early twentieth century. It provided an ideological cement binding a strong and aggressive labor movement to the bourgeois social order. It "maintained California for us and our kind of people," boasted Paul Scharrenberg, state secretary of the American Federation of Labor (AFL). Consequently, the

60. McNeill, *Labor Movement*, 433.

enthusiasm of California's Progressive reformers for Asian exclusion matched that of their southern counterparts for legal segregation of Afro-Americans.[61]

That is the reason the ten thousand Chinese who struck the Central Pacific in 1867 had suffered political as well as geographic isolation. The steady rise in wages that Chinese workers could command after the Chinese Exclusion Act, the successful strike of Chinese cigar makers for a wage increase in 1884, and their futile strike for a closed shop the next year elicited not the support of the white trade unions but, rather, the charge that the Chinese had "begun to feel overbearing in their strength."[62] Similarly, the frequent strikes of Japanese agricultural laborers on the eve of World War I, not to mention the widespread purchase of California farmland by Japanese immigrants, served to intensify the efforts of the state's political leaders to drive them out of the region altogether.[63]

So many Japanese field workers sought to join the AFL in 1903 that the Los Angeles Labor Council was tempted to let them in, but it was summarily taken to task by the AFL's Executive Council. For example, organizer F. C. Wheeler of Los Angeles found eight hundred Japanese and four hundred Mexicans standing firmly together on strike during the sugar-beet harvest near Oxnard. He endorsed their application to the Executive Council for an AFL charter, as did many local unions. The Mexicans made it clear that they would not join the AFL if their Japanese comrades were excluded. But President Gompers stood firm. The charter, he wrote, "is issued to you [Mexicans] with the express understanding that under no circumstances shall you take into your union any Chinese or Japanese."[64]

61. See Alexander Saxton, *The Indispensable Enemy: Labor and the Anti-Chinese Movement in California* (Berkeley, 1971); Nee and Nee, *Longtime Californ'*; Coolidge, *Chinese Immigration;* Linda C. Majka and Theo J. Majka, *Farm Workers, Agribusiness, and the State* (Philadelphia, 1982); Morrison I. Swift, *What a Tramp Learns in California: Social Danger Line* (San Francisco, 1896); George E. Mowry, *The California Progressives* (Berkeley, 1951); Walton Bean, *Boss Ruef's San Francisco* (Berkeley, 1952). The quotation of Paul Scharrenberg is from Michael Kazin, "Barons of Labor: The San Francisco Building Trades, 1896–1922" (unpublished Ph.D. diss., Stanford University, 1982), 358.

62. Saxton, *Indispensable Enemy*, 214–18; the quotation is on p. 218.

63. Cletus E. Daniel, *Bitter Harvest: A History of California Farmworkers, 1870–1941* (Berkeley, 1981), 13–76; Majka and Majka, *Farm Workers*, 37–50.

64. F. C. Wheeler to Frank Morrison, June 2, 1903 (Mitchell Papers, Catholic University of America, Box A3-46). On the Oxnard strike, see Foner, *Labor Movement*, III, 276–8.

To understand the aspirations and actions of laborers during the half century before World War I, we must look outside the domain of the organized labor movement. This is especially important in the case of laborers who did not work in direct subordination to craftsmen. On the construction sites of great engineering projects, on the waterfront, and in the fields, laborers' struggles bore the clear imprint of their rural origins and continuing ties to the land, of the agencies through which they were hired and shaped up into work groups, of the gang nature of their labor and the naked coercion practiced by gang bosses, of the contempt and hostility with which they were regarded by native white Americans, and of the patterns of racism that diversely affected the Europeans, Afro-Americans, and Asians among them.

Sojourners' solidarities

"Roustabout gang members," wrote scientific manager Charles Bedaux, are "taken largely from the drifting class" and are "but casually interested in the welfare of the business."[65] Whether by choice or by necessity, most laborers, as we have seen, moved incessantly from one job to another. They continued to require an elaborate network of employment agencies, *banchieri,* saloonkeepers, politicians, priests, hiring bosses, and kinfolk through which jobs were solicited. Between jobs, they needed to know the techniques for survival in America: when bakeries disposed of stale bread, when overripe fruits and vegetables were cleaned out of the markets, which societies dispensed relief to which nationalities, where a few hours' work might be found distributing circulars or carrying advertisements on sandwich boards, where low tide exposed the least polluted clams and mussels, and which lodging houses charged the lowest prices. Sometimes seasonal bursts of activity in different industries would complement each other conveniently. Summer work in a brickyard or tannery, for example, might be followed by fall employment in a packinghouse and winter in a steel mill. At the Pennsylvania Steel Company near Harrisburg, Croat and Italian laborers regularly left for railroad or farm labor during the summer and returned to the mill the following fall. The steel company tried to stop this practice after 1913 by fingerprinting its laborers so that it would know which job applicants had worked there

65. Charles E. Bedaux, *The Bedaux Efficiency Course for Industrial Application* (Grand Rapids, Mich., 1917), 177. For other arguments that casual labor was a "state of mind," see Lescohier, *Labor Market,* 97–110, 264; Carlton H. Parker, *The Casual Laborer and Other Essays* (New York, 1920).

before. In New Orleans, black men who loaded cotton on the docks during the winter months transported barrels of beer out of the city's breweries or carried hods for bricklayers during the summer. There, as on the New York docks, where new crews were shaped up for each arrival and each departure of a ship and jobless men from everywhere descended on the docks in search of wages, neighborhood saloonkeepers and ward heelers managed to secure most of the jobs for their own loyal patrons.[66]

In periods of depression, the search for jobs became more aggressive. During the summers of 1907 and 1908, small gangs of immigrants marched about upstate New York carrying their own shovels or other tools to beg (or demand) jobs from local farmers and municipal authorities. In Detroit during the 1890s, troops of unemployed workers had chased road-repair crews away from their jobs and demanded a turn for themselves. Physical battles between members of different ethnic groups sometimes erupted over the available work. On one occasion, two hundred Poles with picks and shovels assaulted fifty Italians who were paving a road, charging that Italians "get work all over the city," while the families of Poles were left to starve.[67]

Woe unto the man who stood alone in this pitiless struggle for existence. Walter Wyckoff, Alfred Kolb, Whiting Williams, and other upper-class writers who "put on overalls" to share the experiences of unskilled workers in America quickly discovered that both obtaining jobs and surviving on them required pals, kin, connections. The Immigration Commission correctly noted "the importance of certain laborers among his [sic] fellows, who shapes the personnel of the gang in various ways and is instrumental in securing positions for friends of his own race."[68]

> Sir: [a black worker from Algiers, Louisiana, wrote in 1917] I saw some time ago in the Chicago Defender, that you needed men for

66. Leon Stein and Philip Taft, eds., *Workers Speak: Self-Portraits* (New York, 1971), 13–16; Wyckoff, *West*, 1–39; Nee and Nee, *Longtime Californ'*, 70; William I. Thomas and Florian Znaniecki, *The Polish Peasant in Europe and America* (2 vols., New York, 1927), I, 201; Bodnar, *Immigration and Industrialization*, 54–5; Williams, *Worker's Mind*, 59; U.S. CIR, III, 2053–65.

67. U.S. Immigration Commission, *Immigrants in Industry*, Part 22, 394; Melvin G. Holli, *Reform in Detroit: Hazen S. Pingree and Urban Politics* (New York, 1969), 64–7; Oestreicher, "Solidarity and Fragmentation," 60. Shergold argues that the major depression of 1907–8 had less impact on laborers' wages than did the milder recession of 1903–4, because so many immigrants simply returned to Europe in 1908, thus reducing the American labor surplus. Shergold, *Working-Class Life*, 40–1.

68. U.S. Immigration Commission, *Immigrants in Industry*, Part 22, 386.

different work, would like to state that I can bring you all the men you need, to do any kind of work. or send them, would like to come myself[.] Can recommend all the men I bring to do any kind of work, and will give satisfaction; I have bin foreman for 20 years over some of these men in different work from R.R. work to Boiler Shop[,] machine shop[,] Blacksmith shop, Concreet finishing or putting down pipe or any work to be did. they are all hard working men and will work at any kind of work also plastering[,] anything in the labor line, from Clerical work down. I will not bring a man that is looking for an easy time only hard working men, that want good wages for there work, let me here from you at once.[69]

Once on the job, a laborer found personal friendships and loyalties as important to his psychic and even physical endurance as they had been to locating employment in the first place. Longshoremen usually lifted heavy burdens in pairs and became so accustomed to each other's movements that they needed no verbal communication to coordinate their efforts. For such a working couple to part company created a scandal among their workmates. Kinship was especially important in nurturing personal alliances. As Thomas and Znaniecki have argued, family ties among immigrants need not necessarily have involved much affection, but they did create social obligations that were violated only at the risk of provoking sharp community censure. In Thomas Bell's persuasive fictional portrayal of the life of Slovak immigrants *Out of This Furnace,* once Mike Dobrejak had joined forces with Djura and Kracha on the railroad tracklaying gang, the three of them moved together from job to job thereafter. Before and after each turn at work they would drink together. One needed a very good excuse not to participate in this sociable glass on any occasion. Consider also the photographs left from this epoch by Lewis Hine and others; notice how some individuals in every group leaned toward or touched each other.[70]

Such intimate work groups set the tone on any job in the course of their daily interaction with the curses, threats, and entreaties of the gang

69. Emmett Scott, ed., "Letters of Negro Migrants of 1916–1918," *Journal of Negro History,* 4 (July 1919), 305.

70. Reg Theriault, *Longshoring on the San Francisco Waterfront* (San Pedro, Calif., 1980); Thomas and Znaniecki, *Polish Peasant,* I, 87–106; Puskás, *From Hungary,* 18; Thomas Bell, *Out of This Furnace* (Pittsburgh, 1976); James R. Barrett, "Why Paddy Drank: The Social Importance of Whiskey in Pre-Famine Ireland," *Journal of Popular Culture,* 11 (Summer 1977), 155–66; for photographs by Hine, see Walter Rosenblum, Naomi Rosenblum, Alan Trachtenberg, and Marvin Israel, *America and Lewis Hine: Photographs 1904–1940* (New York, 1977), 51, 62, 113.

bosses. A solitary newcomer was quickly introduced into the gang's own work style, as Whiting Williams discovered his first day in a steel mill:

> When I started in I figured I'd keep going as long as I could and loaf after I was played out. I couldn't get on with the programme. First the little Italian boy tapped me on the shoulder and advised "Lotsa time! Take easy!" I slowed down a notch or two. A little later the Russian, wiping off the sweat as he sat for a moment on a pile of bricks, cautioned: "You keel yourself. Twelve hours long time." Finally, after every one had remonstrated, I got down to a proper gait − so you'd have to sight by a post to see if I was moving. But at that I guess they knew better than I − I'm certainly tired enough as it is.[71]

Ferocious bouts of toil were possible for laborers, but no one could sustain such a pace indefinitely. Asked how he had survived sixty-five years of heavy toil, the Welsh-born miner Tom Benyan replied: "Oh, they can't kill you with work if you have sense enough to go slow." For most laborers, the periods of recuperation were provided by the irregularity of employment itself. "One day he will almost work his life out," said Charles Kiehn of his fellow Hoboken longshoremen, "and the next two or three days have nothing to do except where he has a few spare coins to go into a saloon and spend it." Carleton Parker found that on the Pacific Coast the average job duration in 1914–15, a depressed period, to be sure, was fifteen to thirty days in lumber camps, ten days on construction, sixty days in mining, thirty days in canning, and seven days in harvesting. Chicago's packinghouses slaughtered almost three times as many cattle over Monday, Tuesday, and Wednesday as they did during the remainder of the week, and employment fluctuated accordingly.[72]

But laborers also broke up the toil on their own initiative. "To hell with the money, no can live," Pittsburgh workers told writer Charles Walker. They took their own holidays, be they religious festivals or "Saint Monday," which foremen sometimes punished with dismissal, sometimes simply ignored.[73] Moreover, the sociability of the saloon by no means represented wasted time to laborers. In the saloon, Jack London observed, "men talked with great voices, laughed great laughs, and there

71. Williams, *Worker's Mind*, 15. Compare Wyckoff, *West*, 178, on laborers' "deadly uninterest in their work," and the advice of Taylor and Thompson that "unless they are watched every minute," laborers "will be apt to work simply to kill time." Taylor and Thompson, *Concrete Costs*, 479.

72. "Anise," "The Man Who Worked Sixty-five Years," *Seattle Union Record*, May 7, 1921, 8; U.S. CIR, III, 2121, IV, 3490–1; Paul H. Douglas, "The Problem of Labor Turnover," *American Economic Review*, 8 (June 1918), 310.

73. Walker, *Steel*, 55–6, 114–15; the quotation is on p. 148. See also interview with Dave Hollingsworth (Saposs Papers, Box 24).

was an atmosphere of greatness."[74] There old acquaintances and new exchanged news and views, addressed each other by nicknames, and stood or sat in space implicitly acknowledged as theirs. Indeed, the Hungarian correspondent Emil Zerkowitz found in American saloons a "gentleman consciousness" that made him anxious about the political future of Slovak society when emigrants returned to it. In contrast to the home custom of sharing a glass of cheap schnapps with a few other peasants, Zerkowitz saw Slovaks in American cities and mining towns washing themselves in the evening, dressing up, sitting down in an elaborately decorated saloon, and imbibing great tankards of inexpensive beer, in an atmosphere free of police or religious supervision.[75]

Whether they were working flat out, sleeping behind a furnace or inside a boxcar, getting "quitting mad," enjoying the conviviality of the saloon, or being thrown back into the ranks of the unemployed, however, one thing was clear: For common laborers, work was the biblical curse. It was unavoidable, undependable, and unrewarding. But they had urgent need for money. A lonely Italian boy, found by a consul at a British Columbia railroad camp in the middle of winter, would not go into town, lest he spend his earnings once in the company of women (*la madamigella*); he had already mailed half a year's pay (350 lire) home to his mother.[76] Ewa Morawska observed that eastern European peasants were "certainly peacocks." They tried incessantly to outdo each other, Wincenty Witos wrote, in "the quantity and quality of the land, better and bigger farm buildings, better looking horses and cows, even a new sheepskin coat or a russet, shoes or boots."[77]

Nothing in their background in capitalism's rural periphery had nurtured a programmatic sense of collective or even personal advancement. When confronted with socialist arguments, Croatian villagers responded that "a man who thinks too long freezes."[78] When Catholic reformers,

74. Jack London, *John Barleycorn* (New York, 1913), 42.
75. Glettler, *Pittsburg-Wien-Budapest*, 296–300. People interviewed by the Immigration Commission often observed that Italian laborers drank less alcohol than native-born Americans or Slavs, but the Italians were certainly no less fond than others of masculine conviviality.
76. Harney, "Montreal's King," 83.
77. Wincenty Witos, *Moje Wspomnienia* (Paris, 1964), translated and quoted by Ewa Morawska, "The Internal Status Hierarchy in the East European Immigrant Communities of Johnstown, Pa., 1890–1930's," *Journal of Social History*, 16 (Fall 1982), 77. On the status role of new fashions in Polish villages, see Slomka, *From Serfdom*, 24.
78. Joseph Stipanovich, "Immigrant Workers and Immigrant Intellectuals in Progressive America: A History of the Yugoslav Socialist Federation, 1900–1918" (unpublished Ph.D. diss., University of Minnesota, 1977), 191.

attacking the lethargy and decay that settled over much of rural Galicia after the emancipation of the serfs, told peasants that they could improve their health and their savings by giving up smoking, they were met with this tale: "A man who smoked ceased to smoke and put aside the pennies he had been spending on smoking, until he had economized 9 rubles. With this money he bought a pig and used all his grain in feeding him. The pig died and the man suffered hunger."[79]

The vocabulary learned on the land, where capitalism had appeared like a cruel and invincible foreign conqueror, driving men and women away from their homes and families in a single-minded quest for money, was equally appropriate to their lives in industrial America. The laborer from Italy's *Mezzogiorno* seldom said *"Lavoro"* ("I am working"). He said *"Sto fatigando"* ("I am expending myself"). Said Slovenes, *"Pomali delati, pomali krasti"* ("Work a little, steal a little").[80]

Three important consequences of the fickle quality of laborers' toil and of the personal bonds that held their lives intact shaped their tenuous role in the labor movement. First, virtually all laborers' strikes dealt with one or the other of two questions: wages and abusive treatment by foremen. In the first report on strikes issued by the U.S. Commissioner of Labor, for example, the "laborers and wharf hands" of Chicago were among the most frequently listed groups of strikers; wages were invariably at issue. Collective action for a raise might take the form of mass quitting. When laborers were in high demand, they could simply pack off to another employer. Quite often the cause of a strike was that they had not been paid at all. Such was the case with the two hundred black excavators on Richmond's Church Hill tunnel project in 1873. When they received only one month's pay out of the three that were due them, they struck – and were all quickly replaced. Attempts to impose some sort of piecework on laborers could provoke furious responses. In the depths of the 1890s depression, for example, the Detroit Water Board announced its intention to pay eleven cents per yard for excavation work, instead of the customary daily wages. Five hundred Polish laborers refused to be overawed by the presence of the sheriff, armed deputies, and water board commissioners. In a bloody encounter, the Poles bludgeoned

---

79.   Thomas and Znaniecki, *Polish Peasant*, 249. Slomka, *From Serfdom*, 31–46, graphically describes the degeneration of the rural economy in Galicia after emancipation of the serfs and the self-help movement involved in this episode.

80.   Stipanovich, "Immigrant Workers," 191. I am indebted to Andrea Graziosi for the Italian expression. See also E. De Martino, *Sud e Magia* (Milan, 1959), on the "overwhelming power of the negative" in *Mezzogiorno* life.

the sheriff to death, and police gunfire killed eighteen strikers, but the board abandoned the piecework system.[81]

The routine chiseling, intimidation, and physical abuse practiced by labor contractors and gang bosses on the job were ordinarily accepted by laborers as an inevitable affliction that one had to endure in order to earn some money. At times, however, workers rounded furiously on their immediate masters. During a large strike of tracklayers on the Canadian Northern in 1912, their pent-up venom was set to music by Joe Hill:

> For these gunny-sack contractors have all been dirty actors,
> And they're not our benefactors, as each fellow worker knows.
> So we've got to stick together in fine or dirty weather,
> And we will show no white feather where the Fraser River flows.
>
> Now the boss the law is stretching, bulls and pimps he's fetching,
> And they are a fine collection, as Jesus only knows.
> But why their mothers reared them, and why the devil spared them,
> Are questions we can't answer, where the Fraser River flows.[82]

Demands for raises, whether made by Japanese laborers on the Northern Pacific or Italian freight handlers on the New Haven docks, were presented directly to the contractors themselves. A sudden walkout by Italian track laborers left a *padrone* empty-handed and in default to the railroad company that had hired him. During the 1880s, the Chinese Six Companies were frequently faced with strikes led by secretive *tongs*, which insisted on better terms and more protection than the merchant-contractors would provide. In April and May 1888, solidly unionized switchmen in Chicago's railroad yards struck twice to have obnoxious yardmasters and agents dismissed, and they won both times.[83] "If a foreman of a small gang of men is mean and overbearing," an Oregon track laborer advised his colleagues, "we must consider that it was just this disposition that won him his promotion. . . . Let us find fault with those who seek such men to promote."[84] But when laborers walked angrily off

81. U.S. Commissioner of Labor, *Third Annual Report* (1889), passim; Rachleff, "Black, White, and Gray," 452; Holli, *Reform in Detroit*, 66–7.
82. Joe Hill, "Where the Fraser River Flows," *I.W.W. Songbook* (Chicago, n.d.), 58. See also Irving Abella and David Miller, eds., *The Canadian Worker in the Twentieth Century* (Toronto, 1978), 54–5.
83. Ichioka, "Japanese Immigrant," 344; New Haven *Daily Union*, July 7, 1902; Harney, "Montreal's King," 81–3; Nee and Nee, *Longtime Californ'*, 67–9; Walter N. Fong, "Chinese Labor Unions in America," *Chautauquan*, 23 (June–July 1896), 399–402; Foner, *History of Labor Movement*, III, 275; U.S. Commissioner of Labor, *Tenth Annual Report* (1894), 182–5.
84. A track laborer in The Dalles, Oregon, to *Union Pacific Employees Magazine* (September 1889), 252, quoted in Stromquist, "Generation of Boomers," 423–4.

the job, it was the "overbearing" gang boss who drew their ire and to whom demands were addressed.

Second, when laborers unionized as laborers – that is, neither under the direction of some craftsmen nor in conjunction with other workers in the same factory or mill – their organizations were based on ethnic ties. This was as true of Philadelphia's black hod carriers in the 1870s and Irish freight handlers of the port of New York in the 1880s as it was of the Irish grain shovelers who brought the International Longshoremen's Association to the port of Buffalo by means of a successful strike against a saloon-based hiring system in 1899.[85] Likewise, it was true of the *tongs* and the unions formed by California's Chinese; the context of the exclusion movement also inspired purely Chinese unions of cigar makers, jean makers, and laundrymen.[86] The early building laborers' and subway tunnelers' unions of the twentieth century were Italian creations. For example, the AFL's Laborers' and Excavators' Union No. 11679 of Boston originally bore the name *Unione generale dei lavoratori*, and among its officers were several prominent Italo-American politicians. Their most famous leader, Domenico D'Alessandro, enjoyed the collaboration of Italian consuls in Boston and New York in challenging the grip of local *padroni*, not to mention combating anarchist influence among the immigrants, and he was knighted for his efforts by the king of Italy. The most delicate and difficult questions of union development involved the negotiation of alliances and of job allocation among locals based on different ethnic groups. Those issues assumed special importance in the organization of railroad construction workers in Washington and British Columbia during 1911 and 1912 by the Industrial Workers of the World (IWW) and in the relatively long-lived unions of dockers.[87]

Third, when laborers' unions managed to sustain effective strength past a single strike, they focused their efforts on breaking the grip of hiring agencies, establishing a close shop, and moderating the pace of work. Their challenges to the control of *banchieri*, saloonkeepers, or chiseling

85. Julia Blodgett Curtis, "The Organized Few: Labor in Philadelphia, 1857–1873" (unpublished Ph.D. diss., Bryn Mawr College, 1970), 323–4; Eric Foner, "Class, Ethnicity, and Radicalism in the Gilded Age: The Land League and Irish America," *Marxist Perspectives,* 1 (Summer 1978), 6–55; Jeremiah Murphy testimony, Senate, *Labor and Capital,* II, 678–87; Brenda K. Shelton, "The Grain Shovellers' Strike of 1899," *Labor History,* 9 (Spring 1968), 210–38.
86. Fong, "Chinese Labor Unions"; Nee and Nee, *Longtime Californ',* 67–9.
87. Martellone, *Little Italy,* 375–407; Fenton, *Immigrants and Unions,* 108–9, 209–15, 227–37; Yans-McLaughlin, *Family,* 112–15.

agencies over access to jobs often enjoyed significant support from bourgeois reformers and religious leaders. For example, Buffalo's grain shovelers, who in 1899 broke the domination previously exercised by saloonkeepers and Democratic Party bosses over employment on the docks, were assisted by temperance societies, civic reformers, and the city's Catholic bishop. *Padroni* and immigrant bankers were attacked simultaneously by immigrant socialists, Italian consuls and journalists, American grocery-store owners, and large urban banks, which were establishing their own foreign departments. Small wonder they became a favorite target of muckraking authors: a symbol of primitive and "unAmerican" forms of exploitation. Laws in New York and Massachusetts that required anyone in the banking business to post substantial bonds after 1905 drove many *banchieri* out of operation. The IWW directed its best-known "free-speech" campaigns against employment agencies and their fees, and the first victory of D'Alessandro's laborers' union in Boston was the abolition in 1904 of the *bossatura* charge for jobs building the city's new arsenal. Even the Immigration Commission noted that, in the Northeast at least, the practice of charging fees for jobs had "greatly lessened as the experience of the immigrant has increased."[88]

In place of hiring through fee-charging countrymen, the Boston laborers' union established its own hall as the only route through which jobs could be obtained. The closed shop (or, in IWW language, job control) was another fundamental objective of laborers' unions. Only by regulating the flow of casual laborers onto the job could they hope to raise wages above the level fixed by grim competition among job seekers. Moreover, the high turnover experienced by laborers meant that, for all their petty exploitation, *banchieri* and contractors provided a real service in locating employment. A successful union had to fill that need. For these reasons, in Boston's construction industry the predominantly Irish-American craft unions vigorously supported the Italian union's control of laboring jobs. When the IWW began to win wage increases for its members on the Philadelphia docks between 1913 and 1916, it also patrolled the waterfront to ascertain that only men with union buttons shaped up, and it instituted a twenty-five–dollar initiation fee to discourage occasional longshoremen. IWW members ("Wobblies") in the Agricultural Workers' Organization pursued the more famous practice of challenging

88. Shelton, "Grain Shovellers"; Martellone, *Little Italy*, 385–90; Fenton, *Immigrants and Unions*, 97–109, 132–4; Harney, "Montreal's King"; Carlos A. Schwantes, *Radical Heritage: Labor, Socialism, and Reform in Washington and British Columbia* (Seattle, 1979), 185–6; U.S. Immigration Commission, *Immigrants in Industry*, Part 22, 336–7.

people riding freight cars between jobs, to be sure they were all carrying red cards.[89]

Finally, union strength pulled the fangs of the gang bosses. Union power not only reduced the threats of arbitrary dismissal, chiseling on board and wages, beatings and arrests, but also made it possible to scale down the pace of work. Most examples come from the docks, the domain of resilient, though far from continuous, union power. The same phenomenon was evident when unions in Chicago's packinghouses briefly enrolled workers of all grades (1902–3). A member of the beef luggers' local testified:

> We used to load 60 or 70 cars of beef with 5 or 6 men, and this was certainly slavery, as anyone who understands the work will admit. This was the first thing we changed, and now we load 60 cars a day with 8 men, thereby putting more carriers to work; and where we had only 37 carriers before we organized we now have 53, and they do no more loading than the 37 used to do.[90]

Such dramatic elevation by laborers of their own status was a rare development, one that depended on the support of other unions in the same industry for its success. Understandably it roused the fury of employers – even the Chicago packinghouse unions were wiped out less than a year after the beef lugger had told of his success. These scattered examples of laborers' unionism at work are useful above all because they offer fleeting glimpses of the remedies that laborers advanced for their own problems. All of them appeared in some unusual context that allowed self-organization to outlast a single strike, created some framework of stability around the lives of certain laborers, and encouraged concerted action and programmatic thinking. Even in these settings, however, several influences were always in evidence: the laborers' economic and sentimental ties to the land outside the industrial regions in which they were then working, the personal bonds that linked them to one another, and the transient quality of their arduous work itself.

On the docks

Laborers on the waterfront played a unique role in the development of the union movement. Their persistent struggles in all major ports and the

89. Martellone, *Little Italy*, 380–7; John S. Gambs, *The Decline of the I.W.W.* (New York, 1932), 135–7; Philip S. Foner, *Organized Labor and the Black Worker, 1619–1973* (New York, 1974), 113, 137; Foner, *History of Labor Movement*, IV, 480–5.
90. *Official Journal of the Amalgamated Meat Cutters and Butcher Workmen of America*, 8 (March 1903), 42. Courtesy of James Barrett.

frequency with which they forged durable unions make one hesitate to include them in a discussion of laborers at all. But "human machines" they certainly were, forced to push or pull enormous weights, aided only by the most elementary inclines, pulleys, winches, hooks, and screws, and, above all, by their own teamwork. Bags of flour carried in oceanic shipment at the turn of the century weighed 100 to 150 pounds; those of coffee, up to 200 pounds; those of sugar and fertilizer, 300 pounds. The bales of cotton they stowed in holds averaged 500 pounds, and hogsheads of tobacco could weigh twice that. As late as 1914, not a single dock in New York City was equipped with a moving crane. All work was gang work, and virtually all hiring was casual – for the turnaround of an individual ship. Consequently, the very peculiarities of their lot that allowed them success at unionization to a degree that compared favorably with most skilled crafts also provide the historian with a revealing case study of those aspects of laborers' lives and aspirations that have been identified in this chapter. Particular attention will be paid here to the nation's two largest ports, New York and New Orleans. The forty-five thousand to fifty thousand men who regularly sought work in the harbor of greater New York made up considerably more than half of the waterfront workers in the entire United States.[91]

The waterfront of a great port dramatized both the organizational achievements and the social chaos of industrial capitalism. The movement of vast cargoes of food, coal, fibers, oils, chemicals, and manufactured products between railroad cars or riverboats and transoceanic steamers, by way of weighing stations, warehouses, sorting yards, and customs houses, passing through the management of both petty entrepreneurs and great shipping firms, was in itself a testimonial to the human capacity to orchestrate social activity. That the workers whose efforts were thus orchestrated lived from hand to mouth, enjoying no security of life and limb, let alone of income, revealed the human cost of that achievement.

All dock work was highly seasonal. In New Orleans, the leading commodity, cotton, was moved mostly between November and March. The tonnage leaving New York harbor could be four times as great in some weeks as it was in others. Many of its longshoremen moved off to Great

91. [Anonymous], "Longshore Labor Conditions in the United States," *Monthly Labor Review*, 31 (October 1930), 1–20, and 31 (November 1930), 11–25. The figure 45,000 is from U.S. CIR, III, 2061. Probably no more than 20,000 worked on any given day. New York City, Mayor's Committee on Unemployment, *Report on Dock Employment in New York City and Recommendations for Its Regularization* (New York, 1916, hereafter cited as *N.Y. Dock Employment*), 9.

Lakes ports in search of summer work, just as construction laborers migrated to the waterfront in winter. When a steamer arrived in port, word spread quickly through the grapevine, known as the "Longshore Gazette": keepers of saloons and restaurants, neighbors and kinfolk who scrutinized newspaper announcements of ship arrivals and departures, union "beach walkers," politicians, and charity agents. Men gathered quickly at the pier head, knowing the turnaround time when jobs would be available might last only thirty to forty hours. The shape-up began. Men tried to look conspicuous to the hiring bosses, standing so as to demonstrate strength, bobbing about, making signs of recognition or reminders of favors due. At first, only small gangs were hired to clear hatches and rig the ship for unloading. Then large numbers were needed – perhaps half of the three hundred or so shaping up. They formed into gangs of twelve men in New York harbor, six for the hold and six for the deck, and those gangs would usually work continuously until the ship was unloaded. The others drifted away, but usually they did not go far. Different piers so often shaped up at the same time that a loser at one could seldom try his luck at another on the same day. It was wiser to stay "on the farm" – on the sidewalk or in a saloon nearby, in case a foreman came looking for additional men. When loading began, the crew first hired was often larger than was needed for the cargo on the dock, or else special stevedoring gangs might be used for stowing cargo aboard ship. In either case, many men from the unloading gangs were then dismissed.[92]

So irregular was longshore employment that the high hourly rates at which they were paid seldom yielded comfortable annual incomes. On New York's Chelsea docks in 1914 the hourly rate was thirty-three cents, almost that of a unionized machinist, but the average work week of three to four days produced a pay envelope containing, at best, nine to twelve dollars, somewhat less than a steel-mill laborer then earned. Averages told little about individual experience. Seven experienced longshoremen recording their hours of work for investigators during the busy spring of 1916 turned in totals that ranged from nineteen hours to seventy-eight and a half. Loading oceanic vessels at that time earned forty cents per hour on the best piers, while work on the docks of large warehouse companies brought twenty-seven and a half cents per hour, and that on railroad terminals as little as twenty cents per hour.[93]

Moreover, those who sought a regular living from dock work faced

92.   U.S. CIR, III, 2051–212; Tom Murray, *Waterfront Supercargo* (San Pedro, Calif., 1980).
93.   U.S. CIR, III, 2055–6, 2095; *N.Y. Dock Employment*, 5, 18–19.

two special problems. One problem was that beached sailors, men who sought relief from charitable institutions, those whose addiction for drink permitted them only an occasional day's work ("shenangoes"), and the unemployed generally all appeared at shape-ups. Experienced hiring bosses refrained from hiring the same men every day, because they knew that to do so would discourage others who might someday be needed. Although the frequency with which men alternated between seafaring and dock work often promoted a sense of solidarity between seamen and longshoremen, the regular crews of docked ships were also available to load or unload cargoes if dockers refused to do so.

The second problem was that accidents were common among these men, who put in up to twenty-eight hours of steady toil in dark holds among great weights and fast-moving slings. First-aid facilities on the piers were usually limited to fruit crates to remove the dead or disabled, and hospital emergency staffs regarded their filthy patients with contempt. After New York State instituted workmen's compensation insurance, a record of eighty-six accidents was reported in the loading of a single ship. Cancer, heart disease, and pneumonia also contributed to the fact that 53 percent of longshoremen died at between thirty-five and fifty-four years of age, as compared with an average of 34 percent for all occupations. But the U.S. Supreme Court ruled dockers ineligible for state compensation, because their required crossing of the gangplank before starting work made them "maritime" workers, and consequently outside any state's legal jurisdiction.[94]

Nevertheless, a closer look at the waterfront reveals some order amid the chaos, much of it accomplished by the workers themselves. Rather than being one homogeneous mass, the workers sorted themselves out daily into many different occupations, each of which had its own employers, customs, routes of access, and sometimes unions. The port of New Orleans, for example, needed lightermen, warehousemen, freight handlers at the railroad depots, teamsters and draymen, screwmen to load cotton bales into ships' holds, grain handlers, coal wheelers to move coal to the barges, coal trimmers to load them, barge crews to guide them to their destinations, roustabouts to man riverboats, and longshoremen to move diverse wares on and off ships.[95] Moreover, longshoremen tended to seek work in pairs, and there were also regular gangs of six or twelve

94. U.S. CIR, III, 2128–30, 2150; *N.Y. Dock Employment*, 23; American Association for Labor Legislation, "The Longshore Bill" (circular dated 1926).
95. Eric Arnesen, "Until Such Time as Justice Is Done: Black and White Workers on the New Orleans Waterfront in the Early Twentieth Century" (unpublished M.A. thesis, Yale University, 1982), 11–17.

who were known to particular hiring bosses and were called out of the shape-up with some consistency. Such men were residents of neighborhoods adjacent to the piers, who considered jobs on those docks properly theirs, and among whom the "Longshore Gazette" functioned with special efficiency.

Consequently, despite the casual nature of daily employment and despite the constant flow of strangers through the docks, many longshoremen developed an attachment to particular places of work and residence that was unique among laborers. Among Afro-Americans in New Orleans, Germans in Hoboken, Irish in Jersey City and in New York's Chelsea area, and Italians in Brooklyn's Red Hook, sedentary communities of extended families developed around the piers and persisted for decades, even generations. Here the laborers were not strangers. The nine Chelsea piers of New York often employed more longshoremen than did entire ports in other parts of the country, such as Galveston, Baltimore, Boston, and Seattle. The familiar faces who were known and who obtained places on "good gangs," and even those who stood in reserve, included many from families who had lived there from the 1850s to the 1950s. The docking of passenger boats there was a special attraction, for passengers gave tips. Daniel Sullivan could tell the Commission on Industrial Relations in 1914 of his thirty-two years working there, and Patrick Powers could recount his experiences in the great strike of 1874.[96]

Newcomers from capitalism's periphery swarmed on the waterfront after 1890. The depression in cotton drove many rural Afro-Americans and whites to New Orleans in search of work and destabilized union conditions in that city. Italians arrived in large numbers in both New Orleans and New York, although they were often shunted off to undesirable docks and cargoes, such as bananas, which contained tarantulas. By 1916 their numbers almost equaled those of the Irish in New York harbor. Slavic and black newcomers dominated the port work in Baltimore and Philadelphia by 1910. In all major ports, racism assumed a new importance – in the contempt of New York's unionists for the Italian newcomers, in the effective battles of San Francisco longshoremen to keep all nonwhites off the docks, and in the delicate efforts of New Orleans dockers to maintain biracial unionism in the face of congealing, state-supported segregation. The farms of Europe and America continued to supply this country's harbors with strong and willing men, but the new arrivals encountered neighborhood alliances and work practices previously fashioned by their now sedentary predecessors.

96. Anonymous, "Longshore Labor Conditions" (October 1930), 16–20, (November 1930), 15–25; U.S. CIR, III, 2127–33, 2161–4; *N.Y. Dock Employment*, 10 and passim.

Just as pockets of stability in dock workers' lives allowed their unions a peculiar resilience, the structure of the industry limited the ability of their employers to resist unions. Concentrated capital did make its weight felt on the waterfront, especially around the turn of the century. Its main points of concentration, however, were in the railroads and shipping companies, rather than in the firms that actually worked the docks. Few steamship lines followed the example of the North German Lloyd and Hamburg lines, which directly hired as many as fifteen hundred men at a time in Hoboken. Theirs was one of several pockets of German investment in northern New Jersey after 1890; they had financial links to the German state, and their workers in Hoboken were virtually all German.[97] Most shipping companies, on the contrary, solicited bids from contractors for movement, storage, and loading of the wares they were scheduled to transport.

The complex network of firms involved in these transactions lent itself to separate negotiations and sectoral agreements involving, for example, boss draymen and their drivers, lighter owners and their crews, or stevedoring companies and the men they hired from day to day. In such dealings, some groups of workers were invariably stronger than others, and the contracts their unions had negotiated could prove obstacles to portwide solidarities of workers, just as the very diverse interests of many small employers could frustrate the efforts of boards of trade and of important businessmen who dominated those boards to weld together effective unity against union claims. This sectoralism was clearly evident in New Orleans, where employers in cotton, sugar, "round goods" (packaged cargoes), and fruit-transporting enterprises all tended to deal with their own employees quite independently of each other. New York's peculiar geography, which necessitated many handlings of wares between rail terminals and the Manhattan docks, accentuated contractors' concern for their own immediate interests, at the expense of any larger bourgeois conception of "the welfare of the port."[98]

Moreover, to be engaged in shipping out of either harbor was to be involved in party politics. The office of the collector of the port was the most lucrative nineteenth-century patronage appointment available to the federal government in both New York and New Orleans. A substantial cluster of clerical, inspection, medical, and weighing positions changed when a new party took power, and the collector and his subordinates also had effective control over one question of vital importance to ship-

97. U.S. CIR, III, 2115–24.
98. Arnesen, "Until Such Time," passim; Daniel Bell, *The End of Ideology. On the Exhaustion of Political Ideas in the Fifties* (revised edition, New York, 1961), 175–209.

pers: the length of time needed for a ship to clear port. It was well worth
the while of any shipping company to contract for loading or unloading
with a firm whose officers were in good standing with the collector of
customs. Moreover, a firm in such good standing had many longshoremen's jobs to offer, and being a member of the right political club would
not hurt a worker who wanted one of those jobs. In short, both the votes
and the financial contributions needed by political parties moved about
the docks together with coffee and cotton. Given the uninterrupted control of the New York and New Orleans city governments by the Democrats, and the usual appointments of their port collectors by Republicans
in Washington, political deals could become quite complex.

A glimpse of these arrangements is offered by the career of Peter H.
Walsh, or, more precisely, by the ire roused by Walsh's persistent efforts
to undercut the scales of payment set by both employers' associations
and unions. Walsh was the orphaned son of a longshoreman killed on
the job. He rose to prominence in the 1860s by contracting jobs at less
than the scales set by the Master Stevedores' Association and by helping
Collector of the Port Tom Murphy conduct negotiations between Tammany Hall and the Republican Party, to both of which Walsh belonged.
His firm controlled the loading on all docks between Canal and Houston
streets by 1870, and, a critic wrote, "the North River was dotted with
lighters, each carrying pyramids of bacon and flour with which the Walsh
Brothers filled these ships on their return to Europe."[99] Through his personal political clubs, made up of his foremen and his army of "cousins"
in Longshoremen's Union No. 3, Walsh also became a power to reckon
with in the union itself. His attempt to convince the union to cut its wage
scale on his docks was unsuccessful, however, and the union instead dispatched one of its members to London in an effort to persuade owners
of shipping companies there to dissociate themselves from Walsh and his
ways. The ensuing publicity, coming hard on the heels of the downfall of
the Tweed Ring, shed much light on the workings of waterfront commerce, but it did not save the longshoremen's wages for long. In October
1874, the stevedoring companies united forces to humble the longshoremen's union. After a five-week strike, in depression conditions, the union's
power on the docks was shattered. Wages that had stood at forty cents

99. Joseph Jennings, *The Frauds of New York and the Aristocrats Who Sustain
    Them* (New York, 1874), 21. On Walsh's undercutting of tariffs, see *Mas-
    ter Stevedores' Association v. Peter H. Walsh* 2 Daly 1 (New York Court
    of Common Pleas, 1867). On Tom Murphy, see David Montgomery, *Be-
    yond Equality: Labor and the Radical Republicans, 1862–1872* (New York,
    1967), 374–6.

per hour in the daytime and eighty cents at night were cut to twenty-five cents for days and thirty-five for nights. Union wage scales did not again reach the levels of 1874 until 1916.[100]

The network of business relationships exposed by the Walsh revelations involved small contractors, who urgently needed to hold down wages in order to beat out competitors, but who were also susceptible to negotiating their own deals with their own particular employees, if need be. It also included two centers of concentrated business enterprise. One was found in the railroads, which employed thousands of freight handlers to load and unload the railroad cars and operated many of the coastal shipping lines that operated out of New York. The railroads smashed freight handlers' attempts to unionize in the bitter strike of 1882 in New York and isolated and humbled their union in New Orleans in 1902. In both cities, freight handlers' hourly wages were consistently lower than those of longshoremen proper.[101]

The other center of power lay in the large steamship lines. As has been pointed out, however, the big shipping lines were all European, except the International Mercantile Marine Company formed by the House of Morgan in 1902, which went bankrupt in 1914, and the ships of United Fruit and Standard Oil, which carried the companies' own produce and were mostly registered under foreign flags. Cunard, Inman, North German Lloyd, and the other great lines directly linked large business syndicates with their respective governments, as weapons in an international battle for control of world commerce. The subsidies offered American oceanic steamers by Congress after 1891 proved no match for German and British marriages of capital and the state: Only 15 percent of American imports and 8 percent of exports moved in ships of U.S. registry in 1897. As Alfred Chandler said, "no successful giant shipping concern appeared in the United States."[102]

Because these foreign-owned lines floated huge fleets engaged in intense competition with one another in price and in scheduling, their managers were much less interested in holding down the hourly wages of longshoremen than they were in getting their ships unloaded and loaded quickly. Their own piers in New York boasted both the highest wages

100. Jennings, *Frauds*, 27–39; Charles B. Barnes, *The Longshoremen* (New York, 1915), 77–8; U.S. CIR, III, 2161–2. The 1916 ILA contract is reproduced in part in *N.Y. Dock Employment*, 73.

101. Chandler, *Visible Hand*, 190–1; Jeremiah Murphy testimony, Senate, *Labor and Capital*, II, 678–87; Arnesen, "Until Such Time," 56–64.

102. Chandler, *Visible Hand*, 187–92; the quotation is on p. 192. See also Kirkland, *Industry*, 296, 300.

and the most experienced dockers. In return for spasms of intense toil, those men received a good 30 percent more per hour than longshoremen on coastal shipping. Of the forty-five thousand workers in New York harbor in 1914, only three thousand then belonged to the International Longshoremen's Association (ILA), and most of them worked the piers of European fleets.[103]

Moreover, the large companies could offer very effective resistance to unions when they felt it necessary. During the depression of the 1890s, for example, major British lines circumvented the unions as well as the whole business structure of New Orleans by purchasing "through cotton" in the interior and hiring steady crews by the week to load the cargoes. They stood together especially firmly against union rules that they thought slowed the loading of their ships during the chronic strikes on the Crescent City's waterfront between 1901 and 1907 and successfully maintained control over their own foremen. In both cities they strongly supported efforts of government commissions to rationalize dock labor, through long-term union contracts and through proposals to "decasualize" the labor market by use of centralized employment agencies and more regularized employment.[104]

Decasualization under the auspices of the government or shippers' associations had little appeal to the dockers. They feared that such proposals would exclude thousands of men from employment altogether, while the rest would be forced to toil constantly at their arduous tasks and would probably soon face wage cuts on the grounds that steady work obviated the need for high hourly earnings.[105] The remedy proposed by their unions was as simple in design as it was difficult to achieve: Raise hourly wages to a level that could provide a decent income, no matter how irregular the employment, and regulate the pace of work, the size of gangs, and the behavior of foremen so that a man might survive a reasonable lifetime on the waterfront.

The variety of occupations on the waterfront led to a proliferation of unions, each representing a different group of workers and each negotiating its own wages and rules. By 1914, when New York's various dockers' unions had almost all entered the ILA, that organization had twenty-one locals in the port, each functioning in a different occupational or geographic domain. The situation in New Orleans was even more com-

---

103. *N.Y. Dock Employment*, 5; U.S. CIR, III, 2195.
104. Joy L. Jackson, *New Orleans in the Gilded Age: Politics and Urban Progress, 1880–1896* (Baton Rouge, La., 1969), 224–31; Arnesen, "Until Such Time," 82–132.
105. *N.Y. Dock Employment*, 34–44, 65–70.

plicated. The Dock and Cotton Council formed in 1901 represented black and white yardmen, black and white screwmen, black teamsters and loaders, black coal wheelers, and black and white longshoremen. Unions of railroad freight handlers, of dockers moving round freight, fruit, and sugar, and of sugar-refinery workers, who had collaborated closely with dockers during the city's general strike of 1892, stood outside this structure altogether. Each group bargained for itself, and at times they also made common cause with their particular employers. Between 1890 and 1892, cotton yardmen endorsed the appeal of press owners for increased handling charges, and teamsters helped boss draymen get a higher tariff from ship agents and cotton-press owners. Most notably, during the general strike of 1892, which brought forty-two different unions, even barbers and musicians, off the job in support of embattled sugar scalesmen, teamsters, and warehousemen, the cotton-handling trades remained at work. After 1901, the tendency toward sectoralism was strengthened by the firm opposition of ILA president Daniel J. Keefe and the New Orleans leadership of the AFL to any sympathetic strikes that would involve violation of contracts.[106]

In irrepressible opposition to this tendency, however, stood dockers' keen awareness of how closely all their interests interlocked. This awareness was manifested at the organizational level by the frequent appearance and reappearance of councils of delegates from the many unions that attempted to coordinate common policy. In the mid-1880s, district assemblies of the Knights of Labor and central labor unions played this role in both ports. In New Orleans, the Workingmen's Amalgamated Council, which led the 1892 general strike, assumed this function. A decade later the solidification of legal segregation had led to a complex three-tiered leadership structure for the city's labor movement. The Central Trades and Labor Council, formed in 1899, was open only to unions of white workers affiliated with the AFL. The Central Labor Union was made up of delegates from AFL unions of black workers and was led by James Porter, an international vice-president of the ILA. The Dock and Cotton Council had no organizational links to the AFL; it represented both white and black unions on the cotton docks. Porter was its secretary.[107]

More enduring than these various organizational structures was the dockers' code of "enforcing the card." Union members in any occupation

---

106. Arnesen, "Until Such Time," 35; Joel Sabadasz, "General Strike: New Orleans 1892" (unpublished M.A. paper, University of Pittsburgh, 1979), 10, 31.
107. Arnesen, "Until Such Time," 27–9, 35–7.

were loath to handle work brought to them by men who were not members of appropriate unions, especially by scabs. This principle inspired a round of sympathetic strikes, involving virtually all the waterfront groups in 1885 and 1886, that made New Orleans the most highly unionized and highest-paying port on the Atlantic and Gulf coasts. Then, during January and February 1887, one strike of eighty-five coal handlers and another of two hundred longshoremen in New York spread through a series of sympathetic stoppages – boatmen refusing to transport scab coal, shovelers to load it, grain handlers to load ships stocked with such coal, bag sewers to work where grain handlers would not – until twenty-eight thousand workers were on strike, under the general leadership of Knights of Labor District Assembly 49. Although the coal handlers won their wage demands, thanks to all this support, the spreading strike reached its limits when brewery workers and stationary engineers in carpet factories ignored D.A. 49's order to use no coal (i.e., to close their factories). Longshoremen drifted back to work with nothing gained for themselves, and the city's labor movement sank into a factional bickering.[108]

The demoralization of New York's docks after the 1887 strike and the subsequent inundation of the city's piers by newcomers kept the unionized sector of the port small as the twentieth century began, and the later union leaders, like Keefe, not only opposed sympathetic strikers but also advocated arbitration of all disputes. Not until 1919 did a comparable wave of sympathetic strikes tie up the port, despite the furious opposition of the ILA leadership.[109] Nevertheless, in 1907, a strike in the classic style of immigrant laborers shut down the Brooklyn docks. Italian workers dominated these docks, and many of them loaded cargoes only in winter, spending their summers on more reliable construction projects. A branch of the then independent Longshoremen's Union Protective Association (LUPA) had been formed among them, but it had withdrawn from the LUPA when the latter refused to allow the Italians one of their own countrymen as business agent. A wave of agitation swept the docks in the spring of 1907, when work was plentiful in the port, reaching a climax with a large May Day parade calling everyone out on strike and demanding above all decent treatment by foremen. Although LUPA en-

108. Sabadasz, "General Strike," 6–9; New York Bureau of Statistics of Labor, *Fifth Annual Report . . . 1887* (hereafter cited as N.Y. BSL, 1887), 327–85; Barnes, *Longshoremen*, 93–108; John R. Commons et al., *History of Labour in the United States* (4 vols., New York, 1918–35), II, 420–1.

109. Commons, *History of Labour*, IV, 450–1. On Keefe's union practice, see [National Civic Federation], "Joint Trades Agreement Conference of the National Civic Federation, Held . . . May 7th, 1904 . . . (typescript, Mitchell Papers, Box A3-100), 27–37.

dorsed the strike after it had continued for a few days and then enrolled twelve thousand Italians, the poverty of the strikers soon drove them back to the shape-ups with little to show for their efforts – except the rise to prominence in union circles of the racketeer Paolo Vaccarelli (also known as "Paul Kelly"), who became a vice-president of the ILA after its merger with LUPA.[110]

Decent treatment was as important an issue in New Orleans as it was in Brooklyn. In the Crescent City, however, the issue underlay not one spectacular strike but, rather, a chronic battle between shippers and powerful unions that reached its climax in a general strike of the port six months after Brooklyn's Italian May Day. Every year between 1901 and 1907, New Orleans dockers and their employers had done battle over work rules: the number of men on a hatch, whether foremen would be union members, how many bales might be raised or lowered in a sling, and the maximum number of cotton bales a gang of screwmen could be made to stow in a ship's hold during a single day. Union practice there was to levy fines on foremen or workers who violated the contract, among them fines for abusive conduct. It was not always successful. Riverboat roustabouts, for example, lost the 1901 strike in which one of their key demands had been that any officer who clubbed a worker would be fined $200 for the first offense, $500 for the second, and $1,000 for the third.[111] A major screwmen's strike in 1902, however, ended with a compromise provision:

> Any gang or gangs stowing more than ninety (90) bales of flat cotton with screws or more than one hundred and sixty (160) bales of flat cotton by hand for the day's work shall be fined for the first offense fifty ($50.00) dollars per gang; second offense expelled from the Association to which they belong.[112]

The persistence of intense conflict on the docks strengthened the desire of both white and black dockers for effective cooperation between the two races, despite the rising tide of racism and segregation. Their basic formula was the half-and-half distribution of jobs, worked out by union rules and incorporated into the contracts of screwmen, longshoremen, cotton yardmen, and others. The issue was most delicate in the case of the highly skilled screwmen, who packed cotton and tobacco into ships' hulls with great manual jacks. Work-sharing agreements between unions

110. This complex strike has yet to receive serious historical analysis, but see Fenton, *Immigrants and Unions*, 253–4; Barnes, *Longshoremen*, 115–29; [anonymous], *Ai Socialisti del Re* (New York, 1918), 15.
111. Arnesen, "Until Such Time," 52.
112. Louisiana Bureau of Statistics of Labor, *Report for the State of Louisiana, 1904–1905* (New Orleans, 1906, hereafter cited as La. BSL), 81.

of white and black screwmen dated back to 1872, but they had collapsed in the face of racial conflict during the depressions of the 1870s and the 1890s. An agreement of 1875 equalizing the wages of white and black screwmen, but limiting the latter to no more than twenty gangs (100 men) working at a time, had lasted through the 1880s. Then, in 1894, hungry whites, charging that black workers were violating the agreement, had thrown fellow unionists of the wrong complexion into the harbor. In 1901, a new and enduring formula was reached by the two unions and incorporated into subsequent contracts:

> The walking foreman [a union member] shall hire half and half gangs of the [two] Associations and shall distribute them equally in each hatch abreast of each other. Members of the Screwmen's Benevolent Association [white] shall work on the starboard side and the members of the Screwmen's Benevolent Association No. 1, colored, shall work on the larboard side of all ships arriving in the port of New Orleans.

The contract went on to say that union members shall "not take orders from anyone but the walking foreman," and that any foreman who violated the half-and-half rule would be fined fifty dollars for the first offense and expelled for the second.[113]

The limits of interracial solidarity were clear and precise. The half-and-half rule itself distinctly favored the whites, because there were fewer of them among screwmen, longshoremen, and yardmen. Although the rule guaranteed equal hourly wages, it gave whites access to more hours of work. Attempts to mobilize biracial Labor Day parades foundered in 1902 and 1903 over the insistence of whites that Afro-Americans march in the rear, and the decision of black unions to stage their own separate parades, rather than acquiesce to that insulting position. When the Socialist-led brewery workers were expelled from the AFL in 1907 and raided by the Central Trades and Labor Council, all black unions in town supported the brewery workers, and all white unions except the longshoremen and screwmen backed the AFL. Most serious of all, when black longshoremen tried in 1907 to extend the half-and-half principle to gang foremen, as well as gang members, members of the white union almost turned a joint meeting into a riot in protest. The black longshoremen withdrew the demand, and the two longshoremen's unions subsequently stood together through the biggest strike in the port's history.[114]

The closure of the port by eight thousand white and black workers for three weeks in October 1907, in the immediate aftermath of the bitter

113. Ibid., 77.
114. Arnesen, "Until Such Time," 162–5. On the brewery workers controversy in New Orleans, see Arnesen, 134–61.

brewery workers' dispute and the clash over black foremen and in defiance of outcries from the state legislature about black rule and "amalgamation" in New Orleans, testifies to the devotion of dockers of both races to their unions. Their associations maintained some of the highest hourly wages for dockers in the country, established nine hours as a standard work day from the 1880s on, and rigorously controlled the conduct of gang bosses; they also provided centers of self-organized political activity and influence that were as unusual in the experience of American laborers as the economic standards they had won. White dockers were tightly linked to the city's ruling Democratic Party, and more often than not could depend on the mayor and city council to act more as mediator than as foe during dockers' strikes. Afro-Americans, of course, had been disfranchised in the 1890s, but this development did not make their unions any less political. Leading black longshoremen were also prominent in the Republican Party. Black Labor Day parades were major community events. Black nationalist and "race pride" meetings regularly filled black longshoremen's halls on Sunday afternoons.[115] What better portrayal of black dockers' conception of themselves than the defiant declaration made by one of them during the unsuccessful effort to win a half-and-half rule for foremen:

> White people were screening the colored brother off to himself in the street cars; they would not let him enter the saloons and drink there with them; shoved him closer to the sky in the theater, and generally denied him his rights. . . . [T]he colored man is bound to have equality on the Levee if he can have it no place else.[116]

Toward a second "shortage of laborers"

After the depression of 1907–8 had ended, large and demonstrative strikes of laborers became commonplace. Striking Italian building laborers in Buffalo, Providence, and New York marched through the streets behind red banners and bands playing the "Garibaldi March"; Slovak and Polish laborers walked out of steel mills in McKeesport, Duquesne, and Bethlehem, also accompanied by marches, music, and Socialist rhetoric;

115. See, for example, Sylvia Woods's recollections of her childhood, in Alice and Staughton Lynd, *Rank and File: Personal Histories by Working Class Organizers* (Boston, 1973), 113–4, and the nationalist pamphleteering activity of Robert Charles, in William Ivy Hair, *Carnival of Fury: Robert Charles and the New Orleans Race Riot of 1900* (Baton Rouge, La., 1976).
116. *New Orleans Picayune*, August 29, 1907, quoted in Arnesen, "Until Such Time," 165.

track laborers of a dozen nationalities halted work on the Canadian Northern under the leadership of IWW job delegates. These struggles blended with the more famous militancy of unskilled factory operatives in Lawrence, Paterson, and Passaic and of immigrant coal miners from Westmoreland County, Pennsylvania, to Ludlow, Colorado. Industry journals like *Iron Age* were complaining by 1912 of the "scarcity of common laborers" and placing blame for the more demanding behavior of immigrants on the drying up of their European sources.[117] Socialist Phillips Russell was more optimistic about the same phenomenon. "The day of the common laborer has arrived," he exclaimed. "He holds American industry in the hollow of his hand."[118]

Russell was wrong. Rural sources of transient laborers remained abundant, and workers' treatment in the 1920s on construction sites and docks alike differed little from that of the 1880s. Nevertheless, unskilled workers generally had clearly assumed a new role in American society and in the labor movement by 1910. The new role cannot be understood, however, by examining laborers in isolation from other workers. Both the growth of urban immigrant communities and the reorganization of industrial management were binding the experiences and actions of laborers and factory operatives more tightly together. Those developments must be analyzed before we can return to the struggles of twentieth-century laborers and place them in their proper context.

It is worth noting at this point, however, that just as the May Day strike of Brooklyn's Italian dockers anticipated the emerging militancy of unskilled immigrants, so the settlement of the New Orleans strike in the same year suggested important elements of the context in which that militancy was going to express itself. First, although the shutdown of the port was total, there was no city-wide general strike, as there had been in 1892. This time, the leaders of the local AFL declared sympathetic strikes "antiquated" and pledged to continue working in adherence to their contracts with "all fair employers."[119]

Second, the strike was eventually settled with five-year contracts for the screwmen and longshoremen. The city's seven years of chronic conflict were followed by seven years of industrial peace. Third, as part of

117. *IA,* 90 (October 10, 1912), 855. Peter Stearns has concluded that the rural supply of laborers really was drying up in 1912–13. Stearns, "The Unskilled and Industrialization," *Archiv für Sozialgeschichte,* 16 (1976), 249–82. The strikes mentioned in this paragraph will be discussed in Chapters 6 and 7.

118. Phillips Russell, "Shortage of Common Labor," *New Review,* 1 (July 1913), 650–4; the quotation is on p. 654.

119. Quoted in Arnesen, "Until Such Time," 179.

the settlement mediated by the mayor, a Port Inquiry Commission was established by the state to examine the entire fabric of work relations in the port and to propose remedies for those practices that made shipping from it more expensive than from its rivals, Galveston-Houston, Mobile, and Pensacola. After the major steamship lines, unions, and the mayor proved unable to constitute a civic committee for this purpose, the state legislature created a Port Inquiry Commission of two state senators and three state representatives. It was through this governmental intervention that new contractual rules defining a "fair day's work" were established.

Finally, the commission's final report identified the port's greatest problem as its *lack* of racial segregation. "One of the greatest drawbacks to New Orleans is the working of the white and negro races on terms of equality," it concluded. "The Commission believes that this has been the fruitful source of most of the trouble on the New Orleans Levee." The commission denounced the half-and-half system as "altogether degrading for the white man" and recommended separation of the races on the docks "for sociological reasons."[120]

The role of the state generally, and expert commissions of inquiry especially, in attempting to reshape social relations thus appeared to be as important to New Orleans dockers at the turn of the century as they were to the country's embattled ironworkers and steelworkers. Like the steelworkers' project of "amalgamation," the dockers' scheme of half-and-half was portrayed as an obstruction to be overcome in society's quest for social order and industrial rationalization. Laborers and craftsmen alike were summoned to mend their ways in the name of progress.

120. *Official Journal of the Proceedings of the House of Representatives of the State of Louisiana at the First Regular Session of the Third General Assembly* (May 28, 1908), 198–9.

3

The operative

There were more than four thousand people making electric-light bulbs in eight factories surveyed by the federal government at the end of 1907. The men among them included a small number of skilled metal trades-men and electricians and many laborers, who stoked furnaces, handled freight, and moved cases of lamp components about the factories. Among the workers who actually made the lamps, 94.4 percent, or 2,756, were women. The factories were all located in major urban agglomerations where their wares might be used and where many young women resided and sought employment. Almost 60 percent of the production workers, in fact, were between sixteen and twenty years of age; 35 percent were daughters of American parents, 40 percent had been born in the United States to immigrant parents, and only 25 percent were immigrants them-selves. Plant managers expressed a clear preference for employees who had been born and educated in the United States. Consequently, the typ-ical electric-lamp worker might be described as a seventeen-year-old un-married daughter of German immigrants residing in a middling-sized town adjacent to New York, Boston, Pittsburgh, or Detroit.[1]

In contrast to the common laborer who expended his strength in ways that seemed almost impervious to change, the lamp worker found herself at the very frontier of industrial innovation. The electrical industry was scarcely a generation old and was the product of modern research labo-ratories. Its leading companies had been consolidated by investment bankers in the early 1890s and had joined forces in a patent pool in 1896. Because their complex and diverse production processes made them heavily dependent on skilled workers, these corporations were also pioneers in the quest for new methods of managing everything from the boardroom to the production floor. Tireless promoters of standardized methods, sys-

1. U.S. Congress, Senate, *Report on Condition of Woman and Child Wage Earners in the United States* (19 vols., Senate Document No. 645, 61st Cong., 2nd Sess., Washington, D.C., 1911, hereafter cited as Senate, *Woman and Child Wage Earners*), III, 489–92.

tematic accounting, and control of costs, they changed work processes and materials incessantly. Moreover, during the first forty years of this century, light-bulb production was the most consistently profitable component of the business.[2] Nevertheless, both the workplaces and the hierarchical structure within which young women turned out light bulbs in 1907 were more characteristic of late-nineteenth-century factory production than of the scientifically managed enterprise heralded by Frederick Winslow Taylor and his colleagues. Innovations in personnel management found there were largely confined to experiments in incentive-pay schemes.

The factory buildings were not modern, noted the government investigators. Their ventilation was poor, they lacked fire escapes or fire protection, noxious odors filled the air, and temperatures ranged from chilly to stifling hot at different places within the same departments. Although bulb production was divided into thirty-five operations, most processes were manual or aided only by simple machinery. Payment everywhere was by the piece, but piece rates for operations that were virtually identical varied considerably from one factory to another. Foremen established the rates, in most instances by the most widely practiced of all methods: They observed how many parts a good worker could turn out in a day and divided the prevailing daily wage for women's work in the locality by that figure, in order to determine the price per piece. If some process was new, or if the supervisors thought output was inadequate at some task, a "leader" would be assigned to the work group, who would receive a bonus of 5 percent or so in return for demonstrating how many parts she could produce in a day. Once the new standard had been demonstrated, it was made the norm, and piece rates were reduced accordingly. "We keep the rates so low that they have to keep right at it to make a living," explained one supervisor.[3]

Those who failed to meet the expected day's output consistently were simply fired. Work that failed to pass inspection, the breaking of parts, and violations of company discipline were all punished with the universal bane of operatives' existence: fines. Fines that devoured too large a slice of women's pay could provoke a revolt, as when hub makers in one plant found more than fifty cents of their average weekly earnings of $7.50 withheld and struck in protest. Such actions might reduce or eliminate particular fines, but the system of fines itself proved invincible to direct

2. Chandler, *Visible Hand*, 426–33; Ronald W. Schatz, *The Electrical Workers: A History of Labor at General Electric and Westinghouse, 1923–60* (Urbana, Ill., 1983), 4–9.
3. Senate, *Woman and Child Wage Earners*, III, 480.

action by operatives during the half century that followed the Civil War.[4]

Such traditional economic whips were supplemented in the bulb works of 1907 by newer types of cash incentives. Bonuses were sometimes offered to everyone who met a specified level of output. On occasion, as in the gem-mounting section of one plant, differential piece rates were used, so that women who attached fewer than 900 wires to filaments in the course of ten hours were paid $1.03 per thousand, whereas attaching between 900 and 1,000 earned $1.07 per thousand, between 1,000 and 1,100 earned $1.12 per thousand, and surpassing 1,100 for the day raised the rate per thousand to $1.17. The combined effects of all these techniques had raised hourly output on some tasks as much as 40 percent since 1890, with no change at all in methods or materials used.

As these figures suggest, the lamp makers' pace of work was ferocious. Women who struck General Electric's bulb works in Toledo in 1914 told a committee of local clergymen that they were "obliged to place wet cloths over their eyes nights to stop the aching and enable them to get some sleep."[5] Handling filaments, the government investigators had observed, was like "threading a very fine cambric needle" two thousand to three thousand times a day. A machine run by two women made a flare at the top of the stem and sealed the lead-in wires. They averaged 2,600 parts per day and were paid forty-five cents per thousand, or $1.17 daily for the machine feeder and for the finisher. In one instance, a team turned out 3,500; that is to say, each minute for ten hours they flared and sealed between four and six lamps. For this achievement each of them earned $1.58, or as much for the day as a common laborer. The highest pay was earned by those who could exhaust (the operation that completed the vacuum) 900 bulbs per day with the aid of roaring-hot gas ovens. Toledo strikers claimed that only four of the two hundred young women who had entered that department during the previous year were still there; six had died of tuberculosis and two were recuperating in a fresh-air camp. Those who tested finished bulbs placed about thirty-three per minute against an electrified metal plate. At the start of the day they felt a shock with each one, but soon, in the rush to earn $6\frac{1}{2}$ cents per thousand, they no longer felt anything.[6]

The work of the operative, then, had several distinguishing character-

---

4. Ibid., III, 480–1.
5. *Toledo Union Leader,* March 13, 1914. I am indebted to Neil Basen for this source.
6. Senate, *Woman and Child Wage Earners,* III, 467–89. General Electric and Westinghouse developed newer payment systems, based on minimum take-out rates, standard rates, and bonuses during and after World War I. Schatz, *Electrical Workers,* 18–24.

istics. Unlike either the craft worker, whose training and traditions permitted considerable autonomy in the direction of his own and his helpers' work, or the laborer, who applied his portable muscle power wherever and whenever directed, the operative was a specialist, bound to repetition of the same task in the same place. Because the operative's work was easily defined and measured, it was compensated more often by the piece than by the day or the hour.

No matter what the operative's task or what the method of payment, however, the working hours were subject to the virtually absolute authority of a foreman, overseer, or contractor. Daniel Nelson's description of the nineteenth-century factory as "the foreman's empire" would have rung true to any operative of the time.[7] Hiring and firing, assignment to tasks, setting the pay rate (by day or by piece), determining who got laid off or told to stay overtime, and resolving disputes all lay in the foreman's domain. A foreman could favor those he liked with day rates, generous piece rates, relatively easy or pleasant tasks, permission to miss work to tend sick children or visit aged parents, and early recall from seasonal shutdowns. He could punish pieceworkers not only with fines and dismissal but also by delaying delivery of parts to those who had run out of work or by failing to dispatch troubleshooters or repairmen when a machine had broken down. A major difference between the work of the craftsman and that of the operative lay in their relations with their immediate supervisors, and that difference was clearly reflected in nineteenth-century union practice. Operatives' unions struggled to limit the authority of foremen, whereas unions of craftsmen legislated rules concerning their own members' workplace behavior, and they often included foremen within the same union discipline.

Nevertheless, the line distinguishing craft worker from operative was anything but precise and constantly shifted within particular industries even before twentieth-century managerial reforms fundamentally reshaped the relations of production. An early proponent of scientific management, H. A. Worman, argued that the same personal qualities were needed in a semiskilled worker as in a craftsman: "experience, brain power, [and] adaptability." He stressed the importance of compatibility with the foreman, however, and he warned employers against hiring skilled men on hard times, who were "ready to do anything," for operatives' jobs. The "habits of their regular occupations will assert themselves the moment the urge of necessity vanishes," he warned.[8]

7. Nelson, *Managers and Workers*, 35–43.
8. H. A. Worman, "Recruiting the Working Force. IV – Hiring the Semi-Skilled Workman," *Factory*, 1 (March 1908), 194.

Worman's admonitions alert us to the ambiguities of such terms as "skilled" and "semiskilled" and also to the judgment and experience required by many operatives' tasks, despite their repetitious nature. The archetypal operative was the power-loom weaver, whose work consisted basically of watching for breaks in the yarn that would spoil the machine's output. Yet, as veteran weaver Cora Pellerin said, "You have to have it in you to be a good weaver. You either fit in or you don't." Her fellow weaver Mary Cunion explained:

> We used to have warps in five or six colors. It was not just in your hands. It was in your head too. . . . You had to watch your pattern. . . . Sometimes when the loom would get out of order, a bobbin would drop and sprout a whole warp, and the warp would have to be cut out and you'd have to start all over again . . . in fact, you'd never learn it all.[9]

Although the observations of Pellerin and Cunion are based on their experience in this century, they were describing one of the oldest types of machine tending. Their conception of what they were doing stands in stark contrast to this 1923 managerial description:

> The ability to meet ("to hit") and maintain a constant pace; to be able to eliminate all waste and false motions; to follow without wavering printed instructions emanating from an unseen source lodged in some far off planning department – these constitute the requirements of a successful machine tender.[10]

The contrast suggests that scientific management affected the work of the operative as well as that of the craftsman. Moreover, the activities of the operatives themselves played a crucial role in encouraging employers to restructure the management of their labor forces.

The rise of the specialized worker

Operatives are best understood not as an ideal type or as people whose training and expertise fell into a vague intermediate range between the "skilled" above them and the "unskilled" below but as a historical development of ever increasing importance in the reshaping of the working class as the century progressed. Immediately after the Civil War the textile and clothing industries were their most important theaters of action.

9. Both quotations are from Tamara K. Hareven, *Family Time and Industrial Time: The Relationship between the Family and Work in a New England Industrial Community* (Cambridge, U.K., 1982), 79–80.

10. Charles Reitell, "Machinery and Its Effects upon the Workers in the Automobile Industry," *Annals, American Academy of Political and Social Science,* 116 (November 1924), 39.

Each industry then employed between 7 and 8 percent of the country's industrial wage earners. Although their patterns of development were quite different, both of them depended heavily on the work of operatives, and both can help us understand why operatives appeared and how their toil was organized.

Clothing was fabricated in many different ways from the 1860s onward. Women continued to produce much of it at home for their own families, sewing their own dresses, taking in children's clothes for their younger siblings, and altering secondhand coats and pants for their husbands. Journeyman tailors and dressmakers made the finest of outfits to order. But large-scale production of ready-made clothing had been organized as early as the 1840s by highly capitalized wholesale firms in seaport cities, and inland at Cincinnati. Among the largest was Winchester and Davis of New Haven, which gave out sewing to four thousand women and men in the mid-1850s. By promoting the fabrication of cheap, standardized clothing outside of the tailoring shop, such manufacturers had competed effectively with both artisan production and homemade attire. The widespread introduction of foot-powered sewing machines in the 1850s and then of mechanical cloth-cutting knives in the 1870s, however, had opened the way to a reorganization of clothing production, to a more detailed division of labor, and to the rise of the sewing-machine operator.[11]

Most men's coats were then made in small shops run more often than not by German immigrants who had funds enough to buy a sewing machine or two and who put their families to work by their sides. "A tailor is nothing without a wife and very often a child," in Conrad Carl's words.[12] By contracting with wholesale firms for more work than their families could handle and crowding hired hands into their shops, such tailors gave birth to the sweatshop and to an increasingly complex network of outside contracting. Simultaneously, major department stores employed large numbers of women in their workrooms to make clothes for sale over the counter – until the prolonged depression of the 1870s persuaded them to leave the risks of manufacturing to others – and the sewing of shirts, pants, vests, hoop skirts, and bustles was gathered into manufactories, or "inside shops." New divisions of labor appeared in these shops: Cutting and marking emerged as skilled male crafts; basting, finishing,

11. For information concerning production methods in the clothing trades, I am indebted to Linda Pickard, "The Clothing Trades in the Nineteenth Century: Changes in the Methods of Production. A Working Paper, Being Background to the Research" (unpublished manuscript in author's possession), though my interpretation differs somewhat from hers.

12. Senate, *Labor and Capital*, I, 414.

and pressing became separate hand operations; and sewing-machine operators stitched together the parts that had been made by the cutter and tacked into place by the baster. The finisher and presser then added the final touches. Highly capitalized firms with many specialized workers, and even with their own laundries and starching departments attached, had taken over by 1880 most of the work that garret seamstresses had performed on men's clothes before the Civil War. Still, 88 percent of the workers in women's ready-made clothing and 54 percent of those in men's ready-mades were women, according to the census of 1880.[13]

During the 1880s the trend toward concentrated production was abruptly reversed, but in ways that made the work even more specialized while increasing the proportion of men in the industry. The practice of contracting work out of the shop provided the instrument for pitting tailors in intense competition with each other for orders from the manufacturers, and the heavy migration of Jews and later Italians with tailoring and entrepreneurial experience provided the personnel.

First in men's clothing, then in women's cloaks, and ultimately in many branches of production, manufacturers had the cloth cut in their shops, then distributed in marked bundles to contractors, who bid against each other for the work and then hired other workers to help sew the parts according to the manufacturers' instructions. The work was performed in small rooms hired for the season or even in the contractor's own apartment, where the family was crowded into a corner by bundles of sewing during the production season. Although work carried on in the home led to a resurgence of wage earning by mothers and children, major effects of the contracting system were steady increases in numbers and proportions of male operatives. By 1890, the proportion of women among the workers in men's clothing had fallen to 44 percent, and in women's clothing it was down to 66 percent.[14]

In men's clothing, a so-called task system had made its appearance in outside shops by the end of the 1870s, and its use became increasingly widespread and refined over the next twenty years. Initially, three tailors worked as a team to make coats at a specified price per coat. They arranged themselves as a machine operator, a baster, and a finisher. Each of the men was hired for a weekly wage by the contractor, who usually

13. Virginia Penny, *How Women Can Make Money, Married or Single* (Springfield, Mass., 1870), 301–12; Chandler, *Invisible Hand,* 224–9; Pickard, "Clothing Trades," 47–65; Edith Abbott, *Women in Industry: A Study in American Economic History* (New York, 1910), 123, 241.

14. Abbott, *Women in Industry,* 234–41. A fine description of outside contracting can be found in Abraham Bisno, *Abraham Bisno, Union Pioneer* (Madison, Wisc., 1967).

was one of the three himself at first, and the team then turned out the number of garments needed to earn those wages each week at the price for which the contractor had agreed to sew them. The team also needed to hire its own presser. Competition pushed the prices offered by manufacturers for each coat steadily downward, and those who refused to take work at lower prices simply got no work. Consequently, the number of coats in a week's task moved upward from nine or ten around 1882 to eighteen to twenty by the late 1890s. In addition to stretching their own hours of work ever farther, team members converted themselves into specialists at one or another of the operations and also hired women for additional specialties, such as sewing on buttons or pockets. Because a presser could handle more coats in a day than a team of tailors, shops eventually came to be based on three sewing teams to two pressers, and the contractors removed themselves from the critically important sewing machine to spend more of their time arranging for work for the others to do.[15]

The task system and a simpler contracting arrangement that developed in the manufacture of women's cloaks promoted a proliferation of workshops of ten to twenty employees. In the season of 1894, for example, Hart, Schaffner and Marx in Chicago used eighty-seven contractors, who employed eleven hundred workers. The high productivity of the system is suggested by the employment by this leading company of hardly one-fourth as many people as had sewn for a large firm like Winchester and Davis in the 1850s. Moreover, contractors, in turn, subcontracted to others, so that domestic, sweatshop, and factory productions were all interlocked. In addition to making the operatives specialists, the system made the fate of all of them dependent on the prices received by the contractors from the manufacturers. Consequently, when the Knights of Labor unionized garment workers in the 1880s, it organized contractors' local assemblies, as well as those of cutters, tailors, operators, and pressers. The employment of so few workers directly by the manufacturers in their shops, however, made it impossible for unions to regulate the trade by legislating rules for their own members' behavior. Manufacturers told Knights' representatives that they were welcome to fix whatever hours, wages, and work rules they wanted, but the contractor who made the coats or cloaks would be the one who could underbid the others. In

15. John R. Commons, ed., *Trade Unionism and Labor Problems, First Series* (Boston, 1905), 324–9. Bisno's description of the division of labor within teams differs from that of Commons and includes a presser as a member of the team. There probably were many variations in arrangements made by individuals.

Abraham Bisno's words, "solidarity was punished with starvation."[16]

The key to profits, wages, hours, and even conditions of work in the industry was the price per item paid to the contractor. Nevertheless, the manufacturers were also highly vulnerable to strikes for higher piece prices called at the height of each year's production season. Data collected by the U.S. Commissioner of Labor on strikes between 1881 and 1905 showed clothing manufacture to have been one of the most strike-prone industries in the country. A successful New York strike of 1885, which saw contractors, operators, and pressers standing together, set off ten years of annual confrontations over wages in New York, Chicago, and elsewhere. These strikers drew special strength from the fact that the contracting system had located their workplaces in the midst of their homes, if not right inside them, and facilitated the concentration of those homes in solidly Jewish neighborhoods. Whatever gains were won by strike, however, were undermined by the pressure of competition before the season was out. The threat of hunger observed by Bisno prevailed even through the years when community strike solidarity was most impressive.[17]

There were those, among them the Jewish Workingmen's Association of New York, who raised demands for structural changes. In March 1886, when fifteen hundred cloak makers struck against their contractors and were joined by inside workers, thus bringing forty-five hundred workers out, the strikers adopted the association's demand for an end to outside contracting. Despite the manufacturers' plea that they had neither the space nor the facilities to bring all the workers inside their shops, the Central Labor Union of New York took up the strikers' cause and even got one company to agree. The workers planned a victory parade, with each marcher carrying a broom to symbolize the sweeping away of the sweating system, only to discover that not only the contractors but also the suit and cloak cutters' union openly sided with the manufacturers against any change. Loudly the German and Irish cutters proclaimed that

16. *Second Report of Factory Inspectors of Illinois* (1895), 45–52, cited in Pickard, "Clothing Trades," 51, and Bisno, *Union Pioneer,* 238. Rich data on the structure of the Knights of Labor in the garment industry, especially in smaller cities, can be found in the John W. Hayes Papers, correspondence concerning National Trades Assembly, 231, Catholic University of America.

17. David Montgomery, "Strikes in Nineteenth-Century America," *Social Science History,* 4 (February 1980), 91; Louis Lorwin, *The Women's Garment Workers: A History of the International Ladies' Garment Workers' Union* (New York, 1924), 26–43.

they would not work in the same place with "Columbus tailors" and "funny Jews." An offer by the manufacturers to send work only to well-lighted, ventilated shops and to allow union walking delegates to police the enforcement of wage agreements was scornfully rejected by the strikers, but dire need soon drove them back to work, and their unions collapsed.[18]

By the 1890s, however, the cloak makers of New York were forcing the manufacturers to retreat into their factories. Clothing workers' wage strikes were becoming numerous and unusually successful. Only 27 percent of the strikes of 1881 to 1905 in women's clothing were recorded as "failed" by the commissioner of labor, and a mere 9 percent of those in men's clothing, as compared with, for example, 70 percent "failed" in cotton textile workers' strikes and 30 percent "failed" for building workers. Furthermore, garment workers recorded among the highest percentages of strikes called by unions of any industries on record, 90 percent for men's clothing and 84 percent for women's. Strikes in New York, especially, developed a special style. At the call of unions, workers who wanted a raise left their work, joined the unions, and went to wait at the Market Street docks or to have a picnic in Central Park. If a boss was ready to offer a raise, he came to the park or dock and brought a keg of beer. At times the strikes became large and protracted. With issues so simple, unions so fragile, and community involvement so high, charismatic orators gained great prestige among the workers – none more than Joseph Barondess. Always onstage, this hero of the operatives achieved his greatest triumph in the New York strike of 1890, when the cutters and contractors joined the others on strike. The terms he was able to extract from the humbled manufacturers set a minimum wage for tailors of fifteen dollars per week and required all workers to join unions. They also prohibited not outside contracting but *inside* contracting.[19]

Both the power of workers' influence on wages and the futility of union agreements in this industry contributed to the gradual restructuring of operatives' work that followed that strike. Within a year of their pledge to ban inside contracting, major manufacturers had expanded their facil-

18. Elias Tcherikower, *The Early Jewish Labor Movement in the United States,* translated and revised by Aaron Antonovsky (New York, 1961), 291–3; Lorwin, *Women's Garment Workers,* 39–40. Quite different were the events in Chicago in 1886; there, Jewish strikers marched on the inside shops in an attempt to shut them down. Bisno, *Union Pioneer,* 78–81.

19. U.S. Commissioner of Labor, *Twenty-first Annual Report (1906)* (U.S. Congress, 59th Cong., 2nd Sess., House Document No. 822, Washington, D.C., 1907), 81–2; Lorwin, *Women's Garment Workers,* 42–54.

ities, installed new machines, and set up contractors inside their shops. Desperate outside contractors sought to remain in competition by offering still lower prices, and to do that they had to lower wages by locking out their own workers. Over the ensuing decade, factory production of cloaks grew rapidly, both because manufacturers moved their operations inside and because contractors enlarged their operations to become manufacturers in their own right, selling finished goods directly to the jobbers. To improve on the profits made possible by the interminable hours and frantic pace of the outside-contracting system, manufacturers began to use their investment in more and faster sewing machines and the discipline made possible by contracting units right inside their factories in order to redivide labor on an unprecedented level. Their sewing-machine operators no longer stitched whole garments, but rather specialized in sleeves, lapels, pockets, buttonholes, and other portions. Cutters, basters, pressers, and bushelmen plied their crafts in the same shops.

The rapid enlargement of task shops in men's clothing had similarly promoted further specialization of operatives. Two New York strikes in the fall of 1894 directly opposed this ultimate conversion of tailors into factory operatives – one by the Brotherhood of Tailors demanding abolition of the task system, and one by the cloak makers to control earnings and hours both inside and outside through enforcement of union rules that Barondess called his "ten commandments." Both efforts were in vain. The factory operative was becoming the typical garment worker in both men's and women's clothing, despite the persistence of sweatshop competition, and the proportion of workers who were women was again on the rise.

Paradoxically, the rise of the factory and the decline of the nineteenth-century sweatshop were accompanied by a resurgence of home production, or "married women's work," as it was then appropriately called. The census of 1910 found that 52 percent of all women employed in the manufacture of clothing were not in factories – 447,760 women out of a total of 865,086. Embroidering, some button sewing, and other detailed operations often could be performed more cheaply on consignment in someone's home than in the most efficient factory, and factory owners farmed out those portions of their work. Although the number of non-factory women workers counted by the census fell off rapidly after 1910 – to 235,519 in 1920 and 157,928 in 1930 – careful statisticians always considered counts of home producers dubious. Even the line between an independent dressmaker and a homeworker was shadowy, because many women with children earned some money both ways. Consequently, in Troy, long the center of factory production of shirts, most stitching of collars was done by women at home, and a survey of New York City found "solid blocks ... where by actual count more than three-fourths of the apartments contain home finishers."[20]

In short, the historical path that had led to the predominance of operatives in clothing manufacture had been winding and rocky, and even as it culminated in factory production, it regenerated the most primitive forms of homework. Technology, immigration, strikes, and the chronic decline of prices had all contributed to the shaping and reshaping of the industry's relations of production.

Quite different was the growth of operatives' jobs in the textile industry, where the basic patterns of mechanization, gender division of labor, and payment systems had all been in place by the end of the 1850s. The intricate division of labor, refinement of machinery, and integration of successive operations required to spin yarn and weave cloth within the factory system had been accomplished to such an extent that little basic improvement seemed possible for textile mills during the decades that produced such incessant change in the manufacture of clothing. Although new sources of labor were found, especially Quebec, whose inhabitants gravitated to New England's mills in great numbers after 1870 without breaking their ties to land and family, the total labor force grew much more slowly than that in clothing manufacture – 218 percent between 1870 and 1910 for textiles, as compared with 331 percent for clothing. The enormous demand for cloth stimulated by the growth of output in the clothing industry, however, modified the textile industry in two ways. First, it fostered improvements in looms and carding, spinning, and slashing machines that increased output per worker, especially after 1900. Second, it encouraged the creation of new mills: cotton-spinning mills in the South and huge woolen and silk mills adjacent to the centers of clothing production – Passaic and Paterson, New Jersey, and Lawrence, Massachusetts. The men and women who staffed these new mills were drawn overwhelmingly from capitalism's rural periphery. By contrast, the many cotton mills of Fall River, the Blackstone Valley, and the Delaware Valley seemed to be little different in 1900 from what they had been in 1870, except for the new languages in which some workers greeted each other on the way to their machines. Rustic mill towns often had

20. Pickard, "Clothing Trades," 67–80; Abbott, *Women in Industry*, 234, 244; Lorwin, *Women's Garment Workers*, 78–80; Bisno, *Union Pioneer*, 178; Florence Kelley, *Some Ethical Gains Through Legislation* (New York, 1905), 121–3; Leslie Woodcock Tentler, *Wage-earning Women: Industrial Work and Family Life in the United States, 1900–1930* (New York, 1979), 30–2; U.S. Census, *Occ. Stat.*, 123; Gilson Willets, *Workers of the Nation* (2 vols., New York, 1903), I, 302–3; Senate, *Woman and Child Wage Earners*, II, 218.

grown larger and dirtier, and many company tenements had been bought up privately by workers, but the job went on in the same old way.[21]

The gender division of labor was firmly fixed. Male carders in cotton mills had some female assistants, but the ring spinners and spoolers were women (with some little boys as doffers). Mule spinners, who prepared the best warping threads, were men who struggled tirelessly to keep alive a craft tradition. Warps were prepared by women, but usually dressed by men (slashers). Loom fixers, who both repaired looms and helped weavers set them up and keep them operating, were men, as were overseers and most of their assistants in supervision of departments (second hands). The highest positions to which women could aspire were those of burlers, who mended and finished cloth, and smash piecers, who straightened out messes into which weavers had become entangled. The one job that was not confined to one sex or the other was weaving. As many as seven-eighths of the weavers were women in Manchester's Amoskeag Mills in 1883. A Rhode Island survey in 1889 found that 59 percent of the state's cotton weavers and 46 percent of the worsted weavers were women; the rest were men. Moreover, the piece rates paid men and women seem to have been the same, though there were so many different jobs with so many different prices, not to mention so many ways of varying the amount of work a weaver put out during a month, that differences in earnings between one weaver and another were substantial. Nevertheless, some women usually were among the high earners of a weaving room.[22]

In brief, all production workers in the textile mill were specialized machine tenders, and most were on piecework. Although the men and women who filled the jobs may have changed from American-born children of immigrants to newcomers from industry's European and American periphery between 1870 and 1910, the tasks those operatives performed remained basically the same. As we shall see, however, even in this industry with its long-established patterns of work, employers at the turn

21. Herbert J. Lahne, *The Cotton Mill Worker* (New York, 1944); Broadus Mitchell, *Rise of the Cotton Mills in the South* (Baltimore, 1921); David J. Goldberg, "Immigrants, Intellectuals and Industrial Unions: The 1919 Textile Strikes and the Experience of the Amalgamated Textile Workers of American in Passaic and Paterson, New Jersey and Lawrence, Massachusetts" (unpublished Ph.D. diss., Columbia University, 1983); Lillie B. Chase Wyman, "Studies of Factory Life . . . ," *Atlantic Monthly*, 62 (July 1888), 16–29, 62 (September 1888), 315–21, 62 (November 1888), 605–12, 63 (January 1889), 69–79.

22. Hareven, *Family Time and Industrial Time*, 261–2; Rhode Island, *Third Annual Report of the Commissioner of Industrial Statistics (1889)* (Providence, 1890, hereafter cited as R.I. CIS), 164–7.

of the century were anxiously searching for ways to increase productivity. By turning to the state, with some success, for legislation to limit working hours, reduce child labor, and restrict the use of fines, textile workers had placed the question of productivity per worker-hour at the very top of their employers' agenda.

There were two other important means by which the population of operatives grew. One involved the adding of supplementary operations to an enterprise in which the basic processes remained in the hands of craft workers. The brass mills of Waterbury, Connecticut, for example, depended on highly skilled brass molders and drawers assisted by male laborers well into the twentieth century. Nevertheless, when the Scoville Manufacturing Company expanded its payroll from 304 workers in 1874 to 1,157 in 1892, women then composed more than half of its force. Women were found in new departments, making thimbles, soldering and packing products, and performing other such repetitious, specialized tasks. Similarly, in New England's paper mills, the huge, cantankerous Fourdrinier machines turned out paper under the guidance of notoriously craft-conscious tenders, but the finished paper was trimmed, ruled, stamped, and backed by young women. The clean, quiet character of the work and the flexible hours they were often allowed made such work attractive to native-born women, especially to those who were heads of households.[23]

The other means by which the numbers of operatives grew was direct substitution of specialized tasks for work that had formerly been done by craftsmen. Although developments of this type took place in most industries, they were most notable in woodworking enterprises, especially in the manufacture of furniture, carriages, coffins, and railroad cars. The days when cabinetmakers had carried their own huge toolboxes and even their own workbenches from shop to shop and fashioned furniture to order had largely faded into the past after the Civil War. Small workshops in major cities continued to employ artisans, who formed strong and aggressive craft unions in the 1880s and 1890s, but their counterparts in smaller towns gradually succumbed to the competition of wares imported from major manufacturing centers. Specialized machines, such as compound carvers and mechanical sanders, proved especially effective on soft woods, and factories of 200 workers or more in places like Grand

23. Bucki, *Metals, Minds and Machines*, 44–52; P. W. Bishop, "History of Scoville Manufacturing Company" (unpublished manuscript in Scoville Manufacturing Co. Papers), 200; Dandy Roll (pseudonym), "John Tubbs, Papermaker" (unpublished manuscript in possession of John W. Bennett); Judith A. McGaw, " 'A Good Place to Work,' Industrial Workers and Occupational Choice: The Case of Berkshire Women," *Journal of Interdisciplinary History*, 10 (Autumn 1979), 227–48.

Rapids, Michigan, put local farm youth to work on those machines. Young Oscar Ameringer found "no resemblance" between his work in a Cincinnati furniture factory in 1886 and what he had done in his father's shop. "Here everything was done by machine," he wrote. "Our only task was assembling, gluing together, and finishing at so much a chair or table." Similarly, pieceworkers in the carriage factories of Cincinnati, Detroit, and New Haven spent their hours fashioning identical parts on rotary planers, spoke shavers, spoke facers and taperers, felloe rounders, hollow augers, and other single-operation machines, under a foreman's watchful eye. More than 90 percent of the workers in both furniture and carriage factories were men, with German immigrants and their sons especially prominent in the ranks. Craftsmen fallen on hard times, carpenters who tolerated the sawdust-filled air of the factory because it offered them a steadier income than the construction site, and especially sons of artisans and farmers who saw no future for themselves in those hard-pressed enterprises all set themselves to the specialized tasks of the factories.[24]

A closer look at the largest woodworking factories reveals that many important operations were still as much under the direction of skilled workers as those in the iron and steel mills of the epoch. Moreover, the dividing line between autonomous craftsmen and specialized machine tenders not only was subject to constant change but also was itself an object of workplace struggle. Consider the Pullman Company works in the company town just south of Chicago. Although its force of forty-four hundred to forty-eight hundred workers in 1893 made this one of the nation's largest factories, it was but one of half a dozen plants in which fourteen thousand people worked for the company, whose payroll that year exceeded $7 million. Ties to the nation's railroad system had generated huge firms in this industry, just as they had in steel. In addition to operating its own fleet of cars, Pullman produced an average of 3 sleeping cars, 10 coaches, and 240 freight cars during each week of 1891 and 1892.[25]

The cavernous workshops of Pullman housed so many different kinds

24. Elizabeth A. Ingerman, "Personal Experiences of an Old New York Cabinetmaker," *Antiques*, 84 (November 1963), 576–80; Oestreicher, "Solidarity and Fragmentation," 115–16; Steven J. Ross, "Workers on the Edge: Work, Leisure, and Politics in Industrializing Cincinnati, 1830–1890" (unpublished Ph.D. diss., Princeton University, 1980), 173; Jack Gillette, "The World of the Carriage Workers: New Haven, 1886" (unpublished paper in possession of the author); Oscar Ameringer, *If You Don't Weaken* (New York, 1940), 44; Jentz and Keil, "From Immigrants to Urban Workers," 95; Griffen and Griffen, *Natives and Newcomers*, 7–21, 193–8.
25. Stanley Buder, *Pullman: An Experiment in Industrial Order and Community Planning, 1880–1930* (New York, 1967), 138; U.S. Strike Commis-

of work that when the employees flocked into the ranks of the American Railway Union (ARU) in 1894, they formed nineteen branches at that location, each based on a separate craft or department. The woodworking crafts – car builders, cabinetmakers, and painters – were easily the most numerous, because it was not until 1897 that a freight car was made out of pressed steel in the United States. Truck builders, blacksmiths, and machinists who fabricated metal components and tools totaled fewer than 250 men.

When Pullman Vice-President Thomas H. Wickes, who supervised the factory, described his payroll as of April 1893, he called 2,625 of the workers "journeymen mechanics" and said that their pay ranged from an average of $2.055 per day for shop carpenters to $3.30 per day for carvers, making an overall average of $2.63 per day. The other employees, "excluding journeymen mechanics, superintendents, foremen, and [the] clerical force," numbered 1,808. Their wages averaged $1.665 per day. In other testimony, a union leader described 800 of the workers as common laborers. That would leave around one thousand who were neither craftsmen nor laborers. Within this remainder were blacksmiths' helpers and carvers' apprentices, who clearly belonged to the domain of the crafts, and there must have been enough other apprentices and helpers scattered throughout the plant to leave the actual number of operatives well below one thousand. Perhaps they constituted one-fifth of the production force.[26]

No figures were offered to indicate how many women worked at Pullman. The carpet, upholstery, and linen department – stronghold of the "girls' union," local 269 of the ARU – the glass-embossing department, and the laundry were identified by Wickes as locations of "female employees." Their aggregate payroll, minus journeyman mechanics, was 239 people. In four other departments – mills, wood machine, tinners, and streetcar – wages of nonjourneymen averaging less than $1.40 per day suggest that women held at least some of the jobs. Their total nonjourneyman force was 176. There were also some women elsewhere, like Mary Alice Wood, who testified about the electrical department. The number of women at Pullman must have been somewhere between a low of 250 and a high of 590.[27]

sion, *Report on the Chicago Strike of June–July 1894* (U.S. Congress, 53rd Cong., 3rd Sess., Senate Executive Document No. 7, Washington, D.C., 1895), 545, 592.

26. U.S. Strike Commission, *Report*, 429, 592–3; Willets, *Workers of the Nation*, I, 135.

27. U.S. Strike Commission, *Report*, 592–5, 434, 455; William H. Carwardine, *The Pullman Strike* (Chicago, 1894), 85–6. Carwardine says women were limited by law to eight hours of work per day, but the Illinois law of 1893

In short, the Pullman works' payroll suggests that operatives numbered roughly one-fifth of the total force, craftsmen about three-fifths, and laborers about one-fifth. The company had always proclaimed that its primary purpose in constructing its model town had been to attract and retain first-class mechanics, and these figures indicate how heavily it depended on their skills. Among those who were neither journeymen, laborers, helpers to craftsmen, nor apprentices, a large proportion were women – probably a solid majority.

Although statistical analysis can suggest rough proportions of types of workers, it may also obscure as much as it reveals. In the first place, both the testimony of Jennie Curtis before the United States Strike Commission in 1894 and Wickes's rebuttal of her statements show that her job of sewing new carpets for a sleeping car under repair involved a very high level of judgment and initiative, in addition to the "dexterity" customarily attributed to operatives. Sewing that carpet, which paid $1.80 after the wage cuts of 1894, was considered a sixteen-hour task by the company, and Wickes thought that a "reasonable basis" for computing women's piece rates was an expected earning of one dollar per day. In other words, Curtis's low earnings tell us more about her gender than they do about the technical content of her job. The mattresses, tapestries, and curtains on which she had sewn for the previous five years were also complex undertakings. It is probable that Curtis's supervisor did little more than assign her tasks and try to set piece rates low enough to make her work fast.[28]

Second, the gray area in which the most expert work of operatives resembled the self-directed exertions of journeymen was itself a battleground, where employers contested the craft practices and ethical codes of their skilled hands, using piecework as the main weapon. Evidence from Pullman indicates that the outcome of the battle was decisively influenced by the state of the labor market. There was no straight line of march toward the dilution of skills, but in depressed periods the ablest of craftsmen could be forced to surrender their "manly bearing" and cherished customs, or else to redeem them by a struggle like the one that made the Pullman workers world-famous in 1894.[29]

The battle over piece rates lay at the heart of the great 1894 strike, and it provides important clues as to how tasks became specialized. Although

referred only to manufacturers of clothing, and it was ruled unconstitutional by the state supreme court in 1895. Kelley, *Ethical Gains*, 265–6.

28. U.S. Strike Commission, *Report*, 434–5, 594.
29. On the craftsmen's ethical code, see the section "Workers' control: the craftsmen's style," in Chapter 1.

the U.S. Strike Commission estimated that twenty-eight hundred of the employees were normally on piecework at the time of the strike, by no means was a given individual always paid by the piece or by the day. Not only were there departments, such as the machine woodworking section, where piecework was finally imposed despite workers' resistance only a few months before the strike, but there were others where foremen fixed rates and decided how each worker and each task should be compensated. Such arbitrary power had its worst impact in the repair departments, where long runs – the kind on which pieceworkers were most likely to make good earnings – were rare, and prices might be conjured up by the foremen on the spur of the moment for all sorts of new jobs. "It was only the friends of the foremen that got the day work," car builder Thomas Heathcoate explained.[30]

Heathcoate himself had usually constructed new car bodies. His department, like some others, had first been converted from day rates to piecework during the hard times of 1883–4, and its workers had struck under the banner of the Knights of Labor in May 1886, demanding a restoration of day rates and an eight-hour day. But the strike had been lost, and President Pullman had defended piecework publicly as an "educational tool in that it offered incentive to the worker to improve his skills."[31] Moreover, for the car builders, piecework initially developed as a form of inside contracting that only indirectly threatened the craftsmen's autonomy. Anywhere from two to five men made the body together for a set price, such as twenty-six dollars for a merchant's despatch car in 1890. Heathcoate spoke of the workers' dividing the sum equally among themselves, although the company left the terms of division up to the gang leader's assessment of the skills and contribution of each member. When hard times returned in 1893–4, therefore, prices were cut again and again, and gang leaders were tempted not only to hurry their workmates but also to divide up the price unequally, in order to defend their own incomes. They also found it harder to resist when foremen imposed additional, sometimes inferior, workmen on the crew to hasten completion of cars. The best thing for a gang leader to do with the new men was to assign them to simple, repetitive tasks. Similarly, if some task allowed a reasonable income only to those who practiced it constantly, the foremen could most readily foist it onto workers who lacked self-confidence. In short, piecework and inside contracting by their very nature tended to stimulate specialization even among those who called themselves journeyman mechanics, just as the task system had done

30. U.S. Strike Commission, *Report*, xxxiii, 418.
31. Buder, *Pullman*, 139–42; the quotation is on p. 141.

among tailors. Both confidence in one's own competence and the availability of other jobs in town were needed if craftsmen were to oppose these pressures.

There was one other way in which hard times and piecework could combine to lessen the contrast between the work of the craftsman and that of the operative. When orders from higher management drove foremen not simply to cut specific piece rates or to transfer individuals from day work to piecework but also to slash rates in their departments wholesale, workers naturally became angry and defiant. In turn, the foremen became more coercive and overbearing toward the workers. Testimony from Pullman workers about foremen's punching workers, cursing them, and waving clubs at them appears in connection with foremen's effort to impose new and inferior piece rates. Just as workers individually had to be forced to make the same parts for less money than before, they also had to be prevented from assembling in groups or talking with each other, let alone joining unions for their mutual defense. It was at this point that workers' codes of ethical behavior were put to the acid test. Painter Theodore Rhodie said that Pullman had deprived him not only of his income but also of his "right as an American citizen" freely to espouse and live by his own principles.[32]

In short, the Pullman Company's response to the depression of 1893 had reduced its workers' wages, challenged the values its craftsmen held dear, and narrowed the difference between their work and the work of operatives. Nevertheless, basic differences remained: For all the skill some operatives' jobs required, their toil was specialized and repetitive; whatever initiative and judgment were required of operatives, they did not direct their own work, let alone that of helpers. For all the efforts of nineteenth-century employers to speed up craftsmen's production and reduce costs through piecework and inside contracting, they could not emancipate themselves from their dependence on the skilled crafts. Even contracting was a way to use that dependence to their own advantage. And if hard times, like the depression of the 1890s, might humble their craftsmen or challenge them to strikes they had no chance of winning, returning prosperity put the shoe on the other foot. Between 1899 and 1903, American craftsmen entered the most collectively aggressive phase of their history, prompting their employers to pay close attention to the teachings of Frederick Winslow Taylor: that piecework was not enough, that management had to end its reliance on the workers' "initiative" altogether. Such restructuring of production, as we shall see, involved basic

32.   Ibid., 150–1; U.S. Strike Commission, *Report*, 416–29, 436–44, 457–9, 481–2, 594. The quotation from Rhodie is on p. 418.

changes in the treatment of operatives, as well as an end to craftsmen's dominance over production.

"Praise be the labor turnover!"

The world of the operative was dominated by youth. Although craftsmen whose trades had fallen on hard times or who were too old or infirm to pursue their normal callings, women with households dependent on their earnings, common laborers in search of winter work, and older immigrants without industrial skills were all to be found among nineteenth-century operatives, the typical member of the group was young and unmarried. As we have already noted, industrial output swelled during the last three decades of the century, primarily because of massive inputs of labor power from abroad and from the rapidly rising native-born population. The median age of American nonagricultural workers in 1890 was 33.3 years for men and 24.3 years for women.

Moreover, the customary age for youth raised in American cities to begin full-time employment was around thirteen throughout this epoch. As late as the early 1920s, a majority of urban children left school while between thirteen and fifteen years of age, and less than 12 percent of them finished high school. Although girls, on average, remained in school a few years longer than boys (by 1900, many did so precisely in order to prepare themselves for clerical jobs), most of them were sent out to contribute to their families' coffers, and daughters of the best-off workers were often kept home from school to help their mothers tend house. Boys' parents needed whatever income their sons could bring in, and those who hoped for better jobs for their lads also knew that the route to such jobs passed through apprenticeship and experience, not schoolrooms. In fact, the youth themselves were often contemptuous of the high schools. When Helen Todd, a factory inspector in Chicago, committed the highly unusual act of asking 500 factory workers aged fourteen to sixteen what they thought of schools, 412 of them replied that they would rather be in the factory. Their replies were often vivid:

> They ain't always pickin' on you because you don't know things in a factory.

> The children don't holler at ye and call ye a Christ-killer in a factory.

> You can buy shoes for the baby.

> I got three cards with "excellent" on 'em, an' they never did me no good. My Mother kept 'em in the Bible, an' they never did her no good, neither. They ain't like a pay envelope.

School ain't no good. The Holy Father he can send you to hell, and the boss he can take away yer job er raise yer pay. The teacher she can't do nothing.[33]

In the minds of American workers, "child labor" was the earning of wages by boys and girls under fourteen. Of course, most children had some errands or tasks to bring in a few pennies from a very early age. The number of children working full time in mining and manufacturing, however, rose sharply during the depression of the 1870s and its aftermath, then declined steadily through the 1880s, only to rise again under the combined impact of the depression of the 1890s and the resurgence of domestic production and sweatshops in clothing, artificial flowers, packaging, and other occupations. Depressions always had the effect of pulling youngsters out of school: The harder the times, the more people looked for work. Moreover, there was such an upsurge in employment of children under fourteen in mines, textile mills, glassworks, and woodworking factories between 1878 and 1882 as to give the impression that the working class as a whole was striving desperately to recoup its recent financial losses by every means possible. Unions of coal miners even tried to regularize the employment of miners' children during those years rather than abolish it. But by the end of the decade, the proportion of workers in manufacturing who were under fifteen had fallen from 6.7 percent (1880) to 2.8 percent (1890). Unions of glassblowers, mule spinners, weavers, and coal miners were actively campaigning to stamp out child labor. Although the campaign against child labor had earlier been dominated by middle-class reformers, the labor movement had assumed a decisive role in its development by the end of the century. By then it had clearly become the ethical norm of working-class life that children should not be sent to work before they had finished half a dozen years of elementary education, unless the death, desertion, or disability of the father made it unavoidable. Newcomers from the rural periphery, however, neither shared nor could afford such beliefs, and the sweating system waxed fat on the labors of their families.[34]

33.   John D. Durand, *Labor Force in the United States, 1890–1960* (New York, 1948), 38; Horace M. Kallen, *Education, the Machine, and the Worker: An Essay in the Psychology of Education in Industrial Society* (New York, 1925), 10; Margaret F. Byington, "The Family in a Typical Mill Town," *American Journal of Sociology*, 14 (March 1909), 651. The quotations are all from Edwin Markham, Benjamin B. Lindsey, and George Creel, *Children in Bondage* (New York, 1914), 373–7.

34.   Stanley Lebergott, *Manpower in Economic Growth: The American Record since 1800* (New York, 1964), 53; Harvey, *Best-dressed Miners*, 48–57; Pennsylvania, *Report of the Superintendent of Common Schools . . . for the*

The predominance of youth prevailed only among operatives, not among craftsmen. When Leon Fink analyzed the working populations of four towns in 1880 (Kansas City, Kansas, Richmond, Virginia, Rutland, Vermont, and Rochester, New Hampshire), he concluded that 58 percent of their semiskilled factory, mill, and quarry workers were under thirty years of age. By contrast, 48 percent of their workers in industrial crafts were under thirty years of age, as were 39 percent of their laborers and 35 percent of their handicraft artisans. Similarly, Sally and Clyde Griffen found factory work in Poughkeepsie dominated by American-born children of immigrants who were under thirty and not firmly attached to any particular occupation. Workers who were older, as well as workers who had been born abroad, were more often to be found among craftsmen or laborers than among operatives in the town's highly diversified economy.[35] A thorough survey of Michigan's agricultural-implement and ironworking factories in 1890 found a larger proportion of foreign-borns among the operatives, especially Germans and Poles, but they were on average no older then their counterparts in Poughkeepsie.[36]

With youth came transient attachments to the jobs themselves, a quality that as we shall see, had somewhat different meanings for women and for men. A mayor of Lynn expressed his alarm over the "many young persons, without families or friends here [who] were thronging our city from neighboring places, in search of work, some staying but a short time." Such workers seemed "to think that a certain amount of bravado is necessary to let their consequence be known," he warned. "I have brought from the country within the last fourteen months 230 girls and out of these only 115 are now here," the treasurer of a large Chicopee cotton mill had lamented in 1860. "We are the largest [mill] village in the neighborhood and hence if any person wants a house girl or mill help this place is resorted to at once."[37]

Year Ending June 2, 1873 (Harrisburg, 1874), xxxvi–ix; Grace Abbott, *The Child and the State* (2 vols., Chicago, 1938), I, 413–15; John Spargo, *The Bitter Cry of the Children* (New York, 1906); Yans-McLaughlin, *Family and Community*; Kelley, *Ethical Gains*.

35. Leon Fink, *Workingmen's Democracy: The Knights of Labor and American Politics* (Urbana, Ill., 1983), 222; Griffen and Griffen, *Natives and Newcomers*, 7, 169–76, 193.
36. [Michigan], *Eighth Annual Report of the Bureau of Labor and Industrial Statistics, February 1, 1890* (Lansing, 1891, hereafter cited as Mich. BLIS), 1–189.
37. Alan Dawley, *Class and Community: The Industrial Revolution in Lynn* (Cambridge, Mass., 1976), 106; Vera Shlakman, *Economic History of a Factory Town, A Study of Chicopee, Massachusetts* (Northampton, Mass., 1936), 149.

The high mobility of nineteenth-century Americans generally, and especially those under thirty years of age, has provided a common theme for recent quantitative studies and contemporary commentators alike. "Hundreds and thousands of youth enter our manufacturing establishments [and] are perhaps taught to do one particular portion of the work," noted the Ohio Bureau of Labor Statistics in 1878, "but their proficiency on that one portion seals their fate in that particular establishment." The most common way to vary one's work, learn something new, or seek a better job was to move. Employers tried to slow the departure rate. Many textile mills would give no money to a worker who quit until the next regular monthly payday. Shoe manufacturers in Haverhill tried to force their employees to post fifty-dollar security bonds against quitting during the season, and only a three-month strike dissuaded them. Cornelia Parker's working experience early in the twentieth century taught her that although workers' propensity to quit their jobs might distress plant managers, to "the factory girl, it saves her life like as not. Praise be the labor turnover!"[38]

As early as 1888, a textile-mill owner from Woonsocket, Rhode Island, had delivered a warning not to misinterpret the transience of operatives:

> It is almost universally [said] by those unacquainted with factory populations, that they possess as roving a disposition as the Tartars. The fact is, it is a very large calculation as far as my experience goes, to suppose that one-eighth of a factory village remove in the course of a year. They go, it is true, where they can get the best employment, and the best wages, but few remove because they are fond of changing their locations.[39]

A way to understand the perpetually high turnover on jobs in textile mills without exaggerating its scale or resorting to some imagined "roving disposition" has been suggested by Tamara Hareven's thorough analysis of the payrolls of the huge Amoskeag Mills during the early decades of the twentieth century. The typical worker's career, Hareven concluded, was short and frequently interrupted. Those whose years at Amoskeag were unbroken by any departure from the mills usually did not stay there

---

38. Ohio Bureau of Labor Statistics, *First Annual Report of the Bureau of Labor Statistics . . . 1877* (Columbus, 1878, hereafter cited as Ohio BLS), 302; Cornelia Straton Parker, *Working with the Working Woman* (New York, 1922), 43. See also Stephan Thernstrom, *The Other Bostonians: Poverty and Progress in the American Metropolis, 1880–1970* (Cambridge, Mass., 1973); Howard M. Gitelman, *Workingmen of Waltham: Mobility in American Urban Industrial Development* (Baltimore, 1974).

39. R.I. CIS (1888), 137.

long. The persisters, those whose faces were often to be found among the mill's seventeen thousand or so workers, experienced, according to Hareven, "numerous separations and rehirings, although some separations were initiated by the workers themselves in order to be transferred to a preferred department." The reasons for leaving were many: discharge, desire to try another job, pregnancy, an attempt to get a raise in pay, anger at an overseer, or simply "going crazy" on some machine. In general, however, men left to search for better jobs; women left to care for other members of their families.[40]

The difference is important. For many young men in the late nineteenth century, one or more repetitive, specialized tasks in a factory or sweatshop served as stepping-stones to a skilled craft. The gray zone of conflict that separated semiskilled work from skilled work for men could be traversed in either direction. Because operatives were most often used instead of journeymen in small towns where unions were weak, a youth's move up into skilled trades often also involved a move to the city. For women, the factory offered no prospects of a better job to the pieceworker, aside from a handful of positions as forewoman or troubleshooter in a women's department. Many young women worked themselves to exhaustion without accomplishing the day's production norm, except on rare occasions. Others were helped by relatives or friends to learn the knack or to get assigned to some operation on which they could "break the rate" for weeks at a time by perfecting the motions they repeated so often. Either way, their earnings would rise; but the long-term prospects were limited. In the electric-bulb industry, for example, the average earnings of women rose sharply between the ages of sixteen and twenty, then increased only marginally to age twenty-four and actually fell after age twenty-five. The few women over forty-five in lamp factories took home, on average, the same income as a seventeen-year-old.[41]

Moreover, the plateau at which women's wages leveled off was lower than the lowest normal level for male wages. Women whose wages reached the laborer's level of $1.25 to $1.40 per day were rare in the 1880s, even in highly seasonal industries, and when some sewing-machine operators earned close to two dollars at Pullman, the management concluded that their piece rates were in obvious need of drastic revision downward. In the first decade of the twentieth century, when the Department of Labor investigated women's earnings in six major cities, it concluded that 74.3 percent of the women in factories and 66.2 percent of those in stores

40. Hareven, *Family Time and Industrial Time,* 226–45; the quotation is from p. 234.
41. Senate, *Woman and Child Wage Earners,* III, 496.

earned less than a "living wage." The latter was defined as minimum subsistence and was fixed at eight dollars per week, at a time when economists regularly based "subsistence" or "living wage" for men on the support of a family of five members and set it at eleven to twelve dollars per week.[42]

The low level of women's pay had two interrelated causes. First, although women found employment in more than five hundred occupations, according to Virginia Penny, the tireless chronicler of women's search for wages, virtually all occupations employed either women or men exclusively.[43] Thus, the number of choices available to most women in search of employment was sharply restricted. Moreover, most of the openings were in occupations that represented commercialization of women's household roles: domestic service, textiles and clothing, food processing and serving, and prostitution. In all these undertakings the necessary training was provided by other women – even in textile mills, where weavers, for example, were instructed either by relatives or by other women, with the trainee paying a fee to compensate for the teacher's lost production. Basically, a girl was prepared for the world of wage earning in and by her family – if you will, she was apprenticed to her mother or sister – and she went forth to find many others like herself crowding into a sharply limited number of employments. Furthermore, in each occupation open to her, a woman had to compare the wages offered her not with those men earned but with those she might earn elsewhere. Inexorably, the job that employed by far the largest number of women, domestic service, provided the standard against which all others were measured. Even women's occupations that required high levels of scholastic training, such as teaching and clerical work, could not escape the downward pull that the glut of women in the major fields open to them exerted on the earnings of all women.[44]

42. Senate, *Labor and Capital*, III, 207–8; Pa. BIS (1888), passim; Mary H. Blewett, "The Union of Sex and Craft in the Haverhill Shoe Strike of 1895," *Labor History*, 20 (Summer 1979), 362; U.S. Strike Commission, *Report*, 594; Senate, *Woman and Child Wage Earners*, V, 348–9. On laborers' wages, see E. Abbott, "Wages of Unskilled Labor." For definitions of a living wage, see Louis B. More, *Wage Earners' Budgets: A Study of Standards and Costs of Living in New York City* (New York, 1907); Shergold, *Working-Class Life;* Eudice Glassberg, "Philadelphia's Poverty Line, 1860 and 1880: A Comparison of Earnings and Minimum Standard of Living" (typescript, University of Pennsylvania School of Social Work, 1973).

43. Penny, *How Women Can Make Money;* Kessler-Harris, *Out to Work,* 45–72.

44. On domestic service, see Katzman, *Seven Days a Week;* Lucy M. Salmon, *Domestic Service* (New York, 1897); Daniel E. Sutherland, "Americans and

Second, women expected that marriage, caring for a household, would be their lot and responsibility. Parental strictures, preachers' homilies, husbands' demands, other women's esteem or contempt, and even the powers of government – as evinced in relief payments given to mothers only, or the arrest of ablebodied men who chronically were supported by their wives' wages – all reinforced that expectation. Elizabeth Beardsley Butler wrote:

> "We try to employ girls who are members of families," a box manufacturer said to me, "for we don't pay the girls a living wage in this trade." The social fact of women's customary position in the household, the position of a dependent who receives no wages for her work, thus lies behind the economic fact of her insufficient wage in the industrial field. It is expected that she has men to support her.[45]

Supply considerations (family roles) and demand factors (limited openings) conspired to hold women's wages below subsistence levels. Few women could live on what they alone earned; marriage was as important for survival as it was for social approval and affection. The converse of this relationship, as many historians of family life have demonstrated, is that whereas both men and women from all but the most privileged classes knew that anyone who did not work should not eat, men expected to spend their lives working for wages, but a woman's wage earning was most often limited to the years before the birth of her first child. After that point, her work was largely unpaid – cooking, scrubbing, and feeding the household on the wages the husband and, in time, the children brought home. Much income-producing toil could be brought into the home and combined with the daily chores. Keeping boarders was especially widespread in this period of heavy immigration; clothing was sewn by the piece at home; and laundry was scrubbed, especially before the rise of steam laundries late in the century converted that into a form of factory employment for single women. Although many women found themselves widows or keepers of invalid husbands by their forties and fifties, and were driven to become wage earners once more, rather few

Their Servants, 1800–1920" (unpublished Ph.D. diss., Wayne State University, 1976); Joan Sangster, "Finnish Women in Ontario, 1890–1930," *Polyphony,* 3 (Fall 1981), 46–54. For general studies of women's employment in the nineteenth century, see Kessler-Harris, *Out to Work;* Claudia Goldin, "Female Labor Force Participation: The Origin of Black and White Differences, 1870–1880," *Journal of Economic History,* 37 (March 1977), 87–108; Carroll D. Wright, *The Working Girls of Boston* (Boston, 1889); Louise A. Tilly and Joan W. Scott, *Women, Work, and Family* (New York, 1978); Jane Humphries, "Class Struggle and the Persistence of the Working-Class Family," *Cambridge Journal of Economics,* 1 (1977), 241–58.

45. Elizabeth Beardsley Butler, *Women and the Trades: Pittsburgh, 1907–1908* (New York, 1911), 346.

then faced an "empty nest," with all children grown and gone. Long years of childbearing meant that there was usually some youngster underfoot.[46]

No single behavior pattern could possibly describe all working-class families, to be sure. Cultural norms varied from one nationality to another. Whereas southern Italians feared scandal if women went to work unaccompanied by other family members, English-born textile workers frequently left the household in the care of grandparents, while husband and wife went to separate mill jobs. Location made a difference. Centers of heavy industry offered relatively little industrial employment to women, who could find jobs in abundance in clothing and textile centers. Women who had once worked in a textile mill could later take advantage of contacts with foremen and other workers there, should they wish to return. Although more than half of all black women in the South worked for wages, as compared with fewer than one-fifth of southern white women, less than 3 percent of black women employed in 1890 had industrial jobs. Most of those who did were in tobacco factories. Laundering employed 16 percent of black female wage earners, domestic service 31 percent, and agriculture 39 percent.[47]

A large percentage of working-class families survived on one income only. When E. R. L. Gould investigated the budgets of 2,490 men who worked in coal mines and iron and steel mills in the early 1890s, he found

46. See Hareven, *Family Time and Industrial Time;* John Modell and Tamara K. Hareven, "Urbanization and the Malleable Household: An Examination of Boarding and Lodging in American Families," *Journal of Marriage and the Family,* 35 (August 1973), 467–79. See also Laurence A. Glasco, "The Life Cycles and Household Structure of American Ethnic Groups: Irish, Germans, and Native-born Whites in Buffalo, New York, 1855," in Tamara K. Hareven, ed., *Family and Kin in Urban Communities, 1700–1930* (New York, 1977), 122–43.

47. On English immigrants, see Massachusetts Bureau of the Statistics of Labor, *Report, 1871* (Boston, 1872, hereafter cited as Mass. BSL), 476–80, but compare Daniel J. Walkowitz, *Worker City, Company Town: Iron and Cotton-Worker Protest in Troy and Cohoes, New York, 1855–84* (Urbana, Ill., 1978), 67–74, 113–16. On Italians, see Yans-McLaughlin, *Family and Community;* Judith E. Smith, "Remaking Their Lives: Italian and Jewish Immigrant Family, Work, and Community in Providence, Rhode Island, 1900–1940" (unpublished Ph.D. diss., Brown University, 1980). On Afro-Americans, see Jean C. Brown, "The Negro Woman Worker, 1860–1890," *The Southern Workman,* 60 (October 1931), 430–1; Elizabeth H. Pleck, "A Mother's Wages: Income Earning among Married Black and Indian Women, 1896–1911," in Michael Gordon, ed., *The American Family in Historical Perspective* (second edition, New York, 1978), 490–510.

that slightly more than half of these families reported no income other than that of the father. A decade and half later, the U.S. Immigration Commission discovered that 40.7 percent of the 15,704 families it studied had only one income, and among native-born Americans the figure rose almost to half (48.4 percent). It is safe to assume, however, that most of these families had but one income because their children were too young to hold regular jobs. Only among the best-paid ironworkers and steelworkers, wrote Gould, "was it possible for the husband unaided to support his family," and even there "the margins are so small as to cause one to refrain from congratulation."[48]

The most common way to increase that "margin" was through the earnings of teenaged children. Children of coal miners studied by Gould who earned wages contributed, on average, 22.5 percent of the family income, and even those of well-paid rolling-mill workers contributed an average of 10.9 percent to the family coffers. "When the people own houses," testified printer John Keogh about his native Fall River, "you will generally find that it is a large family all working together." The Italian proverb linking a family's prosperity to the number of its wage earners held true there: "Dal numero delle braccia di una famiglia depende la prosperità della medesima."[49] Many working hands provided not only income but also some freedom for individuals. In the Amoskeag mills in the 1880s, where large families drew five to six dollars per day in pay, absenteeism ran as high as 25 percent. Similarly, the large families of French-Canadian workers after the turn of the century provided many-faceted support for each other. In Tamara Hareven's words:

> Relatives alternated running machinery and taking breaks, substituted for each other during illness, childbirth, and taking trips to Canada, and often helped slower kin complete their piece-work quotas. Out of consideration for each other they rarely exceeded the production quotas that had been informally agreed upon.[50]

Despite all the individual, cultural, regional, industrial, and racial variations in women's employment, both household and factory experiences drove home to daughters a message of interdependence among family members and placed greater value on solidarity and loyalty than on their personal achievements. In this way the nineteenth-century family was a

48. E. R. L. Gould, *The Social Condition of Labor* (Baltimore, 1893); the quotation is on pp. 26–7.
49. Ibid., 18–19; Senate, *Labor and Capital*, III, 488. The proverb "The prosperity of the family depends on the number of arms in it" is from Yans-McLaughlin, *Family and Community*, 180.
50. Senate, *Labor and Capital*, III, 207–8; Hareven, *Family Time and Industrial Time*, 100.

nursery of class consciousness, as well as a school for instruction in women's separate and subordinate sphere. If working men's experience introduced them to class first and foremost through conflict at the workplace, women's lives placed daily before them a panorama of goals and pleasures that required joint efforts, of loyalties to "one's own kind" in defiance of the contempt so freely expressed by one's "social betters," and of interdependence with neighbors, as well as with workmates. If someone had to plead for still more credit from the grocer or coal dealer, the woman did it. If hunger drove the family to beg help from officials of some charity, the woman went. And if angry crowds marched from one workshop to the next, rousing whole neighborhoods to revolt, as they did, for example, in Chicago in May 1867, July 1877, May 1886, and July 1894, women were prominent in the marchers' ranks. Consequently, two images of working women appeared regularly in the literature and press of the Gilded Age: the weeping, abused wife of a drunkard, and the caricatured Irish "Amazon." Both these bourgeois perceptions were incorporated into reformer Helen Campbell's 1886 description of New York's toilworn women as "ignorant, blind, stupid, incompetent in every fibre."[51] Repeated encounters with such disdainful attitudes of society's more fortunate members broadened women's attachments to their families into loyalty to their class.

Two significant consequences derive from the fact that women's wage-earning experience was ordinarily confined to their youthful years and the fact that their sense of class ran through family to neighborhood, spurred by endless reminders of social subordination. First, their awareness of class was intertwined with awareness of their subordination as daughters to their parents and as wives to their husbands. Second, special bonds, almost a distinct subculture, developed among young wage-earning women. The first of these consequences was the focal point of Leslie Woodcock Tentler's history of wage-earning women at the turn of the century. Because most female workers lived under the parental roof and put their earnings into the family pot, Tentler concluded that they were preoccupied far more with "the struggle with parents for social freedom" than by the struggle with employers for higher wages or better conditions of work. This assertion is true, but insufficient. Tamara Hareven's interviews with the women of the Amoskeag Mills abound with stories of painful personal sacrifices made in order to care for parents. Louise Montgomery's sociological survey, *The American Girl in the Stockyards*

51.   Helen Campbell, *Prisoners of Poverty: Women Wage-Earners, Their Trades and Their Lives* (Boston, 1887), 245. I am indebted to Priscilla Murolo for this quotation.

District, found irrepressible tension between parents' rules and daughters' "desire for evening pleasures and some of the novelties and frivolities of fashion," but concluded that "among the 500 girls their instinctive devotion to family claim has been strong enough to keep them obedient."[52] Moreover, many firsthand accounts of factory life support Tentler's argument that the "romantic preoccupations of the work group . . . encouraged many young women to choose an early marriage as the most desirable route to freedom from parental control,"[53] not to mention escape from piecework. Neighbors' scorn for the "old maid" and religious teachings about woman's "true role" as mother reinforced this preoccupation.

Nevertheless, census data indicate that more adult women who never married were born between 1860 and 1900 than at any other time in American history. Among women born between 1865 and 1874 who reached working age during or after the 1880s, 11 percent were listed as never having married by the census of 1940, as compared with 4.5 percent of comparable age groups in 1970. Moreover, early deaths or disabling illnesses of husbands often made the "normal" pattern impossible of attainment.

It was not remarkable to find "Hannah," a Rhode Island widow of 1888, living with her three children and two unmarried sisters. The sisters worked in a textile mill, and Hannah kept house. All-female living arrangements reappeared in many boardinghouses in textile and shoe-manufacturing towns throughout New England. For example, in Haverhill, Massachusetts, where the women's shoe industry dominated the town and was subject to extreme seasonal fluctuations, the "great bulk of the female population," according to a local newspaper, lived "in houses where there is considerable of home life. . . , the head of which is an elderly woman who has, perhaps, in her younger days herself worked in the shoe shops."[54] For young women who found the rules of boarding-

52. Tentler, *Wage-earning Women,* 61; Hareven, *Family Time and Industrial Time,* 104–9; Tamara K. Hareven and Randolph Langenbach, *Amoskeag: Life and Work in an American Factory-City* (New York, 1978), 90; Louise Montgomery, *The American Girl in the Stockyards District* (Chicago, 1913), 90. See also Mary Kingsbury Simkhovitch, *The City Worker's World in America* (New York, 1917); Margaret F. Byington, *Homestead: The Households of a Mill Town* (New York, 1910).
53. Tentler, *Wage-earning Women,* 60–1; Parker, *Working Woman;* Bessie Van Vorst and Marie Van Vorst, *The Woman Who Toils* (New York, 1903).
54. Daniel S. Smith, "Family Limitation, Sexual Control, and Domestic Feminism in Victorian America," in Nancy F. Cott and Elizabeth Pleck, eds., *A Heritage of Her Own: Toward a New Social History of American Women*

houses too restrictive, the Massachusetts Bureau of Statistics of Labor reported in 1873, "the factory girls . . . combine two and two, and hire lodging rooms elsewhere, taking only their meals at the corporation boarding-houses."[55] Even if such women sent much of their earnings to their parents, money in their hands and distance from home allowed them other "preoccupations" than those described by Tentler.

Moreover, even teenagers under the parental roof kicked over the traces. "Chewing-gum chippies" made the rounds of dance halls and nickelodeons after work with boys from neighborhood gangs.[56] Mary Meyer of Chicago outsmarted parents and charity agents alike. Her disabled father had lived off his wife's earnings until the United Charities had had him jailed. The Charities then found Mary, who refused to work as a domestic, a job in a hat factory, only to report:

> Woman in office in great distress; says Mary has not worked at all at the hat factory [as she had pretended]. . . . Has been going with a girl who worked there. The girls say the employer is an evil man and showed them a check book and said they could draw what they liked. . . . Mary [refused to let him kiss her but] stole this check book and on the 29th forged a check for 12 dollars which she brought her mother saying it was her pay. On the 2nd she forged another check for 11 dollars; $6. of this she gave to her mother and $5. she spent at Riverview Park.[57]

Two aspects of this anecdote deserve some thought. First, it was with a friend of her own age that Mary had been "going." Demands of parents had always to compete with appeals and pressures from friends who were the wage earner's own age. Moreover, immigrant parents especially complained that their authority, in competition with peer pressures, had been

(New York, 1979), 223–4; Wyman, "Studies of Factory Life: Among the Women," *Atlantic Monthly,* 62 (September 1888), 316–17; *Haverhill Gazette,* January 19, 1895, quoted in Blewett, "Haverhill Shoe Strike," 360. Note the constantly shifting household arrangements in Wyman's account of "Hannah," and compare them with Tentler's account of the grim options facing "women adrift." Tentler, *Wage-earning Women,* 115–23.

55. Mass. BSL (1873), 285. See also Hareven, *Family Time and Industrial Time,* 24–5, for accounts of boardinghouses feeding many more women than they housed.

56. For example, see the report of the beating of Mary Fox, New Haven *Daily Union,* July 7, 1902. See also Evan Stark, "Gangs and Progress: The Contribution of Delinquency to Progressive Reform" (unpublished paper in possession of author).

57. Thomas and Znaniecki, *The Polish Peasant,* II, 1677–8. The editorial emendations and comments in this passage are those of Thomas and Znaniecki.

undermined by American institutions, including the charities. "[My son Stach] runs away and loafs about," Helena Dabrowskis wrote to her relatives in Poland. "Well, let him run. I had his eyes wiped [had him instructed] as well as I could; he can read, write, and speak English, quite like a gentleman. You say, 'Beat.' In American you are not allowed to beat; they can put you in prison. Give them to eat, and don't beat – such is the law in America."[58]

Second, for wage-earning women, as for most teenaged boys, work was most unlikely to become the central concern of their thoughts and dreams. The dance hall, the nickelodeon, athletic events and clubs, frolicking in the park, and lounging on the corner were above all the activities of youth. "I have noticed young men that before they were married have been doing very well indeed," commented Fall River's observant printer John Keogh, "but after they got married, even when their wives have gone to work in a mill for a short period, they have seemed to go down hill entirely, wear poor clothes and have to stint themselves on many things."[59] Husbands and wives might share a summertime picnic at the end of the streetcar line, an occasional union or fraternal-lodge outing, or a nap and a walk on Sunday afternoon, or might simply watch the youngsters play, but they could afford neither the time nor the money for the many commercial entertainments available in the city. These were the "evening pleasures" at which young wage-earning women appeared, dressed their very best, arm-in-arm together, and met the assembled young men.

The temporary quality of women's work expectations, the power of family ties, and the society of youth all contributed to a distinctive bonding of working women to one another. Women's fondest memories relating to work invariably hinged on conviviality. "We used to dance in the noontime and we used to jump rope," recalled Angelique Laplante of her years at Amoskeag. "Even after I was married we'd go out into the alley at noontime and dance."[60] Cornelia Parker remembered fumbling helplessly with candies and wrapping papers during her first day on a job. Tessie, across the worktable, was fumbling, too.

> Finally [Tessie] puts down the patient piece of chocolate candy and
> takes both hands to the job of separating one cup from the others.
> She places what is left of the chocolate in the middle of what is left

58. Ibid., I, 748. Compare the accounts of immigrant women using domestic-relations courts to their advantage and changing husbands without officially divorcing, in Kate Holladay Claghorn, *The Immigrant's Day in Court* (New York, 1923), 73–95.
59. Senate, *Labor and Capital*, III, 488.
60. Hareven, *Family Time and Industrial Time*, 77.

of the paper, looks at me, and better than any ouija board I know what is going on in her head. I smile at her, she smiles back, and she eats that first chocolate. Tessie and I are friends for life.[61]

Conversation was incessant. Single women talked hopefully of marrying. Married women warned against it. "Sign talk" carried the conversation over the deafening noise of power looms. "Some of the girls were very amusing, especially the Irish," recalled Swedish-born Mary Anderson of a Massachusetts shoe factory. "To me it was great fun and something I needed very badly, because, after all, I was a greenhorn."[62]

Just as Anderson's workmates saw to it that she did not remain a greenhorn long, in factories throughout the land women taught newcomers how to dress and how to behave. "We were proud we were weavers and we dressed well,'" noted Cora Pellerin.[63] Immigrants shed their old-country clothing, and along with it any air of submissiveness with which they had first entered the factory. Newcomers at Amoskeag who brought chocolates to the foreman or smiled too sweetly heard other women hiss *"lecheux"* ("lickers"). Coming under the awesome authority of the foreman, the newcomer in Fall River mills had to be told the ways of each of them: "Now there's French Charlie, he will take only pretty girls; he takes mostly French girls too, of course. But French Charlie, he don't cheat you on your cloth; some supers are terr'ble mean that way."[64]

The young women's work culture thus confronted supervisors with a paradox. On the one hand, the conviviality and even the fantasy world into which pieceworkers often let their minds slip actually provided a lubrication that helped both workers and their employers accomplish their daily tasks. In this sense, Tentler is right: Women workers then had "preoccupations" other than fighting their bosses. On the other hand, the bonds that attached young women to one another also fostered a sense of identity and of self-respect that overseers offended at their peril. Clothes, the fashionable attire that invariably shocked upper-class observers as frivolous, became the outward symbol of that identity, on and off the job. Mary K. Simkhovitch observed early in the twentieth century that the "American born working girl and her foreign-born sister soon catch the habit, and dress as modishly as any woman." Unlike most com-

---

61. Parker, *Working Woman*, 8–9.
62. Mary Anderson, with Mary W. Winslow, *Woman at Work: The Autobiography of Mary Anderson* (Minneapolis, 1951), quoted in Tentler, *Wage-earning Women*, 68. See also Parker, *Working Woman*, 67–8; Gertrude Barnum, "The Story of a Fall River Mill Girl," in Stein and Taft, *Workers Speak*, 28–30.
63. Hareven, *Family Time and Industrial Time*, 72.
64. Tentler, *Wage-earning Women*, 73; Hareven, *Family Time and Industrial Time*, 53. The quotation is from Barnum, "Mill Girl," 29.

mentators of her time, Simkhovitch grasped the significance of those clothes. "Sumptuary laws were intended . . . to prohibit the break-down of class through a common garb," she wrote. "Fashion levels."[65]

The sense of self that was expressed outwardly in dress found other expressions in the comments of women workers to government investigators and in their strike demands. First, because the foreman or forelady was the inescapable embodiment of their exploitation, most grievances and protests were directed to that office. The bitterest memories expressed in Tamara Hareven's interviews with textile workers were those of bosses who "would chase the girls and slap their behinds, . . . send away those they didn't like and not pay them." When women struck, their protests singled out, time after time, "disrespectful remarks" and "improper conduct" by foremen.[66] Second, by the 1880s, women were repeating the same basic litany of complaints whenever they were asked. Fines, rigid rules against absence from work, long periods between pays (often a month), and interminable hours of work drew their ire. For many women, however, the sight that most deeply offended them was child labor. Even those who took their own little daughters to help them at the machines considered it outrageous that they had to do so.

> Poor, puny, weak little children, scantily clad in garments saturated with oil [said a woman spinner in Rhode Island] are kept at work the entire year without intermission of even a month for schooling. The overseers are to them not over kind and sometimes do not hesitate to make them perform more work than the miserable little wretched beings possibly can.[67]

65. Simkhovitch, *City Worker's World*, 131. On the fantasy life of workers on the job, see Parker, *Working Woman*, passim; Barbara Garson, *All the Livelong Day: The Meaning and Demeaning of Routine Work* (Garden City, N.Y., 1975); Margaret Stasik interview in Schatz, *Electrical Workers*, 32. Among the commentators who were shocked by working women's "inappropriately" fashionable dress were Lillian Betts, *The Leaven in a Great City* (New York, 1902), and Marie Van Vorst, *The Woman Who Toils, Being the Experience of Two Ladies as Factory Girls* (New York, 1903). I am indebted to Priscilla Murolo for these references.

66. Hareven, *Family Time and Community Time*, 136. For examples of women's strike protests, see Patricia Ann Cooper, "From Hand Craft to Mass Production: Men, Women and Work Culture in American Cigar Factories, 1900–1919" (unpublished Ph.D. diss., University of Maryland, 1981), 282–9; Nancy Schrom Dye, *As Sisters and As Equals: Feminism, the Labor Movement, and the Women's Trade Union League of New York* (Columbia, Mo., 1980), 22–3, 67.

67. R.I. CIS (1889), 152–3. This entire issue of the Rhode Island CIS reports is devoted to women workers. Compare this attitude with the apparent acceptance of child labor as inevitable among more recent immigrants.

The bearing, the sense of self, the bonding with other young women, and the issues of common concern found clear expression during the 1880s and 1890s in two institutions: the Working Girls' Clubs and the Knights of Labor. The two movements grew simultaneously (1881 was the year when the first club was started and when women were formally admitted to Knights membership) and drew on the same constituency in the Northeast, but the importance of the clubs to working women outlasted that of the Knights. Women who worked in New York City's carpet, silk, jute, box, and cigarette factories provided the membership and much of the initiative for the clubs, which were sponsored by Grace Dodge and other wealthy female philanthropists. Their example inspired such widespread imitation that by 1890 a convention of 225 delegates represented fifty-five clubs in every northeastern city. Their activities included classes in dressmaking, cooking, typing, spelling, physical culture, and first aid, as well as the collection of libraries, and "practical talks." The talks were a favorite occasion among the members. Invited speakers addressed topics ranging from attire, "true friends," health, and letter writing to immigration restriction, strikes, women's wages, and government control of railroads. They opened discussions through which, one silk weaver explained, "we learn to speak quickly and think readily, and . . . put into words the very ideas we never thought would see the light of day." The members' mixed feelings of gratitude toward wealthy benefactresses and their determination to direct their own affairs inevitably caused tensions, especially when the wage earners engaged in public fund-raising activities; but those activities integrated the clubs into neighborhood life, just as did their "helping hand" assistance to needy families and their invitations to men to be guests at select meetings of "our club." Working Girls' Clubs explicitly cultivated the codes of bonding and individual conduct that were implicit in women's workplace culture. "It is natural, though not just, for people to judge a class by the actions of a few of that class," one delegate told the 1890 convention. "Let every one of us, then, so act in a good, true self-respecting way, that the reputation of all of us may be raised."[68]

The key to the clubs' success, most members agreed, was their adherence to the basic principles of "cooperation, self-government, self-support."

68. Priscilla Murolo, "The Working Girls' Clubs of New York City, 1884–1894: Cooperation, Self-Government, Self-Support" (unpublished paper in possession of the author); the quotations are on pp. 9 and 11. See also Clara Sidney Davidge, "Working-Girls' Clubs," *Scribner's Magazine*, 15 (January–March 1894), 619–28. The clubs have often been depicted simply as humanitarian concerns of their sponsors; e.g., Kessler-Harris, *Out to Work*, 93.

And it was those very principles that, for women, gave special meaning to the Knights of Labor. In 1887, the Knights' general investigator for women's work, Leonora M. Barry, estimated that sixty-five thousand women belonged to the order. Most of them had joined during 1885 and 1886, when operatives, laborers, and craft workers alike had flocked into the Knights, and easily two-thirds of the women were enrolled in "ladies' locals." The structure found in Philadelphia's shoe industry was typical of the order's style: Ten local assemblies were organized by trade (cutters, heelers, McKay-machine operators, etc.), and an eleventh – by far the largest – was the Garfield Assembly, No. 1684, composed entirely of women. We have already encountered that pattern in the ARU's locals at Pullman. Not all of Philadelphia's female shoe workers belonged to the Garfield Assembly, however, and many female Knights elsewhere also participated in the same local assemblies with men. There were, as well, local assemblies of domestic servants and of housewives; and one homemaker, Elizabeth Rodgers, presided as "master workman'" over Chicago's fifty-thousand-member District Assembly 24, while raising ten children with her molder husband.[69]

Many trade unions also boasted hundreds or even thousands of female members, although the most important of them, those in the textile and garment industries, usually affiliated en bloc with the Knights during the mid-1880s. Even unions of domestics were not unique to the Knights: They had appeared in black communities in Richmond, Galveston, and other southern cities during the 1860s and 1870s and could still be found in New Orleans and Baton Rouge bearing the label of AFL federal unions in 1904. Nevertheless, the Knights offered women a special quality that organizations based purely on occupation could not duplicate. Knights' local assemblies were available to women at all stages of their adult lives; they incorporated both the bonds that linked young wage-earning women to each other and those that linked married women to their families and neighborhoods. The weapon of the boycott offered especially effective assistance to the struggles of those who fabricated clothing for working-class customers. Knights-sponsored cooperatives not only promised employment (as in the famous Our Girls' Co-operative Clothing Manufacturing Company of Chicago) but also provided "escape for the overtired housekeeper" through "neighborly neighbors working together." More-

69. Susan Levine, "Labor's True Woman: Domesticity and Equal Rights in the Knights of Labor," *Journal of American History,* 70 (September 1983), 323–39; Augusta Emile Galster, *The Labor Movement in the Shoe Industry, With Special Reference to Philadelphia* (New York, 1924), 50–7. See also Levine, "Their Own Sphere."

over, the order enforced its own code of personal behavior through a carefully codified judicial system, which expelled four thousand members between 1880 and 1886. Most of those expelled were simply scabs, to be sure, but seventy-three women were thrown out for violation of their obligation to the order (women's offenses were seldom precisely described in notices of expulsion), and at least that many men were denounced for deserting their wives, abusing their families, failing to pay board bills, rape, and other crimes against women. Finally, between 1886 and 1889, a general investigator, Leonora Barry, directed a special Committee on Women's Work and undertook the staggering task of examining and publicizing the conditions under which American women earned wages.[70] A poem in the *Journal of United Labor* summed up the paradoxical, many-faceted self-image cultivated by both the Knights of Labor and the Working Girls' Clubs:

> We ask not your pity, we charity scorn,
> We ask but the rights to which we were born,
> For the flag of freedom has waved o'er the land,
> We justice and equality claim and demand.
> Then strive for your rights, O, sisters dear,
> And ever remember in your own sphere,
> You may aid the cause of all mankind,
> And be the true woman that God designed.[71]

Piecework

Although the protracted deflation of the last quarter of the nineteenth century spurred employers' unceasing search for lower production costs, that quest was consistently resisted and often thwarted by a working class that enjoyed significant reservoirs of social strength. Among them were the "initiative" of craftsmen, which remained both indispensable to employers' efforts to accumulate capital and a formidable obstacle to their realization of that goal, and the personal and ethnic bonds among laborers, which helped secure a steady flow of "human machines" for

70. Levine, "Labor's True Woman," 329. See also Levine, "Their Own Sphere," 209; Jonathan Garlock, "The Knights of Labor Courts: A 19th Century American Experiment With Popular Justice" (unpublished paper prepared for 1978 meeting of the Social Science History Association). On domestic servants' unions, see Rachleff, "Black, White, and Gray," 225–334; La. BSL (1904–5), 53, 60.
71. *Journal of United Labor,* January 10, 1885, reproduced in Levine, "Labor's True Woman," 330.

industry and provided the basis on which laborers' occasional fierce revolts were mobilized. Similarly, many of the characteristics that enabled
operatives to accommodate to the requirements of the companies that
employed them also provided the basis for intense, if usually sporadic,
resistance to their employers' demands. Operatives drew strength from
the basic attributes of their working lives: their youth, their mobility,
their family and neighborhood ties, and the distinctive bonds that wage-
earning women developed with one another. By the turn of the century,
managerial reformers were concerned as much about their operatives'
behavior as about that of their craftsmen. The prolonged deflation had
swelled the numbers of operatives and also generated many conflicts. The
flash point in these conflicts usually was the piece wage itself. Some consideration of the nature of piecework will show why, and a case study of
textile workers will suggest the main economic, social, and political contours of that conflict.

Payment at a specified amount per unit of production was neither new
in the 1870s nor confined to operatives. Artisans such as cabinetmakers
had long been employed to produce, say, bedsteads, at so much per bed,
and printers had been paid so much per pica of type set at least since the
eighteenth century. Although attempts to introduce piecework into the
payment of machinists, blacksmiths, carpenters, bricklayers, and pattern
makers met fierce resistance from workers, people in some crafts were
paid by the part, by the ton, or by the mile as accepted practice at least
since the 1850s. They included cigar makers, tailors, mule spinners, coal
miners, iron molders, hat finishers, and locomotive engineers. Indeed, in
the iron and steel industry, the tonnage men were the elite; day men were
laborers. Union rules and scales in such crafts were based on the presumption of piecework, not on opposition to it.[72]

Piecework came into increasingly widespread use after the 1860s, and
as it did so, it exposed two interrelated qualities worthy of note. First,
payment by the piece was bound up with the specialization of tasks;
payment became less often for making a bed, and more often for turning
a certain number of bed legs. Second, the basis on which piece rates were
calculated was not the value of the product but rather the locally pre-

72. The classic discussion of piecework is Sidney and Beatrice Webb, *Industrial
    Democracy* (revised edition, London, 1920), 287–346, 402–13. Insightful
    discussions may also be found in Simonetta Ortaggi, "Cottimo e produtti-
    vità nell' industria italiana del primo Novecento," *Rivista di storia contem-
    poranea,* 7 (1978), 15–58; Ortaggi, "Cottimo e organizzazione operaia nell'
    industria del primo Novecento," *Rivista di storia contemporanea,* 7 (1978),
    161–99; W. H. Booth, "Piece-Work," *American Machinist,* 14 (October 8,
    1891), 1–2; Marx, *Capital,* I, 602–11.

vailing rates of wages for women and for men. The way in which rates were fixed at Pullman and in clothing has illustrated this process.[73] From the 1860s on, employers in both Europe and America experimented and debated in the hope of finding the form of payment that would best stimulate workers to higher individual output. Investigators for the U.S. Commission of Labor at the turn of the century found employers "quite generally" claiming "that the piecework system gives them from 15 to 25 percent greater output than they can secure on the day-wage basis," and adding that quality improved along with quantity of output, because pieceworkers received no payment for work not accepted by foremen or inspectors.[74]

Piecework locked a number of factors (specialization, the intensity of work, the length of the working day, and the authority of supervisors) together so tightly with one another and with the level of earnings that a conflict about one of those subjects inevitably put all the others in question. This interrelationship of issues made gains on any one of them especially difficult for operatives. It also meant that although the question most likely to bring operatives out on strike was that of wages (protesting a reduction of their piece rates or demanding an increase), their rhetoric of protest and the support they enjoyed from others in their communities illuminated all these aspects of their exploitation – the whole "wages system." Moreover, whatever style of organization they carried with them back into the workplace had to be able to define and uphold workers' common interests in earnings, hours, intensity of work, and treatment by bosses, as they were manifested in a bewildering array of different individual piece rates.

"Factory C," studied by the U.S. Commission of Labor around 1901, had twenty-two thousand different piece prices for its twenty-seven hundred employees. One department alone boasted more than twelve hundred job rates. All of them were determined by the foreman's estimate of a good day's output and his knowledge of what he had to pay per day to hire

73. Karl Marx wrote, "Piece-wage is the form of wages most in harmony with the capitalist mode of production." *Capital*, I, 608.

74. U.S. Commissioner of Labor, *Eleventh Special Report*, 114, 117. On the spread of piecework, see Arthur Studnitz, *Nordamerikanische Arbeiterverhältnisse* (Leipzig, 1879), 115; Licht, *Working for the Railroad*, 133; Clawson, *Bureaucracy*, 180–3. On the discussion in Europe, see Stearns, *Lives of Labor*, 201–21; E. J. Hobsbawn, "Custom, Wages and Work-Load in Nineteenth-Century Industry," in Hobsbawn, *Labouring Men* (London, 1964), 344–70; Alain Cottereau, "Etude prélable" to Denis Poulot, *Le sublime, ou le travailleur comme il est en 1870 et ce qu'il peut être* (Paris, 1980), 73–4, 77–9.

each type of worker his department needed. The simpler and more repetitious the task, the cheaper the rate at which someone could be hired to perform it. Each fraction of a cent added to or taken off each piece rate influenced who did the job, how fast it was done, and how many "extra" hours before or after the normal day might be involved.[75]

The greatest apparent advantage of piecework to employers was that it made workers drive themselves. Failure to produce at a high level brought direct and instant punishment: loss of pay. Moreover, some types of work lent themselves to group piecework, which gave every worker a stake in the output of the group. The task system in making men's clothes was one example, and another was found among the women who manufactured cheap cigars at specified prices per thousand in Detroit and the Pennsylvania Dutch country. They worked in groups consisting of one buncher, who assembled the filler tobacco with the aid of a wooden mold, and two wrappers, who finished the cigars. Although the system lent itself to conversation, singing, and even pianos in the workshop, it also encouraged women to keep each other at their tasks and to stay together for long extra hours of work. Such workers readily developed what was known as "the piecework gait."[76]

Moreover, piece rates fluctuated so often that a major effort of mule spinners' craft unions and of Knights of Labor assemblies in textiles and in the shoe industry was simply to stabilize them – to fix their level firmly and openly for some specified period of time. Although workers were often able to force up the rates during periods of high demand for their products, temporary gluts on the market and major depressions alike brought reductions of rates in their wake. Every reduction made workers toil harder to preserve their incomes. With cruel irony, slack production also increased the workers' "loafing time," during which they waited for materials to weave or to stitch or for foremen to approve one batch of work before assigning them another task. The burdens of inefficiency in organization and of poor market conditions thus fell on the pieceworker.

Nevertheless, few employers thought the self-discipline imposed on workers by piece rates sufficient. Workers were as well aware as their bosses that if their earnings rose above prevailing daily wage scales, the piece rates would be cut. Payment by the piece both encouraged some workers to earn more than the average and lowered the average. Consequently, it was in the operatives' interest to watch each others' earnings, as well as their own, and to impose a ceiling on everyone's output.

75. U.S. Commissioner of Labor, *Eleventh Special Report*, 208, 211.
76. Cooper, "From Hand Craft," 193–207, 223–60; U.S. Commissioner of Labor, *Eleventh Special Report*, 119.

Unionized crafts did so openly – more openly, it seems, the more the century progressed. They simply stood the method by which foremen set piece rates on its head. By union rule they would determine a proper day's earnings (e.g., three dollars for a wood carver), then forbid any member to earn more than that amount, on pain of fines or expulsion imposed by the union. Metal polishers were even famous for helping each other meet the standard fixed by the group, if necessary, so that everyone's daily earnings ended up within a few cents of the same figure, despite the wide variety of piece rates in their shops. Although female operatives without union protection had to be slier about it, they, too, often showed that they had learned the rules by which rates were fixed. It was common in the shoe factories of Philadelphia, for example, for small groups of women to work slowly and refuse all overtime for as long as two weeks at the peak of a production season until the foreman agreed to raise the rate on their job.[77]

Employers and their foremen struck back against such restriction with discharges, shop rules, and fines, all of which revealed that piecework alone could not discipline the operatives. A Massachusetts leather currier complained in 1878 that the men in his shop were "not allowed to speak to each other though they work close together, on pain of instant discharge." The five hundred workers in the carriage works of James Cunningham and Sons in Rochester, New York, found themselves locked into the factory from starting until quitting time, so that no pieceworker could finish a stint and leave, and they were allowed only one cup of water per day, which the foreman drew at his discretion and gave to the worker. Striking female carpet workers in Yonkers, New York, denounced the surveillance to which they were subjected on the job as worse than incarceration in Sing Sing prison.[78]

Fines were the form of punishment that most enraged the workers, however, because they deprived the operatives directly of what they had earned. Moreover, struggles concerning fines helped instruct operatives that piece rates were not a price paid for the product of their work but simply one way of paying for their labor power while increasing their output. Consider, for example, the experiences of carpet weavers in the 1880s. Because hand-loom weaving had predominated in the carpet industry and had been carried on within large manufactories side by side with the new power looms into the 1870s, customs long associated with hand production of carpets had survived the rise of mechanized factories.

77.   U.S. Commissioner of Labor, *Eleventh Special Report,* 207–22; Galster, *Shoe Industry,* 47n.
78.   Mass. BSL (1879), 133; R. D. Layton testimony in Senate, *Labor and Capital,* I, 9; Levine, "Their Own Sphere," 143–4.

Among those customs was the right of workers whose carpet was rejected by the overseer, and thus not paid for, to buy the defective article at the cost of the materials that had gone into it. By 1884, weavers in the major centers of carpet production were complaining that they had been deprived of that right. Instead, the companies were keeping the defective pieces and fining the weavers for bad work. Rather than having to buy her product that the company did not want, the weaver was punished financially for wasting her time that the company had hired.[79]

The intensity of the piecework gait was of special concern to operatives who were no longer young. If prosperous times found Fall River mill owners complaining that their "carders and spinners went out [of the mill] whenever they wanted to, and many times without asking," the city's most prominent mule spinner, Robert Howard, observed that tending the four stretches made by "long mules" every minute forced the spinner to walk as many as thirty miles per day just to keep up with his machine. No one could endure that pace ten hours a day, six days a week. Four and a half days was closer to what a normal adult could stand, and there was always plenty of "sick help" at the mill gates in the morning ready to replace absentees.[80] Medical studies of industrial life made at the turn of the century confirmed Howard's grim observation. Fatigue, in the vivid words of the Swiss researcher Zaccaria Treves, was the "borderland of illness." A study of causes of unemployment undertaken by the U.S. Commission of Labor in 1901 found sickness ranking with inability to find work as one of the two leading causes. Fifteen times as many workers lost time because of sickness as because of accidents. Moreover, workers' morbidity rates rose rapidly after the age of twenty-five. As John Modell wrote: "Children from middling and poor families were reportedly more healthy than those from wealthier families: *but their parents were less healthy.*" The lower a father's regular earnings, the more likely he was to lose all of his earnings because of illness.[81]

To restrain the pace of work, therefore, was a question of survival, and

79. Pa. BIS, 17 (1889), 1D–52D; Levine, "Their Own Sphere," 52–83, 141–4.
80. Mass. BSL (1882), 365; Senate, *Labor and Capital,* I, 495–6. See also John Golden's testimony, U.S. CIR, I, 988.
81. John Modell, "Changing Risks, Changing Adaptations: American Families in the Nineteenth and Twentieth Centuries," in Allan Lichtman and Joan R. Challenor, eds., *Kin and Communities, Families in America* (Washington, D.C., 1979), 119–44; the quotation is on p. 126. The quotation from Treves is in Josephine Goldmark, *Fatigue and Efficiency* (New York, 1912), 111. Goldmark had to rely primarily on European research into fatigue and its effects, because very little research had been done in the United States before the publication of her book. Goldmark, 115–20.

the pace met by pieceworkers could be restrained only if piece rates were pushed upward. Operatives in highly seasonal industries were the least likely to succeed in establishing effective control over their stints, because they had only a limited time in which to earn their year's income. Workers in clothing shops, box factories, binderies, and breweries moved at a fierce tempo, and they put in days of eleven to twelve hours or more for three or four months at a stretch before entering a time of slack work and slack pay, then encountered their regular annual unemployment. Alfred Kolb found his fellow brewery workers returning to the boarding-house at the season's peak and collapsing onto their beds without washing or changing clothes for days on end. Chronic indigestion, anemia, and tuberculosis dogged their tracks. Only the young and those with only themselves to support, who could quit all work from time to time, could sustain such a pace.[82]

Piece rates and politics in New England milltowns

To do battle over piece rates, therefore, was to seize the whole leviathan of intensity and hours of work, specialization, and discipline by its most vulnerable limb. According to the strike statistics gathered by the U.S. Commissioner of Labor for the period 1881 to 1905, 65.8 percent of all strikes in textiles were about wages, as compared with 56.1 percent of strikes in all industries taken together. In good years, most strikes were for wage increases; in bad years, they were against wage cuts. Whatever the issue involved in the strikes, however, the workers lost 66 percent of the recorded struggles. That was a high loss ratio for the epoch; among eighteen leading industries tabulated by P. K. Edwards, only railroad workers suffered defeat as often, and in proportion to their numbers, they struck much less often than textile workers.

Although textile workers' strikes were frequent, most of them involved only a single mill, or even a single department in a mill. Consequently, a comparison of the total numbers of textile workers engaged in strikes during the twenty-five-year period with the numbers employed by the industry reveals that their overall strike propensity was slightly below the norm for American workers: 23 strikers per thousand workers in textiles, as compared with 25 per thousand in all industries, and, for example, 133 per thousand among miners. Moreover, huge textile strikes toward

82. Goldmark, *Fatigue and Efficiency*, 84–9; Alfred Kolb, *Als Arbeiter in Amerika. Unter deutsch-amerikanischen Grosstadt Proletariern* (Berlin, 1904), 65–8.

the end of the period, such as the Lawrence strike of 1894, the Lowell strike of 1903, and the Fall River strike of 1904, had broken the pattern of highly localized stoppages that had prevailed during most of the period. Two features dominated strike patterns in the late nineteenth century. First, only 24 percent of the recorded strikes were called by unions. That is a very low ratio, especially in contrast to the other leading "women's" industry, clothing, in which 84 to 90 percent of the strikes were led by unions. Second, again in sharp contrast to the situation for most other industries, it made little difference to the outcomes of textile workers' strikes whether they were led by unions or not. In fact, 68.9 percent of the union strikes were lost but only 63.7 percent of the strikes without unions. That level of defeats takes on added significance with the realization that wage strikes were the type that workers were most likely to win during these years, and for industry as a whole, union-led strikes went down to total defeat only 34.6 percent of the time, in comparison with 56.4 percent defeats for strikes without unions.[83]

Textile unions were primarily associated with mule spinners; textile strikes were sparked in most instances by weavers. Among the twenty-three strikes in Lowell and Lawrence between 1882 and 1892, for example, thirteen were undertaken by weavers, and only four involved spinners.[84] Given the predominance of women in most weaving rooms, it is clear that the average striker was a young woman trying to raise or prevent a reduction of her piece rates. Her companions on the picket lines were from the same weaving room; the hands at other mills in the neighborhood, and even workers in other rooms, usually remained on the job. When strikes involved most or all of a mill's employees, they usually spread by contagion from department to department. At the Crompton Company in Rhode Island's Blackstone Valley, for example, 30 velvet cutters struck unsuccessfully for a raise late in January 1888. Two weeks after they had returned to work, 180 weavers demanded an increase from nineteen cents per cut to twenty-one cents, and walked out. The 18 mule spinners remained several days on the job, doing less and less work, until

83. All the strike data in these paragraphs are from P. K. Edwards, *Strikes in the United States, 1881–1974* (Oxford, 1981), 99–101, except the ratios of strikers to workers employed, which are from Montgomery, "Strikes in Nineteenth-Century America," 91. My calculations of propensities to strike are quite different from those in Edwards, 106.

84. Jean-Claude G. Simon, "Textile Workers, Trade Unions, and Politics: Comparative Case Studies, France and the United States, 1885–1914" (unpublished Ph.D. diss., Tufts University, 1980), 42, 278. Perrot noted the prominence of weavers in French strikes also. Perrot, *Les ouvriers en grève*, 349–58.

they too struck, demanding a 10 percent raise. Eighty-seven ring spinners and 70 card-room workers then had meetings of their own and struck for a 10 percent raise, soon to be followed by loom fixers, burlers, and others. By the end of February, 500 workers were out – everyone except the velvet cutters, who had set off all the activity.[85]

One result of this strike behavior was that whatever organizational assistance textile strikers received tended to come from outside their ranks. Central labor unions, the Socialist Labor Party, and between 1878 and 1882 the International Labor Union rushed orators and organizers to the scenes of strikes in Paterson, Fall River, Cohoes, Lawrence, Lowell, and other textile centers. In the South, typically some carpenter, printer, or bricklayer would show up in a strikebound mill town to preach the gospel of labor reform. The message of class solidarity carried through the spoken or printed word found a receptive audience among the many kinfolk and neighbors of the strikers, who participated in the picnics, dances, flea markets, and other fund-raising activities needed to sustain the strikes. Grocers who extended credit, lawyers who counseled arrested strikers, and local politicians who endorsed the workers' cause all served to transform struggles of a few hundred young women into community mobilizations and to provide them with a common vocabulary of protest. During the large Fall River strike of 1879, the workers even organized a "varsity troupe" that gave several benefit shows in the city's opera house, as well as in Brockton, Boston, Lynn, Lowell, and other urban centers in the region. Especially important to strike agitation, however, was the labor press: a Detroit *Labor Leaf,* a Boston *Labor Leader,* a Chicago *Workingman's Advocate, John Swinton's Paper* from New York, or a Fall River (later Paterson) *Labor Standard.* The press carried the strikers' message to the community and to the nation at large, between strikes sustaining a drumbeat of exposures of speedups, long hours, and abusive foremen. So disturbed were mill owners by this activity that their most common way of attacking the labor movement during the early 1880s was by bringing suits for libel against its editors.[86]

The struggles of nineteenth-century operatives invariably interacted with those of craftsmen in the same factories, and textile workers proved no

85. R.I. CIS (1888), 98–100.
86. Herbert G. Gutman, *Work, Culture, and Society in Industrializing America: Essays in American Working-Class and Social History* (New York, 1976), 234–92; Stuart B. Kaufman, *Samuel Gompers and the Origins of the American Federation of Labor* (Westport, Conn., 1973), 90–1; Melton A. McLaurin, *Paternalism and Protest: Southern Cotton Mill Workers and Organized Labor, 1875–1905* (Westport, Conn., 1971), 75–110, 138; Oestreicher, "Solidarity and Fragmentation," 118.

exception to this rule. Although loom fixers, carders, and second hands often formed local unions of their own, it was the mule spinners who injected a forceful, continuous, and cautious craft-union presence into the New England mills. Theirs was one of the earliest crafts created by the Industrial Revolution. Each spinner operated two large machines at once, walking in behind the carriage of the one that was winding thread (called "filling") onto bobbins while the other, behind him, performed its drawing and twisting motion mechanically. Although the "self-acting" mules in use by the 1850s had eliminated the need to crank the mules in by hand and adjust faller wires after every stretch, each spinner still had a personal technique of setting the quadrant control nuts, waxing the belts, and adjusting gear wheels so that all of the hundreds of spindles on his two frames would produce the same grade of thread. He was assisted by a back boy, who cleaned up lint and helped piece broken threads back together. To run the large mules of the Amoskeag Mills, spinners there hired two helpers. Although continual improvements in ring-spinning machinery confronted mule spinners throughout the 1880s with the prospect of being made obsolete by machines that required very little skill to operate, both the quality of their filling and the cost to employers of replacing all their spinning machinery kept the trade alive. By 1894, however, ten mills in Fall River were operating with no mules at all, and others were phasing them out. Realizing that the days of their craft's existence were numbered, the Fall River union persuaded the National Mule Spinners' Association to recruit ring spinners and drop the word "mule" from its name. The epoch of predominance of the mule spinners' craft in textile workers' unionism in New England was coming to a close, leaving behind it only a disproportionate number of former spinners in the officialdom of AFL textile workers' unions.[87]

In upstate New York and in Philadelphia, mule spinners played a less outstanding role in the shaping of textile unionism; knitters and carpet weavers were at least as important there. In the South, ring spinning held sway from the earliest days of the industry, with the result that southern textile workers' unions usually included all employees in the same organization. Within New England itself, Fall River became the headquarters of mule spinners' unionism. Crowded with more than thirty mills employing 100 to 500 workers apiece, this center of high-quality and varied cotton fabrics attracted thousands of experienced British workers during

87. John Golden testimony, U.S. CIR, I, 985–8; Mass. BSL (1871), 482–3; Senate, *Labor and Capital*, I, 631; Freifeld, "Emergence," 188–90; Philip T. Silvia, Jr., "The Spindle City: Labor, Politics, and Religion in Fall River, Massachusetts, 1870–1905" (unpublished Ph.D. diss., Fordham University, 1973), 491–545.

the middle decades of the century, followed by French-Canadians and Portuguese immigrants in later years. Both the organizational style and the rhetorical flavor of its union movement were distinctly British in the 1870s and 1880s. One important aspect of that British influence was that the spinners of Fall River were never parochial. From the 1850s onward, their activists tried to build a union that would control the craft throughout New England.

That ambitious project was launched in October 1858 at a convention in Fall River that established the Benevolent and Protective Association of the United Operative Mule Spinners of New England. The delegates established a fund for the use of strikers and men fired for union activities, declared it the duty of every member to intercede for fellow members in need of jobs, and proclaimed as their objectives "the attainment of our rights, the protection of our interests, and our social elevation in society, as men." Most significantly, they ruled that members could not negotiate for advances in wages or a reduction in any single mill, unless authorized by a two-thirds vote of a general district meeting. From the outset, therefore, the spinners' union tried to establish both a general uniform scale for spinners' piece rates for all of New England (a goal not attained until 1886) and the submission of disputes between members and their employers "to arbitrators agreeable to both parties, their decision to be final." By these means they intended to defend spinners "against the *false political economy*, which declares that a reduction of wages *by giving an impetus to competition,* improves trade."[88]

By the time of the 1870 strike in Fall River, 350 of the city's 430 mule spinners belonged to the union. They had waged a successful campaign for the ten-hour day for all the city's textile workers and had sharply limited child labor by simply refusing to work when children were in the rooms. They led seven thousand workers out of the mills and enjoyed ardent support from "the small help of the mills," who "would assemble at the gates" and "halloo and hurrah" scab spinners and their piecers. Not only youngsters but also women and two local carpenters were arrested for picketing the mills.[89] Nevertheless, even mule spinners lost most of their strikes, especially the fierce Fall River confrontations of 1875, 1884, and 1893, the Lowell strike of 1875, and the Lawrence battle of 1882. Still, the union always revived, "like Banquo's ghost," in the words of its leader Robert Howard, and left its indelible imprint on the wages

88. *Constitution and General By-Laws of the Benevolent and Protective Association of the United Operative Mule Spinners of New England* (Fall River, 1858); the quotations are on pp. 1 and 2.
89. Mass. BSL (1871), 78, 91, 92, 476–85.

and work rules of spinning departments and on the network of labor newspapers, temperance societies, reading rooms, legislative lobbies, and cooperative stores that fanned out toward the north from Fall River, until it reached, and was held at bay by, the great Amoskeag Mills of Manchester, New Hampshire.[90]

In the mid-1880s, the strike militancy of the weavers and the craft-based reformism of the mule spinners found a common home in the Knights of Labor. Both groups were something of latecomers to that order, which had been formed in Philadelphia in 1869 and had grown slowly through the 1870s as it had recruited craftsmen and coal miners, primarily in Pennsylvania. Among the Philadelphia workers who joined the Knights toward the end of the decade were many carpet weavers and shoe workers, whose example reached northward during the early 1880s to persuade textile workers in Cohoes, Yonkers, Amsterdam, the Blackstone Valley of Rhode Island, and Fall River to form their own local assemblies. Moreover, its message proved especially attractive to the shoe workers of New England, who had already experienced powerful unionism, as well as major strike defeats, under the banners of the Knights and the Daughters of St. Crispin between 1867 and 1878. In fact, before 1884, most members of District Assembly 30, which comprised all Knights in Massachusetts outside of Boston, were shoe workers. During the next two years, however, the state's textile workers rushed to join the Knights. A large unsuccessful strike of spinners, back boys, and weavers at Lawrence's Pacific Mills in 1882 had been followed by the founding of an important local assembly, with the support of labor-oriented politicians from both the Greenback and Democratic parties. By June 1886, there were five thousand Knights in Lawrence, organized into seven local assemblies. Although the Knights in Lowell recruited primarily loom fixers and second hands, members from other occupations gave the order ten assemblies in that city by late 1886. In neighboring Rhode Island, the Knights grew on a wave of successful agitation for a legal ten-hour day; weavers constituted an important share of the twelve thousand members during 1886. In Fall River, the spinners' union joined the Knights as a unit, and made its own Robert Howard a leading officer of District Assembly 30.[91]

90. Freifeld, "Emergence," 340, 94; Wyman, "Studies of Factory Life: Black-Listing at Fall River," *Atlantic Monthly*, 62 (November 1888), 605–12. The quotation from Howard is in Freifeld, 394. On Fall River's cooperative stores, see Mass. BSL (1870), 283–4; Mass. BSL (1871), 480–2; George Jacob Holyoake, *Among the Americans* (London, 1881), 52.

91. Jonathan Garlock, *Guide to the Local Assemblies of the Knights of Labor* (Westport, Conn., 1982), xv–xxv, 87, 187, 194; Galster, *Shoe Industry*,

The rapid growth of the Knights during 1885 and 1886 was one of the most spectacular developments in the history of the American labor movement. On May 10, 1886, for example, the *Journal of United Labor* listed 690 new local assemblies that had been founded during the preceding fifteen days alone. Although workers of all types were swept up in this enthusiasm for the order, careful studies of Cincinnati, Chicago, Detroit, Milwaukee, and San Francisco have all noted that large factories had emerged as especially important centers of class mobilization, rather than as the barriers to mobilization they so often represented in the late nineteenth century, and operatives were prominent actors in the unionization of those factories. Textile operatives of the Northeast were no exception to this rule. Consequently, a close examination of the order's role in textiles may serve two purposes: First, it can reveal what the Knights meant to operatives. Second, it can show how operatives tried to reorganize work relations on their own behalf, when they had the chance.

The weavers who struck the nation's largest carpet mill, Alexander Smith Company of Yonkers, in March 1885 raised demands soon to be repeated in factories across the land: "Reinstatement of all employees unjustly discharged, Readjustment of the arbitrary and unjust system of docking and NO MORE BOSS OR SUPERINTENDENT TYRANNY."[92] The strikers wanted twenty women who had been fired as Knights activists reinstated, and they also wanted two overseers, known for their "obnoxious" behavior, dismissed. The Knights warmly endorsed the weavers' call for a boycott of Smith's wares and their practice of social ostracism of any resident of Yonkers who would fill a striker's job. Moreover, the Knights institutionalized the practice of using "outside agitators," which had long been familiar to textile workers, by dispatching officers of district assemblies to assist the strikers and publicize their cause.

When those officers carried their mission so far as to negotiate the actual settlement, they all too often bargained away demands of critical importance to the workers' subsequent power within the factory (e.g., the demand that all employees be required to belong to the order). So women often preferred the practice developed in the Cohoes strikes of 1880 and 1882: They did the negotiating, while male officers made public statements. This arrangement conformed to accepted gender roles,

49–57; McNeill, *Labor Movement,* 196–202; Dawley, *Class and Community,* 175–219; Walkowitz, *Worker City, Company Town,* 226–9; Simon, "Textile Workers," 24–5, 42–7; Paul Buhle, "The Knights of Labor in Rhode Island," *Radical History Review,* 17 (Spring 1978), 48–66; Silvia, "Spindle City," 452–7.

92. Yonkers *Statesman,* March 6, 1885, quoted in Levine, "Their Own Sphere," 141.

and it saved textile workers from the frequent threat of discharge that could result from too much publicity. Nevertheless, the women who constituted so large a proportion of the membership in the shoe and textile assemblies had sent enough delegates to the Knights' General Assembly of 1885 to form their own caucus, and although they failed to place one of their number on the General Board, they persuaded the Richmond General Assembly of 1886 to appoint Leonora Barry (master workman of an Amsterdam, New York, women's mixed assembly) to be general investigator for women's work.[93]

The Knights' message that "no pride of craft, no caste of trade should separate you" had special meaning for workers who had no craft. "Organize each with his particular guild," taught the Knights of Lawrence, "and form in the mass a federation that with the principles formulating the platform of the K of L will become a pride in your midst."[94] The Knights made local political hustings, picnics, parades, and press columns resound with the message of labor reform. Within textile mills, their large membership made it possible to compel the overseers and agents to discuss piece rates, fines, discharges, and other grievances with committees representing the workers. Such committees assumed a variety of forms. Most often in textiles, various departments had their own committees. In the Philadelphia area, however, textile workers tried with varying degrees of success to reproduce the pattern that had proved effective in the city's shoe industry. Different trades and occupations were organized city-wide into separate local assemblies, with a committee in each shop representing all its employees to the factory's owners, and one male and one female "statistician" in each shop kept track of the piece rates. Although shop committees never succeeded in abolishing fines, they were often able to reduce their level and to institute some appeals procedures. In Wansuck, Rhode Island, for example, the chairperson of a weavers' committee inspected all allegedly defective cloth and either personally negotiated a settlement of related fines or called in the whole committee to do so.[95]

Shop committees, supported by local and district assemblies, therefore, were the living embodiment of the Knights' gospel of "organization" in the textile and shoe industries. Although they were based on long-established practices of mule spinners and shoe workers, both of whom

93. Michael A. Gordon, "The Labor Boycott in New York City, 1880–1886," *Labor History*, 16 (Spring 1975), 212–13; Walkowitz, *Worker City, Company Town*, 98–9, 221–9; Levine, "Their Own Sphere," 158–88.
94. Quoted in Simon, "Textile Workers," 88.
95. Levine, "Their Own Sphere," 92–121; Galster, *Shoe Industry*, 55–7; Providence *People*, January 2, 1886, courtesy of Paul Buhle.

had for two decades gained more by solidarity on the job between strikes than they had by going out on strike, shop committees were widely developed by weavers, wool sorters, card-room workers, ring spinners, dyers, and other textile workers only under the umbrella of the Knights. Paradoxically, their success was both dependent on the Knights' teaching of "arbitration" and often in conflict with that message. By "arbitration," the Knights meant simply an established procedure for negotiation of disputes. They hailed any agreement by employers to sit down and talk with representatives of their workers as a step toward their goal. Best of all, in the Knights' view, was an agreement to submit a dispute to people who were not directly involved in it and to abide by whatever ruling those people made. Such outsiders usually were drawn from the ranks of other employers in the industry and officers of the Knights from other factories or other occupations.[96]

"All disputes hereafter arising in the factory shall be submitted to a joint committee of employers and employees for adjustment," said the agreement signed by E. S. Higgins and Company and Carpet Workers' National Trade District Assembly No. 126 in January 1887.[97] Undoubtedly, such a contract provided the most secure basis possible for the functioning of shop committees. Nevertheless, many mill owners considered grievance committees "one of the many nuisances which the Knights of Labor and other trade organizations inflict on manufacturers." Before employers would agree with Philadelphia's carpet workers to end the three-month strike of 1884, therefore, the workers had to renounce their shop committee, though the companies did agree to recognize an outside "arbitration board" to handle subsequent disputes. Small groups of that city's shoe workers, basking in the sense of strength the Knights provided them, but often unwilling to wait for or trust in the results of arbitration, frequently went on so-called vacations to enforce their demands. Responding to a strike of 160 hand-sewing benchmen, the manufacturers locked out all their workers in October and November 1887, thus finally destroying the organization of shoe workers that had provided leadership by example to shoe and textile workers alike.[98]

The ultimate test of arbitration for operatives was its impact on piece rates. Although the Knights had succeeded in standardizing wage scales

96. McNeill, *Labor Movement*, 497–507; Gregory S. Kealey and Bryan D. Palmer, *Dreaming of What Might Be: The Knights of Labor in Ontario, 1880–1900* (Cambridge, 1982), 330–9; Montgomery, *Beyond Equality*, 154–5.
97. N.Y. BSL (1887), 256.
98. *Carpet and Upholstery Trade Review*, July 15, 1887, quoted in Levine, "Their Own Sphere," 164–5; see also p. 150; Galster, *Shoe Industry*, 69–73, 182–8.

in Philadelphia's carpet industry by the spring of 1886, and even winning the praise of some manufacturers because of the barrier that achievement posed to destructive competition, a more severe challenge to the order was posed by New England's highly variegated textile industry. The first accomplishments appeared in Fall River – the handiwork, as one might expect, of the mule spinners. After the spinners had affiliated with the Knights, they arranged a general discussion of wages between three officers of the order and three leaders of the Cotton Manufacturers' Association. There, Robert Howard persuaded the employers to pursue his long-standing goal of "high wages and high prices for commodities." The bargainers attempted to equalize spinners' earnings for more than a hundred different grades of filling by comparing the numbers of spindles tended, the degrees of attention required, and the yards walked on the various grades. They also agreed, in November 1886, on a sliding scale that based the spinners' wages on the difference between the price of cotton and the selling price of print cloth. Mills in Fall River, Lawrence, New Bedford, and other major Massachusetts towns were covered by this complex agreement, which, with regularly negotiated revisions, continued to govern mule spinners' piece rates in the region until World War I. It marked a triumph of the version of "political economy" for which mule spinners had fought since 1858, by tying their fluctuating piece rates formally to the employers' profit margins, rather than to the prevailing wage. It also led Robert Howard, who had always discouraged strikes, thenceforth to wield his influence adamantly against any action by mule spinners that might jeopardize the sliding scale.[99]

Ironically, under the banner of the Knights of Labor the mule spinners had negotiated an agreement that had an unfortunate consequence: Thenceforth, Massachusetts weavers who went on strike could expect no help from the spinners' union. The tensions first became evident in Fall River itself, where the spinners negotiated a 9.5 percent raise in wages for themselves in January 1888, while other grades received only a 4.5 percent increase. True to form, the city's weavers struck in March, only to find the spinners reporting for work every day, making filling that the companies sold to other mills. Although virtually every mule spinner in the city had enrolled in the spinners' association by then, the weavers' strike was not even mentioned at its meetings.

In Lawrence, the local joint executive board of the Knights demanded

99. On carpet weavers, see Levine, "Their Own Sphere," 165. On spinners, see Silvia, "Spindle City," 452–7; U.S. CIR, 985–90. The quotation from Howard is in Senate, *Labor and Capital*, I, 641. For a biography of Howard, see Boston *Labor Leader*, January 15, 1887.

a general wage increase for all mill hands early in 1888, on the basis of the industry's prosperity and rising prices. For three days arbitration proceeded: Representatives of the local assemblies discussed the wage question with a committee of mill agents, but the manufacturers refused to offer a penny. The Knights' executives were stymied. Not only did General Master Workman Powderly "discountenance strikes," but all textile workers knew that they had lost every strike they had attempted recently in Lawrence and Lowell. All the order's leaders could do was to admonish the members "to be cautious and remain unknown" and to shun "any petty strike" that might erupt.[100]

The Lawrence defeat could not have come at a worse time for the order. During the fall months of 1887, the once mighty shoe workers' assemblies in Philadelphia had been crushed, and those in Cincinnati were routed at the very time the wage movement was checked in Lawrence. Blaming their failure on the Knights' structure, which subjected their local assemblies to the leadership of city-wide district assemblies, whose officers knew little of the shoe industry, many shoe workers had first formed National District Assembly No. 216, composed only of their assemblies, then over the course of 1888 and early 1889 had withdrawn from the Knights altogether and affiliated with the new AFL as the Boot and Shoe Workers' International Union. Carpet workers' assemblies had also been driven out of their former strongholds, such as the Alexander Smith Company and the Philadelphia mills, between the end of 1886 and early 1888, despite their having been among the first Knights to group themselves into a national district assembly based on industry rather then geography. By July 1888, Massachusetts' District Assembly 30 no longer had enough members to keep it alive, and it was merged with another district. No textile workers ran for office in the new structure.[101]

The textile workers' moment of power in the workplace had turned out to be brief. Only the mule spinners retained a strong organization, and Robert Howard bluntly summed up his union's position: "We are a trades union and represent our trade. Let the other operatives follow our example and organize for themselves."[102] But it proved impossible for the "other operatives" to imitate the spinners. They could see but two ways to improve their conditions. One was to form an industrial union,

100. Silvia, "Spindle City," 460–8; Simon, "Textile Workers," 87–9, 278; the quotation is on p. 88.
101. Galster, *Shoe Industry*, 59–73; James M. Morris, "The Cincinnati Shoe-Makers' Lockout of 1888," *Labor History*, 13 (Fall 1972), 505–19; Levine, "Their Own Sphere," 168.
102. *New York Times*, March 1, 1889, quoted in Silvia, "Spindle City," 464.

building on the Knights' legacy of recruiting all workers and also making full use of the weavers' well-known readiness to strike as the driving force for the new organization. The other was to reform industry through legislation, thus continuing and intensifying another aspect of the Knights' heritage. Although the two ideas were not mutually exclusive, Howard's mule spinners strongly opposed the first, but approved of the second.

On the last two days of March 1891, textile workers from Fall River, Lawrence, Lowell, and New Bedford, Massachusetts, Dover and Nashua, New Hampshire, and the Providence region of Rhode Island gathered in Lowell for the announced purpose of creating a "national union that would embrace within its folds every textile worker from the card room to the finishing room." The National Union of Textile Workers (NUTW), which they established, proclaimed increased wages and a legal fifty-four-hour week as its main objectives, and the enthusiastic support it received from many local weavers' unions enabled it to grow rapidly. It even supported a few small, but successful, weavers' strikes in Lawrence and Lowell. Hardly had the NUTW launched its career, however, when it ran into the great depression of the 1890s. Even the proud mule spinners then had to accept a 10 percent reduction in their scale. The weavers of Lawrence, however, rebelled against a reduction in their piece rates in 1894 and led twenty-five hundred workers out into the city's first multiplant, all-departments textile strike. The strikers were quickly replaced by men and women desperate for work. Only the mule spinners and loom fixers kept enough organized strength intact to win some concessions. The weavers gave up after eighty-four days of striking, and more than nine hundred of them lost their jobs permanently. Six months later, an even larger number of weavers struck the mills of Fall River to protest reductions in their wages. Despite the support they received from an alliance of all the city's textile unions, they, too, went down to defeat.[103]

The legislative route to reform appeared to hold greater promise of success than did strikes. The campaign for legislation to limit the working day in Massachusetts mills to ten hours had begun in the 1830s and 1840s and reached its initial goal when the legislature adopted a law in 1874 limiting the work of women to ten hours daily. Because few mills, if any, could function long after the women had gone home, the law effectively established a new standard for textiles. In 1885, Rhode Island followed suit, after two years of intensive popular agitation. The effect

103. Simon, "Textile Workers," 96–100; the quotation is on p. 96; Silvia, "Spindle City," 510–16.

of having an hour and a quarter shaved from her day in the mills by the new law was recounted by an "Irish widow" to the writer Lillie B. Chase Wyman:

> Why, the extra quarter hour at noon gives me time to mix my bread; an' then when I comes home at night, at six o'clock, it is ready to be put in the pans, an' I can do that while Katie sets the table; an' after supper, an' the dishes are washed, I can bake; an' then I am through, an' ready to go to bed, mebbe afore it's quite nine o'clock. Oh, it's splendid, the best thing as ever 'appened. I used to be up till way into the night, bakin', after my day's work in the mill was done.[104]

During the Knights of Labor upsurge, the legislative program sought by textile workers called for further reduction of the work week to fifty-eight or even fifty-four hours and was expanded to encompass all the grievances they found so difficult to remedy by arbitration and shop committees. Two bills for which the Knights campaigned were enacted by the Massachusetts legislature in 1887: one requiring corporations to pay their employees every week, and another establishing a state board of arbitration. The latter is especially significant, because many self-reliant craft unions opposed government arbitration in any form. The Massachusetts law empowered the mayor or aldermen of any town to request a board of three members appointed by the governor to send an agent who would mediate a current or pending strike. If both sides agreed, that agent could issue a ruling, binding on both sides for six months. Essentially, the board provided employers with an agency through which to undertake negotiations with dissatisfied employees without formally recognizing their unions. Although textile unions seldom obtained employers' consent to the use of binding arbitration, they quickly came to rely on the board as the most useful instrumentality for opening negotiations after the collapse of the Knights of Labor, although they usually refused its requests that they call off strikes already under way.[105]

Having failed to eliminate fines by workplace action, the movement campaigned aggressively to have them outlawed. The enactment of such a law in May 1891 brought joyous celebration among Lowell's weavers

104. Wyman, "Studies," *Atlantic Monthly*, 62 (September 1888), 321.
105. Simon, "Textile Workers," 200; U.S. Strike Commission, *Report*, 641–3; Blewett, "Union of Sex and Craft," 367; George E. Barnett and David A. McCabe, *Mediation, Investigation and Arbitration in Industrial Disputes* (New York, 1916). On craft-union resistance to governmental arbitration, see Bernard Mandel, *Samuel Gompers* (Yellow Springs, Ohio, 1963), 189–91; John D. French, " 'Reaping the Whirlwind': The Origins of the Allegheny County Greenback Labor Party in 1877," *Western Pennsylvania Historical Magazine*, 64 (April 1981), 15n.

and spinners during the four weeks before the state supreme court ruled it unconstitutional. By that time, candidates who sought labor's votes supported a long list of legislative proposals favored by labor: an end to the poll tax, establishment of a labor holiday, giving state and municipal employees an eight-hour day, prohibiting contract labor, introducing secret-ballot election, providing for women factory inspectors, banning tenement-house manufacture of clothing, raising the state's school-leaving age to fifteen, forbidding manufacturers to discriminate against union members, making employers liable for industrial accidents, retaining annual election of legislators, allowing colored oleomargarine, prohibiting night work by women and children in factories, banning all overtime, and reducing the legal work week to fifty-four hours. Craft organizations, cities' central labor unions, the remnants of the Knights, and the newly formed NUTW and Boot and Shoe Workers' International Union all joined in the lively, if unsuccessful, struggle for these bills.[106]

More precisely, weak unions and Democratic politicians joined forces to reform the textile mills by statute. Pro-labor Democrats were no stronger than the unions, because, as Lillie Wyman pointed out, in mill towns "none of the women and few of the men are voters."[107] The restriction of the suffrage to males over twenty-one who were citizens and could meet residential and poll-tax requirements meant that in Lawrence, for example, only 15 percent of the population were registered voters in 1880. The boards of aldermen in Lawrence and Lowell were ordinarily under Republican control, and vigorous support from the labor press and local unions only occasionally carried a friendly Democrat to the legislature by a narrow margin. Mayor Abbott and state representative M. F. Sullivan of Lowell tied the Democrats of that city closely to the Knights of Labor and its successors. Robert Howard himself was sent to the state legislature in 1880, when his role in preventing a spinners' strike while building union strength won him the endorsement of many employers and of both parties, as well as that of Fall River's unions. In 1885 he was elected to the state senate as a Democrat, and he was still there in 1892 to help put through a new law reducing the working hours of women

106. The list of legislative demands is from the Boston *Labor Leader,* July 30, 1887, October 8, 1887, October 24, 1891 ("Michael J. McEttrick"). On the fines bill, see Simon, "Textile Workers," 204–6. Southern textile unions also battled for state legislation at this time, especially for hours and child-labor limitations. See McLaurin, *Paternalism and Protest,* 124–5, 141–2. Textile unions did not use the argument advanced by cigar makers, printers, and others that protective legislation would reduce the employment of women. For that argument, see Kessler-Harris, *Out to Work,* 201–5.
107. Wyman, "Studies," *Atlantic Monthly,* 62 (July 1888), 18.

and children to fifty-eight per week. Michael McEttrick, from the Democratic stronghold of Boston (Roxbury), however, had enough seniority to serve as dean of the labor-reform contingent in the lower house.[108]

The uphill battle for legislative reform made the labor movement heavily dependent on the efforts of a handful of friendly legislators. It also forged an alliance between AFL unions and New England's Democrats that would still be intact and would shape the responses of local governments when the gospel of revolutionary industrial unionism inspired mass strikes in Massachusetts mill towns between 1912 and 1922. The same circumstances that generated this alliance, however, converted many labor activists in textile centers to socialism. Trade unionism seemed to them to be the "labor of Sisyphus" – pushing a great rock uphill only to have it fall back down again and again. The experiences of people like Thomas Cahill, the Lawrence weaver who became a leading figure in that city's central labor union, and James F. Carey, the future Social Democrat mayor of Haverhill, whose four sisters all worked in the city's shoe factories, had persuaded them that offering support to friendly Democrats was as futile as union struggles. In their minds, the only remedy for working people was to use the machinery of state to reorganize and direct all economic activity toward planned social objectives. Such workers denounced the alliance of trade unionists with local Democrats and vigorously promoted distinctly labor politics, in some towns by running slates of independents, in some places through the People's Party between 1892 and 1895, and elsewhere through the Socialist Labor Party (SLP), or, after 1897, the Social Democracy of America. They proved to be much more influential in the leading councils of the union movement than they were among the electorate at large. In 1894, Populist and SLP candidates in Lawrence and Lowell never won more than 3 percent of the vote, but socialist influence was so strong among the officers and convention delegates of the NUTW that Howard's mule spinners withdrew from the organization after a brief affiliation, and in 1896 only the skillful and impassioned intervention of P. J. McGuire of the AFL stopped the union's convention from voting to affiliate with the Socialist Trades and Labor Alliance. Only in the shoe towns Brockton and Haverhill did socialists control the municipal governments, beginning in 1897 and 1898.[109]

108. Simon, "Textile Workers," 35, 199–201; Boston *Labor Leader*, January 15, 1887 (on Howard), October 24, 1891 (on McEttrick); Silvia, "Spindle City," 483–4; Silvia, "The Position of Workers in a Textile Community: Fall River in the Early 1880s," *Labor History*, 16 (Spring 1975), 230–48.

109. Simon, "Textile Workers," 200–22; Blewett, "Union of Sex and Craft," 368; McLaurin, *Paternalism and Protest*, 133–4, 146–7; Henry F. Bedford, *Socialism and the Workers in Massachusetts, 1886–1912* (Amherst, Mass., 1966). The phrase "labor of Sisyphus" is from August Bebel.

An immediate consequence of the growing controversy over the proper form and objectives of labor's political action in the context of ineffective unionism was the intense ideological factionalism of New England's labor movement during the 1890s. Bitterly fought strikes by textile and shoe operatives during 1894 and 1895 retarded somewhat the downward trend in piece rates, but they could not restore anything like the power within the mills that operatives had often exercised between 1885 and 1887 or the apparent unity of purpose that the Knights of Labor had provided. Their main immediate effect was to stimulate both the popularity of political action and controversy over what form it should take. That debate was articulated primarily by craftsmen and by aspirants to political office rather than by the operatives themselves, but the popularity of one reform in particular revealed the influence of female operatives in provoking the whole discussion: The AFL, Democrats and socialists alike, in the mill towns declared themselves vigorously in favor of woman suffrage.[110]

The return of prosperity at the end of the 1890s brought with it rapid expansion of textile output – of woolens and silks in the Northeast, of carpets and knitwares around Philadelphia, and of cotton, especially in the South. Manufacturers responded to the new demand by enlarging their mills to unprecedented sizes, by installing more productive looms and forcing each weaver to operate many more of them, by demanding increased output from spinners to feed the voracious appetites of the renovated weaving rooms for yarn, and by tapping vast reservoirs of new workers in Europe and the American South. Legal barriers in northeastern states prevented mill owners from simply extending the hours of work or employing more children, as their competitors in the South were doing. The urgent task confronting northern textile manufacturers, therefore, was that of using labor more intensively – of raising productivity.

Textile manufacturers' access to seemingly inexhaustible supplies of labor and their success in beating down the many strikes by French-Canadian, Polish, Greek, and Italian operatives between 1903 and 1906 kept the average weekly wages of operatives in Lowell, Lawrence, and Fall River no higher in 1911 than they had been in 1893, despite the

110. Bedford, *Socialism*, 11–140; J. W. Sullivan and Hayes Robbins, *Socialism as an Incubus on the American Labor Movement* (New York, 1918); John H. M. Laslett, *Labor and the Left: A Study of Socialist and Radical Influences in the American Labor Movement, 1881–1924* (New York, 1970), 54–79; John T. Cumbler, "Labor, Capital, and Community: The Struggle for Power," *Labor History*, 15 (Summer 1974), 395–415. On woman suffrage, see Foner, *Labor Movement*, II, 190–1; Blewett, "Union of Sex and Craft," 373; Simon, "Textile Workers," 201; Montgomery, *Beyond Equality*, 285–7.

increases in both productivity and the cost of living during the interven-
ing years.[111] Nevertheless, the propensity of operatives, and of weavers
in particular, to resist reductions in their piece rates persisted into the
twentieth century, and the alliance of Democrats and craft unionists survived and became more effective in the statehouse and in city hall. Socialism, too, sank its roots deeper into the mill towns, especially among
Germans, Belgians, Italians, Jews, and Lithuanians. All these developments helped set the stage for the successful city-wide strikes of 1912 in
Lawrence and Lowell and for the subsequent spread of enthusiasm for
the IWW into most northeastern textile and shoe towns. In response to
this crisis, mill owners and social reformers alike directed their attention
to the community life, as well as the work patterns, of the operatives.
They recognized a need to do more than simply increase the operatives'
productivity: Social engineering had to be applied to the whole matrix of
work, family, peer-group, and neighborhood bonds that was the breed-
ing ground of class consciousness.

111.   Simon, "Textile Workers," 306–8; Silvia, "Spindle City," 696–705.

4

The art of cutting metals

The protracted deflationary crisis that had beset American industry since the early 1870s took the economy to rock bottom in the depression of 1893–7. For twenty years before the outbreak of the depression, the nation's manufacturing output had grown primarily as a result of ever greater inputs of labor power, despite remarkable technological improvements in some industries. While output per worker increased at a slower rate than the midcentury decades (1840–70) had exhibited, selling prices declined almost steadily, as did the average rates of return on manufacturing investments. Employers in virtually every industry tried to reduce their production costs by lowering wages. That effort was often challenged by workers, whose powers of resistance were strengthened by familial, gender, ethnic, and community loyalties, and especially by the decisive role of skilled craftsmen in the existing relations of production. The contest so pervaded social life that the ideology of acquisitive individualism, which explained and justified a society regulated by market mechanisms and propelled by the accumulation of capital, was challenged by an ideology of mutualism, rooted in working-class bondings and struggles. Chief Justice Paxson had charged the Homestead strikers with "insurrection and rebellion against the Commonwealth of Pennsylvania," and painter Theodore Rhodie accused the Pullman Company of depriving him not only of income but also of his "right as an American citizen" to espouse and live by union principles.[1] Contests over pennies on or off existing piece rates had ignited controversies over the nature and purpose of the American republic itself.

Not all workers fared alike in this contest. Overall, daily real wage rates rose 15 percent between 1873 and 1893, according to the calculations of Donald R. Adams, Jr.,[2] but workers did not share equally in the improvement. Skilled craftsmen in highly capitalized industries often suf-

1. See Chapter 3, footnote 32.
2. Glenn Porter, ed., *Encyclopedia of American Economic History: Studies of the Principal Movements and Ideas* (3 vols., New York, 1980), I, 244.

fered wage reductions as well as unemployment during recessions, only to recover and even improve on their former earnings and workplace power during the ensuing booms. The large enterprise proved to be their nemesis. Railroads and giant steel mills often made concessions to their craftsmen when labor markets were tight, but they usually crushed any union that went on strike against them. Nevertheless, in the great strikes of 1877, railroads became the sources of a general revolt, and during 1885 and 1886, large factories, as well as railroads, were major centers of working-class mobilization. The operatives in large and small factories alike were prominent actors during the peak periods of strike activity. Although their unions were fragile, their strikes both galvanized and depended on community support to a greater degree than those of craftsmen. Even though operatives' earnings crept upward during the more prosperous years, the large proportion of them who were women were paid at rates systematically set far below those for men. Daily wages for laborers, though higher than those for women, were actually lower on average in 1891 than they had been in 1872. Massive migration from capitalism's rural periphery had kept the supply of laborers abundant. What distinguished American industrial wages from those in industrialized Europe by 1900 was not just a higher general average, but especially greater differentials.[3] High returns for skill were both the essence of whatever superiority in living standards American workers enjoyed over western Europeans and a critical challenge to employers hard pressed by falling prices. Manufacturers as small as those producing cloaks in New York and as large as those pouring steel in Pittsburgh committed their ingenuity and their power to overcoming that challenge.

The high unemployment of 1893–6 allowed employers generally to slash their operatives' piece rates and humble their craftsmen, while the shortage of employment for laborers severely reduced the influx of immigrants. Workers' diverse efforts to cope with unemployment through collective self-help soon collapsed under the weight of the great numbers to be fed, leaving the needy dependent on local organized charities. When prosperity revived with the exuberant boom of 1898–1903, however, immigrants arrived in unprecedented numbers, while simultaneously craftsmen joined unions with such enthusiasm that in five years the labor movement grew from the corporal's guard that had survived the depression to a size and stability hardly dreamed of by nineteenth-century labor reformers. The employers' quest for lower labor costs, therefore, had to take into account large wage differentials and collectively aggressive craftsmen, as well as a new institutional context for business itself.

Traversing the depression of the 1890s proved to be a crossing of the

3. Shergold, *Working-Class Life.*

Rubicon for workers and industrialists alike. Although both groups had from time to time during the preceding quarter century displayed styles of organization, forms of struggle, and ideologies that were to dominate the industrial scene after 1898, neither of them could subsequently return to pre-depression ways. The consolidation of industry that had begun with railroad reorganization and early trusts, such as Standard Oil, in the 1870s and 1880s accelerated with the formation of fifty-one holding companies, most of them sponsored by investment bankers, between 1890 and 1893, then slowed down somewhat during the worst of the depression, only to leap forward between 1898 and 1903, when hundreds to thousands of firms disappeared into mergers each year. Many of the mergers failed, especially when the new firms were unable to create marketing structures and to lower labor costs sufficiently to exclude competitors from the field. Nevertheless, as Alfred D. Chandler, Jr., has written, "By the second decade of the century, the shakedown period following the merger movement was over. . . . Modern business enterprises dominated major American industries, and most of these same firms continued to dominate their industries for decades."[4]

Chandler has also shown that all of the newly merged corporations dominating consumer-goods industries (Campbell, Heinz, Borden, American Tobacco, Armour) were geared to international markets, as were many leading manufacturers of machinery (International Harvester, Singer Sewing Machine, Remington Typewriter).[5] Branch plants of American machinery producers invaded Europe on such a scale that by the time of the Chicago machinists' strike in 1900, even moderate-size firms had European operations. Producers of mining machinery, for example, had branches in Britain to give them access to South African mines and other parts of the British Empire. By 1914, American direct foreign investment equaled 7 percent of the nation's gross national product – precisely the same percentage that the foreign investment of 1966 would represent. Moreover, although the bulk of the country's exports were still agricultural commodities, U.S. exports of manufactured wares equaled those of England by 1913. They had been only 21 percent of England's in 1879.[6]

Foreign trade and foreign investment involved imports as much as they

4. Chandler, *Visible Hand*, 332–44; the quotation is on p. 345. See also Naomi R. Lamoreaux, *Great Merger Movement in American Business, 1895–1904* (New York, 1985); H. Roger Grant, *Self-Help in the 1890s Depression* (Ames, Iowa, 1983).
5. Chandler, *Visible Hand*, 351–9.
6. Ibid., 368–72; U.S. Industrial Commission, *Report*, VIII, 11, 17–18, 298; Harold G. Vatter, *The Drive to Industrial Maturity: The U.S. Economy, 1860–1914* (Westport, Conn., 1975), 143.

did exports. Imported raw materials more than doubled in value between 1880 and 1900, and doubled again by 1910, so that they then accounted for one-third of all the country's imports.[7] Asia and Latin America were especially important in this expansion. Investment houses in the United States helped open the mines, improve the plantations, construct the railroads, and operate the port facilities that made the Third World's produce accessible to this country's economy. We have already discussed the shipping lines of United Fruit and Standard Oil that transported such wares to the ports of New Orleans and New York.[8] Victory over Spain in the war of 1898 gave the United States its own overseas colonies. Less than a decade later, armor plate from U.S. Steel, artillery from the works of Bethlehem Steel, and "sea coal" from Maryland's Cumberland fields all helped float the Great White Fleet that was sent around South America and the Pacific Ocean by President Theodore Roosevelt to demonstrate America's ability to police its trade routes.[9]

But America's most significant import after the depression of the 1890s was people. The bridges between the nation's industry and capitalism's rural periphery that had been built during the 1880s provided the routes over which millions of men and women traveled each year after prosperity returned in 1898. As Italian villagers still sang in the 1930s:

> After thirty days in the steamship
> We got to America;
> We slept on the bare earth;
> We ate bread and sausages . . .
> But the industry of us Italians
> Founded towns and cities[10]

So great were the roles of the newcomers as laborers in mills and factories, as hewers and haulers in mines, as diggers of tunnels and layers of track, as stitchers in the burgeoning clothing industry and as operatives in the expanding textile mills that supplied that industry's cloth, as meat cutters and sausage packers – as toilers in both the most modern and the most archaic production settings – that they produced nothing less than an ethnic recomposition of the American working class. After 1900, the customs, ideas, and institutions so carefully cultivated by American workers during the previous forty years remained the possessions of only part of the working class, and a relatively privileged part at that. Symbolically,

7. Gabriel Kolko, *Main Currents in Modern American History* (New York, 1976), 38.
8. See the section "On the docks," Chapter 2.
9. John Morton Blum, *The Republican Roosevelt* (Cambridge, Mass., 1965), 135–7.
10. Ignazio Silone, *Bread and Wine* (New York, 1946), 220.

the term "American worker" came to refer to those who shared that heritage, regardless of the fact that many of them and most of their parents had been born in Germany, Ireland, or England. "There should be a law . . . to give a job to every decent man that's out of work," a poor but generous Irish woman had said as she fed Walter Wyckoff. "And another law . . . to keep all them I-talians from comin' in and takin' the bread out of the mouths of honest people."[11]

Things other than business organization and the working class had undergone irrevocable transformation by the end of the 1890s: Organized society and the state had also been changed. The rapid construction of a new physical infrastructure for urban America, the enthusiasm of business and professional groups for self-organization, the new uses of the state's coercive power to order social relations, and the secure position of the Republican Party as the dominant force in national political affairs were aspects of this change so pertinent to this discussion as to deserve brief mention here.

America's cities had become concentration points for industrial production and, even more significantly, for administration of the new global activities of the business community. Keeping accounts, typing internal and external correspondence, filing information, insuring risks, and creating and managing money involved more Americans in clerical work by 1910 than were employed even in the huge construction industry. At the same time, department stores, emporiums of commerce, emerged as centers of upper- and middle-class social life. If large factories employed ten thousand to fifteen thousand workers by 1905, department stores like Marshall Field of Chicago hired almost as many. Bureaucratically structured hierarchies of management emerged even earlier in such stores and in large offices than they did on the production floor. Capitalism had entered the stage in its development in which the proportion of wage earners who actually made goods had begun to shrink, and it has continued to shrink to the present day.[12]

11. Wyckoff, *West*, 94.
12. Chandler, *Visible Hand*, 224–33; Jurgen Kocka, *White Collar Workers in America, 1890–1940: A Social-Political History in International Perspective* (London, 1980). See also Ileen A. DeVault, "Sons and Daughters of Labor: Class and Clerical Work in Pittsburgh, 1870s–1910s" (unpublished Ph.D. diss., Yale University, 1985). On department stores, see Susan Porter Benson, " 'A Great Theater': Saleswomen, Customers, and Managers in American Department Stores, 1890–1940" (unpublished Ph.D. diss., Brown University, 1983), 27–8 and passim; Harry Braverman, *Labor and Monopoly Capital: The Degradation of Work in the Twentieth Century* (New York, 1974), 306–8.

As the mention of building construction suggests, the new infrastructure required a large physical component. Even during the worst years of the depression, new commercial buildings and urban streetcar lines continued to be constructed with little interruption. After 1898, new skyscrapers, bridges, subways, roadways, and stores reshaped every major urban center. There were two important consequences of this development: First, construction workers developed an especially strong and distinctive style of trade unionism that was of decisive importance in reorienting the behavior and objectives of the labor movement as a whole. Second, huge railway stations, department stores, museums, and theaters, public structures under private control, were placed at the physical center of urban social life. Moreover, among the newer industries were some, most notably in electrical equipment, that had to manufacture a demand for their products, as well as the products themselves. That, in turn, led to a network of power plants, transmission lines, trolley lines, and street lights that could be put in place only as a result of public decision and at public expense. Corporate policy and governmental activity formed new bonds at the level of local government as tight as those railroads had earlier enjoyed with federal developmental and military decision makers.[13]

Second, 245 national professional associations had been formed in the United States between 1870 and 1900. Engineers, architects, historians, economists, lawyers, tuberculosis researchers, urban charities administrators, public accountants, railroad superintendents, and registered nurses were but a few of those who established organizations through which to speak with a single voice in public affairs and to regulate admission to and the professional conduct of their own groups. As Samuel P. Hays and others have argued, those associations played a decisive role in guiding the municipal reform movements of the Progressive Era. Business groups were also better able to create and sustain disciplined organizations of their own after the 1890s than they had been earlier. Both national associations and city-wide employers' associations provided manufacturers with collective power during the first three decades of the twentieth century.

Tentatively, and often reluctantly, American business and professional groups were modifying their earlier acquisitive individualism into capitalist collectivism. Their new watchwords were "organization," "effi-

13. Alan Trachtenberg, *The Incorporation of America: Culture and Society in the Gilded Age* (New York, 1982), 107–39; Samuel P. Hays, "The Politics of Reform in Municipal Government in the Progressive Era," *Pacific Northwest Quarterly*, 55 (October 1964), 157–69; Schatz, *Electrical Workers*, 3–24.

ciency," "responsibility," and "management." Their call to the nation's "most distinguished individuals" to place their talents "at the service of their country" was summed up by philosopher Herbert Croly: "When a nation is sincerely attempting to meet its collective responsibility, the better individuals are inevitably educated into active participation in the collective task."[14]

Third, this collective task demanded that both private associations and the state deliberately seek to reshape human relations so as to make society more orderly, efficient, and united. It required efforts designed to overcome controversies at home and to face international conflict with greater military might and patriotic ardor. This meant, to Croly, finding the means to diminish the worker's " 'class consciousness' by doing away with his grievances" and "in every way" help "to make the individual working man more of an individual."[15] Among the other social goals projected by this ideal and motivating the political debates of the epoch were an "orderly" arrangement of race relations by systematic segregation of black social life from that of whites, control or prohibition of alcoholic drink, and "Americanization" of immigrants. These objectives shaped the reforms of industry's personnel practices as much as they shaped discussion of policy. In particular, the rhetoric of the scientific-management movement attempted to identify its proposals for new workplace practices with all these larger social goals.

Finally, both the interwoven efforts of those who envisaged themselves as the "better individuals" to regulate social and economic life via institutions other than the market and the pervasive mood of optimism, inquiry, experiment, and global influence that informed those efforts needed and found political form. Citizens' leagues, independent of both major parties, reshaped municipal politics. The dominant expression of that form at the national level, however, was the reinvigorated Republican Party, which shook off its defeats of the 1880s and early 1890s to rule the federal government firmly from the congressional elections of 1894 to those of 1910. Under the leadership of Presidents McKinley and Roo-

14. Thomas Bender, "The City and Intellectual Life: Crisis and Reorganization in Nineteenth-Century America" (unpublished paper, Hungarian-American Historical Conference, Budapest, 1982); Hays, "Reform"; Robert H. Wiebe, *Businessmen and Reform: A Study of the Progressive Movement* (Cambridge, Mass., 1962); Clarence E. Bonnett, *Employers' Associations in the United States: A Study of Typical Associations* (New York, 1922); James Weinstein, *The Corporate Ideal in the Liberal State, 1900–1918* (Boston, 1968). The quotation is from Herbert Croly, *The Promise of American Life* (edited by Arthur M. Schlesinger, Jr., Cambridge, Mass., 1965), 407.
15. Croly, *Promise*, 416.

sevelt, the Republicans assured business that the machinery of state was in good hands, and they built a solid electoral base throughout the urbanized North thanks to the loyalty of Protestant voters generally and many immigrant leaders as well. Cartoon imagery of the time regularly portrayed the typical American as a male clerical employee. Vigorous presidents protected him from hostile foreign navies, Caribbean bandits, debt defaulters, immigrant slum dwellers, extortionist labor unions, and the harebrained schemes of populists and socialists, and they encouraged sane and expert investigators to expose and remedy the many social flaws that had appeared during the nation's rapid rise to affluence. The portrayal was appropriate: It symbolized the political ballast that stabilized society against the designs of its less fortunate members while its "better individuals" restructured industrial capitalism.

By 1910, however, the orderliness of this process had given way to turbulent political controversies and merciless journalistic scrutiny of many aspects of American life that had previously been sacrosanct or else ignored. A wave of major strikes between 1909 and 1913, an avalanche of muckraking journalism, the rapidly growing strength of the Socialist Party, the appearance of other working-class–based independent political movements in Pennsylvania, West Virginia, and elsewhere, and finally the split of the Republican Party by the Bull Moose Progressives opened the door to a Democratic administration in Washington that was necessarily quite sensitive to working-class demands. In this context, the "better individuals" redoubled their efforts to control the environments of their factories and local communities. Above all, they intensified their efforts to reshape social institutions and popular thinking in ways that would be suited to the needs of the emerging industrial order.[16]

One aspect of the post-depression interplay between the economic foundations of social life and American ideas about that life was of special importance to wage earners: the crusade for scientific management. The teachings and practice of Frederick Winslow Taylor and his colleagues have had profound influences on work relations in twentieth-century America and on the country's dominant ways of defining what constitutes "progress" in economic life. Their admonitions to employers

16.   See Herbert Croly, *Marcus Alonzo Hanna: His Life and Work* (New York, 1912); Blum, *Roosevelt;* Weinstein, *Corporate Ideal;* Harold U. Faulkner, *Decline of Laissez-Faire* (New York, 1951); Richard Hofstadter, *Age of Reform: From Bryan to F.D.R.* (New York, 1955); George E. Mowry, *Era of Theodore Roosevelt, 1900–1912* (New York, 1958); Gabriel Kolko, *Triumph of Conservatism* (New York, 1963); Arthur S. Link, *Woodrow Wilson and the Progressive Era: 1910–1917* (New York, 1954); J. Joseph Huthmacher, "Urban Liberalism and the Age of Reform," *Mississippi Valley Historical Review,* 49 (September 1962), 231–41.

on ways to make their workshops more "efficient" drew heavily on the reform rhetoric of the Progressive Era and also contributed important themes to that rhetoric. In this sense, Taylor and his disciples provided a self-conscious vanguard of managerial reform, surveying and synthesizing what they considered the most advanced managerial practice of their time and providing that practice with ideological justifications and guidelines that spread their influence far beyond the walls of those factories in which they actually worked as consultants.

The metalworking industries provided the laboratory in which a new style of management was developed. They operated at the forefront of modern technology; indeed, most nineteenth-century members of the American Society of Mechanical Engineers (ASME) were entrepreneurs in machine-building enterprises. But their output was inescapably dependent on the skills and initiative of craftsmen in a variety of trades – machinists, molders, boilermakers, blacksmiths, electricians, pattern makers, metal polishers, draftsmen – each of which dominated one or more shops in any machine-building firm, and none of which ordinarily could be eliminated by mechanization. As we have seen, railroads had led the way in perfecting elaborate administrative structures; chemical and food-processing industries had pioneered continuous-flow production, which minimized the need for skilled workers in production; and textile and shoe factories had basically fixed the division of labor for their operatives by the 1860s.[17] Both the cost and the intractability of skilled labor posed special challenges to the owners of metalworking firms. Even consolidation of firms into huge enterprises helped little, because large metal-fabricating works enjoyed few economies of scale, if any.

To understand scientific management and its impact on American workers, it is necessary to look first at the metalworking enterprises in which it was cultivated, and especially at its relationship to the machinist's trade. The formulas developed by Taylor and his colleagues in that domain were couched in general terms that proved applicable to wage labor in many types of production, clerical, and sales work and were disseminated through academic courses, journals, management societies, and consultants until by the end of the 1920s they had become the new norms of American managerial practice. Their earliest applications, however, confirmed the observation of journalist John G. Brooks in 1903: "In the conflict between employers and employed, the 'storm centre' is largely at this point where science and invention are applied to industry."[18]

17. See "The crisis of competitive capitalism," Chapter 1.
18. John G. Brooks, *The Social Unrest, Studies in Labor and Socialist Movements* (New York, 1903), 6.

Culture and conflict in the machine shop

"We recognize that in the machinists' trade, especially, what may to-day seem impossible is a matter of practice tomorrow," a business agent of the International Association of Machinists (IAM) testified at the turn of the century. "We as a craft can not and do not stand in the way of progress."[19] Modern technology was the machinist's natural habitat, and technological improvements were as often as not their own inventions. Their craft required not only experience and manual dexterity but also abstract reasoning. Whereas machinists' handbooks of 1860 contained little mathematics beyond simple fractions and ratios, those of the early twentieth century included plane, solid, and descriptive geometry and, above all, the trigonometry of right triangles – needed for locating holes with reference to the two calibrated axes of milling, drilling, and boring machines. Paradoxically, the educational requirements of the work rose together with its specialization. By 1900, every issue of the union's organ, *The Machinists' Monthly Journal,* carried discussions of the latest techniques of locomotive assembly and ways to temper tools, along with reports on trade unionism the world over and essays on the need for socialism. Self-improvement for the machinist was a matter of keeping up with the progress of the times.

The ethical codes of machinists and their employers had much in common during the later nineteenth century, though not as much as the employers liked to pretend. The rapid growth in the numbers of metal-trades workers, the increasing specialization of their tasks, and, above all, the spread of piecework payment magnified the differences between bosses and journeymen and stimulated rapid growth of machinists' unions at the end of the 1890s. The same divergence of interests and outlooks made machine-building industries in general, and the ASME in particular, the nursery of scientific management. The reforms advocated by Taylor and his fellow engineers represented their response to industrial conflict in the industry and to the increasingly collective and aggressive forms of self-assertion by metal-trades craftsmen. To attack craft practice through scientific management also required the entrepreneurs to repudiate significant portions of their own earlier work culture. The outraged reaction that elicited from workers led to resurrection of values and vocabulary once taught by their employers, but newly applied in defense of the workers' new form of solidarity.

The machinists were but one of half a dozen trades found in any metal-working establishment, together with some common laborers, appren-

19.   U.S. Commissioner of Labor, *Eleventh Special Report,* 145.

Table 4.1. *Machinists in the United States*

Year	Machinists	Tool and die makers
1870	55,138	No listing
1880	101,130	No listing
1890	186,828	No listing
1900	283,145	No listing
1910	461,344	9,263
1920	801,901	55,092
1930	640,289	78,749

Source: U.S. Census, *Occ. Stat.,* 105. Apprentices were not always listed separately from machinists before 1910.

tices, helpers, and a growing number of operatives. The last group consisted of men and women who, in the words of IAM president James O'Connell in 1903, worked on "automatic machinery where no skill is required of the operator, nut-tapping machines, bolt cutters, small simple drill presses used to rough holes upon common rough work, power saws, and a simple class of machinery," and who were, he insisted, "not admitted" to his union.[20] Moreover, those who qualified as journeyman machinists were themselves a variegated group who stood together as a craft in aggressive strike activity far less often than did some other metal tradesmen, such as molders and boiler-makers, before the last decade of the nineteenth century. Nevertheless, the machinists greatly outnumbered those more militant crafts, and census estimates of the numbers of people working as machinists grew rapidly between 1870 and 1920 – as rapidly and to almost the same decennial totals as those for coal miners (Table 4.1).

The precision of the census figures is deceptive, not only because the boundary between craft work and operative work was itself a cultural boundary that shifted in response to workplace struggles, as we have seen, but also because the nature of the machinist's craft was constantly changing. The pre–Civil War machinist was described by the pioneer trade unionist Jonathan Fincher as "a cross between a millwright and a whitesmith, a fitter, finisher, locksmith, etc."[21] Although by 1900 the

20. *Machinists' Monthly Journal,* 9 (June 1897), 258 (hereafter cited as *MMJ*).
21. J. C. Fincher, "Early History of our Organization," *Machinists and Blacksmiths International Journal* (February 1872), 520. Eastern European immigrants who were machinists in the early twentieth century usually had been trained as locksmiths.

name of the trade usually designated people who cut and shaped metal parts on machine tools, less than half a century earlier it had referred to builders of machinery. One can even encounter suggestive references in the 1870s to "machinists" who worked in small shops with no power-driven machinery. Most machinists of that epoch, however, had used a workbench to lay out cuts to be made on machine tools, as well as to hand finish their work with files, scrapers, and lapping stones. They would move the work to an available lathe, drill press, milling machine, shaper, or planer, as the sequence of operations they had determined required, until they could deliver finished parts or assembled units to the foreman. The latter's instructions to the journeyman were little more than a description of, or consultation about, a mechanical problem to be solved. Desired dimensions or shapes might be chalked on the units or on the shop floor. Fitting parts together in assembly, or "erection" of final products, was as important a part of the trade as was the shaping of the parts.[22]

The various names adopted by machinists to identify their own trade organization underscore its ambiguous nature. An attempted union of 1877 was called the Mechanical Engineers of North America (a title long employed by the British union, the Amalgamated Society of Engineers). The Knights of Labor's national trade district of machinists formed in 1888 bore the label Machine Builders. During the first year of the IAM's existence (1888–9) it had carried the title Order of United Machinists and Mechanical Engineers of America. Most members of that organization, however, would have described their daily work as that of a lathe hand, a vise hand, or a floor man (fitter). By 1897, when the IAM's convention agreed to admit to membership "any competent, sober and industrious machinist" with four years' experience who was of the white race and was paid at least the minimum wage fixed by the union for his locality, it also decided to designate on the member's card which of the various competences applied to him: general machinist, floor hand, lathe hand, vise hand, planer hand, milling-machine hand, shaper hand, slotting-machine hand, die sinker, toolmaker, boring-mill hand.[23] Paradoxically, machinists became increasingly craft conscious as their craft became harder to define.

As we are now well aware, such definitions are shaped by the culture

22. See International Association of Machinists, *Proceedings of the Fourteenth Biennial Convention* (Davenport, Iowa, 1911), 160; *Boston Daily Evening Voice*, December 7, 1864; Fred J. Miller, "The Machinist," *Scribner's Magazine*, 14 (October–December 1893), 314–34.
23. U.S. Commissioner of Labor, *Eleventh Special Report*, 104–5; Mark Perlman, *The Machinists: A New Study in American Trade Unionism* (Cambridge, Mass., 1961), 5, 22–3.

of a craft. Machinists' work culture evolved during these decades through daily interaction between their own experience and traditions and the values espoused by their employers, so that the differences in outlook and behavior between boss and worker can be understood only as they related to each other. That relationship was often intensely personal, and it reflected peculiar characteristics of the production with which both were concerned.

Machinists were employed by small workshops and by large enterprises. More than half of Chicago's 4,887 machinists in 1880, for example, were in eight or nine of the city's 150 machine shops and foundries; two-thirds of the firms had only between six and fifty employees. Many companies of that time were founded to produce but a single type of machine for the market (a governor, an engine, a pump), and even the large concerns that turned out a variety of locomotives, ships, canal gates, artillery pieces, or the like built such products to order. Although the capital invested per worker was considerable their specialty was custom-made producer goods, and their favorite mart for display of those wares was a national or international exposition. Precision work was the key to a manufacturer's reputation, and "accuracy," recalled the famous engineer-entrepreneur C. T. Porter, "depended entirely on the skill of the workman."[24]

The leading entrepreneurs in machinery construction formed a tightly knit group during the post–Civil War decades. Locally, graduates of a city's polytechnic institutes constituted a prominent clique among its shop owners and executives. Nationally, the ASME, which was established in 1880, was well described by its historian Monte Calvert as a "gentlemen's club" of proprietors, superintendents, foremen, designers, and graduates of engineering schools who entered the group through personal recommendation only and who shared what Calvert called a distinctive "shop culture." That shop culture was clearly articulated in the research papers presented to the ASME, as well as in the reminiscences of prominent engineers in the columns of the weekly journal *American Machinist,* and especially in *Chordal's Letters,* which were written by James W. See (a founder of the ASME) and published in a variety of editions by *American Machinist.*[25]

These sources offer a clear image of what constituted a Good Workman in the eyes of the engineer-proprietors of machine-building estab-

24. Hartmut Keil and John B. Jentz, *German Workers in Industrial Chicago, 1850–1910: A Comparative Perspective* (DeKalb, Ill., 1983), 79; Charles T. Porter, *Engineering Reminiscences* (revised and enlarged edition, London, 1908), 31.

25. Roy Rosenzweig, *Eight Hours for What We Will: Workers and Leisure in an Industrial City, 1870–1920* (New York, 1983), 15; Monte A. Calvert,

lishments. In the first place, he had served a rigorously practical apprenticeship. Best of all, wrote Chordal, were the "street boys" (others preferred "country-bred boys") who had revealed their interests and talents by tinkering around idle machinery until they were "kicked out of the shops," and who subsequently had been indentured after they had passed written or oral examinations, which included questions about history, geography, and grammar, as well as arithmetic and mensuration. Editor W. S. Rogers of *American Machinist* later recalled his own apprenticeship as a blend of rough lessons from the journeymen, wise guidance from the boss, and boundless practical experience, all of which gave him the technical knowledge and human wisdom needed to rise in life and to guide others in his turn.[26]

This image of apprenticeship differs sharply from the contempt in which the institution was held by many contemporary academics. Canada's Royal Commission on the Relations Between Labor and Capital reported in 1888 that both employers and young workers had lost interest in apprenticeship, which survived only because of craftsmen's struggles to preserve their professional status. President James H. Smart of Purdue University was scornful of the institution; he claimed that it only encouraged bad work habits and "ancient relics of prejudice and unscientific 'rules of thumb,' handed down by the traditions of the shops."[27] This image also challenges the belief prevalent among historians that apprenticeship was long since dead. In fact, such large enterprises as Hoe Printing Press in New York, Baldwin Locomotive in Philadelphia, and Brown and Sharpe in Providence had many apprentice boys, whom they required in 1890 to study mathematics, mechanical drawing, reading, and spelling in night school while they mastered the basic machine tools during a four-year indenture. A poll of 116 machinery manufacturers six years later found that 85 of them (73 percent) trained apprentices, and 78 of those who did were satisfied with the system.[28]

The Mechanical Engineer in America, 1830–1910: Professional Cultures in Conflict (Baltimore, 1967), 110–13.

26. [James W. See], *Extracts from Chordal's Letters* (New York, 1880, hereafter cited as *Chordal*), 41; Thomas Livermore testimony, Senate, *Labor and Capital*, III, 16; W. S. Rogers, "Sketches of an Apprenticeship," *American Machinist*, 13 (September 18, 1890), 11–12. For a written qualifying examination for apprentice machinists used in 1886 by the Union Pacific Railroad and featuring many liberal-arts questions, see U.S. Circuit Court, District of Nebraska, *Oliver Ames, Second, Et Al. vs. Union Pacific Railway Company, Et Al., Record* (Omaha, 1894), 439–47.

27. Harvey, *Révolution industrielle*, 124–5; R.I. CIS (1888), 163.

28. Rogers, "Sketches"; U.S. Commissioner of Labor, *Seventeenth Annual Report . . . 1902. Trade and Technical Education* (57th Cong., 2nd Sess., House

Nevertheless, even though this conflicting evidence suggests that historians' knowledge of late-nineteenth-century apprenticeship is vague and unreliable, one must beware of accepting *American Machinist*'s image as reality. The Rhode Island Bureau of Industrial Statistics found that only 14 percent of the boys hired in machine shops ever became "first-class workmen." P. J. Conlon later recalled western railroad shops around 1890 in which ninety-six boys, alleged to be apprentices, worked alongside only six journeymen. The first lodges of both the Machinists' and Blacksmiths' International Union (Philadelphia, 1857) and the IAM (Atlanta, 1888) had been established primarily to stop the flooding of workshops by so-called apprentices. Charles Stelzle, who had completed a genuine apprenticeship at Hoe Printing Press that same year, commented that only a few of the American-educated workers he met in the trade "knew how to read a drawing or work to scale." Although native-born Americans were numerous in machine shops, especially in the East, figures provided by the U.S. Immigration Commission suggest that by the dawn of the twentieth century, most journeymen, in the Midwest at least, had been trained in Germany or Britain. Vice-President D. Douglas Wilson of the IAM estimated that 50 percent of his union's membership was foreign-born, largely British, like himself.[29]

The shop culture's image of the apprentice is important because it was a compelling social myth. It stressed the superiority of practical training over purely scholastic training and the need for "wise instruction as boys, and constant study and effort as men," if workers were to become "machinists or mechanics," rather than "specialists, or machine tenders." Above all, wrote W. S. Rogers, "the height of every worthy cub's ambition is to some day be the Old Man [boss] of some plant."[30]

Chordal's descriptions also make it possible to examine the behavior ascribed to the Good Workman between apprenticeship and proprietorship in some detail. First, he changed jobs often: "A machinist who has travelled and worked in a variety of shops, is always a more valuable and

Document No. 18, Washington, D.C. 1902); Calvert, *Mechanical Engineer*, 72–3. Paul Douglas developed the following overall ratios for apprentices to total employed in manufacturing and mining: 1860, 1:33; 1880, 1:87; 1890, 1:62; 1900, 1:88; 1920, 1:98. Paul H. Douglas, *American Apprenticeship and Industrial Education* (New York, 1921), 74.

29. R.I. CIS (1888), 163; Perlman, *Machinists*, 3–4; Curtis, "The Organized Few," 69–71; Charles Stelzle, *A Son of the Bowery: The Life Story of an East Side American* (New York, 1926), 40–1; P. J. Conlon to *MMJ*, 21 (February 1909), 164–5; U.S. Immigration Commission, *Immigrants in Industry*, Part 21, Vol. 1, 4–6; U.S. Industrial Commission, *Report*, VIII, 496.

30. Rogers, "Sketches," *American Machinist*, 14 (May 14, 1891), 3; 13 (September 25, 1890), 11.

desirable man than one who has not done so." Because firms tended to produce only a limited range of machinery and to depend for their success on their journeymen's abilities, they found their best men among those who tramped about through "job after job, shop after shop, year after year." Second, he did not try to impress his employer by racing about on the job. For Chordal, the "lazy machinist" was patently superior to the "lightning machinist." To fall into a frenzied pace was a sign of ignorance and incompetence. The able man made no "false strokes" but took the "sure and certain and effective path." Finally, the model mechanic held posted shop rules in contempt. Directives, notices, and warnings decorating the shop's walls were to him symptoms of inept management and a chaotic workplace. The Good Workman's apprenticeship had set him on the right path, and his technical knowledge, self-direction, and ability to guide others were reinforced by competent and appreciative employers. Broad experience also cultivated his executive abilities and helped him reach what presumably was his ultimate goal. "Is there a mechanic worthy of the name who has not the hope of some day owning a shop of his own?" asked the *Northwestern Mechanic*.[31]

Nevertheless, *Chordal's Letters* also reveals that many journeymen fell far short of this ideal. The flaws in the character and performance of machinists depicted in this literary compendium of proprietors' shop culture provide clues to the dilemmas of late-nineteenth-century machine-shop management as well as hints of another, different work culture – one nurtured by the machinists themselves. Among the misfits of the machine-building establishments was a "certain species of machinist who makes mistakes – always and continuously." Another type, far preferable in Chordal's mind, "works decisively and surely," but on occasion "will make some grand blunder. . . . He will get an engine four inches out of line, but he will never get it a sixteenth out of line." Especially disturbing was the "anxious man," who "calipers a fit, turns his work nearly to size, hesitates, doubts, and goes through the whole calipering process again." Then there was the "mullet head," who had, for all his

31. *Chordal*, 56, 58–61, 137–8, 153; *Northwestern Mechanic*, 1 (March 1889), 8, quoted in Calvert, *Mechanical Engineer*, 192; Miller, "The Machinist." For studies of "self-made" entrepreneurs in the machine-building industry, see Herbert G. Gutman, "The Reality of the Rags-to-Riches 'Myth': The Case of the Paterson, New Jersey, Locomotive, Iron, and Machinery Manufacturers, 1830–1860," in Gutman, *Work, Culture, and Society*, 211–33. For later comments by employers favorable to machinists who traveled from job to job, see H. A. Worman, "Recruiting the Work Force. V – Hiring the Skilled Workman," *Factory*, 1 (April 1908), 231; Studs Terkel, *Working* (New York, 1974), 556.

years in the trade, "no skill, no pride, no taste, no knowledge, no judgement, no nothing." At the other extreme could be found the machinist of remarkable abilities who "has been in the shop so long that he thinks, as the foreman does, that the shop can't exist without him; so he gets ugly, and 'sassy,' and has his regular drunk weeks and his irregular sober ones." And everywhere one found "growlers." There were "a hundred thousand men working in machine shops to-day who cannot show twenty-five cents for the last twenty years' work." The reason usually was not to be found in drink or gambling, but was "simply because they don't know what to do with their pay." It was these men who mismanaged their earnings and were chronically in debt, Chordal concluded, who "kick the hardest for higher pay."[32]

Chordal and his fellow engineer-entrepreneurs suggested two basic remedies for the unfortunate existence of "more bad skillful workmen than good ones." The first was close and careful supervision, based on two of Chordal's "rigid laws": "a place for everything and everything in its place, and specific lines of duty for every man."[33] Because no proprietor could attend well to the sales and design end of his business and to the supervision of many craftsmen with as many quirks, the role of foreman was decisively important – even in production so heavily dependent on the workers' skills. Chordal's own favorite style of supervision was what he called "the Yankee contractor." Inside contracting had spread between 1860 and 1890 to such an extent that a government study found it "practically universal in New England" and commonplace elsewhere.[34] It encouraged some workers to become temporary or long-term employers of other workers while using the firm's machinery and floor space, and it gave the contractor a monetary interest in maximizing the output of a group of his workmates that was small enough to be supervised effectively.

Inside contracting assumed a variety of forms in machine shops, just as it did in rolling mills, carriage works, and clothing factories. At times it was little more than group piecework where several workers shared the income from parts or subassemblies on which they had cooperated, much the way car builders at the Pullman works had done. At other times, the

32. *Chordal*, 112, 210–12, 230–3.
33. Ibid., 71, 242. A similar estimate, that only one-fifth of the ship carpenters and caulkers of New York were "really very valuable men," was offered by industrialist John Roach. Senate, *Labor and Capital*, I, 1011. Remarkably similar estimates were offered by the French machine-shop owner Denis Poulot, *Le sublime.*
34. *Chordal*, 29–35; U.S. Commissioner of Labor, *Eleventh Special Report*, 135.

group leader, who took the contract at so much per unit, hired others on day rates and pocketed the margin between his helpers' wages and the price the company had paid him.

The system could also operate on a grander scale. An individual might contract by the year to manage a particular department. Several times during the year the total value of the department's output would be calculated at current prices and credited to the account of the contractor. From that account would be deducted the department's payroll, charges for materials, tools, and repairs, and any costs that might have arisen for medical treatment, property damage, and so forth. The contractor then would retain a stipulated percentage of the remainder, usually between 10 and 25 percent. In the Winchester Repeating Arms factory at New Haven, five contractors who were in charge of different departments in the 1880s employed forty-three people apiece and earned an average of $4,800 yearly, in contrast to their employees' average of $700. They might also expect to receive liberal gifts from their employees. Here was a way of becoming the "Old Man of some plant" to which the shop culture's Good Workman could realistically aspire, because he did not need to provide the capital equipment. Such a man, wrote Chordal, was a "superintendent getting big pay [who] directs every stroke made by his few men." An Ohio firm he described had "five contractors in their shop on different classes of work, and [the proprietors] see these contractors making more money than the shop; but they are smart enough to see that the shop and the men make money, too, and that the credit is due entirely and solely to the contractors."[35]

The second element in the entrepreneurs' formula for good shop management was found in their celebration of the labor market's "unseen hand." Good machinists deserved good pay, Chordal warned employers, and wise bosses made "some small difference in the pay" of each worker. His advice to journeymen was consistent with his admonitions to their employers:

> Prove your worth in the shop, and you will get your money, and, when you prove more valuable, you will get more. Now comes the golden rule: Keep your mouth shut and don't tell any man, woman, or child on the face of the earth what wages you get, unless you don't

35. John Buttrick, "The Inside Contract System," *Journal of Economic History*, 12 (Summer 1952), 205–11; Will Poyfair, Jr., diary, 1914 Archives of Labor History and Urban Affairs, Wayne State University (description of his work group on last address page). For an informative discussion of inside contracting with an interpretation different from mine, see Clawson, *Bureaucracy and the Labor Process*. Standard contract forms can be found in the Sargent Company Papers, University of Connecticut Library.

get what you are worth, in which case go to the office *alone* and fix
it at once. Remember that. Don't brag about your wages to any soul
as long as you live. If you get a raise and blab about it, the bosses
will kick you out for your lack of sense, or the other boys will freeze
you out for your good luck.[36]

A benign sense of common interest binding "cub," journeyman, and
"the Old Man" to each other in mutual respect and interdependence
pervaded Chordal's philosophy. His utter contempt for those engineers
who lacked practical workshop experience or who were disdainful of
their workers' knowledge, his emphasis on technical problems that challenged bosses and craftsmen to cooperative endeavors, his gruff, earthy
vocabulary, and the scent of cutting oil and iron filings that virtually rises
from the pages of his "letters" all reinforced the impression that Chordal's shop culture belonged to everyone in the shop. The "bad skillful
workmen" he described represented simply a challenge for supervisors to
overcome. Nevertheless, he found that most machinists were in the ranks
of the "bad," rather than the ranks of the Good Workmen, and that their
pathological behavior conformed to patterns that were familiar to employers and workers alike. For example, Chordal warned his readers:

> The average machinist considers all machinists the same, and thinks
> they should all receive the same pay. He has a certain amount of
> bigotry about him, and cannot be convinced that he is not as valu-
> able a man as there is on earth. . . . He will kick, if he gets less wages
> than others, and others will kick if he gets more.[37]

An employer who would champion the "natural law" of supply and
demand in wage determination against this working-class "bigotry" had
to use both stealth and coercion. Moreover, he often found his efforts to
increase output and to assign "specific lines of duty for every man" frustrated by "cliques" among the workers. "There is but one way to circumvent a 'clique,' and that is to stamp out every man composing it," he
wrote, abruptly abandoning his folksy tone. "Be king; be a good king,
deserve loyalty, and remove all disloyal influences."[38]

The youthful Frederick Winslow Taylor had followed that advice when
he became gang boss over the lathes at Midvale Steel within months of
the first publication of *Chordal's Letters*. His later account of the ensuing
conflict between the workers and himself is certainly the best-known
chronicle of workers' defiance of a nineteenth-century boss. "As was usual
then," Taylor wrote in 1911, "the shop was really run by the workmen,
and not by the bosses." Workers "carefully planned just how fast each
job should be done," and when Taylor transferred workers from job to
job, fired "stubborn men" or lowered their wages, cut piece rates, and

36. *Chordal,* 69.　　37. Ibid., 67.　　38. Ibid., 234.

introduced "green men" with promises of future rewards for obeying his instructions, the lathe hands replied by bringing "such pressure to bear (both inside and outside the works) upon all those who started to increase their output that they were finally compelled to do about as the rest did, or else quit."[39]

Taylor later claimed that at the end of three years he had emerged triumphant: He had doubled output on the lathes, rooted out troublemakers, assigned all workers to the special tasks they did best, and even invented and introduced his infamous differential piece-rate system. It is noteworthy, however, that Taylor believed that he was able to prevail only because, although he was a trained machinist, he was *not* from the working class. His bourgeois origins provided him two decisive advantages during the struggle. First, whenever higher officials of the company heard a dispute between Taylor and his workers, they believed and sided with Taylor. Second, Taylor could retire at night to the security of a fine home far from industrial neighborhoods. Had he been an ordinary foreman or contractor, Taylor realized, he and his family would have been subject to irresistible pressures from their neighbors, as well as from his workmates. The patterns of resistance his efforts had encountered were evidence not simply of deviance, underprivilege, or cliques, but of class.

Charles Stelzle knew this because he had been raised (and still lived) in a New York tenement district and had run with street gangs when he began his apprenticeship at the huge Hoe Printing Press Company in 1885. The eager youth found his employers' shop culture most alluring, however, and vowed that "some day I would be boss of that shop." He studied hard, eagerly sought new challenges, and tried to complete assigned tasks in record time. Told to cut keyways on a new shaft, he more than compensated for his inexperience with exuberance, even standing on the moving table of the planer, and completed in only five hours a job the foreman had estimated at twelve hours. Stelzle not only earned the full six-dollar piece price for only five hours of work but also was assured that some day the foremanship would be his. The older machinists, however, cursed him angrily and warned the naive "cub" that the rate for the job would surely be cut when news of his accomplishment reached the office. And so it was: When the next such shaft appeared in the shop, the pay for cutting its keyways had been slashed from six dollars to four.[40]

Stelzle also discovered that one older journeyman in his department was universally despised by the others. This "big Yankee" was definitely

39. Taylor, *Principles*, 48–50. For a slightly different version of the story by Taylor, see U.S. CIR, I, 782.
40. Stelzle, *Son of the Bowery*, 42–3.

a Good Workman. He consistently took the bosses' side in disputes, ground his tools before starting time, turned out gas jets carelessly left burning by other men, and once even engaged the drive belt of his lathe the instant the main engine was fired up and the overhead shafts began to turn, "amid howls of derision from all over the shop." In May 1886, when more than 900 of Hoe's workers joined a city-wide strike for shorter hours, the Yankee reported to work. When he sauntered out at noontime for his regular can of beer, he was viciously beaten by his mates.[41]

From ethical code to craft union

The work culture taught to Stelzle by the older machinists at the Hoe works had much in common with the entrepreneurial shop culture of the times. Machinists celebrated the self-direction of the "practical mechanic," just as Chordal had. They defended their own notoriously migratory propensities as necessary for their self-education and for their economic security. Although machinists of the 1880s suffered less seasonal unemployment than many other craftsmen, and often expressed a preference for working in large enterprises over smaller ones, because of the relatively steady employment offered by big firms, all machinists knew that the best security for their families' incomes was the knowledge and experience that made them attractive to employers. The able man had little fear of losing a job, except in depressed times, because he could always get another. Among railway repair-shop machinists, transient "boomers" were legendary, and resident machinists were expected to stake a newcomer in search of work to a few meals and lodging for a night or so, as well as to provide introductions to foremen and information about local wage scales. As late as 1907, not a single machinist in Edgemont, South Dakota, had been there more than five months, and on one occasion eight boomers hit town on a single day. "Every gaffer of Old Paduke but one has been a traveller," wrote a union correspondent from "old [lodge] 123, gray, but strong in the workers' cause," down in Kentucky:

> Boomers come the firstest
> And skeeters bite the worstest
> in Paducah.[42]

41. Ibid., 44–5.
42. J.D.P. to *MMJ*, 19 (July 1907), 691–2; John Geiger to *MMJ*, 18 (November 1906), 1044–5. On the preference of machinists for large enterprises, see Mass. BSL (1870), 338–9, and on seasonal unemployment, see Lauck and Sydenstricker, *Conditions of Labor*, 96; U.S. Commissioner of Labor, *Report* (1889), 144. For an account of the similar link between skill and

If Chordal had been scornful of academic training and posted regulations, journeymen held them in undisguised contempt. "To most machinists," wrote a worker from the Enterprise Manufacturing Company in Philadelphia, "the variety and extent of the notices, rules, regulations, warnings, etc., that decorate both the interior and exterior of this building would be irritating, but they are really more amusing than anything else."[43]

As for the "lightning machinist," he was regarded as incompetent and a menace to the welfare of the other workers. The cliques Chordal feared as the worst of evils within the shop had developed first and foremost to combat this character, whom Chordal had also held in contempt. That paradox, in turn, reveals that for all its similarities to entrepreneurial shop culture, the work culture of the machinists was collective in its basic orientation, not individualistic. John Morrison, a nineteen-year-old New York machinist, testified in 1883 that he and his mates had "lost all desire to become bosses now," both because "they earn so small wages" that "it takes all they earn to live" and because "it takes so much capital to become a boss that they cannot think of it."[44] Some might still become foremen or inside contractors, to be sure. Walter Wyckoff noted, however, that when a resident of his Chicago boardinghouse was promoted to tool-room supervisor, the other boarders congratulated the man warmly on his success, but thereafter ceased to regard him as one of them.[45]

Moreover, if employers thought of the pace of work in terms of the quantity and quality of their factories' output, workers thought of it in terms of their own health and longevity. Every worker knew from experience the truth of Josephine Goldmark's observation: "Fatigue is the borderland of illness." Moreover, all knew that after the average man passed his mid-thirties, the amount of working time he lost to sickness and injuries rose sharply.[46] Employers could always find new workers, but each worker had only one body and one life. No one could afford to let youthful exuberance set the pace at work.

Finally, at least during the second half of the nineteenth century, machinists often exhibited an awareness that the machine-building enter-

mobility in Russia, see S. I. Kanatchikov, "From the Story of My Life," in Victoria E. Bonnell, ed., *The Russian Worker: Life and Labor under the Tsarist Regime* (Berkeley, 1983), 36–71.

43. "H." to *MMJ*, 14 (June 1902).
44. Senate, *Labor and Capital*, I, 759. For similar arguments from two Massachusetts machinists, see Mass. BSL (1871), 589, 591.
45. Wyckoff, *West*, 161–2.
46. Goldmark, *Fatigue*, 111 (where the expression is attributed to Zaccaria Treves); Modell, "Changing Risks."

prise was an arena of exploitation. In saloon and street-corner conversations, union meetings, pamphlets, and newspapers they explained to each other that their long hours of toil produced far more revenue than they received in wages. As the terms of "Yankee contractors'" agreements made crystal clear, the value added to raw materials by the workers also paid for the firms' buildings and machinery, the salaries of clerks, foremen, and contractors, and the often munificent stipends of the proprietors as well. For some machinists, like John Morrison, only converting all means of production into "the public property of the people" could deliver to workers the "full value of their labor." Many more of them endorsed at least the earliest demand of machinists' unions: the eight-hour day. The influential self-educated machinist-intellectual Ira Steward described the connection between exploitation and the eight-hour demand in 1868:

> The Wages we receive, under the present system, are not a just equivalent for our Labor; and they will not be for what the Products of our Labor in the Eight Hour system will sell for, after allowing a liberal margin for every legitimate expense. . . . The Eight Hour system *may* gradually reduce the profits or the "Wages" of the employers; but are not *our* Wages or "profits" reduced, now and then, when we work by the job or piece? From time to time Employers decide that *we* are making too much money. We have decided that THEY are making too much money! *They* cut down OUR Prices!
> We *shall cut down* THEIR *Hours!*[47]

From the founding of the Machinists' and Blacksmiths' International Union (MBIU) in 1859 to May 1, 1916, when the IAM called six hundred strikes around the country, agitation for the eight-hour day was a consistent and basic theme of all organized efforts of machinists. The Philadelphia machinist Jonathan Fincher had set the tone with the slogan "EIGHT HOURS, A Legal Day's Work for Freemen" that was emblazoned across the masthead of his weekly newspaper. The prominence of machinists among working-class intellectuals, in the Eight-Hour Leagues and Industrial Congresses of the 1870s, in the Knights of Labor, and in the Socialist Labor Party also gave evidence of their awareness that this struggle could not be won by their trade alone. More than one-third of the delegates to the 1874 Industrial Congress in Rochester were machinists, as were eighty-six delegates to the Knights' Richmond General Assembly of 1886.[48]

---

47. Senate, *Labor and Capital*, I, 762; Ira Steward, *The Meaning of the Eight Hour Movement* (Boston, 1868), 6–8.
48. On the Industrial Congress, see *Workingman's Advocate*, April 25, 1874. For O'Connell's recollections of the Richmond General Assembly, see IAM, *14th Convention*, 159. For social-reform arguments couched in terms of

Equally consistent, however, was the insistence of machinists' spokesmen that solid unionization of their trade, and of the working class in general, would institute an age of harmony between labor and capital. As President Isaac Cassin of the MBIU had said in 1860, a "complete affiliation of every interest, and every class of labor into one common cause" would "supersede all strikes, and install an 'Age of Reason' among operators and operatives."[49] As active citizens and articulate propagandists, machinists' leaders hoped to reduce working hours by legislation and by winning over public opinion. In May 1886, Knights' assemblies of machinists in Chicago, Cincinnati, Milwaukee, Boston, and elsewhere joined parades and strikes for the eight-hour day, but they consistently refused to march behind red banners or armed contingents of workers, and later they gave overwhelming support to General Master Workman Powderly's denunciations of the Haymarket anarchists. The hundreds of machinists who erected sawmills and other heavy machinery at the E. P. Allis works in Milwaukee reached a peaceful agreement with the owner to reduce both hours and wages; and later they defended the factory, "armed with hammers, clubs, and three lines of fire hose," against strikers who were closing other plants in the vicinity. Similarly, in Cincinnati's largest machine-building enterprise, the J. A. Fay Company, processions of other workers headed by banners and drummers had to invade the workplace and drive the machinists out.[50]

Not all machinists shared this vision of organized harmony. Prominent members of the Socialist Labor Party worked at the trade – among them,

machinists' experience, see Terence V. Powderly, "Organization of Labor," *North American Review*, 137 (August 1882), 118–26.

49. *Proceedings of the National Union of Machinists and Blacksmiths of the United States of America, Held in Baltimore, Md., Nov., 1860* (Philadelphia, 1861), 11. The theme of organization and harmony also appeared in machinists' testimony, Mass. BSL (1871), 588–92, and in the MBIU's constitution. John H. Randall, *The Problem of Group Responsibility to Society: An Interpretation of the History of American Labor* (New York, 1922), 118.

50. Ross, "Workers on the Edge," 284, 426, 482–517; George Schilling, "History of the Labor Movement in Chicago," in Lucy E. Parsons, *Life of Albert R. Parsons, with a Brief History of the Labor Movement in America* (Chicago, 1889), xiv–xxviii; Wisconsin Bureau of Labor Statistics, *Second Biennial Report, 1885–1886* (Madison, 1886), 314–50 (hereafter cited as Wisc. BLS); Fink, *Workingmen's Democracy*, 190–3. Not all machinists shared this outlook. Compare Joseph R. Buchanan, *Story of a Labor Agitator* (New York, 1903). But note the similar conduct of German machine builders in 1849: P. H. Noyes, *Organization and Revolution: Working-Class Associations in the German Revolutions of 1848–1849* (Princeton, 1966), 273.

Louis Waldinger, Thomas J. Morgan, John Morrison, J. Edward Hall, and Matthew Maguire. All of them coupled their commitment to trade organization with a firm belief that only political struggle to collectivize the means of production could produce a genuine "Age of Reason." Others, virtually all German immigrants, had openly affiliated with the anarcho-communists (or social revolutionaries) whose banners and armed contingents so frightened their English-speaking colleagues. The Metal Workers' Union, which was represented in the anarchist-led Central Labor Union of Chicago, was among the city's largest unions in the spring of 1886. Although most of its members toiled in small workshops, many had found employment at Pullman, McCormick, and other large plants. The metal workers opened their ranks to all workers of all occupations in these firms, and there is no evidence available to indicate how many of their 1,815 members were machinists.[51] Their legacy is evident in the many resolutions submitted to the IAM early in the twentieth century from machinists' lodges in Chicago, Cleveland, Cincinnati, and elsewhere, which bore names like "Freiheit Lodge" or "Einheit Lodge," calling for the federation of metal-trades organizations into a single all-grades union.

More important, the metal workers shared the anarchist belief that pursuit of workers' control under capitalism was futile. Workers who had "massed their forces in labor organizations, principally the Knights of Labor and trades unions," wrote Albert Parsons, "have built their house upon a foundation of sand, which the wind, rain, and storm of poverty now descending upon it will wash away."[52] The call of the Federation of Organized Trades and Labor Unions for "all labor organizations to so direct their laws that eight hours should constitute a legal day's work on and after May 1, 1886"[53] was greeted with contempt by Chicago's anarchists. August Spies mocked those who believed that "if the workmen are organized they will gain the eight hours in their Sunday clothes."[54] Only when he and his comrades became aware of the breadth

---

51. Paul Avrich, *The Haymarket Tragedy* (Princeton, 1984), 89–90; Hartmut Keil and Heinz Ickstadt, "Elemente einer deutschen Arbeiterkultur in Chicago zwischen 1880 und 1890," *Geschichte und Gesellschaft*, 5 (1979), Heft 1, 111–12; Bruce C. Nelson, "We Can't Get Them to Do Aggressive Work: Chicago's Anarchists and the Eight-Hour Movement," *International Labor and Working-Class History*, 29 (Spring 1986), 1–13.

52. Parsons, *Albert R. Parsons*, 45.

53. W. H. Foster, "To the Officers and Members of All Trade and Labor Unions," in Wisc. BLS (1885–6), 315–16.

54. Editorial, *Arbeiter-Zeitung*, May 4, 1886, translated in *American State Trials*, edited by John D. Lawson (St. Louis, 1919), XII, 95.

of popular enthusiasm for the eight-hour—day struggle did they join the cause, escalating its demand to universal adoption of eight hours, with no reduction of pay, and mobilizing demonstrations to rival those of Chicago's Trades and Labor Assembly. Their vision of the "complete affiliation of . . . every class of labor into one common cause" anticipated not an end to strikes, as desired by Isaac Cassin, but a general strike and armed confrontation of classes. The anarchists' gatherings were larger than those of the Trades and Labor Assembly, and they were decked out in revolutionary regalia and boastfully steered "clear of politics and politicians."[55]

In short, machinists involved in the eight-hour—day struggle of 1886 either had negotiated cautiously with their employers or had been swept into the vortex of the battle in the streets. Either way, they had demonstrated the relative uncertainty and ineffectiveness of their efforts to translate their work culture into organized power. The contrast with the cigar makers is instructive. This highly organized trade, a stronghold of socialist sentiments, especially among its German-speaking majority, had been the most successful of all trades in securing the eight-hour day. The union had simply instructed all members to leave the shops after eight hours, and thereafter had fined any member caught working late. But the work culture in quality cigar shops, as Patricia Cooper has shown, easily dominated the life of those shops. All cigar makers did the same work and adhered to the same ethical code.[56] The metalworking establishment was very different. There were "at least a dozen grades of 'society' among the men" in the Hoe Printing Press works, Charles Stelzle recalled. No mechanic would dream of allowing laborers to "eat their sandwiches and drink their beer in the same corner in which they ate. The draftsmen considered themselves much superior to the pattern-makers, the pattern-makers thought they were better than machinists, the machinists looked down upon the tin-smiths, and so it went on."[57] Consider the contrast between the work of machinists and boilermakers in the same locomotive or shipbuilding works. Each machinist shaped his assigned parts at the lathe, bench, shaper, or drill press. Boilermakers toiled in teams, amid deafening noise, covered with sweat and often with filth. An observer described the construction of a boiler in 1851:

> Some men stand inside, holding heavy sledges against the heads of
> the rivets, while others on the outside, with other sledges, beat down

55. Nelson, "Chicago's Anarchists," 1–6. The quotation is from Avrich, *Haymarket*, 93.
56. Algie M. Simons, "A Label and Lives – The Story of Cigar Makers," *Pearson's Magazine*, 37 (January 1917), 69; Cooper, "Hand Craft to Mass Production."
57. Stelzle, *Son of the Bowery*, 44.

the part of the iron which protrudes, so as to form another head to each rivet, on the outside. . . . One man holds up against the under side of the plate a support for the rivet, while two men with hammers form a head above – striking alternatively upon the iron which protrudes.[58]

Consequently, when the president of the MBIU proposed to strengthen the organization in 1874 by admitting boilermakers, an angry broadside from the Buffalo lodge replied, "The admission of Boiler makers would not be advancing in that social and intellectual scale that is desirable." Terence V. Powderly, then a young officer of the union who favored the defeated proposal, responded in verse:

> Aristocrats of labor, we
> Are up on airs and graces.
> We wear clean collars, cuffs, and shirts,
> Likewise we wash our faces.
>
> There's no one quite so good as we
> In all the ranks of labor.
> The boilermaker we despise,
> Although he is our neighbor.[59]

Two goals, "complete affiliation of every . . . class of labor into one common cause" and the craft's advancement in "social and intellectual scale," coexisted uneasily in machinists' unions. At times they were embodied in rival organizations, but more frequently they generated controversy within machinists' unions. Both the Knights of Labor in the 1880s and the American Railway Union in the 1890s enrolled thousands of machinists under their universalistic banners. Early in the twentieth century, the United Metal Workers' International Union and the Industrial Workers of the World similarly attracted many machinists. Conversely, the MBIU, which survived in some places into the 1890s, and the new IAM initially emphasized status. "We ought to preserve our dignity," argued John J. Walsh of Washington in opposition to a proposal to admit operatives to the IAM. There were even disputes about whether every journeyman machinist was eligible. Although a Chicago lodge had Bohemian officers and proposed that union constitutions be printed in Polish, Bohemian, and other languages, an Italian who joined a Brooklyn lodge encountered, wrote one observer, "such a stubborn fight . . . against

58. Jacob Abbott, "The Novelty Works," *Harper's New Monthly Magazine*, 2 (May 1851), 726–7. Courtesy of Iver Bernstein.
59. Machinists' and Blacksmiths' International Union No. 5, printed brochure dated November 28, 1874 (Powderly Papers, microfilm reel 1); Terence V. Powderly, *The Path I Trod*, edited by Harry J. Carman, Henry David, and Paul N. Guthrie (New York, 1940), 41–2.

his application that it was barely voted through, and for no other reason than his nationality."[60]

Afro-Americans were rare in the trade. Nineteenth-century descriptions of black workers in machine shops usually portrayed them in one of two ways: as ingenious mechanics performing amazing repairs with hand tools in small rustic shops, or as helpers who assisted white machinists in preparing and setting up large, cumbersome, and often greasy work, usually in southern railroad repair shops. Southern railroad machinists tended to look on their lodges as citadels of white workingmen's respectability. Several aldermen, sheriffs, and even state legislators from such cities as Vicksburg, Savannah, and Shreveport were IAM members, and correspondence to the union journal from southern towns was drenched in racism.[61]

The self-image of fifty thousand shopmen in the Birmingham, Alabama, region who struck the Southern Railway Company for a nine-hour day and union recognition in 1901 was indelibly stamped on the pages of their paper, *Striking Machinist*. It boasted that they were descendants of "pioneer stock" and included in their ranks "many of the best foremen the company had." It thanked the Birmingham city council for its support and said that the strike showed the importance of those workers whose four-year apprenticeships had enabled them to master the art and science of metalwork. Their struggle, the paper concluded, would keep from America's shores the extremes of wealth and poverty that had brought ruin to Athens and Babylon.[62]

Small as the number of black machinists was, the issue of race was inseparably bound up with the origins of the IAM. The union had held its first-anniversary convention (1889) in the Georgia Senate chamber and declared itself explicitly for social harmony and against strikes. Over the next two years, however, it expanded rapidly in both the South and the Midwest, and at a convention in Pittsburgh, where the name International Association of Machinists was finally adopted, permitted its General Executive Board to authorize strikes, on the condition that 75

60. *MMJ*, 15 (July 1903), 588, 640; *MMJ*, 15 (April 1903), 295.
61. John Day to *MMJ*, 21 (March 1909), 258–9; *MMJ*, 18 (July 1906), 651; John Geigh to *MMJ*, 17 (September 1905), 839. Lorenzo Greene and Carter G. Woodson, *The Negro Wage Earner* (New York, 1930), Appendix Table 50, offered the following figures for numbers of black machinists (the calculations of percentages of total numbers of machinists are mine): 1890, 857 (0.5%); 1900, 1,263 (0.5%); 1910, 3,120 (0.7%); 1920, 10,570 (1.3%).
62. William Hall, in *Striking Machinist* (n.d.). I am indebted to Paul Worthman for bringing this journal to my attention.

percent of the local members involved voted in favor, a cumbersome procedure the union has retained to this day.[63]

Having decided to be a militant craft organization, rather than a southern fraternal lodge, the IAM's leaders were anxious to affiliate with the AFL, but the AFL refused to charter a union whose constitution excluded Afro-Americans. Its founding unions – those of carpenters, typographers, molders, miners, cigar makers, and iron and steel workers – had all formally admitted black workers by then, and its hopes to grow in the South required the support of southern dockers. Indeed, when the admission of the IAM was debated at the AFL's 1890 Detroit convention, a black bricklayer from Cleveland, James F. Moxley, was presiding. Seeking some formula to bring machinists into the AFL, Gompers encouraged fifteen independent local unions to form the International Machinists' Union (IMU) in 1891, with the expectation that it would soon merge with the IAM. The new union declared itself "based upon the principles which recognize the equality of all men working at our trade regardless of religion, race or color." Its leading figures, however, soon became anathema to Gompers on other grounds: Thomas J. Morgan of Chicago and August Waldinger of New York were members of the Socialist Labor Party. In 1893 they proposed to the AFL a political program based on independent political action for collective ownership of the means of production, which Gompers resisted fiercely. So bitter did the controversy over the AFL's political direction become that Gompers was voted out of the AFL's presidency for the year 1895, and he came to regard Morgan and the IMU as mortal foes.[64]

Two other developments also favored the IAM over its new rival. First, despite some serious strike defeats in 1892, the IAM grew much more rapidly than the IMU, and by 1893, when James O'Connell was elected its Grand Master Machinist, it had committed itself firmly to militant craft unionism and to seeking affiliation with the AFL. Its success in wooing thousands of Union Pacific shopmen away from the Knights of Labor in 1892 had been abruptly undone when they and entire lodges of other western railroad machinists had joined the new American Railway Union (ARU). With the destruction of the ARU as a result of the 1894 Pullman boycott, however, the IAM was the union best situated to pick up the pieces, and it seized the initiative that autumn by joining with six other unions (some of them AFL affiliates) to form the Federated Metal Trades.[65]

63. Perlman, *Machinists*, 3–9.
64. Foner, *Labor Movement*, II, 195; Laslett, *Labor and Left*, 144–9. On Moxley, see *Detroit Evening News*, December 11, 1890.
65. P. J. Conlon, "Past, Present and Future of Our Association," *MMJ*, 21 (February 1909), 164–6; *MMJ*, 9 (1897), 141.

Second, the tide of segregationist thinking and segregation laws was rising rapidly. Although prominent members of the IAM, such as D. Douglas Wilson, James O'Connell, Robert Ashe, and P. J. Conlon, tirelessly urged their union to drop its racial barriers and join the AFL on the AFL's terms, other metal-trades unions, such as the boilermakers and the blacksmiths, devised local regulations that kept out black workers, the four railroad brotherhoods had always banned them, and the ARU at its 1894 convention had narrowly but definitely voted to admit whites only to that new all-grades union of railway workers. Biracial unionism survived the 1890s primarily in industries like coal mining and longshore, where black workers were deeply entrenched and fought with some success to preserve their place within the workers' organizations. Even the Knights of Labor had abandoned its earlier defense of black workers. Its General Master Workman James Sovereign spoke publicly in 1894 in favor of deporting all Afro-Americans to Africa, to the horror of many veteran Knights. Consequently, the IAM's members rejected the appeals of their officers and voted in an 1894 referendum by 2,604 to 1,913 to retain the whites-only clause. Two arguments had carried the day for racial discrimination, and the appeal of both underscores the status consciousness prevalent among machinists even as they became more militant in the 1890s. One was that admission of black workers "would be a step toward social equality." The other was couched in terms more appropriate to the union's new economic battles. As one member from Philadelphia expressed it: "Not that [the black machinist] ain't as good a man as many whites, no, but it is not good for us, as he is a born competitor with us, and we will command still less pay than we are getting now."[66]

The compromise that brought the IAM into the AFL in 1895 represented a concession to equality in language only. The machinists' convention removed the exclusionary clause from the union's constitution, thus formally complying with the AFL's demand; but, with the AFL's tacit consent, the ritual of the IAM's lodges incorporated a pledge by each member that he would propose no one else for membership who was not Caucasian — and that ritual was retained until 1948. Soon after the AFL chartered the IAM, and after Gompers returned to the presidency, it resolved the problem of dual unionism it had created by unceremoniously revoking the charter of the IMU. The IAM had become the machinists'

---

66.   Foner and Lewis, *The Black Worker*, IV, 49–57; Nick Salvatore, *Eugene V. Debs: Citizen and Socialist* (Urbana, Ill., 1982), 227; Foner, *Organized Labor and the Black Worker*, 62–3. The quotations are from Foner and Lewis, *The Black Worker*, IV, 52, 53.

union of the AFL, and two years later O'Connell was elected one of the AFL's vice-presidents, symbolizing the decisive importance the union quickly assumed among the AFL's metal-trades workers.[67] For the trade-union movement, an important pattern had been set: Metal-trades unions were to be for whites only. In a more fundamental sense, however, the view of many machinists that preserving their trade's social status required the exclusion of black workers had been powerfully reinforced by the dominant intellectual and political currents of the age, and the counter-argument, based on class solidarity, had been swamped.

It was also evident that machinists envisaged their trade as appropriate only for males. The relationships of their unions with white women were more complex than those with black men; nevertheless, feminist and socialist voices outside as well as inside union ranks supported the efforts of wage-earning women to enlarge their role in the IAM.

Although thousands of women worked in machine-building establishments by the turn of the century, most of them were found where electrical appliances were mass-produced for consumer markets, and they were confined to such repetitive operations as making cores for the foundries, assembling light bulbs, wrapping cables, and winding coils. In the huge Westinghouse works in East Pittsburgh in 1907, for example, 650 of the ten thousand workers were women. Half of them worked in a single room where, wrote Elizabeth Beardsley Butler, at "one side men operate lathes and bor[ing mills]; on the other are girls, row back of row, ... working fast at winding coils by hand or machine, or at pasting mica at long tables at the far end." Many such women belonged to the Allied Metal Mechanics, a union of machine operatives with which the IAM merged in 1904, but the nature of their welcome was soon made clear by President O'Connell. More than a hundred former members of the Allied Metal Mechanics at the Starrett Tool Company in Athol, Massachusetts, refused to join the new union because of the increase in dues and the subordination to journeymen to which they would be subjected. The company forced the rebels back into the union's ranks because it wished to continue using the IAM's union label on its instruments, which were purchased largely by individual machinists. President O'Connell rushed to the scene and fined the dissidents, but he also declared, "The girls are exempt, as we do not want any more women in the machinists' union."[68]

67. Perlman, *Machinists*, 15–22; Laslett, *Labor and Left*, 147–8.
68. Butler, *Women and the Trades*, 216; MMJ, 17 (May 1905), 391–3; the quotation is on p. 392. Some metal-trades unions' constitutions excluded women from membership. Alice Henry, *Women and the Labor Movement* (New York, 1923), 100–1.

Not until 1911, the year the socialists captured the union's leadership, were women officially admitted to the IAM.

Alfred Kolb's description of Monday morning in a Chicago bicycle factory captured the male ambiance of the shop:

> A Monday morning in the factory. Brr! Many stand at their places, worn out, with rings under their eyes, and try to pull themselves together with their work, as well as it goes. The overseer looks in, hung-over; his voice is husky. There is more chatting than usual: about Sunday naturally. A new acquaintance, a pick-up tried without success, some overheard lovemaking, a couple of coarse jokes. Even the married men join in and in naive cynicism raise the curtains of their marriage beds.[69]

Many a male trade unionist considered such an atmosphere "morally corrupting" for women. Their fear of female sexuality was shared by the socialist Gregory Weinstein, who worked together with forty to fifty other unskilled young men and women at the Hoe Company in the early 1880s and found the women's manners "free and easy" – too much so for his taste: "Many of the words used by the girls I could not find in my lexicon at all, and some which I did find were too shocking for my modesty to repeat."[70]

In short, machinists usually regarded women in the workshops as interlopers who threatened both the status and the earnings of journeymen. The IAM's requirement of four years of apprenticeship to qualify for membership was itself enough to exclude practically all women, until the union voted to admit operatives ("handymen") to subordinate status in 1903, in conjunction with the pending merger with the Allied Metal Mechanics. Nevertheless, all machinists' organizations, and the IAM especially, consistently solicited the support of the members' wives and families for the labor-reform cause. The IAM pioneered in the promotion of women's auxiliaries, published a monthly page in its journal entitled "In Woman's World," and campaigned in favor of woman suffrage from the 1890s onward. One of its most famous members was Kate Richards O'Hare, who in fact had completed an apprenticeship in her father's machine shop. Her fame rested not on her talents at the lathe, which were seldom used, but on her ability as a socialist lecturer who was constantly in demand at machinists' meetings. O'Hare never challenged established

69. Kolb, *Als Arbeiter,* 139; my translation. An editorial in *Iron Age* commended "a large manufacturing plant" for banning all pictures, postcards, and calendars from its walls. "The men do not always make a proper choice of subjects," it said. *IA,* 91 (March 13, 1913), 670–1.

70. Gregory Weinstein, *Reminiscences of an Interesting Decade: The Ardent Eighties* (New York, 1928), 22–3.

gender roles, but she summoned machinists and their families alike to commit their skills and their organizations to a new vision of progress: the cooperative commonwealth.[71]

The battle for control of the machine shop

If industry and labor set out during the 1890s on new paths from which there was no turning back, the new departure seemed especially abrupt in the strike behavior of machinists. Before the 1890s, machinists rarely went on strike at all, and those who did were most often either railway repair-shop workers, as in the famous southwestern strikes of 1885–6, or machinists who joined in a general enthusiasm that had been initiated by other working people, as in the New York strike of 1872, the nation-wide revolt of 1877, and the eight-hour–day movement of 1886. The strike statistics published by the U.S. Commissioner of Labor in 1887 and 1896 classified strikers by occupation. Strikes by coal miners, building workers, clothing workers, ironworkers and steelworkers, printers, and others appeared frequently in these data, but not strikes by machinists. Work stoppages that closed metal-fabricating establishments were regularly attributed to molders, and less often to boilermakers and black-smiths. In the Pittsburgh region, for example, strikes by iron puddlers, heaters, and rollers were frequent, but except in 1877, the mills' machine shops customarily continued to operate after the Amalgamated Association of Iron and Steel Workers had marched out. Of the fifty strikes in the city's metal industry (excluding iron and steel smelting and rolling) in 1886, not one was credited to machinists.[72]

Large manufactories of railway cars in Detroit, Pullman, Paterson, and elsewhere were struck often in the 1880s, but most of their employees were woodworkers. In those plants, as in San Francisco shipyards, Connecticut hardware factories, and midwestern agricultural-implement works, where important strikes took place before 1894, machinists may have left their posts along with the others, but there is no hint that they initiated the action. A veteran of Detroit's long-lived MBIU affiliate observed

71. *MMJ* (1897–8), passim. I am indebted to Neil Basen for the information on O'Hare.
72. U.S. Department of the Interior, *Report of the Secretary of the Interior* (50th Cong., 1st Sess., House Executive Document No. 1, Part 5, Washington, D.C., 1887); U.S. Commissioner of Labor, *Tenth Annual Report . . . 1894. Strikes and Lockouts* (2 vols., 54th Cong., 1st Sess., House Document No. 339, Washington, D.C., 1896); B. F. Jones diaries, June 3, 6, 10, 1878.

in 1902 that in "the thirty years of the [union's] existence . . . there was no serious effort made to permanently advance the interests of the machinists, such as shorter work day, card shops, rates of wages, etc."[73] This minor role in nineteenth-century strikes stands in stark contrast to machinists' prominence in strikes after 1899, and especially between 1916 and 1922, when they were consistently among the three occupational groups initiating the largest numbers of strikes. During 1918 and 1919 they led the U.S. Labor Department's list (even ahead of coal miners).[74]

Before the 1890s, the work culture of machinists had encouraged the development of a species of working-class intellectuals whose writings and oratory contributed to the general labor-reform cause and a demanding ethical code governing individual behavior on the job that was enforced by a variety of informal sanctions. Three of these sanctions had appeared in Taylor's account of his troubles at Midvale Steel: social pressures against the deviant (both on and off the job), systematic deception of the boss (e.g., claiming a machine tool had broken down because the foreman had insisted on speeds or cuts that exceeded the machine's capacity), and simple sabotage (e.g., seeing to it that the machine was overloaded). One wonders how many of the "grand blunders" Chordal observed were not accidental.

The moral imperative of a "manly bearing" appeared as often in the discourse of machinists as in that of iron rollers, mule spinners, and other craftsmen. The workers' code celebrated individual self-assertion, but for the collective good, rather than for self-advancement. For example, in stark contrast to Chordal's advice to keep one's wages a secret, the MBIU called on all its members to make their earnings public knowledge. Decades before machinists' unions began to establish "standard rates" through trade agreements, the MBIU detailed its members' work records on union traveling cards, including the wages they had last received and the highest and lowest wages paid in their last places of work. As machinists moved about, therefore, they carried with them information about their own pay rates and those of others. Later, railway lodges of the Knights of Labor demanded that companies publicly post at least the minimum wages to be paid to each craft.[75]

Similarly, the individual was expected to refuse to obey objectionable orders from bosses, even if he had to quit. An employer testified around 1900 that on discovering that each cut taken by "machinist A.B." on a

73. "An Old Subscriber" to *MMJ*, 14 (October 1902), 692.
74. Edwards, *Strikes; Monthly Labor Review*, 14 (May 1922), 181–9.
75. E. J. O'Boyle's MBIU traveling card, dated April 9, 1877, in Powderly Papers, reel 1; *Oliver Ames vs. Union Pacific*, 354–62 and passim.

boring mill took some ten minutes, he had moved a small drill press close to the boring mill and ordered A.B. to drill oil holes in his spare time. "A.B. objected saying that it was two men's work, [reported the employer,] and he quit rather than obey the foreman's orders," claiming "he was carrying out union principles." Although A.B.'s certainty that his skills would soon earn him another job helps to explain his conduct, the fact that the employer quickly and happily replaced him with a less expensive apprentice, who ran both machines, shows the limitations of such "manly" action.[76]

The individual who earned praise from his fellow machinists was "conservative" (i.e., not prone to thoughtless actions), highly competent at his trade, scrupulously observant of the craftsmen's ethical code, and fully prepared, if need be, to sacrifice his personal interests to the common good. By the turn of the century, these virtues had been blended with devotion to the union, as a eulogy to the IAM's Chicago leader Russell Quinn illustrates. "Conservative and prudent, [Quinn] advised against rash or hasty action, and not until every means to effect a settlement had been exhausted did he give his approval for a strike," wrote the secretary of his lodge. "Once into the fight he was in to win." Quinn had been active without respite on picket lines and at meetings during the big strike of 1900, but after the union's victory, the Link Belt Company refused to reinstate him, and he had "nobly sacrificed himself in order that men with families to support might return to work." His skill swiftly earned him employment at Allis-Chalmers, in time for him to lead a thirteen-month strike there. Again, the firm settled the strike on the condition Quinn leave. He went to American Can, "where he soon gained the respect of the firm and the admiration of his shop-mates." On a trip back from his native Canada, however, Quinn's train crashed, and he met his death at age thirty-one while tending to the needs of his fellow victims.[77]

As Quinn had come to realize, individual "manliness" without organized solidarity was quixotic. To be sure, the deliberate, collective action that Quinn had infused by word and deed into the traditional code could also meet defeat. During the depression of 1908, this was learned by 117 machinists in the Louisville and Nashville shops, who all left rather than turn in their union books in return for a raise in pay, only to see unemployed men rush to take the vacant posts. More fortunate was the worker at the Morgan Engineering Works in Alliance, Ohio, who was fired for

76. U.S. Commissioner of Labor, *Eleventh Special Report*, 226–7.
77. "Vale! Russell Quinn," *MMJ*, 15 (March 1903), 217–19. See also R. Quinn to *MMJ*, 14 (January 1902), 28–30.

refusing to run two machines at once, and whose lodgemates all walked out with him. When the company responded by discharging all the lodge's officers and hiring many strikebreakers, trainloads of sympathizers came from nearby cities to picket the plant. One evening a grand torchlight parade led to a rally at the Alliance Opera House that was addressed by IAM leader P. J. Conlon, by a local state senator, and by socialist editor Max Hayes. After two months the company capitulated and reinstated all strikers, while festive meetings of workers throughout the Cuyahoga Valley celebrated the triumph of the craftsmen's code.[78]

The transition from informal social sanctions to highly organized collective struggle had been caused by the rapid transformation of the machinists' working environment during the last two decades of the nineteenth century. Large enterprises had become the employers of most men in the trade, and the number of machinists counted by the census had increased by 180 percent, from 101,130 in 1880 to 283,145 in 1900, on the way to 461,344 in 1910. More important than the trade's growing size was the increasing production by large machine-building firms of standardized products and the use of many standardized parts in their custom-designed machines. Engineering societies promoted nationwide uniformity in screw and pulley sizes, cutting-tool dimensions and shapes, and railroad gauges. Sewing machines, rifles and pistols, clocks and watches, and agricultural machinery were mass-produced by the mid-1880s, and even though printing presses, rolling mills, elevators, machine tools, and ships were still made to customers' specifications, many of their components were machined in large prefabricated batches.

Standardized components and products, in turn, encouraged not only inside contracting but also work specialization, piecework payment, and demands that a worker operate two machines at once. Although "accuracy" in production still depended, as C. T. Porter had observed, "entirely on the skill of the workman," that worker was increasingly often assigned to apply his skills to a single lathe or milling machine, or simply to filing and fitting components on the erection floor. As production runs became longer, employers were tempted to convert his wages to piecework. Conversely, "piece work develops specialists," as an Omaha strike committee argued. "One man learns to do a particular piece of work . . . and can do it rapidly, but he can do nothing else."[79] Workers with lim-

78. H. M. Eskridge to *MMJ*, 20 (January 1908), 544–5; *MMJ*, 20 (November 1908), 995; *MMJ*, 21 (January 1909), 42–3; *MMJ*, 15 (July 1903), 607–16, 656–7; *MMJ*, 15 (August 1903), 727.
79. "Press Committee" to *MMJ*, 15 (May 1903), 354.

ited knowledge and experience also willingly accepted jobs at less than the journeyman's scale. Moreover, it was when workers remained at one machine, rather than moving about from bench to machine and back, the way they had once machined and fitted pulleys, for example, that overseers could easily see machine running time during which a second task might be assigned. The fight against this cluster of innovations provided the main stimulus for creation of a militant craft union.

Many entrepreneurs, steeped in their own shop culture, also objected to these developments. Chordal explicitly associated piecework with shoddy production, arguing that any attempt to lower production costs by putting men on a "piece-work price, which drew the sweat," would only make "the best men" quit, drive "the married men . . . down to corn bread, and the single men . . . to cheap, low boarding houses," and raise the threat of riot and arson, without providing the employer any meaningful reduction in costs. Only the wise supervision of a "Yankee contractor" could accomplish lower costs, he had taught.[80] As late as 1904, the U.S. Commissioner of Labor reported that "no manufacturer of machine tools in the United States . . . has successfully experimented with the piecework system of payment," because to do so "would destroy the reputation of the establishment." The same report quoted an aged employer, who had no union in his shop but had risen through the ranks, as saying: "If I had a man in my shop who would run two or more machines, . . . I should doubt very much whether he [had] ever learned the machinist's trade."[81]

Nevertheless, the chronic decline of selling prices from the early 1870s to the late 1890s spurred employers to take advantage of every opportunity made available to them by standardized parts, long production runs, and large work forces. Even the ASME, the forum of entrepreneurial shop culture, became by the late 1880s an incubator of piecework and premium-payment schemes, each advertised by its creator as a sure cure for workers' slothful behavior. The turning point came in 1886, when Henry R. Towne, senior executive of the Yale and Towne Lock Company, made his inaugural address as president of the ASME. He issued a call for papers dealing with the "questions of organization, responsibility, reports, systems of contract and piece work, and all that relates to the executive management of works."[82] The members' re-

---

80. *Chordal,* 27–8.
81. U.S. Commissioner of Labor, *Eleventh Special Report,* 108, 114.
82. Towne, "The Engineer as Economist," quoted in Chandler, *Visible Hand,* 272.

sponse was a flood of papers concerning incentive pay, the most famous of which during the next ten years were those of Frederick W. Taylor and Frederick A. Halsey.[83]

All these plans used the prevailing machinists' daily wage as their point of departure, just as straight piecework for operatives in other industries did.[84] As had long been evident to their more militant brethren the iron molders, and as became clear to machinists during the 1880s, piece rates were not commensurate with the value of the product but were simply a form of payment for labor time that induced the worker to maximize his output during that time. The general result of piecework was to raise some workers' wages above the average, while lowering the average. It was, wrote machinists' editor Wilson in 1897, a "vile, insidious disease" that "encourages greed, is immoral in its tendencies, and does more to create discord and make a perfect hell out of our craft, than all of the evils that escaped from Pandora's box."[85]

The first wave of confrontations over these managerial innovations came on the railroads, which were the largest employers in the land and familiar terrain to machinists' unions. Although major railroads had elaborate managerial hierarchies and payrolls that could dwarf those of even the largest manufacturing firms, their repair depots were ordinarily divided into boiler shops, machine shops, blacksmith shops, and so forth, each of which was the undisputed domain of a particular craft. Because repair work confronted craftsmen with a variety of problems, and the speed of its completion was influenced more by their skill than by the pace of their work, railroad machinists tended to be paid better than those in factories, and their early unions had seldom been aggressive.

The strikes by shopmen in Moberly and Sedalia, Missouri, against the lines of Jay Gould's southwest system early in 1885 had pitched their machinists into a new type of confrontation with the companies. The strikes themselves had been protests against wage cuts, and strong community support had helped the strikers win quick victories. In their wake, thousands of western shopmen had enrolled in the Knights of Labor.

83. For analyses of various widely used incentive plans, see Paul H. Douglas, C. N. Hitchcock, and W. E. Atkins, *The Worker in Economic Society* (Chicago, 1923), 777–9; Van Dusen Kennedy, *Union Policy and Incentive Wage Methods* (New York, 1945); Robert F. Hoxie, *Scientific Management and Labor* (New York, 1920), 75–9. Differential piece rates were used in French machine shops as early as the 1860s. See Poulot, *Le sublime,* 79–80.

84. See "Piecework," Chapter 3.

85. Editorial, *MMJ,* 9 (May 1897), 139. For an insightful analysis of piecework, see "Strike of Rank and File, Not Agitators," *MMJ,* 15 (May 1903), 352–5.

They supported rallies, press campaigns, and boycotts that brought men and women, black and white workers of many occupations into the railroad towns' various local assemblies, to the increasing anxiety of the local elites. The Knights' gospel of "universal brotherhood" assumed an especially militant aspect when District Assembly 101 was formed, demanded recognition from the southwest lines as agent for all railwaymen, and presented wage demands for yard and section hands. The ensuing strike dragged on from March into May 1886 before it was crushed by the combined weight of Gould's determination, the vigilantism of local Law and Order Leagues, some 600 arrests, and Powderly's timidity.[86]

During the next six years the Knights succumbed to employers' attacks on all western lines but the Union Pacific. As P. J. Conlon recalled, "there was no such thing as a shop committee and the master mechanic as general rule was a czar and monarch of all he surveyed."[87] So-called apprentices and semiskilled specialists were hired in droves, piecework was introduced despite the extreme variations in conditions under which repair work was performed, and foremen's demands for bribes and gifts in return for jobs became widespread. As the intense competition among overbuilt railroads was made still more bitter by steadily declining markets for western grain, cattle, and ores in the 1890s, new rounds of general wage cuts were announced. In response, shopmen struck with increasing frequency, trying to regulate the conditions of their employment, as well as their pay. But the revenge of the railroads was draconic. According to the U.S. Commissioner of Labor's estimates, 60 percent of the shopmen who struck in 1892 never regained their jobs, and in 1894, the year of the Pullman boycott, 75 percent of those who struck were fired.[88] These early struggles explain the prominence of railroad lodges and of veterans of the Knights and the ARU in the early IAM. They also reveal why those veterans exhibited considerable enthusiasm for nationalization of the railroads and for government arbitration of labor disputes, enthusiasm that was not shared by Robert Ashe and other early leaders from eastern factory-based lodges.[89]

It was not only railroad shopmen who faced specialization, piecework, two-machine operations, and arbitrary foremen during the 1890s. The

86. Ruth A. Allen, *The Great Southwest Strike* (Austin, Tex., 1942); Stromquist, "Boomers," 321–413; Michael J. Cassity, "Modernization and Social Crisis: The Knights of Labor and a Midwest Community, 1885–1886," *Journal of American History*, 66 (June 1979), 41–61.
87. *MMJ*, 21 (February 1909), 164.
88. Conlon, "Past," *MMJ*, 21 (February 1909), 164–6; Stromquist, "Boomers," 64–6.
89. Laslett, *Labor and Left*, 148–55.

impact of the depression goaded employers to experiment more widely with these practices while it undermined the workers' resistance. "Manly defiance" resulted only in hungry families. Moreover, for the rest of the decade, many employers put relentless pressure on their inside contractors for cheaper output – lowering contract rates as much as 5 percent each year, making their own cost analyses and limiting the percentage return allowed contractors over the resulting estimates, and abruptly dismissing contractors for disobedience, for padding payrolls with relatives, or for conspiring together to fix the bids they made to the companies. While machinists' unions were trying to eradicate inside contracting, employers themselves often discarded the system at the turn of the century, substituting piecework payment to each individual, group premiums, or the schemes proposed by Taylor and his colleagues.[90]

With the return of prosperity in 1897–98, the machinists struck back. Most commonly, as the U.S. Commissioner of Labor's 1904 report *Regulation and Restriction of Output* documented in detail, machinists simply stood their employers' way of fixing piece rates on its head. They would decide among themselves what was the standard day's earnings for the locality. They then agreed, first, to fight together against any piece rate that could not yield that day's wages for the average worker and, second, to prohibit anyone of their own number from earning more than a day's earnings acceptable to the group. If, for example, they had fixed a day's pay at $2.25, a worker might earn 50 cents more than that, about 25 percent customarily, with impunity. More than that would bring group punishment, often in the form of a fine. Machinists seldom duplicated the practice of metal polishers, who fined "hogs" all their extra earnings and assisted one another to complete the day's work, so that despite a bewildering proliferation of piece rates on different jobs, the highest and lowest daily earnings of polishers fell within pennies of each other. Nevertheless, machinists had turned their long-evident belief that every journeyman should earn the same daily wage into an effective device for placing a stint on output.[91]

This form of workers' control threw machine shops into a state of war. "They steal from us and we steal from them," said one machinist of his employers, "everybody taking every possible advantage in a hog-eat-hog

---

90. Buttrick, "Inside Contract"; U.S. Commissioner of Labor, *Eleventh Special Report*, 204; Elm Lodge to *MMJ*, 15 (August 1903), 731–2. See also the letters from the company executives to their inside contractors during the 1890s in the Sargent Co. Papers.

91. U.S. Commissioner of Labor, *Eleventh Special Report*, 114–231. The Amalgamated Society of Engineers did fine away its members' "excess earnings." *MMJ*, 9 (1897), 139–40.

game."[92] Employers fought back with dismissals of unruly machinists, and that, more than anything else, prompted the workers to join the rapidly growing IAM. More often than not, the stints had preceded the union into the factories during the post-depression years; but the IAM itself demanded of its new members pledges never to work two machines, never to accept employment below the local union's standard wage, not to work by the piece unless that was already the established practice at their place of employment, and, if it was, to struggle for its eradication. The union forced firms as large as Hoe Manufacturing to abandon inside contracting and made companies like Cincinnati's Simmons and Flemming sign agreements to pay machinists a minimum of $2.50 for a ten-hour day, to put none on piecework or on two machines, and to give preference in hiring to union members.[93]

Union power even reimposed the craftsmen's norms on the Union Pacific Railway. In July 1902, IAM officers on that line demanded an end to piecework. While tense negotiations were in progress, the master mechanic of a repair shop in Evanston, Wyoming, set a handyman to work running a large turret lathe. In protest, the shop committee called a halt to all work; its members were promptly fired by the master mechanic, and the IAM replied with a strike against all that railroad's shops. The strike dragged on for almost a year, until the union escalated the action by threatening to strike the shops of two other lines that were also owned by the Harriman banking interests. The threat was effective: All strikers were reinstated by the Union Pacific, piecework was abolished, and a wage increase was granted. Among the many celebrations that followed the settlement was one in Brainerd, Minnesota, where a thousand people marched behind a twenty-piece band under a banner emblazoned "Victory." Along with the town's machinists marched boilermakers, blacksmiths, car men, sheet-metal tradesmen, railway clerks, helpers, teamsters, and plumbers. At the rear of the column came a cannon and caisson ridden by two Civil War veterans, a machinist and a boilermaker, between whom sat the young son of the IAM's vice-president and editor, D. Douglas Wilson. A banner over the gun read "We have fought to teach the young."[94]

By no means did all machinists take the union pledge. There were still many reports of young shipyard workers who had never served apprenticeships and were eager to learn a trade by replacing a journeyman who had quit in "manly indignation," of older hands at the Waltham Watch

92. U.S. Commissioner of Labor, *Eleventh Special Report*, 211.
93. *MMJ*, 10 (September 1898), 556–9; *MMJ*, 11 (October 1899), 577–9; *MMJ*, 10 (December 1898), 711.
94. *MMJ*, 14 (May 1902), 297–9; *MMJ*, 14 (July 1902), 454.

Company who had "life jobs and [were] not taking any chances," and of Good Workmen at Morse Twist Drill who were simply "too aristocratic" to organize. Nevertheless, the president of Western Electric in Chicago testified in 1900 that there simply were not enough nonunion machinists to meet industry's demand for craftsmen. "It is pretty hard to find out whether a union [man] is employed," another Chicago manufacturer added, "until you have a controversy with labor."[95]

Machinists were prominent in the wave of craftsmen's struggles for collective workplace power that characterized the prosperous years 1898 to 1903. Their victorious strike of 1900 in Chicago led to a national trade agreement between the IAM and the National Metal Trades Association that instituted a nine-hour day. Their union power on western railroads put them at the forefront of a revival of craft strength in the repair shops that was to last until the great defeat of 1922. Moreover, in many factories, operatives who had but recently arrived in the United State formed their own unions and demanded that they be recognized, as well as the craftsmen, in metalworking, just as they did in meat packing, textiles, and other industries.[96] The new power of unions had created an intolerable situation, wrote Charles B. Going, editor of *Engineering Magazine*. The IAM, in particular, he warned, not only had demanded shorter hours but also wanted employers to hire only union members. That meant, he explained,

> . . . those who work under union regulations in all things, including a limitation of the number of apprentices; prohibition of piece work; refusal to run more than one machine, to work with non-union men, or to give any instruction to a handy man; dictation of minimum wages, and even limitation of product and of speed of working.[97]

New markets lay open to American machinery builders. Corporate mergers had reduced competition and costs in sales and administration. Prices and profits had reversed their long downward trend and were rising steadily. But although the sizes of factories were increasing spectacularly, in the workshops themselves no economies of scale appeared, wages were increasing, workers were thwarting pay schemes designed to entice greater output from them, and they often imposed their own collective control. It was "not very long," wrote Taylor's colleague Henry Gantt,

95. Holden A. Evans, *One Man's Fight for a Better Navy* (New York, 1940), 184; William Cowgill report, *MMJ*, 9 (March 1897), 63–5; U.S. Industrial Commission, *Report*, VIII, 4, 299.

96. For example, David Montgomery, "Sargent Workers Rediscover 1902 Strike," *UE News*, November 14, 1983, pp. 4–5.

97. Charles B. Going, "Labour Questions in England and America," *Engineering Magazine*, 19 (May 1900), 161–76. On the 1900 strike, see Chapter 6.

"before we began to hear complaints of the increasing inefficiency of labor."[98]

No continuous-flow processes or mechanical remedies were available to rid the employers of their dependence on their craftsmen's skill and initiative. Small wonder they began to pay increasing attention to Taylor's proposals to end that dependence by systematic study and reorganization designed to expropriate the craftsman's skill itself. Their new interest removed scientific management from the realm of experiment and ASME professional papers to the realm of workplace practice – before long, standard American manufacturing practice. To make this transition, however, the entrepreneur-engineers of machine building had to eschew the last remnants of their own nineteenth-century shop culture, and those tattered fragments were commandeered by the enraged journeymen for their own rhetorical defense against the degradation of craft that Taylorism threatened. The defensive and even archaic character of the workers' rhetoric, in turn, disguised the glaring difference between their new organized militancy and their behavior in Chordal's day. Twentieth-century machinists only appeared to be defending tradition. But that appearance itself was incorporated into the arguments of the Taylorites: To them, trade unions were reactionary obstacles to efficiency and progress.

98. Henry L. Gantt, *Work, Wages, and Profits* (second edition, New York, 1919), 228.

5

White shirts and
superior intelligence

The revitalization of industrial capitalism at the end of the 1890s was international in scope, and the optimism and sense of achievement it unleashed in intellectual and political life were exuberant. The French economist Leon Dupriez calculated that the average annual change in physical output per capita for the advanced industrial countries as a group between 1895 and 1913 was double what it had been between 1880 and 1894. The United States, which had already emerged during the 1880s as the world's leading industrial producer, increased its output even more rapidly than its leading rivals, England, Germany, and France. Its factories grew to dwarf the largest works of the nineteenth century. Electrical- and farm-equipment companies, meat-packing firms, woolen and silk mills, and, above all, automobile producers overtook the older, railroad-related giants – steel mills and railroad locomotive and car companies – by employing fifteen thousand to twenty thousand workers in a single complex of factory buildings. Great as the infusion of workers was, however, the new epoch also benefited from dramatic increases in output per worker. Data from the U.S. Census of Manufactures indicate that whereas the number of wage earners in American manufacturing had risen 37 percent between 1899 and 1909, the value added per worker had grown by more than 40 percent.[1]

Much of the vast amount of capital at the disposal of business had been fed back into reinforced-concrete factory buildings and electrically powered machines. Huge cranes and hoists appeared in steel mills, at construction sites, and on docks to supplement and augment the power of laborers' muscles. A new generation of machine tools, many of them designed to cut several surfaces at once, led manufacturers to develop, in the words of *Iron Age*, "millions of dollars in specifications for new machinery," and in particular for "special and semi-special machinery, and the newest types of high-power, high-speed and standard tools." Al-

1. Gordon, Edwards, and Reich, *Segmented Work*, 103; Nelson, *Managers and Workers*, 9; *IA*, 89 (April 18, 1912), 1004.

though plans for such purchases were held in abeyance by the recession of 1908–9, those dull months witnessed a "vast amount of reorganization of shop equipment and methods," and with the return of prosperity, orders flooded the offices of machine-tool manufacturers – especially from automobile makers. In fact, the automobile industry paced the economy's growth. The sixty-five thousand cars produced in 1908, the year in which General Motors was organized and Ford's first Model T appeared, put American production far ahead of that of the world's former leader, France; within seven more years, car output had reached the million mark, and in 1920 no fewer than 2.2 million autos were to come out of American factories.[2]

During this growth period the automobile industry had completely abandoned the methods of production in which craftsmen had made the products while laborers fetched and carried. A 1923 analysis of the industry's production workers found 46.8 percent of them to be machine tenders and 17.6 percent assemblers. In other words, almost two-thirds of the total force (64.4 percent) consisted of operatives on highly specialized tasks, whereas only 9 percent were skilled tradesmen and another 9 percent laborers. According to census counts (which used somewhat different definitions), the number of operatives in the industry grew from 21,091 in 1910 to 121,164 in 1920, and the percentage of them who were women remained small (4 percent in 1910 and 10.6 percent in 1920). Although the numbers of skilled workers remained much larger in the other great growth industry, electrical equipment, there, too, the number of operatives was increasing rapidly: from 26,677 (45 percent women) in 1910 to 64,841 (42 percent women) in 1920.[3]

These figures from leading growth industries illustrate the transformation of work relations brought about during the early twentieth century. Skilled workers in large enterprises did not disappear, but most of them ceased to be production workers. Their tasks became ancillary – setup, troubleshooting, toolmaking, model making – while the actual production was increasingly carried out by specialized operatives. Moreover, no longer did American-born daughters of immigrants constitute the largest group of operatives, as they had in the nineteenth century.

2. "A Model Factory City," *Factory*, 5 (October 1910), 251–8; George M. Price, *The Modern Factory: Safety, Sanitation, and Welfare* (New York, 1914); Vatter, *U.S. Economy*, 139; *IA*, 89 (January 4, 1912), 89; *IA*, 89 (February 22, 1912), 502; Alfred D. Chandler, Jr., *Giant Enterprise: Ford, General Motors, and the Automobile Industry. Sources and Readings* (New York, 1964), 11; Patrick Fridenson, *Histoire des usines Renault: 1. Naissance de la grande enterprise, 1898/1939* (Paris, 1972), 26.
3. Chandler, *Giant Enterprise*, 185; U.S. Census, *Occ. Stat.*, 106–8, 124–6.

Although many thousands of the latter continued to perform specialized tasks, even greater numbers of men and women from capitalism's rural periphery were found not only on laboring gangs and in sweatshops, as before, but also operating machine tools and occupying stations on assembly lines. And the number of supervisory workers swelled accordingly. Between 1910 and 1920, the numbers of wage earners in manufacturing, mining, and transportation grew by 27.7 percent, but the numbers of supervisory employees grew by 66.3 percent.[4] "The breaking up of crafts under scientific management," as the engineer Miner Chipman wrote in 1913, "is also the breaking up of certain of our social formations."[5] Twenty years later, F. J. Roethlisberger and W. J. Dickson could elaborate on what had occurred. The production worker, they wrote, finds himself "at the bottom level of a highly stratified organization," his "established routines of work, his cultural traditions of craftsmanship, his personal interrelations" all "at the mercy of technical specialists."[6]

The role of the pioneers of scientific management was to explain, guide, and justify this transformation. Taylor and his colleagues Henry Gantt, Carl Barth, and Horace Hathaway had their roots in the ASME. Indeed, all of Taylor's famous papers – "A Piece Work System" (1895), "Shop Management" (1903), "On the Art of Cutting Metals" (1906) – were presented before the ASME, and only after its officers refused to publish his "Principles of Scientific Management" (1911), because it was a work of popularization that contained nothing new for engineers, did Taylor seek a publisher outside of that society. By that time, the movement had spread its influence far beyond the circles of metalworking entrepreneur-engineers. Frank and Lillian Gilbreth and Sanford Thompson had carried out time-study experiments in the construction industry. Morris L. Cooke and others had been personally trained by Taylor at the Tabor Manufacturing Company and at his estate in Boxley. By 1911 these men had formed their own Society to Promote the Science of Management (renamed the Taylor Society after his death in 1915), in part to free their teachings from their close association with mechanical engineering. Several journals and an Efficiency Society, which welcomed members who were not engineers, also provided wide popularization for the emerging

4. J. B. S. Hardman, ed., *American Labor Dynamics in the Light of Post-War Developments* (New York, 1928), 60.
5. Quoted in Hugh G. J. Aitken, *Taylorism at Watertown Arsenal: Scientific Management in Action, 1908–1915* (Cambridge, Mass., 1960), 225.
6. F. J. Roethlisberger and W. J. Dickson, *Management and the Worker: Technical vs. Social Organization in an Industrial Plant* (Cambridge, Mass., 1934), 16–17.

science of management. Harrington Emerson had made use of this society to promote his fame as Taylor's leading rival in the field.[7]

Personal rivalries among the early consultants were often bitter, as each of them (Taylor especially) denounced as fraudulent any plan that diverged one iota from his own. Nevertheless, their ideas converged on four essential proposals: (1) centralized planning and routing of the successive phases in fabrication, (2) systematic analysis of each distinct operation, (3) detailed instruction and supervision of each worker in the performance of that worker's discrete task, and (4) wage payments carefully designed to induce each worker to follow those instructions. The underlying theme of these recommendations was summed up by Frank Gilbreth: "the establishment of standards everywhere, including standard instruction cards for standard methods, motion study, time study, time cards, records of individual output."[8]

The first of these proposals was the one most widely followed in business practice. In newer factories, especially, employers often devoted careful attention to plant layout and the routing of work. With increasing frequency, machines were grouped by type and parts, and the tools, gauges, and instructions they needed were dispatched to them from stockrooms and toolrooms as directed by a central planning office. Managers discouraged workers from hunting up their own materials or devising their own tools and fixtures. These were to be delivered and accounted for by clerks. The planning room became the factory's nerve center, and its anonymous instructions were sent to operatives in written form, replacing and supposedly improving on the often vague oral instructions of shop foremen. Time clerks assumed special importance, keeping detailed records of each worker's performance and the whereabouts of each part. More careful routing and record keeping appeared even in foundries, which traditionally had been labyrinths of vessels, sand piles, discarded scrap castings, and molds being rammed, set out, or poured.[9]

---

7. Nelson, *Managers and Workers*, 61–4. See also Daniel Nelson, *Frederick W. Taylor and the Rise of Scientific Management* (Madison, Wisc., 1980); Frank B. Copley, *Frederick W. Taylor, Father of Scientific Management* (2 vols., New York, 1923); Sudhir Kakar, *Frederick W. Taylor, A Study in Personality and Innovation* (Cambridge, Mass., 1970).

8. Frank B. Gilbreth, *Primer of Scientific Management* (second edition, New York, 1914), 36.

9. John Calder, "Overvaluation of Management Science," *IA*, 91 (March 6, 1913), 605–6; Gantt, *Work, Wages, and Profits*, 105–6; [anonymous], "Dispatch System of Norton Grinding Company," *IA*, 98 (July 6, 1916), 1–5; Aitken, *Taylorism*, 85–134; Frederick W. Taylor, "Shop Management," *Trans. ASME*, 24 (1903), 1369–71; U.S. Congress, House of Representa-

The congressional committee investigating the application of the Taylor system to the Watertown Arsenal in 1911 found workers there rather friendly toward better routing and planning, at least when the improvements seemed to be in the hands of "practical men." Like other pieceworkers, the molders had long been aware that their employers had shown little concern for rationalizing the flow of work and that the burden of "making the rate" fell entirely on the worker. An analysis of another foundry's operation that year, for example, had attributed only 18 percent of the "unnecessary time" consumed on the job to chatting, relaxing, or other "inefficiency" on the workers' part, but more than 80 percent of the loss to poor planning that left molders without needed supplies, looking for tools, or waiting for cranes.[10] The foreman's inefficiency had long been a favorite topic in workers' conversation and jokes – as it still is. Early complaints that centralized planning had *reduced* efficiency came largely from foremen, who protested that parts were being sent to machines without jigs, that expensive machines were being kept out of use so that the elaborate setup needed for one job would not have to be performed again, and that they were forbidden to correct obvious mistakes made in the planning room. Many workers, however, shared the sentiment of arsenal machinist Hugo Lueders, who said: "The men would welcome any system. They want it bad." Then he quickly added, "As far as having a man stand back of you and taking all the various operations you go through, that is one thing we do not care for. Outside of that, they would welcome any system."[11]

From Taylor's point of view, however, "system" and the "man standing back of" Lueders were inseparable. The very essence of scientific management, he wrote, was "the deliberate gathering in on the part of

tives, *Hearings before the Special Committee of the House of Representatives to Investigate the Taylor and Other Systems of Shop Management* . . . (Washington, D.C., 1912, hereafter cited as House, *Taylor Hearings*), 956; O. J. Abell, "Making the Ford Motor Car," *IA*, 89 (June 6, 1912), 1383–90; *IA*, 89 (June 13, 1912), 1454–60; H. M. Ramp, "What the Foundry Thinks of the Machine Shop," *IA*, 88 (December 21, 1911), 1350–2.

10. Max H. C. Brombacher, "The Watertown Labor Trouble," *IA*, 89 (January 25, 1912), 249; C. E. Knoeppel, "Systematic Foundry Operations and Foundry Costs, Part VI," *Engineering Magazine*, 41 (April 1911), 49–62; Sumner H. Slichter, *Union Policies and Industrial Management* (Washington, D.C., 1941), 282–344.

11. House, *Taylor Hearings*, 1000; see also pp. 344–6, 383, 390, 405–6, 1507. Harry Ruesskamp at Midvale categorically denied that factories before Taylorism had been less "up to snuff" in routing, etc. House, *Taylor Hearings*, 1819.

those on management's side of all of the great mass of traditional knowledge, which in the past has been in the heads of the workmen, and in the physical skill and knack of the workman, which he has acquired through years of experience."

Harry Ruesskamp described how that "gathering in" had been accomplished when he had been a machinist in Midvale Steel's ordnance department in 1898. Several estimators, all recently graduated from what he called "manual training schools," approached him and his fellow machinists to observe their work, make sketches, time operations with stopwatches, and ask innumerable questions. A machinist, Ruesskamp recalled, might "show the sketcher a piece of work that was laid out" and "would have to practically go over and show this sketcher the operations to be performed to post him on the conditions of the work." Subsequently, the machinist would be confronted with a plan of operation and a time allotted for the job that had been worked out by a "large office force," and there might be several experiments at running the job according to those instructions. The worker would then be offered a bonus in addition to his regular hourly pay if he could finish the job within the assigned time. Those who failed to make the rate "would have to be continuously going backward and forward to the office" and faced certain layoff "if a little slackness arrived" in the company's orders.[12]

Time studies of tasks were acclaimed by Taylorites as the "basis of all modern management."[13] The time-study technique itself had been considerably refined between the 1890s and 1914. Taylor's own research into the loading of pig iron in 1898 had — despite all the fanfare with which he presented his constantly changing accounts of the famous "Schmidt" running up the gangplank — differed little from the studies by Coulomb and Desaguiliers more than a century earlier regarding how much weight an exceptionally strong man could carry in a day. Taylor's disciple Sanford Thompson similarly addressed himself to the classic questions of earth-moving by gangs of men and by workhorses, that is, to the capacities of "human machines" and other beasts of burden.[14]

The attention of Taylor and his colleagues soon shifted from that scientific problem of early capitalism to another that served the needs of modern corporate capitalism: analysis and standardization of skilled labor. Frank and Lillian Gilbreth stood in the forefront of this investiga-

12. House, *Taylor Hearings*, 1393, 1807–8. Compare Taylor's account of the same process, *Principles*, 48–53; Copley, *Frederick W. Taylor*, I, 205–62.
13. Robert T. Kent, "Micro-Motion Study in Industry," *IA*, 91 (January 2, 1913), 37.
14. Taylor and Thompson, *Concrete Costs*. On Coulomb and Desaguiliers, see Chapter 2, footnote 11.

tion. Their attention also fixed early on construction work, but not on the moving of earth or the pouring of concrete. They set out to find the "one best way" to lay bricks. All the complex movements, decisions, and knacks that bricklayers had learned through years of training and experience were analyzed into discrete motions of the hands, arms, back, and legs, so that the Gilbreths might reintegrate those motions into an efficient choreography, which they then taught to the workers and required them to follow. Because teams of bricklayers raised wall sections together, to have all of them working in exactly the same way at exactly the same time and aided by adjustable scaffolds of Gilbreth's design supposedly would make erection of the wall quick and perfectly coordinated.[15]

Taylor's later claim that the Gilbreths had practically tripled the daily output of Boston bricklayers probably was highly exaggerated, as most of his self-advertising was. Faced with fierce competition because of the use of concrete and steel construction in large commercial buildings, bricklayers' unions around the country had acquiesced in steadily rising output quotas since the late 1880s, with or without instruction in the "one best way."[16] Nevertheless, the techniques developed by the Gilbreths in these experiments were quickly applied in machine shops and were further refined in a catalogue the Gilbreths developed to describe the elementary muscular motions that in some combination or other, produce all physical work. These motions they called "therbligs" – an almost backward spelling of their own name. Motion-picture cameras and chronometers allowed them to take a major step closer to their goal of eliminating the "human equation" from job analysis altogether. Their fellow job analyst Robert T. Kent wrote in 1913 that "time-study is the basis of all modern equipment. The provision of a machine to make time-study should be as revolutionary in the art of time-study as was the invention of the power loom in the art of weaving."[17]

Machinists at the New England Bolt Company in Providence, Rhode Island, offered a rather different description of their encounter with this revolutionary mechanism:

> "Cameras to the front of them. Cameras to the rear of them. Cameras to the right of them. Cameras to the left of them." Pictures taken

15. Frank B. Gilbreth, *Bricklaying System* (New York, 1909); Taylor, *Principles,* 77–83.
16. Gordon E. Sands, "Architecture and the Building Trades in Chicago and New York, 1880–1920" (forthcoming Ph.D. diss., Yale University).
17. Kent, "Micro-Motion Study," 37; Braverman, *Labor and Monopoly Capital,* 172–6; Samuel Haber, *Efficiency and Uplift: Scientific Management in the Progressive Era, 1890–1920* (Chicago, 1964), 40.

of every move so as to eliminate "false moves" and drive the worker into a stride that would be as mechanical as the machine he tends. If the "Taylorisers" only had an apparatus that could tell what the mind of the worker was thinking, they would probably develop a greater "efficiency" by making them "cut out" all thoughts of their being men.[18]

The primary symbol of Taylorism in the minds of workers the world over was not the camera but the stopwatch. As Albert J. Berres, secretary-treasurer of the AFL's metal-trades department, said, "I do not think that any man, any young American at least, wants anybody to start him off with the watch and stop him with the watch."[19] The famous walkout of the molders at the Watertown Arsenal that led to the congressional investigation of the Taylor system began when molder Joseph Cooney refused to work under the stopwatch and all his mates left work in his support. The next year, metal polishers in auto plants of Saginaw, Michigan, struck in a successful protest against being timed, and strikes against *le chronométrage* spread from the Berliet and Renault-Billancourt works across the French automobile industry. The U.S. Congress responded to protests from workers in government arsenals and navy yards by prohibiting the use of time studies there in 1915 (a law that remained on the books until 1949), but that restriction did not apply to private industry.[20]

An entry in the 1915 diary of Will Poyfair, Jr., a worker in Buick's Flint works, says simply: "Stop watched today." One week later, the work of his four-man drip-pan gang was divided into separate tasks for each man, each with its own quota and piece rate. His was the most common experience. Workers without unions who saw that they were being timed found many ways to deceive the man with the stopwatch, but they could not wish him away. And the scientific managers held such workers' discomfort in contempt. "We use the stopwatch," explained Taylor's colleague Carl Barth, "because the sun dial will not do."[21]

Management had two persuasive means at its disposal to induce workers to submit to its new instruction: detailed supervision and incentive

18. Providence *Labor Advocate,* November 30, 1913, p. 1. Courtesy of Neil Basen. The effort to instruct workers in the "one best way" to think was, to be sure, already under way.

19. U.S. CIR, I, 900.

20. House, *Taylor Hearings,* 228–30; "Protest Against Stop Watches," San Antonio *Weekly Dispatch,* November 30, 1912; James M. Laux, "Travail et travailleurs dans l'industrie automobile jusqu'en 1914," *Le Mouvement Social,* 81 (October–December 1972), 24; Aitken, *Taylorism,* 239ff.

21. Poyfair diary, May 28, 1915, and undated June 1915 page describing work group; U.S. CIR, I, 897.

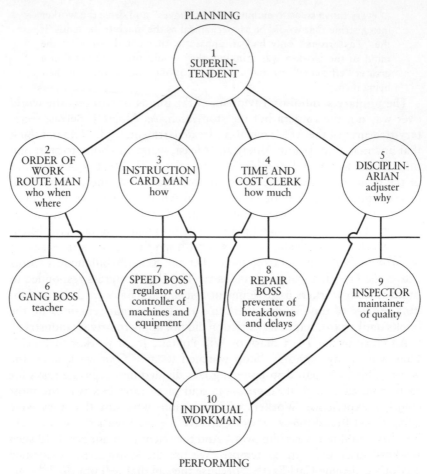

PLANNING

Chart of human organization of a plant

PERFORMING

pay. Taylor analyzed the traditional tasks of the foreman, found eight distinct functions there, and argued that each of the eight should be assigned to a different person. A route clerk, an instruction-card clerk, a time-and-cost clerk, and a disciplinarian (the task Taylor had assumed for himself in Midvale's machine shop) would concern themselves with disseminating the planning room's instructions, while a gang boss, a speed boss, and an inspector would instruct the operative, oversee the settings of his machine, and check the quality of his output, and a repair boss would minimize the loss from breakdowns. It was crucial to Taylor's pet doctrine, "functional foremanship," that each of these individuals give commands directly to the operative in the area of the foreman's particular expertise. Frank and Lillian Gilbreth depicted functional foremanship as shown in the accompanying diagram.[22]

With the worker so carefully instructed and supervised, it would no longer be necessary for him to possess a broad understanding of the processes in which he was engaged. The ablest craftsmen could be promoted from the ranks to the many new foremen's positions, and the rest could be replaced with unskilled men and women, instructed by the foremen in the "one best way" to perform their tasks. After Taylor reformed the machine shop at Bethlehem Steel, 95 percent of the men assigned to roughing work were retrained laborers, as were 25 percent of those on finishing. "The full possibilities of functional foremanship," he explained, "will not have been realized until almost all of the machines in the shop are run by men who are of smaller calibre and attainments, and who are therefore cheaper than those required under the old system." Similarly, at the Tabor Manufacturing Company, where the skills required of the ninety employees to turn out molding machines had required the firm to bid with high wages for the best machinists, thorough application of Taylor's methods enable it to replace almost all its craftsmen with cheaper help. The former machinists were either promoted to supervisory positions or dismissed.[23]

A competent operative could be trained quickly to a specialized task under this arrangement, and, Taylor promised, the increased cost of the "non-productive labor" of supervision would be more than offset by the lower base rates and higher hourly output of each operative. Moreover, paths of social advancement would be opened to all those who were prepared to exert themselves. As the engineer M. Cokely explained:

> Fortunately, through the invention of automatic and semi-automatic machinery and the standardization and specialization of product, avenues have been created through which the common laborer of thirty or forty years ago has advanced himself to a higher position in the industrial world and what is left of the place he vacated is now occupied by what is considered an element of inferior ability from continental Europe.[24]

22. F. B. and L. M. Gilbreth, "The Individual in Modern Management," *IA*, 96 (October 7, 1915), 802–4. The diagram is on p. 803. See also Gilbreth, *Primer*, 10; Taylor, "Shop Management," 1394–400; Gantt, *Work, Wages, and Profits*, 82–9, 262–3.

23. Taylor, "Shop Management," 1395. See also House, *Taylor Hearings*, 1489, 1759; Sterling H. Bunnell, "Right Principles in Works Management," *IA*, 87 (May 4, 1911), 1084–5.

24. Robert M. La Follette, ed., *The Making of America*, Vol. VIII, *Labor* (Chicago, 1905), 361. Compare Taylor, "Shop Management," 1422.

Although Taylor considered functional foremanship the sine qua non of truly "scientific management," very few firms adopted the proposal. It met with considerable opposition from workers and employers alike. For workers, proliferation of "white shirts" served as a constant reminder of their submissive roles. The commands of eight bosses, furthermore, could easily become contradictory and confusing. When Edwin Hatch, a machinist at Tabor, found that the cutters he had been issued for one job had been ground with inadequate clearance for the speed at which he was instructed to run them, he called the problem to the attention of his gang boss. Informed by the route clerk that the toolroom had not the time to correct the error, the gang boss told Hatch to use the cutters, but at a slow speed. Because the speed boss was busy with another man, Hatch could not explain the situation to him. Hardly had he begun to cut when the speed boss yelled from afar, "Speed that machine up." When he ignored the command, Hatch recalled, the enraged speed boss "came over and threw my belt off the pulleys, shifted them back to where he wanted them to be, and I shifted them back." The discomfited boss stormed upstairs to the office of the disciplinarian, who came down and fired Hatch. Later, after consultation with all the foremen, the superintendent reinstated Hatch, but cautioned him that "it was advisable, as a workman, to do as I was told."[25]

Employers' resistance to functional foremanship stemmed largely from their dismay at the prospect of paying an army of administrators. "The essence of successful management," in the opinion of Alba Johnson, superintendent of the huge Baldwin locomotive works next door to Tabor, "is to keep down the overhead or unremunerative labor." Johnson denounced Taylor's method as an unbearably expensive way of producing controls that were themselves illusory. He thought that "many manufacturers wreck themselves" on "the belief that certain information is essential to them, which is not really essential."[26]

His caution proved to be an accurate premonition of the massive falsification of accounts and time cards by operatives and by supervisors seeking to improve their ratings that would in time become routine in American industry. As John Calder of Remington Typewriter observed, corporate executives had been reluctant to allow free rein to professional consultants and were skeptical that any "system" could replace their own personal wisdom and charisma in directing the firm. Taylor's proposals

25. House, *Taylor Hearings*, 1757–8.
26. U.S. CIR, III, 2831. See also E. C. Peck, "Systematic Versus Scientific Management," *IA*, 88 (August 17, 1911), 365–6; W. L. Myles to *IA*, 90 (July 4, 1912), 24–5.

for a managerial hierarchy so structured that it would virtually operate itself led, in his view, "to a curious non-responsibility on the part of any person for the total result."[27] Nevertheless, few of the skeptics defied the rush toward elaborate and thorough record keeping, and even fewer could resist the illusion that an increasing flow of reports into executive offices and orders issuing from them was a sign that the inhabitants of those offices were, in Hugh Aitken's words, "more important people, with greater control over what happened in the plant, than before."[28]

As early as 1914, therefore, a line-and-staff form of management was gaining popularity in business circles. One foreman transmitted all commands to the workers. He was advised by specialists in routing, speed-setting, and so forth, and assisted by skilled workers, who served as troubleshooters, setup men, and inspectors. The disciplinarian, meanwhile, had been elevated to a status of special authority through the developing profession of personnel management. By 1919, even Link-Belt, one of the first firms to embrace Taylorism, had given up its functional foremen.[29]

It is important not to confuse form with substance here. Functional foremanship was a flop, but proliferation of "white shirts" and conversion of craftsmen into supervisors were universal and continuing phenomena. As R. F. Hoxie observed, the new style of management had replaced the lines craftsmen had created between themselves and their laborers with a new division between "the few who rise to managerial positions, and the many who seem bound to remain task workers within a narrow field."[30] Educational credentials came to play an increasingly important role in determining the fate of individual employees. By the early 1920s, many major corporations had developed their own training schools for foremen and for others who were being promoted through the ranks. Such cadre were considered the key to successful operation of the firm.[31]

Finally, all promoters of plans for the reform of management were

27. Calder, "Overvaluation," 606.   28. Aitken, *Taylorism*, 120.
29. George P. Stratton, "The Management of Production in a Great Factory," *Engineering Magazine*, 34 (January 1908), 569–76; C. V. Carpenter, "Committees for Controlling Manufacture," *IA*, 92 (October 8, 1914), 822–3; John R. Commons et al., *Industrial Government* (New York, 1921), 26–34.
30. Hoxie, *Scientific Management*, 93.
31. See David F. Noble, *America by Design: Science, Technology, and the Rise of Corporate Capitalism* (New York, 1977); Samuel Bowles, "Understanding Unequal Economic Opportunity," *American Economic Review*, 63 (May 1973), 346–56.

convinced that some monetary incentive was necessary to persuade workers to abandon their "restrictive" practices and to identify their personal aspirations on the job with those of management. As early as the mid-1880s the ASME heard papers extolling the virtues of one or another payment plan. The Halsey-Towne scheme, which offered bonuses to workers who surpassed their customary norms, was easily grafted onto established shop practice and spread widely in the 1890s. Taylor's own differential-piece-rate system had been developed at Midvale Steel and was presented to the ASME in his famous paper of 1895. What made that paper worthy of its fame, however, was not the payment plan but the more novel and profound idea running through Taylor's argument that no means of payment could solve industry's problems: Only the standardization of work could do that. The function of his pay incentives was to induce workers to participate willingly and actively in the new style to production.[32]

Proponents of the new forms of payment agreed that both day rates and piecework had proved to be failures. Uniform daily wages, Henry Gantt explained, gave the inefficient man more than he was worth, and the good man less, inducing the latter to join unions and providing neither an incentive to produce. Piecework had done no better. Time and again workers had mastered it with stints, and any inducement it might have provided to increased output was eroded by the widespread experience that high piecework earnings led to lowered rates. "It is a lazy, haphazard method of shifting responsibility and direction from employer to employee," argued one engineer before the 1904 ASME convention, "and it gives a long string of broken promises from the former."[33]

Both Taylor's differential-piece-rate plan and Gantt's task-and-bonus plan offered the worker more money per piece once a set production quota had been surpassed. Taylor proposed a rising scale of payments per piece, and women who mounted gems in the lamp factories were among those who worked under this plan.[34] Its use was not common, however, because employers disliked the extreme contrasts between the earnings it provided superior and inferior workers, and because it inhib-

32. House, *Taylor Hearings*, 917; *MMJ*, 10 (May 1898), 260; *MMJ*, 17 (April 1905), 335–6; Frederick W. Taylor, "A Piece Rate System: A Step Toward Partial Solution of the Labor Problem," *Trans. ASME*, 16 (1895), 856–93.
33. Gantt, *Work, Wages, and Profits*, 58–60; Taylor, "Shop Management," 1342; Frank Richards, "Is Anything the Matter with Piecework?" *Trans. ASME*, 25 (1904), 74–5. Taylor thought that a fixed day rate, with the length of the day regulated by an assigned task, was the best plan for employing little children. "Shop Management," 1373–4.
34. See Chapter 3.

ited them from cutting back the really high earners. Gantt's guarantee of a minimum hourly wage near the going scale for the community, which was converted into piecework based on that rate plus a bonus of 20 to 50 percent once the norm had been accomplished, was more attractive to plant managers. It was especially well suited for use among workers who had been accustomed to time wages. Any bonus earned could simply be put in a separate paycheck, which would be issued when the worker asked for it. The conversion of workers to scientific management was "voluntary."[35]

The great appeal of the Halsey-Towne, Emerson, Vickers, and Bedaux plans to employers was that they were all constructed on some mathematical basis that automatically reduced the price per piece as the worker's output rose. Consider, for example, the plan of Harrington Emerson, which workers often said was adopted where the workers were Swedish and might be lulled by the name. A worker with an hourly rate of thirty cents on a job timed at ten parts in ten hours would earn thirty cents per hour if those parts took him fifteen hours, thirty-six cents per hour if he just met the rate, and fifty-six cents per hour if he did them in only six hours. But, in contrast to Taylor's plan, the price he would have earned per piece in these instances would have fallen from 45.3 cents to 36 cents to 33.5 cents. In other words, companies using this plan would no longer need to aggravate high producers by cutting their piece rates; the cut was built into the plan. Emerson and others justified the falling rate by arguing that the worker's high output had been made possible only by the combined impact of the worker's exertion and good management, so that any "saved" production time should be shared between the two parties responsible. The editor of the *Machinists' Monthly Journal* took a less charitable view. "You get all you earn under the piece work system" he growled, "but under this improved method you return fifty percent of what you earn to the employer for allowing you the privilege of working."[36]

The aura of scientific precision in which all these plans were wrapped does not withstand close scrutiny. Different people timing the same task often reached remarkably different estimates. Even when therbligs were used to compute the time needed for bodily and machine motions, a "fatigue allowance" for physical recuperation had to be computed. The lim-

35. Kennedy, *Union Policy*, 36–40.
36. *MMJ*, 19 (June 1907), 569. See the debate over various payment plans in *Trans. ASME*, 24 (1903), 250–63. The Vickers plan was christened the "Vickers-Maxim" plan by shipyard workers because it reminded them of the machine gun. House, *Taylor Hearings*, 1312.

its of that allowance depended on the generosity of the time-study expert. Today, any worker knows that some jobs that come to the shop floor have times that are "murderous" and others are a "piece of cake." Much of the contemporary foreman's authority, in fact, is based on his ability to allocate each kind of job.[37]

Workers' objections to incentive-payment plans forced many employers to give them up during the labor shortages and numerous strikes between 1916 and 1920. The bonus rates Gantt had introduced at Bethlehem Steel were abolished by order of the National War Labor Board in 1918 for having a "serious detrimental effect upon the production of war materials," and the next year at Plimpton Press, where the first marriage of scientific management and collective bargaining had been celebrated, task-and-bonus payment was dropped in favor of straight time wages.[38] Moreover, as the original Plimpton Press contract had revealed, even some members of the Taylor Society, notably Robert Valentine and Morris Cooke, had concluded that despite the "scientific" fixing of tasks, the wage rates to be paid for those tasks were functions of market forces and might appropriately be bargained with unions.[39]

For management, the decisive requirement concerning wages was that they be designed specifically as incentives, not that this or that particular form of incentive be adopted. Even straight time wages could be used as incentives, as the Franklin auto company's plan for fixing them on a "purely individualistic basis" showed. Its formula for determining the hourly wage for each employee had eighteen variables, including absenteeism, spoiled work, output, and the "co-operation or conduct factor." Similarly, the Springfield and Rock Island arsenals ranked each worker every six months on an efficiency scale based on habits, application, adaptability, and quantity and quality of output. Demerits were recorded for talking, idling, absence, and other violations of plant discipline. Bullard Machine's "Maxi-Pay Plan" replaced an earlier premium scheme with an elaborate ladder of pay rates, without corresponding job titles, that workers ascended or descended as management assessed the quality of their performance.[40] Even where incentive pay was in use, the hourly

37. House, *Taylor Hearings*, 505–7; Slichter, *Union Policies*, 400; Roger Tulin, *A Machinist's Semi-Automated Life* (San Pedro, Calif., 1984).
38. *IA*, 95 (June 3, 1915), 1248; U.S. Department of Labor, *U.S. Employment Service Bulletin*, 1 (October 22, 1918), 7; Commons, *Industrial Government*, 158–60.
39. Milton J. Nadworny, *Scientific Management and the Unions, 1900–1932* (Cambridge, Mass., 1955), 76–104; U.S. CIR, I, 834–62, 991–1011.
40. George D. Babcock, "Fixing Individual Wage Rates on Facts," *IA*, 97 (June 8, 1916), 1375–9; *IA*, 91 (April 3, 1913), 811–12; Bullard Machine Com-

base pay of the worker was individually fixed. Workers at Link-Belt, who were paid according to Gantt's scheme, testified that they felt greater anxiety over possible increases or reductions in the hourly base than they felt over the premium.[41] Any "standard wage," declared the officers of Remington Arms during the war, "would destroy discipline," and "the right to classify must be exercised by those directly responsible for maintaining production."[42]

Taylor summed up the purpose of his proposals for routing, job analysis, supervision, and payment precisely and clearly:

> It is only through *enforced* standardization of methods, *enforced* adoption of the best implements and working conditions, and *enforced* cooperation that this faster work can be assured. And the duty of enforcing the adoption of standards and enforcing this cooperation rests with the *management* alone.[43]

Reforming the factory

The historical role of the scientific-management movement was to explain, guide, and justify the changes in the hierarchy of human relations in the workplace that accompanied the turn-of-the-century transformation of American industry. Most studies of Taylorism have been devoted more to the intellectual history of this movement than to its impact on industrial practices.[44] In an important sense, that emphasis has not been misplaced. Taylorism, as an ideology, variously stirred up excitement, great hopes, and deep anxieties in many quarters: commercial newspapers, speeches from the White House, congressional hearings, *Good Housekeeping*, the *Pittsburgh School Bulletin*, immigrant journals from *Denni Hlastel* to *Työmies* and the New York *Volkszeitung*, business periodicals like *Iron Age*, *Oil and Gas Journal*, and *Factory*, and the trade-union press – not to mention lectures at the new schools of business administration established at Dartmouth, Harvard, the University of Pennsylvania, and elsewhere. "Mr. Taylor and his followers," editorial-

pany, *The Maxi-Pay Plan* (n.p., n.d.); *IA*, 89 (January 4, 1912), 1–6; Commons, *Industrial Government*, 13–25.

41. House, *Taylor Hearings*, 1686–7.
42. "Brief Submitted by Remington Arms Union Metallic Cartridge Company, July 12, 1918," 18–19, NWLB Case File 132, Box 21, R.G. 1, National Archives.
43. Taylor, *Principles*, 83 (italics in original).
44. For example, Haber, *Efficiency and Uplift*; Nadworny, *Scientific Management*; Nelson, *Managers and Workers*. Nelson even contends that Taylorism's "direct effects on the workers . . . were probably minimal" (p. 74).

ized the *New Republic,* "have made a major contribution to civilization."[45] In that contribution, ideology and practice were inseparably linked.
Even though only a handful of firms redesigned their operations entirely
in conformity with the advice of a Taylorite consultant, some of them
achieved overnight fame, thus teaching by example. And the many corporate leaders who shared the skepticism of Remington Typewriter's John
Calder toward the dogmatism and exaggerated claims of Taylor and the
other peddlers of the "royal road to success" still read their advice with
care and exhibited an increasingly receptive attitude toward the basic
thrust of the new science of management.[46]

Taylor's own path to international fame was opened up by the experiments he and fellow engineer Maunsel White had conducted at Bethlehem Steel in the hardening of steel for cutting tools. Although this research dealt with the behavior of steel when heated to various temperatures,
rather than with the behavior of workers under various stimuli, it was a
consistent part of Taylor's life work. Taylor and White were in quest of
the "one best way" to temper bits of steel before they were ground to
form cutting tools. Machinists had long known from experience that
heating the metal until it turned "cherry red" and then cooling it quickly
produced the hardest known surfaces for the cutting edges of tools. Heated
beyond that point, the metal was spoiled: It lost its temper.

Taylor and White boldly raised the best available steel (Mushet) to
temperatures far above those that practical experience had ordained. They
learned that at 1,725 degrees Fahrenheit, 225 degrees hotter than "cherry
red," its hardness began to increase once more, and it kept on increasing
until maximum hardness was reached just below the melting point.[47]
This discovery was used by Bethlehem Steel to produce standardized steels
for high-speed tools as early as 1900, and it was unveiled to the world in
Taylor's 1906 paper "On the Art of Cutting Metals." Cutters ground
from this steel could remove metal at four to six times the speed formerly
achieved by machinists, who dubbed it "blue chip steel," after the color
of the shavings produced by cutting at the speeds it allowed. No extrav-
agant claims were needed to make engineers and machinists aware of this
invention's importance. What is noteworthy is that its creation had required not only laboratory experiments but also outrageous violation of
the common sense of practical mechanics – continuing to heat tool steel
that had already been ruined by overheating. In its invention, as in its

45. Quoted in Haber, *Efficiency and Uplift,* 89.
46. Calder, "Overvaluation," 606.
47. Copley, *Frederick W. Taylor,* II, 79–106.

use, high-speed tool steel made possible a new relationship between engineer and machinist.[48]

Taylor and White's technological leap at once rendered the machinists' traditional knowledge of proper cutting speeds and feeds obsolete. Not only was it necessary to retool American industry – to produce machine tools with cone pulleys large enough and bed and toolholder capacities strong enough to bear loads and velocities far in excess of anything previously known – but the operators of those machines found themselves at a loss to know what could be expected of them. Taylor's colleague Carl Barth provided the answer in another set of experiments on cutting speeds and feeds, using high-speed steel, from which he developed a twelve-variable slide rule for use in determining proper machine settings.

Armed with the slide rule, machine-shop employers were in a position to command. And the machinist found his traditional knowledge of little avail in contesting the new science. Undoubtedly, machinists, left to themselves, would in time have adapted their practices to the capacities of the new cutting steel, just as puddlers had slowly but definitely adapted their union rules to new furnace capabilities. But they were not given the chance. A knowledge hiatus of enormous strategic importance to the employers had been created, and they moved quickly into the breach with new standards of output set by time-and-motion studies.

The moment could not have been propitious for metal-trade employers. They were engaged in a fierce international race to provide the machinery for capitalism's dramatic renovation, and they also had to deal with widespread collective self-assertion from their craftsmen, climaxed by the noteworthy power and success of the IAM in the strikes of 1900 and 1901. Two firms that were anxious to refurbish their machinery so as to make optimal use of high-speed–tool steel, firms that had also been hard hit by the union, called in Taylor and Barth to revamp their works. One was Tabor Manufacturing, with ninety employees in Philadelphia. The other was Link-Belt, which had 800 solidly unionized workers in Chicago, 400 in Philadelphia, and another 200 rather weakly unionized employees in Indianapolis.[49] In both places, Taylor introduced the whole package of reforms that he expounded to the ASME in his

48. Hugh G. J. Aitken views Taylorism as fundamentally an adaptation of machine-shop practices to the possibilities offered by high-speed steel. This technological determinism is a misleading aspect of what remains otherwise the best existing study of Taylorism. Aitken, *Taylorism*, 30.

49. U.S. CIR, I, 862–73; House, *Taylor Hearings*, 517, 1628, 1683–99; *IA*, 96 (December 9, 1915), 1368.

1903 paper "Shop Management." There Taylor elaborated his technique of weaning workmen to standardized methods by coaxing them individually, emphasizing instruction in the "right way" rather than simple speed, and putting bonus earnings in a separate check for the worker to collect when he chose. "When they are convinced that a system is offered them which will yield them higher returns than the union can offer they will promptly drop the union," Taylor explained.[50]

Reform in its many guises swept the metalworking industries during the following decade. Machine-tool manufacturers, such as Lodge and Shipley in Cincinnati and Bullard in Bridgeport, thoroughly remodeled themselves in the Taylor pattern. The huge Dodge Brothers plant in Detroit, which produced motors for both Ford and Olds, resembled a showroom for modern machine technology and systematized controls. United Shoe Machinery and National Cash Register supplemented scientific management with elaborate welfare work and also built spacious, airy new plants in beautifully landscaped settings that impressed George Price as "shining examples" of John Ruskin's influence on architecture. The Royal Typewriter Company even instituted Gantt's proposal that foremen and executives have assigned tasks with appropriate bonuses.[51]

Not all employers in the metal trades greeted "shop management" with pure enthusiasm. There were machine-tool manufacturers, such as E. C. Peck of Cleveland Twist Drill, who were dubious that there was a single right way to do any machinist's job and who feared for the industry's fate if it ceased to nurture all-around mechanics. Large multiplant firms, such as International Harvester, Westinghouse, and General Electric, eagerly embraced time study, premium pay, specialized operatives, and time clerks to record work flow and production costs, but they were loath to tamper with their supervisory structures or with the decisive roles of craftsmen in key departments.[52]

Up-to-date managers found especially puzzling Taylor's lack of attention to machine technology per se. Aside from certain machines made at Tabor, which they peddled as "indispensable" for scientific reorganiza-

50. Taylor, "Shop Management," 1477–80; the quotation is on p. 1479.
51. IA, 88 (August 3, 1911), 268–71; IA, 89 (January 4, 1912), 1–6, 24–8; IA, 91 (January 2, 1913), 1–10; IA, 91 (May 15, 1913), 1159–62; Price, Modern Factory, 57; Henry L. Gantt, "A Practical Application of Scientific Management," Engineering Magazine, 41 (April 1911), 1–22.
52. Peck, "Systematic versus Scientific Management"; Robert Ozanne, A Century of Labor-Management Relations at McCormick and International Harvester (Madison, Wisc., 1967), 175, 181–2; Haber, Efficiency and Uplift, 11n; Stratton, "Management of Production"; Schatz, Electrical Workers, 11–14.

tion of factories, Taylor and his disciples had virtually nothing to say about what different machinery might do for efficiency. Their thinking was riveted on commandeering the craftsmen's knowledge. The contrast with the content of the Chicago-based journal *Factory* is sharp. From its first volume in 1907 onward, *Factory*'s pages abounded with "trips through the world's great factories" and articles on electric motors, new milling machines, hoists and cranes, fire prevention, cost analysis, time cards, belting, and plant layouts – but not pay systems or functional foreman-ship. Its columns were not open to miracle cures for inefficiency, nor were those of *Iron Age*. Not until 1910 did *Factory* carry a Taylorite piece on "Planning Jobs for Each Workman."[53] Many more appeared after that, and *Factory*, like *Iron Age*, published eloquent tributes to Tay-lor following his death. At no point, however, did the editors of either business journal allow their interest in managing workers and recording information to become divorced from, let alone overwhelm, their fasci-nation with machine technology.

Here lay the contribution of the automobile industry. Taylor himself commended a body of six hundred Detroit auto-factory superintendents and foremen in 1914 for having been the "first to install the principles of scientific management without the aid of experts."[54] The process of con-verting skilled workers into foremen or toolmakers and assigning pro-duction tasks to untrained operatives who performed minutely subdi-vided tasks under tight supervision was carried to its most extreme form in the auto plants of southern Michigan by the 1910s. But the functions of routing and directing the operatives' tasks not only had been assigned to engineers and supervisors but also to an astonishing degree had been incorporated into the machinery itself. Nowhere was this clearer than in Ford's Highland Park plant, which was opened in 1910 and quickly be-came the engineering marvel of the world.

Although the auto industry's plan to control its workers directly through machine technology carried scientific management in a direction unan-ticipated by Taylor, that particular plan was not applicable to as many work settings as Taylor's teachings were. Ford's circumstances were unique. So great was the demand for the company's Model T that 90 percent of the six hundred or more cars that came off its assembly lines every day

53. Frederick C. Coburn, "Planning Jobs for Each Workman," *Factory*, 5 (Oc-tober 1910), 206–7, 244.
54. Quoted in Stephen Meyer III, *The Five Dollar Day: Labor Management and Social Control in the Ford Motor Company, 1908–1921* (Albany, N.Y., 1981), 20. For a description of the Detroit meeting, see Keith Sward, *The Legend of Henry Ford* (New York, 1948), 33–4n.

by 1914 were shipped immediately to dealers. Ford did not even have a storage lot. Consequently, it was possible to commit fifteen thousand men and women to fabricating a single, if complex, commodity in a plant that was characterized by large and small chain-driven subassembly and final-assembly lines and by thousands of machine tools especially designed for making a single cut on a single part, and capable of doing nothing else. To retool for another product required shutting and reconstructing the entire plant – as Ford did, idling one hundred thousand workers, in 1927.[55]

When Ford hired people to tend these machines, it had "no use for experience." In the words of one engineer: "It desires and prefers machine-tool operators who have nothing to unlearn, who have no theories of correct surface speeds for metal finishing, and will simply do what they are told to do, over and over again, from bell-time to bell-time."[56] One worker reamed bushing T-225 for Stub-Axle Arm, Left T-270, 850 times in an eight-hour day, while three others turned spindles for Stub-Axle T-203 at the rate of one every thirty seconds. The final assembly had forty-five work stations, each with a task like the following:

> 30. Two men. Place motor pans, one each side, under chassis frame, and pan-holding bolts and nuts.
> 31. Four men. Tighten motor-pan-bolt nuts and place split pins in same.

To outfit those machine tools and assembly stations required a staff of 240 toolmakers, 50 tool-fixture draftsmen, and 105 pattern makers, who called the jigs and fixtures they sent to the production floors "farmers' tools," in contemptuous reference to the operatives who would use them. Here were the skilled crafts in their ancillary roles. And no fewer than 255 overseers in the machine shops alone watched the machine tenders, with absolute authority to fire any one of them at will.[57]

With machines and ubiquitous bosses pacing each task, there seemed to be no need for incentive pay. Ford soon discovered, however, that these conditions also produced staggering rates of labor turnover. To maintain an average force of thirteen thousand during the prosperous times between October 1912 and October 1913, Ford had to hire fifty-four thousand people, an annual turnover rate of 416 percent. Moreover, an average of thirteen to fourteen hundred workers were found to be missing from their stations every day. To remedy these problems, the company introduced periodic wage increases based on the recommenda-

55. Horace L. Arnold and Fay L. Faurote, *Ford Methods and Ford Shops* (New York, 1919).
56. Ibid., 41–2.
57. Ibid., 6, 8, 38, 46, 149, 175; Meyer, *Five Dollar Day*, 26.

tions of foremen, and then a personnel department to which a worker might appeal a discharge. A campaign by the IWW at the gates of Detroit's auto plants in 1913 and several IWW-assisted strikes in the tire industry and at smaller auto plants added to the company's anxiety. Consequently, in January 1914, Ford proclaimed an eight-hour day and a new plan of "profit sharing" for all employees. Any man or woman above twenty-two years of age who contributed to the support of others, had worked for the company six months or more, and was pronounced "acceptable" by the firm's Sociological Department was eligible to "share the profits" by earning five dollars per day. A staff of a hundred "sociologists" investigated the habits, home lives, and attitudes of workers to discover who was acceptable and by the end of March 1914 had approved 57 percent of them to receive the magical five dollars.[58]

Instead of individualizing pay rates as incentives, the Ford plan had gone to the other extreme and promised everyone who qualified the same high rate. But the jump between Ford's starting rates (around $2.50 per day for most operatives) and the promised five dollars was every bit as extreme as the difference between what Taylor's differential piecework offered low and high earners. Will Poyfair, who averaged $4.25 per ten-hour day on piecework for Buick at the stint he and his mates had established in 1913, noted in his diary:

> Jany 6th 1914 Ford Motor Co of Detroit announces a plan for an 8 hour day and profit sharing among the 24000 employees amounting to about 10 million dollars a year.
> In return he will have the pick of the best mechanics and will get a big days work besides getting a big amount of advertising.[59]

In fact, there was always a crowd outside the gates of the Highland Park plant looking for work, and so many had gathered the day after the profit-sharing plan had been announced that a riot broke out. Nevertheless, neither Poyfair nor any other member of his Flint drip-pan crew, who worked together for nearly a decade, was among the rioters. Unemployment was severe in Michigan and throughout the country in January 1914, a circumstance that made Ford's announcement all the more sensational, but when short work cut Poyfair's earnings, he left Buick for almost four months to make drip aprons for a small Detroit firm. Those

58. Arnold and Faurote, *Ford Methods*, 46, 61; Sward, *Legend*, 32–8; Chandler, *Giant Enterprise*, 34–45; IA, 93 (January 1, 1914), 48–51 (January 8, 1914), 150–1 (January 29, 1914), 306–9; L.A. "The Automobile Industry," *International Socialist Review*, 13 (September 1912), 255–8; Nelson, *Managers and Workers*, 144–50. On women earning the five dollars, see Arnold and Faurote, *Ford Methods*, 373–4, 398.
59. Poyfair diary, 1914, note on address page.

who flocked to Ford were largely immigrants (71 percent), and a 1914 survey found that 53 percent of all Ford's workers came from Russia, Romania, Italy, and Austria-Hungary. The standards set by the Sociological Department to qualify for the five-dollar day pertained above all to the life-styles of the immigrants. Four days after Ford had announced the profit-sharing plan, it made another dramatic statement: Almost nine hundred men were fired for staying away from work to celebrate the Eastern Orthodox Christmas. If "these men are to make their home in America," explained a company official, "they should observe American holidays."[60]

Ford's much publicized policies represented a convergence of task standardization with mechanization, of incentive pay with personnel management, of work discipline with Americanization, and of mass production with a redefinition of the promise of industrial life. However, the very success of industry in reorganizing the human relations of production, which the automobile industry epitomized, had created a new set of problems for corporate managers, as well as new opportunities. The combined impact of standardization and mechanization had had two interrelated effects: It had shifted craftsmen from production to ancillary tasks, and it had blended the worlds of the laborer and the operative. Villagers from capitalism's rural periphery not only were wielding shovels on construction projects and needles in sweatshops but also were tending the most modern of machines in factories. Rustic styles of behavior that were easily accommodated on railroad track gangs played havoc in the midst of tightly integrated machine processes and assembly lines. The way this problem appeared to managerial reformers was reflected in the writings of economist Don Lescohier. Casual labor, he argued, was a "state of mind" that industry had to replace with "thrift, sobriety, adaptability, [and] initiative."[61]

Just as engineering consultants had spread the "Old Testament" of Taylorism, so another profession had emerged even before Taylor's death to amend his teachings with a new gospel of personnel management. It had a preprofessional ancestry in welfare work, but the uproar in business circles concerning a "turnover crisis" and the "epidemic of strikes"

60. Ibid., April 8 to July 9, 1914; Sward, *Legend*, 53; *IA*, 93 (January 8, 1914), 48–51; Meyer, *Five Dollar Day*, 77; Meyer, "Adapting the Immigrant to the Line: Americanization in the Ford Factory, 1914–1921," *Journal of Social History*, 14 (Fall 1980), 74.

61. Lescohier, *Labor Market*, 268; Graziosi, "Common Laborers," 532–40. Managerial concern with the virtues mentioned by Lescohier in itself had a long history. See Gutman, *Work, Culture, and Society*, 3–78; Sidney Pollard, *Genesis of Modern Management: A Study of the Industrial Revolution in Great Britain* (London, 1965).

between 1911 and 1913 bestowed on the employment manager or the sociological department an important equal to that of the practitioners of time-and-motion study.

Corporate welfare workers had found widespread employment during the first decade of this century. They filtered gradually into industry from the YMCAs, which had a history of working with railroad train crews since the 1870s, from settlement houses, from temperance and public-health movements, and from churches to design and supervise company-sponsored welfare and recreational activities. Although a great deal was written about their work during these early years, the authors who celebrated it made virtually no reference to questions of efficiency or productivity.[62] Conversely, Taylor was contemptuous of the sports clubs, reading and dining rooms, toilets, and infirmaries that they promoted in perhaps two thousand firms, insisting that such innovations "should never be allowed to engross the attention of the superintendent to the detriment of the more important and fundamental elements of management." As if to prove his point, his own Tabor Manufacturing Company had no showers, washstands, or reading rooms, nor even windows on some sides of its cramped quarters.[63]

The pioneering Sociological Department of the Colorado Fuel and Iron Company, established in 1901, illustrates this early style of welfare work in an elaborate form. A physician, R. W. Corwin, supervised a small corps of employees who provided medical services, cooking classes, and temperance dining rooms for miners and their families in the company's widely scattered camps and supplied the state's public schools with a uniform curriculum, so that children moving from one camp to another with their parents would never break educational stride. Corwin described the Greeks, Italians, Croats, and Mexicans who mined coal or smelted ore as "drawn from the lower classes of foreign immigrants" and explained that their "primitive ideas of living and ignorance of hygienic laws [rendered] the department's work along the line of improved housing facilities and instruction in domestic economy of special importance."[64]

62. See, for example, Price, *Modern Factory;* William H. Tolman, *Social Engineering. A Record of Things Done by American Industrialists Employing Upwards of One and One-Half Million of People* (New York, 1909); Crystal Eastman, *Work-Accidents and the Law* (New York, 1910); Gerd Korman, *Industrialization, Immigrants and Americanizers: The View from Milwaukee, 1886–1921* (Madison, Wisc., 1967), 10–11, 74–5; Ozanne, *Century,* 173ff.
63. Taylor, "Shop Management," 1454; House, *Taylor Hearings,* 1523; Hoxie, *Scientific Management,* 91.
64. Quoted in Tolman, *Social Engineering,* 55.

Corwin's twin themes – the immigrants' need for special help and guidance, and the importance of the worker's household, family, and leisure activities – appeared again and again in early explanations of corporate welfare work. "A resort to direct paternalism . . . is necessary or desirable for recent immigrants who in their native lands have been accustomed to the guardianship of superior authority," explained Gertrude Beeks, who was soon to become secretary of the Welfare Department of the National Civic Foundation.[65] C. W. Price, a former clergyman who had become manager of welfare for International Harvester, agreed: "In factories similar to ours, where the great majority of the men are humble foreigners . . . the leadership must come . . . from someone acting in the capacity of social secretary."[66] To be sure, diverse programs of the Pullman type, designed to cultivate the loyalties of the "best mechanics" – company housing or home-purchase plans, company-sponsored medical and burial societies, and even profit sharing – had been found here and there since the late nineteenth century. What was new after 1900 was the emphasis on the recent immigrants and the prominence of men and women with social-service backgrounds in directing the corporate welfare work. Both the numbers of people brought together daily by the modern corporation and the coercive authority the corporation could wield over them made the workplace itself appealing to many social reformers as a more effective agency through which to change popular behavior than legislation or appeals to reason seemed to provide. Even a factory inspector who was endowed with legal responsibility to promote safer work environments wrote in 1914 that although educated mechanics might be taught by example or practical reasoning, such an approach was futile in plants that did "not employ what I term civilized labor." Poles and Italians, he contended, could be persuaded only by punitive layoffs and discharges for hazardous conduct. Because they kept "one eye on the foreman and the other eye on the clock, the only way to educate this class of labor is through their pockets."[67]

The prosperity that followed the economic crisis of 1907–9 added a new dimension to earlier corporate concern about welfare and safety work

65. Quoted in Bruno Ramirez, *When Workers Fight: The Politics of Industrial Relations in the Progressive Era, 1898–1916* (Westport, Conn., 1978), 151. On Beeks's important role, see Marguerite Green, *The National Civic Federation and the American Labor Movement, 1900–1925* (Washington, D.C., 1956).

66. Quoted in Ozanne, *Century*, 169. See also Korman, *Industrialization*, 10–11. Compare the argument of David Brody that welfare policies in steel were directed primarily at the skilled workers. Brody, *Steelworkers*, 87–95.

67. *Safety Engineering*, 28 (November 1914), 401.

among immigrants: the historic discovery of labor turnover. As we have noted, high rates of turnover among workers of all types had been a fact of life since the earliest years of industrialization. The new elements of 1910–14 were the fixation on turnover that seized corporate managers and professional economists alike and the appearance of a new profession whose expertise was directed specifically at its solution. Both the concern of business with the detailed direction of its labor force and the creation of professional associations had by then become integral and familiar parts of American industrial life. The new profession of personnel management, or employment management, as it was styled during the first few years of its existence, was not, however, a simple logical extension of scientific management. Rather, it represented a new awareness among industrialists of some inner contradictions in scientific management and an attempt to do something about those contradictions.

Ford was not the only company to learn that when jobs were plentiful, as they were through much of 1909–10 and 1912–13, workers both stayed off work and quit their jobs with alarming frequency. "The men do not seem to value their jobs as they should," commented a newspaper in Elwood, Indiana, in the spring of 1913 concerning workers at the local American Sheet and Tin Plate Company. "One man recently laid off for two weeks that he might go on a fishing trip. Others have stayed home for several days at a time that they might make a garden or help with the house cleaning."[68] The cost of such absences deserved management's attention, warned International Harvester's Worman: "two or three Monday-idle machines in any group, make serious inroads on the department's earnings."[69] Moreover, when Magnus Alexander, John W. Williams, W. A. Grieves, and other prominent industrialists kept systematic records of the numbers of workers who entered and left their factories between 1911 and 1913, they learned that annual turnover rates ranged anywhere from 100 percent to 250 percent. Twelve metalworking firms studied by Alexander, for example, increased their aggregate payrolls by 6,700 workers during 1913, but to do so they had to hire 42,571 new people.[70]

Alexander's other discoveries were more ominous. First, he observed that the tendency to quit was especially great among operatives on repetitious jobs. Second, those very workers were the most expensive to break

68. Elwood *Call Leader*, May 14, 1913. Courtesy of Errol Wayne Stevens.
69. Worman, "Recruiting . . . Unskilled," *Factory*, 1 (February 1908), 172.
70. Douglas, Hitchcock, and Atkins, *The Worker*, 310–13; Magnus W. Alexander, "Waste in Hiring and Discharging Men," *IA*, 94 (October 29, 1914), 1032–3.

in. "In the case of a first-class mechanic the cost of replacing him is relatively small," confirmed Charles Fouhey of Curtiss Aeroplane. "He is given the blue print and it matters little to a first class man whether he is working on aeroplane parts or on marine engines." But the cost of initiating workers who had to be taught each assignment ranged from $4.05 on drill-press work to $91.13 on production lathes.[71]

Although Alexander's figures were somewhat different, his conclusions were the same. When he reckoned up the total cost of hiring a new employee for General Electric, including the time of the hiring agent, job instruction, wear and tear on equipment from improper use, the substandard output of the novice, and spoiled work, the results were clear. The cost of a new laborer was $8.50, of a clerical worker $29.00, of a highly skilled mechanic $48.00, of an inferior mechanic who needed a year or more to attain a fair proficiency $58.50, and of a semiskilled operative "who can attain a fair proficiency within a few months" $73.50. In short, the worker created by the emerging style of industrial organization and promoted by scientific management was the type most likely to walk out on a job and most expensive to replace. Even rehiring such an employee cost $35.00, Alexander calculated, in contrast to only $10 for rehiring a highly skilled mechanic.[72]

To make matters even worse, laborers and operatives alike engaged in unprecedented levels of collective protest during the period of prewar prosperity. A revolt by textile workers that swept out of Lawrence across New England and New Jersey in 1912 had set off what *Iron Age* called in April 1913 an "epidemic of strikes." Although there are no federal strike statistics for this period, P. K. Edwards's careful calculations have suggested that the ratio of strike participants to the total labor force was higher between 1912 and 1915 than it had ever been before. Unskilled workers, seeking high wages to offset a steadily rising cost of living, constituted a large proportion of those who walked off their jobs collectively, as well as individually.[73]

The remedy seized on by most corporations was the introduction of yet another specialized supervisory position, the employment manager. The role of this new supervisor was far more significant than the role

71. Council of National Defense, "Labor Turnover – First Report," Department of Labor, Chief Clerk's File 20/542, R.G. 174, National Archives; Daniel Bloomfield, *Selected Articles on Employment Management* (New York, 1922), 283.
72. Magnus W. Alexander, "Hiring and Firing: Its Economic Waste and How to Avoid It," *Annals of the American Academy of Political and Social Science*, 65 (May 1916), 128–44.
73. Edwards, *Strikes*, 254.

Taylor had assigned to one of his functional foremen, the "shop disciplinarian." He was to be a major managerial officer who would screen applicants before sending them on to an appropriate foreman for a final decision on hiring and would again interview any worker who was fired or who quit, to determine if that person should and could be persuaded to remain. He kept files of employment histories and often heard grievances, and he quickly took over all the functions previously performed by welfare officers.

The new managers presented themselves as professionals, whose purpose was to contribute decisively to the efficiency of the firm, not as do-gooders camped out in some spare office of the factory. In 1911, fifty of them gathered in Boston to organize the first Employment Managers' Association. By 1918, no fewer than 900 personnel managers were on hand for a national convention, and Dartmouth, Harvard, Rochester, Columbia, and Pennsylvania universities were all offering professional training in the field. Their graduates were demanding salaries, status, and office furnishings equal to those of production managers. Just as Taylor had once claimed that his science would reconcile labor and capital under a "government of facts and law," so the new professional now claimed to represent "on the one hand the desires and the rights of the working force, and on the other hand the desires and the rights of the management. He is the harmonizer and adjuster," in the words of the Dartmouth professor Harlow S. Person.[74]

By 1923, the bubble of enthusiasm for personnel managers had burst. During and even after the depression of 1920–2, there was a chronic buyers' market for industrial labor, which deterred workers from quitting whatever jobs they had. The topic of turnover virtually disappeared from management periodicals, and personnel managers found their suggestions brushed aside again and again by unsympathetic production managers (and often even losing their office carpets). The Employment Managers' Association was taken over by executives determined to counteract what they considered the excessively "altruistic" notions of professionalism that wartime conditions had stimulated within that body. They changed its name to the American Management Association. Its leader,

74. Meyer Bloomfield, "The New Profession of Handling Men," *Annals of the American Academy of Political and Social Science*, 61 (September 1915), 121–6; M. Bloomfield, "A New Profession in American Industry," in D. Bloomfield, *Employment Management*, 113–18; John A. Fitch, "Making the Boss Efficient: The Beginnings of a New Industrial Regime," *Survey* (June 2, 1917), 211–15; Harlow S. Person, "University Schools of Business and the Training of Employment Executives," in D. Bloomfield, *Employment Management*, 128–37; the quotation is on p. 131.

Sam Lewisohn, reviewed the business experience of the previous decade and concluded, "The management of human relations must finally rest in the hands of line officials – the regular production executives. There is no clearly marked boundary dividing personnel from production."[75]

In short, whereas personnel management did not emerge simply as a logical extension of Taylorism, neither did the two simply blend to form the "American Plan" style of corporate welfarism in the 1920s. This was an epoch of intense class conflict in which industrialists made a number of strategic adaptations and changes of emphasis, all within the general context of transformed human relations of production and an enthusiasm for professionalism and expertise that informed all public discourse. The turnover crisis of 1911–13 had produced the new profession, full of vigor and self-confidence. It even captured the attention of Taylor's disciples. When David Van Alstyne wrote "Modern Shop Management" in 1911, it was devoted mostly to personnel questions, and it concluded that every large employer should have a "sociological department." At the 1914 meeting of the Society to Promote Scientific Management, professionalization of personnel management was the absorbing topic.[76]

All this professional attention helped employment managers quickly expand the scope of their own interests and activities. First, as Vice-President R. C. Clothier of Philadelphia's Scott Company observed, they sought to "examine applicants [for employment], carefully, not only with respect to their fitness for the particular tasks, but with respect to their constitutional ability to harmonize with the ideals and underlying principles of the company they are to serve; they must be capable of loyalty as well as efficiency."[77] Both high quit rates and trouble in the works resulted from placing an unsuitable person on the job. It was necessary, therefore, to select workers of the right nationality, race, and sex for each position. All managers seem to have agreed with International Harvester's H. A. Worman that "each race has aptitude for certain kinds of work," even though they often disagreed as to just which "race" was best for what. Worman advised selecting Poles, Hungarians, and Austrians for inside jobs, and Irish, Scandinavians, Germans, and northern Ital-

75. Sanford M. Jacoby, "Industrial Internal Labor Markets during the 1920s," Working Paper Series 69, All-UC Economic History Conference, University of California at Davis, May 1984; Sam A. Lewisohn, *The New Leadership in Industry* (New York, 1926), 89.

76. *IA*, 94 (December 10, 1914), 1369–72; David Van Alstyne, "Modern Shop Management," *IA*, 87 (April 20, 1911), 970–2. Ford abolished its Sociological Department in 1921. Meyer, *Five Dollar Day*, 198–9.

77. R. C. Clothier, "The Function of the Employment Department," in D. Bloomfield, *Employment Management*, 159.

ians for outside work. The Fayette R. Plumb Company of Philadelphia was confident of its selections:

> [*Grinders.*] Polish, Lithuanians or American, experienced grinders, or Americans that want to try it after being told that the job is hard work, wet work and that the majority of the men are Polish, but the job pays good money. . . .
>
> *Handlers.* Americans over twenty-one. Men accustomed to using a hammer preferred. . . .
>
> *Finishers.* Girls sixteen or over. Americans or Italians, former preferred. . . . Neat about clothing, without cheap finery. Better if they are not "flirty" and live at home.
>
> *Handle Belters.* Americans or Italians. Eighteen to twenty-five. Strong wrists and quick movers.[78]

Managers of steel mills were advised by *Iron Age* not to think of immigrants in general terms but to focus on "certain races only" that were "disposed to seek employment" in the industry. At Pittsburgh's Central Tube Company, the personnel manager analyzed the "racial adaptability" of thirty-six different ethnic groups to twenty-four different kinds of work under twelve sets of conditions and plotted them all on a chart to guide his hiring practice. He found Lithuanians good at trucking barrels or cases but mediocre at shoveling materials, suited to outdoor work but poor performers under hot and dry conditions and generally undesirable at night. Ukrainians, on the other hand, were splendid under dusty and smoky conditions and good tank cleaners, but they made poor boilermakers' helpers. The minute detail of this manager's effort may have been unusual, but all employers sought such information as he gathered, and all of them thought in similar ethnic stereotypes.[79]

Second, personnel management extended the purview of scientific management from the factory itself to the surrounding community. In part, this development flowed directly from the concern with recruiting from specific ethnic groups. The head of labor and safety at Illinois Steel's south works observed:

> The superintendent . . . must not only be aware of the location of all the groups of foreign settlements in the community, but he must

78. H. A. Worman, "Recruiting the Working Force. II – The Personal Interview in Hiring Men," *Factory*, 1 (January 1908), 111; John M. Willliams, "An Actual Account of What We Have Done to Reduce Our Labor Turnover," *Annals of the American Academy of Political and Social Science*, 71 (May 1917), 64.

79. Editorial, *IA*, 96 (July 8, 1915), 91; "Racial Adaptability to Various Types of Plant Work," reproduced in Ira DeA. Reid, "The Negro in the Major Industries and Building Trades of Pittsburgh" (unpublished M.A. thesis, University of Pittsburgh, 1925), Appendix 3, p. 54.

become personally acquainted with the individual boarding bosses, steamship agents, clergymen, and other influential agents with whom the immigrant maintains a close contact. These are his supply depots, and only by perpetual, personal reconnoitering can he remain familiar with the quality and quantity of available applicants.[80]

There was another dimension to the new concern. Boyd Fisher, a vice-president of the Detroit Executives' Club and an expert on "hiring and holding" men for the automobile industry, believed that "eighty percent of the causes of labor turnover lie outside the plant." Like Henry Ford, Fisher contended that the employment manager had to become a "co-partner with the teacher, the minister, [and] the social worker in the business of reforming men," and he boasted in 1917 that "it wasn't Billy Sunday, it was the employers of Michigan that put the state in the prohibition column."[81] Efficiency justifications and corporate muscle began to be put behind older welfare causes, such as the closing of bars between the worker's job and his home, preventing immigrants' fraternal lodges from serving liquor, bringing college students to the factories to deliver noon-hour talks on "clean living, character-building and vital religion," and surveying the home living conditions of employees. In basic steel-producing areas, and perhaps elsewhere, corporate executives assumed control of local Americanization efforts, displacing the American grocers, clergymen, and organized nativists who had sponsored earlier campaigns to change immigrants' belief and behavior.[82] All these missions appeared in the boastful description of his achievements recounted by the industrial-relations manager of Youngstown Sheet and Tube:

> ... a reduction in working time lost, a reduction in labor turnover, the elimination of serious labor disputes, the development of esprit de corps, greater production, betterment of physical and social conditions of employees, a reduction of sickness and accidents, and the Americanization of aliens.[83]

80. A. H. Young, "Employing Men for the Steel Mill," *IA*, 98 (November 16, 1916), 1108.

81. Quoted in Noble, *America by Design*, 294.

82. *IA*, 93 (March 12, 1914), 698; *IA*, 95 (March 11, 1915), 554–5; Charles M. Ripley, *Life in a Large Manufacturing Plant* (Schenectady, N.Y., 1919), 62. On the shifting social forces behind Americanization, see Frank H. Serene, "Immigrant Steelworkers in the Monongahela Valley: Their Communities and the Development of a Labor Class Consciousness" (unpublished Ph.D. diss., University of Pittsburgh, 1979), 105–31.

83. E. C. Gould, "A Modern Industrial Relations Department," *IA*, 102 (October 3, 1918), 832–3.

The promise of industrial life

The proud claims from Youngstown echoed the rhetorical tone of most public discussion of scientific management after 1910. Paradoxically, the protests of craftsmen against Taylorism reached their crescendo at the very time that the operatives who were replacing them in production processes were serving as catalysts for modification of the teachings of scientific management. Most published opinion, however, brushed aside the complaints of craft unionists as the irrational grunts of reactionary vested interests. Through controversies over railroad repair shops and government arsenals, metal tradesmen's battles against Taylorism had ironically provided a forum for popularization of the Taylorite gospel.

Although after 1897 America's railroads entered yet another phase of building, involving both spurs and reconstructed truck lines, the industry had lost its leading position in economic growth to the auto and electrical industries, and its management was no longer particularly innovative. Its repair shops were slow to turn to efficiency schemes or even to centralization to repair work. Attempts to reintroduce piecework faced intense resistance from workers. The tasks of dismantling cars and locomotives, outfitting them with new parts, and returning them to the rails were still dominated by craftsmen in the old familiar style. Moreover, craft unions had rapidly regained their hold, at least on western lines, after the return of prosperity. Wage rates and work rules that they negotiated with railroad managers were simply posted as company rules, so that union conditions obtained, even though union shops were rare.[84] Owners of the big locomotive and railroad-car factories, which were mostly nonunion, remained content with the inside-contracting system with which they had long been familiar. Extreme fluctuations in output from year to year also discouraged attempts to substitute systematic organization for knowledgeable and adaptable journeymen. Many of Taylor's critics among mechanical engineers were to be found in these large firms.

The first major systematizing effort on a railroad took place on the Santa Fe line during a strike, when the company's most pressing problem was to organize effective work among new and inexperienced scabs in its repair shops. Harrington Emerson was engaged to revamp the shops, and

84. H. W. Jacobs, *Organization and Economy in the Railway Machine Shop* (New York, 1907); Charles Day, "The Machine Shop Problem," *Trans. ASME*, 24 (1903), 1310; Jacob Hollander and George E. Barnett, *Studies in American Trade Unionism* (New York, 1912), 123–34. For a sample of union-negotiated railway rules, see La. BSL (1904–5), 63–7.

he did so with his customary fanfare. When Louis Brandeis later extolled that effort as a model for the whole railroad industry, shop superintendents were aghast. Railroad shop work, argued one of them, "renders it absolutely essential to successful operation that both the foreman in direct charge of each operation, and the mechanic who is actually performing the work, shall not only be *permitted* but *required* to bring into use their mechanical skill and judgement, which, under the proposed plan of 'scientific management,' they would be prevented from doing."[85]

After the economic crisis of 1907, most railroads faced both intense pressure from shippers to hold down freight rates and effective demands from their workers for wage increases. Many shops then began to introduce piecework once again into the more routine operations, such as "turning tires" (refinishing the running surfaces of wheels), but this time in combination with time study. Six railroads had already faced machinists' strikes over this issue during 1909 and 1910, before the eastern-rates case was considered by the Interstate Commerce Commission (ICC). The story deserves the attention that historians of the Progressive Era have given it.[86] The railroads informed the ICC that the wage raises they had been forced to grant their workers made an increase in rates imperative. Shippers' organizations, representing farmers and manufacturers alike, mobilized intense opposition to the demand, and that in turn brought several railroad unions into public support of their employers' appeal. The long deflation had yielded to thirteen years of rather steadily rising prices, so that protests against the high cost of living were heard from all corners of the land. Into this setting stepped Louis Brandeis, attorney for eastern shippers. Armed with the testimony of Harrington Emerson, Brandeis argued that application of scientific management would allow the railroads to raise wages without raising freight rates: It would save them "a million dollars a day."

As Samuel Haber has pointed out, Brandeis's phrase ran like a shock wave across the printing presses of America. It evoked an image of science in the service of the people, showing the way to hold down the cost of living while raising American wages under the guidance of modern management and experimental method. Only the reactionary railroads and unions opposed the public good. Even the interests of the railroad

85. Wilson Symons, "The Practical Application of Scientific Management to Railway Operations," *Journal of the Franklin Institute*, 172 (January 1912), 14; House, *Taylor Hearings*, 548–60.
86. "Efficiency" (pseudonym), "Railroad Efficiency and the Labor Unions," *IA*, 87 (February 12, 1911), 476–8, (March 23, 1911), 724–5; H. H. Fisher, "The Hypocrisy of the Bonus System," *MMJ*, 19 (August 1907), 755–6.

workers were best represented by enlightened management, not by their unions, which held back output and progress.[87]

Just as the cause of Taylorism was being wrapped in the banner of progress, democracy, and the common welfare, workers mounted a series of well-publicized revolts against the regime of the stopwatch and incentive pay. The American Locomotive Company had ten works, scattered from Montreal and Schenectady to Pittsburgh and Richmond, where its vice-president, David Van Alstyne, wished to introduce standard times and the Emerson premium system. In 1907 he reached an agreement with leaders of both the molders' union and the blacksmiths to guarantee recognition of their unions in return for their cooperation in applying new methods to maximize output. Shop committees reserved the right to contest any job rate, and the plan was to be given a one-year trial starting in January 1908.

According to the testimony of John O'Leary of the molders, his own members required "considerable persuasion," including "use of the 'club,' " to induce them to cooperate. The officers of the boilermakers, all vying with each other for office, feared to enter any such agreement and called strikes in several plants. Machinists at the Pittsburgh works began mass passive resistance, which spread to other locations. When P. J. Conlon of the IAM visited the Pittsburgh shop, he examined the pay envelopes of thirty-eight members of his union and found that altogether they had earned but $6.57 in bonus for a week. Ultimately a strike by machinists at that plant forced the company and the various unions alike to abandon the scheme, and Van Alstyne left American Locomotive for another position.[88]

During the next two years the metal trades experienced what might be called the "Great Fear" of Taylorism, somewhat like the mass anxiety that gripped the French peasantry in 1789. Opposition to scientific management spread much faster than did its practice. The very appearance of stopwatches, time cards, or measurements of machine cutters, beds, or T-bolts that so much as hinted at standardization was enough to trigger anxious caucuses of craftsmen, strikes, or beatings of those who seemed to be collaborating with the systematizers. When Jones and Laughlin Steel in Pittsburgh announced a pay bonus on the Emerson plan, the mill erupted in walkouts, department meetings, and wrecking of machinery. Time cards appeared at the Norfolk Navy Yard a few days after the new commandant, Holden M. Evans, had delivered a speech at the local businessmen's association on how Taylorism could improve the yard's productivity. Ev-

87. Haber, *Efficiency and Uplift*, 51–6.
88. House, *Taylor Hearings*, 568–9, 1236–50, 1660–9; U.S. CIR, I, 874–86.

ans had declared that the slogan of the yard's workers was "Don't give up the ship," and as if to confirm his assessment, the craftsmen held a mass meeting and walked out. While that conflict was in progress, early signs that stopwatches might be introduced into the shops of the Illinois Central railroad prompted its shopmen to form a system federation for joint rank-and-file bargaining by all the crafts. The company's refusal to deal with that organization provoked a bloody strike that lasted until 1914. Molders at the Watertown Arsenal met without the sanction of their union and voted that no one would work under the stopwatch. That decision precipitated the arsenal strike of 1911 that let to a congressional investigation of the Taylor system and to a law banning the use of time study in government workshops.[89]

This agitation made the name Taylor widely known among workers. Dockers in New York, whose piers were totally lacking in system of any sort, described their toil as "Taylorized," because of its intense pace. Machinists who were laid off in Worcester, Massachusetts, blamed their unemployment on "working on short time owing to the adoption of the so-called Taylor System of scientific efficiency." The workers' main source of information was Taylor's own book *Principles of Scientific Management,* copies of which became dog-eared as they were passed from hand to hand, spreading dread of what the bosses had in store for craftsmen.[90] Nels Alifas, a machinist from Davenport, Iowa, put his colleagues' sentiments concisely before the Commission on Industrial Relations:

> Now we object to being reduced to a scientific formula, and we do not want to have the world run on that kind of a basis at all. We would a good deal rather have the world run on the basis that everybody should enjoy some of the good things in it, and if the people of the United States do not want to spend all of their time working, they have a right to say so, even though the scientific engineers claim that they can do five times as much as they are doing now. If they don't want to do it, why should they be compelled to do it?[91]

Although Alifas's statement got to the heart of what was at stake in America's industrial transformation, the very fact that it was a protest,

89. *Survey,* 28 (August 3, 1912), 596; *IA,* 90 (July 18, 1912), 146; Evans, *One Man's Fight,* 141, 181–3; House, *Taylor Hearings,* 1298–369, 1711–12.
90. U.S. CIR, III, 2117; Alexander Keyssar, *Out of Work: The First Century of Unemployment in Massachusetts* (Cambridge, 1986), 71; "Mike" (pseudonym), "Scientific Management," *Architect and Engineer* (July 1911), 92–4; "Efficiency," St. Louis *Melting Pot,* 2 (September 1914), 12–13 (courtesy of Neil Basen).
91. U.S. CIR, I, 944.

rather than a proposal, revealed the weakness of his position. In the first place, the transformation of work effected by scientific managers was irreversible. Even when workers were able to prohibit time study or incentive pay by strike action, as Abraham Bisno observed, that "would not help them very much, . . . for the schedule of time costs was kept in great detail, . . . the memories of the foremen on each particular item were constantly sharpened, and the foremen were told that they could not keep their jobs unless their men kept their speed up to their previously shown capacity."[92] Moreover, workers soon came to realize that scientific management would not take the form of a visit to the factory by some disciple of Taylor's, after which the firm would be fundamentally reorganized for once and for all. On the contrary, the new managerial techniques meant that work relations were subject to incessant reexamination and reorganization. Time-study men in the modern plant were always snooping around somewhere. When one department had been rearranged to their (momentary) satisfaction, they turned to the next. Workers found themselves paid by the hour at some times and on incentive rates at others. New product lines often were initiated by journeyman machinists, then put into the hands of operatives, with some of those journeymen serving as troubleshooters, once production was ready to roll. New designs, changes in work instructions, or a supervisor's belief that a standard was wrong led to retiming. Dynamism, instability, new orders from on high, and angry disputes over those orders, which usually involved only small isolated groups of workers, were endemic to the new regime.

When Henri de Man investigated American industry for the Belgian government during the war, he made the same point in more general terms. Taylorism had often been checked, he observed, because of workers' opposition, its mistaken psychology, and the charlatan character of many efficiency experts. Nevertheless, he added, "even while admitting that Taylorism has met defeat, it is necessary not to conclude that after it was tried, one simply returned to the former methods." Although "Taylorism was liquidated," de Man concluded, " 'scientific management' was not by any means."[93]

In the second place, scientific management was as important an element in the transformation of American ideology as it was in the reshap-

92. Bisno, *Union Pioneer*, 215–16.
93. Kingdom of Belgium, Ministère de l'industrie, du travail et du ravitaillement, *Le travail industriel aux États-Unis: Rapports de la Mission d'Enquête* (Brussels, 1920), I, 215.

ing of industry. Industrial practice and public debate about the purpose of industrial life interacted vigorously as the new century began. As Woodrow Wilson noted during the election campaign of 1912:

> There is one great basic fact which underlies all the questions that are discussed on the political platform at the present moment. That singular fact is that nothing is done in this country as it was done twenty years ago. . . . We have changed our economic conditions, absolutely, from top to bottom; and with our economic society, the organization of our life.[94]

Nineteenth-century celebrations of competition, of the titan of industry, of the unfettered market as the ablest arbiter of relations among competitors, and even of Victorian morality as the noblest guide for the lives of women had all come under a barrage of criticism and scorn from prominent intellectuals and publicists. For all the variety of new ideas under debate, the targets of rhetorical assault were routinely identified as special interests, commercialism, corruption, and waste. The vocabulary of reform celebrated the common (or public) interest, management (as opposed to drift), expertise (rather than experience), and professional (as opposed to commercial) ethics.

Louis Brandeis's advocacy of scientific management in the eastern-rate case touched all these chords. It helped propel an image of social progress directed by incontrovertible "facts," sweeping away the relics of yesterday's ignorance and strife. "Capitalists" and "trusts" were replaced in the public mind by "managers" and "large-scale organizations." Both the grievances and the slothfulness of workers were to be remedied by the guidance of trained professionals. When workers complained of speedup, they were advised that rational organization was making their work easier and eliminating the "waste" of their time and energy. The "time, health, and vitality of our people are as worth conserving, at least, as our forests, minerals, and lands," proclaimed Theodore Roosevelt. "And Scientific Management seems to do even more for the workman than for raw materials."[95] When craftsmen protested that they were being converted into robots, Brandeis had the answer:

> Eagerness and interest take the place of indifference, both because the workman is called upon to do the highest work of which he is capable, and also because in doing this better work he secures appropriate and substantial recognition and reward.[96]

Never one to be outdone, Harrington Emerson hailed his own efforts as unleashing men's "reserve powers," and he argued that "the reason

94. Quoted in Walter Lippmann, *Drift and Mastery: An Attempt to Diagnose the Current Unrest* (New York, 1914), 132.
95. Quoted in Gilbreth, *Primer*, 2.   96. Ibid., vii.

the white men are civilized and have beaten out the savages is because they have utilized their reserve powers to a greater degree than the savage ever thought of doing."[97] Just in case the appeal to imperialism had not sufficed to make his case, Emerson also identified management with masculinity. Woman creates individual life, he explained, while man organizes mass forces; "woman croons her lullaby to her restless baby, but men organize grand opera, develop the phonograph."[98]

It is not enough, however, just to plot the points at which the ideology of scientific management intersected with the dominant themes of bourgeois thought at the time. Taylor and his disciples also made a distinctive contribution to situating a cult of the expert and a compelling definition of what constitutes a "good job" firmly and enduringly in the center of twentieth-century American intellectual life and public policy.

"I can say, without the slightest hesitation," Taylor told a congressional committee, "that the science of handling pig-iron is so great that the man who is ... physically able to handle pig-iron and is sufficiently phlegmatic and stupid to choose this for his occupation is rarely able to comprehend the science of handling pig-iron." Lest anyone believe that he was referring only to common laborers, Taylor elaborated his argument:

> This inability of the man who is fit to do the work to understand the science of doing his work becomes more and more evident as the work becomes more complicated, all the way up the scale. [The] law is almost universal – not entirely so, but nearly so – that the man who is fit to work at any particular trade is unable to understand the science of that trade without the kindly help and cooperation of men of a totally different type of education, men whose education is not necessarily higher but of a different type from his own.[99]

Taylor's admirers elaborated the theme, while emphasizing the authoritarian character of that "kindly help and cooperation." Brandeis welcomed the "perfect team play," which he envisaged when the employer "assumes the burdens of management, and relieves labor of responsibilities not its own."[100] The work of managers and planners themselves certainly could not be subjected to time-and-motion study, wrote President Wilfred Lewis of Tabor Manufacturing, because it was "creative and full of harmonies." Depending "largely, as it does, upon inspiration,

97. U.S. CIR, I, 831.
98. Harrington Emerson, "The Twelve Principles of Efficiency, Part XV," *Engineering Magazine*, 41 (August 1911), 812.
99. House, *Taylor Hearings*, 1397.
100. Louis Brandeis, "Brief before the I.C.C., January 3, 1911," in D. Bloomfield, *Employment Management*, 127.

there is no superior intelligence to direct its progress."[101] As for the "officers of a great corporation," George Perkins of International Harvester told a gathering of Harvard students, "they can look upon all labor questions without bias, without any personal axe to grind, solely from the broadest possible standpoint of what is fair and right between the public's capital, which they represent, and the public's labor, which they employ."[102] Or, as welfare enthusiast William Tolman had expressed it, the employer saw himself as "something more than a producer: an instrument of God for the upbuilding of the race."[103]

The essence of scientific management was systematic separation of the mental component of commodity production from the manual. The functions of thinking and deciding were what management sought to wrest from the worker, so that the manual efforts of wage earners might be directed in detail by a "superior intelligence." Frank Gilbreth contended that work guided by his instructions would be ideal for a "man who had no leaning toward brain work." To the worker who retained cerebral inclinations, it left three options: He might "join the planning department." He might become a teacher on the job of "the other men who prefer the so-called monotonous work." Failing those careers, he could "plan the spending of the extra money that will be in the pay envelope on the next payday, and can consider the intellectual stimulus that the extra pay will purchase."[104]

The apostles of scientific management not only redefined the respective roles of employers and workers but also categorically asserted on behalf of the workers what it was that workers really wanted. In so doing, the reformers offered their own image of a "good job," as though it were the most obvious thing in the world, and linked the attainment of that objective inseparably to ever rising productivity. "What the workmen want from their employers beyond anything else is high wages," Taylor told the ASME, "and what employers want from their workmen most of all is a low labor cost of manufacture." Hence, a possible reconciliation of

101. Wilfred Lewis, "Efficiency Methods of the Tabor Mfg. Company," *IA*, 87 (April 13, 1911), 903.
102. Unidentified press clipping dated April 16, 1910. William Brown Dickson Papers, Pennsylvania State University Library, Box 7.
103. Tolman, *Social Engineering*, 355.
104. Gilbreth, *Primer*, 54. Compare the formula proposed by Henry Ford for enriching life through mass production: "There should be leisure, music and poetry – the five day week, the old-fashioned dance, and the hospitable inn beside the road." Quoted in H. Dubreuil, *Robots or Men?: A French Workman's Experience in American Industry*, translated by Frances and Mason Merrill (New York, 1930), 152.

their interests, and indeed a prosperous and harmonious social order, lay in systematic efforts to overcome "the enormous difference between the amount of work which a first-class man can do under favorable circumstances and the work which is actually done by the average man." He portrayed scientific management as a "great mental revolution" in which "both sides take their eyes off the division of the surplus as the all-important matter, and together turn their attention toward increasing the size of the surplus until this surplus becomes so large that it is unnecessary to quarrel over how it shall be divided."[105] Workers' happiness would come through an abundance of material goods, and that abundance was to be created through ever increasing productivity. Although, as Henry Gantt observed, learning "to obey orders is often the hardest part of a workman's task," the reward for obedience was Taylor's promise that "in the next hundred years the wealth of the world is going to grow per capita . . . to such an extent that the workman of that day will live as well, almost, as the high-class businessman lives now, as far as the necessities of life and most of the luxuries of life are concerned."[106]

When Taylor presented his paper "Shop Management" to the ASME, the first commentator who rose from the audience was the venerable Henry R. Towne, who presented his own written remarks extolling the virtues of inside contracting and traditional piecework, when used in combination with time study. He was followed immediately by Commissioner E. F. Du Brul of the National Metal Trades Association, who warned the assembled engineers not to "reckon without our host." There could be no progress in shop efficiency until businessmen combined to overcome the unions, and in particular the IAM, he argued. Every subsequent speaker echoed Du Brul's theme, virtually ignoring the substance of Taylor's paper, except for Oberlin Smith, who placed his hopes in proper instruction in economics by the public schools, so that workers would grow up knowing that their fate depended on their productivity. The esteemed William Kent closed the discussion with a call for a "Boston Tea Party" to end "union tyranny."[107]

In more public settings, however, Taylor's colleagues preferred to portray themselves not so much as foes of trade unions' as "rival tradesmen trying to sell the same thing to the same people – that is higher wages and shorter hours."[108] With the triumph of scientific management, unions

105. Taylor, "Shop Management," 1343, 1345; House, *Taylor Hearings*, 1388.
106. Gantt, *Work, Wages, and Profits*, 156; Taylor quoted in House, *Taylor Hearings*, 1388.
107. *Trans. ASME*, 24 (1903), 1457–77; the quotations are on pp. 1457, 1467, 1477.
108. Charles Mixter to U.S. CIR, I, 839.

would have nothing left to do, and they would have been cleansed of their most evil feature: the restriction of output. To underscore this idea, Taylor fashioned the myth that "there has never been a strike of men working under scientific management," trying to give it credibility by constant repetition.[109] In similar fashion he incessantly linked his proposals to shorter hours of work, without bothering to produce evidence of Taylorized firms that had reduced working hours, and he revised his famous tale of Schmidt carrying pig iron at Bethlehem Steel at least three times, obscuring some aspects of his study and stressing others, so that each successive version made Schmidt's exertions more impressive, more voluntary, and more rewarding to him that the last.[110] Unlike Emerson, Taylor was not a charlatan, but his ideological message required the suppression of all evidence of workers' dissent, of coercion, or of any human motives or aspirations other than those his vision of progress could encompass. Workers' control, as machinists had exercised it, was simply castigated as "soldiering," "restriction of output," a mindless abuse against the public interest.

The "great mental revolution" preached by Taylor assumed special significance during the "efficiency craze," because the popularization of scientific management coincided with the prewar increases in mass strikes, Socialist votes, and popular agitation for social reform on innumerable fronts that brought to an end eighteen years of undisturbed Republican rule and filled the nation's press with muckraking assaults on many formerly secure centers of power and authority. "Our time . . . believes in change," wrote Walter Lippmann in 1914. In concise reference to the turbulent controversies and social struggles of the epoch, he explained:

> Scientific invention and blind social currents have made the old authority impossible in fact, the artillery fire of the iconoclasts has shattered its prestige. . . . The dominant forces in our world are not the sacredness of property, nor the intellectual leadership of the priest; they are not the divinity of the constitution, the glory of industrial push, Victorian sentiment, New England respectability, the Republican Party, or John D. Rockefeller.[111]

---

109. U.S. CIR, I, 772–3.
110. For a critique of Taylorism on hours, see Goldmark, *Fatigue and Efficiency*, 203–10. The Clothcraft Company of Cleveland, a highly paternalistic garment manufacturer, provided one example of shorter hours that Taylor's group could produce. On Taylor's fabrications in the Schmidt legend, see Charles D. Wrege and Amedeo G. Perroni, "Taylor's Pig-Tale: A Historical Analysis of Frederick W. Taylor's Pig-Iron Experiments," *Academy of Management Journal*, 17 (March 1974), 6–27.
111. Lippmann, *Drift and Mastery*, xviii.

Even millionaires like Henry Ford, William Randolph Hearst, and Thomas A. Edison so well understood their times that they built their fortunes while, and even by, hailing the ascent to power of the working masses. Edison, for example, wrote in 1911 of "The Wonderful New World Ahead of Us," in which he identified the people's hopes and prospects with mass consumerism, and their enemies as tradition, habit, and the outmoded institutions of the Old World. While soaring production would bring harmony in America, he predicted, mass strikes would topple the dynasties of Europe. "I believe . . . that all England will some day stop at one command, and that the command of a workingman."[112] As these three men were aware, industrial growth had made possible a material abundance beyond the wildest dreams of earlier generations of humanity, without bringing prosperity, let alone contentment, to the bulk of the population. Workers' movements, national-independence movements, women's demands for social and political emancipation, and rural rebellions had the industrial world simultaneously glorying in its new splendor and trembling at the prospect of bloody barricades.

Industrial society had emerged from the crisis of the 1890s with a new lease on life. But in what direction would it develop? To what uses would its wondrous productive capacity be put? These were questions people had to answer in the first two decades of the twentieth century. Helen Marot, a Socialist and a leader of the Women's Trade Union League of New York, put her reply in very broad terms:

> In scientifically managed plants there is no change whatever in the status of capital and labor, except the extended enslavement of the latter. Efficiency engineers might successfully promote scientific management by advertising their hope that the management will "share what it gets" if the factory system had been a less efficient teacher. But the factory system has taught the workers by a series of object lessons. Labor unions represent those workers who have learned that they must rely on schemes for relief which they themselves initiate or control.[113]

The reply of the advocate of scientific management was sharp and uncompromising. Employees, wrote Henry Towne, have no "right to control or to participate in the management of the establishment." John Calder added: "The last thing a good manager would think of doing would be to make his possibilities of shop management the subject of a referen-

112. Thomas A. Edison, "The Wonderful New World Ahead of Us," *Cosmopolitan Magazine,* 50 (February 1911), 294–306; the quotation is on p. 306.

113. Helen Marot, *American Labor Unions, By a Member* (New York, 1914), 237–8.

dum."[114] And indeed they should not, seconded economists John Bates Clark and Henry L. Moore. By statistical computations they demonstrated that workers' earnings were correlated not with the cost of subsistence, as earlier economists had taught, but with productivity. In other words, rewards did go "to each according to his work," so that even a socialist society would compensate workers just the way modern corporate capitalism did. Moore concluded: "Concentration of industry is no ground for the socialization of industry, but [my findings] place in clearer light the solidarity of industry and illustrate how the increasing welfare of the laborer is dependent upon the skillful management of large capital."[115]

114. *IA*, 89 (April 11, 1912), 912–14.
115. Henry L. Moore, *Laws of Wages: An Essay in Statistical Economics* (New York, 1911), 194.

6

"Our time . . . believes in change"

The Chicago Civic Federation gathered representatives of those whom its secretary called the "solid, unselfish, humane, Christian, educated element of the nation" for two highly successful conferences as the nineteenth century drew to a close. One, held at Saratoga Springs in 1898, dealt with the future foreign policy of the United States as a world power. The second, convened in Chicago in 1899, dealt with the role of "combinations and trusts" in the emerging economic order.[1]

Among the participants in the latter was M. M. Garland of Pittsburgh, who had left his heating furnace to assume the presidency of the Amalgamated Association of Iron, Steel and Tin Workers just as the Homestead strike was going down to defeat. His speech to the conference was optimistic but cautious. His hopes were based on the fact that with the return of prosperity, wages were rising and his union was growing again; it had even instituted a workday of three eight-hour turns for most of its remaining members in midwestern iron-rolling mills. He had left both the union office and the mills behind him when President McKinley had appointed him Pittsburgh's collector of customs. Addressing himself to the current wave of mergers in the business world, Garland declared that whether or not the nation "tolerated" trusts would depend on their behavior toward workers. Antitrust laws should be avoided, because the courts had applied them unhesitatingly against unions. The great peril was the "wanton" slashing of wages that steel companies had practiced during the depression years. If trusts would secure the earnings of their employees, rather than competing aggressively for customers, and if they would "treat with organizations" of their workers, they could indeed provide the economic foundation of a better society in the century to come.[2]

1. Ralph Easley, quoted in Green, *Civic Federation*, 7; on the two conferences, see pp. 6–10.
2. *National Labor Tribune*, September 21, 1899. On Garland and the three-shift movement, see Fitch, *Steel Workers*, 96–7.

The trade unions, which had sprung from the work cultures and daily struggles of the craftsmen, had entered a period of unprecedented growth after 1897. Nevertheless, they still represented but a small minority even of the skilled workers of the land, and nowhere was this more evident than in the steel industry. Its major corporations had snuffed out the union's major lodges during the previous decade, and the most famous of the trusts, U.S. Steel, was to humble the Amalgamated Association in a nationwide strike less than two years after Garland's speech. Even more important, in that industry and others, sharply contrasting earnings, work practices, life-styles, and even social origins separated the craft workers, unionized or not, from the more numerous operatives and laborers. New technology and new managerial practices were beginning at that very moment to transfer the dominant role in production toward less skilled workers and to blend the diverse experiences and lives of laborers and operatives. In these respects, work experience was being homogenized, although the working class remained anything but homogeneous.

Business executives, who were reshaping work relations as well as merging enterprises into "tight combinations," were often captivated by a new rhetoric that counterposed "efficiency," "organization," "expertise," and the "public interest" to the sins attributed to the recent past: "drift," "waste," and "special interests." Taylor and his colleagues neatly placed their prescriptions for reorganizing the shop floor within the context of these newly acclaimed values. They heralded a "great mental revolution" in which both labor and capital would take "their eyes off the division of the surplus as the all-important matter, and together [turn] their attention toward increasing the size of the surplus until this surplus becomes so large that it is unnecessary to quarrel over how it shall be divided."[3]

Taylor and Herbert Croly had agreed that to harmonize the social order through soaring productivity also meant to diminish the worker's " 'class consciousness' by doing away with his class grievances" and "in every way" making "the individual working man more of an individual."[4] That course of development, however, could only undermine the very social foundations of the workers' organizations, whose future role Garland had identified as the decisive test of whether or not the trusts should be "tolerated" by America. Machinists, construction workers, coal miners, and railway workers were among those Americans who did not wait for management to resolve the course of national development. Their aggressive posture at the time of Garland's speech and over the next two decades forced the issue. The resulting conflict drove American economic

3. House, *Taylor Hearings,* 1388.   4. Croly, *Promise,* 416.

life and political life into paths no one had anticipated at the Chicago Civic Federation's conferences. It also divided the labor movement into mutually antagonistic ideological groupings.

Machinists and the National Civic Federation

A pervasive sense that the great depression of the 1890s had ended infused the delegates to the IAM's 1897 convention with determination to eradicate the evils that afflicted their craft forthwith. May 1, 1898, was the date enthusiastically set to institute the eight-hour day and at last to abolish all piecework. As the day of battle approached, the union's officers and members watched with mounting anxiety the course of the lockout of the Amalgamated Society of Engineers (ASE) in England. The world's largest machinists' organization, powerful enough to have instituted the nine-hour day in 1871 and to have enforced its elaborate rules over most of England's metalworking industries, was engaged for ten months in a nationwide struggle for its very life. In February 1898, the ASE signed terms of surrender, opening all plants to nonunion men, promotion of handymen, and piecework. The Americans' zeal wilted at the news. The ASE, after all, had 78,450 members in 1897, and the IAM scarcely 15,000. May 1 passed without a strike. For excitement, the machinists had to settle for Admiral Dewey's victory in Manila Bay.[5]

Two years later the union's fighting spirit had revived. This time its attention was focused on its four thousand members in Chicago. The leaders were wise to commit themselves to battle in that city, because the workers of Chicago had accomplished a fusion of craft organizations with class solidarity on a level unmatched anywhere in the land. The lament of the manager of Fraser and Chalmers, a part of the Allis-Chalmers chain, concerning his experience during a molders' strike in the fall of 1899 illustrates vividly the role of class consciousness in sustaining craft organization there. The unions, said he,

> . . . had so boycotted our place that we could not buy a pound of castings in any shop in the United States; they had watched the railroads so that we could not ship tools out of the city. They had so picketed us that when we brought a load of men – we brought 202

5. *MMJ*, 9 (June 1897), 214, 247–8, 276–7; 10 (January 1898), 25; 10 (February 1898), 65, 75; 10 (April 1898), 230–1, 237–8; 10 (August 1898), 463–6; 10 (December 1898), 722–5. Only the Pittsburgh lodges struck, and they won the nine-hour day in sixty-six shops. Hollander and Barnett, *American Trade Unionism,* 129. See also Going, "Labour Questions in England and America." On the membership of the ASE and the IAM, see Webb, *Industrial Democracy,* 287; Perlman, *Machinists,* 33.

men to Chicago and we put up a building, we built a restaurant and fed them, and we could not buy bread or food; they would not sell any member of our company or office staff a newspaper in the vicinity; we could not hire a carriage; and they went around and said, "If you sell anything to this house, if you supply this firm with anything for their men, we will withdraw our patronage and you will have to go out of business."[6]

District 8, on behalf of all the IAM lodges of the city, presented 150 machine shops with a proposed agreement in January 1900. A nine-hour day, a closed shop, a seniority rule for layoffs, recognition of shop committees, and a minimum wage of twenty-eight cents per hour were all terms at which the employers balked, and on March 1, five thousand workers went on strike. Because more than forty thousand building-trades workers were on strike at the same time, more work was closed down in Chicago than at the height of the Pullman boycott. Encouraged by Chicago's example, the union's district officers in Cleveland, Detroit, Paterson, and Philadelphia also called out their members.[7]

It soon become apparent to Chicago employers that they could not win a total victory, and seventeen firms affixed their names to the union's terms. But the officers of the Chicago branch of the newly established National Metal Trades Association (NMTA), which grew quickly in membership and prestige by taking command of the employers' side of the battle, searched for a formula that would minimize the cost of capitulation. They had little to quarrel about with the twenty-eight–cent standard rate, because most machinists already earned more than that, and they decided to offer concessions on the nine-hour day and on union recognition. On the other hand, they disliked the idea of reducing their workweek to six hours shorter than that of their competitors in other cities. And they detested the prospect of being bound to settle grievances with what one of them called the "arrogant, dictatorial" unions of Chicago. Because the "average intelligence" of machinists is "not high," explained one manufacturer, formal recognition of their union "becomes license, license. If the local association can once maintain its control there is no end to what it will have afterward." The president of Western Electric concurred: "Well, we should not have a committee or what they call a steward, an official of the union, in our place to represent the union among our employees. We should not have it."[8]

6. U.S. CIR, VIII, 8.
7. *MMJ*, 12 (March 1900), 196–8, 210–12, 235; U.S. Industrial Commission, *Report*, VIII, 6–7, 490–2.
8. U.S. Industrial Commission, *Report*, VIII, cxxiv, 6–7, 180–2, 299, 500–3; the quotations are on pp. 6, 24, and 299. See also *MMJ*, 12 (May 1900), 249–52.

The remedy for all these problems came in one formula: Negotiate a national agreement between the NMTA and the top officers of the IAM. The nine-hour day would then apply to competitors everywhere in the country, and the president of Turner Brass believed that "a man fitted to represent a national organization, or representing a national organization, would be an easier man to do business with."[9] Recognizing the opportunity for the greatest coup in the history of their union, President James O'Connell and organizer Stuart Reid hastened to parlay Chicago's power into national recognition of their union. They reached an agreement to transfer the wage question, apprenticeship rules, and any other unsettled grievances, present or future, to a national board of arbitration composed of union and NMTA representatives. A fifty-seven–hour week was to go into effect in six months, and a fifty-five–hour week in one year – quite a victory on the hours question. But Chicago's local demands were largely sacrificed in the process. There was no mention in the pact of a closed shop, minimum wage, or seniority. Most important for the future, the IAM agreed "that there is to be no limit in any way placed upon the production of the shop."[10] Two weeks of argument among the union leaders ensued before a mass ratification meeting was staged at the Salvation Army hall on March 31. With the help of a bass drum borrowed from the hosts and "beaten with tremendous effect when speeches were being made favorable to the agreement," but "always silent when they were unfavorable," a motion to endorse the contract and return to work carried by a vote of 3,028 to 396.[11]

From May 10 to May 18, New York's Murray Hill Hotel was the scene of intense bargaining, with President James O'Connell, Vice-President D. D. Wilson, and Chicago's venerable Hugh Doran, a veteran of the MBIU, representing the IAM, and President D. McLaren of the U.S. Cast Iron Pipe Company in Cincinnati, W. L. Pierce of Brooklyn's Lidgerwood Manufacturing Company, and Edward Reynolds of the E. P. Allis Company in Milwaukee representing the NMTA. They agreed to improve on the Chicago pact by reducing the work week nationally to fifty-seven hours in six months, and fifty-four hours, rather than fifty-five, in one year. The union agreed to call off the strikes outside of Chicago once a small raise had been granted to the Paterson strikers. No union shop was conceded, the agreement calling only for no discrimination by employers against union members. A machinist was defined in accordance with the union's constitution, but wages for each locality were left to future arbitration. The board of six was to sit permanently to hear

9. U.S. Industrial Commission, *Report*, VIII, 35, 490–2.
10. *MMJ*, 11 (May 1900), 254–5.
11. *MMJ*, 11 (May 1900), 255; 14 (July 1902), 424.

future grievances from all over the country, no strikes were to be called during the life of the agreement, and each association undertook to enforce the settlement on its own members. Finally, the union reiterated its pledge to put no restrictions on production, although the panel never dealt specifically with the questions of piecework, two machines, and handymen that the union side had tried to place before it.[12]

Douglas Wilson, the union's Socialist editor and vice-president, hailed the Murray Hill agreement as pointing "the way out [of industrial strife] by the simple and scientific process of gradual change, so gradual that the movement is almost imperceptible."[13] Samuel Gompers and President O'Connell toured New England to recruit for the IAM on the basis of its achievement of the nine-hour day and the employers' pledge of no discrimination, while the NMTA's officers barnstormed the land to force recalcitrant employers into line on the shorter week. Only a few minor firms left the NMTA when the fifty-seven–hour week went to effect in November.[14]

The NMTA's leader justified their behavior by giving currency to the views of William Phaler, the experienced president of the National Founders' Association, which had reached a national arbitration agreement of its own with the iron molders in 1899. Union officers were more reliable than their members, argued Phaler. Furthermore, unions usually won strikes for wage increases and lost other strikes. Hence there was a need for arbitration machinery to handle wage disputes. Finally, he stressed, labor had to be induced to abandon "the idea that recognition of the union implies more than the agreement to make collective bargains between employer and employee . . . or to insist that it conveys the right to enforce rules and methods in the conduct of the business without the consent or co-operation of the employer."[15]

These developments naturally led officers of the IAM and the NMTA to be the featured guests at the December 1900 conference on industrial arbitration and conciliation convened by the National Civic Federation (NCF). Although its National Conference on Combinations and Trusts in the fall of 1899 had established the NCF's claim to being an institution

12. *MMJ*, 11 (June 1900), 311–49, 386–90; 12 (July 1900), 483–90; 12 (August 1900), 496–9. For the membership of the NMTA, see *MMJ*, 12 (May 1900), 252–4. On the issues that the IAM tried unsuccessfully to raise, see *MMJ*, 12 (May 1900), 290.
13. *MMJ*, 13 (January 1901), 32.
14. *MMJ*, 13 (January 1901), 29–33; 13 (April 1901), 198–202; 13 (May 1901), 261–3.
15. Robert M. La Follette, ed., *The Making of America*, Vol. 8, *Labor* (Chicago, 1905), 88–99; the quotation is on p. 97.

that could gather men of prominence in every walk of life to discuss weighty current issues, its energetic secretary, Ralph M. Easley, was convinced that it could also provide a practical agency for establishment of industrial peace. In June of 1900 he had assembled an advisory council of five hundred members to guide the federation's work and lend the prestige of their names. Wilson of the IAM, President Martin Fox of the iron molders, Secretary-Treasurer William Gilthorp of the boilermakers, and Secretary George Buchanan of the bicycle workers represented the metal trades in a union contingent that also included Gompers, Mitchell, McGuire, and two of the labor movement's ancient warriors, George Schilling and George McNeill. Among the fifty-two representatives of "manufacturing" on the council were no fewer than twenty-two prominent metal-trades employers, including Chicago's William Chalmers and Stanley McCormick, Clem Studebaker, and David M. Parry, who was soon to become the nemesis of the NCF. Judge E. H. Gary was one of the eight participants from steel. Textiles, with five members, was the only other industry heavily represented. Both the NMTA and the National Association of Manufacturers (NAM) were represented as organizations on the council.[16]

The main thrust of the federation's work in this field was to promote stable contractual relationships between unions and associated groups of employers by means of propaganda as well as direct intervention in industrial disputes. It sought to convince employers that the established leaders of major unions were both sufficiently honorable to adhere scrupulously to the terms of any agreement they might negotiate and, thanks to the position accorded them by contractual recognition, firmly enough entrenched to be able to compel their members to do so as well. Labor's vexing demand for shorter hours could be met by coupling a reduction in working time with abandonment of workers' restrictions on output. This formula was called by Easley the essence of the Murray Hill agreement.[17]

It was indispensable to the success of such a policy that the union leaders involved vigorously suppress sympathy strikes and strikes by their members in violation of the "sacred contracts." The employer had to be reassured on two points: First, although union officials might drive a hard bargain on wages and hours from time to time, the terms of settle-

16. The membership of the advisory council is from Franklin H. Head and Ralph M. Easley to John Mitchell, February 4, 1901 (John Mitchell Papers, Box A3–9). See also Green, *Civic Federation*, 11–12.
17. Ralph Easley to John Mitchell, April 27, 1903, and the enclosed clipping from the New York *Independent* (Mitchell Papers, Box A3–10).

ment would apply, through the trade association, to his competitors as well as himself. Second, his production would not subsequently be interrupted by the injection into his plant of "irrational" issues of class solidarity possibly arising from disputes that had nothing directly to do with him. The role of John Mitchell, president of the United Mine Workers of America (UMWA), on this question made him Easley's hero in the labor movement. Mitchell consistently rejected private suggestions that he pare down the demands of the coal miners he represented, even when those suggestions came from Easley. But during the 1902 anthracite strike, he made use of the entire staff of the NCF's conciliation committee to barnstorm locals of the UMWA in bituminous-coal areas to help him suppress the movement among them for a sympathy strike.[18] Similarly, during the 1901 machinists' strike, O'Connell of the IAM called on lodges that had settled with their employers, as well as unions of other metal trades, not to join the strike, in order that employers who had contractual arrangements with the union should not be hurt.[19]

The suppression of sympathy strikes was a critical feature of the federation's conciliation activity. Class solidarity had been the traditional mainspring of craft-union strength. Easley and his colleagues now offered established unions an attractive alternative: national agreements between organized labor and organized business, binding on both sides. Strong unions could improve the conditions of their own members under this formula, without being distracted by the plight of less fortunate workers. There was even room for joint action among such unions, as is illustrated by the gradual evolution of the Federated Metal Trades. Sympathetic action among machinists, molders, metal polishers, blacksmiths, pattern makers, and boilermakers had become commonplace, and a league of their national officers had existed since 1894. But the movement for a formal federation with local affiliated councils, which was initiated in 1901 and ratified by a convention in 1906, aimed to promote arbitration of disputes and joint negotiations and to suppress sympathy strikes, as well as moves to amalgamate the unions. Especially important for metal-working enterprises was the unswerving insistence of the iron-molders union that its locals adhere to their trade agreements no matter who else in the factory went on strike. Throughout the first decade of the twentieth century, molders' leaders regularly ordered their members to cross

18. Green, *Civic Federation,* 43–51. For Mitchell's rejection of Easley's request, see Easley to Mitchell, August 4, 1902; and Mitchell to Easley, August 6, 1902 (Mitchell Papers, Box A3-10).
19. Chicago *Record-Herald,* June 9, 1901.

the picket lines of striking machinists.[20] Such efforts were, indeed, timely because the tendency of workers to engage in sympathy strikes, a tendency that had lain dormant through the late 1890s, reasserted itself vigorously between 1901 and 1904.[21] The NCF could reach its goal only if "uncivilized" behavior by workers could be contained.

But the promise of organized harmony embodied in the Murray Hill agreement did not survive a single year. The November 1900 reduction in hours took place with little ado anywhere, except in St. Louis, where the union demanded an increase in hourly wages to compensate for the loss of hours. The question did not arise elsewhere, because metal-trades employers, still faced with a booming market and a shortage of machinists, tended to dispense raises liberally when hours were reduced. Nevertheless, the St. Louis case sounded an ominous note: The NMTA executives refused to arbitrate it or any other wage question at the national level. Wages, they now contended, were for local determination.

O'Connell and other national union officers had anticipated strikes in plants that were not affiliated with the NMTA and had begun a campaign as early as February 1901 to mobilize union members in such companies for a battle to force their weekly hours down to fifty-four on May 18, in line with those of the NMTA shops. But as that date approached, the IAM leaders found themselves deluged with petitions from lodges that were covered by the Murray Hill agreement, all demanding that the union insist on an hourly raise of 12.5 percent to take effect with the final reduction in hours. On May 11, O'Connell and Wilson met for hours with the NMTA's administrative council in a futile effort to reach a national wage settlement. Convinced that the employers had betrayed the spirit of Murray Hill by demanding a national treaty to settle that local Chicago strike one year and then referring national wage claims back to localities the next, prodded by the insistence of his members that they would not accept a loss of income with the reduction in hours, and confident that his union, which had enrolled more than 32,000 members by that time and clearly would bring at least 150,000 workers into action, could weather any storm, O'Connell called a nationwide strike for May 20, 1901.

The IAM Chicago district, on its own initiative, met with the national

20. On sympathy strikes, see "The battle for control of the machine shop," Chapter 4. On the Federated Metal Trades, see *MMJ*, 9 (1897), 141; 14 (May 1902), 254–5; 18 (April 1906), 354; 8 (May 1906), 452–3. On the molders, see U.S. Commissioner of Labor, *Eleventh Special Report*, 202–8.
21. See Chapter 4.

NMTA officers to propose a compromise local settlement, instead of joining the walkout. When the NMTA reply was an offer of a 5 percent increase, regarded as deliberately insulting, because Chicago employers had already offered 6.25 percent, the district officers left the room calling for a strike. The next morning, Decoration Day, the city's IAM headquarters thronged with machinists eager to show their martial skills once again.[22]

The NMTA was ready to meet the challenge. Throughout the previous year, its officers, too, had been deluged with complaints from their constituents. Emboldened by national recognition of their union, machinists not only had enrolled in the union in great numbers, employers protested, but also had demanded that all their workmates do the same and had refused to work in violation of union rules. Having rejected the demand for a closed shop in negotiations, employers now found their workers establishing it in practice by work stoppages and ostracism of nonunion men. And having traded a reduction in hours for an agreement by the union not to place any limits on production, they encountered adamant refusal by their employees to run two machines, perform piecework, or instruct handymen. Of what value was the written contract, protested President Walter L. Pierce of the NMTA, when "we ran up against this curious proposition that the restriction of production and the freedom of employment was subject to the constitution of the union?"[23]

The Murray Hill agreement of which the NCF had been so proud had broken down in mutual betrayal. Federation officers Wilson and Chalmers were hurling angry press releases at each other from opposite sides of the picket line. To make matters worse, Easley had little time to spare for an effort to resuscitate the pact, because at the same time two other members of his advisory council were engaging in a similar battle: Judge Gary of U.S. Steel and T. J. Shaffer of the Amalgamated Iron and Steel Workers. That embattled union had broken its contracts in the U.S. Steel Hoop Division by calling a general stoppage throughout the new steel corporation and was openly seeking sympathy strikes by coal miners and railroad workers, whose leaders also sat on the NCF advisory council. Working day and night with the aid of Gompers and Mitchell to hold

22. *MMJ*, 12 (February 1901), 63–4; 12 (May 1901), 257–8, 261–3; 14 (July 1902), 30–1, 424–6.
23. U.S. Industrial Commission, *Report*, VIII, 509, 512–13; Chicago *Record-Herald*, June 9, 1901; Harry F. Dawes to Ralph M. Easley, July 8, 1901, copy included in Ralph Easley to John Mitchell, July 13, 1901 (Mitchell Papers, Box A3-10); National Civic Federation, "Joint Trades Agreement Conference of the National Civic Foundation, Held at the Fifth Avenue Hotel, New York City, Saturday, May 7th, 1905 at 10 A.M." (typescript, Mitchell Papers, Box A3-10), 37–45; the quotation is on p. 37.

steel to the NCF's philosophy of labor relations, restrain the other unions, and nullify Shaffer's influence in his own union and ultimately drive him from office, Ralph Easley had little left of his proverbial energy to devote to the metal trades. His dream of organized harmony between labor and capital was fading.[24]

Metal-trades employers had lost all interest in Easley's dream. On May 28, the NMTA administrative council had met in Chicago's Great Northern Hotel to adopt a new declaration of principles. Point one declared, "Since we, as employers, are responsible for the work turned out by our workmen, we must, therefore, have full discretion to designate the men we consider competent to perform the work and to determine the conditions under which that work shall be prosecuted." It went on to proclaim that no employers would deal with men on strike, that each would employ handymen and apprentices as he saw fit, and that hours and wages were to be governed by local conditions. Although it assured readers that the NMTA would not discriminate against workers because of union membership or nonmembership, and would not countenance such premium systems as did not allow an average workman a fair wage, it adamantly asserted the employer's prerogative to use any pay system or production method he chose.[25]

This ringing declaration attracted many manufacturers to an open meeting of the NMTA in New York City at which employers mobilized their side for the battle that was beginning. Former President Pierce (who had signed the Murray Hill agreement for the association) and President Phaler of the National Founders' Association attended, and, Easley later reported, "did everything they could to stem the tide, but every manufacturer was so hot at O'Connell, for his alleged 'treachery,' that they were overwhelmed by the opposition." The "general declaration of war" Easley and his colleagues labored so hard to prevent was enthusiastically carried.[26]

In Chicago, ironically, the employers' bark proved much worse than their bite. Only two thousand machinists were on strike there by the second week in June, because ninety companies had already acceded to

24. Green, *Civic Federation*, 25–33; Brody, *Steelworkers*, 60–8; William Z. Foster, *The Great Steel Strike and Its Lessons* (New York, 1920), 12, 18–20. For Easley's moves against Shaffer, see Easley to Mitchell, November 26, 1901, November 29, 1901 (Mitchell Papers, Box A3-10). Selig Perlman and Philip Taft correctly spoke of this strike as "labor's defeat at the Marne." Commons, *History of Labour*, IV, 97–109.
25. *MMJ*, 14 (June 1902), 329–30; Chicago *Record-Herald*, June 9, 1901.
26. Easley to Mitchell, June 11, 1901. See also Easley to Mitchell, June 12, 1901, June 19, 1901, June 25, 1901 (Mitchell Papers, Box A3-10).

the union's demands. Fraser and Chalmers, however, held out for fifty-four weeks, its president, a member of the NCF council, swearing he would never again deal with the IAM. The molders at Fraser and Chalmers soon joined the strike, with wage demands of their own, and the company responded by hiring strikebreakers and announcing that it was returning to the ten-hour day for all employees. That declaration brought the pattern makers and boilermakers out on strike. The profusion of tents in which scabs were housed earned the plant the name Fort Chalmers.

In June 1902, however, the defeated company signed contracts with all the unions again, granting its machinists an increase of 11 percent, a minimum craft rate of thirty cents per hour, a fifty-five–hour week, and a pledge to reinstate all strikers, except for three leaders. For the next four to five weeks the plant was in turmoil, as workers demonstrated continually to speed up the rehiring of strikers and the dismissal of scabs. On August 5, the union men chased the remaining eight scab machinists down the street from the plant, hurling dire threats. The company fired four men who had been involved in the fracas, and quickly the plant emptied out once more. About a week later, company officials met with union officers and the shop committee, reinstated the discharged men, and agreed to a straight fifty-four–hour week. Work then resumed at Fraser and Chalmers, under union conditions, but hardly those envisaged by the NCF.[27]

All across the country, strikes dragged on into the fall of 1901. In mid-October, President O'Connell reported 3,470 members still walking picket lines from Atlanta to San Francisco.[28] In one respect, however, the defiant stance of the NMTA restored the situation that had existed before Murray Hill: Union power prevailed in Chicago, but the employers had crushed it elsewhere. On the other hand, the Murray Hill–NCF interlude had left both sides much better organized for combat than they had previously been, and although it left some prominent union leaders devoted to the NCF, it convinced metal-trades employers, and soon practically

27. *Chicago Record-Herald*, June 9, 1901; *MMJ*, 14 (January 1902), 28–30; 14 (October 1902), 677–82. A bitter rivalry between the IAM and the Chicago branches of the ASE strengthened the hand of Fraser and Chalmers during the strike. ASE members spoke against the first strike on the picket lines, and during the second walkout the ASE offered to replace IAM strikers with its own members. The British union was consequently ostracized by the Chicago labor movement and, in search of a home, helped found the IWW in 1905. See Lee S. Fisher and J. J. Keppler to *MMJ*, 15 (March 1903), 209–11.

28. James O'Connell to AFL Executive Council, October 15, 1901 (Mitchell Papers, Box A3-46).

the entire business world, of the folly of the NCF philosophy of industrial relations.

The open-shop drive

By September 1903, there were 243,000 trade-union members in Chicago. The city could challenge London for the title of trade-union capital of the world. Possibly one-third of those members worked in the packinghouses, where militant shop committees united the activists of dozens of craft unions to exercise effective job control.[29] The Chicago Federation of Labor defiantly used sympathy strikes as the touchstone of its success. With its help, a coalition of ten unions even brought International Harvester under contract and converted it to the nine-hour day.[30] The policy of sympathy strikes placed the teamsters' union in the forefront of the city's class conflict. Participation by these drivers would carry almost any strike into the streets of working-class neighborhoods, where assaults on scabs became community actions.[31]

Even the business depression of 1903–4 did not destroy the power of Chicago's organized workers, although it undermined that power at several points. By turning a labor shortage into a labor surplus, the depression triggered a general assault on union power throughout the land. The IAM alone faced 134 strikes in 1904, in contrast to 56 the previous year, and 55 of those strikes were in Chicago. In May 1904, the expiration of the Chicago Metal Trades Association's contract covering eighty-two plants allowed the association to demand wage cuts, two-machine operation, and the introduction of "roughers" to perform machinists' tasks of lesser skill at lower than the minimum pay. The union, in turn, demanded Saturday afternoons off, and when the employers responded by instituting a work week of five ten-hour days, the machinists went home en masse at the end of nine hours, starting a general stoppage.

The city's Metal Trades Council brought out all its affiliates in sympathy with the machinists, and union teamsters blacklisted the products of struck plants. But soon the massive unemployment took its toll. Strikebreakers were mustered in large numbers, and the desperate efforts

29. Commons, *Trade Unionism and Labor Problems, First Series,* 36–64, 87–136; Green, *Civic Federation,* 97. I am indebted to Steven Sapolsky for his insights into the Chicago labor movement of that epoch.
30. *MMJ,* 15 (September 1903), 831–3.
31. Commons, *Trade Unionism and Labor Problems,* 36–64; Hollander and Barnett, *American Trade Unionism,* 192–3.

of pickets to keep them out of the plants brought countless arrests and prosecutions of union members. In July, the packinghouses forced all their unions into a long strike, in which the workers were ultimately crushed. In September, International Harvester and Pullman closed completely for two weeks, then reopened on a nonunion basis. With the teamsters' strike in the spring of 1905, the city erupted in class and racial violence, bringing President Roosevelt himself to town to inveigh against apostles of "class hatred" and to threaten the strikers with military occupation of their city. When metal-trades employers began once more to sign contracts with the IAM in April, International Harvester, Link-Belt, Pullman, and others were missing from the roll. But still the union signed pacts with more than four hundred firms.[32]

Outside Chicago, the militant metal-trades employers generally carried the day. In Dayton, Ohio, Sedalia, Missouri, Birmingham, Alabama, Cincinnati, Ohio, and Beloit, Wisconsin, employers' associations mobilized the local business communities to support companies battling the IAM. Their actions initiated a campaign on several fronts that quickly gained momentum throughout the land. The NMTA, guided by Commissioner E. F. Du Brul (sarcastically called its "business agent" in the union press), provided struck employers with advice on strategy, as well as with financial assistance, private detectives, legal assistance, and a card file on every one of the thirty-five thousand workers employed by the association's 325 firms. It organized the Independent Labor League of America, which enrolled machinists and would-be machinists who were ready to go anywhere in the land to replace strikers. By 1911, it had registered sixty-six hundred machinists in Chicago alone.[33] With the aid of such agencies as the Corporations Auxiliary Company, it honeycombed the unions with spies. A sensational exposé in 1904 identified such detectives on the AFL executive council and among the national officers of several unions, federation field organizers, members of city trades assemblies, and union-convention delegates.[34] Such weapons allowed the NMTA in Portland,

32. *MMJ*, 16 (July 1904), 621–2, 637; 16 (September 1904), 821–2; 16 (November 1904), 970; 17 (February 1905), 138–9; 17 (April 1905), 323–5; 17 (October 1905), 916–18. Foner, *Labor Movement*, III, 310–11; Commons, *History of Labour*, IV, 61–70; William M. Tuttle, Jr., "Labor Conflict and Racial Violence: The Black Worker in Chicago, 1894–1919," *Labor History*, 10 (Summer 1969), 411–16.

33. On the NMTA's open-shop drive, see Commons, *History of Labour*, IV, 129–35; Bonnett, *Employers' Associations; MMJ*, 16 (June 1903), 448; 17 (June 1905), 501; *IA*, 87 (March 23, 1911), 740; Hollander and Barnett, *American Trade Unionism*, 198–203, 208–11.

34. Corporations Auxiliary Company to United Brewers Association of New York, October 10, 1906 (Mitchell Papers, Box A3-48); Paul Maas to *MMJ*,

Oregon, to summon each machinist to a central office, where he was confronted with a dossier on his past and forced to tear up his union book.[35]

These undertakings led employers' associations into judicial and political activity on a broad front. Primarily through the agency of the American Anti-Boycott Association they pressed court cases against boycotts and sympathy strikes, establishing judicial precedents for the issuance of injunctions and collection of damages against unions in such cases. Not until the early 1920s did a series of U.S. Supreme Court decisions, among them the Hitchman Coal, Red Jacket Coal, and American Steel Foundries cases, establish a uniform interpretation of federal law controlling boycotting, picketing, and sympathy actions by labor, but state courts and federal rulings in the Danbury hatters case and Bucks Stove and Range case opened the way to widespread issuance of injunctions by local courts. Of the 1,845 injunctions Edwin Witte catalogued that had been issued against union activities between 1880 and 1930, 28 were issued in the 1880s, 122 in the 1890s, 328 in the first decade of the twentieth century, 446 in the second, and 921 in the 1920s.[36]

Much more important than injunctions and the famous court precedents in determining the outcomes of strikes was the behavior of local police and magistrates at the scene of dispute. The laws concerning trespass, traffic obstruction, disorderly conduct, and riot were so ambiguous in their definitions of crimes that the attitudes of law-enforcement officials on the spot in fact determined the atmosphere surrounding picket lines. Awareness of this led militant metal-trades associations to become more active in local politics and in movements for government and police reform. In the midst of the 1900 strike in Chicago, employers' spokesmen had denounced the protection their plants received from police as a "farce" and blamed their troubles on the fact that no fewer than twenty-two "laboring men" occupied important offices in city hall. One of them complained that the police solicited payments from companies wanting

---

16 (February 1904), 117–18; 16 (April 1904), 298–300; 16 (September 1904), 791; 19 (March 1907), 267–8. One enterprising agency offered its services to the AFL Executive Council to ferret out other spies, and anyone else the council might want to watch. B. M. Goldowsky to Samuel Gompers, March 20, 1905, June 3, 1905 (copies in Mitchell Papers, Box A3-47).

35. Ordway Tead, *Instincts in Industry: A Study of Working-Class Psychology* (Boston, 1918), 122–4.

36. Edwin E. Witte, *The Government in Labor Disputes* (New York, 1932), 84. For discussions of injunction law, see Witte, op. cit.; Felix Frankfurter and Nathan Greene, *The Labor Injunction* (New York, 1930).

protection, then "never laid a hand on those men," while strikers shouted insults and threats at scabs.[37]

The employers' crusade for the "open shop" everywhere sought to enlist the participation of concerned citizens from all walks of life. Starting with the Modern Order of the Bees in Dayton and Citizens' Alliances in many towns, local merchants, academics, professional men, supervisory personnel, fraternity boys from universities, and antiunion workers were enrolled in local associations to combat "union tyranny." In Minneapolis, salesmen for the Citizens' Alliance toured the town selling twenty-five–cent antiunion buttons bearing the slogan "Minneapolis Makes Good," while metal-trades employers posted placards in their factories recounting their victories over the unions.[38]

David M. Parry, president of the NAM and head of the Overland Automobile Company, soon emerged as national leader of the crusade. Under his guidance the national Citizens' Industrial Association (CIA) was formed in 1903 to rally all "those who believe in the maintenance of law and order and the perpetuation of our free institutions," first to defend the country's workingmen against "the present programme of violence, boycotting, and tyranny now being carried out by the majority of labor unions," and second to resist "legislation of a socialistic nature."[39] Its leader, C. W. Post of Battle Creek, Michigan, explained the CIA's mission in its first bulletin:

> Do you hear the murmur and the mutterings and see the lightning flashes of the storm of public indignation rolling up in mighty grandeur? It is coming and coming fast. The 14,980,000 decent, upright, peaceful voters who love work and demand liberty are now arising in their might, and the text on the wall, writ by the hand of almighty God, writ in letters of glistening steel, proclaims that the slimy red fingers of anarchy shall be crushed by the mailed hand of the common people and their law.[40]

It has become fashionable for historians to identify the various organizations involved in the open-shop drive as relatively small business concerns concentrated in the Midwest, in contrast with the NCF, which is seen as the agency of the sophisticated leaders of big business. There was much in the rhetoric of the two groups to support that view. Parry and

37. U.S. Industrial Commission, *Report,* VII, 9, 40. Witte, *Government in Labor Disputes,* is one of the few legal studies to stress the importance of local ordinances. See also David Montgomery, " 'Liberty and Union': Workers and Government in America, 1900–1940," in Robert Weible et al., eds., *Essays from the Lowell Conference on Industrial History 1980 and 1981* (Lowell, Mass., 1981), 145–57.
38. *MMJ,* 20 (May 1908), 440.   39. *MMJ,* 16 (January 1904), 9–10.
40. Quoted in Green, *Civic Federation,* 101n.

Post often inveighed against sentimental eastern clergymen and intellectuals who had been duped by Gompers and Mitchell into believing that business could deal honorably with unions. Easley loved to boast that his organization represented "more capital and men that the whole of the Parry outfit."[41]

On examination of the dispute in the metal trades, however, it appears that the difference between the NCF and the open-shop drive was not sociological but tactical. They appealed to the same business groups. Around the time of Murray Hill, Easley's approach won a broad and powerful following. By 1903, however, few manufacturers of any size endorsed his views any longer. The two business groups confronted each other directly, with conventions held almost simultaneously in Chicago in the fall of 1903, and the outcome was disastrous for the NCF. The NMTA openly aligned itself with the NAM and the Citizens' Alliances as six hundred manufacturers from all over the land gathered to demand freedom from union controls. Commissioner Du Brul of the NMTA, who had precipitated the antiunion tirades at the ASME convention after the presentation of Taylor's paper a few months earlier, now scoffed at the NCF. "What do they represent anyway?" he asked. "I have found them a lot of meddlers."[42]

Although Easley still assured Mitchell that "the same employers, and they outnumber the others at the rate of twenty-five to one, are with us,"[43] there was little evidence to support his claim. The employer representatives of the NCF's advisory committee numbered only sixteen at that time, and half of them were from transportation. At the 1905 Trade Agreements Conference, convened by Easley to answer the open-shop drive, only small employers from printing, foundries, and construction participated, and they spent their time furiously berating the AFL representatives present for their sins.[44] By that time, the CIA had adopted as

41. Ralph Easley to John Mitchell, December 8, 1904 (Mitchell Papers, Box A3-10). See also statement of John Kirby, Jr., in Easley to Morris Hillquit (draft), June 26, 1911 (Mitchell Papers, Box A3-11); National Civic Federation, *The National Civic Federation, Its Methods and Its Aims* (New York, 1905). For the usual depiction of the NCF and its rivals, see Thomas C. Cochran, *The American Business Systems: A Historical Perspective, 1900–1955* (Cambridge, Mass., 1957); Wiebe, *Businessmen and Reform;* Weinstein, *Corporate Ideal.* A different view is found in Foner, *Labor Movement,* III, 61–110.

42. Chicago *Daily Tribune,* September 30, 1903; Chicago *Record-Herald,* September 30, 1903.

43. Easley to Mitchell, October 3, 1903 (Mitchell Papers, Box A3-10).

44. NCF, "Joint Trades Agreement Conference ... 1905"; Green, *Civic Federation,* 108–11.

its official platform eight demands against union regulations advanced by the NCF leader, President Charles Eliot of Harvard.[45] In 1906, Easley cautiously put union labels on only those invitations to the annual NCF conference that were intended for labor's representatives.[46]

More important, from 1903 onward, the important manufacturers who were active in the NCF participated in the organization's welfare and safety work but not in its promotion of conciliation and trade agreements. The NAM and the NMTA, however, also approved of this work and engaged in it as heartily as did the NCF. In 1914, only three manufacturers took part in the NCF's committee on collective bargaining – representatives of Otis Elevator, International Paper, and Weinstock and Nichols. Early stalwarts such as U.S. Steel, International Harvester, and National Cash Register had gone over to the open-shop crusade. There were fifty major employers in the NCF's Welfare Department, but fewer than ten of them dealt with unions. Moreover, union representatives were excluded from that department of the NCF.[47]

When a frenzied burst of economic activity in the last quarter of 1906 and the first half of 1907 lent strength once more to the bargaining power of workers, almost as many workers went on strike across the land as had gone out in 1900 and 1901. The NMTA, the Anti-Boycott Association, and the Citizens' Alliances were tested to the limits, but the NCF had no significant role to play. District 6 of the IAM won a raise, a minimum rate, and a fifty-hour week from twenty-two shops in the Pittsburgh area and engaged twenty-five others in long strikes. Parry and Post visited the city, reorganized the Pittsburgh Manufacturers' Association, and boasted of the support they received from U.S. Steel. Large firms such as the Mesta Machine Company of Homestead and the Pressed Steel Car Company of McKees Rocks became the bastions of resistance as the region was flooded with private eyes and state constabulary. The three district leaders of the IAM were all imprisoned, as was only appropriate in a year when Gompers and Mitchell themselves were sentenced to jail for violating an injunction against the Bucks Stove and Range boycott. By December 1907, however, plant closings everywhere had left a tenth of the union's total membership unemployed and another third "on mis-

45. Green, *Civic Federation*, 112. Eliot's demands included no closed shop, no restriction on the use of machinery, no limitation of output, no boycott, no sympathetic strike, and no restrictions on apprentices.

46. See invitations in Mitchell Papers, Box A3-10.

47. Robert F. Hoxie, *Trade Unionism in the United States* (New York, 1936), 202–3; Green, *Civic Federation*, 274n; Ramirez, *When Workers Fight*, 220–34; Committee on Collective Bargaining membership list, 1914 (Mitchell Papers, Box A3-11).

erably short time." Victory once again belonged to the militant employers.[48]

In a word, Easley and the "Parryites," as he called the open-shop leaders, had battled for the minds of the same business constituency, and the Parryites had won. The reason for their victory, quite simply, was that the leaders of the AFL could not control their members sufficiently to end sympathy strikes and stoppages in violation of contracts and traditional work rules. They could not overrule the metal-trades work cultures, which were the sources of their own organizational strength. Both the NCF and the Parryites promised the workers improved working conditions and fair treatment of union members, and to the employers they promised industrial peace and a free hand for the introduction of scientific management. Both business groups feared the collective power of workers at the plant level, but the effort to control that power through agreements with the unions had proved less effective than unilateral exercise of management control, backed by the concerted efforts of all employers in a given locality. The NCF's approach failed abysmally in the metal trades, while in most of the country the open-shop approach was a smashing success. Hand-blown glassworks, potteries, paper factories, bituminous-coal mines, and railroad carrying trades, in all of which traditional work patterns remained unchallenged in this decade, might provide models of collective bargaining as espoused by the NCF. In the building trades, its formula often worked well. But where management fought to restructure work relations, the open-shop approach proved the most effective strategy.

Union leadership and the NCF

The open-shop drive effectively checked the growth of unionism in the metal trades. The IAM had enrolled roughly 11 percent of the country's machinists in its ranks by 1901, and that proportion was to remain constant through 1913. Its rules and standards were upheld, for the most part, in small workshops, where employers were dependent on the skills of their journeymen to turn out short runs of diverse products, in railroad-car shops, where machinists still rebuilt whole sections of lo-

48. *MMJ*, 19 (March 1907), 263; 19 (April 1907), 372; 19 (May 1907), 473, 483–4; 19 (June 1907), 591–2; 19 (July 1907), 666–8, 682–3; 19 (September 1907), 891–2; 20 (January 1908), 64–8; 21 (April 1909), 341–2. On the Bucks Stove and Range case, see Philip Taft, *The A.F. of L. in the Time of Gompers* (New York, 1957), 268–71.

comotives and where the speed of repair work was more important to the companies than the men's hourly wages, and in firms that manufactured tools and instruments for purchase by craftsmen, who looked for union labels. Aside from temporary increases during the bitter strikes of 1904 and 1907, the union had difficulty enlarging its membership during these twelve years; when it did so at all, it was primarily by admitting operatives into its ranks. The average American machinist, especially if he worked for a large enterprise, encountered at least some elements of scientific management each working day in a nonunion setting.

These developments had two important consequences for the nature of metal-trades unions and the consciousness of metalworkers. First, the differentiation between the salaried leaders of the union and the rank and file became more pronounced. Second, the leaders themselves divided into rival factions, one supporting the NCF and the other the Socialist Party.

The officials of the IAM became quite professionalized as the union's membership expanded from eighteen thousand to fifty-six thousand; its treasury swelled, and contractual relationships with many companies became routine after 1900. The union paid annual salaries ranging from one thousand to fifteen hundred dollars (the income of many male clerical employees) to President O'Connell, editor Wilson of the *Machinists' Monthly Journal,* Secretary-Treasurer George Preston, the tightfisted guardian of its funds, and two general organizers. There were seventeen business agents by 1900, elected by districts or by large locals. They were paid half their salaries by their home bodies and half by the Grand Lodge. Additionally, an average of twenty organizers were assigned to specific missions at any one time. In 1901, the constitution was amended to provide for the elections at large of five paid vice-presidents (increased to seven in 1903), each of whom worked in the field as a troubleshooter, under the general direction of the president. Rank-and-file supervision of this salaried leadership was provided in the British fashion, by a general executive board of five machinists from the shops, who were elected by the membership to meet periodically (with lost time at four dollars per day and expenses paid from the union's treasury) and review the actions of the salaried officials.[49]

The national officers were a homogeneous group in important respects. Of the twelve leaders elected to national posts in 1903, eight had been born in the United States, three in Britain, and one in Canada. All but the venerable Hugh Doran, who had been active since the 1870s, were between thirty-five and forty-five years of age. Seven came from

49. *MMJ*, 10 (January 1900), 15; Perlman, *Machinists*, 24, 151–4, 174–89, 206.

railroad shops. Two had been master mechanics in such shops, and another three had at one time or another operated businesses of their own. Seven had been members of the Knights of Labor in their younger days, and one had been prominent in the American Railway Union. Although only two of the twelve were Socialist Party members (George Preston and P. J. Conlon), the most ardent anti-Socialist on the executive board, Robert Ashe, a Massachusetts single taxer, had been driven from his post in 1897. President O'Connell consistently opposed the Socialists in the running battle of resolutions at the AFL conventions, but within his own union during the first years of the century he was more circumspect, and even inclined to declare, "I am as good a Socialist as any man in this hall."[50]

This homogeneity facilitated a general concurrence among the officers on a program of all-grades unionization of the machine shop, increased discretionary authority to the leaders in dealing with management, increased political action, and broad education of the membership on social and economic questions. All of them were hostile toward DeLeon's Socialist Labor Party and venomous toward the IWW.[51] Although resolutions to endorse the Socialist Party or the "co-operative commonwealth" were consistently defeated at IAM conventions, the delegates of 1903 did agree to insert into their constitution the provision that their union encourage "the wisest use of our citizenship based upon the class struggle upon both economic and political lines, with a view to restoring the common weal of our Government to the people and using the natural resources, means of production and distribution for the benefit of all the people."[52]

The IAM's officers had come to view themselves as full-time specialists in labor-management relations. In this respect they were much like the salaried officers of other American unions of the epoch: born to working-class families, veterans of union struggles since their late teens, and successful in their pursuit of careers in union leadership. "Up-to-date unionism," wrote Herbert N. Casson, an American Fabian, in the machinists' paper, "will choose as its leaders men who can hold their own with the lawyers and capitalists – large minded, masterful men, who will every-

50. "Biographical," *MMJ*, 16 (May 1903), 402–8. On Ashe, see *MMJ*, 9 (August 1897), 366–9. On O'Connell, see report of the IAM delegates to the AFL convention, *MMJ*, 15 (January 1903), 25–7. The quotation is from *MMJ*, 9 (June 1899), 362.

51. On the SLP, see P. J. Conlon, "His Reason for Swatting," *MMJ*, 10 (September 1898), 593–6; Stuart Reid to *MMJ*, 11 (March 1899), 147–8. On the IWW, see editorial, *MMJ*, 18 (November 1906), 984–5.

52. *MMJ*, 15 (July 1903), 552.

where command respect."[53] All of them agreed on the need to instill a more profound sense of discipline and calculation into their members, who still were given to walking off their jobs on a fine spring day without prior discussion with either the boss or the union officers, then wiring union headquarters, "Demands refused. Men walked out. Send man at once."[54] More and more leaders came to agree with Adolph Strasser that their task was to "represent the interests of the International Union, regardless of the local instructions of the strike committee." Specifically, that meant "to bring about an amicable and honorable adjustment of the trouble as speedily as possible, thus saving the funds of the International Union, which would otherwise be wasted; and to maintain the honor and reputation of the International Union for fair dealing with union manufacturers."[55]

Some of the most influential unions in the AFL had cultivated the use of union labels as an alternative to strikes. The cigar makers, hatters, restaurant workers, garment workers, and boot and shoe workers had subtly but significantly shifted the late-nineteenth-century practice of boycotting unfair goods toward a new emphasis on promoting the goods of manufacturers who signed up with the union. None had gone farther in this respect than the boot and shoe workers, who awarded labels even to companies that did not pay union scale; others, such as the United Garment Workers, often assigned labels to clothing made in plants where only the male cutters and pressers were unionized, thus ignoring the largely female operatives. Such practices provoked intense criticism from many members. In the case of the boot and shoe workers, there was an election in which President John Tobin was defeated, only to refuse his accession to what he called a "prank of the referendum mode of election" and subsequently to expel the victorious candidate from membership. To Gompers, the union label had provided the most appropriate instrument for the gradual diffusion of union standards. His foes in the AFL religiously shopped only where union labels were displayed, but they were outraged by such practices as that of Tobin, which they said aided employers rather than the workers.[56]

53. H. N. Casson, "Words of Wisdom," *MMJ*, 15 (April 1903), 271; Warren R. Van Tine, *The Making of a Labor Bureaucrat: Union Leadership in the United States, 1870–1920* (Amherst, Mass., 1973).
54. "Unauthorized Strikes," *International Molders' Journal* (May 1900), 277.
55. Strasser quoted in G. M. Janes, *The Control of Strikes in American Trade Unions* (Baltimore, 1916), 118.
56. See Cooper, "From Hand Craft to Mass Production"; David Bensman, *The Practice of Solidarity: American Hat Finishers in the Nineteenth Century* (Urbana, Ill., 1985); Dye, *Women's Trade Union League*; Galster, *Shoe Industry*. The quotation from Tobin is in Galster, 121.

The IAM used union labels, but only as a minor part of its strategy. Few of its members manufactured consumer goods. From the vantage point of its Grand Lodge, which spent $3,626,890.58 to support strikers and their families between 1899 and 1914, the need for a more "progressive" and "civilized" form of industrial relations was inescapable. To make matters worse, police statistics for the three years 1902–4 in Chicago alone listed 8,299 arrests of machine-shop and foundry workers during strikes.[57] The mediation work of the NCF and its promotion of trade agreements between employers and unions seemed to provide the most viable and attractive alternative to picket lines, injunctions, sluggings, and arrests, on the one side, and the growing threat of compulsory arbitration legislation, on the other.[58] Although twenty-five states had followed the example of Massachusetts in creating conciliation and mediation agencies of some sort by 1911, their powers were limited to persuasion; they had staffs far too small for the work facing them; and they were composed primarily of former union officers, appointed for their services to the Democratic or Republican Party, who were received by the employers with frosty suspicion. State mediators created a professional association of their own in 1911, and in 1914 a federal conciliation service came into being. Prior to that time, only railroad workers could and did regularly call on federal mediation agencies with well-defined statutory powers conferred by the Erdman Act of 1898 and the Newlands Act of 1913.[59]

The NCF, therefore, provided trade-union executives with an agency that enjoyed sufficient standing in the business community to escort employers and unionists to the bargaining table in 118 disputes during 1902 and 1903 and 156 in 1905, after which its effectiveness in all sectors of the economy fell off rapidly.[60] In its heyday, the NCF offered a means of settling disputes that was less hazardous than reliance on sympathy strikes and boycotts, and it also imported into industrial controversies the businessmen's style of dealing with one another. For example, Ralph Easley sent a note to John Mitchell of the UMWA during the 1902 anthracite strike asking, "Cant you come on & take dinner with me," and adding that George Perkins of the House of Morgan would join them afterward

57. IAM, *Proceedings of the Fourteenth Biennial Convention* (Davenport, Iowa, 1911), 17; Rhodi Jeffreys-Jones, *Violence and Reform in American History* (New York, 1978), 29 (Table II).
58. Compulsory arbitration was widely discussed between 1900 and 1914. See, for example, LaFollette, *Making of America*, Vol. 8; Commons, *Trade Unionism and Labor Problems*, 195–221; Ramirez, *When Workers Fight*, 160–73.
59. Ramirez, *When Workers Fight*, 180.
60. Green, *Civic Federation*, 65–9, 81.

to "compare notes." Lest the evening appear all work, Easley continued: "If you & your private secy [Miss Morris] want to go to something nice tonight let me know & I will get tickets. 'When Knighthood was in Flower' with Julia Marlow is a lovely thing."[61]

In addition to carrying on efforts at conciliation, the NCF was an instrument for improving sanitary and safety conditions at work, and one that was especially important to union leaders who tried to adhere to the NCF doctrine of the sanctity of contracts. This role was illustrated by a request from President Fox of the iron molders to the NCF welfare secretary, Gertrude Beeks, that she prevail on foundry owners to repair broken windows to reduce wintry drafts, install showers, and give the men lockers for their street clothes. Fox "had his hands full in getting the wage-scale signed up year after year with a provision for reasonable hours," a federation spokesman explained, and "if he undertook to get any physical betterment for the men the employers would contend that he was only trying to stir up trouble and break contracts."[62]

Understandably, the popularity of the NCF was greater and lasted much longer among conservative union leaders than in the business world. No substitute for it was available until Congress established the federal conciliation service in 1914. It is more remarkable that in the fresh glow of the Murray Hill agreement, the activities of the NCF were commended by all officers of the IAM, including the Socialists.[63] The latter looked on both the rising level of Socialist votes and arbitration agreements such as that reached at the Murray Hill Hotel as signs of the "marvelous times." Despite the criticism leveled at the NCF by the Socialist press from 1901 onward, editor D. D. Wilson of the *Machinists' Monthly Journal*, a Socialist Party member, saw no anomaly in placing two disparate items, one directly after the other, in the same column of his paper – the first urging his readers to study socialism, and the second praising Marc Hanna of the NCF for remarks "that would do credit to an advanced trade unionist."[64] Wilson, like Garland, denounced open-shop advocates for

61.   Easley to Mitchell, n.d. (1902 folder, Mitchell Papers, Box A3-10). It is an interesting commentary on the mores of the age that at the social affairs of the NCF, which the wives of capitalists dutifully attended, the wives of the trade unionists were conspicuously absent.

62.   Edward Marshall, "Welfare Work May Conquer Great Labor Problems," *New York Times*, November 17, 1912. See also Green, *Civic Federation*, 272–4; Civic Federation of New England, *Better Workshops*, Bulletin No. 5 (Boston, May 1906).

63.   The Socialist leaders of the brewery workers used the NCF to arrange negotiations with the National Brewers Association as late as 1904. Easley to Mitchell, February 8, 1904 (Mitchell Papers, Box A3-10).

64.   *MMJ*, 15 (January 1903), 5.

their devotion to an individualistic order that had already been undermined by "big modern capitalistic combinations," and he suggested that if businessmen would only "work in harmony with the times, cooperate for the elimination of waste – economic waste – put away their competitive knives and tomahawks, adopt modern methods, they would assist in the industrial and social revolution that is in progress."[65]

The mounting fury and increasing success of the open-shop drive shattered the ideological harmony among the IAM leaders. The union's growth ground to a halt in 1904, but strike expenditures continued to soar, and injunctions, spies, and organized strikebreakers dogged its tracks. To President O'Connell and special counsel Frank Mulholland, former president of the Allied Metal Mechanics, who became O'Connell's closest aide after the merger of the two unions, an alliance with the NCF was vital if they were to combat the "Parryites" of the business world. At the 1907 IAM convention, they pleaded at length with the delegates not to pass a motion denouncing the NCF and got their way in a confusing voice vote. But by the time of the next convention, 1911, a referendum had prohibited any officers of the IAM from belonging to the NCF, by a vote of 11,469 to 8,008.[66]

Toward the cooperative commonwealth

The leaders and beneficiaries of the assault on the NCF were the Socialists. Editor Wilson had hailed Eugene V. Debs's *Unionism and Socialism* in 1904 for its lucid presentation of the need to abolish capitalism and of the separate yet complementary roles of trade unions and socialist political action, without ever mentioning the pamphlet's castigation of union collaboration with the NCF.[67] Within another year, however, Wilson's faith in the work of the NCF had turned to anxiety. The federation's retreat before the rising tide of antiunion sentiment in the business world had culminated in the election of August Belmont as its president. Bel-

---

65. Editorial, *MMJ*, 15 (June 1903), 449–50. Two Socialists, A. M. Simons and T. J. Morgan, and two philosophical anarchists, Benjamin Tucker and George Schilling, had participated in the 1899 National Conference on Combinations and Trusts, at which Garland spoke. Ralph Easley to Morris Hillquit (draft), June 26, 1911 (Mitchell Papers, Box A3-11). For early Socialist criticisms of the NCF, see Easley to Mitchell, November 2, 1902 (Mitchell Papers, Box A3-10).

66. IAM, *Proceedings of the Twelfth Biennial Convention* (St. Louis, 1907; bound with *MMJ*, Vol. 19), 79–80; *MMJ*, 23 (October 1911), 1050.

67. *MMJ*, 16 (August 1904), 735; E. V. Debs, *Unionism and Socialism; A Plea for Both* (Terre Haute, Ind., 1904).

mont, Wilson charged, had "hired and retained the most notorious strike breaker in the country" to defeat the unions on his New York subway lines.[68] The editor's warning to the machinists to be "alert" was underscored by the memory that the national bituminous trade agreement, widely touted by the NCF as the outstanding model of its philosophy of industrial relations in practice, had survived the previous year only at the expense of a 5.5 percent wage cut imposed on miners over the angry protests of the union's convention.[69]

During the ensuing years, Wilson simply stopped writing about the NCF, while his paper gave extensive coverage to the socialist movements of Europe and the electoral activities of IAM members on behalf of the Socialist Party in the United States. There was plenty of such activity for him to describe, and its nature is well illustrated by the case of the cluster of manufacturing towns then known as the Tri-Cities: Rock Island and Moline, Illinois, and Davenport, Iowa. Three machinists' lodges were to be found there, one in the federal arsenal at Rock Island, one in Moline, where the John Deere Company had its farm-machinery works, and one in Davenport.[70] By 1911, when the IAM held its national convention in Davenport, a new railroad lodge had also been formed in the area.

For almost a year, during 1905 and 1906, the Socialist Party locals of the area issued their own ten-cent newspaper, *The Tri-City Workers' Magazine,* which addressed itself directly to the concerns of these workers. Three questions were emphasized in its columns: the insecurity and anxiety of working-class life, the degradation of the craftsman in the modern factory, and the neglect of workers' needs by the Democratic and Republican politicians in local governments.

Debts, mountains of them, provided the rhetorical theme for the first of these issues. Work was so irregular, especially with seasonal layoffs every summer and fall in the farm-equipment industry, and earnings under constantly shifting piece-rate standards were so unreliable that every family was depicted as carrying a heavy tally of credit on the grocer's books, not to speak of those of the butcher, the coal dealer, the clothing

68. *MMJ*, 17 (February 1905), 101–3.
69. On the miners' wage cut and Socialist responses, see E. V. Debs in *Social Democratic Herald,* April 7, 1904, and Chicago *Chronicle,* May 12, 1904; Laslett, *Labor and Left,* 205–7. Mitchell had earlier been roundly attacked by the Socialists of West Virginia for his opposition to a sympathy strike by miners in 1902. Frederick A. Barkey, "The Socialist Party in West Virginia from 1898 to 1920: A Study in Working Class Radicalism" (unpublished Ph.D. diss., University of Pittsburgh, 1971), 38–44.
70. The addition of East Moline later changed the name of the group to the Quad-Cities.

store, and the furniture market. But most agonizing of all was the effort to buy a home of one's own. Convinced that an able and industrious American workman should be entitled to enjoy the security and comfort of his own frame house, the worker described in issue after issue resolutely put his neck into the yoke to take on staggering mortgage payments, only to be foiled cruelly by the next bout of unemployment.[71]

But on the job, matters were even worse, according to *The Tri-City Workers' Magazine*. A layoff of several hundred men at the arsenal early in 1906 reminded its employees once more of the tyranny of its administration, which had battled the IAM through strike after strike over handymen, time study, and incentive pay since 1897, until the 1906 convention of the AFL officially proclaimed the arsenal a "sweatshop." The efficiency-rating system seemed the worst tyranny of all. Twice yearly, each employee was rated for regularity of attendance, skill, accuracy, deportment, and rapidity, and his pay was adjusted according to his performance on these counts during the previous six months. Looking out the window had cost A. A. Gustafson twenty-five cents per day for the next four months, and breaking a toolholder took four points off the score of Nels Alifas, in addition to a fine of $6.12.[72] And even though Alifas consistently scored 100 for deportment and attendance, when he left the arsenal to assume a union post, the army major in charge noted on his record: "This man is a disturber; has been disrespectful to me, and under no circumstances would I employ him in a shop of my own."[73]

At John Deere's vast "cornplanter works," according to the Socialist paper, the workers' lot was even harsher than at the arsenal. Piecework predominated, and in parts of the plant workers subcontracted the construction of machines, rushing and cheating each other. The atmosphere of the plant resembled that of the state penitentiary, but because "the piece work system sets every man at his fellow worker's throat, the corporation has them all in its grasp." There was but one remedy: to deal

---

71. *Tri-City Workers' Magazine* (January 1906), 11–17. Compare Stephen Thernstrom's treatment of the aspiration to home ownership as a deterrent to class consciousness, *Poverty and Progress. Social Mobility in a Nineteenth Century City* (Cambridge, Mass., 1964), and his modification of the argument in John H. M. Laslett and Seymour Martin Lipset, eds., *Failure of a Dream? Essays in the History of American Socialism* (Garden City, N.Y., 1974), 522–3.

72. *Tri-City Workers' Magazine* (February 1906), 13–16; (August 1906), 5–7. My description of the arsenal is based on House, *Taylor Hearings*, 895–922, 1262.

73. Alifas's employment record is reproduced in House, *Taylor Hearings*, 1262–4.

with the bosses "politically as a class. . . . Electing their class to power workers elect themselves."[74]

The indictment of capitalism presented in these local accounts, and the political remedy proposed, echoed the themes of Debs's famous pamphlet of 1904:

> In the capitalist system the soul has no business. It cannot produce profit by any process of capitalist calculation.
> The working hand is what is needed for the capitalist's tool and so the human must be reduced to a hand. . . .
> A thousand hands to one brain – the hands of workingman, the brain of a capitalist.
> A thousand dumb animals, in human form – a thousand slaves in fetters of ignorance, their heads having run to hands – all these owned and worked and fleeced by one stock-dealing, profit-mongering capitalist. This is capitalism![75]

The only meaningful remedy for both the "penitentiary" in which the worker toiled and the want he suffered when the "penitentiary" did not want him was for workers to use their political power to collectivize the factories and introduce a "truly scientific" management by the workers themselves.[76] But the Socialist Party members in the Tri-Cities were as much concerned with their family and community lives as they were with the inside of the factory. Their paper agitated incessantly against the bleak living conditions and barren community life in towns whose sole reason for existence seemed to be to provide hands when needed for the corn-planter works.[77]

Above all, the party campaigned for establishment of free kindergartens at every public school. They argued that capitalist development had transferred one traditional function of the family after another to the "mill and factory, bakeshop, school, dispensary and hospital." But the young child was left to be socialized "in the street," to a sense of subordination and humility, or to its sublimation in gang loyalties, unchallenged by either the former nexus of family activities or any constructive alternative. Despite the evident failure of the city schools to equip young workers with a firm sense of how to contend with the world into which they were soon to be sent, the argument concluded, free kindergartens

74. *Tri-City Workers' Magazine* (September 1906), 6–7. I am indebted to Neil Basen for bringing this magazine to my attention.
75. Debs, *Unionism and Socialism*, 43–4.
76. H. L. Varney, "The Fallacy of Scientific Management," *MMJ*, 24 (January 1912), 22–4.
77. *Tri-City Workers' Magazine* (December 1905), 5; (September 1906), 1–4. The Socialists' ringing denunciations of dance halls may have made them as obnoxious to many young workers as were the local evangelists.

offered the best hope for instilling "community ideals" into the child, developing a sense of solidarity through relationships with other children, and encouraging through "close personal touch" with the teacher "the high instincts latent" in the child's mind, "which under any other method of ordeal and routine lapse into disuse and oblivion." To win this goal, however, an intense political struggle was needed against "the school board, the conservative German element and the Catholic Clergy."[78]

These arguments deserve some attention. There was much truth in their premise that working-class children (especially boys) spent little time at school or at home under their mothers' feet but much time in vacant lots, streets, and hallways and on tenement rooftops, riverbanks, and docks. There they received rough lessons about society. As Pauline Goldmark reported concerning boys of New York's West Side:

> If a wagon nearly runs over him the driver lashes him with a whip to teach him to "watch out." If he plays around a store the proprietor gives him a cuff or a kick to get rid of him. . . . And if he is complained of as a nuisance the policeman wacks him with hand or club to notify him that he must play somewhere else. Moreover, everything that he does seems to be against the law.[79]

The streets provided most of the child's earliest lessons in the meaning of authority, group solidarity, and class. It was there, too, that the child learned to regard the law as the ubiquitous foe of every pleasant activity, let alone of children's frequent but informal contributions to the family's food and fuel. Parents also learned to consider the policeman or the juvenile court as a merciless enemy. The Socialists' Catholic opponents proved to have a better understanding of this pervasive aspect of working-class experience than did the contributors to *The Tri-City Workers' Magazine*. The Catholics wanted no kindergarten teachers to instill "community ideals" in the children, because they were quite content with the ideals that the street and the home were already imposing (with proper interpretation by the church).

78. Floyd Dell, "Socialists and Kindergartens," *Tri-City Workers' Magazine* (February 1906), 7–11. The remarkable similarities of these arguments to those of early nineteenth-century bourgeois educational reformers explains the Socialists' consistent lionizing of Horace Mann and contrasts sharply with recent revisionist critics of educational reform. Compare Michael Katz, *The Irony of Early School Reform: Educational Innovation in Mid-Nineteenth Century Massachusetts* (Cambridge, Mass., 1968).

79. Pauline Goldmark, *West Side Studies: Boyhood and Lawlessness* (New York, 1914), 37. For an insightful study of the contrast between socialist attitudes and working-class experience in Austria, see Reinhard Sieder, "Gassenkinder" (unpublished paper in possession of the author). On Catholic Action and the working-class family, see "Party and Church," Chapter 6.

The crusade for kindergartens reflected the anxiety of skilled workers over the fate of their children in the city's streets as clearly as the paper's treatment of consumer debt and home ownership revealed their problems of economic survival and its castigation of the factory "penitentiaries" reflected their loss of control on the job. In the Tri-Cities, as in Brockton and Haverhill, Massachusetts, Schenectady, New York, Wheeling, Huntington, and the Kanawha mining towns of West Virginia, Pitcairn and Wilmerding, Pennsylvania, and other communities where it has been studied closely, the Socialist Party appealed above all to unionized workmen during the first decade of the twentieth century. In all these towns its program was the "constructive socialism" that linked union struggles over job conditions to community reforms of desperate importance to workers. Nothing could be more misleading than to identify "sewer socialism" with bourgeois influence on the party. The bourgeoisie, and only they, already had good sewers.[80]

Socialism of this sort had no insurrectionary bite and recoiled in fear before "the great slum population," which the IAM's most famous Socialist, Kate Richards O'Hare, called "the greatest danger to our state – the greatest menace to humanity – and civilization."[81] Because of its strong commitment to both parliamentary activity and trade unionism, its local organization resembled a labor party as much as it did a revolutionary organization – if not more so.[82] The party's moderate leader Robert Hunter could argue with considerable merit in 1914 that the Socialist Party "is a labor party, more or less dominated even today by Trade Unionists, and all it needs to make it rank with its capitalist rivals in this country and to make it as powerful as the great labor parties of

80. See Barkey, "Socialist Party in West Virginia"; Bedford, *Socialism and the Workers in Massachusetts;* Bruce M. Stave, ed., *Socialism and the Cities* (Port Washington, N.Y., 1975). See also Ira Kipnis, *American Socialist Movement, 1897–1912* (New York, 1952), 198–201, on the composition of party membership (41% craftsmen and 20% laborers in 1908). For the role of workers in nineteenth-century struggles for public sanitation, see Feinstein, *Stamford in the Gilded Age.*

81. O'Hare speech to IAM Lodge 105, Toledo, in *Toledo Evening News,* June 6, 1903. I am grateful to Neil Basen for this item. Karl Kautsky expressed the same fear of, and contempt for, the "slum proletariat" that was constantly replenished by migrants from the countryside in *The Class Struggle (Erfurt Program)* (translated by William E. Bohn, New York, 1971), 168–70.

82. This tendency is analyzed well in William E. Walling, *Socialism As It Is: A Survey of the World-Wide Revolutionary Movement* (New York, 1912), 350ff.

Europe . . . is the united support of all American labor organizations."[83]

In fact, Socialist votes invariably increased in parallel with union strength, including IWW strength after 1910, and they shrank rapidly when that union base was destroyed.[84] In the Tri-Cities, it was only after the brief triumph of unionization during the war years and the party's very effective local antiwar activity that the Socialists carried Davenport's elections.[85] Moreover, by that time, the members of the national executive board of the party bore a striking resemblance to those of most union executive boards: They were predominantly self-educated and self-confident careerists up from the ranks of the working class.[86]

The fact remains, however, that the ranks of the Socialist Party were infused with a profound class consciousness and an ardent commitment to total change of the social system. Much as they liked to argue that the type of political action pursued by the AFL Executive Council was ineffective according to its own criteria,[87] they ultimately insisted that no measures that did not bring the workers to political power, collectivize industry, and abolish the ethic of competition and greed would suffice to meet workers' needs. Consequently, the party instructed its locals to emphasize street-corner speaking, pamphleteering, bookselling, and other educational work on behalf of socialism. Locals were to avoid meeting in saloons, where the atmosphere would repel women members and impede serious discussion, to rotate the chair regularly, "so that no one gets too much power and becomes the 'boss' of the local," and to make themselves experts in all deliberations concerning their own needs. "If we are to rule the world," the instructions advised, "we must train ourselves to think clearly, talk calmly, debate kindly but forcibly, and the training can be obtained in the Socialist Local as nowhere else."[88]

The Tri-Cities Socialists projected the image of a socialist future in which no individual would gather rent, interest, or profits. At the very least, the eight-hour day would instantly become the practice throughout

83. Robert Hunter, *Labor in Politics* (Chicago, 1915), 179.
84. Barkey, "Socialist Party in West Virginia"; Joseph R. Conlin, "The IWW and the Socialist Party," *Science and Society*, 31 (Winter 1967), 22–36.
85. James Weinstein, *The Decline of Socialism in America, 1912–1925* (New York, 1967), 44, 52. For an account of the party's public antiwar activity in the Tri-Cities, see *International Socialist Review* (June 1917), 758.
86. Sally M. Miller, *Victor Berger and the Promise of Constructive Socialism, 1910–1920* (Westport, Conn., 1973), 47–8, 138 n. 12; Hunter, *Labor in Politics*, 181–2.
87. Hunter, *Labor in Politics*, 31–45, 105.
88. Socialist Party, *How to Organize a Socialist Local or Branch* (Chicago, n.d.); copy in National Archives, R.G. 28, Post Office, Item 529, Box 13.

society, and union scale would be the lowest possible pay. The government would end its interference in people's personal lives, they predicted, and control of all social functions would revert to the smallest social groups that could manage their affairs efficiently. Furthermore, in contrast to the leaders of the IAM, they looked on the new IWW with considerable sympathy, and when Haywood, Moyer, and Pettibone went on trial, all discussion of piecework and kindergartens was sidetracked in favor of a tireless campaign for their release.[89] In short, the intellectual dichotomy of reformism versus revolutionary activity obscures, rather than clarifies, the ideology of these workers.

The Socialist Party had no formula for coping with scientific management on the job. It was the trade unions' task to deal with that problem as best they could, while the party charted the path out of capitalism in all its forms. To be sure, many Socialist leaders of IAM lodges in Toledo, Detroit, Chicago, Schenectady, and elsewhere ardently favored amalgamation of the metal-trades unions and more militant actions to cope effectively with the open-shop drive, but the party's emphasis was on political action. Its most prominent spokesman in the AFL, Max Hayes, asserted in 1907 that "it is absurd for Socialists to waste a lot of valuable time in splitting hairs, over the question of industrial organization."[90]

The fact remains that the open-shop drive and managerial reform together were undermining the traditional bases of craft control, solidifying the local middle class as a whole against the labor movement in town after town (making the opposite sides of the tracks, so vividly depicted in John Steinbeck's novel *East of Eden,* political as well as social antagonists), and through injunctions and police ordinances making the daily functioning of trade unions a political issue. These developments brought the Socialists into control of the IAM.

The economic boom of early 1907 saw more workers out on strike than in any other year between 1904 and 1910, among them the largest number of IAM members who had ever been out in any year in the union's history. New recruits swelled the union's membership by almost 40 percent in a single year. Militant dockers' strikes in Brooklyn and New Or-

89. "The Ideas on Which Socialism Rests: The Cooperative Commonwealth," *Tri-City Workers' Magazine* (December 1905), 13–15. On the Haywood-Moyer-Pettibone case, see *Tri-City Workers' Magazine*, March 1906, 19, and May 1906, passim. Compare Kipnis, *American Socialist Movement*, 325ff., who contends that constructive Socialists held aloof from the case.

90. Quoted in Kipnis, *American Socialist Movement*, 237. On left-wing demands for amalgamation and industrial unionism within the IAM, see IAM, *Proceedings Fourteenth Convention*, 90–2, 137; *MMJ*, 17 (December 1905), 1123, 1125–6; Ramirez, *When Workers Fight*, 116–22.

leans gave a preview of the 1910–13 "revolt of the laborers," and the firm support that black unionists in New Orleans provided for the brewery workers frustrated the effort of the AFL Executive Council to destroy that Socialist-led union. Then, in the fall of the year, the economy collapsed, leading to sweeping layoffs and even more widespread short time for workers in most industries. The open-shop drive was dramatically joined by U.S. Steel, which expelled all remaining unions from its own plants and influenced whatever mines, docks, ships, haulers, and construction operations it could to do the same. As the crisis gave way to renewed prosperity in the summer of 1909, aggressive strikes in McKees Rocks and Newcastle, Pennsylvania, the West Virginia coal fields, and New York's garment markets, all ably conducted under Socialist or IWW leadership, contributed immensely to the prestige of the Left. The general strike of 146,000 workers in Philadelphia in 1910 and the briefly effective fusion of the AFL and Socialist Party efforts in Job Harriman's campaign for the office of mayor in open-shop Los Angeles the next year bore eloquent testimony to the class solidarity the Socialists preached.[91]

The results were evident at the polls and in the trade unions. Socialists won major municipal offices in seventy-four cities in 1911. Among them was Schenectady, where nine of the eighteen party members elected to the city government were members of the IAM.[92] Although Thomas Van Lear had not been successful in his 1910 bid to become mayor of Minneapolis, he emerged from the effort as the most prestigious Socialist in the union and leading strategist of the emerging "progressive" bloc. Two national organizers for the party had toured locals of the IAM and UMWA in 1909, and the party's national executive committee established a trade-union department to systematize the propaganda and recruiting work they began. At the 1908 convention of the miners, John Mitchell was retired from office, and Socialist delegates, who numbered 400 out of the 1,000 miners present, led an assault on the NCF and successfully urged a resolution barring from union membership anyone who joined the army or militia. During 1911 and 1912, conservative leaders of long standing in several unions were driven from their offices by rebel movements under Socialist direction. Among them were James Moffitt of the hatters,

---

91. John H. Griffin, *Strikes: A Study in Quantitative Economics* (New York, 1939), 43. For IAM struggles during these years, see *MMJ*, 21 (April 1909), 341–2; IAM, *Proceedings Fourteenth Convention*, 17. On strikes in other industries, see Arnesen, "Until Such Time," 138–97; David Montgomery, "The 'New Unionism' and the Transformation of Workers' Consciousness in America, 1909–22," *Journal of Social History*, 7 (Summer 1974), 509–29.

92. Weinstein, *Decline of Socialism*, 116–17; Laslett, *Labor and Left*, 161.

Albert Berres of the pattern makers, John Lennon of the journeyman tailors, Hugh Frayne of the sheet-metal tradesmen, William Huber of the carpenters, and James O'Connell of the machinists.[93]

The more than forty Socialist Party members among the delegates to the 1911 convention of the AFL introduced a series of resolutions calling for financial aid to the indicted McNamara brothers and endorsement of Socialist Job Harriman's campaign for mayor of Los Angeles, both of which carried unanimously, and for greater attention to unionization of unskilled workers, which was referred to the Executive Council. Their other proposals, that federation officers be elected by referendum vote (which might have deposed several vice-presidents, and possibly Gompers by 1913) and that the NCF be denounced, lost by the wide margin of five thousand to twelve thousand.[94] Nevertheless, the delegates' vote to "sustain the conception of the labor problem in the United States for which The National Civic Federation stands"[95] gave conservative unionists a frail reed with which to defend themselves after that conception had been repudiated by most leading figures among the manufacturers.

Socialist–conservative factionalism

The IAM had already broken decisively with the NCF's "conception of the labor problem." Referendum votes before the union's 1911 convention had repudiated the NCF and replaced President O'Connell with a Socialist militant from Providence, Rhode Island, William H. Johnston, by a vote of 13,321 to 15,300, with 42 percent of the membership participating.[96] When the 131 convention delegates appeared in Davenport, Iowa, they were aligned in two opposing blocs that were so tightly disciplined that in balloting for convention committees and resolutions, fewer than a dozen delegates ever deviated from the side with which they had voted on the previous issue. James O'Connell directed his faction, and Thomas Van Lear conducted the "progressive" group with precision that was almost military. When the delegate from Rock Island Arsenal Lodge No. 18 was discovered to be voting with the conservatives, his home lodge convened an emergency meeting and recalled him, because he had

93. [Ludwig Lore], "Progress Backward," *The Class Struggle,* II (September–October 1918), 507–12; Kipnis, *American Socialist Movement,* 336–7; Green, *The National Civic Federation,* 144–55; Van Tine, *Making of a Labor Bureaucrat,* 158.

94. Kipnis, *American Socialist Movement,* 341–3.

95. Green, *The National Civic Federation,* 343.

96. *MMJ,* 23 (October 1911), 1025–32.

been under instructions "to vote with the progressives on all questions." Conversely, Lodge 147 of Providence, which had not been able to send a delegate, wired its protest against the "radical proceedings now being carried on by the delegates." Outgoing President O'Connell was openly bitter in his valedictory speech and boasted to the delegates that he had job offers from the metal-trades department of the AFL and from two agencies in Washington, where he could earn ten thousand dollars per year for only two or three hours of work per day. No one moved to extend him a vote of thanks for his twenty-one years of leadership.[97]

One-fourth of Johnston's votes had come from the 162 railroad lodges of Division 1, the lines between the Illinois Central and the Pacific Ocean, which had favored him overwhelmingly. He also enjoyed majorities in most New England lodges, in the battered lodges of the Midwest, where the open-shop drive had done its greatest damage, and in the Chicago lodges. Conservative strength was concentrated in Division 3 (the railroad lodges of the Southeast), in New York City's large lodges (though not the smaller ones of neighboring New Jersey), and in the lodges of Philadelphia and eastern Canada. By the close of the 1911 convention, therefore, members of the Socialist Party were firmly in control of a machinists' union whose 54,300 members were sharply divided along ideological lines. Five years were to pass before the union called another convention, and during the interim, recall votes were used to remove three officers who opposed the new administration.[98] The bitterness of this conflict was both duplicated and reinforced by the leadership conflicts within the AFL as a whole. Understanding this conflict requires that our examination of the Socialists be supplemented by some knowledge, first, of their conservative opponents and, second, of the revolutionary syndicalist challenge that emerged on their left flank between 1911 and 1916.

The AFL's conservatives drew on three sources of strength: their control of the administrative machinery of the AFL and of most unions, the increasingly explicit and forceful role of religious institutions in working-class communities and in unions, and an alliance of trade unionists with the Democratic Party that culminated in the elections of 1916.

Control of the top offices in most unions provided conservatives with effective instruments for dominating union conventions (or postponing them altogether), rewarding loyal activists with desirable jobs, undermin-

---

97. IAM, *Proceedings Fourteenth Convention*, 94, 109, 159–60, and passim.
98. For a detailed analysis of the vote, see David Montgomery, *Workers' Control in America: Studies in the History of Work, Technology, and Labor Struggles* (New York, 1979), 79–82. On the recalls, see Perlman, *Machinists*, 46–50.

ing the relations of dissidents with employers or other unions, and keeping the image of themselves as constructive and indispensable leaders before the eyes of the members. Despite the AFL's frequent claim that it respected the autonomy of member unions, its officers consistently strengthened the positions of conservatives in those unions and attacked Socialists. The demise of the United Metal Workers at the hands of the AFL Executive Council, the harassment of the brewery workers by jurisdictional disputes and their ultimate expulsion for a year, and the council's decisive support of John Tobin's leadership of the boot and shoe workers after he had clearly lost the election are three of the most dramatic instances of the council's important role. By 1907, Secretary Morrison instructed all AFL organizers in the field to keep Socialist leaders of affiliated unions under constant surveillance. On the other hand, when conservative officers of affiliated unions were voted out of office, the council found places for them in the hierarchy of the AFL itself. O'Connell of the machinists became president of the metal-trades department, Moffitt of the hatters was made a legislative agent, and Berres, Lennon, and Frayne all found sinecures with the AFL.[99]

Despite election of the AFL's executive officers by convention votes that usually were dominated by the influence of a handful of individuals who attended year after year and who often cast the bloc votes of larger unions, and despite President Gomper's skillful use of his powers to appoint and co-opt officers and organizers, the fact remains that Gompers was consistently supported by a majority of the votes cast at AFL conventions. Many of these votes came from leaders of label-oriented unions, such as the garment, flint-glass, and boot and shoe workers, who represented but small minorities of the workers in their industries. Interestingly, some votes came from embattled unions of unskilled workers whose leaders were firmly committed to the NCF, such as the longshoremen and street-railway operators. Nevertheless, all those unions combined cast fewer votes than the UMWA in 1913. By that year, most of the miners' 3,708 votes were cast on the Socialist side, as were those of the machinists, brewers, ladies' garment workers, western hard-rock miners, and journeyman tailors, and together they constituted a third of the AFL convention votes. That is why many writers in IWW journals and employers' publications alike considered the Socialists on the verge of taking control

99.   Foner, *Labor Movement,* III, 136–60; Van Tine, *Making of a Labor Bureaucrat,* 113–60; Ramirez, *When Workers Fight,* 104–14; Laslett, *Labor and Left,* 83–5; Frank Morrison to John Mitchell, February 21, 1907 (Mitchell Papers, Box A3-49). On the brewery workers, see the massive record in the AFL Executive Council minutes, January 5, 1907 to January 23, 1908 (Mitchell Papers, Box A3-49).

of the AFL in 1912–13. What prevented that third from combining with the many available scattered votes to form a majority, however, was the solid support given Gompers by the 4,442 votes cast by the building trades that year (22.6 percent of the total voting power).[100] Although many unions of construction workers, and especially the United Brotherhood of Carpenters and Joiners, which was second only to the coal miners in size, caused President Gompers endless worries with their jurisdictional claims that led to frequent defiance of Executive Council rulings and threats of secession, they could be counted on to vote solidly against the Socialists. They also voted to sustain the NCF conception of the labor problem, though they played little role in the NCF itself.

Efficiency engineers and personnel managers were figures alien to American construction sites. As late as 1923, when the U.S. Department of Labor undertook a survey of output in building trades, it could not find a single employer who recorded such information. Despite Gilbreth's experiments with Boston's bricklayers, stopwatches were as uncommon as written job assignments. The general bricklaying practice was simply "keeping in line": No one raised a new course of bricks on any wall until everyone else on the wall had finished work on the lower course. Bosses often put pacesetters on the wall to speed the others along, whereas unions instructed stewards on the job to prevent rushing, laying with both hands, elevating the course more than a line at a time, and so forth. The new technology of poured concrete was subjected to serious Taylor-style studies, leading to the use of precut lengths of wood with designated spots for carpenters to place nails, as well as to competitive pressure on bricklayers to work faster. Such practices intensified local conflicts over work rules, but they did not lead to reorganization of work relations in construction.[101]

Essentially, the line between the craftsman who erected his portion of the building and the laborer who kept that craftsman supplied with materials defined the job in 1910 as it had in 1870. That is not to say that no important changes had taken place. On the contrary, planing mills prefabricated trim, doors, and even staircases by the 1890s, employers introduced piecework, and there was "lumping" or subcontracting of portions of the work openly or by stealth whenever hard times or union weakness allowed. Two changes at the turn of the century were of special importance. One was the proliferation of new architectural styles and

100. My calculations based on voting-strength data in Helen Marot, *American Labor Unions*, 255–60.
101. William Haber, *Industrial Relations in the Building Industry* (Cambridge, Mass., 1930), 207–8, 210–11; Taylor and Thompson, *Concrete Costs*; U.S. CIR, I, 914–16.

building materials, especially in the erection of large buildings, that multiplied the number of skills needed and broke down lines of demarcation between the traditional crafts. The world of carpenters, plasterers, bricklayers, painters, and plumbers was invaded by electricians, elevator riggers, metal lathers, structural-iron and sheet-metal tradesmen, terracotta layers, and hoisting engineers. Each of these trades brought new unions and new contractors into being, and often they installed trim or fixtures where once a carpenter would have worked. Technological innovations made jurisdictional controversies endemic in the industry.[102]

The other major change was in the ethnic origins of big-city laborers. Italian and Polish replaced English and German as the languages of those who carried hods and pushed wheelbarrows around the scaffoldings. Older, predominantly Irish laborers' unions fell into decay in Boston, New York, and elsewhere and were replaced, especially by unions of Italians. Italian laborers staged major strikes in Boston in 1904, Buffalo in 1907, and Providence and Buffalo again in 1910. The International Hod Carriers, Building and Common Laborers Union, chartered by the AFL with the endorsement of the major building-trades unions in 1903, had a membership that was almost entirely Italian, and its president, Domenico D'Alessandro, was knighted by the king of Italy for his services to the king's subjects abroad. The ideological ambiance in laborers' strikes, however, was far different from that seen in the trades. A description in the *Providence Journal* of a parade of hod carriers on strike for better wages captured the diverse currents of the immigrants' community life:

> The Italian Royal March was succeeded by the Socialist Anthem, and the American National Anthem by the Garibaldi March. Whenever the band struck up the well-known strains of the Garibaldi March, all the marchers took their hats off and applauded enthusiastically. Along Knight Street the band played the Socialist hymn "Internationale" but as the members passed in front of the Church of the Holy Ghost, the majority of them uncovered and remained so until they had swung into Atwells Ave. The march was headed by laborers with Italian flags, followed by men with American flags, followed by the Savoia Band, followed by D'Alessandro, followed by officers of the union.[103]

102. Haber, *Building*, 1–48, 152–69; *The Carpenter* (January 1882), 4; (April 1898), 3; (May 1899), 10. I am indebted to Mark Erlich for bringing these articles to my attention.

103. Fenton, *Immigrants and Unions*, 223–37; Smith, "Remaking Their Lives," 224–5; Yans-McLaughlin, *Family and Community*, 112–15, 250; Pedro Castillo, "The Making of the Mexican Working Class in the United States: Los Angeles, California, 1880–1920," in Frost, Meyer, and Vásquez, *El Trabajo*, 511; U.S. CIR, II, 1755–1767. The quotation from the *Providence Journal*, May 2, 1910, is in Smith, 224–5.

Although unions of building tradesmen had been active since the eighteenth century, they had assumed a new importance and adopted new styles of operation between the 1860s and the 1890s. Workers' loyalties were attached to the craft, rather than to the place of work, because few carpenters or bricklayers worked long for any one firm. Several jobs per season were as common as winter unemployment. Successful unions might establish a standard wage for the locality (no matter who the employer), help workers locate jobs and employers locate potential workers, shorten the working day, provide life and accident insurance for members, and cultivate conviviality, debate, and self-improvement among them. Bricklayers' and carpenters' unions by the 1880s often collected libraries for their members, held frequent "smokers" for the men and occasional dances and picnics to involve their lovers, wives, and children, provided major contingents for Labor Day parades, and produced activists who sparked local central labor unions and helped organize local mill and shop workers. The hard, dangerous, and often challenging work made the unions' efforts to "elevate" their members' economic conditions and family lives especially meaningful. As the Boston carpenter and foe of socialist politics Harry Lloyd explained to the 1894 AFL convention:

> I have heard some men here and outside say the trades union is a narrow institution. How narrow? What does it mean to me? It means the complete and utter destruction of the wage system. That is its logical conclusion. Where have you heard any trades union get on a platform and say when we get $3 a day we will stop? When we get eight hours a day we will stop? Not at all. But preach the duty that all that labor earns belongs to the laborer; that wage earners have time to cultivate their intellect; time to study and have all that has been so often denied them. What does it mean to me? It represents my hopes and aspirations to the fullest possible extent. If I cannot be a gentleman the trades union will make me one.[104]

By the time of Lloyd's oration, the major crafts all had functioning international unions with important Canadian as well as U.S. sections. They also had many local building-trades councils and were all affiliated with the AFL, except the bricklayers. Many of them paid walking delegates who patrolled work sites, with authority to call men off if union standards were not being met. The eight-hour day had been won in many cities, especially after the carpenters' May 1 strike movement in 1890. As

104. American Federation of Labor, *A Verbatum* [sic] *Report of the Discussion on the Political Programme of the American Federation of Labor, December 14, 15, 1894* (New York, 1895, hereafter cited as AFL, *Pol. Pgm. Debate*), 59–60. On libraries, see Richard T. Ely, *The Labor Movement in America* (New York, 1886), 125. On building-trades aid to textile workers, see Chapter 3, Footnote 86. See also Frank K. Foster, *The Evolution of a Trade Unionist* (Boston, 1901), 54ff.

organizations became more stable, their officers inveighed against what Peter McGuire called the "hurrah" system of organizing: meeting in a beer garden when jobs were plentiful and declaring "down with the bosses – the capitalists; they are making too much money; now is the time to give them a whack in the back of the neck."[105] Moreover, the bricklayers of both Chicago and New York had emerged from fierce strikes in 1887 with negotiated agreements to arbitrate work rules with master masons' associations and to shun sympathy strikes.[106]

Building tradesmen believed that workers' control could be exercised in the here and now. To do so, however, required unity, increasingly stringent rules, and quasi-military discipline. "That's why it is right almost to force the non-Union men into line," argued Chicago's Anton Johannsen. "Life, when taken right, forces a man to be a good husband. Why not force a scab to be a good citizen, a good member of his class?"[107]

The depression of the 1890s lifted slowly in residential construction, but quickly in the rebuilding of urban commercial centers. Stonecutters, plasterers, lathers, ironworkers, and steam fitters joined carpenters and painters in raising wages, fixing task sizes, prohibiting machinery, rooting out lumping and piecework, and shortening hours of work in New York, Chicago, San Francisco, and other metropolitan centers. Walking delegates halted work for immediate settlement of grievances, and sympathy actions spread the stoppages quickly from trade to trade. Secondary boycotts forced contractors to use union-made or locally manufactured materials. Office buildings, stadiums, department stores, and other huge projects abounded with jurisdictional disputes. Such disputes set groups of contractors, as well as workers, against one another, and they were sometimes settled by fisticuffs or payoffs. Workers' solidarity allowed small unions, especially the steam fitters' helpers and structural ironworkers, to increase the earnings and expand the domains of their members rapidly, but also to extort graft. Journalistic exposés of such practices made the names of "Skinny" Madden and Sam Parks household words.[108]

105. *Carpenter* (January 1892), 4.
106. Robert A. Christie, *Empire in Wood: A History of the Carpenters' Union* (Ithaca, N.Y., 1956), 56–60; Haber, *Building,* 279–80; *Carpenter* (June 1890), 4; Senate, *Labor and Capital,* I, 813–20; James C. Beeks, *30,000 Locked Out: The Great Strike of the Building Trades in Chicago* (Chicago, 1887). I am indebted to Gordon E. Sands for bringing this book to my attention.
107. Hutchins Hapgood, *The Spirit of Labor* (New York, 1907), 349.
108. The classic study of these developments is Haber, *Building;* but see also Foner, *Labor Movement,* III, 136–73; Charles Hoffman, "The Depression

National contracting firms involved in commercial building were prime movers in organizing militant employers' associations that locked out tens of thousands of workers in Chicago in 1900 and New York in 1903, demanding the dissolution of building-trades councils, an end to sympathy strikes, abolition of restrictive practices, and separate negotiations of each craft union with corresponding employers' associations. In Chicago, the Building Contractors' Council, led by the tough Billy O'Brien, who had once been president of the bricklayers' union, drafted principles to guide every craft agreement, escorted scabs onto jobs, shut off supplies to contractors who settled separately with unions, flooded the courts with petitions for injunctions, and organized rival unions to combat those they had locked out. Note that these employers' associations, unlike those in the metal trades, did not try to stamp out the unions. On the contrary, they recognized that though four-fifths of the country's building workers remained unorganized, those in most major cities would not take a job without union protection. Consequently, the contractors offered to pay union scale and sought to sign contracts of their own design with unions. They tried to police and reshape the unions rather than destroy them. Often they succeeded, even to the point of getting AFL unions to charter or to merge with rival unions that the employers had created. No fewer than seven of the twenty-nine unions dealt with by New York's Building Trades Employers Association in 1903 were dual unions created by the contractors themselves.[109]

The paradoxical juxtaposition of intense worker loyalty to the union cause, persistent enforcement of craft codes and rules, effective intervention by employers in the shaping of union practices, and the interlocked fates of some twenty crafts with one another and with their own particular employers produced a style of unionism that was effective, authoritarian, and, though still tolerant of diverse ideological currents, quite inhospitable soil for Socialist politics. Building-trades councils existed separately from the central labor unions in major cities, symbolizing the separate world of construction craftsmen, though they often participated in both institutions. Despite the growth of some nationwide construction firms, networks of subcontracting produced swarms of small employers. San Francisco in 1910, for example, had 1,113 building contractors, most

of the Nineties," *Quarterly Journal of Economics*, 16 (June 1956), 145–8; Luke Grant, *The National Erectors' Association and the International Association of Bridge and Structural Ironworkers* (Washington, D.C., 1915).

109. E. M. Craig, "Building Conditions in Chicago: A Survey of the Actual Developments in Dealing with the Labor Problem from 1900 to the Present Time," serialized in *The American Contractor*, 44 (January 6, 1923), passim. On dual unions, see U.S. CIR, II, 1585.

of them immigrants or children of immigrants, just like their employees. Rivalry with one another and urgent needs to meet deadlines for work made it difficult for them to stand united against unions. Instead, they usually cultivated sectoral alliances, akin to those found on the docks, between particular craft unions and associations of contractors in the relevant trades. In New York City, almost 90 percent of building trades-men (163,000) were union members by 1914–16, and even among paint-ers and structural ironworkers, who had neither closed shops nor formal trade agreements, union scales and rules prevailed. Jurisdictional wars kept the loyalties of carpenters' locals attached directly to the Indianap-olis headquarters of their powerful brotherhood, but local officers, local agreements, and local building-trades councils exercised decisive roles in most other trades.

Paradoxically, the sectoralism of the building trades simultaneously undermined employers' attempts at united fronts and nurtured union corruption that in some places was shameless. Chicago's Building Con-tractors' Council, having forced all the city's unions to abandon the building-trades council led by "Skinny" Madden, by the fierce lockout of 1900, found that within five years a new board of business agents under Madden's leadership was operating effectively, whereas the contractors' association had crumbled. By 1910, they faced the even more formidable menace of a building-trades council under middle-of-the-road leadership that was militant and was opposed to Madden's efforts to rule the whole movement from his hotel suite, a council that led a series of major strikes between 1911 and 1915 that placed the contractors right back where they had been before their 1900 victory.[110] It was a crucial element of employers' disunity that every jurisdictional dispute involved questions not only of which workers should get a job but also of which bosses. Moreover, unions and contractors regularly approached city officials to urge that civic projects use local firms and local materials. Under such circumstances, sectoral alliances easily undermined both unions' and em-ployers' class loyalties.

Sectoralism also bred corruption. When, for example, sixty "house-smiths" (structural ironworkers) helping to build New York's Polo Grounds stadium struck the Turner Construction Company, the firm contracted with a metallic-lathers union to do the work. When the Tampa conven-tion of the AFL decreed that the ironworkers should do the work, the metallic lathers ignored the decision, formed a Cement League with four other unions and five contractors' bodies, and were supported by the New York Board of Business Agents. The same AFL convention had also

110.   Craig, "Building Conditions," passim; Kazin, "Barons of Labor," 140; U.S. CIR, II, 1598.

decided that sheet-metal tradesmen should install trim on wooden doors. The carpenters defied the decision and won the support of the employers by agreeing to install trim from nonunion shops.[111] It was corruption of this sort that most roused the ire of middle-of-the-road building-trades unionists, such as Chicago's John Metz and Anton Johannsen, not the better-known forms of extortion, such as strike-protection payments or fines for jurisdictional violations on work that had already been completed, that were trumpeted by the muckrakers and by legislative investigators. Growled Johannsen, "The labor movement is more in need of intelligence than it is of honesty."[112]

Moreover, a fixation on building-trades scandals diverted attention from the power and significance of middle-of-the-road activists. Officials who were feathering their own nests were neither the only nor the most important antagonists of the Socialists in the building trades. Consider San Francisco, where the building-trades council resembled a French or Italian *bourse du travail*. It had a large building that served as library, meeting hall, and hiring center for all construction workers of that compact city. All job permits were issued by the council, rather than by individual unions – a practice that seems to have been found in the United States only on the Pacific Coast and that strongly countered sectoral impulses. The council fielded its own cadre of business agents, directed by its authoritarian president Patrick H. McCarthy, who was also elected mayor of the city on the Union Labor ticket in 1909. The council also published *Organized Labor,* a weekly newspaper with a circulation of fifty thousand by 1915. Its editor Olaf Tveitmoe packed the journal with news of the world labor movement and editorials indicating how united, disciplined unions would improve workers' lives today and put an end to capitalism tomorrow. Michael Kazin's insightful history of the San Francisco movement calls this combination of practical unionism with utopian vision "business syndicalism." The union, not the Socialist Party (which ran candidates against the Union Labor Party), was depicted as the agency of social transformation. "A wide variety of radical and conservative notions was permitted within the BTC," wrote Kazin, "as long as one did not challenge the decisions of the McCarthy machine in practical affairs."[113]

111. U.S. CIR, II, 1686–705.

112. Hapgood, *Spirit of Labor,* 260. Johannsen was actually a shop worker, but he belonged to the United Brotherhood of Carpenters and was a field organizer for that union in California after 1914. For a fine fictional portrayal of construction unionism at the time, see Leroy Scott, *The Walking Delegate* (New York, 1905).

113. Kazin, "Barons of Labor," 223–6; the quotation is from p. 317. On the *bourses du travail,* see Peter Schottler, "Politique sociale ou lutte des classes:

Direct democracy (through popular initiative and referendums), taxation of the fruits of land speculation, and public ownership of utilities were goals as dear to Tveitmoe and McCarthy in San Francisco as they were to Metz and Johannsen in Chicago. Their connection with the union cause was made explicit in a pamphlet, *Common Sense on the Labor Question,* written by the Fabian Herbert N. Casson in the same year as Debs's *Unionism and Socialism* and very widely distributed by AFL unions. It may be taken as a summary of favorite beliefs of militant, committed, non-Socialist, middle-of-the-road building-trades activists.

Casson celebrated the accomplishments of American unions. *"Workers get as much of their product as their combined, organized intelligence and courage deserve,"* he wrote, paraphrasing the early philosopher of the eight-hour movement, Ira Steward.[114] Unions had restricted individual rights to prevent "social injury," and in doing so had not only provided the purchasing power that had made the expansion of American industry possible but also provided the basic freedom of industrial life: *"something to say about the conditions under which* [one] *works."* They stood against both the tyranny of monopolies and the menace of "class war." Union leaders knew, Casson explained, "that in the long march towards the new socialized civilization, class-war and revolution would mean delay and disaster." Marx, Guesde, Jaurès, and Kautsky were "great and useful men in their own countries," but *"not one of them has ever been in America or knows the facts about American industrial evolution."*

The "American plan" was to organize every worker, skilled and unskilled alike, into unions, to "always ask for the [union] label," to build up strike funds, to educate the membership in social issues, and to put legislative committees vigorously to work. Those committees should campaign for prohibition of child labor, initiative and referendum, restriction of immigration (and exclusion of Chinese), employers' liability for accidents, land reform, income and inheritance taxes, public ownership of railroads and telegraphs, and municipal ownership of utilities. But unions should also avoid party politics: "Again and again a flourishing union has been broken up by a few members who were rabid Republican, Democratic or Socialist politicians." Casson warned that *"Party*

notes sur le syndicalisme 'apolitique' des Bourses du Travail," *Le Mouvement Social,* 116 (July–September 1981), 3–20.

114. Herbert N. Casson, *Common Sense on the Labor Question* (New York, n.d.), 8. I am indebted to Steven Sapolsky for bringing this pamphlet to my attention. On Ira Steward, see Montgomery, *Beyond Equality,* 249–60.

politics is like war — all the jobs and all the glory go to the few, while the rank and file get nothing but empty praise and promises. The trade union movement is the only one in which every man gets an equal share of the benefits."[115]

Echoes of Anton Johannsen's contempt for the "Socialist Tammany Hall" resound through these arguments. "Socialism is only a word," wrote Casson. "It should neither frighten us nor send us into spasms of delight. . . . The wise thing to do is to *suspend judgement.* Let the experiment go on."[116]

As these comments suggest, Socialist Party members played important roles in many building-trades unions. It was not until the United States entered World War I that those who were loyal union members faced ostracism for their Socialist Party views. They were especially numerous among German and Scandinavian carpenters and painters. In fact, Charles Leinenweber's analysis of the 1904 membership lists of the Socialist Party in New York City revealed that almost a third of them were German-born building-trades workers. Twelve of the city's sixty locals of the United Brotherhood of Carpenters and Joiners regularly endorsed Socialist candidates, contributed to the party press, and sent participants to its parades. By 1915, the median age of German building-trades party members, however, was fifty-five, and they were not being replaced by younger recruits. Moreover, a large proportion of the party members in the brotherhood worked in furniture and machine woodworking shops, where union practice was very different from what it was on building sites. Furniture workers were in small shops, usually with German-born employers who were themselves so hard-pressed by the competition of larger factories that the union could win little improvement in the members' economic status. Mutual assistance, the preservation of a Germanic atmosphere, and socialist education, therefore, were the local unions' main functions. Their aging Socialist members were accepted as members of the brotherhood but exerted little influence on its general tone and policies.[117]

115. Casson, *Common Sense,* 27, 30, 47. Italics in original.
116. Ibid., 50.
117. Charles Leinenweber, "The Class and Ethnic Bases of New York City Socialism, 1904–1915," *Labor History,* 22 (Winter 1981). On woodworking shops, see Kazin, "Barons of Labor," 151–2; John B. Jentz, "Skilled Workers and Industrialization: Chicago's German Cabinetmakers and Machinists, 1800–1900," in Keil and Jentz, *German Workers in Industrial Chicago,* 73–85; Hartmut Keil, ed., *Deutsche Arbeiterkultur in Chicago von 1850 bis zum Ersten Weltkrieg* (Ostfildern, 1984), 63–70. For a revealing fictional description of ideological tendencies in German-American unions, see Elias Tobenkin, *The House of Conrad* (New York, 1918).

What is noteworthy about the dominant middle-of-the-road ideology is its continuity with mainstream labor-reform doctrines of the nineteenth century. These workers were overwhelmingly of the Irish, German, and British stocks that had shaped the movement of the previous century. They battled for workers' control within the existing social order, much as the Amalgamated Association of Iron and Steel Workers had done in the 1880s. Local politicians still courted them, as did figures of national prominence. In the midst of Chicago's 1900 lockout, the city's Labor Day parade featured Vice-President Roosevelt, William Jennings Bryan, and the two major-party candidates for governor (Samuel Alschuler and Richard C. Yates) on the reviewing platform. Yet those marchers were as familiar with the harsh face of the law as the Homestead strikers had been. Injunctions were familiar fare to them, and in 1902 alone, 1,268 Chicago carpenters and plasterers were arrested during strikes.[118] Just as labor reformers like George McNeill had written during the 1880s that "the wage-laborer [was] attempting to save the government, and the capitalist class ignorantly attempting to subvert it," so Casson wrote in 1904 that the trade union was "doing the work for which this republic was founded" and "deserves the support of every right-minded man and woman, because it is battling against those *secessionists of wealth* who are endeavoring to Europeanize the United States."[119]

Party and church

This traditional, secular, gradualist, trade-union–oriented vision of social reform aligned most building-trades militants in the Gompers camp, along with the many AFL officials who owed their careers directly to the president. It also blended nicely with Gompers's policy of rewarding political friends and punishing enemies regardless of their party affiliations. As the Socialist pamphleteer Robert Hunter argued so persuasively in 1915, most trade-union leaders who protested Socialist efforts to "inject politics into the union" were themselves up to their ears in local politics.[120] With the formation of the federation's Labor Representation Committee in 1906, however, the AFL began to move openly toward a national alliance with the Democratic Party. Long-standing Republican connections of many trade-union officers and the genuine conviction of

118. Craig, "Building Conditions," *American Contractor*, 44 (May 12, 1923), 26; Jeffreys-Jones, *Violence and Reform*, 29.
119. McNeill, *Labor Movement*, 459; Casson, *Common Sense*, 56.
120. Hunter, *Labor in Politics*, 102–30.

others that involvement in either party should be studiously avoided retarded the consummation of the alliance as effectively, at least, as did the protests of the Socialists. Of course, the generous and widespread activities of Martin M. Mulhall in trade-union circles on behalf of the Republicans encouraged this resistance, until they were sensationally exposed by a congressional investigation in 1913. After 1913, however, the Democratic administration provided a conciliation service that mediated 1,780 cases between 1915 and 1919 (in contrast to the 274 mediated by the NCF in its 1902–5 heyday), in addition to desired legislation and abundant patronage. The government assumed the role that the NCF had tried to play earlier and with less success.[121]

The historical basis of the Democratic Party's role was the long-standing loyalty it had enjoyed among German and Irish Catholics. This fealty had been based on the party's persistent defense of their religious institutions and their cultural values against the homogenizing efforts of Protestants, especially in connection with liquor licensing, parochial schools, Catholic charities, and sabbatarian legislation. The major business interests in the northern wing of the party – export-import merchants, brewers and distillers, impresarios of mass entertainments, and contractors on municipal projects – readily made common cause with Catholic working people on these issues.[122] To this historic defense of "popular liberties" against oppressive government, the Democrats in many localities had followed the lead of those in Massachusetts textile towns in adding labor-reform legislation and protests against police and judicial repression of strikes and boycotts to the party's program. During the open-shop drive, this theme assumed increasing importance the party's propaganda. The emerging alliance of the Democratic Party with the leadership of the AFL only supplemented an old partisan loyalty of two ethnic groups of decisive importance among union members. That old attachment, furthermore, was based on cultural values to which clerical leaders could effectively appeal against the rising tide of socialism. By 1911, this appeal had also been organized as an effective force in the labor movement.

The most significant clerical influences in the labor movement during the heyday of the NCF had come from the seminary and episcopal or presbytery level of leadership in Protestant denominations. Twenty-three Protestant clergymen and editors sat on the 1901 advisory council of the

---

121. Ibid., 45–96; Foner, *Labor Movement*, III, 335–66; John S. Smith, "Organized Labor and Government during the Wilson Era: Some Conclusions," *Labor History*, 3 (Fall 1962), 265–86.

122. Paul Kleppner, *The Cross of Culture: A Social Analysis of Midwestern Politics, 1850–1900* (New York, 1970); Rosenzweig, *Eight Hours;* Holli, *Pingree*.

NCF, along with only Archbishop John Ireland and two editors from the Catholic church. YMCAs and YWCAs sponsored many noon-hour factory and department-store services at the invitation of employers during the early years of this century, but such Presbyterian ministers who were on good terms with local unionists as Charles Stelzle, Raymond Robbins, and Alexander Irvine had also organized "people's churches" designed especially to draw northern Protestant working-class men into the activities of the churches, where they had become conspicuously absent. In 1906, Stelzle, who had been a member of the IAM, was seated in the AFL convention as fraternal delegate from the year-old Department of Church and Labor of the Presbyterian church – a status equal to that of delegates from the National Women's Trade Union League, the Farmers' Educational and Cooperative Union, and the British Trades Union Congress. Three years later he was seated as fraternal delegate from the Federated Council of the Churches of Christ in America, which was then engaged in a strenuous public campaign to persuade steel manufacturers to let their men off work on Sunday. Stelzle frequently lectured both the AFL and the IAM on the dangers of Socialists and of foreigners.[123]

This early activity prepared the way for a wave of joint religious-revival/trade-union–recruiting campaigns known as the Labor and Religion Forward movement that touched 150 cities between 1911 and 1916. Evangelical rallies for Christianity were coupled with celebration of the virtues of union craftsmen, promotion of union-label products, and often systematic canvassing of working-class neighborhoods by AFL recruiters. The pioneering researches of Elizabeth and Kenneth Fones-Wolf have begun to reveal the scope of this activity and its place in American intellectual life, but much remains obscure. Their research has made it clear that trade unionists were the initiators of such activities more often than were clergymen. Although Stelzle's early activities in collaboration with the central labor unions of Minneapolis and Philadelphia had shown the potentialities of such crusades, it was the specific endorsement by the 1912 AFL convention that opened the floodgates. Moreover, Catholic unionists were conspicuous on the platforms of these Protestant rallies. John Mitchell, Hugh Frayne, James O'Connell, and others encouraged the Labor and Religion Forward movement and the Catholic Militia of Christ simultaneously. They hoped for three rewards from their efforts: to re-

123. Stelzle, *Son of the Bowery;* Advisory Council of the National Civic Federation (Mitchell Papers, Box A3-9); Taft, *AFL,* 334–41; George H. Nash III, "Charles Stelzle: Apostle to Labor," *Labor History,* 2 (Spring 1970), 151–74; Charles Stelzle to *MMJ,* 19 (May 1907), 445–7. The Protestant campaign against Sunday work in steel was thoroughly reported in *Survey,* but see also Eggert, *Steelmasters.*

cruit Protestant craftsmen, who had often been reluctant to unionize; to wean local businessmen and molders of public opinion away from the open-shop drive; and to combat the rising popularity of socialism. The open class conflict that accompanied the large strikes of immigrants, especially in the textile, garment, mining, and steel industries between 1909 and 1913 and the sensational boost to antiunion propaganda provided by the conviction of J. S. McNamara and other leaders of the Bridge and Structural Iron Workers on charges of dynamiting the Los Angeles *Times* building in 1911 served to make the evangelical route attractive to AFL leaders. And the chiliastic enthusiasm of contemporary middle-class reformers, epitomized by the signing of the "Doxology" at the nominating convention of the Bull Moose Progressives, made it seem promising.[124]

Socialists were well aware of the new movement's significance. A general strike involving 140,000 workers called by Philadelphia's AFL unions to support embattled streetcar drivers in 1910 had abruptly increased both the size of the city's union movement and the prestige of Socialists within it. Their conservative foes, such as Frank Feeney, W. J. Tracy, and William Boyle, were the prime movers of the subsequent revivals. Later, in Indianapolis, the Socialist Party again mobilized widespread community support for striking street-railway workers with the slogan "We walk. Vote for Socialism and Ride Your Own Cars." The union's own rallies, however, featured clergymen and a rabbi as speakers and called for arbitration. "Sickening," commented a Socialist correspondent.[125]

Nevertheless, the explicit Protestant influence was short-lived and left no clear ideological legacy. In Philadelphia and in other Pennsylvania cities, employers frightened by the growth of unions and the increase in strikes promoted antiunion revivals, and especially tours by Billy Sunday, to encourage workers to be "more faithful to their duties."[126] Some clergymen friendly to labor joined the Socialist Party, rather than opposing it, and New Haven's Alexander Irvine served on its national executive committee after 1912. Moreover, the evangelists' enthusiasm for Prohibition provoked counter-organizing within the AFL by the brewery-

124. Elizabeth and Kenneth Fones-Wolf, "Trade Union Evangelism: Religion and the AFL in the Labor Forward Movement, 1912–16," in Michael H. Frisch and Daniel J. Walkowitz, eds., *Working-Class America: Essays on Labor, Community, and American Society* (Urbana, Ill., 1983), 153–84.

125. Elizabeth and Kenneth Fones-Wolf, "Protestantism, Welfare Capitalism, and Labor Activism in Progressive-Era Philadelphia" (unpublished manuscript); *International Socialist Review*, 14 (December 1913), 340–2 (hereafter cited as *ISR*).

126. Phillips Russell, "Billy Sunday as a Social Symptom," *New Review*, 3 (May 15, 1915), 36 (hereafter cited as *NR*).

sponsored Trades Union Liberty League that so seriously threatened to split the movement that Gompers persuaded Stelzle to forgo his plans for temperance rallies at AFL conventions. By 1919, in fact, the AFL convention was the scene of a serious movement for a general strike against Prohibition. Most important, as Mary K. Simkhovitch remarked in her 1916 commentaries on working-class religiosity, Protestantism may have provided the vocabulary for much nineteenth-century protest, but it lacked the organic or corporatist vision out of which a coherent social program for industrial society might be constructed.[127] Perhaps its most pervasive role in twentieth-century union circles was to strengthen the identification of the movement and its goals with "assimilated" white Americans of Old Immigrant stock. As early as 1899, the poet Edwin Markham had played that note in an appeal for Christian brotherhood that he wrote for the *Machinists' Monthly Journal*. In it, he denounced greedy plutocrats for bringing Finns, Slavs, and Sicilians – "brothers to the ox" – to America's shores: "Not content with the negro, we call these hordes into our beloved land to hinder the growth of democratic and social justice."[128]

The Catholic contribution, on the other hand, provided trade unionists with a more coherent anti-Socialist ideology. Effective Catholic intervention in labor affairs and appeared early in the century at the parish level, with resounding denunciations of socialism from the pulpit and from lay organizations in Brockton, Haverhill, Lynn, and other Massachusetts towns, in Schenectady and Buffalo, New York, in Butte, Montana, and in St. Louis. By 1906, the German Catholic Central Verein had undertaken to coordinate this struggle, drawing especially on the experience of worker-priests who had battled the Socialist leadership of the brewery workers' union in St. Louis. Its activity propelled Reverend Peter E. Dietz of Elyria, Ohio, into the national limelight when he came to the 1909 AFL convention in Toronto, determined to enroll the "class-conscious children of our Holy Mother Church" within the union movement, which he envisaged as the "classic battleground of socialism in this country."[129]

127. Kipnis, *American Socialist Movement*, 385n; Stelzle, *Son of the Bowery*, 197–9; Nuala M. Drescher, "Organized Labor and the Eighteenth Amendment," *Labor History*, 8 (Fall 1967), 280–99; Simkhovitch, *City Worker's World*, 221–31. Compare Herbert G. Gutman, "Protestantism and the American Labor Movement: The Christian Spirit in the Gilded Age," in Gutman, *Work, Culture, and Society*, 79–117.
128. *MMJ*, 11 (December 1899), 769.
129. Bedford, *Socialism and Workers*, 181–219; Kipnis, *American Socialist Movement*, 268; Daniel DeLeon, *The Vatican in Politics: Ultramontanism* (New York, 1954), 31–4 and passim; Peter E. Dietz, *Social Service: A*

Although it is clearly foolish to depict the Catholic church as single-handedly halting the rise of socialism, the Catholic effort was important in two ways. First, it helped organize a deliberate, coordinated antisocialist bloc in the leadership of the unions. Although the Militia of Christ for Social Service, launched with great fanfare at the 1910 convention of the AFL, was strictly an organization of high union officers and was dissolved by Reverend Dietz after only a year's existence, the Catholic caucus at Executive Council meetings, the Labor Mass at each convention of the AFL, and the effective presence of Father Dietz in the lobbies became regular and important features in the lives and activities of many top leaders of the AFL. Between 1910 and 1916, at least, those efforts strongly supported Gompers's leadership.[130]

Second, the Catholic Action movement provided an ideological antidote to socialism that appealed to the sentiments of many American workers. In contrast to the NCF's celebration of big business as organized labor's potential ally, the sermons of Dietz, Archbishop John Glennon of St. Louis, and other priests who involved themselves in the labor movement stressed the church's defense of "her children," the workers, against the rapacity of the rich. They drew on the church's traditional hostility toward materialism when they challenged the Taylorite doctrine that the best society is one that maximizes productivity.[131] Although Dietz needed some careful instruction from John Mitchell to convince him that a union could not open its doors to all social classes or abhor strikes and boycotts, he learned to denounce the "sham competition of individual bargaining between master and working man" and to uphold unions as a check against the "parasitic industries that take and use up the lifeblood of the successive relays of working men, casting the worn-out toiler

Summary Review of the Social Position of Catholicism (Vol. 1, No. 1, Oberlin, Ohio, 1911), 66, 68; Marc Karson, *American Labor Unions and Politics, 1900–1918* (Carbondale, Ill., 1958), 212–84; Karson, "Catholic Anti-Socialism," in Laslett and Lipset, *Failure,* 164–84.

130. Lore, "Progress Backward." See also Karson, "Catholic Anti-Socialism," and the reply by Henry Browne labeling the Militia of Christ a "one man show" (Laslett and Lipset, *Failure,* 185–94); *ISR,* 14 (January 1914), 414–15. By 1917–18, the alliance between Gompers and the Catholic Actionists had given way to bitter rivalry. See Lore, "Progress Backward"; Taft, *AFL,* 346, 362–3.

131. Dietz, *Social Service,* 63. See John A. Ryan, *A Living Wage* (Washington, D.C., 1906), 10–19 and passim, for a telling attack on the cult of productivity. For its roots in Catholic doctrine, see Pius IX, *Syllabus of Errors,* in Anne Freemantle, ed., *The Papal Encyclicals in Their Historical Context* (New York, 1956), 135–52.

upon the scrap heap." He pledged his church's aid to the struggle for "the living wage, reasonable hours and fair conditions."[132]

Above all, the clergy who were engaged in this battle rested their case on a defense of the patriarchal family and on warnings against the growing power of the state in modern life. The doctrine of the "living wage," as developed by American Catholic thinkers, had two important features. First, the wage to which every workingman was entitled by "natural right" was based not on his productivity but on his need as a person for "reasonable and frugal comfort." Second, it would be a wage sufficient for a father to support a family without any contribution by his wife or young children. "The welfare of the whole family, and that of society likewise," wrote John A. Ryan, "renders it imperative that the wife and mother should not engage in any labor except that of the household."[133] He cited with approval the declaration of a French congress of Christian workingmen that the "wife become a wage worker is no longer a wife."[134]

The aspiration so widely shared among workers for homes of their own, where the wife would remain, caring for the needs of the family, was elevated to the level of a doctrinal imperative that ruled out such socialist proposals as kindergartens. "We have . . . to preserve, without state control, our homes," preached Archbishop Glennon to the AFL delegates assembled in his city of St. Louis. "We utterly abhor the idea that the children are the wards of the state: — common property."[135]

The admonitions against the expanding domain of governmental activity suggested in these remarks was often spelled out explicitly. Archbishop Glennon warned his listeners:

> There is a strong tendency to obliterate individuality in the state. The state is the cure, the panacea for all our ills. Capital wants the state

132.   Dietz, *Social Service*, 61, 65. For Dietz's early ideas, see Dietz to Mitchell, April 10, 1911; Mitchell to Dietz, April 12, 1911; and passim in file No. 108, Mitchell Papers, Box A3-14. Dietz was roused to come to the 1909 AFL convention by the news that the Executive Council had passed a resolution protesting the execution of the Spanish anarchist Francisco Ferrer.

133.   Ryan, *Living Wage*, 132. The phrase "reasonable and frugal comfort" was from Pope Leo XIII, *Rerum Novarum*.

134.   Ryan, *Living Wage*, 133n. These ideas blended easily with the crusade of the influential National German Alliance, which was founded in 1907 and funded by the United Brewers' Association against what it targeted as the twin menaces of Prohibition and woman suffrage. See Carl Wittke, *German-Americans and the World War (With Special Emphasis on Ohio's German-Language Press)* (Columbus, Ohio, 1936), 163–7.

135.   Dietz, *Social Service*, 64. At the 1894 AFL convention, many delegates vigorously attacked a proposal for state inspection of their homes. AFL, *Pol. Pgm. Debate*, 21–5.

to affirm its banking systems, to guard their interests through an interstate law. There are some of our laboring people preaching a gospel that wants us to throw our lives, our homes and our children into the state, making the state our mother and father.[136]

To workers already anxious about business's increasing use of the government to control more and more aspects of social life, the archbishop was saying that the socialist remedy was only more of the same. To those in fear of scientific management of the factory, he warned that the revolutionaries would bring a scientifically managed society. In that respect he echoed John Mitchell's famous denunciation of governmental paternalism:

> The American-bred wage worker does not wish to be the ward of any man or system – classified, numbered, tagged, and obliged to carry a card of identification, or be subject to police control or employing class supervision. In fact the American wage worker who is the product of our general system of education is about the equal of his fellow-citizens and needs only the fair opportunities promised in the principles of our republic to work out his own economic salvation.[137]

It is true that Catholic social doctrine did not always bear this anti-statist bias. In fact, the first articulate Catholic social thought in America turned impulsively to welfare legislation as the cure of social ills, and by the 1920s that theme would once again be dominant.[138] Moreover, the ideas outlined here were by no means articulated by all of the clergy, even during that period. Most clerics either ignored the labor question altogether or contented themselves with admonitions to the faithful, such as those of Cardinal Gibbons, to "foster habits of economy and self-denial" and shun "the slightest invasion of the rights and autonomy of employers."[139] Nor can anyone argue that the Socialists had no success

---

136. Dietz, *Social Service*, 64. For evidence of the celebration of the state by Progressive Era reformers concerned with child care, see Mary Madeleine Ladd-Taylor, "Mother-Work: Ideology, Public Policy, and the Mothers' Movement, 1890–1930" (unpublished Ph.D. diss., Yale University, 1986), 70–134.

137. John Mitchell, *The Wage Earner and His Problems* (Washington, D.C., 1913), 129.

138. Vincent A. McQuade, O.S.A., *The American Catholic Attitude on Child Labor since 1891* (Washington, D.C., 1938). See also Aaron Abell, *American Catholicism and Social Action: A Search for Social Justice, 1865–1950* (Garden City, N.Y., 1960); Pope Pius XI, *Quadragessimo Anno*.

139. James Cardinal Gibbons, "Organized Labor," in Leon Stein and Philip Taft, eds., *Wages, Hours, and Strikes: Labor Panaceas in the Twentieth Century* (New York, 1969), 18, 23.

among Catholic workers. In Milwaukee, their candidates carried the city's Polish wards in 1910, and the secretary of the Connecticut state branch claimed that 70 percent of the Socialist Party members there were Catholics.[140] Moreover, the largest bloc of right-wing votes in the IAM came from the predominantly Protestant railroad lodges of the South, while many heavily Catholic lodges in the Northeast went for the Socialists.

The point is that at this critical moment in the development of the labor movement there were Catholic thinkers in close touch with trade unionists who attacked the Socialists with arguments bound to be convincing to large numbers of workers. The clearest statement of their position appeared in Hilaire Belloc's provocative book *The Servile State,* published in 1912. This work, which clearly influenced both Father John Ryan and the Guild Socialists of England, argued that the inherent tendency of modern capitalism was toward a society in which the whole working class more or less willingly submitted to state direction in all its affairs, in return for relief from the brutal insecurity it had suffered under nineteenth-century capitalism. Corporate reformers and socialists stood together in the vanguard of this trend, said Belloc. Clear echoes of his arguments were to be heard in the 1916 convention of the IAM, when Catholic conservatives, who by then were in opposition, defended syndicalist rebels against the union's Socialist leadership. Belloc, however, was no syndicalist. Modern society and especially its workers suffered, he argued, from "suppressed catholicity." Spiritual unity required universal acceptance of hierarchy, authority, and mutual obligations. It was within that context that trade unions had to play their proper role. His doctrines provided reinforcement for the existing patterns of everyday plebeian life, not a revolutionary critique.[141]

The gospel of direct action

Revolutionary syndicalism extracted from the solidarities and ethical code of workers' daily lives a merciless critique of the existing structures of exploitation, power, and authority. It did not spare the institutions that workers had created for themselves, but depicted the trade unions and

140. Miller, *Victor Berger,* 21; *ISR,* 14 (March 1914), 562–3.
141. Hilaire Belloc, *The Servile State* (London, 1913). For Belloc's influence on Ryan, see Patrick W. Gearty, *The Economic Thought of Monsignor John A. Ryan* (Washington, D.C., 1953), 271–2. For his influence on British shop stewards and Guild Socialists, see James Hinton, *The First Shop Stewards' Movement* (London, 1973). On the Person case in the IAM, see IAM, *Proceedings, 1916,* 142–4.

even the Socialist Party as so deeply embedded in the fabric of capitalist life that they had become obstacles to the revolutionary efforts of workers to create a new society. New industrial structures required a new workers' movement. As the manifesto that summoned delegates to the 1905 convention to found the IWW argued:

> Social relations and groupings only reflect mechanical and industrial conditions. The *great facts* of present industry are the displacement of human skill by machines and the increase of capitalist power through concentration in the possession of the tools with which wealth is produced and distributed. . . .
>
> Universal economic evils afflicting the working class can be eradicated only by a universal working class movement. Such a movement is impossible while separate craft and wage agreements are made favoring the employer against other crafts in the same industry, and while energies are wasted in fruitless jurisdictional struggles which serve only to further the personal aggrandizement of union officials.
>
> A movement to fulfill these conditions must consist of one great industrial union embracing all industries. . . . It must be founded on the class struggle, and its general administration must be conducted in harmony with the recognition of the irrepressible conflict between the capitalist class and the working class.[142]

Metalworkers played a prominent role in the early career of the IWW, but they soon extended the ideal of "one great industrial union . . . founded on the class struggle" far beyond the confines of that institution. Although the prime movers in bringing the IWW into existence had been the Western Federation of Miners and the Socialist Labor Party (SLP), its first president, Charles O. Sherman, was the leader of the United Metal Workers Industrial Union. That organization had fourteen thousand members in Chicago in 1903, among whom were pattern makers, wire workers, surgical-instrument makers, coppersmiths and machinists, all committed to the buildings of a single union for all grades of metalworkers under socialist leadership. Although the United Metal Workers had friendly relations with the IAM in Chicago, they were anathema to the Executive Council of the AFL. Small as the union was, it conjured up an image of metalworkers' unions in Germany, Italy, and France – socialist strongholds whose size and militancy were making them dominant forces in their countries' labor movements. Every meeting of the Executive Council during 1902 and 1903 wrestled with the future of the metal trades. By 1904, the AFL had resolved the issue by awarding virtually all workers within the United Metal Workers' jurisdiction to some other union

142. Industrial Workers of the World, *Proceedings of the First Convention of the Industrial Workers of the World* (New York, 1905; hereafter cited as IWW, *First Convention*), 3, 5–6.

(most of them to the Structural Iron Workers or the Allied Metal Mechanics), then arranging a merger between the IAM and the Allied Metal Mechanics, which obliged the IAM to break its Chicago alliance with the metalworkers. In a word, the AFL had consigned the United Metal Workers to extinction.[143]

The United Metal Workers struck back by joining the IWW, being awarded its presidency, and making the main activity of the IWW during the first year of its existence a raid on the membership of the IAM. During the six months that followed the founding convention, IWW organizers toured IAM lodges and showered metal-fabricating shops with leaflets in Youngstown, Buffalo, Cleveland, Cincinnati, Schenectady, and Chicago. The effort was especially intense in Chicago, the main base of both the IWW's president Sherman and the American lodges of the British Amalgamated Society of Engineers, which had also joined the IWW. The IAM responded by announcing that any member who joined the IWW would be expelled from the machinists' union, sending an agent to observe the IWW convention from the inside, mobilizing its own officers for an all-out fight in the contested lodges, and filling the columns of its journal with tributes to Kier Hardie, John Burns, and other exemplary British advocates of trade unionism and parliamentary socialism. By the time of the IWW's second convention, in September 1906, the IAM's leaders could breathe more easily. A coalition of western advocates of direct action and followers of Daniel DeLeon's SLP had not only removed Sherman from the IWW presidency but also expelled him from the organization as a "corrupt opportunist." The Western Federation of Miners had withdrawn its support from the IWW, as had Eugene V. Debs. Editor Wilson of the *Machinists' Monthly Journal* gloated that the IWW had "fallen to pieces," confirming what he and other "constructive socialists" had always argued, "that greater haste is made by going slowly and surely" and by being "wisely conscious of our class interest."[144]

As it turned out, however, the influence of revolutionary syndicalism among machinists had only begun to grow. Debates about industrial unionism, general strikes, and the true path to socialism resounded through machinists' lodges, bars, and lunchrooms. Russia's revolution and Chicago's massive teamsters' strike, in which the central issue was the em-

143. Ramirez, *When Workers Fight*, 104–14; AFL Executive Council minutes, 1902–4 (Mitchell Papers, Box A3-47); Melvyn Dubofsky, *We Shall Be All: A History of the Industrial Workers of the World* (Chicago, 1969), 76–7.

144. *MMJ*, 18 (February 1906), 139; (July 1906), 637–9; (December 1906), 1108–11; Foner, *Labor Movement*, IV, 71–7. The quotation is from *MMJ*, 18 (November 1906), 985.

ployers' determination to stamp out sympathy strikes and force the drivers' union to concern itself only with its own members, and the exhilarating
debate in European socialist parties over the "mass strike" as a political
weapon made the IWW's ideology timely, just as the transformation of
production justified its critique of craft unionism. Consequently, the first
highly visible manifestation of the IWW's influence among machinists
came after the IWW's disheartening second convention and in a stronghold of both craft unionism and the Socialist Party: the General Electric
(GE) works of Schenectady.

Schenectady's Lodge 704 had entered the IAM as part of the merger
with the Allied Metal Mechanics. The men and women who composed it
were operatives, largely on hand-screw machines. They enrolled en masse
in the IWW and were joined by some of the journeyman machinists from
Lodge 204, among them its former president Henry Jackson, who ruled
from the chair of the city's trades assembly that IWW delegates were
welcome to join that body. Five locals of other crafts had also affiliated
with the IWW by the end of 1905, bringing its total membership to twelve
hundred and promoting collaboration between the city's Socialist Party
and the SLP. Vice-President John J. Keegan of the IAM and organizer
Stuart Reid (a prominent Socialist) hastened to Schenectady to expel
Jackson from the IAM, persuade the trades assembly to reverse itself and
ostracize the IWW, and build up the ranks of journeymen in Lodge 204
as a counterweight to the growing popularity of revolutionary industrial
unionism. But the idea that all GE's workers should enroll in one big
union refused to die. In fact, it caught fire among the draftsmen as well
as the production workers. They were aware of President Sherman's closing words to the founding convention:

> We don't propose to organize only the common man with the callous
> hands, but we want the clerical force, we want the soft hands that
> only get $40 a month, those fellows with No. 10 cuffs and collars.
> We want them all, so that when a strike is called we can strike the
> whole business at once.[145]

In December 1905, management fired three draftsmen who were recruiting their workmates into the IWW. The IWW demanded their reinstatement, rejected management's offer to transfer the men to another
department, and then organized a sit-down strike by some twenty-seven

145. IWW, *First Convention,* 586. This account of the Schenectady struggle is
based on *MMJ,* 18 (January 1906), 42–3; (February 1906), 139; 19 (January 1907), 59–60; (February 1907), 162; (September 1907), 983–94;
Foner, *Labor Movement,* IV, 88–9; *New York Labor Bulletin,* 9 (March
1907), 14; Fred Thompson, "Digging into IWW History: The Schenectady
Sit-Down," *Industrial Worker* (August 1975), 6.

hundred of the plant's fifteen thousand workers. After occupying several parts of the GE plant for three days, the strikers left the plant to picket from the outside for another week. Gradually the strike disintegrated as the IAM vigorously denounced it and the company replaced possibly two hundred militants. The operatives' Lodge 704 was subsequently reorganized under new leadership by the IAM.

The GE strike revealed the determination of the AFL's leaders, including members of the Socialist Party, to stamp out the IWW. The fact that it took place after the IWW's drive on machine shops had ended, however, also suggested that revolutionary unionism as an ideal might prove attractive to many more metalworkers than would the IWW itself. And so it did. Resolutions favoring the amalgamation of all metal-trades unions into a single metalworkers' union and urging greater autonomy of metal-trades locals from their craft internationals, so that they might better combine for local struggles, came to the AFL from city metal-trades councils in Detroit, Toledo, Grand Rapids, and other midwestern centers. Machinists, steam fitters, car men, sheet-metal tradesmen, boilermakers, blacksmiths, painters, laborers, and clerks in the repair shops of the Illinois Central railroad formed a "system federation" and then launched a strike to force management to deal with that new unified body – a strike that lasted four years. The IAM lodges that initiated these efforts all supported the Socialist bloc in 1911, and their call for a more aggressive, unified, class-conscious unionism reflected a growing ideological schism over trade unionism within the Socialist Party itself. The IAM could never unionize the automobile industry, or others like it, in which specialists were coming to perform almost all of the work, wrote Hugo Lenz in the *International Socialist Review*. As a craft organization it "is doomed." The hope of the future lay in a single industrial union of all metal and machinery workers.[146]

At the very moment when Socialist Party members were gaining the leadership of major craft unions and winning elections to local offices in unprecedented numbers, an important minority within the party were questioning the validity of the strategy on which these "successes" were based. Journals like the *International Socialist Review* and the *New Review*, the major outlets for Marxist discussion within the party, carried a vigorous debate over the significance of the strike wave that followed the return of prosperity in 1909. Side by side with a new union aggressiveness in the metal, mining, and building trades came thrilling revolts by

146. Ramirez, *When Workers Fight*, 104–22; *MMJ*, 23 (March 1911), 254–5; Hugo Lenz, "The Passing of the Skilled Mechanic," *ISR*, 13 (March 1913), 668–70. On the systems federations, see Montgomery, *Workers' Control*, 107–8; Foner, *Labor Movement*, V, 164–81.

the operatives and laborers in the garment, textile, maritime, and steel industries. In 1910, when machinists struck Bethlehem Steel's shops to demand the elimination of Henry Gantt's task-and-bonus payment system and a reduction of working hours, Hungarian and Slavic blast-furnace laborers walked out too. Within days, everyone had joined the strike, and then each group met separately under AFL guidance to formulate its own demands. Across the country, in Los Angeles, all the metal trades struck together, but they made no effort to enlist the Mexican, Italian, and Ukrainian laborers of the city in their campaign. Why perpetuate such divisions? Austin Lewis later asked in the *New Review*. The Mexicans, he noted, had organized themselves and marched in a great parade behind the craft unionists, carrying a simple placard: "Workers of the World Unite!"[147]

New working-class practice was forcing these Marxists to revise Debs's conception of America's path to socialism. In the first place, they began to talk about the revolutionary significance of workplace organization. To them, industrial unions were not simply agencies to provide workers with a more effective defense of their interests than craft unions offered; they were more than a vehicle for the dissemination of socialist education on a mass scale: They mobilized direct attacks on capitalism. Unlike committed anarcho-syndicalists, these Socialists did not consider party activity useless, let alone detrimental, to the struggle. They did, however, agree with the Dutch socialist Anton Pannekoek, a favorite contributor to the *New Review* by 1913, that the "labor union has just as great a revolutionary significance as the political party."[148] Moreover, that conclusion demanded that the party itself play a role in directing strike and union activity. The Pittsburgh editor Fred Merrick, who was soon to lead two thousand Lithuanian, Polish, and Slovak workers on strike against the National Tube Company of U.S. Steel, described his new orientation in this way:

> If the political organization has not attracted the proper quota to its standard in the past, it is . . . because [the workers] think we are following some kind of utopian, Sunday school program. Let it become clear to the Pittsburgh worker that the party wants to protect the worker while he organizes in a militant manner . . . and is not

147. On the strike wave, see Montgomery, "New Unionism." On Bethlehem, see U.S. Congress, Senate, *Report on the Strike at Bethlehem Steel Works*, Senate Document No. 521, 61st Cong., 2nd Sess. (Washington, D.C., 1910). On Los Angeles, see Austin Lewis, "The Basis of Solidarity," *NR*, 3 (August 15, 1915), 186.

148. Anton Pannekoek, "Socialism and Labor Unionism," *NR*, 1 (July 1913), 622–3.

seeking to advance another group of politicians [and the party will enjoy an] avalanche of support.[149]

Revolutionary tactics based on the strike and workplace organization were linked, in the minds of Lenz, Pannekoek, Lewis, John Macy, William English Walling, Louis Fraina, and other contributors, to a new awareness of how capitalism was changing under their feet. Their party, they argued, was still combating the laissez-faire capitalism of the nineteenth century and was too prone to hail every piece of welfare legislation as a step toward socialism, or to scorn it as a meaningless sop to the hungry workers. Walling believed that the bourgeoisie had jettisoned individualism and replaced it with "capitalist collectivism," or, as he sometimes said, less felicitously, "state socialism." Capitalism's "new reform programme" that Walling saw "being put into execution" in some fashion in every industrial country was intended to link large blocs of the population to the state through subsidies, transfer payments, public works, and nationalization of key sectors of the economy, so as to create "a privileged majority." He considered this prospect "the nightmare of every democrat for whom democracy is anything more than an empty political reform." It would produce "an iron-bound society solidly entrenched in majority rule" whose "very essence" was the goal that "the share of the total profits which goes to the ruling class should not be decreased, and if possible should be augmented."[150]

Walling thus dissented sharply from Casson's repudiation of class war, not to mention Reverend John Ryan's prescriptions for social harmony. He found much that was attractive in the IWW, and he considered the seizure of initiative by unskilled workers away from the craftsmen *"nothing less than a revolution in the labor movement."*[151] Nevertheless, he also feared that the energizing charge of revolutionary syndicalism would be grounded in the quest for immediate gains, if it were isolated from political action:

> If we are advancing toward socialism, [he concluded,] it is not because the non-capitalist classes, when compared with the capitalists, are gradually gaining a greater share of wealth or more power in society. It is because they are gradually gaining that capacity for or-

149. Fred H. Merrick, " 'Justice' in Pittsburgh," *ISR*, 12 (September 1911), 163 (courtesy of Paul Buhle). On the National Tube strike, see *Survey*, 28 (July 6, 1912), 487–8; (August 3, 1912), 595–6.

150. Walling, *Socialism As It Is*, 45, 109. Similar views may be found in John Macy, *Socialism in America* (Garden City, N.Y., 1916); S. J. Rutgers, "The Left Wing: Imperialism," *ISR*, 16 (June, 1916), 728–31.

151. W. E. Walling, "Industrialism or Revolutionary Unionism," *NR*, 1 (Jan. 11, 1913), 45–51; (Jan. 18, 1913), 83–91. The quotation is on p. 88.

ganized political and economic action which, though useless except for defensive purposes to-day, will enable them to take possession of industry and government *when their organization has become stronger than that of the capitalists.*[152]

If workplace organization could have revolutionary significance, it was obligatory for revolutionaries to devote painstaking attention to how the workplace – the modern workplace – might best be organized for workers' control. To "roast" craft unions from the soapbox was fun, but it did not organize industrial workers. At the huge headquarters plant of Westinghouse Electric in the Turtle Creek Valley, east of Pittsburgh, workers created just such a movement as Walling and Pannekoek had in mind. Merrick was its spiritual mentor, but it was the men and women entering the factory's buildings daily who devised the organizational forms and tactics appropriate to an up-to-date enterprise.

The company had moved its production facilities to the new suburban plant in 1894. Turbines and electric motors were its main products, and because of the demand for power and public transportation in American cities, its payroll grew from three thousand at the plant's opening to thirteen thousand in 1913. Standardization of parts and methods allowed the firm to hire large numbers of young women, migrants from the countryside, and European immigrants and to defeat handily the efforts of its craftsmen to win union recognition in 1903 and 1907. A cluster of related firms also dotted the region: Westinghouse Air Brake, Westinghouse Meter Works, Union Switch and Signal, among others. Small towns such as Wilmerding, East Pittsburgh, Turtle Creek, and Pitcairn housed many of the workers' families, while other employees quickly occupied the new housing in the nearby Homewood section of Pittsburgh. In the immediate vicinity of the factory, families and boarders were virtually stacked on top of each other. Just around the bend of Turtle Creek from Westinghouse, largely hidden by a bluff, except for its smoke, lay the huge Edgar Thompson works of U.S. Steel and the town of Braddock.

The Socialist Party was strong in the smaller residential towns of the valley. In fact, it outpolled both major parties during the elections of 1910 and 1912, although it faced stiff competition first from the Keystone Party and then from the Progressive (Bull Moose) Republicans, who attracted the protest votes of many Protestant workers in Pennsylvania. By 1912, however, the region's Socialists were sharply divided between the dominant advocates of "constructive socialism" and a large, very vocal minority centered on the newspaper *Justice,* which was edited

---

152. Walling, *Socialism As It Is,* 426. A similar view, written before the war but published after it, is Emile Vandervelde, *Socialism versus the State* (translated by Charles H. Kerr, Chicago, 1919).

by Frederick H. Merrick. *Justice* strongly supported the IWW in the 1913 strike of Pittsburgh's stogie makers and was enraged by the party's constitutional amendment to bar advocates of direct action. Party members in the Homewood area, where Merrick lived, had supplemented their electoral work for Debs in 1912 with a sustained "free-speech" campaign at plant gates and street corners, during which many members were jailed for agitating in public places against conditions inside the Westinghouse factories. Most of those who appeared in group photos of the activists were young Jewish women. Veterans of this period also remember many German and Croatian activists, young as well as old, some attached to the Socialist Party and others to the SLP.[153]

During the boom years of 1912 and 1913, when machinists in other urban centers launched many strikes and the IAM targeted Los Angeles and Buffalo for organizing drives, production continued without interruption in the Turtle Creek Valley. Westinghouse itself recruited a thousand workers, foremen, and superintendents into a "progress union," and it also created a Veteran Employees Association for those with twenty years of experience, in preparation for instituting a pension program.[154] Then, as 1913 ended, the economy slipped into a severe decline. Workers' militancy shriveled as the crowds of unemployed outside the plant gates grew. At the April 1914 convention of the NMTA, outgoing President Layman assured his colleagues: "One year ago the I.W.W. movement had attained alarming proportions. To-day we believe the menace of it, in a large sense, has passed." The reason, he explained, was not simply that unemployment had made obstreperous workers easy to replace, but also that the middle class, prodded by the rising cost of living, was involving itself in labor controversies on business's side. The defeats of unions in Calumet, Michigan, Ludlow, Colorado, Leeds, England, and the South African mines, and on New Zealand's waterfront, had all illus-

153.   Schatz, *Electrical Workers*, 4–9; Patrick M. Lynch, "Pittsburgh, the I.W.W., and the Stogie Workers," in Joseph R. Conlin, ed., *At the Point of Production: The Local History of the I.W.W.* (Westport, Conn., 1981), 79–94; Jacob Margolis, "The Streets of Pittsburgh," *ISR*, 13 (October 1912), 313–20; *Smull's Pennsylvania Manual, 1912* (Harrisburg, 1912); Michael Nash, *Conflict and Accommodation; Coal Miners, Steel Workers, and Socialism, 1890–1920* (Westport, Conn., 1982), 116–17; Margaret Nelson to author, December 21, 1983.

154.   R. M. Easley to W. B. Wilson, July 7, 1914, in Federal Mediation and Conciliation Service File 33-37 (U.S. National Archives, R.G. 280, hereafter cited as FMCS); *IA*, 91 (May 22, 1913), 1261; *IA*, 93 (March 5, 1914), 609.

trated the same sense of social solidarity against strikes. The great peril of the hour, he concluded, was not radical unions but labor legislation. The widespread defeat of political reformers of all stripes in the following year's local elections seemed to NMTA members to corroborate Layman's judgment.[155]

Not six weeks after Layman's speech, however, the Westinghouse complex was shut by a strike. The hard times were the immediate cause, because the company had reduced working hours from fifty-four to forty-eight per week, dismissed many workers, including a reported two thousand salaried employees, and slashed incentive rates on jobs all over the factory. For five months the workers endured these blows, while quietly recruiting members into the Allegheny Congenial Industrial Union. That all-grades organization copied the IWW by devoting itself to organizing struggles around demands, rather than negotiating contracts, and charged only twenty-five cents per month for dues, but it also used a system of departmental delegates inside the plant as its basic structure. The three thousand workers who responded to the strike call on June 5 were soon joined by all but about fifteen hundred of the eighty-two hundred women and men then employed, as well as by many people from smaller firms in the valley that were economically linked to Westinghouse. The strikers demanded a rotation system for handling layoffs and abolition of all piecework and incentive-pay plans. Never, replied the company's president, E. M. Herr: "The pay of skillful and productive Westinghouse employees shall not be regulated by the pay of the inefficient and less productive."[156]

Washington's newly created conciliation service wheeled into action, sending to the scene Charles W. Mills, a Philadelphia coal and iron dealer, and Patrick Gilday, the recently defeated president of UMWA District 2. Mills assured the strikers of his friendship to their cause, while he drafted replies for President Herr to make to their demands and asked Secretary of Labor Wilson for help from the "secret service." "I realize perfectly well the foothold which Socialism has acquired in the Turtle Creek Valley," Mills wrote to Herr. "I also realize that this must be stamped out to secure any continued industrial peace, but I believe this can be better

---

155. *IA*, 93 (April 30, 1914), 1074–6; the quotation is on p. 1074. On the 1915 elections and business's satisfaction, see *IA*, 95 (April 22, 1915), 890–3; *NR*, 5 (November 6, 1915), 1–2.

156. FMCS, 33-37; E. M. Herr to Chas. W. Mills, June 29, 1914 (draft) in FMCS, 33-37; *IA*, 93 (January 22, 1914), 285; 93 (June 11, 1914), 1496; 94 (July 2, 1914), 56; 94 (July 16, 1914), 180.

stamped out by the removal from the district of the more radical element and the toning down of those less radical, than by a continuance of the strike."[157] Although company officials met with committees of "the better employees," they refused to make concessions to either the union or the mediators. After four weeks, the clerical workers voted to join the strike, but the union's members decided to return to work soon after that. Despite the company's public rejection of all their demands, the strikers proclaimed that they had forced Westinghouse to recognize their union, and they marched in formation into the plant to resume their jobs.[158]

For the next two years Westinghouse dealt with the union, which soon changed its name to the American Industrial Union (AIU). It also dealt with its own creation – the progress union – as well as with the IAM, the International Brotherhood of Electrical Workers, and others from time to time. Official company policy was that any employee could belong to any organization and could bring a grievance to a supervisor. Meanwhile, war in Europe had created boom conditions in the Turtle Creek Valley. As industry leaders had predicted, South American markets were cleared of European competition. Then machine-tool orders came from the belligerent powers themselves, so that the United States produced more machine tools in the first three months of 1915 than it had in all of 1914. Most important of all, the opening months of 1915 brought enormous orders for shrapnel shells. In short, all types of production increased in the valley, but shell production gave special impetus to highly specialized, repetitive lathe work, often carried on in new buildings hastily erected for the purpose. Westinghouse returned to the fifty-four–hour workweek and soon doubled its work force as well. Moreover, news of an insatiable demand for labor in the automobile and truck industries in Michigan and Ohio lured off machinists and unskilled workers alike and made Pittsburghers aware that the hour had arrived to demand more for their own work.[159]

By midsummer, a wave of largely spontaneous strikes rolled across the munitions and metalworking plants of New England and began to spread

157. C. W. Mills to E. M. Herr, June 29, 1914; Mills to W. B. Wilson, July 6, 1914; R. M. Easley to W. B. Wilson, July 7, 1914 (FMCS, 33-37).
158. Pittsburgh *Post,* July 7, 1914; R. M. Easley to W. B. Wilson, July 14, 1914 (FMCS, 33-37).
159. *IA*, 94 (August 13, 1914), 8; (August 27, 1914), 510; (October 29, 1914), 1038; 95 (April 8, 1915), 827; (May 6, 1915), 1023, 1092; (August 26, 1915), 494. On the munitions strikes and their sequel, see Cecelia F. Bucki, "Dilution and Craft Tradition: Bridgeport, Connecticut, Munitions Workers, 1915–1919," *Social Science History*, 4 (February 1980), 105–24.

into the West. Both the AIU and the AFL stepped up their activities at Westinghouse, and Gompers assigned a young field representative, John L. Lewis, to organize its workers into craft unions. In September, however, the company entered negotiations with a committee of twelve of its employees – six selected by management and six by the workers – to whom it offered a reduction in working hours to a fifty-two–hour week, with no loss of earnings, plus a bonus of 6 percent on all wages, payable after October 1 in quarterly installments. Lewis worked hard to persuade a mass meeting of the workers to reject the offer and strike for the eight-hour day under AFL leadership. But the Westinghouse employees were more favorably impressed by their committee's work than by the AFL. They voted to accept the offer by a margin of 7,073 to 2,495.[160]

Special roles were played in the Westinghouse unions by two groups of workers who were products of the twentieth-century style of factory operation: the toolmakers and the operatives. The name "toolmaker" had first entered everyday speech in the 1890s, and they were first counted separately from other machinists in the 1910 census. At that time they numbered 9,263, and the spread of scientific management increased the membership attributed to this new trade to 55,092 by 1920. They fabricated the jigs, fixtures, prototypes, and form tools that were necessary if closely instructed operatives were to replace journeyman machinists in the shaping of parts on machine tools. There were about two thousand toolmakers and tool grinders at Westinghouse by 1916, and they clearly envisaged themselves as the elite of the work force. They exercised fine judgment in their tasks, virtually never encountered piecework, related to their foremen the way nineteenth-century machinists had done, and worked in a setting in which, as two engineers wrote of Ford's Highland Park toolroom, "nothing [was] scamped or hurried."[161] Nevertheless, union sentiment was widespread among them. They had no standard wage; there was extreme and often inexplicable variety in their earnings. They hungered for such traditional union goals as the eight-hour day and protection against arbitrary treatment. Moreover, as war production increased, they often learned of unskilled pieceworkers mastering some repetitive operations so well that they earned more than anyone in the toolrooms. It is not surprising, therefore, that by April 1916, some five

160. *IA*, 96 (October 7, 1915), 853 (where the vote is reported as 9,000 to 2,000); Melvyn Dubofsky and Warren Van Tine, *John L. Lewis: A Biography* (New York, 1977), 28–9. Machinists at Westinghouse's newly acquired arms factory in Chicopee Falls, Massachusetts, struck in December. *IA*, 96 (December 23, 1915), 1496.

161. Arnold and Faurote, *Ford Methods*, 41. The census figures are from U.S. Census, *Occ. Stat.*, 106.

hundred of Westinghouse's toolmakers had enrolled in the IAM and negotiated a 10 percent raise for themselves, and they eagerly awaited May
1, the date set by the IAM for a nationwide strike of machinists for the
eight-hour day.[162]

There was also among the toolmakers a revolutionary minority, epitomized by John Hall, who actually worked in the huge shell-turning
building. These men favored the AIU, consulted with Merrick and circulated *Justice,* and held the IAM in contempt. They believed that only a
union of all its employees could deal effectively with a concern like Westinghouse. It was, they noted, the production workers who actually turned
out the motors and artillery shells sold by the company; the toolmakers'
role was only ancillary. They also believed that workers needed and would
use the power of the strike, as well as the ballot, in order to overthrow
capitalism. Although they generally supported the special demands of
their fellow toolmakers, including exemptions from the draft in 1918,
Hall and his comrades tried to persuade their colleagues that their interests were one with those of the operatives. Their demands were couched
in aggressive rhetoric, and their motto, "Organization, Education, Solidarity," was borrowed from the "Detroit IWW" (i.e., the SLP). Within
the toolmakers' ranks, therefore, tension persisted between these broad
aspirations and the parochial struggle to protect the privileges and wage
differentials of the machinists' elite. Both the company and the government mediators were aware of this tension and played on it. On April
20, the same day that Westinghouse raised the wages of its toolmakers,
it fired Hall.

The protest strike that began the next day was supported at first by far
more production workers than toolmakers. Their role was symbolized
by Anna Katherine Bell of Braddock, a 21-year-old worker with three
years' experience at Westinghouse, who was to appear prominently in
every strikers' parade during the next two weeks and ultimately be indicted on riot charges along with Hall and Merrick. The factory's nearly
three thousand female employees, like the farm youth and immigrants'
children who constituted the rest of the production force, had no craft
heritage or privileges to protect. Experience at Westinghouse had taught
them that they needed an in-plant organization made up of their own
elected delegates who not only could formulate general demands but also
could deal with the reality of their work experience at Westinghouse.

The key to that experience was that scientific management, as we have

162. [Clifton Reeves] to William B. Wilson, August 15, 1916, in FMCS, 33-
      202 (hereafter cited as Reeves Report).

seen, did not reorganize production methods and work relations once and for all; rather, it reorganized them incessantly. Scientific management was by its very nature discontented management. Its efficiency experts and time-study men moved about tirelessly from one department to the next, and then back to those they had already reorganized once or twice before. New product lines might first be produced by journeyman machinists before they were handed over to less skilled workers using jigs, fixtures, and setups made by craftsmen especially assigned to those ancillary tasks. Unlike the Highland Park plant, with its single product and its engineering cast in steel, the Westinghouse works turned out a cornucopia of generators, flatirons, streetcars, and shells for the voracious appetite of Europe's cannon. Different standard work times and base and incentive rates existed for the various components of these products. New designs, changes in work instructions, or a supervisor's belief that a standard was wrong would lead to retiming. Continual changes in products and departmental organization meant ongoing hiring, layoff, and transfer within the plant, and all that meant a broad scope for favoritism or reprisals by foremen. And everywhere, always, there was the pressure to produce faster!

Such a setting made a mockery of craft-union practice. What meaning had a standard machinist's wage there? What worker could pledge to abide honorably by union work rules? What use was the traditional IAM steward, whose tasks had been to see that members kept their dues paid up and to report infractions of union rules to headquarters? Mass-production workers needed the permanent presence of an active group representative right there on the production floor, all day every day, and they had to be prepared to defend those representatives against management's reprisals. Personal or group grievances over job rates could be negotiated when and where they appeared. And for the workers as a whole, the remedy for their intensive toil was the eight-hour day.

At the call of the AIU, two thousand men and women walked out of the shell-turning buildings to protest Hall's dismissal at three o'clock Friday afternoon. The next morning they and many more linked hands to form a huge human chain around the Westinghouse complex and increased the number of strikers to thirteen thousand. Meeting in the Turtle Creek playgrounds, they heard speeches by Merrick, Hall, and Bell; then they formulated four demands: reinstatement of all employees discharged "on account of activity in connection with the formation of an industrial union"; an eight-hour day for all workers; continuation of the 6 percent bonus offered the previous September; and a company guarantee that no one would be victimized after the return to work. Bell's appearance at the meeting was especially dramatic. She arrived with a suitcase in hand, explaining that her parents had thrown her out of the house for refusing to return to work.[163]

During the next week, the strikers were constantly in the streets. Huge processions of men and women with eight-hour-day cards in their hats, one of them led by a mysterious "girl in the paper mask," broke up a meeting convened by the company at the YMCA to rally loyal employees, marched on Air Brake, Switch and Signal, Pittsburgh Meter, and other companies in the area again and again, and gradually closed down the entire valley. Only a few dozen members of the Westinghouse Air Brake Veterans Association who could prove to the pickets that they were almost eligible for pensions were given work permits signed by the strike committee, a grim testimonial to the recognized importance of the new welfare benefits.

The AFL dispatched Secretary Frank Morrison and more than a dozen of its best organizers to the region, though perhaps its most influential figure there was the IAM's Andrew McNamara, who was to remain a prominent figure in the Turtle Creek Valley through the 1920s. The region's unionized iron molders had been on strike since the previous fall, and the IAM, as part of its national campaign, addressed a circular to all employers of machinists in the Pittsburgh area to "respectfully request that you establish not later than May 1, 1916, an 8-hour work day with no reduction in pay per day." In contrast to the three locals recruiting for the AIU, each from a different company, the AFL's organizers asked workers to join one of sixteen craft locals that were to be coordinated by a local metal-trades council, as was done by the GE workers in Schenectady. Although some six hundred machinists' strikes erupted around the United States on May 1 in response to employers' rejections of the IAM's appeal, the AFL officers in the Pittsburgh region knew that the decisive battle was already under way and had begun under auspices hostile to them. They decided not to oppose the strike in progress but, rather, to offer the strikers their support, to join AIU representatives on speakers' platforms, to urge their own members to attend the rallies, and to play for the opportunity to seize control of the struggle.

That opportunity was not long in coming. On May 1, a huge parade, bedecked with red flags and led by a Lithuanian band, moved through the valley and then around to Braddock and Rankin, where marchers invaded steel mills, chain works, and machinery companies, bringing some thirty-six thousand workers out. Another parade the next day sent off contingents to picket everything in the valley, while others returned to

163. FMCS, 33-202; Pittsburgh *Daily Dispatch*, April 24, 1916.

the steel towns. The ethnic antagonisms that have absorbed the attention of most historians studying the region's workers seemed to melt away, as the angry and joyous tide of humanity poured through the streets. The great crowds confronted an army of railroad detectives, coal and iron police, and other company guards, estimated by the press at seventeen hundred in number and armed with clubs, rifles, shotguns, and machine guns. In a bloody battle around the gates of the Edgar Thompson steelworks, three men were killed and probably fifty to sixty men and women wounded, although people's fear that going to a hospital would invite arrest prevented an accurate count of the casualties. The next day, Governor Martin Brumbaugh dispatched more than a thousand infantry and cavalry soldiers to place the region under their rule, and the police arrested Merrick, Hall, Bell, and twenty-seven other strike leaders, along with dozens of Slovak and Rusyn residents of Braddock, on charges of riot and being accessories to murder. Mediators Clifton Reeves from Washington and Patrick Gilday, then head of Pennsylvania's conciliation service, assembled a negotiating committee of twenty workers that included five AIU members and five from the IAM, but Westinghouse refused to meet with them. By means of a bridge erected over the picket lines, the company lured back thousands of workers in the stunned aftermath of the Braddock riots, and by May 5 the satellite plants of the valley were largely back in operation. The AFL toiled vigorously to hold the strikers out under its leadership. Mass rallies convened almost daily by McNamara featured marching contingents of molders from struck foundries and women organizers like Mary Kules and Mary Schully. Increasing numbers of the seventy-three hundred workers still on the streets signed up in craft unions, but they could not stop the swelling tide of those who returned to their jobs in the face of company threats to terminate seniority privileges and bonus payments for those who were late in coming back. Amid stormy and conflicting meetings on May 15 and 16, the strike simply collapsed. The next day, the IAM officially called it off.[164]

Although many strikers, including Bell, were ultimately acquitted by juries, Merrick drew three and a half years in prison, along with his Socialist comrades Anna Goldberg and Rudolph Bloom, and nine immigrants received shorter sentences. Although Merrick was to emerge from

164. This account of the 1916 strike is based on material in FMCS, 33-202, especially the Reeves Report, and on the thorough survey of the Pittsburgh press found in Dianne Kanitra, "The Westinghouse Strike of 1916" (unpublished M.A. thesis, University of Pittsburgh, 1971, in possession of the author).

jail to become the most prominent Communist of western Pennsylvania in the early 1920s, his health had been shattered by his prison experience. When he was arrested in 1923 and the judge offered him the choice between returning to prison and retiring from politics and returning to his native West Virginia, Merrick chose to become a solitary farmer. Meanwhile, his organization, though decapitated, had not been killed off in the Westinghouse works. The IAM also kept open an office in the valley, but it had won the eight-hour day only for some 322 machinists in small shops around the county.[165]

During the first week of the strikes in the valley, the Manufacturers' Association of Pittsburgh had convened a special meeting and changed its name to the Employers' Association of Pittsburgh. Although the association did not publish the names of its officers, it delegated Isaac W. Frank, president of the United States Engineering and Foundry Company, to be its spokesman. "The new organization will handle wage and labor matters," reported *Iron Age*, "and is regarded as very strong, its membership being composed of the most representative manufacturing concerns in the Pittsburgh district."[166] It moved vigorously into the fray, publishing a series of newspaper advertisements arguing that it would be "suicide" to Pittsburgh's growth to concede the eight-hour day. Interviewed by journalist Dante Barton, Frank lost his composure, blamed the whole agitation for the shorter day on the head of the U.S. Commission on Industrial Relations, Frank P. Walsh, and declared that Walsh "should be assassinated."[167] Although Frank hastily retracted that statement as "unrational," it immediately entered into the discourse of the region's workers. After the end of the strike, the association circulated among its members lists of machinists, teachers, saleswomen, stenographers, laborers, and others whom it considered dangerous, asking, "HAVE YOU ANY OF THESE PERSONS IN YOUR EMPLOY? . . . Check these names against your pay roll and telephone any developments to our Mr. Horn without loss of time."[168]

An eerie calm had descended on the Pittsburgh region during a period of months when strikes reached unprecedented levels elsewhere in the country and rapidly rising prices combined with high levels of employment to produce soaring labor turnover and induce U.S. Steel to raise the wage rate for common labor no fewer than three times within the year.

165. Kanitra, "Westinghouse Strike," 29–34; *IA*, 98 (July 13, 1916), 112; Steve Nelson to the author, December 20, 1983; IAM, *Proceedings, 1916*, 14.
166. *IA*, 97 (May 4, 1916), 1104.
167. "What the 8 Hour Day Means," Pittsburgh *Post*, May 6, 1916; Dante Barton, "The Pittsburgh Strikes," *ISR*, 16 (June 1916), 15.
168. "To All Members of the Employers' Assn. of Pittsburgh. September 6, 1917" (in possession of author).

America's entry into the war provided the occasion for establishing more effective control mechanisms to preserve that calm. Mediator Clifton Reeves wrote Secretary of Labor Wilson in August 1917:

> I find that while there are no strikes of any importance actually on in Pittsburgh at the present time in the machinist's trade, there is considerable unrest out in East Pittsburgh and the vicinity of the Westinghouse Company's plant. Socialistic agitators are making speeches against the Government and everyone else.[169]

As evidence, Reeves enclosed an unsigned leaflet warning workers to beware the "labor fakers" of the AFL.

BEWARE   WATCH   BEWARE
MCNAMARA WILL BETRAY YOU

The vocabulary of the leaflet linked it to the SLP, whose Sunday-night meetings in Braddock attracted many workers from the valley. But the IWW and the local Socialist Party, which had firmly opposed the war, were also busy among the workers whose dreams of 1916 had been so rudely crushed. Reeves's remedy was to establish a local committee of the Council of National Defense. He obtained the participation of President Herr of Westinghouse, President A. L. Humphrey of Westinghouse Air Brake (then president of the employers' association), and President George Mesta of Mesta Machine, as well as Philip Murray of the UMWA, President John Williams of the Amalgamated Association of Iron and Steel Workers, and Andrew McNamara of the IAM. Despite the evident irony that none of the employers involved recognized the unions represented by their labor colleagues, a government council appeared to have realized the NCF's ideal of labor relations. Whether such collaboration would in time benefit the AFL unions remained to be seen; the acid test came two years later during the great steel strike. But the Turtle Creek Valley did not stir during that strike or during the 1918–19 rising of the GE workers. Many of its residents still debated ardently, and often secretly in their political clubs, and veterans of 1916 were prominent activists in the United Electrical Workers, affiliated with the Congress of Industrial Organizations, when it came to the valley in the 1930s, but they would not again strike on such a scale until 1946.[170]

Democracy, Taylorism, and workers

The reorganization of American industry after the 1890s had broken down the nineteenth-century partitions between craftsmen, operatives, and la-

169. Clifton Reeves to W. B. Wilson, August 3, 1917 (FMCS, 33-374).
170. Ibid.; Schatz, *Electrical Workers*, 83, 90–2.

borers. In this important sense it had homogenized the labor force. But that homogenization had not unified the working class. The diversity of daily experience among women and men, the different races, the many nationalities, the toolmakers and the machine tenders, and the construction workers and the dockers continued to produce a plethora of attitudes and interests in working people's everyday encounters with one another. Many strikes in the century's second decade retaught the lesson of the Turtle Creek Valley: that militant unity was possible on a massive scale despite that diversity. Although it was made up of millions of individuals, dozens of nationalities and religions, several races, and two sexes, the working class was a formidable fact of American life.

Nevertheless, within that working class, the differential impact of the restructuring of capitalism on different groups of workers and workers' organizations had nurtured a variety of ideologies. More than that, despite the recognizable grounding of Gompers's craft unionism, middle-of-the-road building-trades practice, socialism, Catholic action, syndicalism, and feminism in the same soil of working-class experience and the same celebration of mutualism over competitive individualism, these ideologies and the institutions in which they were embodied not only were different from one another but also were often bitterly antagonistic toward one another. Moreover, the antagonists were not minuscule doctrinaire sects but large, historically influential bodies of working people.

The Turtle Creek strike had revealed their size the importance for all America to behold. Its participants had organized inside Westinghouse and conducted themselves in the streets in ways that would become commonplace in American manufacturing centers between 1918 and 1922. So would the militant mobilization of local business, the hostility of the middle classes toward the strikers, and the use of governmental apparatus both to suppress the strikers and to nurture alternative mechanisms for industrial harmony be as important in the later strike wave as they had been at Westinghouse. This hostile social and political context was clearly understood by the valley's workers. During the last days of the great strike, a certain resolution was adopted with thunderous acclaim at an AFL meeting in Pittsburgh's downtown Labor Temple and at a large rally in the Turtle Creek playground. The only existing copy of this resolution is a wretchedly typed draft in the files of the conciliation service. Its many typographical errors magnify the poignancy of its contents. Addressed "To The Honorable William, B, Wilson," secretary of labor, it was a cry from the heart of the hundreds of thousands of men and women who had come from the four corners of Europe and America to earn a living in the region.

> Wheras We the striking workers, of the Pittsburgh Valley have been
> deprived of the right of free speech, and free assemblage in all places,

in this region xxx controlled, by the elected, officials who owe their
offices and are subject to the will of thier corporate masters,
and
Whereas, Because of the suppression of these rights, acts of violence
have occured, which have been aggravated, bybthe , private police,
in the pay, of the corporation, assisted by the,army of railroad detectives, and deupty sheriffs, who receive their, compensation, from, the
same source, that now proposes to crush the workers into subjugation. . . .
Wheras We fear for the future of rights as citizens, when Issac Frank
President of the Pittsburgh Employers Association, expresses xxxx
hinself to the effect "That Frank Walsh should be assasinsated," because he indorsed the eight hour movement. . . .

Therefore, be it resolved that the workers "petition you to use your
good office" for a federal investigation into this abuse of corporate power
"to the end that Justice may prevail for all those, on whom this country
must depend for its National Defense." The ominous conclusion not only
reflected the approaching clouds of war but also proposed a workers'
agenda for the crisis through which the country was passing: "Injustice
has dulled our patriotism, Mans equality before the law will make us
patriots instead of paupers."[171]

171.   "To the Honorable William, B, Wilson," typescript in FMCS 33-202. On
the meetings where the resolution was adopted, see "Strikers Protest Holding
of Rioters," Pittsburgh *Post,* May 15, 1916.

7

Patriots or paupers

"War is the health of the state," wrote Randolph Bourne in 1917.[1] The lines of communication linking America's places of work to the command center in Washington became increasingly important after the Great War erupted in Europe, and they assumed decisive importance when the United States officially entered the war. During the public debate over "preparedness" that filled the press in late 1915 and early 1916, Taylor's disciple C. E. Knoeppel redirected his attention from improving the management of foundries to "industrial preparedness." As usual, Knoeppel's publisher was the influential *Engineering Magazine,* but his latest contribution to its Industrial Management Library was a volume packed with quotations from prominent politicians, writers, and businessmen, all dealing with the question how Germany had managed to sustain two years of war against an alliance of major European powers and then emerge as military master of the Continent. The answer lay in German efficiency, and the secret of that efficiency was German organization, not simply of the workplace but of the entire society. Government in Germany, wrote Senator Gilbert Hitchcock, was a "working partnership with the people for the promotion of prosperity."

"That's it," exclaimed engineer Knoeppel. Such a partnership involved organization and "expert guidance," "cohesion and unity of purpose," a "reasonable distribution of wealth," and proper "direction and encouragement of big business." Moreover, it required both "freedom from costly industrial disputes" and "elimination of politics from things influencing the welfare of the people."[2]

Knoeppel had come a long way from the planning of foundry work flows and the one best way to make molds, but he had not traveled alone. By 1918, even his last two proposals would evoke a friendly response from the War Labor Policies Committee and from such military leaders

1. R. Bourne, "The State," quoted in Christopher Lasch, *The New Radicalism in America: The Intellectual as a Social Type* (New York, 1965), 210.
2. Charles E. Knoeppel, *Industrial Preparedness* (New York, 1916), 105–7.

as General Enoch Crowder, director of the draft. The "mental revolution" implicit in the enlarged appeal to national "efficiency" enjoyed ardent support in the ranks of business leaders and social reformers alike. At the 1915 convention of the NMTA, for example, one speaker after another expressed joy over the growth of collaboration among different manufacturers' organizations and of tangible public friendship toward business's leadership and goals. So happy were the convention delegates, reported *Iron Age,* that at the banquet they had all joined vigorously in singing "It's a Long Way to Tipperary," and then "Die Wacht am Rhein."[3] By the next year, German war songs were no longer in vogue, but war mobilization was the NMTA's all-absorbing topic. The task facing America, argued President James Emery, was not simply to be prepared for possible military action, but above all to be ready for the "world contest of peace succeeding that of war." That economic contest would be won by the most efficient producers, he warned. Consequently, "it is no hour for watered capital or watered labor, but for management trained to the moment and operatives conscious that harmonious cooperation and intelligent self-interest can alone insure the joint industrial success of employer and employee."[4]

At the time Emery spoke, social reformer George Creel was engaged in rallying public opinion against the NMTA's assaults on unions and on welfare legislation. Yet it was Creel whom President Wilson asked to head the Committee on Public Information in its wartime campaign to secure the support of all segments of American society for the war effort. In his subsequent report, *How We Advertised America,* Creel reflected with satisfaction on the social solidarity inspired by the war: "When I think of the many voices that were heard before the war and are still heard, interpreting America from a class or sectional or selfish standpoint, I am not sure that, if the war had to come, it did not come at the right time for the preservation and reinterpretation of American ideals."[5]

The war had indeed permitted – or rather climaxed – a "reinterpretation of American ideals." Nevertheless, the process was by no means as benign and harmonious as his words suggested. In fact, the wartime measures of the government borrowed heavily from Knoeppel's agenda, were supported by most of labor's leadership with arguments akin to those of Creel, and had the results Emery wanted. For America's work-

---

3. *IA,* 95 (April 22, 1915), 890–3. For Crowder's thoughts on the role of labor in social reconstruction, see E. Crowder, *Spirit of Selective Service* (New York, 1920), 251–3.
4. *IA,* 97 (May 4, 1916), 1074–5.
5. George Creel, *How We Advertised America* (New York, 1920), 105.

ers, however, these were years of soaring hopes, fierce class conflict, and ultimate subordination to business's "reinterpretation" of the nation's needs and goals.

The abundance of employment between early 1916 and the summer of 1920 gave millions of workers the confidence to quit jobs and search for better ones and to go on strike on a scale that dwarfed all previously recorded turnover and strike activity. Union membership almost doubled, rising from 2,607,000 in 1915 to 5,110,000 in 1920, leaving a larger proportion of American workers unionized than is the case in the 1980s. More important than the overall size of the union movement was the influx of workers who had previously been on the margins of union organization, at best: recent immigrants in textiles, steel, longshore, maritime, railroad construction, and other activities; workers in the open-shop strongholds of metal fabrication; and 396,000 women, whose prominence among the clothing and textile workers, railway clerks, and electrical workers swelled union ranks and brought their proportion of total union membership up to 7.8 percent, roughly what it had been in 1886–7. Constantly rising prices kept workers fighting for higher wages and also brought urban mothers into marketplace struggles over the cost of food, a development that had been quite rare since the 1860s. Conversely, when the boom turned to depression between the middle of 1920 and the end of 1922, workers faced an effective counterattack against their recent gains in wages and unionization.

The dense concentration of workers in class-segregated neighborhoods made economic struggles community mobilizations. And the quickening and refocusing of wage earners' aspirations for a better life led to confrontations over pay and treatment that rang with the rhetoric of social reconstruction. This blending of immediate demands with dreams of an altogether different social existence became the hallmark of the postwar years. It distressed Gompers as much as it did Emery, Knoeppel, and Creel. "Our movement is passing through a critical stage," Gompers wrote in 1920:

> The minds of men are not working in a normal manner. The struggles, the sacrifices, the enthusiasm, the highly nervous strain induced by the World War, have brought about a state of almost mental hysteria and our movement and our country require the counsel and services of those, who, while looking forward, yet have maintained a mental balance that will help to tide over the abnormal, troublesome times until the hysteria shall have been stilled and yet the energy which it has evoked shall have been directed into a constructive, rational, natural advance upward and onward.[6]

6. Samuel Gompers to James Duncan, May 4, 1920, quoted in Smith, "Labor and Government During the Wilson Era," 282.

War and peace in the coalfields

All these developments, including the efforts of AFL leaders to "tide over the . . . troublesome times," are illustrated by the experience of coal miners and their union. There were 785,000 coal miners in the United States in 1920, and more than half of them were enrolled in the UMWA. In spite of numerous and often catastrophic defeats in strikes since the 1860s, miners' unions had demonstrated a resilience that had placed them consistently among the most influential organizations in the labor movement. That resilience derived from three sources: the bonds among the men at the coal face, the cohesiveness of the women in the mining towns, and the impact of a vast and complex union structure with which those personal loyalties interacted.

The coal miner of 1910 was an unusual blend of a craftsman and a laborer. Easily half of his working time was spent shoveling coal into a wagon. To bring down that coal so that it could be loaded required artistry, judgment, and self-reliance. Although different types of coal, different slopes and widths of seams, and the various adjacent rock formations required different mining techniques, most miners, especially in bituminous pits, toiled in pairs at a section of coal face (their "room") and were paid by the ton for the coal they loaded. By 1915, the difficult task of undercutting the section of coal to be blasted was done by machines for 50 percent of the bituminous extracted nationwide, and when machine cutting was combined with the presence of specialized shot firers and tracklayers, the experience required to mine the coal face was sharply reduced. Nevertheless, supervision was so meager that many foremen visited rooms less often than once a day, and decisions about drilling shot holes, placing charges, shoring up the roof with timbers, and advancing track for the wagons were made by the miners themselves. Life and death hung on those decisions, and rockfalls, gas, and crushing by vehicles provided daily perils, in between the catastrophic explosions and fires underground. Consequently, coal miners insisted on speaking of their "craft" and worked with an independence that was the envy of other workers. It was no rare event for miners who had finished the day's task they had set for themselves simply to leave.

> By quitting time in some towns, [noted an observer in the early 1920s,] most of the miners will be out of the mine and many of them will be washed up and down town again. [He] may quit to butcher a calf, for example, or to help cook the dinner for the boarders on the night shift, or simply because he "knows when he is tired," or because he has earned what seems to him enough for the day.[7]

7. Carter Goodrich, *The Miner's Freedom. A Study of the Working Life in a Changing Industry* (Boston, 1925), 42. See also Keith Dix, *Work Relations*

Tonnage miners constituted 90 percent of the work force in the bituminous mines of Pennsylvania during the 1890s. The remainder were "company men": outside laborers and mechanics, breaker boys, underground stable and track hands, and others who were paid by the day. Although the development of undercutting machines and the use of shot firers and other specialists had raised the proportion of company men to almost one-fourth of the employees by 1930, three of four workers loosened and loaded coal and were paid by the ton for what they sent to the surface. Ironically, therefore, the UMWA, which enrolled all workers in and about the mines and was thus considered the AFL's leading industrial union, represented a more homogeneous occupational group than did the IAM, the cigar makers, or many other leading craft unions of the time.

Among the 145,000 anthracite miners, however, the persistence of subcontracting made a sharper division between miners and laborers than was customary among the 640,000 bituminous miners. Before the resurgence of the union in 1897, as many as 80 percent of the laborers were hired by the day in groups ranging from two to twelve by a single tonnage miner. The miner was usually British, Irish, or German, and the laborers Polish, Slovak, or Italian. That division was not obliterated by the rise of the UMWA but was continued along with other past practices in arbitration awards in the decade following the 1902 strike, and it remained the source of much friction until large numbers of Italians, enrolled in the IWW, fought for the suppression of the contract system in 1916. By that time, however, as Selig Perlman discovered in his investigations for the Commission on Industrial Relations, the ethnic dimensions of the system had changed, though its economics remained the same. Wrote Perlman, "This contractor is more often a Pole than he is an English-speaking person. The contractor gets as many cars as he needs and the bona fide contract [tonnage] miner is often short of cars. Very frequently the contractor runs a saloon or a boarding house and is not a miner himself."[8]

in the Coal Industry: The Hand-Loading Era, 1880–1930 (Morgantown, W.Va., 1977).

8. Interview with J. J. Kajawski, in Selig Perlman, "The Immigrant and the Agreement in the Pittsburgh District" (unpublished manuscript, CIR Case Studies – BLS, Department of Labor R.G. 174, Box 2, National Archives), 11. The correct spelling of Kajawski's name appears on p. 24. On earlier subcontracting, see Frank J. Warne, "The Anthracite Coal Strike," *Annals of the American Academy of Political and Social Science*, 17 (January 1901), 32–3. On the past-practices agreement, see Anthracite Board of Conciliation, *Report*, Vol. 9 (Wilkes-Barre, Pa., 1922). I am indebted to the late Carter Goodrich for the gift of this volume.

In both the bituminous and anthracite fields the mines employed many experienced miners, usually from the British Isles, as well as newcomers of rural origins. Between 1895 and 1905 the UMWA had lobbied successfully for a Pennsylvania tax of three cents per day for each immigrant on a mine payroll, and other laws in Illinois and Indiana requiring inexperienced men to work as helpers for one year before they could obtain a state license to mine rooms of their own.[9] Such laws were widely ignored and usually were eventually struck down by the courts. The Pennsylvania law had the ironic effect of helping to bring thousands of immigrants into the union that had advocated it. When it went into effect in 1897, the companies simply deducted the tax from the immigrant's pay. The result was a strike, followed by the massacre of nineteen marching immigrants at Latimer, and a general strike in protest against the shooting, which resulted in a wage increase and massive enrollment of workers into the union.[10]

By 1916, American coal towns housed a mosaic of nationalities and religions. Long-settled British communities, like Braidwood, Illinois, and Frostburg, Maryland, remained quite intact, as did the famous *kleine deutsches Athen in Amerika*, Belleville, Illinois. Although there were many Slavic and Italian miners in Alabama and northern West Virginia, the mines of the southern Appalachians were worked primarily by migrants from the region's own farms – in stark contrast to the rest of the country, where few local farmers joined the immigrants in the mines. Twenty-six percent of the southeastern coal miners in 1910 were Afro-Americans. Although their numbers grew from 11,237 that year to 42,666 in 1920, a huge influx of white immigrants into West Virginia during the same period slightly reduced the proportion of the region's black miners to 23 percent. The notion that English-speaking miners in the North had been driven westward by the influx of recent immigrants is widely believed, but of dubious validity. Western mines had been opened, usually by railroads, during the 1870s and 1890s and attracted both white and Chinese miners. By 1908 in Rock Springs, Wyoming, scene of the bloody massacre of Chinese miners by white Knights of Labor in 1885, Chinese members attended UMWA meetings, according to one reporter, together with "nearly every nation of Europe." The labor force in Colorado blended Chicanos with Slavic, Greek, Italian, British, and Mexican immigrants

---

9. Dix, *Work Relations*, 79–81; Harold W. Aurand, *From the Molly Maguires to the United Mine Workers: The Social Ecology of an Industrial Union, 1869–1897* (Philadelphia, 1971), 137–41.

10. Aurand, *Molly Maguires*, 137–41; Victor Greene, *The Slavic Community on Strike: Immigrant Labor in Pennsylvania Anthracite* (Note Dame, Ind., 1968), 133–8.

and a few westward-driven Anglos. Conversely, union grievance forms submitted to the Anthracite Board of Conciliation in 1917–20 showed many Irish and English names among those of Poles, Slovaks, and Lithuanians.[11]

Whatever the nationality or race of the miners, work practices and work relations were much the same. Workers' concerns focused on earnings and survival, and both inspired solidarity. Because wages were the heart of coal production costs, companies sought every opportunity to reduce tonnage rates, screen out small coals for which they did not want to pay, and announce weights for carloads that were too low for miners to believe. Few issues evoked more chronic controversy in the coalfields than miners' demands for checkweighmen, selected by themselves to assure proper weighing of the coal. From Pennsylvania to Colorado, state laws providing for checkweighmen were widely ignored by operators, provoking many strikes from the 1870s through the 1920s. Most important in union mines, however, was the role of the pit committee. The committee usually consisted of three miners, whose task it was to see to it that a checkweighman was doing his job, and also that cars were made available for loading to all miners as they needed them and without partiality, that "dead work" (excavation of rock to reach the coal) was fairly distributed and compensated, that undercutters were dispatched to rooms as they were needed, and that roofs that growled and rumbled dangerously were made safe by pulling down adjacent pillars and roof to lessen the strain. As Carter Goodrich learned in his study of Pennsylvania mines, the pit committee was responsible not only for keeping miners safe from accident or abuse but also for making the operation efficient, so that tonnage miners could earn a reasonable income in a reasonable amount of time. It was the living embodiment of the miners' cohesiveness and group self-discipline. It was also the pedagogue of correct behavior for new miners and the key to understanding miners' widespread belief that they could "run coal" better than the capitalists.[12]

11. I am indebted to Paul Nyden for the calculations concerning black miners, based on U.S. Census data. On British communities, see John H. M. Laslett, *Nature's Noblemen: The Fortunes of the Independent Collier in Scotland and the American Midwest, 1855–1889* (Los Angeles, 1984); Harvey, *Best-dressed Miners.* On Chinese in Rock Springs, see A. M. Simons, "The Miners' Union – A Doer of Big Deeds," *Pearson's Magazine,* 37 (February 1917), 132. For grievance forms, see Anthracite Board of Conciliation, *Report,* 10, passim.

12. Goodrich, *Miner's Freedom,* 78–86; Mary Van Kleeck, *Miners and Management: A Study of the Collective Agreement Between the United Mine Workers of America and the Rocky Mountain Fuel Company and an Analysis of the Problem of Coal in the United States* (New York, 1934), 364.

The solidarity of miners underground was reinforced powerfully by that of women aboveground. Their two worlds were sharply separated. So few women worked the coal face in this epoch that those who did became legends. Moreover, most of what miners' wives and daughters knew about the dark world underground they seem to have learned from other women, not from conversation with the men. The awful wail of the disaster siren that brought them running to the pithead in search of husbands, fathers, and brothers was their main contact with the subterranean world. Yet their lives revolved around it from birth to death.

The worst thing that could happen in a coal town, a West Virginia woman told historian David Corbin, was for a clothesline to break on wash day. Consider her point. Clothes – the shirts and trousers of coal diggers – were scrubbed, usually in a galvanized tub with water carried from a stream and with the help of soap only during those rare periods when work was plentiful for the husband. Sometimes two days of scrubbing were needed before clothes were hung on the line to dry. If the line then broke, what was on the ground beneath it? Coal dust.[13]

The home economy was so visible in mining towns that only with serious effort could an observer miss its relationship to the extraction of coal. Gardens and livestock were everywhere. Boarders, husbands, and sons ate huge meals and came home needing to be scrubbed at all hours. Or, all too often, they did not, because there was no work. Between 1890 and the 1918 peak of war output, bituminous miners experienced, on average, between 104 and 137 days of unemployment each year. In slack times, special effort was needed to stretch the food budget. At all times, miners' ethics required that an extra plate be set for even the chance visitor. Many anthracite mines were close enough to urban centers, such as Hazleton and Scranton, for wage employment to be available there for miners' daughters. The silk manufacturing in the anthracite region was an economic complement to the production of coal. Elsewhere, however, and in most bituminous regions, a few restaurants, hospitals, put-out needlework, and domestic service in managers' homes provided the few occasions for women to earn cash. Widows often opened small candy stores or saloons that were patronized by their former husbands' friends. Indeed, the making and sale of liquor may have been as important a part of women's economic activity in American mining towns as elsewhere in the world.[14]

13. David A. Corbin, *Life, Work, and Rebellion in the Coal Fields: The Southern West Virginia Miners, 1880–1922* (Urbana, Ill., 1981), 92.
14. Harvey, *Best-dressed Miners*, 74–125; Joseph F. Patterson, "Old W.B.A. Days," *Publications of the Schuylkill County Historical Society*, II (1910), 355–84; John Bodnar, *Anthracite People: Families, Unions and Work, 1900–1940* (Harrisburg, Pa., 1983).

Lodge, church, and union activities provided the core of community life and often involved the whole family. Violins, accordions, and wind instruments were everywhere, and pianos were often bought by organizations. To be a musician let a man or woman entertain neighbors and also earn extra money. Ceremonial occasions also built on and nurtured the links between households that were necessary for survival, but were also woman's work. At times they were joyous, as in a wedding procession, a union parade and picnic, or a procession to dedicate a church or a lodge's new flags. Other occasions were more solemn. The death of a miner underground brought all work to a halt and the whole town to the funeral. Then Catholics, Protestants, Orthodox, and secularists sang and prayed together.

The acid test of women's solidarity, however, came during strikes. The flow of husbands' earnings stopped altogether and often for many months at a time – during the bituminous strike of 1922–3 for sixteen months in some regions. Evictions from company houses came quickly, and the women set up housekeeping in tent colonies, usually on the land of a friendly farmer, but often strategically situated near the main entrances to the struck mines. Blocking the roads to scabs became the most dangerous activity of miners' families, but simple survival on the meager relief made available by the union became the everyday challenge. On occasion, women might march with their children in a demonstration, perhaps at the state capital, to publicize their cause, or attend meetings where orators such as Mother Jones were especially popular. In between one such event and the next came the staffing of committees to distribute food and clothing, arrange Christmas or Easter celebrations, care for the sick, and assist neighbors in childbirth. Swaggering soldiers and mine guards posed a constant menace: "the women that have been insulted in Ludlow – it is terrible," testified Welsh-born Mary Thomas. They murdered all three children of her neighbor Mary Petrucci. In those tent colonies there was no question who was everyone's enemy: the company.[15]

Their bulwark – almost their secular church – was the union. No other AFL union of the 1910s evoked such loyalty from members, such fervent responses to strike calls from miners who were not members, such rank-and-file fury at leaders' misdeeds, such factionalism, or such a blend of locally directed struggle with conviction that outside the international

15. Priscilla Long, "The Women of the Colorado Fuel and Iron Strike, 1913–1914," in Ruth Milkman, ed., *Women, Work and Protest: A Century of US Women's Labor History* (Boston, 1985), 62–85; the quotation is on p. 74. On women's roles in strike relief, see Ernest T. Hiller, *The Strike: A Study in Collective Action* (Chicago, 1928); minutes of UMWA Local 445, April 19, 1911, in possession of the author.

union there was no salvation as did the UMWA. It had emerged from the depression of the 1890s with 9,700 U.S. members in 1897, almost all of them in Ohio or western Pennsylvania, and it had grown by 1913 to 377,700 on the way to its all-time peak of 425,700 in 1921. Between 1898 and 1915, the union collected and spent $21,774,791, of which $16,451,832 went for strike relief. Much of the rest went to pay the salaries of a staff, which included international officers, executive-board members, and 150 field representatives, by 1919, who did no negotiating of contracts or grievances but dedicated their time to organizing new locals, visiting old ones, instructing members on the proper transaction of business and keeping of books, and advancing the program and interests of the incumbent international leadership. The field organizers were of many nationalities and races, including an occasional Chinese or Japanese. A meeting of Local 445 in Arona, Pennsylvania, during the bitter Westmoreland County strike of 1910–11 was addressed by three international representatives, listed by the local's recording secretary as "Bro John Vernatti of Ill [who] addressed the Itialian Bros[,] Bro Johnas Gautt of Iowa [who] gave a lengthy and interesting talk to the English Bros [and] Bro Paul Stolpa of Herminie [who] addressed the Slavish Bros in there languish."[16]

Staff work involved more than lecturing to and supervising locals. A major task during strikes was to compile lists of deputy sheriffs, militiamen, and certified jurors, detailing their occupations, politics, arrest records, and company connections for the use of lawyers and friendly politicians during the inevitable arrests and trials of strikers. Instant alarms had to be raised at the moment of arrest so that observers could be on hand at police headquarters when the apprehended men or women were brought in. Lobbies were constantly busy in state legislatures promoting bills to deal with safety, checkweighmen, child labor, police and militia regulations, company stores and scrip payment, hours of work, woman suffrage (a cause early championed by miners' unions), and state mediation services. In the United States, as in Europe, coal miners' unions were as strongly committed to political action and legislative reform as they were to collective bargaining, and Vice-Presidents William Green and William Wilson were not the only union leaders to hold or seek legislative offices. When the NCF's Gertude Beeks asked John Mitchell for in-

16. Leo Wolman, *The Growth of American Trade Unions, 1880–1923* (New York, 1924), 110; Austin K. Kerr, "Labor-Management Cooperation: An 1897 Case," *Pennsylvania Magazine of History and Biography* (January 1975), 58; Simons, "Miners' Union"; interview with John L. Lewis, January 21, 1919 (Saposs Papers, Box 21, Folder 5); minutes of UMWA Local 445, April 19, 1911.

troductions to union officers in the three anthracite districts in October 1906, Mitchell replied that she was unlikely to find UMWA leaders in the region with time to see her. In District 1, President T. D. Nichols was running for Congress as a Democrat; in District 7, W. H. Dettry was running for Congress, and Charles P. Gildea for lieutenant governor, both as Socialists; and in District 9, John Fahy and Miles Dougherty were Democratic candidates for the legislature.[17]

Union miners, left, right, and center, were more concerned with sustaining an effective fighting organization than with democratic procedures. The biennial conventions of a thousand delegates by 1908 and two thousand by 1922 routinely voted sweeping authority to the international officers. A sense of quasi-military discipline was easily and often evoked by those officers to quell dissent or shroud their work in secrecy. During the presidency of T. L. Lewis, who replaced Mitchell with Socialist support in 1908, the appointment of field organizers was instituted. During the next decade, district officers began to select the locals' checkweighmen, and pit committees were increasingly often elected by local meetings, rather than by the miners in the particular pits. When a serious effort was made at the union's 1919 convention to have the organizers chosen by election, black and foreign-born delegates rallied to the administration's side, convinced that only the appointment system could secure them proper representation on the staff.

As factional battles among powerful international and district officials flared, fraudulent telegrams concerning the deeds of rivals, prostitutes planted in delegates' rooms for private detectives with cameras to discover, and stormy physical confrontations became common fare at UMWA conventions. Rebel movements grew in importance together with the size and bureaucracy of the UMWA, most notably the IWW in anthracite, the West Virginia Miners Organization between 1912 and 1916, and the Illinois wildcat strike movement of 1919. None of these movements dislodged miners' commitment to the UMWA for long. In fact, they were overshadowed by the readiness of miners in Colorado, southern West Virginia, Alabama, the Pennsylvania coke regions, and elsewhere outside the organized domain of union strength to respond to UMWA strike

17. On staff work, see Adolph Germer Papers, Box 23, Folder 53. On Candidates, see John Mitchell to Gertrude Beeks, October 1, 1906 (Mitchell Papers, Box A3-11). On the UMWA's political program, see Laslett, *Labor and Left*, 192–231. Compare Rolande Trempé, "Le réformisme des mineurs français à la fin du XIXe siècle," *Le Mouvement Social*, 65 (October–December 1968), 93–107.

calls. It was the great prestige of this giant union that made it the touchstone of Socialist hopes.[18]

As we have noted, however, the UMWA had also been the apple of Ralph Easley's eye and the NCF's model of proper collective bargaining. Indeed, the NCF's trade-agreement department, which had a purely propagandistic role (in contrast to the mediation work of its conciliation department), was headed in 1903 jointly by John Mitchell and President Francis Robbins of the Pittsburgh Coal Company. The explanation of this paradox lies in the 1898 trade agreement for the "Central Competitive Field" (CCF). Bituminous miners had long recognized that competition among their employers clustered around clearly definable, often large, market regions. As early as 1859, miners in the three counties whose waterways led to Pittsburgh had struck jointly to establish payment by the ton rather than by the carload. Ten years later, a union of anthracite miners undertook to regulate tonnage payments and output on a uniform basis for the entire region. By 1882, a "Pittsburgh scale" was established by a master agreement, and three years later a miners' union attempted to extend that scale all the way to St. Louis – throughout the whole of the CCF, between the Ohio River and the Great Lakes. Although that effort failed and union defeats in 1894–5 had virtually obliterated union influence outside of Ohio, the great strike of 1897 made possible the realization of the dream of union-enforced wage uniformity over the heartland of America's bituminous output.[19]

What a strike it was! A summons from the officers of a union with 10,000 members brought an estimated 150,000 men out of the pits starting July 4. The conflicting interests of railroads, steel companies, urban coal merchants, and other business groups frustrated all efforts at an employers' united front and even encouraged the governors of Ohio, Indiana, and Illinois to proclaim their support for the strikers. The aging Knights of Labor teamed up with Eugene Debs's youthful Social Democracy of America to extend the strike into West Virginia. Ten years later, an IWW pamphlet denouncing the leaders and practices of the UMWA began with a reference to "1897, a year that almost every coal miner

18. McAlister Coleman, *Men and Coal* (New York, 1943), 79–105; Heber Blankenhorn, *The Strike for Union* (New York, 1924), 7–10; Dubofsky and Van Tine, *John L. Lewis*, 51; Simons, "Miners' Union."

19. Green, *Civic Federation*, 85–8; Montgomery, "Strikes in Nineteenth-Century America," 90–1; Jon Amsden and Stephen Brier, "Coal Miners on Strike: The Transformation of Strike Demands and the Formation of a National Union," *Journal of Interdisciplinary History*, 7 (Spring 1977), 583–616.

points to with pride, and well he may." Leading coal dealers and mine operators bargained through the first two weeks of September with UMWA officers to produce an agreement for an immediate raise in the Pittsburgh region, as prelude to a convention the following January of industry and union representatives from the entire CCF. At the 1898 gathering, an elaborate scale of payments, designed more to equalize employers' labor costs than to equalize wages per se, was coupled with a general wage advance, a formal eight-hour day, and a checkoff of union dues. It was evident that the operators signing the agreement had a vested interest in a large union strike fund, because strikes were the only means to bring recalcitrant employers into the agreement. Mine operators in bituminous had been unable to organize themselves to stabilize prices, because powerful buyers of coal, such as the railroads and the steel industry, owned mines of their own, which helped them hold down prices. The UMWA thus provided a rationalizing agency for the industry. The agreement also provided for periodic conventions of union and industry representatives in the future, at which adjustments of wages and work rules could be made only by unanimous consent, which meant, in practice, by complex bargaining spiced by workers' threats to strike and operators' threats to withdraw. Over time, the operators won provisions to restrict the conduct of miners and their pit committees and even an agreement by the union not to seek any legislation that had not been approved by the joint convention.[20]

The CCF agreement was the foundation of the UMWA's accomplishments, income, and bureaucracy. In return for important concessions to the region's bituminous miners, it made their union the economic policeman for a highly competitive industry. But almost from the day the 1898 trade agreement was signed it suffered erosion at the geographic frontiers of the CCF. Nonunion coal was available from Colorado and Alabama, and above all from West Virginia. One stimulus that had made Pittsburgh operators offer concessions to end the 1897 strike had been the knowledge that the House of Morgan was building a new rail network to make the vast coal deposits of southern West Virginia easily accessible to northern markets. Union strength in that state had largely been restricted to Kanawha County during the strike, and subsequently the com-

20. Kerr, "Labor-Management Cooperation"; Van Kleeck, *Miners and Management,* 179–90; Industrial Union Leaflet No. 12, "An Address to Coal Miners"; NCF, Joint Trades Agreement Conference, May 7, 1904, 5–13 (typescript in John Mitchell Papers, Box A3-10); Illinois Miners Contract 1908 (John Mitchell Papers, Box A3-10); Henry Demarest Lloyd, *Men, the Workers* (New York, 1909), 217; Commons, *Trade Unionism and Labor Problems, First Series,* 11–12.

pany towns to the south of there proved effective barriers to union recruiting. By the 1910s, 94 percent of the state's miners lived in company towns – towns without elected local government, where Baldwin-Felts guards were the law. To dispel any doubts, the state legislature enacted a measure in 1901 giving mine-company rules the force of law. Booming production made the miners' annual earnings higher than those union men enjoyed in the CCF and attracted migrants from Galicia and Alabama alike. But all those migrants were effectively sealed off from "outside agitators."[21]

The rising volume of coal from the South made CCF operators increasingly restive. In 1904 they demanded and won a wage reduction as the price of continuing the agreement. Two years later they forced Mitchell to break the CCF into several regions, each with its own agreement. Enraged UMWA members responded by ousting Mitchell from the presidency and repudiating the NCF. Within the union's heartland, Socialist strength grew rapidly. In 1908, at least 400 of the 1,000 delegates to the union's biennial convention held party cards; by 1910, Presidents John Walker of the Illinois district, Francis Feehan of the Pittsburgh district, and W. D. Van Horn of the Indiana district were all party members. Adolph Germer of the party's executive board and Duncan McDonald were also leading figures in the Illinois district. As the new leaders restored all of the CCF except Illinois to one master agreement and launched increasingly aggressive organizing strikes in nonunion pockets in the CCF (such as Pennsylvania's Westmorland coke region) and on the CCF fringes in West Virginia and Colorado, miners' votes for the Socialist Party rose rapidly. Michael Nash's survey of voting in seventy-three Westmoreland County coal towns in 1910 revealed that the Socialists had outpolled the Democrats (2,339 to 1,102) and had almost matched the Republicans (2,467). He also concluded, however, that most Socialist votes came from those Slavic and Italian miners who were entitled to vote. English-speaking miners more often cast their protest votes for the reformist Keystone Party, a predecessor of the Bull Moose Progressives, which swept the field with 3,628 votes. Evidently, intense class struggle stimulated more political activity among workers, but not any one single kind of activity. Socialists, Democrats, and independents were all competing effectively for the votes of workers in search of a new political regime.[22]

The miners' new leadership and their political alliances were put to the test in their confrontations of 1913–14 with the Colorado Fuel and Iron

21. Corbin, *Life, Work,* 25–60.
22. Coleman, *Men and Coal,* 59–82; Nash, *Conflict and Accommodation,* 87, 137.

Company (CFI). This huge concern was basically a steel producer, but almost twelve thousand of its workers were coal miners. They mined inward from canyon walls, rather than sinking deep shafts, and they represented at least thirty-two different nationalities. Miners of Mexican, Italian, Croatian, Greek, and British origins were especially numerous. The desolate company towns scattered over a thousand miles, but especially heavily concentrated in Las Animas and Huerfano counties, were tightly controlled by two CFI institutions: the company guards and the welfare department. It is noteworthy that this Rockefeller-owned company, which was to play so prominent a role in proposing new plans of union-free employee representation to American business and intellectual leaders after 1915, had already established a reputation as an innovator in corporate welfare practices before the strike. It was especially concerned with teaching "domestic economy" to women who had left behind the gardens, livestock, and social networks that had earlier shaped their lives in distant villages. The welfare manager, Dr. R. W. Corwin, considered the miners and their wives "drawn from the lower classes of foreign immigrants" and entrapped by "primitive ideas of living and ignorance of hygienic laws."[23] As the strike made clear, the mine guards and most of the state's electorate regarded them with the same disdain.

The UMWA dispatched Vice-President Frank J. Hayes to the region in 1913, and he quickly organized a district policy committee dominated by socialists of British and Irish birth and a network of mine committees, where Spanish, Croatian, Slovenian, Polish, and Italian were the most common languages. The Yugoslav Socialist Alliance (YSA) was especially strong and influential in these fields, though the miners' best-known leader, Louis Tikas, was Greek. Company towns left little space for an immigrant bourgeoisie, so that socialist-organized lodges provided not only centers of family conviviality but also political orientation in the mine patches. The first nationally distributed newspaper of the YSA, *Glas svobode,* came from Pueblo, in the heart of the CFI domain. Mihajlo Livoda and his Serbian comrade Peter Kokatovíc were but two socialist miners from this region whose roles in the 1913–14 strike were the beginnings of long careers of organizing immigrants into the union fold.[24]

The union's prospects were promising. It enjoyed the support of an effective network of men and women in the mining towns, and the state

23. Tolman, *Social Engineering,* 37–42, 54–5, 258–61; the quotations are on pp. 54–5. See also Sarah Jane Deutsch, "Culture, Class and Gender: Chicanas and Chicanos in Colorado and New Mexico, 1900–1940" (unpublished Ph.D. diss., Yale University, 1985).
24. Stipanovich, "Immigrant Workers," 164–76.

government was in ostensibly friendly hands: Democratic Governor Elias Ammons had come from the Farmers' Union, which was often allied with the politically active Colorado Federation of Labor. Mary Bradford of the Women's Trade Union League was state superintendent of instruction. Nineteen members of the state legislature held union cards, and one other listed herself as the wife of a union machinist. True, Ammons was no match for astute and aggressive Populist Davis H. "Bloody Bridles" Waite, who had occupied the governor's chair in the 1890s, but the Populist epoch had left laws on the statute books forbidding interference with a worker's joining a union and requiring mining companies to allow their employees to elect checkweighmen. Moreover, both the state's constitution and its statutes limited miners' hours to eight per day. CFI smashed a strike to enforce these laws in 1904 and continued to flout them until the UMWA drive got under way. Then it announced dates for election of checkweighmen, in which no miners dared take part, and in March 1913 instituted an eight-hour day. Moreover, a strike had been under way in the northern coalfields of the state since 1910.[25]

The UMWA's demands summarized the miners' aspirations: recognition of the union and its grievance committees, removal of armed guards, abolition of company scrip and of obligatory trading at company stores, enforcement of safety regulations, the right of miners to choose boardinghouses and doctors for themselves, the eight-hour day and elected checkweighmen as provided by law, and a 10 percent increase in wages. When its proposals were rejected contemptuously by CFI, the union called a strike for September 23, 1913. Company guards instantly evicted the strikers from the company-owned housing, and close to ten thousand miners and their families trudged through rain and sleet down the canyons to tent colonies that the union had established near the canyon mouths. The rest of the story is well known. Although many miners moved elsewhere, thousands remained in the tent colonies, where the women joined the men in picket duty, set up housekeeping, and organized multinational support networks. Mother Jones rushed to the scene to make daily rounds "cheering the women, inspiring the men" and entertaining the children. Deadly clashes with company guards flared at once, leading Governor Ammons to dispatch units of the Colorado National Guard to the scene, where they were welcomed by children dressed in white wav-

25. Hunter, *Labor in Politics*, 126; George P. West, *United States Commission on Industrial Relations Report on the Colorado Strike* (Washington, D.C., 1915), 63–6, 77–8. On the 1904 strike, see Benjamin M. Rastall, *Labor History of the Cripple Creek District: A Study in Industrial Evolution* (Madison, Wisc., 1908).

ing American flags. The governor had ordered the troops not to escort strikebreakers who came from out of the state.[26]

Company officials mobilized the state's business community, its bankers, who extended the credit to pay the troops, and most of its press to mount relentless pressure on the man they called "the cowboy governor" to change that order. They portrayed the state as languishing in the grip of foreign anarchists and warned that its householders faced a winter without coal for their homes. On December 1, the governor yielded to their demands and ordered the troops to protect anyone who wanted to cross the picket lines and go to work. The company's board chairman, Lamont M. Bowers, triumphantly wrote to Rockefeller in New York:

> If the governor had acted on September 23 as he has been forced to act during the past few weeks, the strike would never have existed ten days.
>
> We used every possible weapon to drive him into action, but he was hand-in-glove with the labor leaders and is today, but the big men of affairs have helped the operators in whipping the agitators, including the governor.[27]

Arrests and armed clashes became routine as national guard and company guards jointly enforced martial law over the canyons' mouths, despite widespread efforts of railroad workers to impede the movement of troops. During the winter months the men and women of the tent colonies supplemented their parades and petitions with the digging of slit trenches and dugouts, which were put to use April 20, 1914. The previous day had been Greek Easter, and all strikers had joined in the celebration. Most families were sleeping late, and some bachelors were still dancing and playing music, when the guardsmen's rifles and machine guns opened up on the tents of Ludlow. The strikers raced to the trenches with their rifles and fired back until they ran out of ammunition late in the afternoon. Then the guards entered, burning tents, shooting people, and smashing accordions and violins. In all, thirteen women and children were killed, and Tikas and two other strikers were seized and executed on the spot.

Two days later a memorable meeting took place. Leaders of the UMWA, the Colorado Federation of Labor, and the Western Federation of Miners

26. On demands, see U.S. CIR, VII, 7017. On tent colonies, see Long, "Women"; Mary Field Parton, ed., *Autobiography of Mother Jones* (Chicago, 1925), 178–204; Edward J. Boughton, *The Military Occupation of the Coal Strike Zone of Colorado by the Colorado National Guard, 1913–1914* (Denver, 1914), 8–14.

27. L. M. Bowers to J. D. Rockefeller, Jr., December 22, 1913, in West, *U.S. Commission*, 136. This letter appears in a series subpoenaed by the U.S. CIR and reprinted in West, 111–15.

jointly and formally called their members to arms. Strikers and their allies swept down on scabs and guards, burned mine tipples, and sealed pits. As a federal investigator reported: "Responsible union officials planned the movement of their men, set about collecting and distributing arms and ammunition, and openly justified their acts."[28] All told, 66 people were killed between September 1913 and April 29, 1914: 18 strikers, 10 guards, 19 scabs, 2 militiamen, 3 noncombatants, 2 women, and 12 children. On April 30, federal troops arrived on orders from President Woodrow Wilson. The fighting stopped, but the strike continued.

Corporate leadership and social order

Although the appearance of the U.S. Army after the workers had defeated mine guards and state troops, especially in several battles on April 29, resembled the summoning of state militia to Homestead after the surrender of the Pinkertons to the workers, there were two major differences between 1892 and 1914. First, UMWA and other AFL leaders in Colorado had publicly advocated the use of federal troops, as had the Denver Chamber of Commerce, the state's entire all-Democratic congressional delegation, and a thousand women described by the *New York Times* as "the cream of Denver's society," who refused to leave Governor Ammons's office until he formally requested federal intervention.[29] Second, the America of competitive capitalism, in which the state could "restore order" and then consider its task completed, no longer existed. The new context of tightly structured corporate capitalism, systematic reshaping of work relations, trade-union movements six to seven times larger than they had been in 1892, and the world's great powers on the brink of war meant that governmental forces had to provide not simply suppression of "industrial unrest," but also solutions. That necessity, in turn, made both business and union leaders determined to define the terms of those solutions. Their efforts to do so in Colorado cast a long shadow over the country's future.

President Wilson was eager to find a remedy quickly. The states-rights traditions of his party, to which he had been committed all his public life and of which he was reminded sharply by southern congressional leaders such as South Carolina's James Byrnes, held that state authorities were

28. West, *U.S. Commission*, 136. The call to arms is reproduced in Walter H. Fink, *The Ludlow Massacre* (n.p., 1914), 19–20.
29. Billie Barnes Jensen, "Woodrow Wilson's Intervention in the Coal Strike of 1914," *Labor History*, 15 (Winter 1974), 63–77; the quotation is on p. 69.

exclusively responsible for securing domestic order. Moreover, the day after the Ludlow massacre, U.S. Marines had taken the city of Tampico in Mexico, after the navy had shelled it. On the day the Colorado Federation of Labor issued its call to arms, Congress authorized the president to employ whatever force he deemed necessary to avenge the recent arrest of a shore party of marines by Mexican authorities. It was no time to have America's small army tied up in Colorado's canyons.[30]

In fact, Secretary of Labor Wilson had been making futile efforts to persuade the Rockefeller interests to accept mediation even before the strike began. Between May and September, the army attempted to be evenhanded: It disarmed everyone, prohibited picketing, and prohibited the hiring of new miners from out of state, but also allowed resumption of operations with whatever local miners CFI could get. A new mediation team met with no success in its efforts to bring the company to the table with the UMWA, but it did recommend a settlement that President Wilson officially transmitted to the two parties in September. It called for a three-year truce, during which "all striking miners who have not been found guilty of violation of the law shall be given employment"; state laws were to be enforced, the union would waive all claims to recognition and stage no demonstrations or interferences with production, and a grievance committee would be instituted at each mine elected by the votes of all employees except company officials. A commission appointed by the president would serve as umpires for any disputes concerning "wages, working and social conditions" not resolved by a grievance committee and local management. A district union convention, meeting only one week short of a year after the strike had begun, voted overwhelmingly to accept the proposal. The company flatly refused. In particular, it objected to interference by government-appointed commissioners in its affairs and to the dismissal of loyal employees that reinstatement of strikers would require.[31]

John D. Rockefeller, Jr., and the executives of CFI had meanwhile devoted a great deal of thought to the issues involved in the president's proposal. Their plans were based on a keen awareness of the role of the modern state, the world crisis, and the importance of public relations to a successful corporation. Ivy L. Lee, publicity agent for the Pennsylvania Railroad, was hired immediately after the massacre to enlist writers and academics in the service of CFI's public image, and the former Canadian minister of labor, W. L. Mackenzie King, was asked to propose a long-

30. Ibid. See also Byrnes's dissent, U.S. Congress, House of Representatives, *Report on the Colorado Strike Investigation* (63rd Cong., 3rd Sess., House Document No. 1630, Washington, D.C., 1915), 45–50.

31. West, *U.S. Commission*, 94–9.

term remedy for the company's problems.[32] King's letter of acceptance in August 1914 revealed the farsighted view with which he approached the assignment. He warned that the outbreak of war had created conditions under which astute public leadership might create industrial peace. It also presented the peril that labor leaders might take the "short-sighted" view that

> ... the opportunities which may come to American capital through the crippled condition of industries elsewhere, will induce a recognition [of unions] which under less favorable circumstances might not be granted. This is almost certain to be the immediate effect, and I think you are wise, therefore, in dismissing altogether from your mind the possibility of the United Mine Workers calling off the strike.

The newly created Rockefeller Foundation, King continued, should look for "a means of restoring industrial peace" in the context of the changed conditions brought about by Europe's war. He suggested two basic considerations. First, although labor markets would be tight during the immediate future, heavy unemployment was bound to follow the war. At that time unions would become aware that recognition per se was "less pressing as an immediate end" than the maintenance of "standards already existing." In that context, unions might "come to regard as their friends and allies companies and corporations large enough and fair enough to maintain these standards of their own accord." The concept was breathtaking: The wages and working conditions established by open-shop big business not only could provide its employees with the conditions unions demanded but also could underwrite the efforts of unions in other sectors of the economy to preserve their standards against the attacks of smaller enterprises. An alliance of the future between union-free corporations and the trade-union movement was, to say the least, an imaginative reconciliation of the goals of the open-shoppers and the NCF.

King's second suggestion was to become basic doctrine to personnel managers of the 1920s. Corporations could no longer manage their affairs, let alone fend off unionization, by dealing with each employee individually. There was another way:

> Between the extreme of individual agreements [with employees] on the one side, and an agreement involving recognition of unions of national and international character on the other, lies the straight acceptance of the principle of Collective Bargaining between capital and labour immediately concerned in any certain industry ... and the construction of machinery which will afford opportunity of easy and constant conference between employees and employed with reference to matters of concern to both, such machinery to be avowedly constructed as a means on the one hand of preventing labour from

32. Ibid., 151–65.

being exploited, and on the other, of ensuring that cordial cooperation which is likely to further industrial efficiency.

The aim, King concluded concisely, was to secure "a maximum of publicity with a minimum of interference in all that pertains to the conditions
of employment."[33]

The Colorado Industrial Plan, as King's scheme came to be known,
was not America's first employee-representation plan or company union.
Straiton and Storm had developed a similar plan for its many cigar makers in the late 1870s, and both Philadelphia and New York had instituted
representation plans for their transit workers in the wake of general strike
movements in 1910 and 1916.[34] What was new in the Colorado Industrial Plan was the public attention it attracted, the foundation research it
inspired, and its formative role in American business's designs for the
postwar world.

The managers in Colorado had been reluctant to institute any workers'
representation, lest it look like a victory for the union, but President Wilson's proposal called for a countermove. President Welborn of CFI
promised Wilson "an even more comprehensive plan [than his own], em-
bodying the results of our practical experience."[35] The moment for reform arrived on December 10, when exhausted delegates to a special
UMWA conference called off the strike. As federal troops left the region
early in January, CFI posted notices inviting its miners to cast ballots for
representatives who would present their grievances to the company and
staff special committees on safety, housing, recreation, and education.
There had, to be sure, been no commitment to reinstate strikers or to
refer unresolved grievances to any agency outside the company. When
John Fitch visited the mines on an inspection trip for the government in
1917, he found the atmosphere quite open. He also noted, however, that
a majority of miners still paid dues to the UMWA and were aware that
the union had won recognition from the Victor-American Fuel Company, which had also been involved in the 1913–14 strike. The contest
for the minds and loyalties of the workers was by no means over.[36]

33. Ibid., 162–3. See also John D. Rockefeller, Jr., *The Personal Relation in
    Industry* (1917), reproduced in Leon Stein and Philip Taft, eds., *The Man-
    agement of Workers. Selected Arguments* (New York, 1971).
34. On Straiton and Storm, see Senate, *Labor and Capital,* 803–27. On the
    Philadelphia and New York plans, see Commons, *History of Labour,* IV,
    343–52.
35. West, *U.S. Commission,* 175.
36. Ibid., 184–5; Valerie Jean Conner, *The National War Labor Board: Sta-
    bility, Social Justice, and the Voluntary State in World War I* (Chapel Hill,
    N.C., 1983), 110–11; Benjamin Selekman and Mary Van Kleeck, *Employ-*

One feature of King's proposals that made them especially attractive to corporate executives was that his style of collective bargaining was restricted to the employees and officials of the individual firm. Not only "outside unions" were to be excluded; so were government agencies. There was no way such isolation from "external" influences could be secured, however, without appropriate behavior on the part of government. Rockefeller's awareness of this relationship is evident from the intense public-relations effort he assigned to Ivy Lee. Within Colorado, it was also necessary to cleanse the state government of Ammons and other unreliable officials. The company committed 150 of its personnel to a campaign to restore "law and order" to the state in the fall of 1914, and it effectively linked that slogan to a crusade for prohibition of liquor sales. What these undertakings allegedly had in common was that their antagonists were foreign-born labor radicals. The effort was a total success. Prohibition carried the election handsomely, and the Republicans took all state offices except that of Democratic Attorney General Farrar, who had openly championed CFI's demands for military repression throughout the strike. The triumph was a tribute to the company's ability to rally the votes of farmers and the urban middle class. Most miners, after all, were not eligible to vote. General John Chase, who commanded the national guard forces, declared that even in the town of Forbes, most of whose strikers had been born in the British Isles and had lived twenty to thirty years in the United States, only three were citizens. Moreover, the sweep at the polls was seconded by the lower courts. They indicted 124 miners for the April battles and after election day sentenced Lawson to life imprisonment on charges that he had been responsible for the death of a mine guard at Ludlow. The state supreme court, in the hands of the state's older political leadership, ultimately reversed all these decisions.[37]

The rightward swing of Colorado's elections was part of a nationwide harvest for business's political campaigning for a more secure local political climate, as well as a preview of greater triumphs to come. Local elections in the spring and fall of 1915 were largely disasters for labor-backed candidates, and especially for Socialists. A mournful survey by the *New Republic* revealed that old-guard Democrats and Republicans had carried New York City, Philadelphia, and Massachusetts and that woman suffrage had been voted down in four states. Socialist adminis-

ees' *Representation in Coal Mines* (New York, 1924); *Denver Post*, March 25, 1917.
37. West, *U.S. Commission*, 19–26, 114–16; Boughton, *Military Occupation*, 34; Commons, *History of Labour*, IV, 341.

trations had lost control of Butte, Milwaukee, and every one of the five towns previously held in Colorado. Schenectady was the only bright spot for the Socialists, and its victorious Mayor Lunn was to be expelled from the party early in 1916. To take a longer view, the tabulation of Socialist mayors compiled by James Weinstein shows 74 elected in 1911, 32 in 1913, 22 in 1915, and only 17 in 1917.[38]

Consequently, in the fall of 1915, the editors of *Iron Age* were simultaneously worried that labor's growing economic strength might place "permanent hobbles on the industry" and pleased with the current of politically effective public opinion.[39] Like the delegates to the 1915 NMTA convention who had celebrated the election news by singing both "Tipperary" and *"Die Wacht am Rhein,"* *Iron Age* had already concluded that the vital question of the hour was not which side was winning the war in Europe but how American industry might emerge from the conflict as master of all the belligerents. Business's concern for the "trade war" to follow the military engagement was reinforced by the rapid conversion of leading forces of the prewar peace movement, such as Elihu Root and the Carnegie Foundation, away from any effort to halt the war and toward consideration of how the "trustees of civilization" might reorganize international order. The formation in 1915 of the League to Enforce Peace, headed by former President William H. Taft and supported, as C. Roland Marchand's analysis has revealed, by virtually all the dignitaries of prewar campaigns for arbitration of international disputes, signaled the change. Statements from the league made it quite clear that it "does NOT seek to end the present war," but rather looked forward to a league of nations through which great powers after the end of this war might maintain order through "their united economic and military power."[40]

While mounting war tensions fanned the patriotic fervor of law-and-order committees against foreigners, radicals, and strikes, leading figures from the corporate and engineering worlds built closer institutional con-

38. *New Republic,* 5 (November 6, 1915), 1–2; *NR,* 4 (May 1916), 147; *IA,* 95 (April 22, 1915), 890–3; James Weinstein, *Decline of Socialism,* 116–18. The New York Consumers' League reported an unprecedented campaign against labor laws in state legislatures in 1915. See William L. O'Neill, *Everyone Was Brave: The Rise and Fall of Feminism in America* (Chicago, 1969), 218.

39. *IA,* 95 (April 22, 1915), 890–3; 96 (November 11, 1915), 1131.

40. C. Roland Marchand, *The American Peace Movement and Social Reform, 1898–1918* (Princeton, 1972), 147–75; Missouri General Committee of the League to Enforce Peace to Frank P. Walsh, March 1, 1917 (Walsh Papers, Box 4).

nections with administrative agencies of the federal government. Immediately after the sinking of the *Lusitania,* Secretary of the Navy Josephus Daniels and Thomas A. Edison met to plan a Naval Consulting Board. Its members were selected by the country's five largest engineering societies, and its most important undertaking was an "industrial preparedness inventory" of America's industrial capacity, directed by Vice-President Howard E. Coffin of the Hudson Motor Company and W. S. Gifford, chief statistician of American Telephone and Telegraph. The 245 engineers participating in the project were reminded by Chairman Bascom Little of the National Defense Committee of the Chamber of Commerce that an order placed with his company for 250,000 three-inch high-explosive shells represented "less than one day's supply of shells for France or England or Russia." The goals of the inventory were to discover where war orders might best be placed and to avoid the European experience of having skilled workers shipped to the front "only to be pulled back later, more or less demoralized, to tasks from which they never should have been taken." It was this mobilizing of engineers that had inspired the publication by *Engineering Magazine* of Knoeppel's *Industrial Preparedness.*[41]

Between the time when Mackenzie King had urged his vision of a future alliance of open-shop corporations with craft unions based in more competitive sectors of the economy and the time the engineers began their inventory of American industry, a number of informal gatherings of corporate leaders at the Yama Farms Inn in the Catskill Mountains had paved the way for the creation of a single institution to speak for American manufacturing. The leading figures came, as one might expect, from the electrical industry. Magnus Alexander and E. W. Rice, Jr., respectively the director of personnel and president of GE, and Vice-President Loyall Osborne of Westinghouse were joined by Frederick P. Fish, former president of American Telephone and Telegraph, and Frank Vanderlip, president of the National City Bank of New York, in setting up a National Industrial Conference Board (NICB). Its members were the National Founders' Association, the NMTA, the NAM, the National Erectors' Association, the National Association of Cotton Manufacturers (northern), the American Cotton Manufacturers' Association (southern), the National Association of Wool Manufacturers, the Silk Association of America, the United Typothetae, the American Paper and Pulp Association, and the Rubber Club of America, representing in all the fifteen thousand employers of the "7,036,337 wage earners in the manufactur-

41. *IA,* 97 (March 23, 1916), 718; (March 30, 1916), 794; Noble, *America by Design,* 148–50. All quotations are from *IA,* 97 (March 30, 1916), 794.

ing industry." The NICB was nothing less than a holding company for the major manufacturers' associations of the United States – the logical culmination of the process of industrial consolidation begun in the 1890s. Its purpose, explained Magnus Alexander, was to be a "clearing house of information" to "analyze and present the essential elements in the situation, suggest methods and inspire united and intelligent action." Realization of its goals would require, first, "the sympathetic support of the public," second, "the co-operation of the Government," and, third, business acting "intelligently and definitely on its own account."[42]

After the presidential election, the NICB formally presented itself to the world at the November 1916 convention of the National Founders' Association. There Alexander spoke extemporaneously to reveal his vision of the future. He imagined a meeting of the NICB "in a commodious office in one of New York's skyscrapers" almost five years hence, in May 1921. Bankers had now joined the conference board, from which they had initially held aloof. The secretary "read a communication from the White House, asking for suggestions for membership in the Federal Trade Commission," a request that was efficiently granted thanks to a "card index of qualified people for Federal and State governmental commissions." Cabinet officers often turned to the board for consultation, "because of the unapproachable character and non-political bias of the advisors." Its careful studies of "economic and legal matters" had produced "sound laws," and "it had come to be an axiom that society should assume the direct supervision over the morals, health and safety of the people."

When Alexander had finished his reverie, GE's President Rice offered a more formal address that like his colleague's, resounded with the ideological themes Knoeppel and King had already suggested. When "the great war ends our troubles in this country will begin," Rice warned. Germany had shown the way to discipline and efficiency, and England was "copying as rapidly as possible whatever seems to be good in the German industrial system." Their societies would, therefore, be "united to compete with us, not only in neutral markets, but if possible in our own market." Efficient enterprise, loyal workers, a sympathetic public, and cooperative government would not come about of themselves, but had to be created by effective and united business leadership. Rice concluded:

> The day of extreme individualism is past. The problems pressing for solution are so great that no single manufacturer, no matter how powerful, or group of manufacturers, no matter how numerous, is

42. All quotations from *IA*, 98 (November 16, 1916), 1118–20; Noble, *America by Design*, 236–8.

able to stand alone to the exclusion of other manufacturers or groups of manufacturers. The time has come when co-operation in the broadest sense is essential to the maintenance of our industrial prosperity.[43]

The NICB never fulfilled Alexander's dreams. Its most prominent political accomplishments were the creation of a National War Labor Board (NWLB) to end the strike crisis of the summer of 1917 and the selection of business's representatives on that board. As we shall see, business soon recoiled from the NWLB, claiming that it had been captured by labor, and clamored for its abolition after the German surrender. Moreover, the determination of prominent NICB members, such as William H. Barr of the founders' association, to drive unions out of the competitive as well as the oligopolistic sectors of American industry made it difficult for the NICB to formulate a single strategy toward labor. Consequently, Alexander and men like him continued to exchange views informally in the Yama Farms Inn and in 1919 created the Special Conference Committee as the agency to promote their own labor strategies. Its secretary, Clarence J. Hicks, was basically a troubleshooter for the Rockefellers who carried the Colorado Industrial Plan to strikebound oil refineries in Bayonne, New Jersey, and thence into the policies of GE, Westinghouse, DuPont, International Harvester, General Motors, and Goodyear Tire. The NICB was left with the important but less ambitious role of business's leading research and study group. American manufacturers neither created nor agreed on an urgent need for a disciplined organizational leadership, such as was then represented by Le Patronat in France, Confindustria in Italy, or the Federation of British Industries.[44]

Nevertheless, the coordination of industrial and governmental administration advocated by Alexander and Rice had, in fact, been institutionalized less than two months before their speeches when President Wilson established a Council of National Defense (CND), made up of six cabinet members and headed by Secretary of War Newton D. Baker. The council's work was performed mainly by its Advisory Commission of seven members: Daniel Willard (Baltimore and Ohio Railroad), Julius Rosenwald (Sears and Roebuck), Franklin Martin (American College of Sur-

43. *IA*, 98 (November 23, 1916), 1172–3. Note the similarity to the views of Charles P. Steinmetz, *America and the New Epoch* (New York, 1916).
44. Clarence J. Hicks, *My Life in Industrial Relations: Fifty Years in the Growth of a Profession* (New York, 1941); "Report of the Special Conference Committee, Revising and Supplementing the Progress Report Published July 24, 1919, and Including the Annual Reports Dated December 15, 1922, and December 6, 1923" (n.d., "for confidential circulation," library of the Graduate School of Business Administration, Harvard University).

geons), Bernard Baruch (Wall Street), Hollis Godfrey (Drexel Institute), Howard Coffin (Hudson Motors), who had directed the industrial-preparedness inventory, and Samuel Gompers (AFL). Seven months after the armistice, a congressional critic reported that the minutes of the Advisory Commission revealed the workings of a "secret government," which had

> ... devised the entire system of purchasing war supplies, planned a press censorship, designed a system of food control and selected Herbert Hoover as its director, determined on a daylight-saving scheme, and in a word designed practically every war measure which the Congress subsequently enacted, and did all this behind closed doors, weeks and even months before the Congress of the United States declared war against Germany.[45]

Grosvenor B. Clarkson, who had kept those minutes for the commission, reprinted the report in his own history of war mobilization, with the comment that the "only fault, aside from its bitterly depreciative tone," to be found with this summary "is that, broad as it is, it does not tell the whole story." Moreover, Clarkson added, the only possible cause the nation might have for regretting the commission's work would be that it had not been "even more inclusive, specific, and compelling."[46]

A forward-looking party

Wage earners could not shape the nation's future by conferring at the Yama Farms Inn or directing military preparedness. Nevertheless, because they could strike and change jobs at a time when economic mobilization placed their services in high demand, and because many of them possessed the right to vote, at a time when intense partisan competition for political office placed their votes in high demand, workers enjoyed an unprecedented ability to influence events that was constantly on the minds of policymakers. Moreover, workers' awareness of their growing might stimulated their appetite for fundamental changes in the way they lived and worked, as well as intense debate among themselves about what changes were most to be desired. It was evident to all parties involved in this debate that the machinery of state would play at least as important a role in shaping their future as their own activities in the workplace. But the decisive question for the workers' movement remained: Was the drift

45. Grosvenor B. Clarkson, *Industrial America in the World War: The Strategy Behind the Line, 1917–1918* (Boston, 1923), 24; Noble, *America by Design,* 149–50.
46. Clarkson, *Industrial America,* 26.

of national policy toward military preparedness and probable war an opportunity or a menace for the workers' rising aspirations?

Samuel Gompers quickly concluded that preparedness mobilization under a Democratic administration offered a golden opportunity to secure an influential and enduring position for trade unions within the machinery of social management then being consolidated. He had worked closely with the Wilson administration and congressional Democratic leaders during the enactment of the Clayton Act, whose provisions promised to limit the use of federal injunctions in industrial disputes, as well as the La Follette Seamen's Act, which emancipated sailors from the restrictions imposed by earlier mutiny and desertion laws, while it also excluded Asians from the crews of American ships and barred noncitizens from many licensed maritime trades. Moreover, Secretary of Labor William B. Wilson, a former leader of the UMWA who had served in Congress as a Democrat until a large Socialist vote in his district in 1912 tipped the scales in favor of the Republican candidate, served as an effective and influential intermediary for the AFL in the cabinet. Secretary Wilson arranged for frequent consultations between Gompers and other members of the cabinet, as well as for his appointment to the CND's Advisory Commission. Most of all, however, was the work of Secretary Wilson's conciliation service. The federal government's mediation work in industrial disputes after 1913 dwarfed the earlier private efforts of the NCF. The consistent theme guiding Wilson's work was that employers should be encouraged to negotiate with legitimate unions and to shun the IWW and other groups deemed "outlaw" by the AFL. Here was the appearance in embryonic form of the doctrine of a certified bargaining agent, which was to be incorporated into the law of the land in 1935. But in Wilson's day, the certification was to be done not by a national labor-relations board but by the AFL itself.[47]

Before 1914, these activities of the Wilson administration would have represented everything Gompers desired from the government, but the outbreak of war in Europe had added a new dimension to his thinking. Gompers quickly realized that the industrial-mobilization policies of England, France, and Germany after the munitions crisis of late 1914 had

47. Simeon Larson, "The American Federation of Labor and the Preparedness Controversy," *The Historian*, 37 (November 1974); Melvyn Dubofsky, "Abortive Reform: The Wilson Administration and Organized Labor, 1913–20," in James E. Cronin and Carmen Sirianni, eds., *Work, Community, and Power: The Experience of Labor in Europe and America, 1900–1925* (Philadelphia, 1983), 197–220; David Montgomery, "New Tendencies in Union Struggles and Strategies in Europe and the United States, 1916–1922," in Cronin and Sirianni, eds., *Work, Community*, 92–3.

given union standards and often union membership the backing of state decrees. He also observed that opponents of those governments' war efforts had been quickly crushed and, moreover, had enjoyed little support from their countries' workers.

> The present war has proved that one of the strongest emotions in men is patriotism [Gompers wrote in March 1915]. . . . It was stronger than the fundamental tenet of socialism, stronger than the ideals of international peace, stronger than religion, stronger than love of life and family.[48]

For the AFL, to oppose the government's war preparations would be to invite destruction, Gompers reasoned, whereas to participate actively in mobilization might ensure governmental support for union standards and union growth. Consequently, Gompers endorsed the League to Enforce Peace and told it in May 1916 that he would not stop the present war even if he could. Two years later, when the United States was fully involved as a belligerent, Gompers described the war as the "most wonderful crusade ever entered upon in the whole history of the world."[49]

Other leaders of the AFL were by no means convinced by Gompers's reasoning. To the members of the Socialist Party, the war was the greatest disaster that could have befallen civilization. The party quickly mobilized everyone it could influence in a campaign to keep the United States neutral; to "starve the war" in Europe by denying the belligerents credit, munitions, and even food from the United States; to resist the government's attempts to use the crisis to strengthen its military and economic grip on Latin America; and to persuade President Wilson to use his good offices to mediate the European conflict.[50] The Irish Race Convention and the conservative National German Alliance, both of which influenced the thinking of many AFL members, also demanded strict neutrality, although the National German Alliance and most of the non-Socialist German-language press hailed the military victories of imperial Germany and had no wish to end the war as long as these victories continued. Moreover, many AFL officers who had been in the Gompers camp on matters of trade-union policy had no desire to fight for the British Empire and were worried about the ease with which preparedness campaigns blended with business's propaganda for law and order and the open shop.

48. *Harper's Weekly,* March 10, 1915, quoted in Samuel Gompers, *Labor and the Common Welfare* (New York, 1919), 214.

49. Simeon Larson, *Labor and Foreign Policy: Gompers, the AFL, and the First World War, 1914–1918* (Teaneck, N.J., 1975), 20–5; the quotation is on p. 25.

50. Alexander Trachtenberg, *The American Socialist and the War* (New York, 1917).

No Democratic politician was closer to the thinking of this group of AFL leaders than Frank P. Walsh of Kansas City, Missouri. After President Wilson initiated his own preparedness campaign (November 1915), Walsh wired the president's advisor Joseph Tumulty, urging that Wilson avoid any association with "security leagues, protective organizations, peace associations, or anything of that character, especially in the West." Such groups, which might also "appear in the guise of chambers of commerce, commercial clubs, and civic bodies," would capitalize on the president's speaking tours for their own local reactionary purposes, Walsh warned.[51]

The sinking of the *Lusitania* by a German submarine in May 1915 stimulated both the advocates and the foes of military mobilization to intense activity. When William Jennings Bryan resigned as secretary of state rather than sign an ultimatum to Germany, he provided the rallying point for the formation of Labor's National Peace Council. The council's public meeting in New York's Cooper Union was sponsored by the city's Central Federated Union and featured its president, Ernest Bohm, Congressman Frank Buchanan (former president of the structural iron workers), Joseph Cannon of the Western Federation of Miners, Homer D. Call of the butcher workmen, John Golden of the textile workers, and Henry Weissman, a former head of the bakery workers who had become head of the baking employers' association. On May 27, a few weeks before the New York rally, officers of nine international unions with headquarters in Indianapolis met in that city to plan a joint strategy of opposition to war preparations and arms shipments. Among them were the coal miners, the carpenters, the teamsters, the bookbinders, the stonecutters, the structural iron-workers, and the typographers. The assembled officers could find no clear way to formulate just what national policy they wanted, aside from continued nonintervention. They could not bring themselves, for example, to endorse the call of Labor's National Peace Council for an embargo on arms shipments to Europe or its denunciation of Britain's naval blockade. Consequently, the meeting's chairman, Daniel J. Tobin of the teamsters, simply wired Gompers to propose that if the United States seemed about to enter the war, the AFL should convene a special meeting to formulate labor's position.[52]

It was clear that the war was changing the character of political align-

51. Wittke, *German-Americans and World War;* James H. Maurer, *It Can Be Done* (New York, 1938), 213–18; Rosenzweig, *Eight Hours,* 162; telegram, F. P. Walsh to Joseph Tumulty, January 21, 1916 (Walsh Papers, Box 3).
52. Lewis L. Lorwin, *The American Federation of Labor: History, Policies, and Prospects* (Washington, D.C., 1933), 139–40; *The Outlook,* 110 (June 30, 1915), 482–3; *NR,* 3 (July 15, 1915), 123–4.

ments within the AFL. Many leaders of the Indianapolis group had once been active in the Militia of Christ, though the new movement scrupulously avoided any confessional flavor. The Socialist Party viewed it with a jaundiced eye, because its own members within all the Indianapolis unions were open foes of the officers who convened the May gathering. Moreover, many Socialists were just as fully convinced as Gompers was that German money subsidized the New York movement, and the Socialists certainly had no more love for German imperialism than they had for British or American imperialism. By September, the Socialists' executive committee refused to participate in a national peace conference supported by Labor's National Peace Council, and Gompers easily persuaded the AFL convention not to vote in favor of an embargo on arms shipments to Europe.[53]

Despite Gompers's triumph at the 1915 convention, anxiety over military mobilization continued to mount within the ranks of the AFL and to cross the lines of political allegiances. The Indianapolis group was to deal Gompers his first serious rebuffs only after the declaration of war in 1917, first when President William D. Hutcheson of the carpenters repudiated Gompers's pledge to the government to forgo closed-shop claims on military construction projects, and then the following fall when Tobin defeated Gompers's candidate, John B. Lennon, in the elections for treasurer of the AFL — the first time in the twentieth century a candidate supported by Gompers was defeated. Amorphous as the group was, its patriotic but anti-British posture reflected the anxieties of millions of workers whose Irish and German forebears had been so prominent in building the industry of the Ohio Valley — Great Lakes heartland. That same constituency, however, also provided a social base for an influential laborite caucus within the Democratic Party whose most prominent voice was Frank P. Walsh.

Walsh was an attorney from Kansas City, Missouri, who had grown up in poverty and studied law at night. By the time President Wilson selected him to chair the U.S. Commission on Industrial Relations, he had become an active Democratic politician with close ties to the Midwest's networks of single taxers, the Catholic benevolent order of the Knights of Columbus, proponents of woman suffrage, movements to reform municipal government and to suppress commercial prostitution,

53. *NR,* 3 (July 15, 1915), 123–4; (September 15, 1915), 246; (October 1, 1915), 263–4; 4 (January 15, 1916), 27–8; Lorwin, *AFL,* 141. For a fictional depiction of socialist fears of German involvement in peace struggles, see Upton Sinclair, *Jimmie Higgins, A Story* (1918, reprinted Lexington, Ky., 1970), 1–55.

advocates of Irish independence, and trade unionists. As head of the commission, Walsh played an increasingly aggressive and partisan role, overriding both the representatives of business and the self-styled impartial social scientists selected by John R. Commons to make the commission the tribune for the oppressed American worker. The culmination of his efforts came after the Ludlow massacre, when Walsh summoned John D. Rockefeller, Jr., before the commission and denounced him publicly as the embodiment of all that was evil in the corporate world. When Congress refused to appropriate funds for further investigation, Walsh wrote on behalf of himself and the labor members of the commission a report that was nothing less than a platform for an American labor party. Walsh's report circulated widely to the loud acclaim of trade unionists, socialists, and even Wobblies.

After dissolving the commission, he formed a Committee on Industrial Relations, together with colleagues such as Dante Barton, Basil Manly, and George West, so that they might continue privately the work they had begun under government auspices. Walsh returned to Kansas City to take control of the *Kansas City Post,* and while he was there throughout 1916 his mailbox was packed with friendly letters from socialists, trade unionists, suffragists, and even Emma Goldman and Vincent St. John (to whom Walsh lent money to open a gold mine when he left the IWW) – but not from Gompers. Prisoners wrote pleas from their cells, musicians asked for and received introductions to the wealthy of New York, whom Walsh had met as head of the commission, and a group of impoverished farmers asked him to help them get jobs at Ford. He had become, wrote K. C. Adams of the UMWA staff, the coal miners' "ideal in public life." No other political figure of his time, or perhaps of any time in American history, so clearly personified the possibility and the potential character of a labor party as did Frank Walsh. His strategy for creating such a party, however, was to mobilize a hegemonic labor caucus among the Democrats.[54]

When Walsh appeared before the convention of the UMWA in January 1916, he spoke at length about the commission, about Ludlow, and about the bitter struggles of labor all over America, all pointing to the need for federal legislation to halt corporate resistance to unions. Then he turned his listeners' attention to the war in Europe, describing the "incomprehensible" spectacle of men, "brothers in blood, religion, and history [springing] at the throats of each other at the command of rulers." Amid

54. This biographical sketch is based on materials in the Walsh Papers. The quotation is from K. C. Adams to William P. Harvey, October 6, 1916 (Walsh Papers, Box 3).

all this horror, however, there had appeared a great hope, a hope that he, like Knoeppel and Alexander, saw in Germany's survival despite the blockade:

> Every engine of production, every man and every instrumentality is hooked up into one co-operative drive. For what? For the salvation of the nation; for the life of the people. . . . We see all the great manufacturing and industrial organizations put under the same co-operative control; every ounce of raw material in the mine, in the field, in the factory and in the home, put into this great hopper of co-operative life.

Walsh heralded not the suppression of individualism sought by American business leaders but, rather, the dawn of industrial production guided by social needs, a spectacle "fraught with such importance as to thrill the human heart." The collective energies now harnessed "for hatred and death" could be "hooked up for love and life." Here was a prospect to unify "workers of all lines of thought" and "leaders of every school of economic belief" who had come before his commission: "one beautiful song, I may say, whose motif was that the producer should have the result of his own labor . . . a democracy, industrious and political, based upon enduring justice."[55]

The applause that greeted Walsh and the resolution to publish his speech were among the precious few manifestations of unity at that miners' convention. Socialist attacks on the administration of President John White had begun almost before the meeting was called to order and continued to the last day of the two-week gathering. White, Vice-President Frank Hayes, who had quit the Socialist Party two years earlier, and the young John L. Lewis, who was released from his duties as an AFL organizer to preside, charged their foes with every perfidious betrayal of the miners' cause and used all the powers of the platform to control the stormy debates. For a day and a half the hall rang with charges by Socialist leaders McDonald and Germer that White had misspent the union's money, and countercharges by White that they had accepted money from coal operators. The furor ended only when Mother Jones took the platform to scold her "boys" for their folly and make McDonald and Germer come forward and shake hands with White and Hayes, to the uproarious laughter of the assembled miners.[56]

55. United Mine Workers of America, *Proceedings of the Twenty-Fifth Consecutive and Second Biennial Convention . . . 1916* (2 vols., Indianapolis, 1916), 540–2.
56. Ibid., 228–318. Jones's speech is on pp. 311–18. The delegate's poem about it is on pp. 512–13. The fact that Jones had already praised Wilson as the greatest president since Lincoln for his role in Colorado makes her interven-

The preparedness controversy haunted the convention. Germer, Pennsylvania's John Brophy, and other Socialists introduced resolutions to prohibit union members from belonging to the national guard or state constabulary. There were, in fact, precedents for union prohibitions against enrollment of members in the military. The American Railway Union had excluded soldiers and militiamen in the 1890s, as had the unions of painters, stonecutters, and brewery workers. Nevertheless, the dominant position in the twentieth-century AFL was that union members should participate in a "citizens' army" in order to win allies among the men with guns and to block the formation of a "military caste." Gompers used that logic vigorously in support of President Wilson's enlargement of the army during 1916. The Socialists' resolutions were clearly so popular among the delegates, however, that more was needed to close off debate than John L. Lewis's sarcasm and heavy gavel. The decisive claim of White was that such exclusion would be illegal, and he produced a telegram from Walsh to support that position. White genuinely feared walking into a legal trap, as he wired Walsh: "We cannot afford to make a mistake at this time especially in view of our stand against preparedness."[57]

White had made his own fears about war mobilization explicit in his president's report to the convention. In Colorado, West Virginia, and Michigan he saw soldiers attacking American workers, and he feared that "standing armies" and "powerful battleships" would tend to carry the country into the war, rather than protect against it. "When people are taught to fight they never rest content until the opportunity is presented to them to demonstrate their prowess," White warned, "and in this age of commercialism no opportunity should be given that would in the slightest degree cause us to be placed at variance with the long established principles of our government." He earnestly hoped "that the plans to make our country an armed camp which may be used to extend commercialism abroad and exploit labor at home will be defeated."[58]

The dilemma for White, for Walsh, for the Indianapolis group, and probably for most organized workers in America was how to accelerate labor's entry into government, bringing the dawn of "production for use," without becoming tools of those who would militarize America precisely in order to "extend commercialism abroad and exploit labor at home."

tion a portent of her open shift of loyalties from the Socialists to the Democrats during 1916.

57. Ibid., 989–1029; telegram, White to Walsh, January 30, 1916 (Walsh Papers, Box 3). On union rules concerning militia membership, see Jeffreys-Jones, *Violence and Reform*, 139; *Railway Times*, July 2, 1894; Morton A. Aldrich, *The American Federation of Labor* (New York, 1898), 225.
58. UMWA, *Proceedings 1916*, 90–1.

Throughout the spring and summer of 1916, Walsh collaborated vigorously with the American Union Against Militarism (headed by Crystal Eastman), with like-minded Democrats such as George Creel, Stephen S. Wise, and Zona Gale, and with Socialists such as James H. Maurer and Marian Wharton, to rally labor and the general public against preparedness and the drift toward war. They drew comfort from the electoral success of a most unexpected ally, Henry Ford, running as a peace candidate in the Republican primaries in Michigan and Nebraska. They shuddered at the preparedness-day parade in Chicago, where thousands of workers marched to patriotic themes ranked by the industries that employed them, but praised the central labor unions of St. Louis and Kansas City, which refused to participate at all in such parades. Everything they feared materialized with a single bomb explosion at San Francisco's parade. Tom Mooney, revolutionary syndicalist leader of the molders' union, and his wife, Rena, a music teacher, were arrested and charged with planting the bomb; swept into the police dragnet with them were Warren K. Billings of the boot and shoe workers, Israel Weinberg of the jitney drivers, and the prominent Edward D. Nolan of the bricklayers.[59]

All the energies of Walsh and his reformist colleagues became concentrated on one desperate hope: to secure the reelection of Woodrow Wilson on a platform committing the Democratic Party to peace and to the defense of "democracy" against "privilege." The fusion of open-shop groups, preparedness leagues, and law-and-order committees; the growing roster of prosecutions of labor activists (such as Mooney and Billings, Tresca and six other Wobblies in Minnesota's iron range, Kaplan and Schmidt in San Francisco, Merrick and Bell in Pittsburgh); and the upholding of fines against the Danbury hatters (1915) and of yellow-dog contracts in West Virginia (1917) by the U.S. Supreme Court posed threats to the working class that could be offset only by a friendly administration in Washington. The Socialist Party simply did not have the electoral strength to provide such an administration. The Wilson administration was increasingly supportive of labor legislation and the AFL, but the difficulty was that the administration was also orchestrating its own preparedness campaign, sustaining an invasion of Mexico by six thousand American soldiers, and publicly discussing America's new role as creditor and financier to the entire world.

59. Crystal Eastman to Frank P. Walsh, March 15, 1916; telegram, Walsh to Carl Beck, July 1, 1916; Walsh to Judson King, May 6, 1916; Stephen S. Wise to Walsh, April 19, 1916 (Walsh Papers, Box 3); Gary M. Fink, *Labor's Search for Political Order: The Political Behavior of the Missouri Labor Movement* (Columbia, Mo., 1973), 61; *ISR*, 17 (July 1916), 7; (October 1916), 216–17.

Consequently, the Democrats' adoption of a platform that drew heavily on the legislative recommendations of Walsh's Commission on Industrial Relations and stressed the administration's role in keeping us out of war rallied many Socialists, along with former Bull Moose Progressives and AFL militants, to the Democratic banner. Walsh spent most of October on the campaign trail in the industrial and mining centers of the Midwest. Reports reached him from Cainsville, Missouri, of Socialist and Republican miners who were "leaning toward Wilson" and of thousands of " 'red card' Socialists" in Kansas who were ready to vote Democratic despite the vigorous efforts of their party to hold them in line. Prominent party members such as Mother Jones, Helen Marot, and Carol Beck stumped for Wilson, and Schenectady's Mayor Lunn, formerly a Socialist, directed the Wilson campaign in the upper Hudson Valley. In West Virginia, the Socialists' heaviest losses of votes to the Democrats were in the mine fields. *Pearson's Magazine,* which had provided a literary common ground for Socialists, Democrats, and Progressives during this convergence, estimated after the elections that 250,000 Socialists had voted for Wilson, primarily because of their fear of militarism and because of the president's public posture of friendship to organized labor.[60] Helen Marot wrote to Walsh that if "Hughes had been elected I would have gone to China as the only civilized place on the globe but as it is I am reassured that America is the great hope of the world. Thank God for your West."[61] And Rabbi Stephen S. Wise, also attributing the victory to the working people of middle America, exulted: "To think that we can have a great forward-looking Party and free that Party from the racial and social Toryism of the South and the industrial and economic reactionism of the East!"[62]

A decisive role in this political realignment within the labor movement and at the polls had been played by railroad workers, in particular by the members of the brotherhoods. A long history of standing aloof from the rest of the labor movement had made the four unions of train service workers (engineers, firemen, trainmen, and conductors) unlikely candidates to lead twentieth-century labor politics. Their membership was entirely white and was composed more markedly of men of American, often rural, parentage than that of any other major union. They represented less than one-fifth of all railroad workers, leaving the shop crafts, section hands, switchmen, telegraphers, clerks, and freight handlers to their own

60. J. D. McDaniel to Frank P. Walsh, September 19, 1916 (Walsh Papers, Box 3); C.S. to National Democratic Headquarters, October 17, 1916; W. P. Harvey to Walsh, October 11, 1916 (Walsh Papers, Box 4); Barkey, "Socialist Party," 193; *Pearson's Magazine,* 37 (January 1917), 92.
61. Marot to Walsh, November 16, 1916 (Walsh Papers, Box 4).
62. Wise to Walsh, November 15, 1916 (Walsh Papers, Box 4).

craft organizations, if they were organized at all. The brotherhoods had grown during the 1880s primarily by providing their members with insurance against death and disability in their accident-filled occupations. During that decade, rapid expansion of railroad employment had given their members some bargaining power, despite their policy of refusing to strike, but crowding at the top of the trades by the late 1880s prompted increasingly bitter disputes, some major lost strikes, and finally the movement toward a single union for all railwaymen, the American Railway Union (ARU). After the ARU had been crushed in the Pullman boycott of 1894 and its militants fired by the thousands, the brotherhoods resumed their earlier cautious practices and started to grow again. Recognizing their importance as a counterweight to militant unionism on the railroads, Richard Olney, who had led the legal attack on the ARU, guided Congress toward enactment of the Erdman Act of 1898. This measure secured the insurance funds of the brotherhoods, prohibited dismissal of a worker for union membership (a provision overruled by the Supreme Court), and established machinery for voluntary arbitration of disputes.[63]

The brotherhoods grew under this special nurturing from an aggregate membership of 100,700 in 1897 to 357,800 in 1916. Their leaders, who preferred the name railway labor executives, were prominent members of the NCF. Warren S. Stone, Grand Chief of the Brotherhood of Locomotive Engineers, became a member of the NCF's executive committee and remained one until 1925. The trainmen's president, P. H. Morrissey, also headed the American Railroad Employees and Investors' Association, through which the executives of the brotherhoods and the railroads lobbied together for commerce-commission rulings favorable to the lines. When delegates to the 1909 trainmen's convention repudiated that organization, Morrissey left his union post to remain in charge of the association. "It is good business for employees to keep a watch on the fund from which their wages are paid," Morrissey explained, "and to note the signs which may curtail them. They are vitally interested in the earnings of the roads."[64]

By the time Morrissey wrote that argument in 1911, however, relations between the brotherhoods and major lines were becoming strained. The unions had learned to make use of the arbitration machinery provided first by the Erdman Act, and in 1913 by the Newlands Act, to

63.   Stromquist, "Generation of Boomers"; Licht, *Working for the Railroad;* Gerald G. Eggert, *Railway Labor Disputes: The Beginning of Federal Strike Policy* (Ann Arbor, 1967), 221–2.

64.   Green, *Civic Federation,* 427, 463–4; William Z. Foster, *Misleaders of Labor* (n.p., 1927), 47–8; P. H. Morrissey, *Views of a Committee of Railway Employes* (Chicago, 1911), 6.

conduct concerted movements for standardization of wages and improvement of conditions over large geographic regions. Although they hired well-trained researchers and confronted the umpires with sophisticated arguments based on scholarly studies of the cost of living and estimates of their growing productivity, the brotherhoods also coupled their "wage movements" with overwhelming membership votes to strike if they did not receive satisfactory awards. In more than sixty arbitration cases between 1908 and 1912, they made substantial gains, whereas weaker unions, such as telegraphers and maintenance-of-way workers, wrung little from umpires. The famous Eastern Freight case of 1910 was a watershed in this development because it showed that federal commissions had become more susceptible to pressure from shippers to restrain railroad fees. At the same time, the constantly rising cost of living made brotherhood members increasingly restive about the time arbitrators took in processing claims for wage increases – let alone the huge costs such proceedings levied against the railroaders' dues.[65]

By 1914, unofficial strikes had begun to involve growing numbers of train service workers. Despite the consistency with which brotherhood members kept trains operating while shop workers and others engaged in bitter strikes, the spirit of militancy and unity exhibited in shop-craft system federations was infectious. In the spring of 1914, Pennsylvania Railroad engine crews struck in sympathy with shopmen near Altoona and with coal miners (themselves wildcatters) near California, Pennsylvania. Eugene V. Debs found himself addressing large crowds of railwaymen once again. Talk of one big union and of a united drive to win the eight-hour day was widely reported by local Socialists.[66] The wave of strikes for shorter hours by machinists, textile workers, and clothing workers during 1915 and 1916 led the New Jersey Bureau of Labor Statistics to conclude that "the universal adoption of the eight-hour schedule in the near future seems all but assured."[67] Train service workers wanted it for themselves.

On the last day of October 1915, close to a thousand railway workers

65. J. Noble Stockett, Jr., *The Arbitral Determination of Railway Wages* (Boston, 1918); Marot, *American Labor Unions*, 34, 42–7; *IA*, 94 (February 20, 1913), 478–82.

66. Eugene V. Debs, "Revolt of the Railroad Workers," *ISR*, 14 (June 1914), 736–8; Comrade H. of St. Clair, Pa., to *ISR*, 14 (May 1914), 687–8; Wade Shurtleff, "One Big Union," *ISR*, 15 (July 1914), 29–30; *ISR*, 15 (July 1914), 62; series of three articles by Carl Sandburg, "Fixing the Pay of Railroad Men," *ISR*, 15 (April 1915), 589–93; (May 1915), 656–8; (June 1915), 709–13.

67. Bureau of Industrial Statistics of New Jersey, *Thirty-ninth Annual Report* (Camden, 1916, hereafter cited as N.J. BIS), 187.

gathered at Boston's Faneuil Hall to demand cooperation among all four of their brotherhoods to win a "maximum eight-hour day in all classes of service" and to insist they would "never again submit to an arbitrator in any move for the increase of wages or the betterment of conditions."[68] Little more than a month later, the officers of the brotherhoods announced that they were jointly presenting a demand to fifty-two railroad lines for an eight-hour day, with time-and-a-half pay to begin after eight hours or 100 miles of train operation, whichever came first. They would not submit the question to arbitration. On March 30 they formally presented the demands to the railroad executives and began the long process of negotiations, union conventions, and strike ballots that concluded with a national-strike deadline set for September 4. During the spring and summer, joint committees of railroad workers sprang up all over the country, women's auxiliaries of the brotherhoods saturated many communities with publicity, Labor Forward movements resumed operations in Virginia and Massachusetts towns, and of course, Frank Walsh was deluged with invitations to speak on May 1: Sapulpa, Oklahoma, Roadhouse, Illinois, St. Joseph, Missouri, the Pittsburgh Labor Forum, Chicago, Buffalo, and points west. President Wilson attempted personal mediation in August, but failed to reach a settlement. Consequently, on August 29 he went before both houses of Congress to ask for a law granting the brotherhoods' demands. Congress passed the Adamson Act within a week, and Wilson signed it into law two days before the strike deadline.[69]

One more strike threat was needed before the eight-hour day was secured. The railroads immediately challenged the constitutionality of the Adamson Act, and the brotherhoods subsequently set March 15, 1917, as a deadline for compliance with the new law. The Council of National Defense arranged a settlement on the unions' terms on that date, and a few hours later the Supreme Court upheld the law. Ralph Easley was horrified at "the evil effect of letting the rank and file discover their own power and the impotency of the public," and Republican candidates charged the president with surrendering to the unions.[70] But for most working-class voters, one note sounded above all the clamor: The president of the United States had told Congress that "the eight-hour day

68.   *ISR,* 16 (January 1916), 390.
69.   Jack Phillips, "Will the Rail Strike Be Side-tracked?" *ISR,* 161 (May 1916), 657–61; Green, *Civic Federation,* 233–5; folders April–July, Walsh Papers, Box 3.
70.   Lorwin, *AFL,* 133; Easley to Seth Low, August 28, 1916, quoted in Green, *Civic Federation,* 235. On business's rage at Wilson's action, see George Creel, *Rebel at Large: Recollections of Fifty Crowded Years* (New York, 1947), 239; Ozanne, *McCormick,* 114.

now, undoubtedly, has the sanction of the judgement of society in its favor."[71]

Two aspects of the struggle of the train service workers epitomized the labor scene in 1916: First, in a year in which far more American workers had gone on strike than in any previous year, the threat of nationwide strike action had wrung speedy passage of legislation securing the workers' demands. Second, the richly endowed and conservatively led railroad brotherhoods had joined the Democratic political camp, along with Samuel Gompers, the UMWA, Mother Jones, and possibly 250,000 socialists. The brotherhoods had also mobilized a political machine of national scope, staffed by working people who had long been familiar with both public debate and local politics in a thousand towns and cities. Railroad workers, as business journals never ceased to lament, had plenty of time for conversation. When they were out on the road, there were others to do political organizing: An organizer for the United Labor Woodrow Wilson League in Los Angeles wrote to Walsh that almost all of the league's officers were women, mostly from the women's auxiliaries of the railroad brotherhoods. Moreover, by early 1917, leaders of the engineers, at least, were seriously discussing ways to ally with organized farmers and to enlist Walsh's coterie of reformers and publicists to woo popular support for the workers in their struggles against the railroad companies. In short, they had shifted their allegiances 180 degrees since the days of the Railroad Employees and Investors' Association. It was this shift that opened the door to the brotherhoods' prominent role in postwar labor politics. The Plumb plan for nationalization of railroads, to be administered jointly by railroad workers and shippers, the brotherhoods' alliance with the mine workers and the machinists to lead a "progressive bloc" in the labor movement, and the 1922 Conference for Progressive Political Action all were made possible by the railway workers' struggles of 1915–16.[72]

71. *IA*, 98 (August 24, 1916), 406.
72. John Murray to Walsh, October 25, 1916; C. G. Brittingham to W. S. Stone, March 26, 1916; John Reed to Walsh, n.d. [June 1917] (Walsh Papers, Box 4); Erik Olssen, "The Making of a Political Machine: The Railroad Unions Enter Politics," *Labor History*, 19 (Summer 1978), 273–96.

8

"This great struggle for democracy"

By Election Day in 1916, the economy of the United States had been partially mobilized for war production. In this context, business not only had perfected new leadership structures, such as the NICB, and new labor strategies, such as the Colorado Industrial Plan, but also had institutionalized an economic directorate within the machinery of the federal government, most notably in the Council of National Defense (CND). Simultaneously, the unprecedented demand for labor and for workers' votes had given a new lease on life to a union movement earlier stymied by the open-shop drive and had reshaped political alliances within that movement. The formal declaration of war in April 1917 merely accelerated all these developments, paving the way for a decisive confrontation between the working class and the state in the years 1919–22.

Paradoxically, during March and April 1917, although the cost of living soared, provoking food riots in New York and Philadelphia, unemployment also rose. The collapse of the tsar's armies had cost the munitions industry a major market. But soon domestic demand picked up the slack, and the combined impact of rising prices and full employment unleashed the largest strike wave the United States had seen up to that time. Between April 6 and October 5, 1917, statisticians of the NICB calculated that 6,285,519 workdays were lost because of strikes, a figure that dwarfed even the record militancy of 1912–13 and 1915–16. The metal trades topped the list, accounting for almost one-fifth of workdays lost and more than 27 percent of the striking workers. Shipbuilding, counted separately, ranked second, with coal mining third, copper mining fourth, and then, at lower but still significant levels, textiles and lumber. Moreover, sixty-seven of the strikes involved more than ten thousand workers each. Fully one-sixth of the lost workdays were in strikes led by the IWW, among them those in northwestern timber fields, Butte's copper mines, Arizona's mines, Philadelphia's docks and sugar refineries, Rockford's machinery works, and the Dakota wheat fields. Many strikers elsewhere had no union affiliations, but in the three leading strike domains, metal trades, shipbuilding, and coal mining, more than 75 percent of the strikers belonged to the AFL.[1]

Neighborhood solidarities were especially conspicuous during this upsurge in workplace struggle. The congested tenements adjacent to the Chicago stockyards stirred with such enthusiasm that 90 percent of the immigrant workers enrolled in the AFL, and John Kikulski, head of the Polish Falcons, became the union's most influential leader, until he was murdered in 1920. During the major strikes in textiles, munitions, and metallurgy, neighborhood benevolent societies of Italians, Poles, Jews, Croats, and Lithuanians frequently provided the bases from which efforts to unionize the factories were launched. Conversely, highly visible strikes could enjoy overwhelming community support. When striking streetcar workers in Springfield, Illinois, had their demonstrations dispersed by the police in September 1917, the region's coal miners led a local general strike that resulted in pledges by city authorities to uphold the streetcar workers' liberties and to dismiss obnoxious deputy sheriffs. Other general strikes followed in 1918: one in Waco, Texas, again in support of streetcar workers, and two in Kansas City, one in the spring to help laundry workers organize and one in the fall to assist striking streetcar men and women. The vast working-class neighborhoods of the early twentieth century could make life unbearable for scabs, mount large funeral processions for slain strikers, and involve entire families in marketplace as well as workplace struggles.[2]

Opposition to the war often reverberated through these neighborhoods. The Socialist Party's emergency convention of April 1917 denounced the government's declaration of war and called for "an even more vigorous prosecution of the class struggle" to protect living stan-

1. National Industrial Conference Board, Research Report No. 3, March, 1918, "Strikes in American Industry in Wartime, April 6 to October 6, 1917"; Alexander Trachtenberg, ed., *American Labor Year Book, 1919–1920* (New York, 1920, hereafter cited as *Am. Labor Year Book, 1919–20*), 163–4; Gambs, *Decline of the IWW*, 35.
2. James R. Barrett, "Work and Community in 'The Jungle': Chicago's Packing House Workers, 1894–1922" (unpublished Ph.D. diss., University of Pittsburgh, 1981), 305–6, 365–6; documents on 1919 Lawrence, Massachusetts, strike in Anthony Capraro Papers (Immigration History Research Center, University of Minnesota); Gladys Palmer, *Union Tactics and Economic Change: A Case Study of Three Philadelphia Textile Unions* (Philadelphia, 1932); Alexander Bing, *War-Time Strikes and Their Adjustment* (New York, 1921), 30n, 203–9. For a more ambivalent view of the role of ethnic neighborhoods in strikes, see Foster, *Great Steel Strike*.

dards and civil liberties against war and conscription. A referendum of the membership upheld that position by a margin of 21,639 to 2,752, in preference to a minority report that would have recognized the war as an inescapable fact and committed the party to seizing "the opportunity presented by war conditions to advance our program of democratic collectivism." No, responded the party's majority:

> The much talked of "War-Socialism" is not Socialism at all. There can be no Socialism apart from democracy. But the collectivism which has been linked to militarism in the war is wrong application of a great and beneficial principle of social action which must be redeemed from misuse. . . . The collectivism of war must be made into the Socialism of humanity.[3]

Although the party's antiwar stance was very different from that of European socialist parties, among whom only the parties in Serbia and Italy had resisted their countries' war efforts, it was encouraged by the recent departures of socialist ministers from the governments of France and Germany, the mounting protests of European workers against continuation of the war, and the revolution in Russia. Moreover, it often met with favorable responses. Although many native-born workers quit the party, the municipal elections of 1917 gave several Socialist candidates from Elmwood, Indiana, to New York City the largest votes they had ever received.[4]

Socialist activity was funneled into the People's Council of America for Democracy and Peace. The council enjoyed considerable support during 1917, when it campaigned for immediate negotiation of peace on the basis of no annexation, no indemnities, and "free development for all nationalities" and for preservation of political liberties and conscription of wealth rather than of men. The trade unionists on its organizing committee included Joseph Cannon, Rose Schneiderman, Duncan McDonald, and President James Maurer of the Pennsylvania Federation of Labor, all of whom remained loyal to the party despite the pressures to which they were subjected, and Joseph Schlossberg of the SLP. Among their prominent allies were Emily G. Balch, Fola La Follette, H. W. L. Dana, and Judah P. Magnes, but the council's optimistic and relentless efforts to win the support of Frank Walsh were in vain. Walsh declined to attend the national meeting planned for Minneapolis on August 31; worse yet, the government of Minnesota banned the gathering. Invited to meet in Chicago by an ardently anti-British Mayor William H.

3. Trachtenberg, *American Socialist and the War*, 32, 34, 39–45; Weinstein, *Decline*, 124, 127, 134–54.
4. Interview with Jack Piper, July 30 [1919] (David Saposs Papers, Box 26); Weinstein, *Decline*, 316–17.

Thompson, the council's delegates were dispersed by three companies of the Illinois National Guard ordered in by the governor.[5]

As the dispersal of the convention of the People's Council made evident, the government had lost no time in installing a complete panoply of political as well as economic regulations for the war effort. New espionage and sedition laws were already on the books, repressive state committees of public safety were at work, especially in Pennsylvania and Minnesota, and speedy enactment of conscription within a month of the declaration of war had made possible the first draft calls on July 20. Statutes placing food, cattle feeds, clothing, fuel, and other commodities under national agencies followed the creation of the War Industries Board in July 1917, with powers to build new facilities, convert existing ones, make purchases for the Allies, and, most important of all, determine priorities for the allocation of raw materials. The Shipping Board's Emergency Fleet Corporation and the U.S. Housing Corporation made the government itself a major employer, and the railroad, telegraph, and telephone systems were placed under government administration.[6]

The summer strike wave of 1917, and especially the possibility that workplace struggles and the antiwar movement might blend, led federal authorities to devote special attention to workers. The Shipping Board, Ordnance Department, and Railway Administration were quick to offer wage increases and reinstatement of fired union activists as the price of keeping workers in the job. Prominent reformers from women's movements, such as Grace Abbott, Pauline Goldmark, and Florence Kelley, were placed on defense advisory boards, and Mary Van Kleeck, the industrial sociologist, and Mary Anderson, long a leader of shoe workers and the Women's Trade Union League, exercised very real powers on behalf of the Ordnance Department in its efforts to integrate female workers into scientifically managed munitions industries. Two months before the end of the war, the Railway Administration also created its Women's Service Section, headed by Pauline Goldmark. It became the common

5. "The People's Council of America Invites You to Send Delegates to the First Constituent Assembly in Minneapolis, September 1, 1917" (File 50206, R.G. 28, National Archives); Lella Fay Secor to Frank P. Walsh, May 3, 1917; Louis Lochner to Walsh, May 5, 1917; telegram, Lochner to Walsh, May 18, 1917; Walsh to Lochner, May 26, 1917; Lochner to Walsh, June 15, 1917; Walsh to Lochner, June 20, 1917; telegram, Secor to Walsh, June 27, 1917; telegram, Walsh to Secor, June 28, 1917 (Walsh Papers, Box 4); Frank L. Grubbs, Jr., *Struggle for Labor Loyalty: Gompers, the A. F. of L., and the Pacifists, 1917–1920* (Durham, N.C., 1968), 62–3. Grubbs mistakenly suggests that Walsh had joined the council (p. 81).
6. Warne, *Workers at War;* Clarkson, *America in the World War.*

practice of all these agencies to advocate – or, where they could, award – especially generous wage increases to the lower-paid employees, thereby reinforcing the effects inflation had of diminishing wage differentials, and at times, as in Bridgeport's strike-torn factories in the summer of 1918, leaving militant craftsmen without the support of relatively satisfied men and women operatives.[7]

An NICB study of the 1917 work stoppages led the board to propose that the government create an agency with general powers to settle industrial disputes. The CND endorsed the proposal, and in January 1918, on its suggestion, President Wilson invited both the NICB and the AFL to appoint five members each to a War Labor Conference Board, a body that formulated some policies and then reincarnated itself as the National War Labor Board (NWLB), cochaired by former President William H. Taft and Frank Walsh. The NWLB was to have advisory powers only, but as the NICB's James Emery suggested, wartime conditions gave its recommendations a "powerful moral sanction." In the sixteen months before it dissolved itself in August 1919, the board considered 1,250 cases and made awards in 500 of them. Although those awards were sometimes defied, more often by business than by workers, the president's wartime powers to seize factories and draft workers made its sanctions more than simply "moral" by the last months of the war.

The labor policies developed by the government were derived from two basic principles. First, it would solicit the cooperation of the trade unions. Second, it would demand that both industry and labor refrain from using the crisis to "change existing standards." These decisions were based on lessons drawn from the British experience – where the 1915 Treasury Agreement to suspend union rules and shopfloor practices had opened the door to a militant shop stewards' movement – and on the consistent support that Samuel Gompers and the AFL Executive Council had offered the CND since 1916.[8]

7.   Marchand, *American Peace Movement*, 262; Maurine Weiner Greenwald, *Women, War, and Work: The Impact of World War I on Women Workers in the United States* (Westport, Conn., 1980), 46–86; V. W. Lanfear, *Business Fluctuations and the American Labor Movement, 1915–1922* (New York, 1924), 30–41; David Montgomery, "Whose Standards? Workers and the Reorganization of Production in the United States, 1900–20," in Montgomery, *Workers' Control*, 120–2, 127–34.

8.   James A. Emery, "War Labor Board for Increasing Production," *New York Times*, April 14, 1918; Loyall A. Osborne to William H. Taft (records of the National War Labor Board, R.G. 2, Administrative Files E15, National Archives); Conner, *The NWLB*, x–xi, 27–32; Taft, *Time of Gompers*, 343–60.

Gompers had pressed forward relentlessly with his design of incorporating the AFL into the administrative machinery of the war, regardless of the qualms of the Indianapolis group, let alone the protests of the Socialists. He never convened a deliberative conference of union leaders to deal with the war crisis, as the Indianapolis meeting of 1915 had requested, but rather assembled a one-day meeting of heads of AFL unions and railroad brotherhoods on March 12, 1917, at which he rammed through a prepared statement of total approval of the administration's course toward war, linked to a declaration that only organized labor could represent the workers in the agencies necessary for economic mobilization. Tobin, of the teamsters, furious at this parody of his 1915 demand, filibustered in hopes of having the question submitted to the unions for a vote, but he was ultimately gaveled down. As soon as Congress had declared war, Gompers made a personal statement, under the auspices of the CND, committing labor to the council's rule that "neither employers nor employees shall endeavor to take advantage of the country's necessities to change existing standards."[9]

Existing standards

Contrary to common belief, the AFL never gave a no-strike pledge during World War I. The Executive Council repudiated Gompers's CND statement at the insistence of carpenters' leader Hutcheson, and Tobin protested so loudly that Gompers wrote him denying that he had "made any promise to any one in any form that 'there shall be no strikes of any kind during the war.' "[10] Nevertheless, the crucial matters for Gompers were to secure the political loyalty of the AFL to the war effort, to place union leaders in administrative agencies, and to write union wage and work standards into government decrees. In all these efforts he enjoyed the overwhelming support of other AFL leaders. Challenges from the Indianapolis group and others hinged not on the federation's support for the war but on how much unions should demand in exchange for that support.

The government assigned the task of whipping up enthusiasm for the war to its Committee on Public Information, headed by Frank Walsh's long-time ally George Creel. The committee won the agreement of the major wire services and most of the press to voluntary censorship, turned

9. Larson, *Labor and Foreign Policy,* 83–5, 95–8.
10. Gompers to Tobin, April 17, 1917, quoted in Larson, *Labor and Foreign Policy,* 98.

out a small library of books and articles on patriotic themes, enlisted seventy-five thousand volunteer "four minute men" as public speakers (later boasting that by Armistice Day they had delivered 7,555,190 four-minute speeches), and energized loyalty committees within each of fourteen immigrant nationalities to argue the links between their national causes and America's victory in the war. On July 4, 1918, Creel's committee organized parades and rallies in industrial centers throughout the country, where large groups of foreign-borns paraded in their national costumes and listened to speakers in many languages advocate loyalty to the United States. A pilgrimage of two representatives of each of thirty-five nationalities (Albanians, Armenians, . . . , Syrians, Ukrainians) traveled on the riverboat *Mayflower* to Mount Vernon that day, there to be welcomed by President and Mrs. Wilson. In all these efforts, men and women with reputations of friendship toward labor were prominent. Their endeavors were supplemented by a vast expansion of the Secret Service and enrollment of 250,000 citizen volunteers into the American Protective League to ferret out disloyal activities in every factory and neighborhood of the land, as well as by compulsory registration of all aliens, six thousand of whom were detained under presidential warrants. The aliens were joined in federal jails by 1,532 persons arrested for disloyalty under the Espionage Act, 10 for sabotage, 65 for threatening the president, and 540 for refusing the draft.[11] Parallel efforts of authorities in many states, including Pennsylvania, Minnesota, Washington, and California, brought many more people up on criminal charges, but lacked the liberal veneer of federal agencies.

AFL executives were especially concerned about the attitudes of union members in New York City, where both the People's Council and Labor's National Peace Council were strong. With the help of former peace advocate Ernest Bohm and former Socialist Robert Maisel, the Central Federated Union launched a campaign "to Americanize the labor movement in greater New York." Despite the effort's patent lack of success, especially in the Jewish neighborhoods of the Lower East Side, it gave rise to the American Alliance for Labor and Democracy, which was endorsed and financed by Creel's committee. The alliance held a convention in Minneapolis on the day the banned gathering of the People's Council had been scheduled, and it was formally endorsed by the AFL at its November convention, after President Wilson had appeared, flanked by soldiers and flags, to make the first address ever by an American president to a labor convention.[12]

11. Creel, *How We Advertised America*, 85, 100, 166–99, 200–8; Robert J. Goldstein, *Political Repression in Modern America, From 1870 to the Present* (Cambridge, Mass., 1978), 113.
12. Grubbs, *Struggle*, 30–45, 62–72, 91–2; the quotation is on p. 39.

It is difficult to assess the impact of all this oratory and pageantry on working people, especially because the more effective police scrutiny of disloyalty became, the less likely were ordinary people to express their opinions in public regarding the war. Critical press commentary was silenced by denial of postal privileges or simple orders to foreign-language journals to shut down. "War! The United States Attorney-General of free America has decreed: 'Keep your mouth shut.' And America shut up," wrote Z. Libin in the *Daily Forward.* "Even my woman neighbor's baby, which used to cry all night, is now quiet."[13]

Former Socialists rounded fiercely on their erstwhile comrades who supported the People's Council. When IAM Secretary-Treasurer E. C. Davidson, for example, received by mail a People's Council circular entitled "Tax the Rich to Pay for the War," he forwarded it quickly to the Post Office Department with the hope it might prove useful in "breaking up schemes of this kind."[14] John Walker, president of the Illinois district of the UMWA, quit the party and wrote Adolph Germer, with whom Walker had joined in so many attacks on UMWA presidents from Mitchell to White, "I want you and your like, who want to bring about improvements for the working people through making the German Kaiser the Emperor of the WORLD . . . to know that there isn't anything I can think of or do, that I won't do, to prevent you from accomplishing your purposes."[15]

As might be expected in such an emotional cauldron of hopes and fears, workers' day-to-day conduct failed to conform neatly to the desires of either the People's Council or Gompers's American Alliance. Mario Manzardo later recalled that political debate was incessant in his Chicago suburb of Kensington, where available jobs at Pullman, Harvester, Griffin Wheel, and other huge enterprises had drawn Italians, Germans, Swedes, Poles, and Dutch to dwell cheek by jowl, the town council always had Socialist members, and speeches by Debs filled Turner Hall to capacity. There were many who denounced the imperialist war, but many more regularly bought Liberty Bonds, and someone singing "The Yanks Are Coming" could always be heard on the streets. Scores of young Italians returned home to volunteer for the Italian Army. In West Virginia, coal miners outdid their neighbors in purchasing Liberty Bonds, and UMWA members at Thayer declared, "Everyone here is attempting to

13. Quoted in Robert E. Park, *The Immigrant Press and Its Control* (New York, 1922), 171–2.
14. E. C. Davidson to Post Office Department, February 5, 1918 (File 50206, R.G. 28, National Archives).
15. John H. M. Laslett, "End of an Alliance: Selected Correspondence between Socialist Party Secretary Adolph Germer, and U.M.W. of A. Leaders in World War One," *Labor History,* 12 (Fall 1971), 579.

do their bit in support of this great struggle for democracy." In Norwalk, Connecticut, a rubber worker who denounced Liberty Bonds was chased by two hundred irate fellow employees, who forced him to kiss the flag. And Robert Paul Prager, a German-born coal miner of Maryville, Illinois, was lynched and killed by fellow miners and union brothers for having criticized President Wilson.[16]

Perhaps the recollections of Freda Maurer sum up the paradoxes of the war years. As a seventeen-year-old helper on knitting machines in Philadelphia, she joined a local union despite her anger at the male knitters, who were incessantly calling strikes over grievances without consulting the women who assisted them on the machines. Like all her workmates, Freda wanted the eight-hour day, and from January until March 1918 they struck thirteen hosiery mills to win that goal. Thereafter, they carefully limited their output to forty dozen stockings per day, and she recalled:

> Things ran smoothly for a while. We were getting good wages, buying bonds, giving a day's wages for the war chest, observing heatless, meatless, wheatless, and other days. As our boys left for camp we went to see them off. We laid down our tools and paraded with our boys to the railroad station, and ate our lunch when they were gone, and took the afternoon off to show our patriotism. The next day we went back to show our patriotism. Didn't Uncle Sam need hosiery to help win the war?[17]

Two things are certain: The workers did not join in Gompers's pledge not to "take advantage of the country's necessities to change existing standards," and usually they expressed their aspirations and demands in the rhetoric of America's ostensible war aims. Every group of working people in America exhibited a desire for a life different from the life they had been leading. None showed more determination to "change existing standards" than the more than 450,000 Afro-Americans who moved from the South to northern cities during the years 1916 to 1918. It is not difficult to discern the economic reasons for the migration: The rapid expansion of demand for labor in the North coincided with the closing off of immigration from Europe. It also followed close on the heels of an absolute decline in the acreage planted in cotton, as a result of spreading infestation by boll weevils. Between 1910 and 1920, the number of black people employed in agriculture fell from 2,835,000 to 2,133,000 leaving tillers of the soil a minority in the black population.[18]

16. Mario Manzardo, "Un decennio di sviluppo: un periodo di contrasti," *La Parola del Popolo*, 124 (July–August 1974), 117; Corbin, *Life, Work*, 182, 189; *Bridgeport Standard American*, April 5, 1918.
17. Palmer, *Union Tactics*, 148–50; the quotation is on p. 150.
18. Emmett J. Scott, *Negro Migration During the War* (New York, 1920), 102;

But the letters reaching northern black newspapers from the South linked the writers' economic aspirations to a determination to pry themselves loose from racial bondage. A man wrote from Birmingham: "i am in the darkness of the south and i am trying my best to get out. . . . o please help me to get out of this low down county i am counted no more than a dog." Another Alabamian wrote, "I am enclosing a clipping of a lynching again which speaks for itself. . . . So many of our people here are almost starving." A story invented by the *Chicago Defender,* largely to help build its circulation, that on May 15, 1917, there would be a "great northern drive" brought letters pouring into the paper's Chicago office from all parts of the South: "It is a rumor all over town to be ready for the 15th of May to go in the drive." "So many women here are wanting to go that day." A woman in Mobile summed up the excitement in her own appeal:

> I was reading in theat paper about the Colored race and while read-
> ing it I seen in it where cars would be here for the 15 of May which
> is one month from to day. Will you be so kind as to let me know
> where they are coming to and I will be glad to know because I am a
> poor woman and have a husband and five children living and three
> dead . . . and my husband can hardly make bread for them in Mo-
> bile. This is my native home but it is not fit to live in. . . . I want to
> get out of this dog hold because I don't know what I am raising [my
> children] up for in this place and I want to get to Chicago where I
> know they will be raised and my husband crazy to get there because
> he know he can get more to raise his children.[19]

Although many sought the opportunity to leave a "native home" that was "not fit to live in," many Afro-Americans who remained in the South organized their own concerted activities in hopes of improving life there. A conference called in 1918 by the governor of North Carolina and the federal Department of Labor to deal with the "scarcity of Negro labor in the state" heard reports of black workers in tobacco, guano, and cotton-oil factories subverting their twelve-hour shifts by "laying off" on Saturdays and Mondays, and in one case striking to abolish Saturday work; of employers in hosiery knitting mills offering black women special bonuses and insurance policies in return for steady attendance at work; and of women in a Rocky Mount mill striking successfully to force the dismissal of a white floor manager who had cursed and abused them. Track-

Pete Daniel, *Breaking the Land: The Transformation of Cotton, Tobacco, and Rice Cultures since 1880* (Urbana, Ill., 1985), 18; Francis M. Vreeland and Edward J. Fitzgerald, *Farm-City Migration and Industry's Labor Reserve* (WPA National Research Project Report No. 1–7, Philadelphia, 1939), 33.

19. Emmett J. Scott, ed., "Additional Letters of Negro Migrants of 1916–1918," *Journal of Negro History,* 4 (October 1919), 440, 418.

layers on the Texas Pacific Railroad struck for higher wages near New Orleans in 1918, only to have their leader sentenced to prison for violation of the Espionage Act because he had interfered with the movement of troops. Early the next year, black building laborers in St. Petersburg, Florida, went on strike, demanding an increase in wages, the right to vote, and equal rights before the law. Their attempt to use the strike weapon for social and political reform paralleled the behavior of innumerable white workers at the war's end, and it was seconded by the field secretary of the National Association for the Advancement of Colored People, James Weldon Johnson. He declared that "the mightiest weapon in the hands of the colored people is the 'strike,' " and he advised Afro-Americans in Jacksonville, Florida, to organize and demand "abolition of the jim crow conditions," with the threat that otherwise they would not "iron or do a stitch of work."[20]

Perhaps the best-sustained and most effectively organized wartime struggle of black workers took place on the waterfront and in the shipyards of the Norfolk–Portsmouth–Newport News area in Virginia. Almost half of the 24,648 black workers who found employment in shipyards worked in this region, and although most of them held unskilled jobs, the bulk of the country's skilled black shipyard workers were employed there. As early as 1917, more than a thousand black union members marched through Norfolk behind the white contingents in a festive Labor Day parade. Later that September, three hundred black women staged a month-long strike against the American Cigar Company, and machinists' helpers also struck for a wage increase, only to be replaced by white scabs. The influence of black workers in local unions and in the Virginia Federation of Labor grew significantly and provoked intense opposition among white union members, leading the IAM to enroll the white scabs of the machinists' helpers' strike and two thousand Richmond members to quit the state federation when it seated a black delegate from Newport News in June 1919. Later that month, however, Virginians were prominent among the twenty-three black delegates to the AFL's Atlantic City convention, and they pushed through a set of resolutions committing the federation, on paper at least, to special efforts to organize black workers.[21]

20. Foner and Lewis, *Black Worker*, V, 382–3, 431–2, 444–5, 531; Judith Stein, *The World of Marcus Garvey: Race and Class in Modern Society* (Baton Rouge, La., 1986), 56.
21. Foner and Lewis, *Black Worker*, V, 399–400, 434–6, 437–9, 445, 480; Sterling D. Spero and Abram L. Harris, *The Black Worker: The Negro and the Labor Movement* (New York, 1931, reprinted New York, 1968), 105–11.

By that time, the National Brotherhood Workers of America had become the organizing center of the Virginia region's black workers. Its founder, R. T. Sims, was a former SLP member who had organized for the IWW in its early years and who envisaged an institution that could do for black workers what the United Hebrew Trades had done for New York's Jews: promote unionization in all occupations. The brotherhood quickly won the support of Socialists A. Philip Randolph and Chandler Owen, who sat on its board of directors. In their journal *The Messenger*, Randolph and Owen saluted the organization for its "sound, union principles and militant, revolutionary methods."[22] A year later, however, the combined impact of heavy layoffs in the shipyards and aggressive organizing of black longshoremen by AFL officers hostile to the revolutionary message of the brotherhood had depleted its ranks. The forms of southern black trade unionism that had reached into new domains and assumed a militant posture during the war had been crippled even before the depression of 1920–2 snuffed out their last glow.

Although these southern workplace struggles have yet to receive close attention from historians, they seem to have consisted mainly of vigorous efforts by committed activists to organize black wage earners, among whom wartime conditions had awakened a glimmer of hope that they might effect some real improvement in their daily lives. The northward migration evoked the same hope, but in a different form. It was, as sociologist Charles S. Johnson observed, a "leaderless mass movement."[23] The ideological manifestations of that movement were shaped not only by the history and desires of the participants but also by the conditions they encountered in the North. This migratory push was concentrated into a very short period of time. It crested before the end of 1917 and tapered off as the labor demands of industry stabilized during the last year of the war, to be renewed after 1922. Moreover, the industries and firms that hired black workers in the North were not numerous. Virtually no black workers were hired in northern metal-fabricating or munitions works, to which white men and women were drawn in huge numbers from other occupations, aside from chemicals plants. In Chicago, no less than half of all adult black workers held jobs in the packinghouses and stockyards. A survey of midwestern industrial centers at the end of the war found clear patterns of concentration in black employment: steel, meat packing, automobile (mostly at Ford), and Pullman shops and yards.

22. Foner and Lewis, *Black Worker*, V, 448. See also William H. Harris, *Keeping the Faith: A. Philip Randolph, Milton P. Webster, and the Brotherhood of Sleeping Car Porters, 1925–37* (Urbana, Ill., 1977), 14.

23. Quoted in William M. Tuttle, Jr., *Race Riot: Chicago in the Red Summer of 1919* (New York, 1970), 93.

The employers were primarily large, open-shop corporations, and such companies tended to employ either many black workers or virtually none. In this epoch characterized generally by high turnover and relatively widespread choices for white workers, the fates of black workers were inexorably linked to certain specific firms in each locality. Moreover, those companies cultivated networks of efficiency clubs, urban leagues, and YMCAs that guided black workers toward prospective jobs and conducted welfare work among the migrants.[24]

Second, the reception accorded the migrants by northern whites was hostile, often violent. Segregated patterns of housing were rigidly enforced, or, if need be, created, as happened in Gary, Indiana, in the face of a rapidly expanding population; Democratic politicians, in Chicago and East St. Louis at least, denounced the newcomers as corrupters of an urban life for white workers that was already desolate enough; unions in the building trades and railroads barred black workers from membership and employment in domains where previous experience would otherwise have sent many of these migrants; and gangs of white teenagers expelled the newcomers from "their" streets and beaches. The bloody riot in East St. Louis on July 2, 1917, featured white workers gathering in their union hall to march on black neighborhoods and resulted in physical expulsion of many Afro-Americans from the city. Mob confrontations recurred in as many as fifteen cities in the summer of 1919, most murderously in Chicago.

In all these battles, Afro-Americans exhibited a readiness to do armed battle in defense of their neighborhoods against white attackers. This assertiveness was widely noted by commentators on race riots of the time. It prompted Frank Custer, who worked in a cattle-killing gang in strife-ridden Chicago and was a loyal union member, to tell a federal umpire, "Supposing trouble starts – I am a colored man and I love my family tree, and I ain't going to stand for no white man to come imposing on my color. . . . there is going to be a fight."[25]

It was in Chicago's packinghouses that the question of trade unionism

24. Cochran, *American Business Systems*, 133; Walter A. Fogel, *The Negro in the Meat Industry* (Philadelphia, 1970), 29; Alma Herbst, *The Negro in the Slaughtering and Meat-Packing Industry in Chicago* (Boston, 1932); T. J. Woofter, "The Negro and Industrial Peace," *Survey*, 45 (December 18, 1920), 420–1.

25. Elliott Rudwick, *Race Riot at East St. Louis July 2, 1917* (New York, 1964), 2–30; Tuttle, *Race Riot*, 184–207; Lee E. Williams and Lee E. Williams II, *Anatomy of Four Race Riots: Racial Conflict in Knoxville, Elaine (Arkansas), Tulsa, and Chicago, 1919–1921* (Jackson, Miss., 1972), 15. The Custer quotation is in Barrett, "Work and Community," 331.

was most ardently debated among black workers, because their numbers rose to fifteen thousand men and women just as enthusiasm for unions swept the ranks of the European immigrants. During 1916 and 1917, social worker Mary McDowell observed that "the workers, mostly Poles, Slovaks, and Lithuanians, became conscious of the undersupply of labor" and engaged in incessant "sporadic, unorganized strikes."[26] A Stockyards Labor Council created by the Chicago Federation of Labor recruited workers so rapidly into its member unions that the federal government dispatched Judge Samuel Alschuler to serve as "Administrator to Adjust Labor Differences" in the meat-packing complex. Alschuler's decision in March 1918 granted the full dollar-a-week raise for common labor demanded by the unions and comparable piecework increases, which made the contrast between the wages black workers earned in Chicago and the wages they had known in the South breathtaking.

The Stockyards Labor Council made a major effort to recruit black workers, even though some of its constituent locals would not admit black members, and neighborhood-based Butcher Workmen's Local 651 received most of those who joined. Black organizers were dispatched from the UMWA and other AFL unions to aid in the effort, George W. Downing of Local 651 was made vice-president of the council, and recruits were constantly solicited on the streetcars that traveled between the packinghouses and the black neighborhood. Such efforts were opposed by important black churches and community organizations that denounced the AFL, as well as by an American Unity Labor Union, which warned migrants not to "join any white man's union." That union was able to recruit heavily because of its access to employment offices and the powerful appeal of its call for a "square deal with your own race." Other prominent Chicago Afro-Americans endorsed the Stockyards Labor Council. Among them were the editors of the *Chicago Defender*. The many "floor committees" activated by workers independent of the AFL and in defiance of Alschuler's arbitration decrees that banned them were especially active among Poles and Afro-Americans. They triggered a wave of departmental strikes in the spring of 1919 as the union was preparing its formal campaign for official recognition.

Nevertheless, even at its peak, the council had recruited little more than 15 percent of the black workers, as contrasted with 90 percent of the Poles and Slovaks, and most of the black workers who joined probably were long-time residents of the city. Whatever hopes it had for an interracial movement died in the riots of July 1919, which claimed the lives of twenty-three Afro-Americans and fifteen whites and brought mili-

26. Barrett, "Work and Community," 299.

tary occupation of the stockyards. From that time until they installed employee-representation plans and wiped out the AFL in the strike of 1921–2, the packinghouses handily played antagonistic white and black workers off against each other.[27] The determination of black migrants to seek a chance to raise their children in decency had met conditions in the urban North that lent themselves more readily at that moment to movements for black pride and community self-help than to trade unionism.

The situation of the Slavic immigrants of packingtown was very different. They had envisaged a new life won by their collective power on the killing floors. When Judge Alschuler awarded the eight-hour day, these workers named a row of park benches near the University of Chicago Settlement House "Eight Hour Benches." There they could sit with their children while the sun was shining. A new desire animated their souls, a sense kindled by an unprecedented awareness of their ability to change the circumstances of their lives and linked to the union cause. Immigrants enrolled in trade unions in such numbers that total membership in metal fabricating rose by 280 percent between 1915 and 1920 (from 220,400 to 836,500) and by 368 percent in textiles (from 23,300 to 109,000). At the same time that they joined unions, they often defied official union practice and demands. When, for example, in February 1919, the United Textile Workers announced a national strike movement for the forty-eight–hour week, silk workers in Paterson scoffed at the call, formed their own coalition of immigrant societies and revolutionary groups, and struck for a forty-four–hour week.[28] Immigrants often expressed their desire in profoundly revealing terms that borrowed heavily from the vocabulary of wartime patriotism. A Polish steelworker took the floor at a union meeting in the Monongahela Valley to say:

> Mr. Chairman – just like a horse and wagon, work all day. Take horse out of wagon – put in stable. Take horse out of stable, put in wagon. Same way like mills. Work all day. Come home – go sleep. Get up – go work in mills – come home. Wife say, "John, children sick, You help with children." You say, "Oh, go to hell" – go sleep. Wife say, "John, you go town." You say, "No" – go sleep. No know what the hell you do. For why this war? For why we buy Liberty

27. Ibid., 316–35; Tuttle, *Race Riot*, 108–55.
28. Barrett, "Work and Community," 312–13; *Monthly Labor Review*, 15 (July 1922), 167; David J. Goldberg, "Immigrants, Intellectuals and Industrial Unions: The 1919 Textile Strikes and the Experience of the Amalgamated Textile Workers of America in Passaic and Paterson, New Jersey and Lawrence, Massachusetts" (unpublished Ph.D. diss., Columbia University, 1983), 104–35.

bonds? For the mills? No, for freedom and America – for everybody. No more horse and wagon. For eight-hour day.[29]

How to run coal

Coal miners' traditions and union organization equipped them to shape their desires into clear programmatic form. The vocabulary they used in that expression drew from both patriotic and revolutionary rhetoric. Between 1917 and 1922 the UMWA grew to a size it never duplicated before or since that time, engaged in some of the largest, longest, and most violent strikes of its history, and experienced within a few short years, first, participation in government planning and, later, the full weight of state power used against it. The embattled miners were not isolated from the rest of the working class during this half decade. Quite the contrary, many men moved about between mining and manufacturing, and the militancy of textile, clothing, maritime, and metal-fabricating workers paralleled and sustained that of the miners, while the UMWA developed close alliances with other unions, especially the railroad brotherhoods and the IAM. This fusion of efforts encouraged official union support for imaginative programs of social reconstruction, as well as widespread adherence of miners in their coal patches to revolutionary organizations and ideals.

Gompers's efforts in the spring of 1917 to commit the labor movement to the policy of upholding "existing standards" as proposed by the CND were sharply rebuffed by the miners, and by the Indianapolis group generally. Bituminous coal had posed special problems for government planners. Unlike the situation in munitions, in which new factories had to be created rapidly, there were more than enough mines in operation to supply the economy's voracious appetite for fuel. The problem was to keep existing mines in constant operation. To achieve that goal it was necessary to increase the supply of railway cars and to iron out the chaotic shipping patterns that the free market had produced over the years and that now threatened the country with a coal famine, to entice miners to go underground faithfully day after day, when good earnings in the mines tempted them to take days off and high pay in other industries lured them off to the cities, and to adjudicate disputes in this strike-prone industry. The CND convened a committee with no labor representatives, but sev-

29. John A. Fitch, "The Closed Shop," *Survey,* 43 (November 8, 1919), 91. I am indebted to Frank Serene for calling this article to my attention.

eral operators of nonunion mines, to make regulations to reduce worker turnover and absenteeism. Furious protests by the UMWA led to the appointment on June 15 of seven union representatives to the committee, the first labor members of wartime planning agencies aside from Gompers himself.[30]

Gompers's embarrassment was compounded a few days later by the irate reaction of the United Brotherhood of Carpenters to the agreement he had made with Secretary of War Newton Baker providing for union wages but no closed shop on military construction projects. President Hutcheson of the carpenters was outraged by this violation of the AFL's craft-autonomy policy and refused to concede the open shop at a time when the prospects for union growth were so promising. Hutcheson drove through the next AFL Executive Council meeting a demand for "direct representation by workers, co-equal with other interests, upon all agencies . . . entrusted with war work," and later called on Washington to imitate the policy of the French government in giving open preference to unionized firms in placing war contracts. "Workers cannot do efficient work on a diet of loyalty," his journal editorialized.[31]

At the November convention of the AFL, where Wilson's appearance helped Gompers win endorsement for the American Alliance for Labor and Democracy, the Indianapolis unions handed Gompers his worst defeats since he was voted out of office in 1894. Frank Hayes of the UMWA, who had quit the Socialist Party, nominated Tobin of the teamsters for AFL treasurer and relished his victory over Gompers's trusted aide John Lennon, 13,478 to 9,102. Two of Gompers's candidates for the Executive Council also went down to defeat before the Indianapolis alliance. The next year, William Johnston of the IAM, who had also left the socialist ranks, at last replaced James O'Connell as AFL vice-president, and one more Gompers man was defeated for the Executive Council by the garment workers' Thomas Rickert. This top-level maneuvering revealed both the determination of some of the AFL's most powerful executives to pursue policies that would maximize their gains from the war and the dissolution of the federation's prewar ideological alignments.[32] The Indianapolis-based opposition had a special affinity for Frank Walsh's conception of using war agencies to introduce industrial democracy. They were America's counterparts of Europe's war socialists. In comparison

30. Bing, *War-Time Strikes*, 95–6; Lorwin, *AFL*, 156–7.
31. Maxwell C. Raddock, *Portrait of an American Labor Leader: William L. Hutcheson* (New York, 1955), 87–108; the quotations are on pp. 92 and 89. On French wartime policy, see Patrick Fridenson, *1914–1918 l'autre front* (Paris, 1977), 111–44.
32. Lore, "Progress Backward," 507–12; Taft, *Time of Gompers*, 346, 362–3.

with these trade unionists, the former party intellectuals, such as John Spargo and Upton Sinclair, who formed the patriotic Social Democratic League lacked any meaningful social base and spent most of the war squabbling with one another.[33]

The coal miners' determination to carry a "fight against Kaiserism" to both Europe's trenches and America's coalfields could be felt from the top of the union to the bottom. It led the UMWA into negotiations with the government that were to have far-reaching implications. In August 1917, Congress passed the Lever Act, giving the president authority to control the production and distribution of food and fuel. The United States Fuel Administration was established pursuant to this act, with Harry A. Garfield as administrator. In 1918, President White of the UMWA resigned to become codirector of the fuel administration's bureau of labor, leaving Frank Hayes the union's president and the ambitious John L. Lewis its new vice-president. Meanwhile, Garfield had undertaken to settle several actual and threatened miners' strikes by reopening the 1916 CCF agreement to allow a general wage increase linked to a rise in coal prices. The October 1917 settlement known as the Washington agreement had three important provisions. First, it set the pattern for agreements in other territories, all of which prohibited discharge of miners for union membership and thus encouraged rapid spread of unionism in areas formerly under tight company control, such as southern West Virginia and Alabama. Second, each agreement had to contain a provision levying a fine of one dollar per day on any miner who went on strike. In Illinois, the UMWA lent vigorous support to this rule. In Kansas, the revolutionary district leader Alexander Howat led a strike against it, but ultimately yielded, so that the antistrike fines had become the rule everywhere the union had contracts. Third, the Washington agreement was to run until the end of the war, or April 1, 1920, whichever should come first.[34]

The Washington agreement greatly strengthened the UMWA, but it also laid the basis for membership rebellions against the union and for the decisive strike of 1919–20. Constantly rising prices soon overtook the wage gains provided by the agreement, leaving steadier work the only possible means to raise miners' incomes. Anthracite miners left the pits in droves for industrial centers, creating, among other things, a large Polish community in Philadelphia. A special raise was allowed for anthracite miners in October 1918 to stem the tide, but none for bitumi-

33. Kenneth E. Hendrickson, Jr., "The Pro-War Socialists, The Social Democratic League and the Ill-fated Drive for Industrial Democracy in America, 1917–1920," *Labor History*, 11 (Summer 1970), 304–22.
34. Corbin, *Life, Work*, 184; Bing, *War-Time Strikes*, 96–101.

nous miners, who often increased their income by inducing operators to offer them bonuses, either by moving from job to job or by collectively stopping work. All the decrees of the Fuel Administration could not prevent operators from offering such bonuses, but the more bonuses were offered, the greater the turnover rates became. Finally, to resolve local disputes and replace the UMWA's lost ability to handle local issues by local strikes, the Fuel Administration ordered the creation of elected grievance committees in every mine. Disputes the committees could not resolve were to be submitted to arbitrators appointed by the Fuel Administration.[35] At a time when official union action was contractually prohibited until 1920, the government had revitalized pit committees!

The cessation of war orders after November 11, 1918, brought rapid declines in manufacturing output, employment, and wholesale prices. By May and June 1919, however, output began to rise again in a postwar boom that lasted about a year. Consumer prices had fallen very little, if at all, even during the slack months, and through the last two-thirds of 1919 they soared upward more rapidly than they had during the war itself. From the successful strike by the Amalgamated Clothing Workers of America for a forty-four–hour week that began on Armistice Day through the national coal and steel strikes a year later, more than 4 million workers walked off their jobs demanding pay increases, shorter hours, and formal recognition of the unions they had built up during the war. Workers in metal fabrication conducted more of these strikes than any other group, just as they had been doing ever since 1916, but those in building construction, clothing, textiles, and mining were not far behind.[36]

Counting up the numbers of strikes, strikers, and workdays lost can reveal the scale of the 1919–20 strike movement but not the content of working-class aspirations that propelled it. The desire for a new way of living nurtured by the war had produced a fusion of immediate demands with grandiose social and political goals that simply confounded the union leadership. Ever since the 1880s, at least, organized labor movements in Europe and America had carefully distinguished between economic and political demands. The former were considered the proper domain of unions, and the latter of labor and socialist parties. The dichotomy was so deeply entrenched in socialist thinking that the Socialist Party of Italy actually held an emergency convention during the 1920 factory occupa-

35. Golab, *Immigrant Destinations;* Bing, *War-Time Strikes,* 96–102; John R. Commons, ed., *Trade Unionism and Labor Problems, Second Series* (Boston, 1921), 499–500.
36. Eugene Rotwein, "Post–World War I Price Movements and Price Policy," *Journal of Political Economy,* 53 (1945), 234–57; *Am. Labor Year Book, 1919–20,* 182–4; *Monthly Labor Review,* 14 (May 1922), 181–9.

tions by the country's metalworkers to debate whether the struggle was economic (to be led by the unions toward the best possible settlement) or political (to be led by the party toward overthrow of the capitalist system). The convention voted that the strike was economic.[37]

The actions and thinking of American (and Italian) workers in 1919 and 1920 simply could not be poured into that categorical mold. Even though the American situation was not revolutionary, bold visions of social change and strikes for a few more pennies per hour fed on each other. During Seattle's February general strike, for example, a committee of three hundred workers, with an executive committee of fifteen, organized twenty-one community kitchens, decided which telephone exchanges, dairies, and hospitals might remain open, and established collective butcher shops and laundries. The city was charged with excitement as uniformed war veterans enrolled by the strike committee patrolled the streets, shipyard workers insisted that pay scales had to be both raised and equalized, and the strike committee boasted that workers were "learning to manage" the economy.[38] Across the country in Lawrence, Massachusetts, at the same time, men, women, and children attended packed meetings in the halls of their national lodges, expressed nostalgia for the old country, along with anger at the new, and opened their meetings by singing "The International." Lithuanians, Italians, Poles, Jews, and Belgians celebrated their various national causes on some occasions and marched all together behind American and red flags to assert their common cause on others. The leaders of the strike, such as Ime Kaplan, Sam Bramhall, Joseph Salerno, Mike Bolis, Annie Trina, and Carl Vogt, had all shared a first youthful experience in the famous strike of 1912, though none of them were any longer in the IWW. They conducted what reporter John A. Fitch called "a strike for wages carried on in a revolutionary atmosphere."[39]

This mood had inspired the 1,182 trade unionists who assembled in Chicago January 14–17, 1919, to chart actions that might bring freedom for Tom Mooney and Warren Billings. Their conviction on charges of planting a bomb to explode during the San Francisco Preparedness Day parade of 1916 had aroused the ire of virtually everyone in the labor movement, except some of the most conservative leaders in their own state. Although Mooney had been sentenced to be hanged on May 17,

37. Paolo Spriano, *The Occupation of the Factories: Italy 1920* (translated by Gwyn A. Williams, London, 1975), 81–96.
38. History Committee of the General Strike Committee, *The Seattle General Strike* (Seattle, 1919), 5 and passim.
39. John A. Fitch, "Lawrence: A Strike for Wages or Bolshevism?" *Survey*, 42 (April 5, 1919), 45; Goldberg, "Immigrants, Intellectuals," 255–381.

1917, public protests and legal appeals and pleas from President Wilson had stayed the execution and by November 1918 had persuaded California's governor to commute his sentence to life imprisonment. The delegates who came to Chicago the following January wanted Mooney and Billings set free. Among them were leading AFL figures such as President Andrew Furuseth of the seamen's union, Vice-President J. F. Anderson of the IAM, two UMWA district presidents, Alexander Howat and Martin Flysik, and John Fitzpatrick of the Chicago Federation of Labor. The convention delegates distanced themselves from revolutionaries by barring six representatives of IWW locals and four from Socialist Party branches, and they were roused by the oratory of Tammany's own Senator W. Bourke Cockran, who had been Mooney's trial lawyer and was a leader in Irish-American affairs. The IAM, carpenters, and UMWA had the largest representation among the delegates, who resolved unanimously:

> We hold that in this day of world changes when empires are crumbling before the onward advance of democracy, that the Mooney case symbolizes all the oppression and bitterness of the struggle of the toiling masses of humanity to rise up and shake off the shackles that have kept in bondage the toilers of the world.[40]

They voted to send a committee of prominent union leaders to ask Washington to intervene. But in the event that effort did not open the doors of California's jails, the convention also called for a national general strike from July 4 through July 8, 1919. To prepare for this strike, it authorized the International Workers' Defense League to distribute strike ballots through every local union and have those ballots sent not to the international unions but directly to the Mooney Federal Intervention Committee in Chicago. The logic of this approach, as the league explained in a brochure that went out with the ballots, was that "old methods" of strike authorization were "too slow and cumbersome," and furthermore that "all forms of secret diplomacy are dead and buried with the past, as far as the masses are concerned, and the rank and file of the common people all over the world are determined to speak for themselves and decide what is best for the masses."[41]

The AFL convention in June called a new trial for Mooney an "imper-

40. [Mooney Convention], "Resolution on National Policies Affecting Labor"; "Report of A. Johannsen to the Officers and Delegates of the Carpenters' District Council of Chicago, Jan. 19, 1919" (Walsh Papers, Box 25); *MMJ*, 31 (February 1919), 135–6. See also Richard H. Frost, *The Mooney Case* (Stanford, Calif., 1968).

41. "Labor Declares War on the California Frame Up" (n.p., n.d., Item 532, Box 13, Post Office Records, R.G. 28, National Archives); "Report of A. Johannsen."

ative necessity," but it denounced the movement for a general strike and the ballot that circumvented constitutional union procedures. It also dissented from the Mooney convention's appeal for the release of "all political and industrial prisoners," as well as "prisoners of war."[42] Given this opposition, it is probable that the claim of the Workers' Defense League that a million workers had struck, 200,000 of them in Chicago alone, was a gross exaggeration. Nevertheless, 60,000 of those who did leave their jobs for Tom Mooney were coal miners in the Illinois Belleville subdistrict. When they returned to work, they found that they had been fined a dollar per day in accordance with the 1917 Washington agreement.

The fines triggered a protest strike that spread rapidly across the mines of central and southern Illinois by caravans of motorized "crusaders." Meetings at one mine town after another denounced the efforts of District President Frank Farrington to suppress the strike, and especially the assaults on crusaders by strong-arm squads loyal to the administration. They also condemned the UMWA leadership for having won no general wage increase for bituminous miners since the fall of 1917. On August 19, insurgent delegates from 141 locals, claiming to represent 57,700 UMWA members, assembled in Springfield, in response to a call from crusaders to "demand of the capitalist class that all instruments of industries be turned over to the working class." The delegates formulated a very specific program. It demanded a thirty-hour week, a pay increase, reform of the contracting system, and transfer of "the mines to the miners."[43]

Although the leading spokesman of this movement, Henry Schilling of Belleville, was a member of the SLP, and he infused its resolutions with that party's vocabulary, which enjoyed great popularity among American revolutionaries in 1919, most of the movement's demands had been anticipated by the UMWA's National Policy Committee when it had met the previous March to consider possible termination of the Washington agreement. An exception was the "mines to the miners" demand – the policy committee had called for "nationalization" of the coal industry. When the UMWA gathered more than two thousand miners at its official convention three weeks after the insurgents' meeting, it barred the delegates of thirty rebellious Illinois locals from participation and approved

---

42. *Am. Labor Year Book 1919–20*, 157; Mooney Convention, "Resolution." Secretary Davidson of the IAM warned all lodges not to participate in the balloting. *MMJ*, 31 (May 1919), 460.

43. *Am. Labor Year Book 1919–20*, 177; Sylvia Kopald, *Rebellion in Labor Unions* (New York, 1924), 50–123; the quotations are on pp. 74–5 and 121.

Farrington's repressive measures. It also adopted a scale-committee report setting November 1, 1919, as the deadline for a national bituminous strike. The demands were a 60 percent wage increase, a six-hour day at the face and a five-day week, and abolition of the penalty fines. The same convention summoned the UMWA's officers to open negotiations with railroad unions for a formal alliance and to convene representatives of unions, cooperatives, farmers' organizations, and North Dakota's Nonpartisan League for the purpose of establishing a labor party.[44]

While the miners were developing their ambitious program, leading toward the November strike, America's business leaders had also sorted out their stance, not simply toward the miners but toward labor generally. During the last months of the military conflict, prominent government planners like Robert Brookings of the War Industries Board and Felix Frankfurter of the War Labor Policies Committee had devised schemes for continued federal control of the economy after the end of the war in order to avoid a collapse of prices and unmanageable industrial strife. None of these ideas for managed reconversion of the economy was accepted by the CND, however, and President Wilson was quick to make a virtue of the country's lack of a plan. He told Congress in December 1918:

> Our people . . . do not want to be coached and led. They know their own business, and are quick and resourceful at every readjustment, definite in purpose and self-reliant in action. . . . I have heard much counsel as to the plans that should be formed . . . but from no quarter have I seen any general scheme of "reconstruction" emerge which I thought it likely we could force our spirited businessmen and self-reliant laborers to accept with due pliancy and obedience.[45]

The "spirited businessmen" did indeed have a program. It included quick dismantling of federal agencies like the National War Labor Board and the Fuel Administration, which had been established at business's requests and then turned under pressure from labor into Frankenstein monsters – encouraging unions, fixing wages, and infringing on business executives' discretionary powers at every turn. Although they wanted an end to price controls, they also wanted to tame inflation, which was mak-

44. Kopald, *Rebellion*, 74–123; Dubofsky and Van Tine, *John L. Lewis*, 45, 49–50.
45. Rotwein, "Post–World War," 242; for governmental discussion of reconversion plans, see pp. 235–43; unpublished interview of Felix Frankfurter for the *New York World* in Charles Wood to Frankfurter, October 14, 1918; Frankfurter to Wood, November 4, 1918 (records of the War Labor Policies Board, Entry 2, Correspondence of the Chairman and of the Executive Secretary, Folder B-1-a Metal Trades, R.G. 1, National Archives).

ing them load up inventories to a danger point in order to avoid higher purchase prices in the future. The key to deflation, they concluded, was to hold down wages. Moreover, as industry's delegates to the president's National Industrial Conference in the autumn of 1919 made clear, they were willing to accept employee representation and welfare programs administered at the level of the individual enterprise, but they unequivocally refused to tolerate "outside interference" from either unions or social legislation. The American Railway Executives Association demanded that rail lines be returned to private hands and, when they were reprivatized in 1920, endorsed the principle of no contracts with labor organizations and abrogation of the national agreements that had been negotiated on behalf of the 90 percent of their workers who were union members.[46]

The results of the 1918 congressional elections had helped persuade political leaders to endorse business's proposals. The Republicans had swept into control of Congress, campaigning everywhere against the high cost of living and obnoxious government regulations of everyday life. Wilson's closest advisor, Joseph Tumulty, warned the president that most Americans who could vote wanted lower prices, even if that meant lower wages. What the administration had already provided labor would ensure its electoral support in 1920, Tumulty argued; to offer more would make "the country at large think that we are making a special appeal to labor at this time." The Democrats' quest for workers' votes subsided simultaneously with employers' demand for their work. The combination of the law-and-order electorate already evident in 1916 with the lower-prices electorate of 1918 had brought to life William English Walling's nightmare of 1912: an "iron-bound class society solidly entrenched in majority rule."[47]

That society had already unleashed its full fury against the IWW during the war. From the vigilante deportation of 1,186 striking copper miners from Bisbee, Arizona, in 1917, through the lynching of Frank Little and raids by soldiers and sailors who demolished IWW halls, to the trial and conviction of 116 leaders in Chicago, patriotic mobs and due process

46. Rotwein, "Post–World War," 247–57; Haggai Hurvitz, "Ideology and Industrial Conflict: President Wilson's First Industrial Conference of October, 1919," *Labor History*, 18 (Fall 1977), 509–27; Bing, *War-Time Strikes*, 116–32; Federico Romero, *Il Sindicato come Istituzione: La Regolamentazione del Conflitta Industriale negli Stati Uniti* (Turin, 1981), 196–224; American Federation of Labor, Railway Employees' Department, *The Case of the Railway Shopmen* (Chicago, 1922), 14, 35–7.

47. Dubofsky, "Abortive Reform," 214–15. On Walling, see Chapter 6, footnote 150.

of law had collaborated to stamp out Wobbly activity. Federal authorities had created the Loyal League of Loggers and Lumbermen to substitute for the IWW as a "union" in the Northwest, and with less success had promoted the UMWA and the Mine, Mill and Smelter Workers in the mines of the Southwest. Although many officials in the Wilson administration, among them Undersecretary of Labor Louis Post and George Creel, abhorred vigilante attacks in the name of patriotism and thought that they were obstructing the effort to win the workers over to the war, rather than helping, the decisive weight of Justice Department and Labor Department activity was devoted to the imprisonment or deportation of "dangerous radicals." A national police agency could cast a far wider net than local sheriffs or law-and-order committees could conjure up. Justice Department files reveal, for example, that when Jesus Romo wrote a letter to the *Los Angeles Record* refuting that paper's editorial charge that Wobblies were dynamite bombers who threatened civilization, the Bureau of Investigation seized him for deportation, then sought out his brother Cleofas, who was an IWW activist at Arizona Copper in Morenci, and another brother Guadelupe and his wife Francisca in Cleveland, so as to dispatch all of them back to Mexico.[48]

Business's emphasis on maximizing the managerial autonomy of the individual enterprise did not mean that it anticipated no important role for the government. On the contrary, business both endorsed and benefited greatly from the public policy of dismantling agencies and trying to deflate the economy, from the repression of radical activities, and from the general strategy pursued by both the Wilson and Harding administrations of postponing decisions in the face of formidable union movements for higher wages. Government and corporate leaders alike were convinced that the high prices of 1919 would soon collapse and that concession of wage increases at that time would inhibit industry's ability to cope with the coming deflation.

Wartime restrictions on speech and public assembly remained in force for years after the armistice. By 1921, only eleven of eighty-eight major cities had removed their wartime bans on street meetings. Post Office censorship of revolutionary publications continued openly until May 1921, and Italy's *Avanti* was still barred from American mails the following August. After Attorney General Palmer's notorious arrests and deportations of alien radicals in 1919 and 1920, the Immigration Bureau of the

48. Dufofsky, *We Shall Be All,* 376–444; Vernon L. Jensen, *Lumber and Labor* (New York, 1945), 125–47; Robert K. Murray, *Red Scare: A Study in National Hysteria, 1919–1920* (Minneapolis, 1955); Creel, *Rebel at Large,* 196–7; Bureau of Investigation, File 363737, Cleofas L. Romo (courtesy of Jeremy Brecher).

Department of Labor settled into routine scrutiny of foreign-born workers in cooperation with local police, employers, and patriotic societies. In fact, more than three-fourths of the employees of the department dealt with immigration and deportation after 1920, and the number of people they expelled annually rose to more than thirty-eight thousand by the end of the 1920s.[49]

This was the context that shaped President Wilson's response to the miners' demands in the fall of 1919. He reactivated the Fuel Administration, which had been shut down in the spring, and denounced the pending strike as an illegal violation of the 1917 Washington agreement. Federal injunctions prevented UMWA officers from organizing the strike or dispensing strike funds, but more than 400,000 miners walked out anyway. On November 11, another court order commanded the UMWA to call off the strike, and President Lewis and the executive board capitulated. Again the miners did not. The government then offered the operators 100,000 troops to help them resume production, saturated the coalfields with Bureau of Investigation agents, put taps on the phones of all union offices, rounded up alien agitators, and cited eighty-four UMWA officers for contempt of court. That done, the Fuel Administration then brought leaders of the operators and union together and negotiated a settlement: The miners received an immediate wage increase of 14 percent, and all other questions were referred to a Bituminous Coal Commission with power to decide on all remaining issues.[50]

In February 1920, the commission awarded tonnage men a raise of 27 percent, and day men 20 percent, and decreed no change in the hours of labor or the hated penalty clause. The agreement was to run until March 31, 1922.[51] This outcome left the CCF highly unionized but seething with rebellious members and factious leaders, while the adjacent regions were ablaze with battles for union recognition. That situation in itself was far from new, but the size of the UMWA and the determination of miners to follow the Great War with social reconstruction gave the virtually continuous strikes of 1920–3 and the union's internal battles over ideology and leadership a ferocity that was remarkable even in comparison with the earlier experience of American coal miners.

49. Editorial, *New York Call*, April 17, 1921; *New York World*, May 26, 1921; *Avanti* file (Post Office Records, R.G. 28, Box 20, National Archives); William Preston, Jr., *Aliens and Dissenters: Federal Suppression of Radicals, 1903–1933* (Cambridge, Mass., 1963), 181–272; Jonathan Grossman, *The Department of Labor* (New York, 1973), 23–6; *Hist. Stat. U.S.*, 114.

50. Bing, *War-Time Strikes*, 99–100; Dubofsky and Van Tine, *John L. Lewis*, 53–63.

51. Douglas, Hitchcock, and Atkins, *Worker in Economic Society*, 365–83.

Newly elected president John L. Lewis enjoyed the support of most officers from the anthracite districts, western Pennsylvania, Ohio, and Indiana, as well as the union's large staff – enough to assure him roughly half of the delegate votes during the tumultuous 1921 and 1922 conventions. The huge Illinois district was headed by Frank Farrington, possibly the most conservative prominent official in the union, but one whose hunger for Lewis's job led him into frequent alliances with more radical activists. Frank Keeney of West Virginia District 17 and Alexander Howat of Kansas District 14 championed the innumerable wildcat strikes led by pit committees in their districts, a stance that led Howat to prison for his violations of the new Kansas law requiring disputes to be submitted to a state industrial court. The Nova Scotia district, led by the astute Communist J. B. McLachlan, declared its adherence to the Red International of Labor Unions (Profintern) in 1920. The UMWA did not try to undermine McLachlan before 1923, however, because the union's most serious rival in the Glace Bay mines was the revolutionary One Big Union, which the Communists opposed. Finally, District 2 in west-central Pennsylvania was led by John Brophy. His commitment to mine nationalization, a labor party, and workers' education attracted an impressive coterie of intellectuals who had been radicalized by wartime contact with the left wing of the British labor movement (Arthur Gleason, Carter Goodrich, George Soule, etc.). Lewis's control of the union rested largely on his remarkable talent for dividing his foes and laying traps for them. At the 1921 convention, for example, he easily rallied the most militant delegates to his side against Farrington's attempts to win greater autonomy for the Illinois district: Who could deny that the miners of the CCF had to fight for a single agreement under a unified command? Lewis then made Howat the first of his many foes to be expelled during the 1920s, by charging him with failure to uphold union contracts. The vote on that expulsion was extremely close, and Brophy's group had been won to Lewis's side by being authorized to devise specific plans to implement the union's commitment to government ownership of the industry.[52]

For all his famous "tiger instinct," however, Lewis's success would not have been possible without the miners' own determination to display a united front toward their employers. The continuing inflation of 1919– 20 kept wage demands constantly in the forefront of workers' struggles,

52. Dubofsky and Van Tine, *John L. Lewis,* 112–24; Coleman, *Men and Coal,* 94–125; David A. Frank, "The Cape Breton Miners, 1917–1926" (unpublished Ph.D. diss., Dalhousie University, 1979); Henry J. Allen, *The Party of the Third Part: The Story of the Kansas Industrial Relations Court* (New York, 1921), 48–61; Winthrop D. Lane, *Civil War in West Virginia: A Story of the Industrial Conflict in the Coal Mines* (New York, 1921).

however many other issues might have been linked to them. Wage campaigns were precisely the type that union officialdom was best equipped to lead. Pit committees might provide the best agency for workers' control, and militant district leaders might pioneer in the preparation and popularization of nationalization plans, but local wage negotiations could at best only supplement the standards established by national unions over large market areas. Only Lewis was in a position to reopen negotiations in the CCF and win a general wage increase in August 1920. The resulting scale for day men was $7.50, at a time when Ford could boast only a six-dollar day and railroad machinists had union scales around $7.00. Already frequent shutdowns of mines sharply limited miners' annual earnings, but wage scales in the CCF were high – dangerously so in comparison with those in nonunion fields. When operators demanded major reductions in the contract to take effect April 1, 1922, delegates from miners' locals insisted that Lewis make no concessions. But again, the character of the conflict accentuated the importance and authority of national officers.[53]

Outside the CCF, most mining companies had simply refused to adhere to the government's April 1920 award. Miners in Alabama and southern West Virginia struck to bring their fields under the agreement. Although the Alabama efforts were soon defeated, the West Virginia miners, whose output had grown to decisive importance in the bituminous industry by 1921, made effective use of three things they had inherited from the war: a vast increase in membership made possible by wartime protections against dismissal, an ideological appeal to the battle for democracy against the "industrial Kaiserism" of the company towns, and military experience. The strikers waged fierce attacks on company guards, state militia, and scabs and had the guidance of enough veterans of the Western Front in their ranks to defeat their enemies time and again. To cleanse Logan County of its hated mine guards, the union mobilized between ten thousand and fourteen thousand armed men who waged a week-long war in the mountains, until the region was occupied by the U.S. Army, supported by the 88th Bomber Squadron under General "Billy" Mitchell.[54]

The soldiers and aircraft sent to West Virginia by President Harding

53. Dubofsky and Van Tine, *John L. Lewis*, 62–3, 78–81; Vertrees J. Wyckoff, *The Wage Policies of Labor Organizations in a Period of Industrial Depression* (Baltimore, 1926), 88–9. On comparative wages, see Lanfear, *Business Fluctuations*, 29–33; Meyer, *Five Dollar Day*, 167–8.

54. On Alabama, see Wyckoff, *Wage Policies*, 80–2. On West Virginia, see Corbin, *Life, Work*, 195–252; Lane, *Civil War*, 99–110; Dubofsky and Van Tine, *John L. Lewis*, 77–8.

allowed the operators to reopen their mines and put an end to the UMWA's hopes of expanding into the country's most rapidly growing bituminous fields. By the time the armed forces arrived, however, the economic boom of 1919–20 had already turned into a major depression. Production and employment levels had fallen in virtually all sectors of the economy since July 1920, and the collapse of high prices, so long anticipated by business and government leaders, had arrived. Detroit's auto manufacturers, who had employed 208,000 workers in March 1920, found jobs for only 135,000 that November, and by the January seasonal layoffs, 25,339. Employment on the country's major railroads fell from 2,197,824 on August 1920 to 1,593,068 the following March, even though the tonnage they hauled remained near record highs. The average coal miner with a job received no call to report to work on almost one-half the days of 1921. Prospects for miners were worst in unionized bituminous fields adjacent to West Virginia, which were seriously undercut by low-wage competition from the South.[55]

During 1921, therefore, mines not covered by the April 1920 contract slashed tonnage rates severely. A strike at CFI against such a reduction gave Rockefeller's company the chance to complete the work it had begun in 1913 and rid itself of UMWA members. More urgent for the union's leadership was the open effort of many operators covered by the 1920 agreement to break away from it. As the termination date, April 1, 1922, approached, the CCF companies demanded arbitration of any new agreement, an end to checkoff of dues, separate settlements for different districts of the field, and a reduction of wages to prewar levels. A defiant UMWA convention unanimously resolved to strike in order to maintain "the present [1920–2] basic wage schedules" and keep the CCF intact. By a rather narrow margin it also voted, against Lewis's advice, to demand again the thirty-hour week. As the convention prepared for combat, it directed the officers to negotiate a pact of unity with the railroad workers.[56]

The impulse uniting coal miners and railroad workers arose as much from a convergence of ideas as from the quest for more successful strikes. Those ideas circulated more widely among local activists and secondary leaders than they did in statements from headquarters of international

55. Zaragosa Vargas, "Mexican Auto Workers at Ford Motor Company, 1918–1933" (unpublished Ph.D. diss., University of Michigan, 1984), 235–6; Stuart Daggett, "The Railroad Labor Controversy of 1921," *University of California Chronicle* (January 1922), 46; Van Kleeck, *Miners and Management*, 364; Wyckoff, *Wage Policies*, 82–8.
56. Wyckoff, *Wage Policies*, 89–91; Harry Laidler, "The Month," *Labor Age*, 11 (March 1922), 24–5.

unions, but the decision of the UMWA's 1921 convention authorizing a committee consisting of John Brophy, William Mitch of Indiana, and Christ Golden of the anthracite fields to spell out the meaning of the union's commitment to "immediate nationalization of the coal industry" allowed them a highly articulate presentation in 1922. The report, *How to Run Coal,* was sent to President Lewis at the end of the summer. It linked the ideals of "production for use" and workers' control. Capitalist management had placed the pursuit of profits above both those goals, the report argued, but to "have a group of politicians at Washington manage coal would be as distasteful to the miner as it would be to the long-suffering public." The alternative was "democratic management": "coal shall be run by the people who mine it, who apply their scientific knowledge to its problems, who transport it, who sell it, who use it."

A major role for trained engineers appeared in the plan: They were to collect statistics of output and demand, to pursue research and inspections, and to fix prices. Mine administration was to be entrusted to a council with representatives of technical personnel, miners, and consumers. Wages were to be fixed by collective bargaining on a national scale, leaving mine managers free of "wage haggling and market-juggling" to devote their energies to organizing production, in collaboration with committees of miners. Nationalization might all too easily become "the control of the industry by a group of businessmen in the interest of private enterprise," the committee observed. To avoid this danger required total unionization, competent technicians and administrators, a large labor representation in "all departments of Government," and a labor party. Consequently, miners had to collaborate with others in forming a new political movement. In this effort, the report concluded, their relationship to railroad workers assumed special importance: "The coal industry is so dependent on transportation that the miners' program is one with the program of the railroad workers for nationalization of the railroads."[57]

Labor's progressives

By 1922, the mine and railway unions stood in the forefront of a postwar "progressive bloc" in the labor movement. The existence of that bloc was a testimonial to the aspirations that the war had unleashed among workers, just as its tortuous career betrayed the anxiety those aspirations aroused

57. Nationalization Research Committee, United Mine Workers of America, *How to Run Coal: Suggestions for a Plan of Public Control and Democratic Management in the Coal Industry* (n.p., 1922); the quotations are on pp. 10, 11, 14, and 17.

among their union leaders. Moreover, unlike the coal miners, whose 500,000-member union provided a lodestone for the workers' loyalties and consequently the theater within which the many ideological tendencies contested with each other, railroad workers had sixteen unions, most of them with highly exclusive membership qualifications. Under government administration during the war, all sixteen had waxed fat, giving their officers salaries, contracts, and lines of demarcation to protect, and also making possible extraordinary new ventures into union banking, real estate, cooperatives, and even foreign-trading companies. Virtually overnight the railway unions had become rich and powerful institutions, strongly oriented toward social reform. Nowhere was this more evident than in the pages of the *Locomotive Engineers' Journal,* which was edited after 1921 by Yale Divinity School graduate Albert F. Coyle. Its pages were filled with essays by Mary and Charles Beard, Paul Douglas, Carter Goodrich, and other scholars, discussing workers' control, labor parties, imperialism, revolutionary movements around the world, and union strategies. Train service workers had long served as well-read convenors of interminable discussions about national and world affairs; now they had a union journal worthy of that heritage.

The experience of the wartime federal railway administration had taught the value of coordinated bargaining to the union leaders and the virtues of nationalized railroads to the members. It had also magnified the tendency of workers to act together, independent of their union officers, when complex contractual arrangements delayed the settlement of grievances. During 1919, the shop-craft workers were especially restive. Like the bituminous miners, they had obtained a wage increase when the government first took charge of their industry but nothing since then. A cooperative railway administration had enabled them to unionize virtually all machinists, molders, blacksmiths, and others in the repair shops and, best of all, to vote on whether they wished to abolish piecework. In one triumphant deluge of ballots they wiped out Harrington Emerson's handiwork. As the summer of 1919 dragged on without a raise, however, local protest strikes had become common. Moreover, the tenor of congressional debate over the railroads' future made it evident that the legislators intended to return the lines to private owners and, moreover, to make it a crime to advocate a railway strike. Lobbying against these proposals was jeopardized by a decree from the new director general Walter Hines forbidding political activity by railroad workers – a remarkable reversal of the Democratic administration's posture since its reelection in 1916. The IAM responded with a membership referendum authorizing a national work stoppage if either house of Congress passed a prohibition against strikes. At the end of December, the Senate adopted a strike ban as part of its version of the reprivatization bill, but the conference committee removed the criminal sanctions and substituted arbitration, and the amended measure was finally enacted in February 1920.[58]

The alternative to reprivatization endorsed by all railway unions during 1919 was the plan proposed by Glenn E. Plumb for government ownership of all lines and a tripartite administration drawn equally from the workers' unions, shippers' organizations, and bondholders.[59] Because the Plumb plan meshed nicely with the miners' demands for nationalization of coal under an administration representing both the miners and the users, and because it offered a clear formulation of common interest between workers and farmers in the future management of America's transportation system, it became a rallying point for all reformists advocating a new social program for the AFL. The progressive bloc's greatest postwar triumph was achieved at the 1920 AFL convention when the delegates overrode the objections of Gompers to endorse public ownership and democratic management of the railroads by a vote of 29,159 to 8,349, after listening to a rousing speech by Glenn Plumb.[60]

While the legislative controversy was mounting, the shop-craft unions voted jointly in favor of a national strike on September 2, 1919, if they had not won a wage increase. On the eve of the strike deadline, President Wilson made a public appeal very different from the one he had made in support of the train service workers' eight-hour demand in 1916. He called on the workers to take a "second thought" and "postpone questions of this sort until normal conditions come again." The government's efforts to reduce prices were beginning to take effect, Wilson argued, and a wage increase at that time "would inevitably raise, not lower, the cost of living."[61] Wilson's appeal to the shopmen succeeded where his calls to steelworkers and coal miners for forbearance had failed. During September, the unions negotiated with the government the first national agreement covering all 425,000 shop employees but settled for a mere four cents per hour as its wage increase. One of the IAM's more militant vice-presidents, J. F. Anderson, justified the decision: "No one can doubt that a strike, with our Government arrayed against us, would have meant

58. *MMJ*, 31 (February 1919), 137, 150; (September 1919), 807–8, 837; *Labor*, November 15, 1919, November 22, 1919, December 27, 1919, February 21, 1920, February 28, 1920.

59. Glenn E. Plumb and William G. Roylance, *Industrial Democracy: A Plan for Its Achievement* (New York, 1923); G. E. Plumb, *Industrial Democracy* (Washington, 1921).

60. *MMJ*, 31 (September 1919), 808; *AFL Proceedings*, 1920, 399–420.

61. Warne, "Anthracite Strike," 163, 165. The lines were reprivatized on March 1, 1920.

defeat, and in all likelihood we would have come out of it an unorganized mass, much to the pleasure of many of the private owners, to whom the railroads will be returned."[62]

Incessant negotiations between unions and the railway administration at the beginning of 1920 failed to produce a smooth transition to private ownership, let alone wage increases. At the beginning of April, strikes began to spread across the Midwest. This time, switchmen were the prime movers, although they enjoyed the support of as many as fifty thousand workers of all categories by April 14. This rebellion shattered all lines of union demarcation, not to mention authorized procedures, and it gave rise to several new unions, all led by rank and filers and all facing the stern opposition of the brotherhoods, the AFL, and the government. In New York, where waterfront workers walked out together with rebellious railway men and women, leaflets circulated denouncing the September surrender to Wilson and advising the strikers as follows:

> **Form Transport Workers' Committees in all your shops and docks.** Link them up into local, district and national councils, to take over the management of the industry. Agitate for One Big Union and Shop Committees and Workers' Councils in all the industries. Make it a single **revolutionary** organization, prepared to fight for the overthrow of the rule of the bosses – the millionaires of Wall Street.[63]

Federal authorities arrested the strike's two prominent Chicago leaders for violation of the Lever and Sherman acts and raided strikers' offices in New Orleans, Cleveland, and elsewhere, while the brotherhoods expelled thirty thousand members and revoked the charters of fifty lodges to stem the rebellious tide. A quickly constituted Railway Labor Board organized bargaining between the railway managers' association and the sixteen unions, resulting in wage increases in July, together with a commitment to continue the work rules established under government management.[64] The rebellious strikes of railwaymen and coal miners in early 1920 had not been unique. On the contrary, national strike statistics reveal that 253 of that year's strikes lacked union authorization. That was only 7.4 percent of the strikes, but they involved 850,837 workers, or 58 percent of all the year's strikers. By way of contrast, only 6 percent of the strikers in 1921 (66,804) lacked official union sanction. By then, the depression had unleashed employers' attacks on union contracts and wage scales,

62. *MMJ*, 31 (October 1919), 931.
63. *MMJ*, 32 (March 1920), 226–40; Kopald, *Rebellion*, 124–9; "Railwaymen and Port Workers!" (Item 251, Post Office Files, R.G. 28, National Archives).
64. Kopald, *Rebellion*, 155–77.

provoking huge, official union strikes and rallied yesterday's rebels around the threatened union banners.[65]

With the railway workers, as with the bituminous miners, the wage increases offered union leaders in the summer of 1920 to stem the wildcat strikes of their members were granted just as the bottom fell out of the economy. Railroad companies could not persuade the Interstate Commerce Commission to raise their rates under deflationary conditions, government subsidies to ease reprivatization ran out after six months, and private investors found the lines' low rate of return very unattractive. Early in 1921, therefore, major companies were appealing to the Railway Labor Board for wage cuts and a waiving of work rules, while the pivotal Pennsylvania Railroad simply repudiated all its union contracts and instituted an employee-representation plan, in defiance of the government's board. When the board granted major concessions to the companies, shopmen voted to strike, and they were soon joined by the engineers, firemen, conductors, and switchmen, who all set a joint strike date for October 30, 1921. A frantic round of board hearings as the deadline approached revealed that the large numbers of men and women hungry for jobs all over the country, the frenzy of the press, and the government's hostile preparation of injunction procedures and soldiers had once more undermined the unions' resolve.[66]

Despite their bold front, the unionists had seen the government smash the maritime unions at the very time the railway workers were taking strike votes. The International Seamen's Union had elected, in January 1921, a militant new leadership that sought to federate all the waterfront workers for a common struggle. When Admiral William S. Benson, commissioner of the U.S. Shipping Board, announced wage cuts and an end to hiring through union halls as of May 1, he also mustered the government's wartime merchant fleet back into service and ordered all seamen to sign the board's terms as individuals, "or get off." A strike by 125,000 sailors and longshoremen had shut down all three coasts between May and June, but later it began to crumble. East Coast ports opened first, then scab longshoremen were recruited through new "blue book" halls on the Pacific Coast, the proud dockers of New Orleans were humbled, and the marine engineers negotiated a separate truce. Ultimately, even the steam-schooner crews, the last to capitulate, had to accept a wage cut, along with an agreement to let nonunion dockers load their ships.[67]

65. *Monthly Labor Review*, 16 (June 1923), 239.
66. Daggett, "Railroad Labor," 43–64.
67. Joseph B. Nelson, "Maritime Unionism and Class Consciousness in the 1930s" (unpublished Ph.D. diss., University of California, Berkeley, 1982), 98–

The railway leaders did not share the One Big Union fervor of the waterfront. Nine days before their strike deadline, the AFL shop crafts announced they would remain at work. The next day, western brakemen and switchmen started out on their own initiative, while the railway clerks were forbidden by their union to join them. Finally, on October 28, when the railway board promised that there would be no further wage reductions until it had resolved the many disputes over work rules, the four brotherhoods withdrew from what was left of the strike movement.[68] Railroad workers' unity had been shattered almost a year before the great shop-craft strike of 1922 began.

Understandably, then, the efforts of the unions of miners, engineers, and machinists to form a united front between 1920 and 1922 yielded more results in the realm of trade-union politics than in coordinated bargaining and strike action. Defeats on the economic front, however, undercut their efforts to reshape the leadership and program of the AFL, so that the high-water mark of progressive influence in the AFL turned out to be the federation's convention of 1921.

As usual at AFL conventions, the resolutions committee was composed almost entirely of Gompers's allies, and it made full use of its powers to recommend negative votes on resolutions from the left, or to select the most obscurely drafted from among them for presentation to the floor. The bloc votes of major unions allowed 60 to 70 of the 600 or so delegates to cast as many as four-fifths of the votes on a roll call. There was nothing new about that. What was new in 1921 was the fact that the progressive bloc, unlike the prewar Socialists, included several of the men with the largest fistfuls of votes to cast. As the delegates assembled, wrote a reporter for the *Seattle Union Record*, they were astir with predictions of "the coal miners, the railroad workers and the metal trades forming a powerful coalition to secure control of the federation" and to promote "a sweeping program" of "government ownership and democratic control" of American industry.[69] John L. Lewis solicited the support of these delegates for his candidacy to unseat Gompers, and his effort was vigorously backed in all corners of the land by the newspaper chain of William Randolph Hearst. Lewis announced: "I stand for Government ownership of the railroad, nationalization of the mines and other progressive legis-

127; Paul S. Taylor, *The Sailor's Union of the Pacific* (New York, 1923), 134–46, 167–83; *Am. Labor Year Book, 1919–20*, 168–70; *Seattle Union Record*, April 30, May 2, 3, 6, 9, 10, 18, June 14, 20, July 21, 1921. On Benson, see *Who's Who in America*, 17 (Chicago, 1932), 293.

68. Daggett, "Railroad Labor," 59–60.
69. *Seattle Union Record*, June 21, 1921.

lation . . . for health insurance, old-age pensions and unemployment insurance, all progressive measures for the working masses."[70]

Because of the unusually open character of the convention, its debates exposed a great deal about the thinking of trade unionists in 1921, as well as the difficulties encountered by new ideas at AFL conventions. Support for an independent Irish republic was overwhelming, but few delegates were prepared to commit themselves to the Sinn Fein proposal that American unions declare a boycott on all English goods. Only a single delegate, President Benjamin Schlesinger of the International Ladies' Garment Workers' Union, rose to defend Soviet Russia against the Executive Council's denunciations. A resolution proposed by black delegates calling for government action against the growing power of the Ku Klux Klan was brushed aside. More attention was devoted to an appeal from the Women's League for Industrial Rights asking that all unions open their doors to women, but most of the men present were quite content when Anna Fitzgerald of the Label League called the proposal "silly." Lady Barbers Local No. 1 of Seattle fired off a furious telegram responding to Fitzgerald, but it was not represented at the convention. A proposal from the IAM that all metal trades merge into "one compact union" was denounced by the Metal Trades Department as "red." Major debate centered on a vaguely worded resolution from the railroad unions calling for legislation to assure that "those men who contribute their effort to the industry shall enjoy all of the rights, privileges and immunities granted those men who contribute capital . . . in order that the government be instituted for the common good and not for the profit of a class." That zombie-like resurrection of Knights of Labor doctrine passed on a resounding voice vote despite Gompers's opposition.[71]

The event everyone had awaited was the presidential election. In this conflict, Gompers showed that he had not lost his touch as a political manipulator, and the progressive bloc revealed that it had none of the cohesiveness of the prewar Socialist opposition. Gompers and his aides, especially George Perkins, flailed Lewis as a pawn of Hearst, an agent of the IWW and of Judge Gary, and a coward who had cravenly capitulated to federal injunctions in 1919. In all, it was oratorical treatment comparable to that Lewis dealt his foes in UMWA conventions. Gompers divided the ranks of the railroad and metal trades by astute promises of

70. *New York World*, June 24, 1921.
71. *AFL Proceedings*, 1921, 224, 363, 371; *Seattle Union Record*, June 9, 11, 13, 14, 15, 17, 18, 20, 22, 23, 25, 1921; *MMJ*, 33 (September 1921), 748–56; David Saposs, "Out of the Beaten Path," *Survey*, 46 (July 16, 1921), 514–15.

seats on the Executive Council. Most important of all, he drew Socialists of the needle trades to his side, helped by earlier expressions of anti-Semitism from the Indianapolis group, and split the votes of the miners. Delegates Farrington, Howat, and Robert Harlin (who had opposed Lewis for UMWA president in 1920) ignored the frantic pleas of Brophy for unity on behalf of nationalization and used their 1,596 votes to help stop their old enemy from becoming president of the AFL. Gompers was re-elected by a margin of 25,022 to 12,324. He had held solid his support in the building trades (except for the mighty carpenters, who went for Lewis) and the many smaller unions, while splitting the huge blocs that had seemed destined to favor Lewis.[72]

In the long run, however, the devastating impact of the depression on unions in mass-production industries turned Gompers's convention success into a permanent and decisive defeat for progressives in the AFL. By 1923, when the AFL devoted its Portland convention to a celebration of American capitalism and a summons to the movement to drive out its radicals, union membership in America had fallen 25 percent since its 1920 peak. Losses in coal mining cannot be calculated, because the UMWA carried thousands of miners who had been forgiven dues payments so that the union's voting power at AFL conventions might be preserved. In transportation, once the most highly unionized sector of the economy, total union membership had declined 25 percent, the IAM had lost 70 percent of its 1920 members, and textile unions had declined by 75 percent.[73]

To stem this adverse tide, leaders of the machinists, railroad brotherhoods, and stationary engineers sent out to progressive unions and sympathetic organizations a call that led to the formation of the Conference for Progressive Political Action (CPPA). Its executive committee included Johnston of the IAM, Stone of the engineers, Vice-President Green of the miners, Sidney Hillman of the clothing workers, Agnes Nestor of the Women's Trade Union League, and leaders of the Nonpartisan League, the Minnesota Farmer-Labor Party, and the League of Women Voters. What remained of the Socialist Party endorsed the movement, and Morris Hillquit also sat on the executive committee. Although the CPPA made the program of the AFL's progressives its own, calling for nationalization of rails and mines, restoration of civil liberties, and an end to U.S. military intervention in the Caribbean and Central America, it decided against creating a new party. Its mission was to support the election of friendly

72. *AFL Proceedings, 1921,* 449–56; *Seattle Union Record,* June 22, 23, 25, 27, 1921; Saposs, "Beaten Path."
73. My calculations from data in Wolman, *Growth,* 110–19.

Democrats, Republicans, Farmer-Laborites, and Socialists to Congress in the fall elections, an undertaking that turned out to be quite successful. At a meeting of UMWA and railroad-union officials held on February 21, immediately after the end of the CPPA meeting, the sixteen unions represented pledged support to one another but declined to negotiate a pact of mutual strike assistance.[74]

Each union stood alone during the brutal strikes of 1922. No fewer than 1,613,000 men and women struck that year. That number was even greater than the strike turnout of 1916, but the moods surrounding the two strike waves could hardly have been more different. In 1916 there had been great hopes, and the abundance of jobs had unleashed thousands of different strikes, many without union support and many more betraying contagious action, such as the six hundred strikes for an eight-hour day on May 1. Whether they had won or lost in 1916, workers proved more than ready to go out again, and they enlisted still more recruits for an even larger wave in 1917. But 1922 was a year of grimly determined defensive warfare for strikers and was followed by an abrupt decline in strike activity. Strikes were not numerous, but they were huge. They were called by union officials in defense of wages, hours, and union rights that employers were stamping out.[75] City streets, flophouses, and shantytowns teemed with unemployed. All strikers knew that there were many workers eager for employment at the lowered wages the strikers were resisting. The harsh reality they faced was depicted by the poet of Nova Scotia's mines, Dawn Fraser:

> When the mines closed down that winter
> He had nothing left to eat,
> And he starved, he starved, I tell you,
> On your dirty, damned street.[76]

To recount those nearly forgotten battles would require, and deserve, another book. Even before 1922 began, the packinghouse workers had been locked out. The hard winter months soon drove those who could regain their jobs to return to work without a union. Strikes dragged on from January to October in most northern textile centers and some southern urban centers and ended with many proposed wage cuts revoked but with the unions decimated and a fifty-four–hour week restored in much of Rhode Island and New Hampshire. The CCF shut down April 1, and once again tens of thousands of miners who were not covered by the agreement walked out together with those in union

74. *Labor Age*, 11 (March 1922), 24–5; Weinstein, *Decline*, 274–8.
75. *Monthly Labor Review*, 16 (June 1923), 231–9.
76. Dawn Fraser, *Echoes from Labor's War: Industrial Cape Breton in the 1920s* (Toronto, 1976), 29.

strongholds. In the coke regions of Pennsylvania's Somerset County, where control of mines by steel and railroad corporations had preserved the open shop, roving organizers from Brophy's District 2 raced from one mine patch to another, often standing four people back to back to speak in different languages, before mine guards dispersed them. Between sixty thousand and seventy thousand previously unorganized miners and their families responded, many leaving the region, the rest moving to union tent colonies. In July, 400,000 railway workers walked out in the first nationwide rail strike since 1894.[77]

Soldiers swarmed over American industrial towns that spring and summer, patrolling the streets and escorting strikebreakers through angry crowds. In July, President Harding called on mine operators to reopen their pits and offered, in his inimitable style, "such assurances of maintained order and the protection of lawful effort as will give assurance to everybody concerned."[78] A month later his attorney general sought and obtained an injunction prohibiting any assistance by unions to the railroad strikers. Because the unions of train crews, trackmen, and switchyard workers alike had refused to join the shop workers in strike, the injunctions had a devastating impact.[79]

Nevertheless, the strikes were not futile. Although the mine, rail, and especially textile unions suffered prodigious losses of members and contracts, they were not wiped out by the battles of 1922. The fate of the miners illustrates a more general pattern of settlements. In August, the UMWA was able to bring enough large operators in the CCF to the bargaining table to sign an agreement – moreover, an agreement that preserved the 1921 scales, including the $7.50 rate for day men. The price paid for that accomplishment was twofold. First, the international union abandoned the previously unorganized miners who had struck in response to its call, leaving Brophy's district to carry on alone until July 1923, when it finally surrendered after sixteen months of striking. Second, the maintenance of high wage scales in the CCF not only accelerated the shift in production southward but also drove unionized mines to rapid mechanization, or out of business. By 1925, only 40 percent of the country's bituminous coal was mined under union contract, as compared with 72 percent in 1919, and the unionized sector remained under intense

77. Barrett, "Work and Community," 370–414; *Monthly Labor Review,* 16 (May 1923), 13–36; Wyckoff, *Wage Policies,* 88–98; Blankenhorn, *Strike for Union;* Commons, *History of Labour,* IV, 515–25; Perlman, *Machinists,* 56–60.
78. Quoted in Wyckoff, *Wage Policies,* 95.
79. Commons, *History of Labour,* IV, 519–22; Lecht, *Railway Labor Legislation,* 42–4.

pressure to reduce labor costs.[80] To preserve his agreements with the unionized firms, President Lewis abruptly jettisoned all talk of nationalization and thirty-hour weeks and drove his more radical rivals out of office – indeed, out of the union. On September 15, 1922, the *United Mine Workers' Journal* initiated a six-part series entitled "Exposé of Communist Revolutionary Movement in Effort to Seize America." The first target of the campaign was Brophy. As for the report *How to Run Coal,* Lewis publicly ignored it, while leaving *Journal* editor Ellis Searles to denounce it as "prepared largely by a bunch of Greenwich Village reds who do not belong to the United Mine Workers of America."[81]

In short, the UMWA remained larger in 1923 than it had been before 1916, but the steam of working-class hopes and daring had gone out of its engines. Like other unions that had ridden the currents of desire unleashed among working people by the war, it now sought self-preservation in tight collaboration with those companies that still bargained with it. The major unions in textiles and clothing encouraged efficiency schemes that labor had once universally denounced, in an effort to keep union-label firms in operation.[82] The Baltimore and Ohio plan, by which the IAM and other shop-craft unions committed their members to participate in productivity committees at every level in return for that railroad's agreement to maintain union standards and perform repair work in its own shops, emerged from the rail strike of 1922 to provide the new model for up-to-date union practice.[83] The plan enjoyed special popularity in unions of the progressive bloc. It offered them hope for survival while they pursued political action aimed at restoring the type of friendly government they had known in 1917 and 1918.

80. Blankenhorn, *Strike for Union,* 115–72; Wyckoff, *Wage Policies,* 95–8; Harry A. Millis, *How Collective Bargaining Works: A Survey of Experience in Leading American Industries* (New York, 1942), 264.

81. Statement to press from Ellis Searles, January 29, 1923 (Brophy Papers, Box A5-1, Catholic University of America). Oscar Ameringer remarked that "the impetuous Ellis Searles" had never been inside a coal mine. *Illinois Miner,* February 3, 1923.

82. Steve Fraser, "Dress Rehearsal for the New Deal: Shop-Floor Insurgents, Political Elites, and Industrial Democracy in the Amalgamated Clothing Workers," in Frisch and Walkowitz, *Working-Class America,* 212–55; Jesse T. Carpenter, *Competition and Collective Bargaining in the Needle Trades, 1910–1967* (Ithaca, N.Y., 1972), 72–89, 462–513, 535–45; Nadworny, *Scientific Management,* 120–37.

83. *Bulletin of the Taylor Society,* 11 (February 1926), 6–25; H. Dubreuil, *Standards: le travail américain vu par un ouvrier français* (Paris, 1929), 350–88; Thomas R. Brooks, *Clint: A Biography of a Labor Intellectual, Clinton S. Golden* (New York, 1978), 100–6.

Because so many of their activists refused to abandon the dreams that had inspired them in the heady postwar days, however, international officers pursuing this Fabian strategy resorted to autocratic control of their own organizations. Beleaguered unions clinging to minority sectors of their industries, surrounded by a hostile open-shop environment and governed by ruthless suppression of dissent within their own ranks – that was the legacy of 1922. Most men and women who punched in daily to tightly supervised jobs where no union steward was to be found at all felt lucky to have the income. Business's successful mobilization for the "world contest of peace succeeding that of war" had persuaded them that to desire more was folly.

9

"A maximum of publicity with a minimum of interference"

From East Pittsburgh to Ludlow, the maturing of modern corporate management had stimulated various forms of employee organization within the workplace. The government's wartime quest for total mobilization of the American people's hearts, minds, and energies had prompted its administrative agencies not only to promote national standards of wages and hours but also to encourage corporate managers to bargain with elected representatives of their employees. In one form or another, the shop committee or works council had appeared in many enterprises by 1920 as the unanticipated companion of the efficiency expert. It was cultivated simultaneously by corporate executives, officials of the federal government, AFL leaders, and socialist militants. Because each of those promoters had quite different purposes in mind, the shop committee emerged at the close of the war as a theater within which struggles for workers' control based on total organization of all workers at the point of production clashed with employers' efforts to exclude unions from their enterprises, and both clashed with the government's search for a mechanism to mediate industrial disputes and improve productivity. The consolidation of scientific management was thus achieved in a manner far different from what Frederick Winslow Taylor had predicted, but one that decisively shaped the contours of American social life during the 1920s and the nature of the industrial unionism that ultimately emerged in the 1930s.

Although 225 works councils were in operation by the fall of 1919, a survey of eighteen major corporations undertaken by the Bureau of Industrial Research in 1919 described their development as "still unproved and tentative" and recognized that their "relation to the spontaneously democratic activities of organized labor [was] still unsettled."[1] Despite the uncertainty, however, many leading corporate executives had been persuaded of the wisdom of Mackenzie King's 1915 advice to Rockefel-

---

1. Bing, *War-Time Strikes*, 164n; Bureau of Industrial Research, *American Company Shop Committee Plans* (New York, 1919), iii.

ler that some institution of collective consultation between representatives of the workers and local works managers could ensure "that cordial cooperation which is likely to further industrial efficiency" and provide the company "a maximum of publicity with a minimum of interference in all that pertains to the conditions of employment."[2]

King's ideas had been recast in wartime rhetoric by Walter Gordon Merritt in a series of articles written first for *Iron Age* and then published in book form under the title *Factory Solidarity or Class Solidarity?* Merritt framed his argument with a critique of both Taylorism and trade unions. Taylor's attempt to end employers' dependence on their workers' initiative had proved futile, he contended, because one "cannot standardize or commandeer carefulness." National unions, for their part, were a "more or less bureaucratic agency" that attempted to impose on the enterprise from without the "conditions which the outsiders believe to be for their best interest." This depiction of a union as a third party, interfering in the relations between employees and managers, was buttressed by arguments learned from revolutionary syndicalists, including quotations from Hubert Lagardelle. Industrial democracy had to be built "from the ground up," starting with the workplace. The manufacturing establishment, Merritt concluded,

> ... is the normal unit of economic self-interest for the workers. If, by reason of closer co-operation and greater mutuality of interest, the workers' loyalty to the individual company were to become stronger than his sense of class consciousness and class solidarity, then ipso facto the class conflict and social disunion as we now see it will disappear.[3]

For him, as for King, mechanisms for employee representation could function properly only to the degree that they were decentralized, unencumbered by outside agencies like unions or arbitrators, which impeded resolution of disputes on the spot, and guided by up-to-date local managers who realized the value of a steady flow of information from the front office to acquaint both the employees and the community in which they lived with the goals, problems, and larger plans of the firm. Merritt had no more desire than John Calder had had before the war to make the employer's "possibilities of shop management the subject of a referendum," but he did believe that once managers had imposed standards everywhere, the "perfect team play" that Brandeis had predicted did not come about of its own accord: It had to be deliberately organized as part

2. West, *Colorado Strike*, 161–3.
3. Walter G. Merritt, *Factory Solidarity or Class Solidarity?* (second edition, reprinted from *Iron Age*, n.p., n.d.); the quotations are on pp. 21, 34, and 49.

of the enterprise's managerial apparatus. His way of thinking was reinforced by the writings of industrial psychologists, such as Frank Watts, Ordway Tead, and Henri de Man, who repudiated Taylor's fixation on the pursuit of monetary gain by the individual worker and stressed instead the role of "irrational" drives and of the "herd instinct" in workers' motivation. The war had exposed workers' desire to "participate" in the direction of the enterprise and to perceive their own place in the larger scheme of things. It had also revealed that mere wage increases did not leave workers contented, but tempted them to demand more. Employers should learn to harness workers' irrepressible sense of "common purpose" to the welfare of the firm and to solid citizenship in the community, wrote Frank Watts: "For the manager, then, who dislikes the mob, the way to counteract its evil influences is to organize groups of various kinds within his works, or better, to encourage his workers to join suitable clubs, circles or societies outside."[4]

Reason, which had been celebrated by nineteenth-century liberals and socialists alike as the human capacity to comprehend and deliberately transform material and social reality, was reduced by Tead and his colleagues to the "instinct of curiosity." It took a proper place among the instincts that managers had to manipulate, along with the "instinct of workmanship" and the "instinct of self-assertion." Two other "innate drives" were especially noteworthy. One was the "instinct of acquisitiveness," which inspired in workers not the aspiration to become shop owners, as nineteenth-century writers would have had it, but the "sense of property rights in jobs," which was manifested by unions' struggles for the closed shop and control of layoffs. The other was the "instinct of submissiveness," which de Man considered erotic in nature. This instinct explained for Tead the entrapment of the working class within the obsolete formulas of the AFL or the chiliasm of socialists. The "discontent among manual workers" and the "underlying trend to orthodoxy and submissiveness in working-class opinion" were for Tead "really obverse sides of the same phenomenon."[5]

In short, to those in business who were enthusiasts for employee rep-

---

4. Frank Watts, *An Introduction to the Psychological Problems of Industry* (London, 1921), as reproduced in Douglas, Hitchcock, and Atkins, *Worker in Economic Society*, 35. For the quotations from Calder and Brandeis, see Chapter 5, footnotes 100 and 114. See also Alberto Cambrosio, "Quand le psychologie fait son entrée a l'usine: sélection et contrôle des ouvriers aux Etats-Unis pendant les années 1910," *Le Mouvement Social*, 113 (October–December 1980), 37–65.

5. Tead, *Instincts*, 11, 70–1, 200; Henri de Man, *Joy in Work*, translated by Eden and Cedar Paul (London, 1929), 43–5.

resentation, works councils and managers trained in industrial psychology were inseparable. Both were as important to the firm's productivity as they were to its harmonious operation. A report from the Special Conference Committee in 1929 summed up the experience of the previous decade:

> No representation plan is good enough to run itself. .... The plans which have the highest measure of success are those in which responsible executives have taken an active and continuing interest and to which they have furnished enlightened guidance. Employee representation, in fact, furnishes an effective means through which management can exercise its normal function of leadership over the working force.[6]

The problem that confronted such "responsible executives" in 1919, however, was that government agencies, the AFL, and revolutionary activists were also furnishing guidance to representation plans. Each group placed its conception of workplace organization in the context of its own larger social objectives. The NWLB established eighty-six shop committees during 1918, and the Shipbuilding Labor Adjustment Board another thirty-one, in addition to various forms of worker representation encouraged by the railroad, fuel, and army clothing administrations. Those created by the NWLB were the most controversial, because they were in private rather than government-operated enterprises, and because they appeared to be permanent innovations in industrial relations, rather than simply emergency war measures.[7] In fact, most of the corporate employee-representation plans that existed in 1920 had been instituted under government orders and subsequently modified to conform to the pattern preferred by management.

The NWLB was committed to the principles of no change in existing standards and no discrimination against employees because of union membership. The latter rule encouraged rapid growth of union membership in major corporations, despite their frequent violations of it. The former prevented even Cochairman Frank Walsh from insisting that firms recognize unions, where they had not done so before the war. It quickly became apparent to the board members, however, that grievances over wages, dismissals, and transfers were difficult to resolve without some bargaining among the people directly involved. Especially at Bethlehem Steel, the largest ordnance works in the land, the complex wage structures created since the days of Taylor and Gantt confounded efforts to resolve them by administrative decrees from Washington, and the incessant strikes of early 1918 were stimulated as much by the company's refusal to bargain with the workers as by monetary demands. Conse-

6. Quoted in Jacoby, "Industrial Internal Labor Markets," 29.
7. Bing, *War-Time Strikes*, 161–4; Conner, *NWLB*, 108–25.

quently, when the board handed down its award on July 31, it not only abolished the hated bonus system and issued guidelines for wage increases but also ordered the election of a shop committee, which was mandated to negotiate with management the application of the award's wage guidelines to specific groups of workers.

Elections for representatives were conducted at work, but under the supervision of NWLB examiners, in each of the many machine shops, blast furnaces, forges, and other departments of Bethlehem Steel. The elected men and women were commissioned to deal with grievances in their own departments and to establish departmental committees, and also to select from among their number three representatives to sit on a joint board with three company representatives, hear unresolved disputes, and work out the details of applying the July award. The chairman of that board was the NWLB examiner, R. B. Gregg. Five days after the armistice, however, President Grace of Bethlehem Steel informed the examiner that the award, in his opinion, "was dead." At that time, fewer than five hundred of the thirty-two thousand workers had actually had their new wage rates and benefits put into effect. Grace refused outright to meet with the machinists' committee, because it was constituted almost entirely of IAM members, and later he protested that the workers' three representatives to the joint board were also union-controlled. Bethlehem Steel, Grace explained, was about to establish its own employee-representation plan and would welcome no interference from Washington.[8]

A protracted battle subsequently began with the postwar layoffs of thousands of workers, including many committee members, and ended only with the great strike of September 1919. Although a shop-committee structure acceptable to the company and the expiring NWLB was finally worked out by May 1, 1919, its inability to resolve any major issues led the committee's members to declare their adherence to the National Committee for Organizing the Iron and Steel Workers and subsequently to make the Bethlehem mills one of the strongholds of the national strike. When the strike was defeated, however, the company re-formed the committee without governmental or union interference. In the new structure, 125 representatives were selected by departments, and they elected an executive committee. That committee was divided into five functional groups, each of which met with an equal number of management repre-

8. E. B. Woods, "Memorandum Regarding Bethlehem Steel Company Award" (Sweeney files); telegram, R. B. Gregg to W. H. Taft, December 6, 1918; memorandum, Lieut. F. H. Bird, Office of the Chief of Ordnance, to Dr. Lucien W. Cheney, n.d., all in NWLB Administrative File B56, R.G. 2, National Archives.

sentatives. In this way, safety, housing, athletics, and welfare were assigned to separate channels of negotiation. There was no NWLB examiner to oversee and arbitrate. There were no government standards of
wages and hours to apply.[9]

The crucial features of the NWLB plans to which business objected
were the oversight role of government examiners and the general standards developed by the board in its attempt to infuse some coherence
into its many awards and to reduce labor turnover by making wages
similar everywhere. By July 1918, its quest for uniformity had led the
board to decree equal pay for men and women on equivalent jobs and to
calculate a minimum wage and a "comfort budget" based on cost-of-
living surveys, for application in subsequent awards. Moreover, at the
instigation of Felix Frankfurter of the War Labor Policies Committee,
representatives of the Metal Trades Department of the AFL and of the
National Industrial Conference Board (NICB) negotiated between May
and August 1918 a plan for a federal board to stabilize and control wages,
hours, and conditions in the metal trades nationally. Again the armistice
brought the scheme to a halt. On November 21 the NICB withdrew its
nominees and its approval from the proposed board.[10]

Government sponsorship of labor standards and shop committees thus
met with delaying operations from business before the armistice and open
repudiation afterward. It was enthusiastically acclaimed, however, by many
progressive writers and by the reconstruction committees of the Catholic
and Protestant churches. Ray Stannard Baker reminded his readers in 1920
of "that sudden lift of common effort, common enthusiasm, which for a
moment fired the soul of America," and assured them that while one
might "mourn over the reaction, and the present wave of unrest, . . .
nothing can ever rob us of that great moment, nor wipe out the effect of
it." Former NWLB examiner W. L. Stoddard foresaw in June 1919 shop
committees and joint industrial councils "sooner or later covering the
nation." The "appalling menace of Bolshevism has called a truce to the
internecine strife between labor and capital," he explained, "and all our
energies are bent rather to the task of cooperation."[11] Similar reasoning

9. Interviews with J. W. Hendricks, Mr. McConlogue, and Max Connor (Sa-
    poss Papers, Box 21); Robert Peles, "Labor Interlude – Johnstown 1919"
    (unpublished M.A. paper, University of Pittsburgh, n.d.).
10. Conner, *NWLB*, 51–67; Metal Trades Board, Entry 2, Correspondence of
    the Chairman and of the Executive Secretary. Records of the War Policies
    Board, R.G. 1, National Archives.
11. Ray Stannard Baker, *The New Industrial Unrest: Reasons and Remedies*
    (Garden City, N.Y., 1920), 151–2; W. L. Stoddard, "Committee System in
    American Shops," in Daniel Bloomfield, ed., *Selected Articles on Modern
    Industrial Movements* (New York, 1920), 170–1.

led the National Catholic War Council to urge that both the NWLB and shop committees be continued after the end of the war. A legal minimum wage, social-security legislation, government housing, grants of land to war veterans, and removal of women workers from industry were its other proposals for postwar social peace.[12] A study sponsored by the Federal Council of Churches of Christ in America and the General War-Time Commission of Churches put more stress on enlightened business leadership and less on the dismissal of women workers than the Catholics had done. It welcomed the initiatives of Rockefeller and King toward reducing the conflict "between classes – which is obviously unserviceable and disastrous." Public works, payment of "a living wage," and protection of women in industry through good management, wage and hour laws, and union involvement were the proposals Protestants appended to a call for "democratic management" and collective bargaining in any form – with or without trade-union participation.[13]

To leaders of the AFL, the nature of union participation was the essential criterion by which they judged all shop committees. A resolution introduced by the AFL Executive Council at the 1918 convention voiced approval of new forms of workplace organization and linked them explicitly to wartime drives for higher productivity. It called for a "committee of the workers" to be established "in all large permanent shops," with the two tasks of conferring with the management "over matters of production" and carrying "any important grievance" over wages, hours, or conditions beyond the foreman to the general manager's office. The resolution's mention of the workers' interest in "increasing output" sounded a novel note in AFL deliberations, but the emphasis was on the workers' initiative, not that of management. "Control brings with it responsibility," the Executive Council declared.[14] Its way of thinking was evidently in harmony with those of Felix Frankfurter, Frank Walsh, and the National Catholic War Council.

Nevertheless, the reconstruction program adopted by the AFL convention made no mention of shop committees or of continuing the operation of agencies like the NWLB. Rather, it contrasted the principles of democratic citizenship that governed America's political life with the autocracy prevailing in industry. Working life could be democratized only by trade unions, the program asserted. It was, therefore, "essential that

12. National Catholic War Council, "Reconstruction Program," in Bloomfield, *Modern Industrial Movements,* 335–52.
13. Committee on the War and Religious Outlook, *The Church and Industrial Reconstruction* (New York, 1920); the quotations are on pp. 102 and 156. It is noteworthy that this document did not equate "the living wage" with a male wage. It took women's wage earning for granted.
14. Commons, *Trade Unionism and Labor Problems, Second Series,* 345–6.

workers everywhere should insist upon their right to organize into trade-unions, and that effective legislation should be enacted which would make it a criminal offense for any employer to interfere with or hamper the exercise of this right or to interfere with the legitimate activities of trade-unions."[15]

Prosperity and social welfare depended, according to the program, on "a living wage for all wage-earners, skilled or unskilled – a wage which will enable the worker and his family to live in health and comfort, provide a competence for illness and old age, and afford to all the opportunity of cultivating the best that is within mankind."[16] In contrast to the Catholic program, there was no call for legislated social insurance here, nor was there a demand for the expulsion of women from industry. Rather, the AFL program reasserted the demand for "equal pay" to women performing "equal work." It coupled that call, however, with an emphasis on women's "potential motherhood," which should not be jeopardized by "tasks disproportionate to their physical strength," and which had clearly been implicit in the formulation of the "living wage" demand. Central to the AFL's approach, therefore, was the conviction that the standards to be introduced into the workplace should be determined and enforced by trade unions, not by governmental agencies. The program had been drafted by five of the most articulate traditionalists in the AFL leadership (Matthew Woll, John Frey, Bert Jewell, John Moore, and George W. Perkins), as its strong denunciation of a labor party and its avoidance of the issue of government ownership of mines and railroads made clear.[17]

AFL leaders who remained devoted to the "tried and true ways" of Gompers and the Executive Council believed that the decisive contribution of the government to their wartime gains in membership were its agencies' reliance on union wage scales to set local standards and its protection against dismissal for union membership. Taken together, those measures had made it less rewarding and more difficult for employers to combat unions. By comparison, government sponsorship of shop committees offered them little. No such committees operated in the building trades, and few in the printing trades or textiles. State encouragement to pit committees in the mines had been far more useful to left-wing rebel movements than to the UMWA's officialdom. Because the needle trades had major garment centers well unionized by 1917, the government had worked through the unions to foster labor peace and productivity. It was

15. Ibid., 563.   16. Ibid., 565.
17. Ibid., 565, 568–9; Taft, *AFL*, 369. Some points in the AFL program, such as the housing proposals and the demands for land for veterans, did echo the Catholic program.

above all the metal-trades unions that had to cope directly with the shop committees instituted by the NWLB and the Shipbuilding Labor Adjustment Board.

Economists Paul H. Douglas and F. E. Wolfe examined the committees of the shipyards and concluded, "They cannot be said to have been a success, in actual operation, except in one district."[18] Employment in the yards under government supervision had soared from 88,000 when the Emergency Fleet Corporation was created in October 1917 to 385,000 in November 1918. Despite their energetic and successful recruiting efforts, trade unionists in the yards felt themselves in peril of being swamped by newcomers – as happened to union carpenters in East Coast yards where wooden antisubmarine craft were built. Consequently, they suspected employers of using committee elections to elevate antiunion representatives. Moreover, everyone foresaw an abrupt decline in employment at the war's end, which would make it easy for a company to dismiss union members if they did not have some contractual control over the layoff process. And finally, the craft jurisdictions of the unions were threatened by the departmental form of representation found in the board's plans. Members of many crafts worked virtually side by side in building ships, not separated into different buildings or shops. Consequently, at the war's end, the Metal Trades Department opened a major campaign to convert shop committees into craft committees corresponding to union jurisdictions and to wrest formal union recognition from the employers. Bethlehem Shipbuilding and American Shipbuilding were among the companies then added, for a few years, to the older closed-shop domain of San Francisco and Puget Sound.[19]

Trade unionists' proclivity to perceive shop committees as employers' instruments, to be infiltrated, smashed, and replaced with closed-shop craft unionism wherever possible, gained strength during the battles of 1919. It was openly expressed in a resolution adopted by that year's AFL convention. The resolution was introduced by the National Committee for Organizing the Iron and Steel Workers, and its denunciation of shop committees as they had developed in the steel industry followed exactly the lines of criticism that many workers at Bethlehem Steel later offered investigators from the Interchurch World Movement. It singled out "the Rockefeller plan" as the enemy. Committees based on that model were "a snare and a delusion . . . and we advise our members to have nothing

---

18.   Commons, *Trade Unionism and Labor Problems, Second Series,* 319.

19.   Ibid., 311–44; Commons, *Industrial Government,* 353–5; Bruce Scavuzzo, "The United Brotherhood of Carpenters and Joiners of America: A Case Study, Essex County, New Jersey, 1915–1919" (unpublished senior history essay, Yale University, 1985).

to do with them." The resolution continued, "We demand the right to
bargain collectively through the only kind of organization fitted for this
purpose – the trade-union – and we stand loyally together until this right
is conceded us."[20]

A perceptibly more optimistic response to both shop committees and
governmental standards was to be found among union leaders of the
progressive bloc. By the end of the war, as we have seen, important leaders of the unions of miners, railway workers, garment workers, electricians, and machinists, as well as leaders of city trades assemblies in Chicago, Seattle, Minneapolis, and elsewhere, had committed their efforts to
the general goals of creating a labor party, nationalizing mines and railroads, pushing welfare legislation through Congress, coordinating the
bargaining and strike activities of different unions, and enrolling relatively unskilled men and women from their industries into union ranks.
During the war they had found most federal agencies helpful to their
goals – with the notable exception of the adamantly antiunion postmas-
ter general's office. In open-shop metal-fabricating enterprises, especially,
the NWLB's shop committees provided a vehicle for enlarging the scope
of craft unions beyond the exclusive boundaries of their nineteenth-century
constitutions. The pattern illustrated by Bridgeport's city-wide elections
for worker representatives under NWLB auspices was often repeated:
Prominent trade unionists were elected to the dominant positions in the
committees. Moreover, metal-trade activists often succeeded in making
local metal-trades councils into effective agencies for coordinating the
various craft unions. Under those circumstances, shop committees provided a vehicle through which craft unions were linked to the nonunion
majority of employees, every worker had access to some representation
in dealing with the company, and the more progressively minded and
experienced trade unionists among the skilled men had organized channels of communication with the women and unskilled men of their factories.[21]

20. Commons, *Trade Unionism and Labor Problems, Second Series*, 347–8;
     the quotations are on p. 348. Secretary Foster of the national committee
     later told investigators of the Interchurch World Movement that "trade
     unions [could] function in connection" with shop committees that were
     genuinely elected by the workers, even if the companies would not meet
     with union officers in negotiations. "Testimony before the Interchurch
     Commission," typescript in Saposs Papers, Box 26, p. 11. O. F. Carpenter
     described the destruction of a shop committee by a union. Commons, *In-
     dustrial Government*, 114–24.
21. On Bridgeport, see Bucki, "Dilution and Craft Tradition"; Montgomery,
     Workers' Control, 127–34.

This broadening of the trade unions' base through workplace organization met an enthusiastic welcome not only from people like Frank Walsh and Ray Stannard Baker but also from noteworthy industrial psychologists who were simultaneously active in personnel-management circles, and even members of the Taylor Society. Ordway Tead, for example, was a regular participant in conferences of the Intercollegiate Socialist Society and its successor, the League for Industrial Democracy, where he praised both management's encouragement of "worker participation" and the program of AFL progressives. Both developments seemed to him to foreshadow a future organization of decentralized joint government of industrial life by workers and corporate managers, as suggested by Britain's Guild Socialist movement.[22] Arthur Gleason, Robert Bruère, Evans Clark, and Stuart Chase had similar hopes. More remarkable was the drift of Morris L. Cooke, Otto Beyer, Fred J. Miller, and even, in his own crusty way, Henry Gantt to the conviction that a thoroughly unionized work force led by officers of broad social vision might be the key to organized collaboration of managers and workers for the elimination of waste and inefficiency. Ironically, once scientific management had become standard industrial practice and blended with professionalized personnel management, the handful of pioneers still meeting in the Taylor Society had become friends of progressive unionism.[23]

As early as the war years, the Amalgamated Clothing Workers of America (ACWA) had effectively linked thorough unionization, workplace organization, standardization of methods and pay, cooperation with employers to improve productivity, militant strikes to improve conditions, and a political program embracing both welfare legislation and friendship for revolutionary Russia. Despite widespread protests, especially from older cutters, pressers, and tailors, that their union's encouragement of standardization was undermining, not increasing, their collective power in the shops, the union's 1920 convention endorsed the program as a step toward workers' control of the industry. Mary Gawthorpe, educational director from the Rochester stronghold of the ACWA, argued that the union was "bringing to the workers' hands and brains every experience that is necessary to full and complete responsibility and ownership of the industry." The coupling of scientific management to workplace organization under union direction, she explained, "leads directly through the progressive steps of recognition of the union, increased

22. *Intercollegiate Socialist,* 7 (February–March 1919), 31–3. On Guild Socialism, see G. D. H. Cole, *Chaos and Order in Industry* (New York, 1920); Cole, *Workshop Organization* (Oxford, 1923).
23. Haber, *Efficiency and Uplift,* 134–67; Nadworny, *Scientific Management;* Henry L. Gantt, *Organizing for Work* (New York, 1919).

wages, shorter hours, voice and vote in the shop as well as in the union, practical education through shop and union committees, to a desire for more and more education and the larger life."[24]

The paradoxical marriage of progressive unionism and scientific management produced its most famous offspring in the Baltimore and Ohio plan. Progressives among the local and national officers of the sixteen unions of railway workers, as we have seen, had committed their energies by the war's end to public ownership of the railroads, alliances among railway unions and between those unions and the mine workers, union-owned banks and insurance companies to mobilize the financial resources provided by the members' dues and savings, promotion of cooperative stores and factories, and above all, a political alliance of workers and farmers, out of which they hoped would emerge an effective farmer-labor party. No matter how irate progressives like J. F. Anderson and Andrew McNamara of the IAM may have been at the conservatism of Gompers and the AFL Executive Council, they remained unequivocally committed to seeking their goals through the existing trade unions. They viewed the celebration of workers' "mass action" by Wobblies and early Communists as mindless adventurism that would only make it easy for open-shop businessmen to destroy everything organized workers had accomplished for themselves during this century, and experience had convinced them that only the mantle of legitimacy provided by membership in the AFL could bring more conservative trade unionists to their support during bitter struggles. Between the end of the war and the formation of the Conference for Progressive Political Action in February 1922, their strategy seemed to be working, despite the shop-craft unions' heavy loss of membership in the manufacturing sector during the depression. The shop-craft strike of 1922 changed all that. Despite the refusal of the brotherhoods and the maintenance-of-way unions to join the action, 400,000 members of six shop crafts, led by the IAM, struck every major railroad in the land. Within two weeks the federal Railway Labor Board had branded the strike illegal, urged the railroads to form company unions, and deprived every striker who refused to return to work of all seniority rights. At the end of August, Attorney General Harry Daugherty applied for his famous injunction that prohibited any activity encouraging the strike. In this context, President Daniel Willard of the Baltimore and Ohio

24. *Socialist Review,* 9 (August 1920), 108–9; William M. Leiserson, "Collective Bargaining and Its Effects on Production," in Furnis, *Labor Problems,* 354–67; Steve Fraser, "Dress Rehearsal for the New Deal: Shop-Floor Insurgents, Political Elites, and Industrial Democracy in the Amalgamated Clothing Workers," in Frisch and Walkowitz, *Working-Class America,* 212–55.

(B&O) proposed that each union negotiate separately with each railroad on the basis of restoring seniority rights and earnings as they had existed on the eve of the strike. Reluctantly the union leaders agreed, and enough major lines signed contracts one by one to save the jobs and unions of 225,000 strikers. Another 175,000, however, were forced to renounce their unions and join employee-representation plans, in a pattern set by the Pennsylvania Railroad.[25]

As was typical of the great strikes of 1922, workers' militancy in the face of depression and a hostile government had saved their unions from destruction, but those unions emerged shrunken and humbled, in an open-shop environment. Even where repair workers had retained their unions, they saw work systematically sent out of their shops to nonunion sub-contractors. This context lent special significance to President Willard's larger design. Since 1921, he had been discussing with various union leaders proposals of the Taylor Society's Otto S. Beyer, Jr., for drawing on the workers' collective wisdom in order to eliminate waste and reduce costs in B&O repair work. Legitimate unions were a better agency for institutionalizing cooperation between labor and management than company unions, Beyer argued, because the latter lacked both the strength to assure workers that they would not suffer from increased productivity and the "capacity, leadership and power of initiative to mobilize the collective facilities of their members to cooperate effectively with management."[26] Beyer's plan was to authorize a committee of union members from each craft in each shop of the B&O to bring to the local managers its proposals for saving materials, fuel, and work time, improving safety and sanitation, and reforming work methods, while district and international officers of the union would discuss topics such as transfer and retrenchment policies with their designated counterparts in management. The plan offered two widely celebrated advantages for the workers: Company pledges not to subcontract repair work out of the shops gave them some job security, and anyone who wished to participate in the plan had to join a union to do it. Complaints from many workers that the railroad consistently refused to translate any of its savings into wage increases and that the company secured the employment of some workers by designating many others as temporary hands without seniority rights failed to deter quite widespread worker participation in the plan, which continued to function into the 1930s. Although opposition to the scheme from both radicals and conservatives in the IAM almost cost President

25. Commons, *History of Labour*, IV, 517–23.
26. *Bulletin of the Taylor Society*, 11 (February 1926), 7; Dubreuil, *Standards*, 350–88. The tone of Dubreuil's account of the plan was changed in the English translation: Dubreuil, *Robots or Men?*

Johnston reelection in 1925, the AFL hailed it as the model for future cooperation between organized labor and business. After 1925, federation officers openly approached General Electric, Ford, and other large corporations with offers to improve their efficiency through unionization. Company executives were not interested.[27]

What is noteworthy, especially in view of the fierce denunciations of "class collaboration" heaped on the B&O plan by the Left after 1923, is that its earliest champions were not AFL traditionalists, but progressives. Clinton Golden and Emil John "Jack" Lever of the IAM in Philadelphia, who were leading advocates of nationalization, a labor party, amalgamation of crafts into industrial unions, and the workers' education movement, defended the B&O plan in rhetoric similar to that used to justify the ACWA program by Gawthorpe: as a means for "teaching workers the technique and management of their own industry," and revealing through their systematic attack on waste in industry "the validity of their attack on the present Capitalist System." Although the "fundamental conflict" between workers and employers could never be eliminated "as long as the present system endures," President Jewell of the AFL Railway Employees Department added, there were other daily questions, "not so fundamental, where there can be a degree of cooperation between worker and employer that may result in *some measure* of benefits to both."[28] In a speech to the Taylor Society in 1926, Jewell linked the plan to the railway unions' political action in a way that anticipated the New Deal. If Congress were to enact the bill then before it to institutionalize collective bargaining on the railroads (the Railway Labor Act of 1926), he said, it would lay the foundation "for the most far-reaching development yet achieved in any industry through genuine cooperation between employees and managements."[29]

---

27. *Bulletin of the Taylor Society,* 11 (February 1926), 6–29; Slichter, *Union Policies and Industrial Management,* 437–79; *AFL Proceedings, 1923,* 31–4; William English Walling, *American Labor and American Democracy* (2 vols. bound as one, New York, 1926), II, 42–7; Foster, *Misleaders of Labor,* 75–80.

28. All quotations are from Brooks, *Clint,* 101, 104. On Golden and Lever, see Solon De Leon, ed., *American Labor Who's Who* (New York, 1925), 88, 135.

29. *Bulletin of the Taylor Society,* 11 (February 1926), 21. On the influence of the B&O plan, see also Benjamin Stolberg, "Some Neglected Factors in Trade Union Capitalism," in Harry W. Laidler and Norman Thomas, eds., *New Tactics in Social Conflict* (New York, 1926), 52–64.

Shop stewards and revolution

The left wing of the workers' movement shared the progressives' enthusiasm for workplace organization, but its conception of the political significance and purpose of shop committees diverged more sharply from that of the progressives with each passing year. Since the prewar heyday of the IWW in the United States and revolutionary syndicalism in Europe, many politicized workers had been convinced that the great modern factory was not only the ultimate achievement of capitalism but also its Achilles' heel. Like Fred Merrick's comrades at Westinghouse, they thought that the exploitation of tens of thousands of men and women by a single firm in one place had made possible the mobilization of direct action on a scale that would eclipse the role of electoral politics or even armed insurrections in bringing about socialism. They also believed that the modern enterprise had rendered craft unions obsolete and their "tried and true ways" only a contemptible deterrent to the revolutionary potentialities seething inside the factory gates. The appearance of workers' councils in Russia and Germany, and even in the creameries of Limerick in Ireland, had strengthened that faith, and the wartime rise of a shop stewards' movement in Britain's factories and shipyards impressed many as a model of workplace organization suited to American conditions. By 1919, "council" and "delegate" were words with revolutionary resonance similar to what "convention" and "citizen" had carried in 1789.

Charles Ruthenberg, the Ohio Socialist leader and future communist, caught this mood in his 1917 pamphlet *Are We Growing Toward Socialism?* He inverted the familiar Debsian argument that the democratic character of American government should be extended to industrial life through state-sponsored collectivization. "Collectivism is the inevitable outcome of the existing system of production," said Ruthenberg. "Democracy must be fought for and won through the power of the working class." That task could not be accomplished without a political movement to control the police, military, and legislative powers of the state, but it also required a campaign to establish democratic rule in the workplace itself. So potent had workers' struggles for "control of industry" become "that the great capitalists themselves are organizing the workers within various industries and giving them some small share in the management," as illustrated by a current rage for representation schemes in Cleveland. Whatever their origins, "the industrial organizations . . . will assume greater and greater power, as they realize their strength, and play a large part in establishing the future industrial democracy," just as Europe's parliaments had steadily wrested more and more power from the monarchs.[30]

When the Communist Party of America was founded in 1919, its first program rang with calls for "mass action," which was "industrial in its origin," but acquired "political character . . . in the form of general political strikes and demonstrations," and for "councils of workers" to "be organized in the shops as circumstances allow, for the purpose of carrying on the industrial union struggle within the old unions."[31] The summons to workers to organize on the job and select their own delegates resounded not only from the two communist parties but also from the "crusaders" of the Illinois coalfields, the shop delegates' movement among women's garment workers, striking railway switchmen and maritime workers in 1919, Brooklyn's Micrometer Lodge of the IAM, and the new United Automobile, Aircraft, and Vehicle Workers Union, which recruited forty thousand members in 1919.[32] Some of its advocates adhered to the disintegrating Socialist Party, others to the SLP, to the Wobblies, to the Russian Workers' Union, or to the One Big Union; many moved freely about between one group and another. Party manifestos of the time, to be sure, emphasized the lines of demarcation among political groups, and they could attack each other fiercely indeed. Nevertheless, a perceptive analysis by the Office of Naval Intelligence of its spies' reports from Baltimore, Boston, New York, Buffalo, Erie, Seattle, and other ports in 1918 had concluded that "mixed locals" had sprung up in all those cities, inspired by a common optimism and encouraged to local self-reliance and minimization of party loyalties by the government's effective suppression of communications between national headquarters and their members.

> No matter whether a man's pet hobby be "Home Rule," bolshevism, sabotage, political socialism or industrial socialism, [the intelligence report concluded,] the belief among them seems to be that to help the other man attain his object is to advance one's own ends. In line with this idea, meetings are held, attended by members of the I.W.W.,

30. Charles E. Ruthenberg, *Are We Growing Toward Socialism?* (Cleveland, 1917), 34, 41, 43.
31. Communist Party of America, *Manifesto and Program. Constitution. Report to the Communist International* (Chicago, 1919), 11, 17. See also Central Executive Committee of the Communist Party of America, "Coal Miners of America" (n.p., 1920).
32. On crusaders and maritime and railway workers, see Chapter 8. On shop delegates, see Lorwin, *Women's Garment Workers*, 354–7. On the Micrometer Lodge, see *MMJ*, 32 (June 1920), 546–7. On the automobile workers, see Meyer, *Five Dollar Day*, 171.

W.I.I.U., Socialist Labor Party, Sinn Feiners, Bolsheviki, National-
ists, and other radical parties.[33]

One movement did arise in Canada in the spring of 1919 that so neatly
captured the spirit and the essential common beliefs of these working-
class militants as to suggest that a unified movement based on workplace
organization might be in the offing: the One Big Union (OBU). The 250
delegates at its founding convention in Calgary in March were all officers
or members of trade unions, the largest contingent coming from the IAM.
Their proclaimed objectives were as simple as they were free of partisan
cant. Their goal was "abolition of the present system of production for
profit and the substitution therefor of production for use." To reach that
end, they proposed a systematic campaign of agitation among the newly
enlarged memberships of existing unions for the purpose of transforming
those organizations into industrial unions built on the foundation of shop
stewards within the various places of work.[34]

The idea met an enthusiastic reception from many AFL members in the
Northwest, among whom were past and current Wobblies, as well as
postwar immigrants from the British Isles, who had had personal experience with the shop stewards' movement there. The experience of Seattle's February general strike had generated receptive audiences for frequent visitors from Canada, such as President Jack Kavanagh of the British
Columbia Federation of Labor, who had chaired the resolutions committee at the Calgary convention. William F. Dunne of Butte also visited
Seattle on behalf of the new movement. Although the OBU envisaged a
future labor movement very different from that represented by the AFL,
it did not call on individuals to quit the federation and join something
new, as the IWW had done. Moreover, the resolutions of the Calgary
convention had stressed workplace organization and had been silent concerning socialist, communist, or labor parties, thus permitting cooperation with any and all of them. As Harry Wright, a Tacoma longshoreman
who was prominent among OBU advocates in Washington argued, the

33. Office of Naval Intelligence, "Investigation of the Marine Transport Work-
     ers and the Alleged Threatened Combination Between Them and the Bol-
     sheviki and Sinn Feiners" (December 23, 1918, Confidential) (Department
     of Labor, R.G. 174, Chief Clerk's File 20/580, National Archives), 9–10.
     Elsewhere, intelligence officers also found members of the Polish League for
     Industrial Freedom, Russian Revolutionists, and "Soviets" involved in sim-
     ilar meetings.
34. Norman Penner, ed., *Winnipeg, 1919: The Strikers' Own History of the
     Winnipeg General Strike* (second edition, Toronto, 1975), 26–7. See also
     Mary J. Jordan, *Survival: Labour's Trials and Tribulations in Canada* (To-
     ronto, 1975), 39–47.

movement was not secessionist, and it offered a common ground to progressives and revolutionaries in the unions. Wright proclaimed, in the vocabulary of his region's movement, that a reorganized trade-union movement would have a place for "radicals" and for "conservatives" – but "reactionists" would be driven out.[35]

The proposal was elaborated in a series of lectures given, under the auspices of the Seattle metal-trades council, to shipyard workers following the February general strike by James Robertson, a member of the AFL boilermakers from Portland. Efforts to reform the union movement by resolutions at AFL conventions, such as the IAM's incessant appeals for amalgamation of metal-trades unions, were futile, said Robertson:

> The natural development of the labor movement in America will not be a reform instituted at the "top" for the "bottom," but a transforming process, now taking place in the rank and file of labor in the workshop, an organic development which consciously strives toward the conscious co-operation of the whole working class – One Big Union.[36]

This country "is not Russia," Robertson warned, and insurrection by "senseless mobs" would only be cut down, because "the parasites possess machine guns." The "dynamic strike" was the workers' weapon of modern times and "the only hope of a bloodless change from the old order to the new." To wield that weapon, workers had to repudiate archaic practices of collective bargaining and follow the British example:

> Working Men and Women:
>
> Call a meeting of your shop group at once; elect your shop steward. Large shop groups will elect several shop stewards. Let conditions and circumstances determine the nature and selection of representation.
>
> Deal "directly" with the conditions under which you work, "Safety First" for life and limb. Deal directly with questions of abolishing piece or contract work, also all jurisdictional disputes. Work for efficiency in production and efficiency in the union, for efficiency in organization will promote the discipline necessary to mass action.[37]

35. *Seattle Union Record*, June 21, 1919 (hereafter cited as *SUR*). On Kavanagh, see Penner, *Winnipeg*, 25; Jordan, *Survival*, 70; #106 Reports, May 5, 1919, in Broussais C. Beck Papers, Box 1, University of Washington. I am deeply indebted to Dana Frank for making available these reports, as well as minutes of the Seattle Central Labor Council.

36. James Robertson, *Labor Unionism, Based upon the American Shop Steward System* (n.p., n.d.), 1. Copy in Department of Labor library. I am indebted to Steven Sapolsky for bringing this pamphlet to my attention.

37. Ibid., 8, 14. Note the similarity between Robertson's treatment of efficiency and the analysis of Turin's factory councils made by Antonio Gramsci. See

During the summer of 1919, the large Seattle boilermakers Local 104, spurred on by its lack of success in the recent strike, instituted a shop stewards' network within the shipyards, as Robertson had suggested. But his desire to reshape the whole state federation of labor into workplace organizations, industrial unions, and district councils, all based on delegates directly elected and subject to recall by their workmates, had proved less successful. The convention of the state federation, held in Bellingham in mid-June 1919, was attended by full delegations from the large local unions for the first time in memory. Boilermakers Local 104 alone gave credentials to 142 members. Women were especially prominent among the delegates, and when they heard a proposal to denounce the employment of married women, in the words of one reporter, they "beat it to a frazzle." Worker-farmer alliances for political action received overwhelming support, as did the proposal, introduced by the longshoremen's Harry Wright, for a membership ballot on the restructuring of the state federation. Over the objections of the resolutions committee and the more conservative state officers, the following resolution passed by a handsome margin:

> Resolved, That the State Federation of Labor, in convention assembled, recommend that each local affiliated vote upon the advisability of forming one big union along industrial lines, and that should the majority of the numerical vote of the rank and file vote in favor of industrial unionism, that the State Federation of Labor issue a call for a special conference to be held in the city of Seattle not less than 60 days after the final count of votes to outline the form of organization.[38]

The majority supporting the resolution soon turned out to be more apparent than real. Many Seattle leftists, tired of waiting for a reformation of the federation and enraged by incessant police raids against radical groups, had already seceded from the city's central labor council to form their own industrial movement, and they met with fierce resistance from progressives (like council secretary James Duncan) and conservatives alike. Duncan and other progressives, for their part, feared that if Washington's trade unionists reorganized their state structure as they planned, they would face excommunication by the AFL and a consequent attack by the national organization on their locals. Confronted with direct orders from AFL secretary Morrison in August to call off the referendum, the executive council of the Washington state federation first wavered, then capitulated. Over the furious protests of their more radical

Gwyn A. Williams, *Proletarian Order: Antonio Gramsci and the Origins of Communism in Italy* (London, 1975), 96–136.
38. *SUR*, June 23, 1919.

members, the state federation and the Seattle labor council both agreed
to cancel the referendum. In its place they called for each local union in
the state to select one delegate for a state-wide meeting to formulate "closer
affiliation" among the unions, promote political action, and mobilize
support for the Plumb plan.[39]

The discipline of the AFL had thus forced Washington's progressive
unionists to break with the OBU plan and leave it the exclusive property
of the Left. Meanwhile, everything the movement stood for had materialized in the Winnipeg general strike of May 15 to June 25, in which
demands of building workers for higher wages and of metal-trades workers for union recognition had been supported by city-wide class solidarity
in a total strike, led by the Trades and Labor Council. The Winnipeg
strike had catapulted the OBU's ideas and leadership to international
fame. But thorough mobilization of military force and business-led citizens' committees ultimately defeated the workers. The prestige of the
OBU wilted when the strike was called off – three days after the vote of
the Washington Federation of Labor – with nothing won, and its leading
figures were soon sentenced to prison. AFL officers moved into the breach
with a vigorous campaign to reassert their control over locals in Winnipeg and elsewhere in Canada and in the United States where OBU sentiment had proved strong. The movement was thus cut off from its roots
in existing trade unions and became, by the time its second convention
met in Chicago in 1920, just what its early advocates had wished not to
be: an organizational rival to the AFL. In Lawrence, Massachusetts, and
among the miners of Glace Bay, Nova Scotia, the OBU remained a potent
force until 1924 or 1925; but it no longer represented the dream espoused by Robertson, Kavanagh, and Wright of an AFL redesigned to
suit the needs and desires of its new membership in mass-production
industry.[40]

That ideal was rescued from oblivion by the Workers' (Communist)
Party but not until 1922–3, when the AFL was rapidly losing the new
membership and the place in modern industry on which the OBU plan
had been based. Despite their many resolutions, both of the two com-

39. #106 Reports, May 5, 9, 14, 15, 21, July 17, 27, August 4, 14, 20, 21,
    1919; Seattle Central Labor Council minutes, May 21, 1919; *SUR*, July 10,
    14, 1919; Harvey O'Connor, *Revolution in Seattle: A Memoir* (New York,
    1964), 148–61. For a different evaluation of this movement, see David Jay
    Bercuson, "The One Big Union in Washington," *Pacific Northwest Quar-
    terly*, 69 (July 1978), 127–34.
40. Jordan, *Survival*, 176–87, 213–17. On the OBU after 1919, see also Pen-
    ner, *Winnipeg;* Goldberg, "Immigrants, Intellectuals and Industrial Unions";
    Frank, "Cape Breton Miners."

munist parties formed in 1919 were too small, inexperienced, sectarian, and beleagured by government attacks to exert a significant influence on the postwar strike wave or the unions' new militants. Most of their members were affiliated through language federations, and circulating underground literature was their main activity. The rather large membership that they had drawn out of the Socialist Party in the revolutionary enthusiasm of 1919 declined rapidly thereafter, leaving militant workers far more likely to attend a meeting of the IWW, Socialist Party, SLP, or OBU than a meeting of communists during 1920 and 1921.[41] In the summer of 1921, however, communist construction workers in San Francisco organized a revolt of local activists against the leadership of the building trades council in an impressive, if unsuccessful, effort to prevent the imposition of the open shop on P. H. McCarthy's crumbling autocracy. At the same time, the Jewish and Finnish federations and the Workers' Council group, frustrated in their long efforts to persuade the Socialist Party to affiliate with the new Communist International, seceded and began the negotiations that resulted in their affiliation with a new open organization established by the communists in December 1921, the Workers' Party. The new party announced its purpose "to co-ordinate the entire left wing of the American labor movement within the existing unions."[42]

The most important vehicle for this effort was the Trade Union Educational League (TUEL). Formed in November 1920 under the leadership of William Z. Foster, the TUEL sought to reorganize a united front of leftists and progressives around systematic campaigns for a labor party and the amalgamation of related craft unions. The next July, Foster joined seven Americans affiliated with the Wobblies, communists, and OBU at the founding convention of the Red International of Labor Unions (RILU)

---

41. Malcolm Sylvers, *Sinistra politica e movimento operaio negli Stati Uniti, Dal primo dopoguerra alla repressione liberal-maccartista* (Naples, 1984), 35–7, 83–7; Anthony Capraro to Romildo Galotte, July 20, 1920 (Capraro Papers, Box 3); Vera B. Weisbord, *A Radical Life* (Bloomington, Ind., 1977), 89–90.

42. Kazin, "Barons of Labor," 498–529; James P. Cannon, *History of American Trotskyism* (New York, 1944), 1–22; [H. W. Laidler], "The United Communist Party," *Socialist Review*, 9 (August 1920), 92–4; *SUR*, April 26, 1921; Workers' Council, *Go to the Masses! A Manifesto of the Third Congress of the Third International, also the Withdrawal Statement of the Committee for the Third International of the Socialist Party to the Members of the Socialist Party* (New York, n.d.); David J. Saposs, *Left Wing Unionism: A Study of Radical Policies and Tactics* (New York, 1926), 49–51. The quotation is from J. Louis Engdahl, "The Workers' Party Is Launched," *Labor Age*, 11 (February 1922), 14.

in Moscow, affiliated his league with the RILU, and, after his return, joined the newly created Workers' Party. Despite the close connections of its leaders with the optimistic new party, the TUEL tried to recruit activists of many political complexions, charged no dues, and required its members only to uphold its declared principles, which were those of most progressives, and to subscribe to its journal, the *Labor Herald*. Its program more often than not consisted of demands taken from resolutions already passed at union conventions. Its 1923 Conference of Progressive Miners, for example, called for nationalization of the industry "under the direction of union miners," a labor party, restoration of nationwide trade agreements, a pact of unity between miners and railway unions, and industrial unionism, while denouncing the UMWA's "timid and incompetent leaders" for their retreat from these declared policies of their own organization. Like other groups on labor's postwar left wing, the TUEL incorporated workplace organization into its larger design for mobilizing the working class. As economist Earl R. Beckner summarized the *Labor Herald*'s arguments: "The League favors the shop-delegate system of local union organization in all industries where such a plan can be worked out effectively, since this form of organization brings into play one of the sources of latent solidarity which the prevailing system of organizing leaves untouched, namely, the natural cohesion of workers on the same job."[43]

The TUEL was most influential in unions that had shown a progressive orientation by 1921, especially the miners, ladies' garment workers, amalgamated clothing workers, carpenters, and machinists. The ebb tide of progressivism, however, had left those unions' international officers loath to undertake aggressive new campaigns for causes they now considered hopeless and increasingly prepared to use disciplinary sanctions against members who tried to make them do so. In the International Ladies' Garment Workers' Union (ILGWU), where the TUEL was heir to a postwar shop delegates' movement, comparable to the shop stewards' movements in the metal trades, as well as to widespread membership admiration for the Russian Revolution, its candidates for office in the largest locals and the joint boards in New York, Philadelphia, and Chicago were remarkably successful during the elections of 1922. Their victories brought strong retribution from the international's general execu-

43. Jay Fox, *Amalgamation* (Chicago, 1923); Theodore Draper, *Roots of American Communism* (New York, 1957), 316; *Program of the Progressive International Committee of the United Mine Workers of America* (Pittsburgh, 1923); Earl R. Beckner, "The Trade Union Educational League and the American Labor Movement," *Journal of Political Economy*, 33 (August 1925), 419.

tive board, which ordered all "leagues" dissolved in the fall of 1923, then reorganized local unions whose officers had failed to obey its orders to cease and desist from activities of the TUEL. Following the progressive miners' convention in June 1923, the UMWA had decreed the expulsion of all communists. Trials and expulsions from the carpenters and machinists followed in 1924 and 1925.[44]

What miners and garment workers had begun received official sanction by the AFL at its October 1923 convention. A resolution was introduced from the platform denouncing the Federated Press, a news agency that served seventy-five radical and progressive publications, for calumnies against the leaders of the AFL. The resolution passed unanimously, but during the debate Matthew Woll pointed out that William F. Dunne, a communist delegate from Butte, Montana, was the personification of all that was evil in the Federated Press and demanded Dunne's expulsion from the convention. For the next two hours, denunciations were poured on Dunne's head by Philip Murray and William Green of the UMWA, Fred Mooney, who had led the coal miners' armed march in West Virginia only two years earlier, and William Hutcheson of the carpenters, who also insisted that every delegate stand up and be counted in a roll-call vote. The vote to evict the convention's only member from the Worker's Party was 27,837 to 108. Among those duly voting for expulsion were all delegates from the UMWA, the IAM, and the ILGWU, except Luigi Antonini, who abstained. James Duncan, secretary of the Seattle central labor council, was among the nine delegates who publicly voted no. The next year he was forced out of office.[45]

After the vote against Dunne had been tallied, Samuel Gompers observed from the chair that this was the "second episode where a delegate has been expelled from the Convention of the American Federation of Labor."[46] He did not comment, however, on the difference between the two episodes. When Lucien Saniel had been denied a seat at the 1891 convention, the ruling had been based on the narrow technical grounds that he represented a political party, not a trade union. Gompers had spoken passionately at the time about the openness of the federation to all political opinions – socialist, greenback, anarchist, whatever – provided the delegate who held those views was a properly credentialed delegate from a union.[47] The expulsion of Dunne in 1923 had been based explicitly on his political views: There was no question that he was a

44. Lorwin, *Women's Garment Workers*, 354–7; Beckner, "Trade Union Educational League," 425–6; Perlman, *Machinists*, 64–5.
45. *AFL Proceedings*, 1923, 130–4, 254–9; O'Connor, *Revolution in Seattle*, 214.
46. *AFL Proceedings*, 1923, 259.   47. Mandel, *Gompers*, 113–15.

union member and carried proper credentials from the Silver Bow Trades and Labor Council. The convention's action, and above all the lynch-mob atmosphere in which it was taken, signaled for all to see that the house of labor in 1923 required ideological as well as organizational orthodoxy of its members.

The almost total isolation of Dunne at the convention also revealed that the TUEL had, in Foster's words, "largely lost the leadership over the so-called progressive elements which played such an important part in its early activities." Most of its meetings, he observed, now consisted "merely of communists and their closest sympathisers."[48] In contrast to the congress of railroad workers organized by the TUEL in December 1922, which drew 425 delegates, only 143 people showed up at the league's national convention held on the eve of the 1923 AFL convention.[49] Progressive union leaders had turned against the communists primarily because the leaders' sense of what was necessary for survival of their beleaguered unions called for a moratorium on militant struggles until a more congenial political climate had been restored. Ironically, their emphasis on political action also led most progressives away from their postwar eagerness to form a labor party.

The Conference for Progressive Political Action (CPPA) had become the repository of their hopes. Although the CPPA entered the election campaigns of 1922 with a nonpartisan approach, its alliance of trade-union, socialist, farmers', and women's organizations persuaded those of its officers who wanted an eventual labor or farmer-labor party that this was the first step, and the only realistic first step, toward the creation of such a party. Not all progressives agreed with this Fabian approach by any means. When the CPPA barred participation by the Workers' Party and refused to proceed immediately to the formation of a party, the Farmer-Labor Party of Minnesota, which was then by far the most successful and self-confident such party actually functioning, withdrew in disgust and openly cultivated a united front with the communists on its home turf. Nevertheless, the CPPA's policy of supporting favored candidates from major parties and third parties alike, depending on local situations, won the support of Warren Stone, William Johnston, Sidney Hillman, and William Green, as well as of Secretary Jay G. Brown of the Chicago-based Farmer-Labor Party (who had briefly been an officer of the TUEL), Morris Hillquit, and James Maurer of the Socialist Party, and editors

48. Quoted in Saposs, *Left Wing Unionism,* 80.
49. William Z. Foster, *History of the Communist Party of the United States* (New York, 1952), 204; Foster, *American Trade Unionism: Principles and Organization, Strategy and Tactics* (New York, 1947), 142.

Frederic C. Howe and Edward Keating of the Plumb Plan League's paper, *Labor*. Although the AFL Executive Council refused to endorse the CPPA, it launched its own National Non-Partisan Campaign Committee to assist a long list of endorsed candidates.[50]

Labor's vigorous campaigning paid off handsomely. Of the twenty-seven candidates for the U.S. Senate endorsed by the CPPA and the AFL, twenty-three were elected, among them Robert La Follette, Henrick Shipstead, and Burton K. Wheeler, whereas prominent champions of the open shop, such as Albert Beveridge, Miles Poindexter, and Frank B. Kellogg, went down to defeat. Moreover, 170 labor-endorsed candidates won seats in the House of Representatives, and the CPPA could take special delight in the defeat of many Republicans who had supported the Harding administration's repressive actions against the coal and railroad strikers. Gubernatorial elections also went well for labor, with such avowed friends as Gifford Pinchot of Pennsylvania, Alfred Smith of New York, J. J. Blaine of Wisconsin, and G. W. P. Hunt of Arizona among the twelve endorsed victors. In Kansas, Governor Henry J. Allen, whose Court of Industrial Relations law had prohibited strikes and sent the UMWA's Alex Howat to jail, was removed from office by the voters.[51]

Never before had the American working class asserted itself so decisively at the polls. The conservative tide that had grown ever stronger in local and congressional elections since 1914 had been reversed. At the 1924 convention of the AFL, the Executive Council could boast that the current Congress had

> . . . stopped the flood of immigration. It blocked the sales-tax gouge. It blocked the Mellon burdensome tax plan. It exposed the Veterans' Bureau Graft. It forced [Attorney General] Daugherty out. It drove [Secretary of the Interior] Fall into retirement. It gave the people the facts about the oil scandals.
>
> *Not one measure opposed by labor was enacted into law by the present Congress.*[52]

The elections of 1922 gave the AFL and the railroad brotherhoods the political breathing space needed to stabilize their membership and their contracts at the new, lower levels. The boundaries of the unionized and nonunion sectors of the economy thereafter remained essentially un-

50. Saposs, *Left Wing Unionism*, 60–2; Weinstein, *Decline*, 274–7; *Labor Age*, 11 (December 1922), 15–17.
51. Walling, *American Labor and American Democracy*, I, 98–100; *Labor Age*, 11 (December 1922), 15–17; Robert H. Zieger, *Republicans and Labor*, *1919–1929* (Lexington, Ky., 1969), 152–77; Allen, *Party of the Third Part*.
52. Quoted in Walling, *American Labor and American Democracy*, I, 101. Italics in original.

changed for the rest of the decade, while measures that conservative unionists considered essential to their cause, such as the severe restriction of immigration from Europe and Asia (1924) and a new railway labor act (1926), could move successfully through Congress.

But what lessons about political action were workers to draw from this accomplishment? The movement's success in mobilizing working-class voters, and especially the notable achievements of the Minnesota Farmer-Labor Party and North Dakota's Nonpartisan League and its off-shoot in Oklahoma, rekindled the conviction of many trade-union progressives that the moment to form a labor party had arrived. Gompers had found abundant evidence for exactly the opposite conclusion. He wrote to editors of the labor press:

> Labor has never participated in a political campaign with such favorable results. There never was such a complete and satisfying vindication of the wisdom of labor's non-partisan political policy. It was proven on November 7 as never before that labor's proper course is to be partisan to principles and not to political organizations.[53]

Two things were certain. First, the labor-endorsed candidates were a heterogeneous group, most of whom (with the major exception of the Minnesotans) not only were committed Republicans or Democrats but also were quite outspoken in their belief that a labor party would appear to most American voters to be a special-interest group or, even worse, a fomenter of class antagonisms that would never win elections. Second, the heartland of labor's electoral strength had been the West – from Wisconsin to Washington. The person who most clearly represented both resistance to a class party and the farmer-labor voting strength of that region was the one whom *Labor* was calling the "strongest political figure in the Nation": Senator Robert M. La Follette.[54]

Consequently, when the CPPA leaders met to assess the election results in February 1923, they voted sixty-four to fifty-two against creating a new party. All the railroad unions, including the IAM, and even the socialists who were present, supported the nonpartisan course of action. Advocates of an independent party, led by J. G. Brown of the Chicago farmer-laborites, quit the CPPA and called a national convention for July to found the new party. So intense was the pressure from the AFL and CPPA against that move, however, that few prominent progressives attended. As a result, the convention was easily dominated by the communists, who captured the determination of those people who had come

53. *Labor Age*, 11 (December 1922), 17.
54. Zieger, *Republicans and Labor*, 171–2, 187–8; *Labor* quoted in *Labor Age*, 11 (December 1922), 15; Belle Case and Fola La Follette, *Robert M. La Follette* (2 vols., New York, 1953), II, 1156.

for immediate action and brushed aside the hesitant leaders of the Chicago Federation of Labor. The latter abruptly abandoned the movement. Although the Minnesota Farmer-Labor Party attempted to revive the effort at the end of the year, the CPPA and the AFL's Executive Council outflanked them easily, boosting a campaign for the White House by La Follette and Burton K. Wheeler, who ran in 1924 as progressives appealing to the independent voters of the land.[55]

In short, the Workers' (Communist) Party had lost its allies on the political front as well as the trade-union front by the time of the 1923 AFL convention and could exert no effective influence on the next year's campaigns, despite a resurgence of conservative strength in both major parties that year.[56] Having failed in the hope expressed at the founding of the Workers' Party, "to co-ordinate the entire left wing of the American labor movement within the existing unions," the communists joined the OBU, IWW, SLP, and what remained of the Socialist Party as another small political grouping building its own organization but lacking a mass ferment of working-class hopes and struggles that might allow its party building to have an influence on national events. Relentless harassment by the "red squads" of municipal police in every city throughout the 1920s reinforced the communists' sense of isolation.[57]

As far as most workers were concerned, the only version of workplace organization they might have encountered by 1923 was one favored by corporate executives. Most enterprises did not even have that, and many of the representation plans that had been instituted during the strike wave fell into disuse after 1922. As William Leiserson reminded his readers,

55. James Weinstein, "Radicalism in the Midst of Normalcy," *Journal of American History,* 52 (March 1966), 773–90. The Workers' Party's decision to field its own presidential candidate against La Follette in 1924 completed its isolation from the remaining AFL progressives. Beckner, "Trade Union Educational League," 428.

56. Walling, *American Labor and American Democracy,* I, 125–36; Zieger, *Republicans and Labor,* 179–83.

57. For lives of communists during the 1920s, see Fred E. Beal, *Proletarian Journey: New England, Gastonia, Moscow* (New York, 1937); James P. Cannon, *First Ten Years of American Communism: Report of a Participant* (New York, 1962); Peggy Dennis, *Autobiography of an American Communist: A Personal View of a Political Life 1925–1975* (Berkeley, Calif., 1977); Kenneth Kann, *Joe Rappaport: The Life of a Jewish Radical* (Philadelphia, 1981); Saul Kreas, *My Life and Struggle for a Better World* (New Haven, 1977); Steve Nelson, James R. Barrett, and Rob Ruck, *Steve Nelson: American Radical* (Pittsburgh, 1981); Al Richmond, *A Long View from the Left: Memoirs of an American Revolutionary* (New York, 1972).

far more workers still belonged to unions than participated in employee-representation plans. But the unions had been virtually banished from larger manufacturing and commercial enterprises, with the famous exceptions of Hart, Schaffner and Marx clothing and the B&O railroad. Among the four hundred firms that had representation plans by 1928, as in other large and small firms where most Americans worked under open-shop conditions, only a managerial rhetoric that celebrated "employee participation" and industry's "new humanism" remained as a ghostly echo of the organizing schemes and lofty aspirations that had flourished within the enlarged labor movements of 1918–21.[58] Just what this meant can be shown by the experience of the workers at General Electric.

General Electric

Virtually all of the corporate practices associated with modern management were on exhibit at General Electric (GE). As we have already noted, the company had been created by leading investment bankers, had generated a wide range of products as essential to the energy and transportation systems of the new urban world as they were to the celebrated consumer durables that decorated its households, and was deeply involved in shaping developmental and social policies of the government, in war as in peace. Its leading executives, such as Magnus Alexander, Gerard Swope, and Owen D. Young, were as much at home in Washington as in Schenectady or Lynn, and through the NICB and the Special Conference Committee they fashioned policy positions for corporate America as a whole. Consequently, an examination of the battle over workplace organization in GE can reveal not the experience of the average American worker or company, by any means, but rather the shape that scientific management had given to workers' aspirations and company practice in the most innovative sector of American industry.

The electrical industry also offers a useful perspective on the changes in character and objectives that scientific management had forced on workers' organization. No nineteenth-century–style craft-union rules, ethnic organizations of laborers, or departmental strikes of operatives could prevail against GE, although traces of all three precedents were visible in the workers' mobilizations of 1916–22. Just as the corporation's strategies for chastening its workers provided a highly publicized model for the open-shop "American Plan" of the 1920s, so the styles of

58. Leiserson, "Collective Bargaining," 357; Jacoby, "Industrial Internal Labor Markets during the 1920s"; Sanford M. Jacoby, "Industrial Labor Mobility in Historical Perspective," *Industrial Relations* (Spring 1983), 261–82.

organization developed by GE's employees in the 1918–19 foreshadowed the practice by which the CIO's United Electrical, Radio and Machine Workers were to bring unionization in the 1930s. In fact, quite a few individuals were involved in both union efforts.[59] Part of the explanation for this continuity lies in the vigorous expansion of the electrical industry through the 1920s, whereas coal mining, railroads, textiles, and other traditional centers of unionism reached their historic peaks of employment early in the decade and declined steadily thereafter. Although the number of production workers in manufacturing remained virtually unchanged at 8.5 million between 1919 and 1929, the number for the electrical industry rose from 128,000 in 1914 to 241,000 in 1919 and 343,000 in 1929. In this respect, electrical manufacturing stood with automobiles, oil, chemicals, and trucking as an industry of the future. Unlike the other growth industries, however, electrical manufacturing had a production force that was almost entirely white and roughly 40 percent female in the 1920s.[60]

GE employed 57,500 workers in the United States in 1917, when its public-relations officer George M. Ripley described it in a series of articles for *General Electric Review*. Forty percent of them (22,600) were at the Schenectady headquarters plant, 12,644 at Lynn, 7,050 at Pittsfield, Massachusetts, 4,372 at Fort Wayne, Indiana, and 3,500 at Erie, Pennsylvania. Peterboro, Ontario, was already the center of its Canadian operations. The company boasted an elaborate array of mutual-benefit associations, safety committees, apprentice schools, women's clubs, and engineers' societies. Their purpose, Ripley wrote, was to make "steady workers." Steadiness, he explained, was what made civilizations great, as was proved by the superiority of peoples from temperate climes. Men and women who had been in the company's employ for five years were eligible for bonuses, those who lasted ten years got a week's vacation with pay, and veterans of twenty years were eligible for a small pension, available to men at age seventy and to women at age sixty. In fact, almost half of the workers at Schenectady and 35 percent of those at Lynn received the five-year-service bonus, though the proportion fell drastically to 27 percent at Pittsfield and only 9 percent at Erie. The company showed concern for municipal politics and civic life, as well as for conditions within the plants. Lynn, Ripley boasted, was "a 'dry' city," and Schenectady had "no 'red light district.'"[61] Not content with the elaborate

59. Ronald W. Schatz, "Union Pioneers: The Founders of Local Unions at General Electric and Westinghouse, 1933–1937," *Journal of American History*, 66 (December 1979), 586–602.
60. *Hist. Stat. U.S.*, 666, 679.
61. Ripley, *Large Manufacturing Plant*; quotations are on pp. 9 and 121.

Americanization program conducted by sociologist Peter Roberts and his corps of teachers for foreign-born employees of the Schenectady works, one of the company's vice-presidents, E. W. Rice, also participated in the 1919 founding of the Inter-Racial Council. Among the proclaimed purposes of the council were

> To apply American business methods to the foreign born press by building up an American advertising base under it. To reduce unrest and disorder through plant analyses. ... To decrease radicalism through the issuances of information and counter education in the foreign language press dealing with attacks on American institutions, law and order, and industry.[62]

Scientific management at GE had been strongly influenced by the French Taylorite, Charles Bedaux. Although Bedaux had publicized his own "efficiency course" by 1917, and his pay system was introduced into meatpacking houses in the early 1920s, his ideas did not generally come into their own until the 1930s. So widely were they adopted then that one might call the Bedaux system the Taylorism of the Great Depression. As usual, GE was in the managerial vanguard. Bedaux advised that motion study be substituted for time study wherever possible. The man standing by the machine with a stopwatch made workers angry, and he was often inexact. The "decomposition of compound operations" into their constituent muscular motions could be studied in a laboratory and could provide, Bedaux argued, an exact measure of the time necessary to complete a set of motions. That time should be augmented by "non-productive time" determined by fatigue studies in order to calculate the number of "points" in an hour's output of any task. Each worker was paid a "minimum take out" or hourly rate, but if he or she managed to produce at a faster rate than the points prescribed, there would be a premium waiting for the "time saved." That is to say, the premium was 75 percent of whatever proportion of the minimum hourly wage the worker had "saved" – the other 25 percent went to foremen, stock handlers, and other indirect laborers for their parts in making the operative's faster production possible.[63]

Bedaux also agreed with Ripley on the importance of steadiness – so much so that, in addition to advocating numerous welfare schemes, he warned that "roustabout gang members" should wear identifying badges

62. Quoted in David E. Nye, *Image Worlds: Corporate Identities at General Electric, 1890–1930* (Cambridge, Mass., 1985), 79.
63. Bedaux, *Bedaux Efficiency Course*, 187–206, 285–91; Louis F. Budenz, "Jehu's Driving at West Lynn," *Labor Age*, 16 (April 1927), 16; Schatz, *Electrical Workers*, 22. On the Bedaux system in packinghouses, see Herbst, *The Negro*, 116–18.

and be isolated from production workers as much as possible, because they were "taken largely from the drifting class" and were "but casually interested in the welfare of the business." The best device for weeding out tardy, negligent, and absentee employees, he added, would be committees of other workers concerned with safety and with maximizing premium earnings.[64]

The flagship plant in Schenectady had long been a stronghold of both the AFL and the Socialist Party. Craft unions had survived the IWW challenge of 1906, but after 1911 a metal-trades council had coordinated the activities of the twenty-five unions represented in the factory. An important precedent for postwar struggles had been set in November 1913, when the company laid off many workers. Among those dismissed were two union activists, Frank Dujay and Mable Leslie, who had recently been prominent in recruiting women into the International Brotherhood of Electrical Workers (IBEW). The metal-trades council called a strike despite the protest of international union officers, and fourteen thousand workers walked out. Socialist Mayor Lunn immediately opened municipal relief stations for the strikers and called both parties to his office to negotiate a settlement. Within four days the strike was over, with both militants reinstated and the company committed for the first time to a formal policy on layoffs. If anyone had to be let go, the management pledged, people from out of town would be discharged first, and those without dependents would be put on part time. The distinction between transient and regular employees, the preference of short time over layoffs, and the policy that among the regulars the first to be cut back should be unmarried women and men were all important elements of company policy as well as workers' demands after the war.[65]

The growth of Schenectady's work force to double its 1906 size by 1917 strengthened the unions, but did little to allay workers' anxieties about losing their jobs after the war. In May, forty-five hundred machinists struck for a wage increase, but returned to work when the IAM agreed to a joint survey and adjustment of rates. Scarcely a month later twice that many workers walked out for a month protesting that the company was opening its machine shops to southern black workers. In fact, one black man had started operating a drill press; but the company got the strikers back by persuading them that he was not a southerner, but a

---

64. Bedaux, *Bedaux Course,* 177, 305–7.
65. *IA,* 92 (November 27, 1913), 1241; (December 4, 1913), 1308; Kenneth E. Hendrickson, Jr., "Tribune of the People: George R. Lunn and the Fall of Christian Socialism in Schenectady," in Stave, *Socialism and the Cities,* 87–8; Ella Reeve Bloor, *We Are Many* (New York, 1940), 118–20.

college student hired as part of a regular summer program. May 1918 saw a short strike by almost twenty-two thousand workers, united for wage increases. That strike put Schenectady's workers on the docket of the NWLB. Most important of all, some fifty office workers formed a union, affiliated with the metal-trades council in June 1918, and successfully joined the appeal to the NWLB for a wage increase. By December, the office workers' union had 900 members, out of 2,000 eligible employees.[66]

By the war's end, therefore, GE's employees at Schenectady were thoroughly unionized, with a metal-trades council coordinating the activities not only of men and women in production but also of organized office workers. They were keenly aware, however, that open-shop conditions prevailed at the company's other plants and that those conditions made Schenectady isolated and vulnerable. Moreover, taking their case to the NWLB had an important consequence: It put Schenectady's delegates in Washington directly in contact with representatives of the Lynn, Pittsfield, Erie, and Fort Wayne workers, who also had cases pending. In this sense, the Washington bureaucracy opened the channels of communication, which paved the way for the attempt at a company-wide union and strike at the end of 1918.

Pittsfield, in northwestern Massachusetts, had been an open-shop stronghold before the war. Many workers had joined unions during the munitions strike wave of 1916, and GE's local management had responded by firing activists and refusing to meet with a delegation of workers who sought to discuss union recognition and a wage increase. A strike began on Saturday, September 2, and over the next two weeks brought out nearly all the employees. Despite mediation efforts by the Massachusetts State Board of Conciliation and Arbitration and threats by unions to call out their Schenectady members, the company held firm against union recognition, agreeing only to a 5 percent wage increase and a ballot by the workers on reduction of hours. By early October, dejected strikers began drifting back to their jobs.[67]

Returning workers were obliged to sign individual contracts, of the

66. FMCS file 33/403, Department of Labor, R.G. 280, National Archives; Bing, *War-Time Strikes*, 158n; *Am. Labor Year Book 1919*, 189; Atherton Brownell, "Report of an investigation into industrial conditions in the several plants of the General Electric Company, together with recommendations of a plan to improve them," in Owen D. Young Papers, Van Hornesville, N.Y., box labeled "G.E. Labor Relations." I am indebted to Ronald W. Schatz for bringing this report to my attention.

67. *IA*, 98 (August 31, 1916), 463; (September 7, 1916), 561; (September 14, 1916), 620; (September 28, 1916), 737; (October 5, 1916), 803.

type the United Shoe Machinery Company was soon to make famous. The agreements met workers' fears of unemployment by guaranteeing them work for one year. In return, the workers pledged not to join unions or engage in strikes. The supreme judicial court of Massachusetts later ruled such contracts legal. As Atherton Brownell later reported when he surveyed the GE plants, however, the "hostility" of Pittsfield's workers toward local management "was not even veiled." He added, "Acrimony, the smart of outraged feelings, a bitter sense of injustice, a complete lack of belief in friendly intentions on the part of management – all of these become apparent at once to the most casual observer."[68]

In May 1918, the Pittsfield plant was struck again by six thousand of its men and women. This time the NWLB intervened, held hearings, and on August 1 awarded a minimum wage for unskilled and semiskilled workers, equal pay for equal work regardless of sex, abolition of the individual contract, and a substantial general wage increase. It also ordered elections to be held for a shop committee, which would function with an NWLB examiner as arbitrator. Although all parties agreed that the shop committee made settlement of routine grievances much smoother, the workers began to want much more. They gave strong support to the campaign of one of their number, David Kevlin, secretary of the metal-trades council, for mayor of Pittsfield. In a town so staunchly Republican that the Democrats seldom bothered to make local nominations, the labor candidate carried four of the seven wards and almost won the election. Simultaneously, local union activists raised the argument that they could never cope effectively with major issues, such as wages, let alone with postwar reductions in force, if they did not have some way to link up with other GE workers and to carry negotiations over the head of local management to the corporation's national headquarters.[69]

The movement for a new type of union that could deal with GE nationally was also gaining strength in Lynn, Fort Wayne, and Erie. The river works in West Lynn had grown to forty buildings by 1918, and its close ties to the nearby Massachusetts Institute of Technology facilitated its development of products ranging in size from giant generators to tiny instruments. As we have noted, unions had been weak there since the 1890s, despite some effective shop-floor struggles against piecework. A recruiting drive by the AFL was begun early in 1917 and soon came

68. Brownell, "Report," 21; Warne, "Anthracite Coal Strike," 137; [IAM], *The Truth about the Individual Contract* (n.p., n.d.), copy in Department of Labor files, R.G. 280, National Archives.
69. Brownell, "Report," 24–8, 34–5; CPI press releases, May 15, 1918, August 1, 1918, in NWLB administrative file B.54, R.G. 2, National Archives.

under the leadership of a gifted organizer, Charles D. Keaveney, who was transferred there from Schenectady by the IBEW. On Wednesday morning, July 10, machinist John J. Connolly was given a discharge slip, and during the next three days several more union members were let go. When Joseph Glassert was fired late Friday, some fifty women and men from his department quit work and came to the IBEW office to inform Keaveney. Together they planned a protest rally for Saturday night, and when fifteen hundred angry workers showed up, they decided to strike. On Monday morning, foremen rapidly dismissed many more activists, while workers in two departments sat down in protest. Early in the afternoon, union sound trucks outside the buildings blared fighting songs and calls to down tools. Within an hour the GE river works were empty.[70]

The strike lasted three turbulent weeks. More than ten thousand workers, 40 percent of them women, picketed, paraded, and signed up in craft unions – among them, four thousand each in the IAM and IBEW – while foremen canvassed the town, searching for people loyal to the company. The strike leaders were combative and effective but not as radical politically as those who came to the fore in Pittsfield, Erie, and Fort Wayne. The company later identified three of them in an internal memorandum as "intensely loyal to their fellow [workers] and consequently to their unions," but among the "more liberal minded" trade unionists, not revolutionaries.[71] The strike was supported by editorials in Hearst's *Boston American,* which called on the government to protect the right of the workers to organize, or else to seize the works, whose manager Walter C. Fish, it said, spent "so much of his time in vain attempts to run the policies of Massachusetts upon medieval principles."[72] Although there was enough left-wing sentiment in Lynn that when Ella Reeve "Mother" Bloor appeared at the victory rally to speak against the war and for Eugene Debs's defense, she was carried to the speakers' platform on strikers' shoulders amid clamorous cheers, Keaveney, Connolly, and the other leaders who had the struggle well in hand appear to have been Walsh-type Democrats.[73]

The confidence in the NWLB that these leaders showed was to be of decisive importance to the future of unionism in GE nationally, because

70. Louis F. Budenz, "Genesis at West Lynn," *Labor Age,* 16 (February 1927), 15–17; Budenz, "Jonah's Whale at West Lynn," *Labor Age,* 16 (March 1927), 15–17.
71. FMCS file 33/1702, Department of Labor, R.G. 280, National Archives; Brownell, "Report," 42, 53.
72. Editorial, Boston *American,* July 21, 1918; Stuart J. Reid, "Conquest of West Lynn," *MMJ,* 30 (November 1918), 999–1000.
73. Bloor, *We Are Many,* 145–6.

the board settled the dispute in a way that separated Lynn's workers from those in the rest of the chain. The state board of conciliation and arbitration had intervened first, sending Henry J. Skeffington to the scene, where he joined another superannuated warrior of nineteenth-century labor struggles, Joseph Buchanan, then a Federal Mediation Service agent. On July 27, the state board recommended that the strikers return to work and allow the board subsequently to decide questions of reinstatement and wages according to NWLB principles. It also suggested that the company recognize "committees of employees chosen inside the works by substantially all the employees." Both manager Fish and the strikers rejected arbitration by the state board. The NWLB was prompted to rush to the scene by delegates of Schenectady and Pittsfield workers, who were then in Washington and threatened to shut down those GE factories in sympathy with Lynn. As soon as the NWLB offered to take up all issues involved in the strike, a triumphant mass meeting of strikers voted to resume work. Six days later, August 8, more than four thousand workers walked out again because more unionists had been fired, and delegates from Schenectady came to join them in presenting their grievances to the mediator, but the NWLB quickly convinced everyone to end the strikes.[74]

The NWLB's award was handed down October 24, 1918. It adjusted wages to levels "comparable with those awarded by the board in the Schenectady case," ordered the reinstatement of eleven fired workers, including Connolly, established a minimum pay for women of $15 per week (50 percent higher than what most women then earned), and almost doubled the pay of female clerical workers by making $16.50 their weekly minimum. It also ordered the election of shop committees and of a general committee of three worker and three management representatives plus an NWLB examiner. The workers were jubilant. Almost 95 percent of them now belonged to one union or another of the AFL, leading unionists had been reinstated, and the company was under orders to work out with the shop committees the restructuring of wage rates necessary to put a large raise into effect. Few protested the more ominous features of the award. Two workers had not been reinstated, because on the first day of the strike they had called on their colleagues not to walk out, but to sit down. The board would not have that! And the examiner soon decided that committee elections should be held in the plants, despite union protests. Nevertheless, union candidates were elected overwhelmingly, and three prominent AFL activists became the workers' representatives on the general committee. It is important to remember,

74. Massachusetts State Board of Conciliation and Arbitration, *Annual Report . . . 1918* (Boston, 1919), 62–3; FMCS file 33/1702.

however, that the future operation of the shop committee and its slotting of the ordered wage increases into the complicated Bedaux system depended on the support and arbitration of the NWLB.[75]

Fort Wayne was more peaceful than Lynn, paradoxically, because the Indiana industrial center was a union town. The Full Fashion Hosiery Workers and the IAM were both influential, and the machinists' business agent Ed Yeargens was a prominent socialist and considered a "bad actor" by local business. The forty-three hundred workers at GE included many union members, but local management kept the peace by dealing openly with union representatives. Although there was far less hostility between the employees and management than was found at Pittsfield and Lynn, pay scales were lower than those at Schenectady. Consequently, the Fort Wayne unions filed a complaint with the NWLB asking for the same wage levels that it awarded workers at the headquarters plant. Like the workers at Pittsfield, the men and women of Fort Wayne also wanted a way to take such issues past the local management to GE nationally.[76]

The decisive initiative for a company-wide movement came from Erie. In that northwestern Pennsylvania city a militant employers' association kept alive an intransigent hostility to unions, and the GE management shared that attitude. It lured thousands of newcomers to the plant during the war by circulating widely news of the high wages and fine houses available there. Although membership in both the IAM and the IBEW grew rapidly, there were no strikes to bring the NWLB into the plant.

The Erie unions were strongholds of both socialist and revolutionary syndicalist sentiment, and despite the surveillance of employers and the city police, the wartime influx of workers increased the openness of the unions to ideas from the left. The Gompersite president of the city's central labor union asserted that "Bolshevist or 'Red' literature" was to be found "in abundance after all union meetings," and he considered "this element ... largely in control of the Machinists." A naval intelligence officer, who had been involved in the study of revolutionary "mixed locals" in port cities, told a representative of GE that "Socialists, the Russian Labor Union, I.W.W., the anarchists, the Bolsheviki and the more radical men within the established unions" had "colonized" Erie during the war.[77] Even allowing for some degree of fantasy in that report, the fact remains that revolutionary militants were numerous in Erie, as were progressives. The first convention of the Pennsylvania state lodge of the

75. "National War Labor Board Decisions," *MMJ*, 31 (January 1919), 11–13; Budenz, "Jonah's Whale," 15; Conner, *NWLB*, 134–6; Robert W. Bruère, "West Lynn," *Survey*, 56 (April 1926), 24; Brownell, "Report," 42–4.

76. Brownell, "Report," 56–8.   77. Ibid., 54.

IAM in May 1919 strongly endorsed amalgamation of all metal-trades unions, public ownership of railroads and other utilities, and a labor party — with only the Socialist delegates offering formal protest that theirs already was the labor party, before allowing the vote on the last point to be made unanimous.[78] Progressives and revolutionary syndicalists in the city's labor movement were encouraged to work together by the president of the Pennsylvania Federation of Labor, James H. Maurer, who had been the most important officer of the AFL to oppose America's participation in the war consistently and openly. Consequently, the IAM in Erie was awash with all the ideological currents let loose by the war. Its float in the 1918 Labor Day parade featured a union-made cannon bearing a placard reading, "This Is The Gun That Will Get The Huns. Come and Join 101," while literature tables in the lodge hall pointed the way to revolution. The previous January, it had hosted a meeting of machinists from all of the country's GE plants, which had unanimously proposed that the IAM create a district lodge that could present a common front to the national corporation.[79]

On November 25, 1918, delegates from the GE plants gathered once again under the auspices of the Erie IAM. The conference exuded the spirit that the OBU convention in Calgary was to crystallize four months later. It founded an Electrical Manufacturing Industry Labor Federation, which the Socialist press later described as the "first thoroughgoing shop stewards' industrial organization in this country, similar to the British working shop management idea." Among the resolutions passed by the convention were demands for a forty-four–hour week, federal unemployment compensation, release of "all political prisoners in this country," and inclusion of labor representatives as half the country's delegation to the Versailles peace conference.[80]

The most urgent question confronting the new movement was the company's abrupt reduction of personnel. Layoffs came in all plants at the end of the war, but they were especially severe and arbitrary at Erie because no union agreements to control them were in place. Although the local management reiterated publicly the force-reduction policies negotiated at Schenectady in 1913, foremen paid little attention to them. Senior workers were let go in departments where newcomers were kept,

78. *MMJ*, 31 (July 1919), 639–42.
79. Ibid., 30 (November 1918), 1041; 30 (January 1918), 56.
80. "Employees vs. General Electric Company, Erie, Pa.," docket No. 20–127. NWLB administrative file B.56, R.G. 2, National Archives; New York *Call*, February 20, 1919; [anonymous], "The 1918 Strike at Erie General Electric," *UE 506 News*, January 1980, 2–3.

and many others were dismissed and then quickly rehired at lower wages. Ten active unionists were among those dismissed. Representatives of the new federation demanded that everyone who had been lured to Erie with the promise of a job be reinstated, along with all men and women dismissed for union activity, and that work hours be reduced for everyone before any layoffs took place.[81]

Mathew Griswold, the plant manager, responded to the crisis by hastily ordering elections for a shop committee, which was to be established on the "Rockefeller plan." Workers greeted the elections with such contempt that an inquiry later undertaken by GE concluded that Erie's workers lacked "confidence in all the plans offered by the management." Consequently, the workers refused to bring their grievances to the "Rockefeller plan" committee; Griswold conceded nothing to the AFL officers who protested to him, and on the morning of December 10, sixteen hundred workers struck. Before the end of the week, the strikers' ranks had been augmented to twenty-three hundred by a steady round of parades, rallies, and dances. A committee of the federation that sought to carry the grievances to President E. W. Rice, Jr., at national headquarters was rebuffed and referred back to the despised "Rockefeller plan" committee. The next day, December 19, all the workers at Schenectady and Fort Wayne and most of those at Pittsfield joined the walkout. They added their own demands – rotation of available work and recognition of the new federation – to their expressions of sympathy with strikers in Erie.[82]

The NWLB broke the strike. Its examiners quickly warned the Lynn workers that if they stopped work, the award of October 24 would be null and void: no wage increases, no shop committee, no arbitration. Lynn's IBEW voted not to strike, and its IAM voted to "defer action." It was then Pittsfield's turn to be warned that continuation of the strike would put its functioning shop committee in jeopardy. On January 3, all strikers there agreed to resume work and allow the NWLB to settle their grievances. The response of GE was blunt: The armistice had ended the authority of the NWLB; moreover, its new representation plan met all the requirements of the board's awards. It added that a "shrinkage of business" had reduced the number of jobs available in any event, so that strikers would be notified individually if and when they could return. Not until January 17 did the unions call off the disintegrating national strike, describing a new pledge by the NWLB to send examiners to all GE plants as a victory. By that time the company had initiated a thorough house-

81. Brownell, "Report," 17–18, 28–31, 50–1.
82. "Employees vs. General Electric"; "1918 Strike"; Brownell, "Report," 8–12; Bridgeport *Labor Leader*, December 26, 1918.

cleaning. Appeals to the NWLB named hundreds of workers who had not been reinstated, and the Pittsfield management especially settled old scores. Among the 262 men and women dismissed there were all union officers, including Kevlin, the recent candidate for mayor. An ironic twist to the dismissals soon caught the company's attention. The IWW had not approved the strike, and its members had remained at work, thus qualifying for first preference in employment. Word came to Pittsfield managers of workers joining the IWW to keep their jobs.[83] Even company loyalists felt insecure in the wake of the strike. As one nonstriker from Erie wrote his Lutheran pastor:

> Work here is very bad – the whole shop on short time and a man don't dare be caught without a job or he gets fired even after we have stood by them all thru the rush we stayed on short time and then through the strike we stood pat, and now they would tie a can on a man on the smallest pretense they could find and still they expect the men to be loyal – some joke I'll say.[84]

The doors of possibility that wartime experience had opened slammed shut for GE workers even more quickly than they did for coal miners, railway employees, and textile-mill hands. Faltering union leadership made management's seizure of the initiative all the more effective. The Electrical Manufacturing Industry Federation held a convention in Schenectady in February and announced its intention to bring its "shop stewards' industrial organization" to 150,000 AFL members in the industry. Atherton Brownell, surveying the situation for GE, considered the new movement "fraught with danger" for the company. The animosity its delegates evinced toward AFL unions for their refusal to sanction strike benefits after the NWLB intervention, offered little comfort to GE, in his opinion, because if the former strikers withdrew from Gompers's organization, it would only be "in order to affiliate . . . with the more radical organization that is steadily making inroads from the more conservative body."[85]

Although President Johnston of the IAM had attended the Schenectady convention and expressed his approval of the new "federation and solidarity of labor," he was also determined to keep shop stewards' activity within boundaries prescribed by the craft unions' bylaws. The bitter prewar clashes of the IAM's officers with the IWW had elevated their devotion to the constitutional procedures and discipline of the international unions to the level of a fetish, and the steady, tangible improvements in wages, hours, and union protection their members had experienced since

83. "Employees vs. General Electric"; "1918 Strike"; *MMJ*, 31 (January 1919), 35; *Springfield Republican*, February 20, 1919; Brownell, "Report," 33–5.
84. Quoted in Brownell, "Report," 53.
85. New York *Call*, February 20, 1919; Brownell, "Report," 19.

1915 made even the more progressive among them wary of actions that would risk all they had built. Officers widely respected for their militancy, like Andrew T. McNamara and J. F. Anderson, argued that Bolsheviks and socialists were undermining struggles for a labor party and nationalization of industries and inadvertently helping the open-shop drive. "Agitate, Educate, and Organize," McNamara admonished machinists, "always keeping your feet on the ground."[86] President Johnston reported to the machinists' convention that the union's membership had more than doubled in 1918 alone, rising to 305,680, but he warned of a "growing tendency" among members to disregard the IAM's laws, especially where new federations and metal-trades councils assumed the power to direct strikes. The Grand Lodge would combat such usurpation of authority no matter how unpopular its action might be at the time.[87]

True to his word, Johnston lifted the charter of Lodge 30 in Bridgeport for its disregard of union rules and jurisdictions during the city's metal-trades strikes of the previous summer, and at the end of the year he summoned union organizers and business agents to two conferences – one for the East and one for the West – to mobilize them for struggle against "the One Big Union; the I.W.W.; the W.I.I.U. and their activities within our ranks." Members of those organizations, he declared, "have no place in the International Association of Machinists." He charged the organizers to cultivate "greater discipline in our Association," a "strict observance of our laws when calling strikes," and "greater interest in politics."[88] In May 1920, Grand Lodge representatives purged radical "disrupters" from three lodges in New York City, at the same time that railroad brotherhoods expelled thousands for participating in the wildcat switchmen's strike. At the IAM's convention the following September, Johnston devoted much of his opening speech to an attack on machinists who had participated in the recent Chicago convention of the OBU, reminding delegates of how the Knights of Labor, American Railway Union, and IWW had all divided the labor movement and represented "reaction rather than progress."[89]

At the same time that they were suppressing "One Big Unionists," however, the officers of the IAM also initiated new campaigns to organize the electrical industry and to amalgamate the metal-trades unions.

86. *MMJ*, 31 (May 1919), 457. Compare editorial, *MMJ*, 31 (May 1919), 454–5.

87. *MMJ*, 31 (June 1919), 511–12. See also "Important Information. Metal Trades Department, A.F. of L.," *MMJ*, 31 (March 1919), 233.

88. *MMJ*, 32 (January 1920), 70.

89. *MMJ*, 32 (June 1920), 546–7; (October 1920), 897–9; Oklahoma *Leader*, September 30, 1920. I am indebted to Neil Basen for the last item.

At the June 1919 meeting of the AFL's Metal Trades Department, special attention was devoted to planning a campaign for uniform wages and conditions and for the forty-four–hour week at GE, now that the NWLB had been dissolved. The IAM's five delegates, one of whom was Lynn's John J. Connolly, also introduced a resolution that virtually repeated the IWW's reasoning of 1905. New methods, tools, and processes in metal-fabricating industries had rendered craft jurisdictions obsolete, it argued, leaving "the amalgamation of the metal trades organizations into one compact, efficient union" the only way to safeguard workers' interests. The resolution called for a conference of metal-trades unions in October to form a single union and submit its plans "to the entire affiliated membership for a referendum vote." It was soundly defeated: 1,178 votes to 2,964. Charles Sehl of Philadelphia subsequently suggested to his fellow machinists that the decision of Wobblies and One Big Unionists to "bore from within" the trade unions confirmed that the only effective course of action was to carry propaganda for amalgamation to other metal-trades unions that were not yet ready.[90] His colleague Vincent Gilbert, writing about Britain's shop stewards' movement, called on the IAM to steal a march on the revolutionaries:

> It is clear that if the American labor unions do not take the first step, they may find themselves facing a bitterly hostile group of radical agitators with all the prestige of the shop steward behind them. The great chance is for the unions to initiate the system, and become the protectors of the stewards, cooperating with them and finding a proper place for them in the labor union structure.[91]

Amalgamation of craft unions and the development of stewards within the shops had thus taken their place in the program of progressives, along with a labor party, the Plumb plan, welfare legislation, and pacts of mutual assistance among unions of miners and railway workers. Although all of these proposals challenged the positions of Gompers and the Executive Council, they were also linked to a ruthless battle against "IWWs and One Big Unionists." The fate of the progressives also hinged, however, on the ability of unions like the IAM to reverse the swelling tide of business's open-shop drive. In the summer of 1920, GE's Canadian workers struck at Peterboro, and five organizers of different metal trades in Erie opened a highly publicized recruiting drive that concentrated its fire on the long and unpredictable hours of work in that city. GE responded by instituting a forty-eight–hour week, which was soon imitated by other Erie companies.

The depressed state of the economy had many men and women work-

90. *MMJ*, 31 (July 1919), 625–7, 814; 32 (January 1920), 28–9.
91. *MMJ*, 31 (May 1919), 426–7. Italics in original.

ing far fewer than forty-eight hours weekly and all fearing for their jobs. Workers who were already union members often struck during the next year and a half, as did the miners, textile workers, railway workers. The molders at GE in Schenectady waged a craft strike for more than three months in the fall of 1920. But few new recruits came into union ranks under depression conditions. By early 1923, the IAM had lost no less than 70 percent of its 1920 membership. David Saposs's team of investigators touring steel-mill towns in 1920 found workers often mumbling about the need for one big union or nationalization of their industry, but very few prepared to act on those sentiments. A year later, Scott Nearing traveled extensively around America's industrial heartland and found workers everywhere cautious and secretive. "The radicalism in the Middle West is under men's hats," Nearing concluded. "When chance gives it an opening, one finds it on all sides, but to date it remains acquiescent."[92]

Quiescence spelled the doom of progressivism in the AFL. In June 1921, on the eve of the convention at which Lewis made his unsuccessful bid for presidency of the federation, the Metal Trades Department once again – and finally – voted down the IAM's proposals for amalgamation. This time the vote went three-to-one against them (3,370 to 1,071), while Connolly and his fellow delegates from the IAM had their turn to be hooted down as "disruptionists" and "One Big Unionists." A prominent official of the department charged IAM President Johnston with trying "to bring Russia over here," and added that when "that notorious scoundrel, Big Bill Haywood, fled the country to avoid the penitentiary, I hoped we had heard the last of this sort of talk." Four months later the united front of railway unions collapsed on the eve of a proposed national strike. As we have noted, railway shopmen, miners, textile workers, and packinghouse workers all fought their battles of 1922 separately. Observing the rapid hardening of orthodoxy in AFL councils, the IAM's editor concluded that the effort to amalgamate trades through convention resolutions was futile: "If closer affiliation between the metal trades is to be accomplished, the movement in that direction must start at the bottom – not at the top." Had not the OBU's James Robertson said that to Seattle's boilermakers in 1919?[93]

92. *MMJ*, 32 (August 1920), 727, 743; 32 (October 1920), 939–40; Mary Senior, "Report," 12–13, and D. J. Saposs, untitled notes, both in Saposs Papers, Box 26; Scott Nearing, "Taking Stock of American Labor," *Labor Age*, 11 (February 1922), 13. See also Mary Heaton Vorse, "Derelicts of the Steel Strike," *Survey*, 45 (December 4, 1920), 355–8.
93. *MMJ*, 33 (July 1921), 602–3; 33 (August 1921), 677–80. On Robertson and the OBU, see "Shop Stewards and Revolution," Chapter 9.

One must conclude, therefore, that GE's defeat of unionization in 1919 was not simply the result of brilliant management strategies. It is important for historians not to be dazzled by GE's image makers and cosmopolitan executives, or to believe, in larger terms, that corporate welfare practices explain the exclusion of unions from America's major corporations during the 1920s. The hostile stance of the state toward labor's demands after 1918, its policies of deregulation and deflation, the ubiquitous repression by local, state, and federal police, and above all the mounting toll of unemployed – first at the end of 1918, more devastatingly during the 1920–2 depression, and then endemic to industrial life through the Coolidge Prosperity – all fostered an environment in which open-shop drives could hurl back the union tide in virtually every city of the land.

A reformation of trade-union policies along the lines advocated by the AFL's progressive wing might have minimized labor's losses, and it would certainly have left the federation better prepared to take advantage of the resurgence of economic activity in 1923, but such a renaissance was not to be. Their proposal to amalgamate related crafts meant something quite different in 1920 than it had to ironworkers and steelworkers of the 1880s. The earlier amalgamaters had sought to fuse the organizations of those workers who controlled various portions of the production process, such as rollers, puddlers, and nailers, leaving aside the growing body of "alien" laborers. By 1920, the restructuring of industry had concentrated metal-trades production in the hands of semiskilled men and women, leaving the tasks of most craftsmen ancillary and their union structures patently archaic, divisive, and exclusionary. In the new context, amalgamation was the most direct route to industrial unionism, and it was explicitly linked by progressives to the direct representation of workers on the production floor by shop stewards drawn from their own ranks. Consequently, amalgamation posed a clear threat to both the offices of many craft-union leaders and the occupational and ethnic enclaves that their members had managed to secure. There was an important element of truth to economist William Leiserson's observation in 1927: "the reason the employee representation movement has grown is because the trade unions have not succeeded in doing their jobs among specialized workers in the large-scale industries."[94]

Gompers and his colleagues ossified the embattled AFL, leaving craft unionism, in Selig Perlman's words, "the all-important 'regularity' principle, upon which the internal order of the Federation depends." The "psychology of a big majority of its leaders," he wrote in 1928, was a

94. Leiserson, quoted in Hicks, *My Life*, 83.

"curious blending of 'defeatism' with complacency."[95] The eased political climate in which the AFL functioned after the 1922 elections allowed
such a labor federation to survive, but not to grow. Even when the New
Deal context brought industrial workers once again into the AFL, it proved
unable to absorb the newcomers without splitting.

The success of corporate welfarism in the 1920s was thus made easy
by the economic, social, and political environment of postwar American
capitalism. To say that is not to denigrate the sophistication of such corporate executives as those who gathered in the Special Conference Committee or the American Management Association. Those at GE moved
quickly to repair the breach in their defenses opened by the 1918–19
strike. General counsel and future board chairman Owen D. Young commissioned Atherton Brownell, until lately editor of the NAM organ
American Industries, to tour the recently struck plants in the guise of an
author for *McClure's Magazine* and write a candid report for Young on
the mood of the workers, the quality of local managers, and the reforms
the corporation should undertake. Brownell summed up his findings by
stating that the company's renowned efforts to cultivate "esprit de corps"
had not been effective, and in particular the workers were "not greatly
impressed" by the activities of the welfare department. The reputations
of individual managers for fairness or abusiveness weighed far more heavily
in workers' attitudes than benefits or programs provided by the company. Although Brownell thought that most (80 percent) of the employees were "conservative," he found "a very strong feeling of solidarity
among them." That feeling posed a major problem for the company because, in the absence of any established mechanisms for communication
with the employees, the conservatives had no way to express themselves
"until an acute antagonism arises, at which time the unions are fulfilling
their original functions as fighting weapons of the men." At such mo-
ments, Brownell concluded, conservative workers would support the militants who came forward as the voice of the workers, and management
would be able to negotiate with its employees only through the agency
of its worst enemies.[96]

Brownell's remedy was similar to that of Mackenzie King: Put an employee representation plan in place, and devote tireless attention to public relations. To make that project succeed, it was necessary for the management to solicit the participation of workers who were highly respected
by their mates, even if those workers were trade unionists. In fact, it was

95. Selig Perlman, *A Theory of the Labor Movement* (New York, 1928), 204,
232.
96. Brownell, "Report," 2, 5, 6.

precisely "the more liberal minded men *among the labor organizations*" who had to be involved if the plan was to win support from any significant body of employees. Brownell went on to name the individuals he had in mind, such as J. Edwin Doyle, John E. Gillon, and Hugh Morrison of Lynn, active but nonradical AFL members, who could "be of the greatest possible service to the company, provided they are not spoiled and their usefulness destroyed through being asked to place their loyalty to the company higher than their loyalty to their fellows." He also advised the company to rehire David Kevlin at Pittsfield and try to use him, and he thought that if the representation plan was first broached in *McClure's Magazine,* rather than a company source, it might even secure an endorsement from Gompers.[97]

For a company plan to succeed, government agencies had to be excluded. Although fear of the NWLB, not loyalty to the company, had kept Lynn at work during the strike, he conceded, the board had developed such dangerous precedents in its wartime rulings that it was "sowing the wind" and could not easily reverse course. The public hearings of state arbitration boards had drawn crowds of workers to jeer management's spokesmen and thus destroyed the workers' morale. Labor peace in large corporations, Brownell believed, in common with most businessmen of his time, could best be preserved at the enterprise level. The most important supplements to employee-representation plans at that point would be public-relations work in the community at large as well as among the employees, and a consistent policy on layoffs. The Schenectady policy was a model that should be proclaimed and practiced. Seniority and the "employee's economical situation" should determine who was selected for layoff in any department.[98] Later reports on GE practice during the depression of 1920–2 suggest that company officials did pay considerable attention to those criteria, with the result that the reductions in force fell most heavily on single women – company policy in the 1920s barred any employment of married women.[99]

The minor role Brownell accorded welfare programs reflected company thinking generally: No major new programs were introduced at GE during the 1920s. In fact, there was little advance in corporate welfare practice anywhere in American industry after 1921. The creative years for mutual-benefit societies, pension plans, stock options, company newspapers, and sporting clubs were the years of labor militancy, 1916–22. Thereafter, a strong reassertion of the authority of production super-

97. Ibid., 34–5, 44, 63, 74.   98. Ibid., 33, 38.
99. "Our Experience with Women Workers. The Policy Followed in 36 Lines of Industry," *Factory,* 29 (December 1922), 660–1.

visors and especially systematic training for foremen and other front-line supervisors were the salient elements of managerial reform.[100]

What, then, happened to GE's shop committees? The best information comes from Lynn, where they suddenly became the subject of journalistic controversy in 1926 and 1927. Gillon, Doyle, and Morrison had all assumed dominant roles on the joint adjustment committee, just as Brownell had urged. All of them remained active union members, and the Lynn metal-trades council initially shaped much of the activity of the shop committees. Bit by bit, management persuaded committee members to make their own decision without "dictation" from the metal-trades council and offered them the use of company chambers, paid time off, and dinners to spare them the trouble of trudging to the union hall after work. A variety of joint committees, dealing with safety, health, social activities, production standards, and other issues on a "nonadversarial basis," whittled down the tasks of the joint adjustment committee, while a new rules committee was charged with reviewing every decision the shop committee made. A 1921 decision by the joint committee guaranteeing that no incentive rates would be cut for six months no matter how much workers produced inspired a flurry of stint-busting on the machines. When many jobs were retired after the expiration of the agreements, enraged workers ousted Gillon and Doyle from the committee, while the management drove the more militant Wright Greggson off the board – among other things by bringing in state policemen to charge him with being a member of the SLP. Thereafter, the joint committee shared the role of the special committees: a transmission belt for presentation of company policies to the employees.

With Lynn's committee tamed by early 1922 and metal-trades unions nationally in the doldrums, management opened a major campaign to persuade Schenectady's workers to accept a similar plan. That old union stronghold voted down the proposal 5,704 to 3,549. But two years later the combined force of company persistence and AFL defeatism had turned the tide: Schenectady's management instituted a company union without putting it to a vote. The Schenectady *Works News* could then proclaim:

100. Schatz, *Electrical Workers*, 21; Jacoby, "Industrial Internal Labor Markets," 8–36; Jacquelyn Hall, Robert Korstad, and James Leloudis, "Cotton Mill People: Work, Community, and Protest in the Textile South, 1880–1940," *American Historical Review*, 91 (April 1986), 245–86. For comparable development of supervisors in France, see Ingo Kolboom, "Patronat et cadres: la contribution patronale à la formation du groupe des cadres (1936–1938)," *Le Mouvement Social*, 121 (October–December 1982), 71–95.

So you see we G. E. girls work and play and enjoy it under the pro-
tecting wing of the Company – every one working, thinking, planning and helping in the manufacture and distribution of those electrical products which put light where darkness should not exist, and
which make easier the work in the factory, the store and the home –
this is the duty as well as the pleasure of the G. E. girl.[101]

Bricks for a new house

Only ten years passed between the subsidence of labor militancy at the
end of 1922 and the resurgence of workplace struggles in the 1930s. In
those ten years, the economic system that had had its origins in the long
deflation of the late nineteenth century reached maturity and then collapsed. Both the revived labor movement and the government's attitude
toward it were significantly different from their earlier counterparts, although in many ways the struggles of 1916–22 had presaged those of at
least the early 1930s, that is, before the founding of the Committee for
Industrial Organization and the enactment of the Wagner Act.

The world of work continued to change throughout the 1920s, but it
evolved within patterns established earlier in the century. Coal mining
and northern textiles were among the older industries that reduced their
work forces sharply, and railroad managers learned by 1929 how to produce the same operating revenue as they had enjoyed before the war with
20 percent fewer employees, in what Secretary of Commerce Hoover called
"probably the most outstanding industrial accomplishment since the
war."[102] Employment in sectors of manufacturing clearly dominated by
new managerial practice, such as electrical appliances, motor vehicles,
chemicals, and rubber, rose during the Coolidge years, as it did in building construction. Overall, however, the steady increase in manufacturing
output was caused by new production methods, in sharp contrast to the

101. Budenz, "Jonah's Whale"; Budenz, "Jehu's Drive"; Budenz, " 'Democracy' a la General Electric," *Labor Age*, 16 (July 1927), 15–16; *Works
News*, January 18, 1924, quoted in Robert W. Dunn, *Americanization of
Labor: The Employer's Offensive Against the Trade Unions* (New York,
1927), 253. After his removal from the joint committee, Doyle was employed in the Lynn-works employee-relations department and by the 1940s
had become its director. Morrison remained highly respected by his fellow
workers and later became active in the United Electrical Workers (UE).
Donald Tormey to author, February 28, 1986.
102. Quoted in Cochran, *American Business Systems*, 35.

last third of the nineteenth century, when new inputs of labor had been the primary cause of rising output of goods. Most new jobs were created in offices and stores, and they were filled primarily by daughters and sons of industrial workers, who had been trained by this country's school system.[103] Both the continuities and changes exhibited by the economy were important. Close to half of all men in the labor force were manual workers in production in the 1920s, as they had been in 1900 and would still be in 1960; but they represented a declining share of the gainfully employed population as a whole. The relative importance of manufacturing in the American economy had reached its historical peak. Thereafter, it would slowly but steadily cede precedence to the clerical, sales, and service sectors, which finally overtook it in the 1950s.[104]

The wage-earning experience of women was changing more profoundly than that of men, though at a gradual pace. As early as the census of 1920, over 25 percent of all female employees were in clerical or sales work, slightly more than the proportion in manufacturing (24 percent), and significantly more than the historically dominant category, domestic service (18 percent). Within manufacturing, a postwar survey revealed that few new jobs had been permanently opened to women. The important development had been the advent of systematic analysis of which tasks were appropriate to women and which to men. Such analysis was based on the assumption that virtually all jobs should be assigned specifically either to men or to women, while the task of scientific management was to determine which operations should be assigned to which sex. Although lines of gender demarcation were equally strict in the office and store, working people were keenly aware of the rapid growth of employment there. Thus, employers in Paterson, New Jersey, for example, explained the absence of American-born youth in the silk mills by the determination of their parents to keep them in school in preparation for work in offices or department stores. Equally important was the steady rise in the proportion of wage-earning women who were married, from 22.8 percent in 1920 to 28.8 percent in 1930. Those statistics reflected the vehemence with which Seattle's female trade unionists in 1919 had denounced proposals that they leave their jobs when they married.[105]

103. See DeVault, "Sons and Daughters"; Benson, " 'A Great Theater' "; Sharon Strom, "Beyond the Typewriter: The Feminization of Bookkeeping, 1910–1940" (unpublished paper).
104. Albert Szymanski, "Trends in the American Class Structure," *Socialist Revolution*, 10 (July–August 1972), 101–22.
105. Kessler-Harris, *Out to Work*, 224–9; "Our Experience with Women Workers"; NWLB case file 1123, Transcript of Proceedings, 99, R.G. 2, National Archives. See also the extensive debate over married women's

For men and women alike, the encounter with scientific management was no longer a novelty. Its tenets informed work relations in the department store or insurance office, as well as the factory. Personnel managers and their welfare schemes, having found widespread favor in business circles during the labor militancy before 1922, ceased to attract as much attention or experimentation thereafter, while systematic training of foremen as the front line of modern management assumed top priority. By the end of the 1920s, however, Stanley B. Mathewson found employers as widely concerned about their workers' "restriction of output" as they had been in Taylor's day. Workers' collective efforts to ease the pace of their work were largely covert, informal, and rarely supported by unions, which were seldom present in any case. Elton Mayo's studies of work relations at Western Electric's Hawthorne works in Chicago reintroduced the concept of "alienation" into the academic lexicon. Louis Adamic's experience as a youth working in various factories in the Scranton area led him to concur with Mathewson and Mayo. "After the suppression of the organized radical movement in 1922 or thereabout," he wrote, the "workers' radicalism now found individual, personal expression in doing as little as possible for the wages they received and wasting as much material as possible."[106]

Although these investigations of worker alienation are revealing, they leave unsaid much that was important about industrial life in the 1920s. In the first place, as Sanford Jacoby has argued persuasively, turnover rates were much lower between 1923 and 1929 than they had been before the war. They had been reduced in part by corporate policies that had linked pay, benefits, and job security to seniority. The impact of such efforts was increased by the rise in the average age of workers, caused by the closing off of immigration and by falling birthrates. Most important of all, even during the Coolidge prosperity, the numbers of unemployed remained chronically higher than they had been in all but recession periods before the war. Workers, especially older workers, became reluctant to quit jobs, because other jobs were hard to find. Highly seasonal manufacturing, such as automobile production, still whirled people in and out of its revolving doors in astonishing numbers. By and large, however, workers of the 1920s were more likely to link their plans for the

wage earning in the Ruth Ridgway columns of *SUR*, January–February 1921.

106. Stanley B. Mathewson, *Restriction of Output Among Unorganized Workers* (New York, 1931); Elton Mayo, *Human Problems of an Industrial Civilization* (Cambridge, Mass., 1933); Louis Adamic, *Dynamite: The Story of Class Violence in America* (revised edition, New York, 1934), 392–3.

future to a particular company, and less likely to tie them to some particular occupation, than their parents or grandparents had been.[107]

Job security remained elusive for the millions of new migrants from the farming regions of the United States and Mexico. Between 1920 and 1929, 19,436,000 people left farms in this country for the urban world. Their ties to rural life often remained strong, so that many returned to the land and were joined in that movement by immigrants who bought farms in this country, rather than returning to their homelands, and by unemployed workers who took up submarginal plots. In all, 13,140,000 urban residents moved to farms during the decade. The two-way flow, especially the net urban migration averaging almost 620,000 people per year, produced men and women in abundance for the constantly expanding and contracting numbers of jobs at the bottom of the industrial hierarchy. As they had during 1916 and 1917, black migrants found themselves especially highly concentrated in particular industries. By 1927, they constituted 20 percent or more of the steelworkers in the Pittsburgh region, the building laborers in northern New Jersey, the packinghouse workers in Chicago, and the dockers in Philadelphia, not to mention all of the Pullman porters. At every AFL convention of the decade, some black dockers, porters, hod carriers, or boilermakers' helpers challenged the racial exclusiveness of many affiliated craft unions, always without success. Despite the persistent difficulties they faced in securing a foothold in northern industry, however, black migrants were fashioning workplace and neighborhood networks of decisive importance for the struggles of the next decade.[108]

Workers' tendency to become more sedentary was accentuated by the most important legislation of the decade, the immigration restriction acts. The emergency limitation enacted in 1919, the quota law of 1921, and finally the law of 1924, which revised the quotas and also provided for the national-origins system, which finally went into effect in 1929, had three basic effects. First, they reduced the total number of newcomers allowed to enter the United States annually to 150,000 after 1924. Second, they put tight limits on entrance of southern and eastern Europeans and prohibited the admission of Asian workers altogether. Nevertheless, by permitting virtually unlimited entrance of North Americans, they institutionalized a revolving door for migrant field workers from Mexico, who numbered at harvest time as many as all immigrants from the rest

107. Jacoby, "Industrial Internal Labor Markets," 1–13.
108. Vreeland and Fitzgerald, *Farm-City Migration*, 6; Thomas L. Dabney, "Negro Workers at the Crossroads," *Labor Age*, 16 (February 1927), 8–10; Dabney, "Bringing the Message to the Negro," *Labor Age*, 16 (July 1927), 6–7; 16 (August 1927), 11.

of the world combined but could be, and were, returned to Mexico en masse when large growers did not need their labor. Third, the Department of Labor, no longer much concerned with tasks such as as mediation of strikes, assigned three-quarters of its staff to the detection and expulsion of illegal immigrants. The numbers deported or otherwise required to depart rose to the vicinity of thirty thousand per year by 1933, making the numbers expelled for political reasons by the Palmer raids appear minuscule in comparison.[109]

Although the AFL welcomed the quota law of 1924, it had little influence on the form the law finally took. From 1919 onward, the federation had appealed for a halt to all immigration whatsoever, arguing that only if the influx of newcomers was prevented could the earnings of all American workers rise to the level of the "living wage" demanded by the AFL's reconstruction program. Business's successful opposition to such a law allowed 805,000 immigrants to enter the country in 1920, more than a quarter of them from Italy and another 119,000 Jews from strife-torn eastern Europe.[110] Protests of nativists like Washington's Senator Albert Johnson that the newcomers were "filthy, un-American, and often dangerous in their habits,"[111] were seconded by Warren Harding, who pledged that as president he would be "more concerned with the making of citizens than . . . with adding to the man power of industry." He promised, "such a policy relating to those who come among us as will guarantee not only assimilability of alien born but the adoption by all who come of American standards, economic and otherwise, and a full consecration to American practices and ideals."[112]

Backed by scholarly treatises on eugenics and "racial traits," congressmen like Johnson and William Dillingham set out on a four-year quest for legislation that would exclude people of "undesirable" nationalities, without closing the doors to northern Europeans or depriving western farm operators of migrant hands. By 1923, the National Industrial Conference Board's leaders had concluded that immigration was "essentially a race question – a question of the kind of citizenship and national life

---

109. Higham, *Strangers*, 308–24; Camille Guerin-Gonzales, "Cycles of Immigration and Repatriation: Mexican Farm Workers in California Industrial Agriculture, 1900–1940" (unpublished Ph.D. diss., University of California, Riverside, 1985); *Hist. Stat. U.S.*, 114; Grossman, *Department of Labor*, 23.

110. American Federation of Labor, *History, Encyclopedia, Reference Book* (2 vols., Washington, D.C., 1919, 1924), II, 97; *Hist. Stat. U.S.*, 105; Higham, *Strangers*, 105.

111. Quoted in Higham, *Strangers*, 309.

112. *Survey*, 45 (November 20, 1920), 278.

we desire to develop in the United States." Although the NAM wanted a larger influx, it, too, had by then accepted the idea of national quotas, and the editors of the *American Contractor* assured building-trades employers that recent migration patterns had shown that they could get all the new workers they needed from northern Europe.[113] In short, Congress and the Department of Labor had undertaken the scientific management of society's entire labor force.

The AFL did not exert itself greatly to secure passage of the 1924 law, partly because its goal of reducing immigration was so powerfully advanced by others, and partly because no fewer than half of the senators elected as friends of labor in 1922 openly opposed the quota bills. Bourke Cochran, Adolph Sabath, Fiorello La Guardia, and other loyal friends of labor in Congress despised the racist logic that pronounced some Americans more desirable than others. This may explain why the speakers' handbook put out by the Eastern District LaFollette–Wheeler Campaign Committee in 1924 contained nothing whatever on the subject of immigration.[114]

Closing the door to Europeans accelerated the stabilization of ethnic communities in industrial towns and cities. It reduced the rate of return to Europe to less than half its prewar level, increased the proportion of women among those who were let in to roughly half the total, and encouraged foreign-born residents to apply for citizenship as some protection against deportation. Just as the outcome of postwar labor struggles had persuaded most older immigrants to abandon whatever dreams they might ever have harbored of together reforming society, so the quota laws made any possible return home an irrevocable act. Reports from those who had returned to Europe in 1919–20 of the devastation found there were enough to snuff out illusions that a better life was being born in the homeland. An older Serb in Johnstown, Pennsylvania, concluded: "Here in America, when things were good, they were better than in the [old] country, but when they turned bad, maybe it was worse. . . . It was just that over there they never seemed to get better."[115]

Immigrants' hopes thus tended to focus on what seemed within reach: a healthy family, a steady job, the purchase of a house, and "respect

113.   Higham, *Strangers*, 317; [anonymous], "Northern Europeans Again Immigrate," *American Contractor*, 44 (September 8, 1923), 17–19.

114.   Walling, *American Labor and American Democracy*, I, 116–17; Higham, *Strangers*, 321–3; Eastern District La Follette-Wheeler Campaign Committee, *The Facts about La Follette and Wheeler* (New York, 1924).

115.   Quoted in Ewa Morawska, *For Bread with Butter: The Life-Worlds of East Central Europeans in Johnstown, Pennsylvania, 1890–1940* (New York, 1985), 3.

among people." Their children, as many oral histories suggest, were more likely to seek advancement in jobs within the mills than in business ventures, had fewer children than their parents, and saved to supply their houses with running water, gas stoves, electric lights and radios, and perhaps even a car. Deference to their elders, wrote Ewa Morawska, was confined to family and cultural life; at work "they did not hide their dislike for the drudgery of their labor and openly used means of avoiding physical exhaustion on the job."[116] And they smarted under the disdain of those, such as Ku Klux Klansmen, who burned crosses on hillsides above their neighborhoods, and the president of the United States who labeled them less than desirable members of American society. On August 25, 1923, Imperial Wizard Hiram Evans led thousands of robed Klansmen on a march acclaiming Protestant America in the Pennsylvania mill town of Carnegie. Massed local workers assaulted the marchers with clubs, stones, and guns and sent them fleeing from the town. Thereafter, although the Klan held many large gatherings in western Pennsylvania, it did so only where most local workers were Protestants. Immigrants' votes for Al Smith were so numerous as to challenge Republican dominance in western Pennsylvania politics only five years later. In Carnegie, where Democrats had secured only 245 votes in 1924 to the Republicans' 1,684, Smith got 1,928 votes to Hoover's 2,099.[117]

Consequently, there was one issue that linked the beleaguered Left to the sentiments of millions of working people, and that was the defense of Sacco and Vanzetti. By the summer of 1927, when the campaign to prevent execution of the two Italian anarchists by the state of Massachusetts reached a fever pitch, they had come to symbolize for foreign-born workers and their children the contemptuous treatment dealt them by Anglo-Saxon America. During July and August, demonstrations and strikes erupted from New York's garment district to midwestern coal towns. Even the miners of Colorado Fuel and Iron struck en masse at the behest of the IWW in protest against the pending execution. The young Slovenian American Louis Adamic was working in a lace mill near Scranton, where he found the operatives "in a bad mood." As he tells the tale:

> The management was speeding up the machines, forcing the employees to work faster and faster for the same pay, with the result that there was much sabotage on the machinery. Looms were injured; on the large machines leather bands were cut with safety-razor blades.

116. Ibid., 273. See also Hareven, *Family Time and Industrial Time;* John Bodnar, *Worker's World: Kinship, Community, and Protest in Industrial Society, 1900–1940* (Baltimore, 1982).

117. Emerson H. Loucks, *Ku Klux Klan in Pennsylvania: A Study in Nativism* (New York, 1936), 43–58, 112.

The foreman blamed these things on "those Communist bastards." On several of the cut leather bands one morning "Sacco-Vanzetti" was inscribed in white chalk.[118]

In the tight repression of the Coolidge era, all but a radicalized handful of workers reported quietly to whatever jobs they managed to hold, discarding their wartime aspirations as the folly of youth and directing their hopes and energies toward their homes, their children, and the esteem of their neighbors. Neither workers nor their employers created any significantly new designs for reshaping the patterns of group life that produced goods and services each day and distributed them in grossly unequal measure. Taylor's prescriptions for the organization of work had become standard business practice without generating the social harmony he had promised. The union movement, though comprising many more workers and officials than it had before the war, was like a great ship becalmed in a shark-infested sea. Slogans like "workers' control" and "production for use," which had only recently come so easily to the lips of its militants, were seldom heard any longer, except ironically in the rhetoric of corporate public relations.

Widespread experimentation with employee organization in the workplace had appeared as a consequence of the restructuring of industrial production that the early advocates of scientific management had never anticipated. Business executives, government agencies, social reformers, trade-union officials, and revolutionaries had all tried to guide this development in accordance with their own particular social goals. By the mid-1920s, the designs of corporate management had clearly prevailed over those of its rivals. No historical resolution of the conflict between wage labor and capital, however, has enjoyed a permanent lease on life. Less than a decade ensued before the economy collapsed and a resurgence of worker militancy reopened the irrepressible question that Frank Walsh had posed in 1916: how "workers of all lines of thought" might combine their forces to create "a democracy, industrious and political, based on enduring justice."[119]

118. Adamic, *Dynamite,* 390. On Sacco-Vanzetti strikes, see *Labor Defender* (August 2, 1927), 115–17; Gambs, *Decline,* 145–53; Fred Thompson, *The I.W.W.: Its First Fifty Years* (Chicago, 1955), 152–3; Leonard Craig, "State Troopers Again Amuck," *Labor Age,* 16 (November 1927), 18–20.

119. See Chapter 7, footnote 55.

Index